Why Do You Need this New Edition?

8 good reasons why you should buy this new Second Edition of *American Stories*!

P9-CBF-143

1. This edition is tied more closely than ever to the innovative website, MyHistoryLab, which helps you save time and improve results as you study history (www.myhistorylab.com). Improved MyHistoryLab icons throughout the book connect the main narrative of each chapter to a powerful array of MyHistoryLab resources, including primary source documents, analytical video segments, interactive maps, and more. Also tied to each chapter of the textbook, a powerful and personalized Study Plan is available on MyHistoryLab that will help you build a deeper and more critical understanding of the subject.

2. Every one of the more than 80 maps in the Second Edition has been redrawn for greater clarity and visual impact, making it easier for you to read and understand the book.

3. The text of the Second Edition has been extensively edited and rewritten to bring the story of American history into sharper focus. For example, all maps, figures, and tables are now numbered for easier reference and to integrate them more closely to the text. Chapter 2 discusses the founding of New Jersey, Delaware, and North Carolina; Chapter 1 has a new discussion and table about the Columbian Exchange; and Chapters 21 and 24 have more detail on empire and American foreign policy in the decades before World War I.

4. The coverage of Native Americans has been increased throughout the text. New sections discuss the diverse life-ways of native peoples in North America before the arrival of the Europeans (Chapter 1); the role of Native Americans in the American Revolution (Chapter 5); the infamous Trail of Tears in the 1830s (Chapter 10); reservation life and the efforts at forced assimilation in the late 19th and early 20th centuries (Chapter 17); and the role of Native American troops in World War II (Chapter 27).

5. The discussion of the Spanish role in the American story has been enhanced with new coverage of Spanish colonization and Spanish interaction with the Native Americans (Chapters 1 and 4); Spain's role in the American Revolution (Chapter 5); and life in the Spanish-speaking borderlands of the Southwest (Chapter 17). . . .

6. The history of African Americans has been expanded with new graphics in Chapter 11 and a major new section in Chapter 19 on the spread of Jim Crowe in both the South and North after Reconstruction.

7. Chapters 31 and 32 have been rewritten to bring the American Story up to 2011 with new sections on the elections of 2008 and 2010, health care reform, the Great Recession, and gay marriage and gays in the military.

8. Many other changes have been made in light of new scholarship, and to incorporate new perspectives into the American story. See, for instance, the discussions of Jacksonian democracy in Chapter 10 and minority issues in Chapters 31 and 32.

PEARSON

American Stories

American Stories

A History of the United States

Volume 1

Second Edition

H. W. Brands
University of Texas

T. H. Breen
Northwestern University

R. Hal Williams
Southern Methodist University

Ariela J. Gross
University of Southern California

PEARSON

Boston   Columbus   Indianapolis   New York   San Francisco   Upper Saddle River
Amsterdam   Cape Town   Dubai   London   Madrid   Milan   Munich   Paris   Montréal   Toronto
Delhi   Mexico City   São Paulo   Sydney   Hong Kong   Seoul   Singapore   Taipei   Tokyo

Editorial Director: Craig Campanella
Editor-in-Chief: Dickson Musslewhite
Executive Editor: Ed Parsons
Assistant Editor: Alex Rabinowitz
Editorial Assistant: Emily Tamburri
Senior Manufacturing and Operations
  Manager for Arts & Sciences: Mary Fischer
Operations Specialist: Christina Amato
Director of Marketing: Brandy Dawson
Senior Marketing Manager: Maureen E. Prado Roberts
Marketing Assistant: Samantha Bennett
Senior Managing Editor: Ann Marie McCarthy
Senior Project Manager: Denise Forlow
Director of Media and Assessment: Brian Hyland

Media Project Manager: Nikhil Bramhavar
Digital Media Editor: Andrea Messineo
Senior Art Director: Maria Lange
Cover and Interior Design: T-9 Design
Cover Image: Bottom, ArtPix/Alamy; top, Lebrecht Music and
  Arts Photo Library/Alamy
Cartographer: Maps.com
AV Project Manager: Mirella Signoretto
Cartographer: Maps.com
Full-Service Production, Interior Design,
  and Composition: PreMediaGlobal
Printer/Binder: Quad Graphics
Cover Printer: Lehigh-Phoenix Color/Hagerstown
Text Font: 10/12.5 Minion Pro

Credits and acknowledgments borrowed from other sources and reproduced, with permission, in this textbook appear on appropriate page within text (or on pages C-1–C-2).

Library of Congress Cataloging-in-Publication Data

American stories : a history of the United States / H.W. Brands . . . [et al.].—2nd ed.
  p. cm.
Includes index.
ISBN 978-0-205-24361-7 (combined)
978-0-205-03656-1 (vol. 1)
978-0-205-03655-4 (vol. 2)
1. United States—History.   I. Brands, H. W.
E178.A5544 2011
973—dc23

2011023657

10 9 8 7 6 5 4 3 2 1

Combined Volume
ISBN 10: 0-205-24361-4
ISBN 13: 978-0-205-24361-7

Examination Copy
ISBN 10: 0: 0-205-06483-3
ISBN 13: 978-0-205-06483-0

Volume 1
ISBN 10: 0-205-03656-2
ISBN 13: 978-0-205-03656-1

Books a la carte Volume 1
ISBN 10: 0-205-20642-5
ISBN 13: 978-0-205-20642-1

Volume 2
ISBN 10: 0-205-03655-4
ISBN 13: 978-0-205-03655-4

Books a la carte Volume 2
ISBN 10: 0-205-20645-X
ISBN 13: 978-0-205-20645-2

PEARSON

Brief Contents

CHAPTER 1   New World Encounters,
             Preconquest–1608 2

CHAPTER 2   England's New World
             Experiments, 1607–1732 30

CHAPTER 3   Putting Down Roots: Opportunity
             and Oppression in Colonial
             Society, 1619–1692 60

CHAPTER 4   Experience of Empire:
             Eighteenth-Century America,
             1680–1763 82

CHAPTER 5   The American Revolution: From
             Elite Protest to Popular Revolt,
             1763–1783 110

CHAPTER 6   The Republican Experiment,
             1783–1788 140

CHAPTER 7   Democracy and Dissent: The
             Violence of Party Politics,
             1788–1800 168

CHAPTER 8   Republican Ascendancy: The
             Jeffersonian Vision, 1800–1814 194

CHAPTER 9   Nation Building and Nationalism,
             1815–1825 220

CHAPTER 10   The Triumph of White Men's
             Democracy, 1824–1840 244

CHAPTER 11   Slaves and Masters,
             1793–1861 268

CHAPTER 12   The Pursuit of Perfection,
             1800–1861 290

CHAPTER 13   An Age of Expansionism,
             1830–1861 312

CHAPTER 14   The Sectional Crisis,
             1846–1861 334

CHAPTER 15   Secession and the Civil War,
             1860–1865 358

CHAPTER 16   The Agony of Reconstruction,
             1863–1877 386

Contents

Maps, Figures, and Tables xiv

New to this Edition (Vol.1) xv

A Note to My Fellow Teachers xvi

A Note to Students: Tips for Studying History xix

Supplements xxi

Acknowledgments xxv

About the Authors xxix

CHAPTER 1

NEW WORLD ENCOUNTERS, PRECONQUEST–1608 2

Diverse Cultures: De Vaca's Journey Through Native America 3

NATIVE AMERICANS BEFORE THE CONQUEST 5

The Environmental Challenge: Food, Climate, and Culture 6

Aztec Dominance 7

Eastern Woodland Cultures 9

CONDITIONS OF CONQUEST 10

Cultural Negotiations 10

Threats to Survival: Columbian Exchange 12

WEST AFRICA: ANCIENT AND COMPLEX SOCIETIES 13

EUROPE ON THE EVE OF CONQUEST 16

Spanish Expansion 16

The Strange Career of Christopher Columbus17

SPAIN IN THE AMERICAS 18

The *Conquistadores*: Faith and Greed 19

From Plunder to Settlement 19

THE FRENCH CLAIM CANADA 22

THE ENGLISH TAKE UP THE CHALLENGE 23

Birth of English Protestantism 24

Religion, War, and Nationalism 26

CONCLUSION: CAMPAIGN TO SELL AMERICA 26

▼ **Study Resources** 27
TIMELINE
CHAPTER REVIEW
KEY TERM QUESTIONS

CHAPTER 2

ENGLAND'S NEW WORLD EXPERIMENTS, 1607–1732 30

Profit and Piety: Competing Visions for English Settlement 31

BREAKING AWAY: DECISIONS TO MOVE TO AMERICA 32

The Chesapeake: Dreams of Wealth 33

Entrepreneurs in Virginia 33

Threat of Anarchy 34

Tobacco Saves Virginia 36

Time of Reckoning 37

Maryland: A Catholic Refuge 38

A "NEW" ENGLAND IN AMERICA 41

The Puritan Migration to Massachusetts 42

"A City on a Hill" 44

Competing Truths in New England 45

Mobility and Division 47

DIVERSITY IN THE MIDDLE COLONIES 48

Anglo-Dutch Rivalry on the Hudson 48

Confusion in New Jersey 50

Quakers in America 51

Penn's "Holy Experiment" 51

PLANTING THE SOUTHERN COLONIES 53

Founding the Carolinas 53

Founding of Georgia 55

CONCLUSION: LIVING WITH DIVERSITY 57

▼ **Study Resources** 57
TIMELINE
KEY TERM QUESTIONS
CHAPTER REVIEW

CHAPTER 3

PUTTING DOWN ROOTS: OPPORTUNITY AND OPPRESSION IN COLONIAL SOCIETY, 1619–1692 60

Families in an Atlantic Empire 61

SOCIAL STABILITY: NEW ENGLAND COLONIES OF THE SEVENTEENTH CENTURY 63

Immigrant Families and New Social Order 63

Puritan Women in New England   64

Establishing a New Social Order   65

THE CHALLENGE OF THE CHESAPEAKE
ENVIRONMENT   66

Families at Risk   66

The Structure of Planter Society   67

RACE AND FREEDOM IN BRITISH AMERICA   69

Roots of Slavery   69

Constructing African American Identities   71

BLUEPRINT FOR EMPIRE   73

Response to Economic Competition   72

Regulating Colonial Trade   74

COLONIAL POLITICAL REVOLTS   75

Civil War in Virginia: Bacon's Rebellion   76

The Glorious Revolution in the Bay Colony   77

Contagion of Witchcraft   78

CONCLUSION: FOUNDATIONS OF
AN ATLANTIC EMPIRE   79

▼ **Study Resources   80**

TIMELINE

CHAPTER REVIEW

KEY TERM QUESTIONS

CHAPTER 4

EXPERIENCE OF EMPIRE: EIGHTEENTH-
CENTURY AMERICA, 1680–1763   82

*Constructing an Anglo-American Identity: The Journal of
William Byrd   84*

TENSIONS IN THE BACKCOUNTRY   85

Scots-Irish Flee English Oppression   86

Germans Search for a Better Life   86

Native Americans Stake Out a Middle
Ground   87

SPANISH BORDERLANDS OF THE EIGHTEENTH
CENTURY   89

Conquering the Northern Frontier   89

Peoples of the Spanish Borderlands   90

THE IMPACT OF EUROPEAN IDEAS ON AMERICAN
CULTURE   91

American Enlightenment   91

Benjamin Franklin   96

Economic Transformation   93

Birth of a Consumer Society   94

RELIGIOUS REVIVALS IN PROVINCIAL SOCIETIES   96

The Great Awakening   96

Evangelical Religion   97

CLASH OF POLITICAL CULTURES   98

Governing the Colonies: The American
Experience   98

Colonial Assemblies   100

CENTURY OF IMPERIAL WAR   101

The French Threat   101

King George's War and Its Aftermath   102

Seven Years' War   104

Perceptions of War   106

CONCLUSION: RULE BRITANNIA?   107

▼ **Study Resources   107**

TIMELINE

CHAPTER REVIEW

KEY TERM QUESTIONS

CHAPTER 5

THE AMERICAN REVOLUTION: FROM
ELITE PROTEST TO POPULAR REVOLT,
1763–1783   110

Moment of Decision: Commitment and Sacrifice   111

STRUCTURE OF COLONIAL SOCIETY   113

Breakdown of Political Trust   113

No Taxation Without Representation: The
American Perspective   114

Justifying Resistance   115

ERODING THE BONDS OF EMPIRE   116

Paying Off the National Debt   117

The Protest Spreads   118

Fueling the Crisis   121

Surge of Force   122

The Final Provocation: The Boston Tea Party   123

STEPS TOWARD INDEPENDENCE   125

Shots Heard Around the World   125

Beginning "The World Over Again"   126

FIGHTING FOR INDEPENDENCE   128

Building a Professional Army   129

"Times That Try Men's Souls"   130

Victory in a Year of Defeat   132

The French Alliance   133

The Final Campaign   134

The Loyalist Dilemma   136

CONCLUSION: PRESERVING INDEPENDENCE   137

▼ **Study Resources   137**

TIMELINE

CHAPTER REVIEW

KEY TERM QUESTIONS

CHAPTER 6

THE REPUBLICAN EXPERIMENT, 1783–1788   140

A New Political Morality 141

DEFINING REPUBLICAN CULTURE   142

Social and Political Reform   143
African Americans in the New Republic   145
The Challenge of Women's Rights   147
The States: Experiments in Republicanism   149

STUMBLING TOWARD A NEW NATIONAL GOVERNMENT   150

Articles of Confederation   150
Western Land: Key to the First Constitution   151
Northwest Ordinance: The Confederation's Major Achievement   152

"HAVE WE FOUGHT FOR THIS?"   153

The Genius of James Madison   154
Constitutional Reform   155
The Philadelphia Convention   157
Inventing a Federal Republic   157
Compromise Saves the Convention   158
The Last Details   159
We the People   160

WHOSE CONSTITUTION? STRUGGLE FOR RATIFICATION   161

Federalists and Antifederalists   161
Adding the Bill of Rights   163

CONCLUSION: SUCCESS DEPENDS ON THE PEOPLE   165

▼ **Study Resources   166**
TIMELINE
CHAPTER REVIEW
KEY TERM QUESTIONS

CHAPTER 7

DEMOCRACY AND DISSENT: THE VIOLENCE OF PARTY POLITICS, 1788–1800   168

Force of Public Opinion 169

PRINCIPLE AND PRAGMATISM: ESTABLISHING A NEW GOVERNMENT   171

Getting Started   171
Conflicting Visions: Jefferson and Hamilton   172

HAMILTON'S PLAN FOR PROSPERITY AND SECURITY   173

Debt as a Source of National Strength   174
Interpreting the Constitution: The Bank Controversy   175
Setback for Hamilton   176

CHARGES OF TREASON: THE BATTLE OVER FOREIGN AFFAIRS   176

The Peril of Neutrality   177
Jay's Treaty Sparks Domestic Unrest   178
Pushing the Native Americans Aside   180

POPULAR POLITICAL CULTURE   181

Whiskey Rebellion: Charges of Republican Conspiracy   182
Washington's Farewell   182

THE ADAMS PRESIDENCY: POLITICS OF MISTRUST   183

The XYZ Affair and Domestic Politics   184
Crushing Political Dissent   186
Silencing Political Opposition: The Alien and Sedition Acts   187
Kentucky and Virginia Resolutions   188
Adams's Finest Hour   189
The Peaceful Revolution: The Election of 1800   191

CONCLUSION: DANGER OF POLITICAL EXTREMISM   191

▼ **Study Resources   191**
TIMELINE
CHAPTER REVIEW
KEY TERM QUESTIONS

CHAPTER 8

REPUBLICAN ASCENDANCY: THE JEFFERSONIAN VISION, 1800–1814   194

Limits of Equality 195

THE REPUBLIC EXPANDS   196

Westward the Course of Empire   197
Native American Resistance   198
Commercial Life in the Cities   199

JEFFERSON AS PRESIDENT   200

Political Reforms   201
The Louisiana Purchase   202
The Lewis and Clark Expedition   203

RACE AND DISSENT UNDER JEFFERSON   203

Attack on the Judges   205
The Slave Trade   207

EMBARRASSMENTS OVERSEAS 208
    Embargo Divides the Nation 209
    A New Administration Goes to War 210
    Fumbling Toward Conflict 211

THE STRANGE WAR OF 1812 213
    Fighting the British 213
    Hartford Convention: The Demise of the
    Federalists 214

CONCLUSION: THE "SECOND WAR OF
INDEPENDENCE" 216

    ▼ **Study Resources 216**
        TIMELINE
        CHAPTER REVIEW
        KEY TERM QUESTIONS

CHAPTER 9

NATION BUILDING AND NATIONALISM,
1815–1825 220
    A Revolutionary War Hero Revisits America in 1824 221

EXPANSION AND MIGRATION 222
    Extending the Boundaries 223
    Native American Societies Under
    Pressure 225

TRANSPORTATION AND THE MARKET ECONOMY 228
    Roads and Steamboats 228
    Emergence of a Market Economy 230
    Early Industrialism 232

THE POLITICS OF NATION BUILDING AFTER THE WAR
OF 1812 234
    The Missouri Compromise 235
    Postwar Nationalism and the
    Supreme Court 237
    Nationalism in Foreign Policy: The Monroe
    Doctrine 239

CONCLUSION: THE END OF THE ERA OF GOOD
FEELING 241

    ▼ **Study Resources 241**
        TIMELINE
        CHAPTER REVIEW
        KEY TERM QUESTIONS

CHAPTER 10

THE TRIUMPH OF WHITE MEN'S
DEMOCRACY, 1824–1840 244
    Democratic Space: The New Hotels 245

DEMOCRACY IN THEORY AND PRACTICE 247
    Democratic Culture 247
    Democratic Political Institutions 249
    Economic Issues 250

JACKSON AND THE POLITICS
OF DEMOCRACY 251
    Jackson Comes to Power 251
    Indian Removal 254
    The Nullification Crisis 257

THE BANK WAR AND THE
SECOND-PARTY SYSTEM 259
    The Bank Veto and the Election of 1832 259
    Killing the Bank 260
    The Emergence of the Whigs 261

HEYDAY OF THE SECOND-PARTY SYSTEM 263

CONCLUSION: TOCQUEVILLE'S WISDOM 265

    ▼ **Study Resources 265**
        TIMELINE
        CHAPTER REVIEW
        KEY TERM QUESTIONS

CHAPTER 11

SLAVES AND MASTERS, 1793–1861 268
    Nat Turner's Rebellion: A Turning Point
    in the Slave South 269

THE WORLD OF SOUTHERN BLACKS 270
    Slaves' Daily Life and Labor 271
    Slave Families, Kinship, and Community 272
    Resistance and Rebellion 273
    Free Blacks in the Old South 275

WHITE SOCIETY IN THE ANTEBELLUM SOUTH 276
    The Planters' World 277
    Planters, Racism, and Paternalism 278
    Small Slaveholders 280
    Yeoman Farmers 280
    A Closed Mind and a Closed Society 282

SLAVERY AND THE SOUTHERN ECONOMY 284
    The Internal Slave Trade 284
    The Rise of the Cotton Kingdom 285

CONCLUSION: WORLDS IN CONFLICT 287

    ▼ **Study Resources 288**
        TIMELINE
        CHAPTER REVIEW
        KEY TERM QUESTIONS

CHAPTER 12

THE PURSUIT OF PERFECTION, 1800–1861   290

Redeeming the Middle Class   291

THE RISE OF EVANGELICALISM   292
- The Second Great Awakening   292
- From Revivalism to Reform   294

DOMESTICITY AND CHANGES IN THE AMERICAN FAMILY   297
- The Cult of Domesticity   297
- The Discovery of Childhood   299
- The Extension of Education   300

REFORM TURNS RADICAL   302
- The Rise of Radical Abolitionism   303
- Black Abolitionists   305
- From Abolitionism to Women's Rights   307

CONCLUSION: COUNTERPOINT ON REFORM   308

▼ **Study Resources   309**
- TIMELINE
- CHAPTER REVIEW
- KEY TERM QUESTIONS

CHAPTER 13

AN AGE OF EXPANSIONISM, 1830–1861   312

The Spirit of Young America   313

TEXAS, MANIFEST DESTINY, AND THE MEXICAN-AMERICAN WAR   315
- The Texas Revolution   315
- The Republic of Texas   316
- The Annexation of Texas   318
- The Doctrine of Manifest Destiny   320
- War with Mexico   320
- Settlement of the Mexican-American War   321

INTERNAL EXPANSIONISM AND THE INDUSTRIAL REVOLUTION   324
- The Triumph of the Railroad   324
- The Industrial Revolution Takes Off   325
- Mass Immigration Begins   328
- The New Working Class   330

CONCLUSION: THE COSTS OF EXPANSION   331

▼ **Study Resources   331**
- TIMELINE
- CHAPTER REVIEW
- KEY TERM QUESTIONS

CHAPTER 14

THE SECTIONAL CRISIS, 1846–1861   334

Brooks Assaults Sumner in Congress   335

THE COMPROMISE OF 1850   336
- The Problem of Slavery in the Mexican Cession   336
- The Wilmot Proviso Launches the Free-Soil Movement   337
- Forging a Compromise   338

POLITICAL UPHEAVAL, 1852–1856   341
- The Party System in Crisis   342
- The Kansas-Nebraska Act Raises a Storm   343
- Kansas and the Rise of the Republicans   345
- Sectional Division in the Election of 1856   346

THE HOUSE DIVIDED, 1857–1860   347
- Cultural Sectionalism   347
- The Dred Scott Case   348
- Debating the Morality of Slavery   349
- The Election of 1860   351

CONCLUSION: EXPLAINING THE CRISIS   353

▼ **Study Resources   355**
- TIMELINE
- CHAPTER REVIEW
- KEY TERM QUESTIONS

CHAPTER 15

SECESSION AND THE CIVIL WAR, 1860–1865   358

The Emergence of Lincoln   359

THE STORM GATHERS   361
- The Deep South Secedes   361
- The Failure of Compromise   362
- And the War Came   364

ADJUSTING TO TOTAL WAR   367
- Mobilizing the Home Fronts   367
- Political Leadership: Northern Success and Southern Failure   368
- Early Campaigns and Battles   370

FIGHT TO THE FINISH   371
- The Coming of Emancipation   372
- African Americans and the War   374
- The Tide Turns   375
- Last Stages of the Conflict   377

EFFECTS OF THE WAR 380

CONCLUSION: AN ORGANIZATIONAL
REVOLUTION 382

▼ **Study Resources 383**

TIMELINE

CHAPTER REVIEW

KEY TERM QUESTIONS

CHAPTER 16

THE AGONY OF RECONSTRUCTION, 1863–1877 386

Robert Smalls and Black Politicians during Reconstruction 387

THE PRESIDENT VERSUS CONGRESS 389

Wartime Reconstruction 389

Andrew Johnson at the Helm 390

Congress Takes the Initiative 392

Congressional Reconstruction
Plan Enacted 394

The Impeachment Crisis 396

RECONSTRUCTING SOUTHERN SOCIETY 397

Reorganizing Land and Labor 398

Black Codes: A New Name for Slavery? 400

Republican Rule in the South 401

Claiming Public and Private Rights 404

RETREAT FROM RECONSTRUCTION 405

Final Efforts of Reconstruction 405

A Reign of Terror Against Blacks 407

REUNION AND THE NEW SOUTH 409

The Compromise of 1877 409

"Redeeming" a New South 410

The Rise of Jim Crow 411

CONCLUSION: HENRY MCNEAL TURNER AND THE
"UNFINISHED REVOLUTION" 412

▼ **Study Resources 414**

TIMELINE

CHAPTER REVIEW

KEY TERM QUESTIONS

Appendix A-1
The Declaration of Independence A-3
The Articles of Confederation A-5
The Constitution of the
United States of America A-9
Amendments to the Constitution A-15
Presidential Elections A-19
Presidents and Vice Presidents A-24

Glossary G-1

Credits C-1

Index I-1

Maps, Figures, and Tables

MAPS

Page

1.1 Routes of the First Americans 6
1.2 The First Americans: Location of Major Indian Groups and Culture Areas in the 1600s 8
1.3 Trade Routes in Africa 15
1.4 Voyages of European Exploration 20
2.1 Chesapeake Colonies, 1640 39
2.2 New England Colonies, 1650 47
2.3 Middle Colonies, 1685 49
2.4 The Carolinas and Georgia 54
3.1 Origins and Destinations of African Slaves, 1619–1760 71
4.1 Distribution of European and African Immigrants in the Thirteen Colonies 86
4.2 The Spanish Borderlands, ca. 1770 89
4.3 The Great Wagon Road 95
4.4 North America, 1750 103
4.5 The Seven Years' War, 1756–1763 Major battle sites 105
4.6 North America After 1763 106
5.1 Colonial Products and Trade 120
5.2 The American Revolution, 1775–1781 131
5.2 Spain entered the Revolutionary war as an ally of France in 1779 133
6.1 Northwest Territory 152
6.2 Western Land 154
6.3 Ratification of the Constitution 164
7.1 Conquest of the West 181
8.1 The Louisiana Purchase and the Route of Lewis and Clark 204
8.2 The War of 1812 213
9.1 The Missouri Compromise, 1820–1821 236
10.1 Election of 1828 254
10.2 Indian Removal 257
10.3 Election of 1840 263
13.1 Territorial Expansion by the Mid-Nineteenth Century 315
13.2 Major Battles of the Texas Revolution 317
13.3 The Mexican-American War 323
13.4 Railroads, 1850 and 1860 325
14.1 The Compromise of 1850 340
14.2 The Kansas-Nebraska Act of 1854 344
14.3 Election of 1860 353
15.1 Secession 365
15.2 Civil War, 1861–1865 379
16.1 Reconstruction 395
16.2 Election of 1876 409

FIGURES

11.1 Cotton Exports as a Percentage of All U.S. Exports, 1800–1860 287
13.1 Immigration to the United States, 1820–1860 328
15.1 Resources of the Union and Confederacy, 1861 367
15.2 Casualties of War 376

TABLES

1.1 New Opportunities, New Threats: The Columbian Exchange 13
2.1 England's Principal Mainland Colonies 56
4.1 A Century of Conflict: Major Wars, 1689–1763 101
5.1 Chronicle of Colonial-British Tension 127
6.1 Revolution or Reform? The Articles of Confederation and the Constitution Compared 162
7.1 The Election of 1796 184
7.2 The Election of 1800 190
8.1 The Election of 1804 205
8.2 The Election of 1808 211
8.3 The Election of 1812 212
10.1 The Election of 1824 252
10.2 The Election of 1832 259
10.3 The Election of 1836 262
11.1 U.S. Slave Population, 1820 and 1860 286
13.1 The Liberty Party Swings an Election 319
13.2 The Election of 1844 319
13.3 The Age of Practical Invention 327
14.1 The Election of 1848 338
14.2 The Election of 1852 343
14.3 The Election of 1856 347
15.1 The Election of 1864 378
16.1 Reconstruction Amendments, 1865–1870 394

New to this Edition

■ **Better Integration with MyHistoryLab** This edition is tied more closely to *My-HistoryLab* than ever before. *MyHistoryLab* icons appear throughout the text, connecting the main narrative to a strong array of *MyHistoryLab* resources, including primary source documents, analytical video segments, interactive maps, and more. A new *MyHistoryLab Connections* feature at the end of each chapter prompts students to follow the Study Plan for the chapter. Central to the new release of *MyHistoryLab*, the Study Plan guides students through activities that develop higher order thinking.

■ **New Format** The Second Edition appears in a new compact format that is more affordable and easier for students to carry and handle.

■ **New Map Program** Every map in the Second Edition has been redrawn for greater clarity and visual impact.

■ **New Key Term Questions** Building on the innovative instructional design of its predecessor, the Second Edition now treats the key terms for each chapter in a unique way. A list of *Key Term Questions* appears at the end of each chapter, placing each key term in the context of a probing question. These encourage students to think critically about the term, rather than simply memorize it. Page references connect the term to where it is first discussed in the text.

■ **Improved Narrative** The narrative has been extensively edited and rewritten to bring the story of American history into sharper focus. For example, all maps, figures, and tables are now numbered for easier reference and to integrate them more closely to the text. Content has been added or refined in every chapter. For instance, Chapter 1 now features a new discussion and table about the Columbian Exchange, and Chapter 2 discusses the founding of the colonies of New Jersey, Delaware, New Hampshire, and North Carolina. Other substantive changes are described below.

■ **Greater Emphasis on Native Americans** The coverage of Native Americans has been increased throughout the text. New sections discuss the diverse life-ways of native peoples in North America before the arrival of the Europeans (Chapter 1); the role of Native Americans in the American Revolution (Chapter 5); and the infamous Trail of Tears in the 1830s (Chapter 10).

■ **Greater Emphasis on the Spanish** The discussion of the Spanish role in the American Story has been enhanced with new coverage of Spanish colonization and Spanish interaction with the Native Americans (Chapters 1 and 4), and Spain's role in the American Revolution (Chapter 5).

■ **Greater Emphasis on African Americans** The history of African Americans has been expanded with new graphics in Chapter 11.

A Note to my Fellow Teachers

From H. W. Brands

I've been teaching American history for thirty years now (I started young—really), and in that time I've noticed something that almost certainly has occurred to many of you: that our students come to our classrooms with increasingly varied backgrounds. Some students are better prepared than ever, having taken advanced placement courses and acquired a solid grounding in historical facts, interpretations, and methods. Other students arrive less well prepared. Many of these are international students; some are students for whom English is a second or third language. Some of these, and some others, simply never took American history in high school. Some, finally, just didn't do well in the history courses they did take.

Different students require different methods of teaching, including different textbooks. Students well versed in American history do best with a book that presupposes their preparation and takes them beyond it. Students for whom the subject is new or otherwise challenging are more likely to succeed with a book that is more selective in its coverage, that focuses on essential themes, and that offers features designed to facilitate the learning process. Any textbook can be intimidating, as even my best students have reminded me over the years. The hundreds of pages and thousands of facts can put anyone off. For that reason, whatever reduces the intimidation factor can help students succeed.

This is the philosophy behind *American Stories: A History of the United States*. A single purpose has motivated the creation of this book: to enhance the accessibility of American history and thereby increase students' chances of success. This goal is what brought me to the classroom, it's what keeps me there, and it's one I think I share with you. If *American Stories: A History of the United States* contributes to achieving this goal, we all—teachers and students—will be the winners.

APPROACH AND THEMES

The most frequent complaint I get from students regarding history textbooks is that the mass of information is overwhelming. There are too many facts and ideas, and it is difficult to determine what to focus on. Many students need help pulling the key concepts from the narrative. This complaint provided the starting point for *American Stories*, which differs from standard textbooks in two fundamental respects.

First, we reduced the number of topics covered, retaining the essential elements of the American story while eliminating others. We surveyed over five hundred instructors from across the country to find out what topics were most commonly covered in a typical survey classroom. Every subject in the U.S. history course was rated according to what respondents thought must be covered. Once we received the results, we culled the most commonly taught topics and selected them for inclusion in *American Stories*. Making choices wasn't easy; at times it was painful. But we considered it necessary. Some topics are simply not taught as often as others, and our job as historians is to let students know what they need to know.

Second, we integrated a variety of study aids into the text. These were originally developed with the assistance of Dr. Kathleen T. McWhorter and Debby Kalk. Kathleen is a professor and author with more than 40 years of experience at both two- and four-year colleges, including Niagara Community College, and specializes in developmental reading, writing, composition, and study skills. Debby is an instructional designer and author with more than 20 years of experience producing materials for educational publishers, corporate training, and public education and who speaks frequently on instructional design at workshops and conferences. With the help of both Kathleen and Debby, *American Stories* is the first college-level U.S. history survey completely designed to meet the needs of the instructor and the student.

Beyond this, *American Stories* places great emphasis on a compelling narrative. We—I and my fellow authors—have used significant incidents and episodes to reflect the dilemmas, the choices, and the decisions made by the American people as well as by their leaders. Our story of the American past includes the major events that have shaped the nation—the wars fought, the presidents elected, the legislation enacted, the treaties signed—but it doesn't stop there. We examine the ways in which the big events influenced the lives of ordinary people. How did the American Revolution alter the fortunes and prospects of men, women, and children around the country? What was it like for blacks and whites to live in a plantation society? How did the shift from an agrarian to an industrial economy transform daily life? What impact did technology, in such forms as the automobile and computer, have on patterns of living in the twentieth century?

Each chapter begins with a vignette that launches the narrative of that chapter and identifies its themes. Some of the vignettes have special meaning for the authors. The account in Chapter 18 of the 1876 Centennial Exposition in Philadelphia, for example, recalls to my mind the 1962 World's Fair in Seattle. I and my brother and sisters traveled by train with my grandfather from our home in Portland to Seattle to see the fair. I remember riding the Monorail and ascending the Space Needle; these two icons of the fair were supposed to point the way to the future of urban life. Things didn't work out quite that way, just as the forecasts from the 1876 exposition missed the mark in some respects. But the excitement the world's fair brought to my eight-year-old life was similar to that experienced by the children who attended the exposition.

The vignette that opens Chapter 26, on the Great Depression of the 1930s, reminds me of the stories my father used to tell about his experiences during that trying decade. His family wasn't nearly as hard hit as many in the 1930s; like Pauline Kael, he was a college student. And like her, he saw how hard it was for many of his classmates to stay in school. He himself was always working at odd jobs, trying to make ends meet. Times were hard, yet he learned the value of a dollar—something he impressed on me as I was growing up.

By these means and others, I and my fellow authors have attempted to bring history to life for students. We believe that while history rarely repeats itself, the story of the American past is profoundly relevant to the problems and challenges facing the nation today.

PEDAGOGICAL FEATURES

The pedagogical elements in *American Stories* have been carefully constructed to be accessible to students and to support a better, deeper understanding of U.S. history. These elements fall into two categories, Textual Pedagogy that appears throughout the main body of each chapter, and Study Resources collected at the ends of chapters.

■ **Textual Pedagogy** Each chapter follows a consistent pedagogy that maximizes student learning. *Spotlight Questions* in the chapter openers preview the main idea for each major section and provide a framework for the entire chapter. As a reminder to students, these questions are repeated in the margins after each major section. *Quick Check Questions* follow each subsection for immediate reinforcement of key ideas presented in each section. If students are unable to answer these questions, they know to go back and reread the subsection for the main idea. *Key Terms* are highlighted throughout each chapter and are defined in the text's glossary. *MyHistoryLab Icons* appear in the margins, identifying additional resources that students may find in the program. (See below for more on *MyHistoryLab*.)

■ **Study Resources** Each chapter concludes with a series of study resources. A chapter *Timeline* surveys the chronology of key events, with page references for easy look-up of information. The *Chapter Review* connects back to the Spotlight Questions, providing brief answers that summarize the main points of each section. *Key Term Questions* place each key term in the context of a probing question, encouraging students to think critically about the term, rather than simply memorizing it. Here too, page references support easy look-up of information. A *MyHistoryLab Connections* feature caps off the study resources for each chapter. These provide questions for analysis drawn from the chapter Study Plan in *MyHistoryLab*.

A FINAL WORD

My fellow authors and I, with the assistance of the professionals at Pearson, have devoted a great deal of effort to making a textbook of which we are all very proud. Our goal with *American Stories* is to convey our excitement for history to our students in the most accessible manner possible. We've done what we can toward this goal, but we realize that our success depends on you, the classroom instructors. Our job is to make your job easier. All of us—authors and instructors—are in this together. So keep up the good work, and thanks!

A Note to Students: Tips for Studying History

Every autumn for many years I have taught an introductory course in American history. Over that time I've come to appreciate the value of devoting the first class session to the fundamentals of studying and learning history. Every subject—mathematics, chemistry, psychology, English, art—has its peculiarities; each reveals itself to students in particular ways. And different students have different learning styles. But the experiences of the many students I've taught have convinced me that certain general techniques produce good results.

I always tell students that these techniques aren't the only way to study; they may have their own methods. But I also tell them that these techniques have worked for a lot of students in the past, and might work for them. Here they are:

1. **History is a *story*,** not just an assortment of facts. The connections are critical. How do the events and people you are reading or hearing about relate to one another? This is what historians want to know, and what distinguishes them from chroniclers, who simply list events and leave it at that.
   Therefore:
   Find the story line, the plot. Identify the main characters, the turning points. How did the story—or the part of the story you are studying in a given chapter or lecture—turn out? Why did it turn out that way and not some other?

2. **Dates matter, but order matters more.** Students often get the idea that history is all about dates. It's not. It's about what caused what (as in a story: see Rule 1 above). Dates are useful only in that they help you remember what happened before what else. This is crucial, because the thing that came first might have caused, or at least influenced, the thing that came later.
   Therefore:
   Concentrate on the order of events. If you do, the dates will fall into place by themselves.

3. **History takes time**—to happen, and to learn. History is nothing more or less than how people deal with each other (again, it's a story). But like any richly detailed story, it can take time to absorb.
   Therefore:
   Spread out your studying. If you have three hours of reading to do, do it over three days for an hour a day. If you have a test coming up, give yourself two weeks to study, allocating a half hour each day. You'll learn more easily; you'll retain more. And you'll have a better chance to enjoy the story.

4. **History's stories are both spoken and written.** That's why most classes involve both lectures and readings. In the typical syllabus, readings—chapters of the text, supplementary documents and articles—are keyed to the lectures, with the readings chosen to complement the lectures, and vice versa.
   Therefore:

Read the assigned materials before the corresponding lectures. It's tempting not to—to let the reading slide. But resist the temptation. Advance reading makes the lectures far more understandable—and far more enjoyable.

5. **Less is more,** at least in note-taking. Not every word in the text or other reading is equally important; not every word uttered by your instructor in a lecture has equal value. The point of notes is to distill a chapter or a lecture into a smaller, more manageable size.

Therefore:

Hit the high points. Focus on where the text and lecture overlap. Write down key phrases and words; don't write complete sentences. And if you are using a highlighter on a book, be sparing. If yellow (or pink or whatever color you prefer) starts to become the prevailing motif of your pages, you've gone too far.

6. **History is a twice-told tale.** History is both what happened and how we've remembered what happened. Think of your first exposure to a particular historical topic as history *happening*, and your second exposure as history *being remembered*. An awareness of both is necessary to making the history stick in your head.

Therefore:

Take a rest after reading a chapter or attending a lecture. **Then go back and review.** Your class notes should not be comprehensive (see Rule 5), but as you go back over them, you will remember details that will help you fill out your notes. While you are reviewing a chapter, ask yourself what your notes on the chapter mean, and why you highlighted this particular phrase or that.

To summarize, when approaching a history course:

- **Find the story line.**
- **Concentrate on the order of events.**
- **Spread out your studying.**
- **Read the assignments before the lectures.**
- **Hit the high points in taking notes.**
- **Take a rest, then review.**

A final suggestion: Allow enough time for this course so you aren't rushed. If you give yourself time to get into the story, you'll come to enjoy it. And what you enjoy, you'll remember.

Best wishes,

H. W. Brands

Supplements for Qualified College Adopters	Supplements for Students
MyHistoryLab	**My**HistoryLab
MyHistoryLab (www.myhistorylab.com) The moment you know Educators know it. Students know it. It's that inspired moment when something that was difficult to understand suddenly makes perfect sense. Our MyLab products have been designed and refined with a single purpose in mind: to help educators create that moment of understanding with their students.	**MyHistoryLab (www.myhistorylab.com) The moment you know** Educators know it. Students know it. It's that inspired moment when something that was difficult to understand suddenly makes perfect sense. Our MyLab products have been designed and refined with a single purpose in mind: to help educators create that moment of understanding with their students.
Instructor's Resource Manual with Test Bank Available at the Instructor's Resource Center, at **www.pearsonhighered.com/irc**, the Instructor's Resource Manual with Test Bank contains chapter outlines, summaries, key points and vital concepts, and information on audio-visual resources that can be used in developing and preparing lecture presentations. The Test Bank includes multiple choice questions and essay questions and is text specific.	**CourseSmart** www.coursemart.com CourseSmart eTextbooks offer the same content as the printed text in a convenient online format—with highlighting, online search, and printing capabilities. You **save 60% over the list price** of the traditional book.
PowerPoint Presentation Available at the Instructor's Resource Center, at **www.pearsonhighered.com/irc**, the PowerPoints contain chapter outlines and full-color images of maps and arts. They are text specific and available for download.	**Books à la Carte** Books à la Carte editions feature the exact same content as the traditional printed text in a convenient, three-hole-punched, loose-leaf version at a discounted price—allowing you to take only what you need to class. You'll **save 35% over the net price** of the traditional book. V1 - **ISBN: 0205206425; ISBN-13: 9780205206421; V2 - ISBN: 020520645X; ISBN-13: 9780205206452**
MyTest Available at **www.pearsonmytest.com**, MyTest is a powerful assessment generation program that helps instructors easily create and print quizzes and exams. Questions and tests can be authored online, allowing instructors ultimate flexibility and the ability to efficiently manage assessments anytime, anywhere! Instructors can easily access existing questions and edit, create, and store using simple drag-and-drop and Word-like controls.	**Library of American Biography** Series **www.pearsonhighered.com/educator/series/Library-of-American-Biography/10493.page** Pearson's renowned series of biographies spotlighting figures who had a significant impact on American history. Included in the series are Edmund Morgan's *The Puritan Dilemma: The Story of John Winthrop,* B. Davis Edmund's *Tecumseh and the Quest for Indian Leadership,* J. William T. Youngs, *Eleanor Roosevelt: A Personal and Public Life,* John R. M. Wilson's *Jackie Robinson and the American Dilemma* and Sandra Opdycke's *Jane Addams and her Vision for America.*

Supplements for Qualified College Adopters	Supplements for Students
Retreiving the American Past Available through the Pearson Custom Library (**www.pearsoncustom.com**, keyword search | rtap), the *Retrieving the American Past* (RTAP) program lets you create a textbook or reader that meets your needs and the needs of your course. RTAP gives you the freedom and flexibility to add chapters from several best-selling Pearson textbooks, in addition to *The American Nation, 14/e*, and/or 100 topical reading units written by the History Department of Ohio State University, all under one cover. Choose the content you want to teach in depth, in the sequence you want, at the price you want your students to pay.	**Penguin Valuepacks www.pearsonhighered.com/penguin** A variety of Penguin-Putnam texts is available at discounted prices when bundled with *American Stories, 2/e*. Texts include Benjamin Franklin's *Autobiography and Other Writings*, Nathaniel Hawthorne's *The Scarlet Letter*, Thomas Jefferson's *Notes on the State of Virginia*, and George Orwell's *1984*.
	A Short Guide to Writing About History, 7/e Written by Richard Marius, late of Harvard University, and Melvin E. Page, Eastern Tennessee State University, this engaging and practical text helps students get beyond merely compiling dates and facts. Covering both brief essays and the documented resource paper, the text explores the writing and researching processes, identifies different modes of historical writing, including argument, and concludes with guidelines for improving style. **ISBN-10: 0205118607; ISBN-13: 9780205118601**
	Longman American History Atlas This full-color historical atlas designed especially for college students is a valuable reference tool and visual guide to American history. This atlas includes maps covering the scope of American history from the lives of the Native Americans to the 1990s. Produced by a renowned cartographic firm and a team of respected historians, the Longman American History Atlas will enhance any American history survey course. **ISBN: 0321004868; ISBN-13: 9780321004864**

MyHistoryLab (www.myhistorylab.com)

The Moment You Know

Educators know it. Students know it. It's that inspired moment when something that was difficult to understand suddenly makes perfect sense. MyHistoryLab has been designed and refined with a single purpose in mind: to help history teachers create that moment of understanding with their students.

Features of MyHistoryLab

MyHistoryLab provides **engaging experiences** that personalize, stimulate, and measure learning for each student.

- *Closer Look tours*—walk students through a variety of images, maps, and primary sources in detail, helping them to uncover their meaning and understand their context.
- **A History Bookshelf**—enables students to read, download, or print up to 100 of the most commonly assigned history works, like Thomas Paine's, *Common Sense*, Booker T. Washington's, *Up From Slavery*, and Andrew Carnegie's, *Autobiography*.
- **The Pearson eText**— lets students access their textbook anytime, anywhere, and any way they want—including listening online or downloading to their iPad.
- **A personalized study plan** for each student, based on a chapter Pre-Test, arranges content from less complex thinking—like remembering basic facts—to more complex critical thinking—like understanding connections and analyzing the past. This layered approach promotes better critical-thinking skills, and helps students succeed in the course and beyond.
- **Assessment** tied to every chapter enables both instructors and students to track progress and get immediate feedback. With results flowing into a powerful gradebook, the assessment program helps instructors identify student challenges early—and find the best resources with which to help students.
- **An assignment calendar** allows instructors to assign graded activities, with specific deadlines, and measure student progress.
- *ClassPrep* collects the very best class presentation resources in one convenient online destination, so instructors can keep students engaged throughout every class.
- **Audio Files**—Full audio of the entire text is included to suit the varied learning styles of today's students. In addition there are audio clips of speeches, readings, and music that provide another engaging way to experience history.
- **Text and Visual Documents**—Over 1,500 primary source documents, images, and maps are available organized by chapter in the text. Primary source documents are also available in

the MyHistoryLibrary and can be searched by author, title, theme, and topic. Many of these documents include critical thinking questions.

■ **Lecture and Archival Videos**—Lectures by leading scholars on provocative topics give students a critical look at key points in history. Videos of speeches, news footage, key historical events, and other archival video take students back to the moment in history.

■ **MySearchLab**—This website provides students access to a number of reliable sources for online research, as well as clear guidance on the research and writing process.

■ **Gradebook**—Students can follow their own progress and instructors can monitor the work of the entire class. Automated grading of quizzes and assignments helps both instructors and students save time and monitor their results throughout the course.

NEW In-text References to MyHistoryLab Resources

Read, View, See, Watch, Hear, Study, and Review Icons integrated in the text connect resources on MyHistoryLab to specific topics within the chapters. The icons are not exhaustive; many more resources are available than those highlighted in the book, but the icons draw attention to some of the most high-interest resources available on MyHistoryLab.

Read the **Document** on **myhistorylab.com** Points students to primary and secondary source documents related to the chapter.

View the **Image** on **myhistorylab.com** Identifies primary and secondary source images, including photographs, fine art, and artifacts to provide students with a visual perspective on history.

View the **Map** on **myhistorylab.com** Directs students to atlas and interactive maps; these present both broad overviews and detailed examinations of historical developments.

Watch the **Video** on **myhistorylab.com** Notes pertinent archival videos and videos of Pearson History authors that probe various topics.

Listen to the **Audio File** on **myhistorylab.com** Marks audio clips from historically significant songs and speeches that enrich students' engagement with history.

View the **Closer Look** on **myhistorylab.com** Alerts students to study resources for each chapter of the textbook available online through www.myhistorylab.com. These resources include practice tests and flashcards.

NEW MyHistoryLab Connections

At the end of each chapter a new feature called *MyHistoryLab Connections* prompts students to follow the Study Plan for the chapter, and provides a list of the resources that are marked with icons in the text.

Acknowledgments

The authors acknowledge with special gratitude the contribution of Kathleen T. McWhorter and Debby Kalk for their work in developing a sound pedagogical plan. We are also most grateful to our consultants and reviewers whose thoughtful and constructive work contributed greatly to this edition. Their many helpful suggestions led to significant improvements in the final product.

Jeffrey Adler, *University of Florida*; Edward Andrews, *University of New Hampshire*; Guy Aronoff, *California State University–Channel Islands*; Andrew Bacha, *Harrisburg Area Community College*; Frank M. Baglione, *Tallahassee Community College*; John Baick, *Western New England College*; Brett Barker, *University of Wisconsin–Marathon County*; Jonathan Beagle, *Western New England College*; Marjorie Berman, *Red Rocks Community College*; David Darryl Bibb, *University of Great Falls*; Brian Black, *Penn State Altoona*; Deborah Blackwell, *Texas A&M International University*; Marcia Schmidt Blaine, *Plymouth State University*; Chuck Boening, *Shelton State Community College*; Edward Bond, *Alabama A&M University*; Barbara Booth, *Santa Ana College*; Wesley Borucki, *Palm Beach Atlantic University*; Jeff Bremer, *Stephen F. Austin State University*; Jeff Broadwater, *Barton College*; Robert E. Brown, *Tunxis Community College*; John Burch, *Campbellsville University*; J. Michael Butler, *South Georgia College*; Don Butts, *Gordon College*; Shvonnie R. Caffey, *Bishop State Community College*; Jeff Carlisle, *Oklahoma City Community College*; Roger Carpenter, *University of Louisiana, Monroe*; Charles L. Cohen, *University of Wisconsin–Madison*; John Condon, *Merrimack College*; P. Scott Corbett, *Ventura College*; Robert Cray, *Montclair State University*; Andria Crosson, *University of Texas at San Antonio*; Thomas A. DeBlack, *Arkansas Tech University*; Andrea DeKoter, *State University of New York at Cortland*; Terrence Delaney, *Three Rivers Community College*; Rick Dodgson, *Lakeland College*; Dean Dohrman, *University of Central Missouri*; Gary Donato, *Massachusetts Bay Community College*; Lisa Linquist Dorr, *University of Alabama*; Shawn Dry, *Oakland Community College*; David Dzurec, *University of Scranton*; Scotty Edler, *North Central Texas College*; Damon Eubank, *Campbellsville University*; Gabrielle Everett, *Jefferson College*; Richard M. Filipink, *Western Illinois University*; Daniel Finn, *Seminole State College*; Michael Fitzgerald, *Franciscan University*; Amy Forss, *Metropolitan Community College*; Arthur Friedman, *Montclair State University*; Hal M. Friedman, *Henry Ford Community College*; Michael Gabriel, *Kutztown University*; Jeff Gall, *Truman State University;*George Gerdow, *Northeastern Illinois University*; Michael Gherke, *Glenville State College*; John Glen, *St. Louis Community College, Wildwood Campus*; Janet Golden, *Rutgers University*; Susan Gonda, *Grossmont College*; Larry Goodrich, *Northwest Vista College*; Kathleen Gorman, *Minnesota State University, Mankato*; Matthew Greider, *Lake Land College*; Aldo Garcia Guevara, *Worcester State College*; Edward Gutierrez, *University of Hartford*; Karen Hagan, *The Victoria College*; Dixie Ray Haggard, *Valdosta State University*; Charlotte Haller, *Worcester State College*; Gregory M. Havrilcsak, *The University of Michigan–Flint*; David M. Head, *John Tyler Community College*; Matthew Hiner, *Lakeland Community College*; Andrew G. Hollinger, *Tarrant County College*; Charles W. Hope, *Tarrant County College–Southeast Campus*; Wallace H. Hutcheon, *Northern Virginia Community College*; Ross Huxoll, *University of Nebraska–Kearney*; Diane B. Jackson, *Los Angeles Trade Technical College*; Thomas Jodziewicz, *University of Dallas*; Andrew Johns, *Brigham Young University*; Juli A. Jones, *San Diego Mesa*

College; Russell Jones, *Eastern Michigan University*; Sandra Jowers-Barber, *University of the District of Columbia*; Mark S. Joy, *Jamestown College*; Jennifer Fish Kashay, *Colorado State University*; John S. Kemp, *Truckee Meadows Community College*; Don Knox, *Wayland Baptist University*; Raymond Krohn, *University of Northern Colorado*; Melissa LaPrelle, *Collin County Community College*; William P. Leeman, *Providence College*; Daniel Lewis, *California State Polytechnic University, Pomona*; Stephen Lowe, *Olivet Nazarene University*; John Maddox, *Los Angeles Valley Community College*; Robert W. Malick, *Harrisburg Area Community College*; Evelyn DeLong Mangie, *University of South Florida*; Edwin Martini, *Western Michigan University*; Louis McDermott, *Solano Community College*; Brian McKnight, *Angelo State University*; Peter C. Messer, *Mississippi State University*; Michael Messner, *Skyline College*; Mary M. McClendon, *Chipola College*; Greg Miller, *Hillsborough Community College*; Sarah E. Miller, *University of South Carolina–Salkehatchie*; Russell Mitchell, *Tarrant County College Southeast*; Caryn Neumann, *Miami University of Ohio*; Dave O'Grady, *University of Southern Indiana*; Gary B. Ostrower, *Alfred University*; Edgar Pacas, *Pasadena City College*; Chris Padgett, *American River College*; David Parker, *Kennesaw State University*; Donald Parkerson, *East Carolina University*; Elaine Pascale, *Suffolk University*; Ronnie Peacock, *Metropolitan State College of Denver*; Katherine Pierce, *Sam Houston State University*; Jeffrey J. Pilz, *North Iowa Area Community College*; Ann Marie Plane, *University of California at Santa Barbara*; Brian K. Plummer, *Azusa Pacific University*; Charlotte Power, *Black River Technical College*; William Price, *North Country Community College*; Daniel Prosterman, *Salem College*; Steven Rauch, *Augusta State University*; David B. Raymond, *Northern Maine Community College*; Jonathan Rees, *Colorado State University, Pueblo*; Miriam Reumann, *The University of Rhode Island*; Paul Rorvig, *University of Central Missouri*; Rodney Ross, *Harrisburg Area Community College*; Tara Ross, *Onondaga Community College*; Mary Ellen Rowe, *University of Central Missouri*; Wendy Maier Sarti, *Oakton Community College*; John C. Savagian, *Alverno College*; Sandra Schackel, *Boise State University*; James Schick, *Pittsburg State University*; Don Schwegler, *SUNY New Paltz*; Earl A. Shoemaker, *University of Wisconsin–Eau Claire*; Terry L. Shoptaugh, *Minnesota State University Moorhead*; James Showalter, *Langston University*; Jeffrey Smith, *Lindenwood University*; Kris Smith, *Lindenwood University*; David L. Snead, *Liberty University*; Jean A. Stuntz, *West Texas A&M University*; James Taw, *Valdosta State University*; Jon Taylor, *University of Central Missouri*; Brad Tennant, *Presentation College*; James Treu, *North Central Missouri College*; John Turner, *University of Southern Alabama*; Marcus S. Turner, *San Jacinto College Central*; Jennifer Wallach, *University of North Texas*; Kenneth A. Watras, *Park University's College of Distance Learning*; Paul Weinstein, *The University of Akron Wayne College*; Pam West, *Jefferson State Community College*; Cheryl White, *Louisiana State University Shreveport*; Scott M. Williams, *Weatherford College*; David Williams, *Valdosta State University*; Larry C. Wilson, *San Jacinto College*; Julie Winch, *University of Massachusetts–Boston*; Deborah Wood, *SUNY Brockport*; Chad Wooley, *Tarrant County College*; Cristina Zaccarini, *Adelphi University*; Colleen Shaughnessy Zeena, *Endicott College*; and Patricia Zelman, *Tarleton State University*.

This book owes much to the many conscientious historians who reviewed previous editions of *America Past and Present* and offered valuable suggestions that led to many improvements in the text. We acknowledge with gratitude the contributions of the following:

Frank W. Abbott, *University of Houston*; Joseph L. Adams, *St. Louis Community College at Meramec*; Frank Alduino, *Anne Arundel Community College*; Kenneth G. Alfers, *Mountain View College*; Elizabeth Ansnes, *San Jose State University*; Thomas Archdeacon, *University of Wisconsin*; James Axtell, *College of William and Mary*; Kenneth R. Bain,

Northwestern University; James Banks, *Cuyahoga Community College;* Lois W. Banner, *Hamilton College;* Samantha Barbas, *Chapman University;* Donald Scott Barton, *East Central University;* James Baumgardner, *Carson-Newman College;* David Bernstein, *California State University, Long Beach;* Chad Berry, *Maryville College;* Joseph E. Bisson, *San Joaquin Delta College;* Kent Blaser, *Wayne State College;* Eric J. Bolsterli, *University of Texas at Arlington;* James D. Border, *Berkshire Community College;* Alexander O. Boulton, *Villa Julie College;* Mary C. Brennan, *Ohio State University;* Blanche Brick, *Blinn College;* Daniel Patrick Brown, *Moorpark College;* Thomas Camfield, *Sam Houston State University;* Clayborne Carson, *Stanford University;* Cynthia Carter, *Florida Community College at Jacksonville;* Kathleen S. Carter, *High Point University;* Raphael Cassimere, Jr., *University of New Orleans;* Katherine Chavigny, *Sweet Briar College;* Francis Coan, *Central Connecticut State University;* Charles L. Cohen, *University of Wisconsin;* Jerald Combs, *San Francisco State University;* John Cooper, *University of Wisconsin;* Yvonne Sutton Cornelius, *Nashville State Community College;* Nancy F. Cott, *Yale University;* Virginia Crane, *University of Wisconsin, Oshkosh;* Edward R. Crowther, *Adams State University;* James C. Curtis, *University of Delaware;* Roger P. Davis, *University of Nebraska at Kearney;* Cole Dawson, *Warner Pacific College;* James Denham, *Florida Southern College;* Patricia Norred Derr, *Kutztown University;* Bruce J. Dierenfield, *Canisius College;* Charles Douglass, *Florida Community College at Jacksonville;* Thomas Dublin, *State University of New York at Binghamton;* Perry R. Duis, *University of Illinois at Chicago;* Richard Ellis, *State University of New York at Buffalo;* John P. Farr, *Chattanooga State Technical Community College;* Kathleen Feely, *University of Redlands;* James E. Fell, Jr., *University of Colorado, Denver;* Eric Foner, *Columbia University;* Stephen Foster, *Northern Illinois University;* William W. Freehling, *Johns Hopkins University;* Fred E. Freidel, *Bellevue Community College;* Richard Frey, *Southern Oregon State College;* Jennifer Fry, *King's College;* Gary

W. Gallagher, *Pennsylvania State University;* Sara E. Gallaway, *Oxnard College;* Don R. Gerlach, *University of Akron;* August W. Giebelhaus, *Georgia Institute of Technology;* Louis S. Gomolak, *Southwest Texas State University;* Lewis L. Gould, *University of Texas;* Lawrence Grear, *Langston University;* Richard C. Haney, *University of Wisconsin, Whitewater;* George Harrison, *Jones County Junior College;* Edward F. Hass, *Wright State University;* Paul B. Hatley, *Rogers State University;* Sarah Heath, *Texas A&M University–Corpus Christi;* Tim Heinrichs, *Bellevue Community College;* Mary Ann Heiss, *Kent State University;* Kenneth E. Hendrickson, *Sam Houston State University;* Sondra Herman, *De Anza Community College;* Wallace Hettle, *University of Northern Iowa;* Anne Hickling, *San Jose City College;* James Hollingsworth, *Pasco-Hernando Community College;* Ranford Hopkins, *Moorpark College;* Brian Hosmer, *University of Delaware;* John R. Howe, *University of Minnesota;* Nathan I. Huggins, *Harvard University;* Susan Hult, *Houston Community College;* James A. Hurst, *Northwest Missouri State University;* Wallace S. Hutcheon, *Northern Virginia Community College;* Robert M. Ireland, *University of Kentucky;* Virginia G. Jelatis, *Western Illinois University;* Carol E. Jenson, *University of Wisconsin, La Crosse;* Ben Johnson, *Southern Arkansas University;* Juli A. Jones, *St. Charles County Community College;* Robert R. Jones, *University of Southwestern Louisiana;* Carol Keller, *San Antonio College;* John Kelley, *Shawnee State Community College;* Richard S. Kirkendall, *University of Washington;* I. E. Kirkpatrick, *Tyler Junior College;* Fred Koestler, *Tarleton State University;* Lawrence F. Kohl, *University of Alabama;* Elizabeth Kuebler-Wolf, *Indiana University–Purdue University Fort Wayne;* Steven Lawson, *Rutgers University;* Edward Lee, *Winthrop University;* Kathy Long, *Chattanooga State Technical Community College;* Henry Louis, *Kansas City Kansas Community College;* Warren Mackey, *Chattanooga State Technical Community College;* Thomas R. Mandeville, *Clinton Community College;* Karen Marcotte, *Palo Alto College;* Herbert F. Margulies, *University of Hawaii;* Myron Marty,

National Endowment for the Humanities; Robert C. McMath, Jr., *Georgia Institute of Technology;* T. Ronald Melton, *Brewton-Parker College;* James H. Merrell, *Vassar College;* Joseph C. Miller, *University of Virginia;* William G. Morris, *Midland College;* Harmon Mothershead, *Northwest Missouri State University;* Timothy Moy, *University of New Mexico;* Peter Murray, *Methodist College;* Rick Murray, *College of the Canyons;* John M. Murrin, *Princeton University;* John K. Nelson, *University of North Carolina;* Roger L. Nichols, *University of Arizona;* Elizabeth R. Osborne, *Indiana University–Purdue University at Indianapolis;* Elliot Pasternack, *Middlesex County College;* J'Nell L. Pate, *Tarrant County Junior College;* Michael Perman, *University of Illinois, Chicago;* Charles A. Pilant, *Cumberland College;* Carrie Pritchett, *Northeast Texas Community College;* Nora Ramirez, *San Antonio Community College;* Marlette Rebhorn, *Austin Community College;* Thomas S. Reid, *Valencia Community College;* Douglas W. Richmond, *University of Texas, Arlington;* Andrew W. Robertson, *Louisiana State University;* David Sandoval, *University of Southern Colorado;* Mark Schmellor, *Binghamton University;* Howard Schonberger, *University of Maine;* Ingrid Winther Scobie, *Texas Women's University;* Rebecca S. Shoemaker, *Indiana State University;* C. Edward Skeen, *University of Memphis;* Kathryn Kish Sklar, *State University of New York at Binghamton;* Allan Spetter, *Wright State University;* Ronald Spiller, *Edinboro University of Pennsylvania;* Cherry L. Spruill, *Indiana University–Purdue University at Indianapolis;* Mark J. Stegmaier, *Cameron University;* George G. Suggs, Jr., *Southeast Missouri State University;* H. Micheal Tarver, *McNeese State University;* Paul F. Taylor, *Augusta College;* Michael E. Thompson, *South Seattle Community College;* Pat Thompson, *University of Texas, San Antonio;* Stephen Tootle, *University of Northern Colorado;* George Torok, *El Paso Community College;* Clyde D. Tyson, *Niagara County Community College;* Nancy C. Unger, *San Francisco State University;* Richard Vanderpool, *Umpqua Community College;* Donna L. VanRaaphorst, *Cuyahoga Community College;* Russell Veeder, *Dickinson State University;* Daniel C. Vogt, *Jackson State University;* Sandra Wagner-Wright, *University of Hawaii at Hilo;* Forrest A. Walker, *Eastern New Mexico State University;* James P. Walsh, *Central Connecticut State University;* Ronald Walters, *Johns Hopkins University;* Stephen Warren, *Augustana College;* Stephen Webre, *Louisiana Tech University;* Marli Weiner, *University of Maine;* Frank Wetta, *Galveston Community College;* James C. Williams, *De Anza College;* James M. Woods, *Georgia Southern University;* David Yancey, *San Jose City College;* Rosemarie Zagarri, *Catholic University;* and Robert F. Zeidel, *University of Wisconsin, Stout*

The staff at Pearson continued its generous support and assistance for our efforts. We thank our Executive Editor Ed Parsons for his attention, support, and thoughtful guidance throughout this revision; Development Editor Gerald Lombardi, who helped us augment and enhance the appeal of the text; and Executive Marketing Manager Maureen Prado Roberts, who worked zealously to convey the message and vision of the authors to the Pearson sales force and to the marketplace. Production Manager Denise Forlow, Cover Design Manager/Cover Designer Maria Lange, and Lindsay Bethoney and the staff at PreMediaGlobal put the finishing touches on this new edition and deftly guided it through the many phases of production.

Finally, each author received aid and encouragement from many colleagues, friends, and family members. T. H. Breen thanks Strother Roberts for his splendid help with this edition. Hal Williams extends thanks to Carole S. Cohen, Jacqueline Bradley, and Susan Harper-Bisso for their help with revisions for this edition. Ariela Gross extends thanks to Riaz Tejani for invaluable help with this edition.

H. W. Brands
T. H. Breen
R. Hal Williams
Ariela J. Gross

About the **Authors**

H. W. Brands

H. W. Brands is the Dickson Allen Anderson Centennial Professor of History at the University of Texas at Austin. He is the author of numerous works of history and international affairs, including *The Devil We Knew: Americans and the Cold War* (1993), *Into the Labyrinth: The United States and the Middle East* (1994), *The Reckless Decade: America in the 1890s* (1995), *TR: The Last Romantic* (a biography of Theodore Roosevelt) (1997), *What America Owes the World: The Struggle for the Soul of Foreign Policy* (1998), *The First American: The Life and Times of Benjamin Franklin* (2000), *The Strange Death of American Liberalism* (2001), *The Age of Gold: The California Gold Rush and the New American Dream* (2002), *Woodrow Wilson* (2003), *Andrew Jackson* (2005), *Traitor to His Class: The Privileged Life and Radical Presidency of Franklin Delano Roosevelt* (2008), and *American Colossus: The Triumph of Capitalism, 1865–1900* (2010). His writing has received popular and critical acclaim; several of his books have been bestsellers, and *The First American* and *Traitor to His Class* were finalists for the Pulitzer Prize. He lectures frequently across North America and in Europe. His essays and reviews have appeared in the *New York Times*, the *Wall Street Journal*, the *Washington Post*, the *Los Angeles Times*, *Atlantic Monthly*, and elsewhere. He is a regular guest on radio and television, and has participated in several historical documentary films.

T. H. Breen

T. H. Breen is the Director of the Nicholas D. Chabraja Center for Historical Studies and William Smith Mason Professor of American History at Northwestern University. He received his Ph.D. from Yale University in 1968. He has taught at Northwestern since 1970. Breen's major books include *The Character of the Good Ruler: A Study of Puritan Political Ideas in New England* (1974); *Puritans and Adventurers: Change and Persistence in Early America* (1980); *Tobacco Culture: The Mentality of the Great Tidewater Planters on the Eve of Revolution* (1985); *Marketplace of Revolution: How Consumer Politics Shaped American Independence* (2004); and, with Stephen Innes of the University of Virginia, *"Myne Owne Ground": Race and Freedom on Virginia's Eastern Shore* (1980). His *Imagining the Past* (1989) won the 1990 Historic Preservation Book Award. In addition to receiving several awards for outstanding teaching at Northwestern, Breen has been the recipient of research grants from the American Council of Learned Societies, the Guggenheim Foundation, the Institute for Advanced Study (Princeton), the National Humanities Center, and the Huntington Library. He has served as the Fowler Hamilton Fellow at Christ Church, Oxford University (1987–1988), the Pitt Professor of American History and Institutions, Cambridge University (1990–1991), the Harmsworth Professor of American History at Oxford University (2000–2001), and was a recipient of the Humboldt Prize (Germany). He has recently published *American Insurgents, American Patriots: The Revolution of the People* (2010). He is now working on a book to be entitled *Journey to a Nation: George Washington's Campaign to Bring the New Federal Government to the People, 1789–1791.*

R. Hal Williams

R. Hal Williams is professor of history at Southern Methodist University. He received his A.B. from Princeton University in 1963 and his Ph.D. from Yale University in 1968. His books include *The Democratic Party and California Politics, 1880–1896* (1973); *Years of Decision: American Politics in the 1890s* (1978); *The Manhattan Project: A Documentary Introduction to the Atomic Age* (1990); and *Realigning America: McKinley, Bryan, and the Remarkable Election of 1896* (2010). A specialist in American political history, he taught at Yale University from 1968 to 1975 and came to SMU in 1975 as chair of the Department of History. From 1980 to 1988, he served as dean of Dedman College, the school of humanities and sciences, at SMU, and from 2002 to 2006 as dean of Research and Graduate Studies. In 1980, he was a visiting professor at University College, Oxford University. Williams has received grants from the American Philosophical Society and the National Endowment for the Humanities, and he has served on the Texas Committee for the Humanities. He is currently working on a biography of James G. Blaine, the late-nineteenth-century speaker of the House, secretary of state, and Republican presidential candidate.

Ariela J. Gross

Ariela Gross is John B. and Alice R. Sharp Professor of Law and History, and Co-Director of the Center for Law, History and Culture, at the University of Southern California. She has been a visiting Professor at Tel Aviv University, the École des Hautes Études en Sciences Sociales, and Kyoto University. She is the author of *Double Character: Slavery and Mastery in the Antebellum Southern Courtroom* (2000) and *What Blood Won't Tell: A History of Race on Trial in America* (2008), winner of the Willard Hurst Prize from the Law and Society Association; the Lillian Smith Award for the best book on the South, and the American Political Science Association Best Book on Race, Ethnicity, and Politics. Gross has received fellowships from the American Council of Learned Societies, the Guggenheim Foundation, and the National Endowment for the Humanities, and is now working on several comparative projects about law, race, and slavery in the Americas, and law, contemporary politics, and the memory of slavery in the U.S. and Europe.

American Stories

Contents and Spotlight Questions

NATIVE AMERICANS BEFORE THE CONQUEST PG. 5

What explains cultural differences among Native American groups before European conquest?

CONDITIONS OF CONQUEST PG. 10

How did Europeans and Native Americans interact during the period of first contact?

WEST AFRICA: ANCIENT AND COMPLEX SOCIETIES PG. 13

What was the character of the West African societies that European traders first encountered?

EUROPE ON THE EVE OF CONQUEST PG. 15

What factors explain Spain's central role in New World exploration and colonization?

SPAIN IN THE AMERICAS PG. 18

How did Spanish conquest of Central and South America transform Native American cultures?

THE FRENCH CLAIM CANADA PG. 22

What was the character of the French empire in Canada?

THE ENGLISH TAKE UP THE CHALLENGE PG. 23

Why did England not participate in the early competition for New World colonies?

((•—⎰Listen to the **Chapter Audio** for Chapter 1 on **myhistorylab.com**

DIVERSE CULTURES: DE VACA'S JOURNEY THROUGH NATIVE AMERICA

The diversity of Native American peoples astonished the Europeans who first voyaged to the New World. Early sixteenth-century Spanish adventurer Álvar Núñez Cabeza de Vaca offered a sample of this

De Vaca and His Fellow Shipwreck Survivors In 1528, a hurricane destroyed a fleet transporting over 300 Spanish soldiers from Florida to Cuba. Shipwrecked on the Florida coast, the survivors set out over land for Spain's holdings in Mexico. Eight years later only De Vaca and three companions survived to stumble into the Spanish outpost at Culiacán.

striking diversity in his La *Relacion (The Account)*. Shipwrecked in Florida in 1528, De Vaca had made his way overland to Texas. During his eight year trek, De Vaca met and lived among Indians belonging to over twenty unique cultures.

The Apalachees of Florida cultivated "great fields of maize" as well as beans and squash. "The Indians of southeastern Texas, whom De Vaca called "the People of the Figs," did not cultivate the soil." Instead, they relied upon fishing and gathering the fruit of the prickly pear cactus, which De Vaca called "figs." To harvest this fruit, the "fig" people traveled great distances, trading with other Indians along their journey. On the plains of northern Mexico, De Vaca encountered the "People of the Cows," who hunted bison for food and clothing.

Other Europeans echoed De Vaca's observations. Throughout the Americas they encountered rich cultural diversity. Language, physical attributes, social organization, and local foodways separated the Indians of North America into unique nations. Each of these nations, in its own way, would have to come to terms with the arrival of Europeans.

Europeans sailing in the wake of Admiral Christopher Columbus—explorers and conquerors like De Vaca—constructed a narrative of superiority that survived long after they themselves passed from the scene. The standard narrative recounted first in Europe and then in the United States depicted heroic adventurers, missionaries, and soldiers sharing Western civilization with the peoples of the New World and opening a vast virgin land to economic development. This familiar tale celebrated material progress, the inevitable spread of European values, and the taming of frontiers. It was a history crafted by the victors and their descendants to explain how they had come to inherit the land.

This narrative of events no longer provides an adequate explanation for European conquest and settlement. It is not so much wrong as partisan, incomplete, even offensive. History recounted from the perspective of the victors inevitably silences the voices of the victims, the peoples who, in the victors' view, foolishly resisted economic and technological progress. Heroic tales of the advance of Western values only deflect modern attention away from the rich cultural and racial diversity that characterized North American societies for a very long time. More disturbing, traditional tales of European conquest also obscure the sufferings of the millions of Native Americans who perished and the millions of Africans sold in the New World as slaves.

By placing these complex, often unsettling, experiences within an interpretive framework of *creative adaptations*—rather than of *exploration* or *settlement*—we go a long way toward recapturing the full human dimensions of conquest and resistance. While the New World often witnessed tragic violence and systematic betrayal, it allowed ordinary people of three different races and many different ethnic identities opportunities to shape their own lives as best they could within diverse, often hostile environments.

Neither the Native Americans nor the Africans were passive victims of European exploitation. Within their own families and communities, they made choices, sometimes rebelling, sometimes accommodating, but always trying to make sense in terms of their own cultures of what was happening to them.

NATIVE AMERICANS BEFORE THE CONQUEST

As almost any Native American could have informed the first European adventurers, the peopling of America did not begin in 1492. In fact, although the Spanish invaders who followed Columbus proclaimed the discovery of a "New World," they really brought into contact three worlds—Europe, Africa, and the Americas—that had existed for thousands years. Indeed, the first migrants reached the North American continent some 15,000–20,000 years ago.

Environmental conditions played a major part in this great human trek. Twenty thousand years ago, during the last Ice Age, the earth's climate was colder than it is today. Huge glaciers, often more than a mile thick, extended as far south as the present states of Illinois and Ohio and covered much of western Canada. Much of the world's moisture was transformed into ice, and the oceans dropped hundreds of feet below their current levels. The receding waters created a land bridge connecting Asia and North America, a region now submerged beneath the Bering Sea that archaeologists named Beringia.

Even at the height of the last Ice Age, much of the far north remained free of glaciers. Small bands of spear-throwing Paleo-Indians pursued giant mammals (megafauna)—woolly mammoths and mastodons, for example—across the vast tundra of Beringia. These hunters were the first human beings to set foot on a vast, uninhabited continent. Because these migrations took place over a long time and involved small, independent bands of highly nomadic people, the Paleo-Indians never developed a sense of common identity. Each group focused on its own immediate survival, adjusting to the opportunities presented by various microenvironments.

The tools and weapons of the Paleo-Indians differed little from those of other Stone Age peoples found in Asia, Africa, and Europe. In terms of human health, however, something occurred on the Beringian tundra that forever altered the history of Native Americans. The members of these small migrating groups stopped hosting a number of communicable diseases—smallpox and measles being the deadliest. Although Native Americans experienced illnesses such as tuberculosis, they no longer suffered the major epidemics that under normal conditions would have killed much of their population every year. The physical isolation of these bands may have protected them from the spread of contagious disease. Another theory notes that epidemics have frequently been associated with prolonged contact with domestic animals such as cattle and pigs. Since the Paleo-Indians did not domesticate animals, not even horses, they may have avoided the microbes that caused virulent European and African diseases.

Whatever the explanation for this curious epidemiological record, Native American populations lost immunities that later might have protected them from many contagious germs. Thus, when they first came into contact with Europeans and Africans, Native Americans had no defense against the great killers of the Early Modern World. And, as medical researchers have discovered, dislocations resulting from war and famine made the Indians even more vulnerable to infectious disease.

What explains cultural differences among Native American groups before European conquest?

View the **Image**
Clovis Points on **myhistorylab.com**

The Environmental Challenge: Food, Climate, and Culture

Some 12,000 years ago, global warming reduced the glaciers, allowing nomadic hunters to pour into the heart of the North America (see Map 1.1). Within just a few thousand years, Native Americans had journeyed from Colorado to the southern tip of South America.

Blessed with a seemingly inexhaustible supply of meat, the early migrants experienced rapid population growth. As archaeologists have discovered, however, the sudden expansion of human population coincided with the loss of scores of large mammal species, many of them the spear-throwers' favorite sources of food: mammoths and mastodons, camels, and, amazingly, horses were eradicated from the land. The peoples of the Great Plains did not obtain horses until the Spanish reintroduced them in the New World in 1547. Some archaeologists have suggested that the early Paleo-Indian hunters were responsible for the mass extinction of so many animals. However, climatic warming, which transformed well-watered regions into arid territories, probably put the large mammals under severe stress. Early humans simply contributed to an ecological process over which they ultimately had little control.

The Indian peoples adjusted to the changing environment. As they dispersed across North America, they developed new food sources, at first smaller mammals and fish, nuts and berries, and then about 5,000 years ago, they discovered how to cultivate certain plants. Knowledge of maize (corn), squash, and beans spread north from central Mexico. The peoples living in the Southwest acquired cultivation skills long before the bands living along the Atlantic Coast. The shift to basic crops—a transformation that is sometimes termed the Agricultural Revolution—profoundly altered Native American societies.

View the **Map**
Pre-Columbian Societies of the Americas on
myhistorylab.com

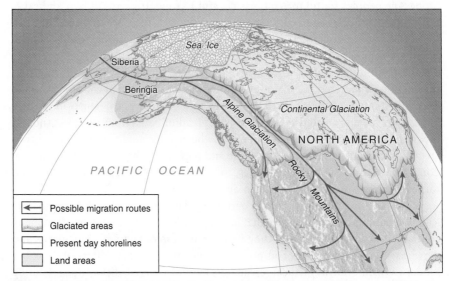

Map 1.1   *Routes of the First Americans*   The peopling of North America began about 20,000 years ago, during the last Ice Age, and continued for millennia.

The availability of a more reliable store of food helped liberate nomadic groups from the insecurities of hunting and gathering. During this period, Native Americans began to produce ceramics, a valuable technology for storing grain. The harvest made permanent villages possible, which often were governed by clearly defined hierarchies of elders and kings, and as the food supply increased, the population greatly expanded, especially around urban centers in the Southwest and the Mississippi Valley. Although the evidence is patchy, scholars currently estimate that approximately 4 million Native Americans lived north of Mexico when the Europeans arrived.

The vast distances and varied climates of North America gave rise to a great diversity of human cultures employing a wide variety of ingenuous strategies for dealing with their unique regional environments. (See Map 1.2.) Some native peoples were unable to take advantage of the Agricultural Revolution. In the harsh climate of the far north, Inuit living in small autonomous kin-based bands developed watertight vessels called kayaks that allowed them to travel and hunt seals in frigid Arctic waters. Many Indian peoples, like those of the Great Plains, combined agriculture with hunting, living most of the year in permanent villages built along river valleys with the men dispersing to seasonal hunting camps at certain times. To attract game animals, especially the buffalo, Plains Indian communities burned the grasslands annually to promote the growth of fresh, green vegetation. Some Native American groups were even more dramatic in their efforts to reshape their natural environment. In the southwest, in what would become New Mexico, the Anasazi culture built massive pueblo villages and overcame the aridity of their desert home by developing a complex society that could sustain a huge, technologically sophisticated network of irrigation canals.

Quick Check

✓ What was life like for the first humans living in North America and what role did the Earth's climate play in shaping their experiences?

Aztec Dominance

As with the Anasazi, the stability the Agricultural Revolution brought allowed the Indians of Mexico and Central America to structure more complex societies. Like the Inca, who lived in what is now Ecuador, Peru, and northern Chile, the Mayan and Toltec peoples of Central Mexico built vast cities, formed government bureaucracies that dominated large tributary populations, and developed hieroglyphic writing and an accurate solar calendar. Their cities, which housed several hundred thousand people, impressed the Spanish conquerors. Bernal Díaz del Castillo reported, "When we saw all those [Aztec] towns and villages built in the water, and other great towns on dry land, and that

The Aztecs This image from the *Codex Magliabechiano* depicts Aztec priests engaged in human sacrifice.

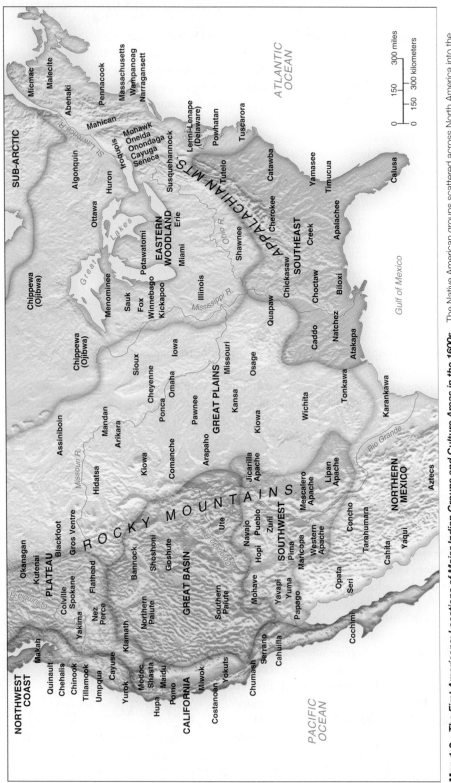

Map 1.2 *The First Americans: Locations of Major Indian Groups and Culture Areas in the 1600s*   The Native American groups scattered across North America into the 1600s had strikingly diverse cultures.

straight and level causeway leading to Mexico, we were astounded.... Indeed, some of our soldiers asked whether it was not all a dream."

Not long before Columbus's first voyage across the Atlantic, the Aztec, an aggressive, warlike people, swept through the Valley of Mexico, conquering the great cities that their enemies had constructed. Aztec warriors ruled by force, reducing defeated rivals to tributary status. In 1519, the Aztecs' main ceremonial center, Tenochtitlán (on the site of modern Mexico City), contained as many as 250,000 people, compared with only 50,000 in Seville, the port from which the early Spanish explorers of the Americas had sailed. Elaborate human sacrifice associated with Huitzilopochtli, the Aztec sun god, horrified Europeans, who apparently did not find the savagery of their own civilization so objectionable. The Aztec ritual killings were connected to the agricultural cycle, and the Indians believed the blood of their victims possessed extraordinary fertility powers. A fragment of an Aztec song-poem captures the indomitable spirit that once pervaded this militant culture:

Proud of itself

is the city of Mexico—Tenochtitlán.

Here no one fears to die in war.

This is our glory. . . .

Who could conquer Tenochtitlán?

Who could shake the foundation of heaven?

> **Quick Check**
>
> ✓ What most impressed Spanish explorers about Aztec culture?

Eastern Woodland Cultures

In northeastern North America along the Atlantic coast, the Indians did not practice intensive agriculture. These peoples, numbering less than a million at the time of conquest, generally supplemented farming with seasonal hunting and gathering. Most belonged to what ethnographers term the Eastern Woodland Cultures. Small bands formed villages during the summer. The women cultivated maize and other crops while the men hunted and fished. During the winter, difficulties associated with feeding so many people forced the communities to disperse. Each family lived off the land as best it could.

Seventeenth-century English settlers were most likely to have encountered the Algonquian-speaking peoples who occupied much of the Atlantic coast from North Carolina to Maine. Included in this large linguistic family were the Powhatan of Tidewater, Virginia, the Narragansett of Rhode Island, and the Abenaki of northern New England.

Algonquian groups exploited different resources in different regions and spoke different dialects. They did not develop strong ties of mutual identity. When their own interests were involved, they were more than willing to ally themselves with Europeans or "foreign" Indians against other Algonquian speakers. Divisions among Indian groups would facilitate European conquest. Native American peoples greatly outnumbered the first settlers, and had the Europeans not forged alliances with the Indians, they could not so easily have gained a foothold on the continent.

However divided the Indians of eastern North America may have been, they shared many cultural values and assumptions. Most Native Americans, for example, defined their place in society through kinship. Such personal bonds determined the character of economic and political relations. The farming bands living in areas eventually claimed by England were often matrilineal, which meant in effect that the women owned the fields and houses, maintained tribal customs, and had a role in tribal government. Among the native communities of Canada and the northern Great Lakes, patrilineal forms were more common. In these groups, the men owned the hunting grounds that the family needed to survive.

Eastern Woodland communities organized diplomacy, trade, and war around reciprocal relationships that impressed Europeans as being extraordinarily egalitarian, even democratic. Chains of native authority were loosely structured. Native leaders were such renowned public speakers because persuasive rhetoric was often their only effective source of power. It required considerable oratorical skills for an Indian leader to persuade independent-minded warriors to support a proposed policy.

Before the arrival of the white settlers, Indian wars were seldom very lethal. Young warriors attacked neighboring bands largely to exact revenge for an insult or the death of a relative, or to secure captives. Fatalities, when they did occur, sparked cycles of revenge. Some captives were tortured to death; others were adopted into the community to replace fallen relatives.

Quick Check

✓ How was society structured among the Eastern Woodland Indians before the arrival of Europeans?

CONDITIONS OF CONQUEST

How did Europeans and Native Americans interact during the period of first contact?

The arrival of large numbers of white men and women on the North American continent profoundly altered Native American cultures. Change did not occur at the same rates in all places. Indian villages on the Atlantic coast came under severe pressure almost immediately; inland groups had more time to adjust. Wherever Indians lived, however, conquest strained traditional ways of life, and as daily patterns of experience changed almost beyond recognition, native peoples had to devise new answers, responses, and ways to survive in physical and social environments that eroded tradition.

Cultural Negotiations

Native Americans were not passive victims of geopolitical forces beyond their control. So long as they remained healthy, they held their own in the early exchanges, and although they eagerly accepted certain trade goods, they generally resisted other aspects of European cultures. The earliest recorded contacts between Indians and explorers suggest curiosity and surprise rather than hostility.

What Indians desired most was peaceful trade. The earliest French explorers reported that natives waved from shore, urging the Europeans to exchange metal items for beaver skins. In fact, the Indians did not perceive themselves at a disadvantage in these dealings. They could readily see the technological advantage of guns over bows and arrows. Metal knives made daily tasks much easier. And to acquire such goods they gave up pelts, which to them seemed in abundant supply. "The English have no sense," one Indian informed a French priest. "They give us twenty knives like this for one Beaver skin." Another native announced that "the Beaver does everything perfectly well: it makes kettles, hatchets, swords, knives, bread … in short, it makes everything." The man who recorded these observations reminded French readers—in case they had missed the point—that the Indian was "making sport of us Europeans."

Trading sessions along the eastern frontier were really cultural seminars. The Europeans tried to make sense out of Indian customs, and although they may have called the natives "savages," they quickly discovered that the Indians drove hard bargains. They demanded gifts; they set the time and place of trade.

Communicating with the Indians was always difficult for the Europeans, who did not understand the alien sounds and gestures of the Native American cultures. In the absence of meaningful conversation, Europeans often concluded that the Indians held them in high regard, perhaps seeing the newcomers as gods. Such one-sided encounters involved a lot of projection, a mental process of translating alien sounds and gestures into what Europeans wanted to hear. Sometimes the adventurers did not even try to communicate with the Indians, assuming from superficial observation—as did the sixteenth-century explorer Giovanni da Verrazzano—"that they have no religion, and that they live in absolute freedom, and that everything they do proceeds from Ignorance."

Ethnocentric Europeans tried repeatedly to "civilize" the Indians. In practice that meant persuading natives to dress like the colonists, attend white schools, live in permanent structures, and, most important, accept Christianity. The Indians listened more or less patiently, but in the end, they usually rejected European values. One South Carolina trader explained that when Indians were asked to become more English, they said no, "for they thought it hard, that we should desire them to change their manners and customs, since they did not desire us to turn Indians."

Some Indians were attracted to Christianity, but most paid it lip service or found it irrelevant to their needs. As one Huron told a French priest, "It would be useless for me to repent having sinned, seeing that I never have sinned." Another Huron announced that he did not fear punishment after death since "we cannot tell whether everything that appears faulty to Men, is so in the Eyes of God."

Among some Indian groups, gender figured significantly in a person's willingness to convert to Christianity. Native men who traded animal skins for European goods had more frequent contact with the whites and proved more receptive to the missionaries' arguments. But native women jealously guarded traditional culture, a system that often sanctioned polygamy—a husband having several wives—and gave women substantial authority over the distribution of food within the village.

The white settlers' educational system proved no more successful than their religion in winning cultural converts. Young Indians deserted stuffy classrooms at the first opportunity. In 1744, Virginia offered several Iroquois boys a free education at the College of William and Mary. The Iroquois leaders rejected the invitation because they found that boys who had gone to college "were absolutely good for nothing being neither acquainted with the true methods of killing deer, catching Beaver, or surprising an enemy."

Even matrimony seldom eroded the Indians' attachment to their own customs. When Native Americans and whites married—unions the English found less desirable

Read the **Document**
Thomas Hariot, The Algonquian Peoples on **myhistorylab.com**

View the **Image**
English Trade with Indians on **myhistorylab.com**

Quick Check

✓ Why did Europeans insist on trying to "civilize" the Indians?

than did the French or Spanish—the European partner usually elected to live among the Indians. Impatient settlers who regarded the Indians simply as an obstruction to progress sometimes developed more coercive methods, such as enslavement, to achieve cultural conversion. Again, from the white perspective, the results were disappointing. Indian slaves ran away or died. In either case, they did not become Europeans.

Threats to Survival: Columbian Exchange

Over time, cooperative encounters between the Native Americans and Europeans became less frequent. The Europeans found it almost impossible to understand the Indians' relation to the land and other natural resources. English planters cleared the forests and fenced the fields and, in the process, radically altered the ecological systems on which the Indians depended. The European system of land use inevitably reduced the supply of deer and other animals essential to traditional native cultures.

Dependency also came in more subtle forms. The Indians welcomed European commerce, but like so many consumers throughout history, they discovered that the objects they most coveted inevitably brought them into debt. To pay for the trade goods, the Indians hunted more aggressively and even further reduced the population of fur-bearing mammals.

Commerce eroded Indian independence in other ways. After several disastrous wars—the Yamasee War in South Carolina (1715), for example—the natives learned that demonstrations of force usually resulted in the suspension of normal trade, on which the Indians had grown dependent for guns and ammunition, among other things. A hardened English businessman made the point bluntly. When asked if the Catawba Indians would harm his traders, he responded that "the danger would be … little from them, because they are too fond of our trade to lose it for the pleasure of shedding a little English blood."

It was disease, however, that ultimately destroyed the cultural integrity of many North American tribes. European adventurers exposed the Indians to bacteria and viruses against which they possessed no natural immunity. Smallpox, measles, and influenza decimated the Native American population. Other diseases such as alcoholism took a terrible toll.

The decimation of Native American peoples was an aspect of ecological transformation known as the Columbian Exchange. European conquerors exposed the Indians to new fatal diseases; the Indians adopted European plants and domestic animals and introduced the invaders to marvelous plants such as corn and potatoes that changed European history. (See Table 1.1.)

The Algonquian communities of New England experienced appalling death rates. One Massachusetts colonist reported in 1630 that the Indian peoples of his region "above twelve years since were swept away by a great & grievous Plague … so that there are verie few left to inhabit the Country." Settlers possessed no knowledge of germ theory—it was not formulated until the mid-nineteenth century—and speculated that the Christian God had providentially cleared the wilderness of heathens.

TABLE 1.1 New Opportunities, New Threats: The Columbian Exchange

From the Americas to Eurasia and Africa

Maize, Potatoes, Sweet Potatoes, Tomatoes, Beans, Cinchona Tree (the source of quinine), Many Types of Beans, Pineapples, Blueberries, Papaya, Pecans, Tobacco, Cacao, Vanilla, Peanuts, Peppers, Cassava, Squash, Avocadoes, Sunflowers, Turkeys, and (maybe) Syphilis

From Eurasia and Africa to the Americas

Cereals (wheat, rice, barley, etc.), Sugar, Bananas, Coconuts, Orchard Trees (apples, oranges, lemons, etc.), Olives, Wine Grapes, Coffee, Lettuces, Black Pepper, Livestock (horses, sheep, swine, cattle, goats, chickens, etc.), Honey Bees, Many Epidemic Diseases (smallpox, influenza, chicken pox, etc.)

Historical demographers now estimate that some tribes suffered a 90 to 95 percent population loss within the first century of European contact. The population of the Arawak Indians of the island of Hispaniola (modern Haiti and the Dominican Republic), for example, dropped from about 3,770,000 in 1496 to only 125 in 1570. The death of so many Indians decreased the supply of indigenous laborers, whom the Europeans needed to work the mines and grow staple crops such as sugar and tobacco. The decimation of native populations may have persuaded colonists throughout the New World to seek a substitute labor force in Africa. Indeed, the enslavement of blacks has been described as an effort by Europeans to "repopulate" the New World.

Indians who survived the epidemics often found that the fabric of traditional culture had come unraveled. The enormity of the death toll and the agony that accompanied it called traditional religious beliefs and practices into question. The survivors lost not only members of their families, but also elders who might have told them how to bury the dead properly and give spiritual comfort to the living.

Some native peoples, such as the Iroquois, who lived a long way from the coast and thus had more time to adjust to the challenge, withstood the crisis better than did those who immediately confronted the Europeans and Africans. Refugee Indians from the hardest-hit eastern communities were absorbed into healthier western groups. However horrific the crisis may have been, it demonstrated just how much the environment—a source of opportunity as well as devastation—shaped human encounters throughout the New World.

View the **Map**
Native American Population Loss, 1500–1700 on **myhistorylab.com**

Quick Check

✓ What effect did the introduction of Old World diseases such as smallpox have on Native American societies and cultures?

WEST AFRICA: ANCIENT AND COMPLEX SOCIETIES

The first Portuguese who explored the African coast during the fifteenth century encountered many different political and religious cultures. Centuries earlier, Africans in this region had come into contact with Islam, the religion the Prophet Muhammad founded in the seventh century. Islam spread slowly from Arabia into West Africa. Not until A.D. 1030 did a kingdom in the Senegal Valley accept Islam. Many other West Africans, such as those in ancient Ghana, continued to observe traditional religions.

What was the character of the West African societies that European traders first encountered?

As Muslim traders from North Africa and the Middle East brought a new religion to West Africa, they expanded sophisticated trade networks that linked the villagers of Senegambia with urban centers in northwest Africa, Morocco, Tunisia, and Libya. Camel caravans regularly crossed the Sahara carrying goods that were exchanged for gold and slaves. Sub-Saharan Africa's well-developed links with Islam surprised a French priest who in 1686 observed African pilgrims going "to visit Mecca to visit Mahomet's tomb, although they are eleven or twelve hundred leagues distance from it."

West Africans spoke many languages and organized themselves into diverse political systems. Several populous states, sometimes termed "empires," exercised loose control over large areas. Ancient African empires such as Ghana were vulnerable to external attack and internal rebellion, and the oral and written histories of this region record the rise and fall of several large kingdoms. When European traders first arrived, the major states would have included Mali, Benin, and Kongo. Many other Africans lived in what are known as stateless societies, largely autonomous communities organized around lineage structures. In these respects, African and Native American cultures had much in common.

The Portuguese journeyed to Africa in search of gold and slaves. Mali and Joloff officials (see Map 1.3) were willing partners in this commerce but insisted that Europeans respect African trade regulations. They required the Europeans to pay tolls and other fees and restricted the conduct of their business to small forts or castles on the coast. Local merchants acquired slaves and gold in the interior and transported them to the coast, where they exchanged them for European manufactures. Transactions were calculated in local African currencies: A slave would be offered to a European trader for so many bars of iron or ounces of gold.

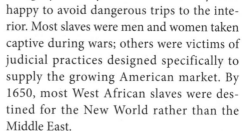

Read the **Document**
Ghana and its People in the Eleventh Century on **myhistorylab.com**

European slave traders accepted these terms, largely because they had no other choice. The African states fielded formidable armies, and outsiders soon discovered they could not impose their will on the region simply through force. Moreover, local diseases such as malaria and yellow fever proved so lethal for Europeans—six out of ten of whom would die within a single year's stay in Africa—that they were happy to avoid dangerous trips to the interior. Most slaves were men and women taken captive during wars; others were victims of judicial practices designed specifically to supply the growing American market. By 1650, most West African slaves were destined for the New World rather than the Middle East.

Even before Europeans colonized the New World, the Portuguese were purchasing almost 1,000 slaves a year on the West African coast. The slaves were frequently forced to work on the sugar plantations of Madeira (Portuguese) and the Canaries (Spanish), Atlantic islands on which Europeans experimented with forms of unfree labor

Slave Factories Cape Coast Castle was one of many so-called slave factories European traders built on the West African coast.

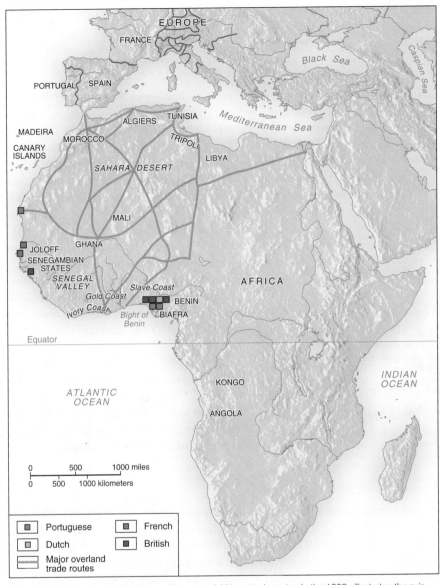

EUROPE

FRANCE

Black Sea

Caspian Sea

PORTUGAL SPAIN

MADEIRA

CANARY
ISLANDS

MOROCCO

ALGIERS TUNISIA

TRIPOLI

Mediterranean Sea

SAHARA DESERT

LIBYA

MALI

GHANA

JOLOFF

SENEGAMBIAN
STATES

*SENEGAL
VALLEY*

Gold Coast Slave Coast

Ivory Coast

Bight of
Benin

BENIN

BIAFRA

AFRICA

Equator

ATLANTIC
OCEAN

KONGO

ANGOLA

INDIAN
OCEAN

| 0 | 500 | 1000 miles |
| 0 | 500 | 1000 kilometers |

☐ Portuguese   ☐ French

☐ Dutch   ☐ British

☐ Major overland
  trade routes

Map 1.3 **Trade Routes in Africa**   This map of African trade routes in the 1600s illustrates the existence of a complex economic system.

that would later be more fully and ruthlessly established in the American colonies. Approximately 10.7 million Africans were taken to the New World as slaves. The figure for the eighteenth century alone is about 5.5 million, of which more than one-third came from West Central Africa. The Bight of Benin, the Bight of Biafra, and the Gold Coast supplied most of the others.

The peopling of the New World is usually seen as a story of European migrations. But in fact, during every year between 1650 and 1831, more Africans than Europeans came to the Americas. As historian Davis Eltis wrote, "In terms of

🔍 **View** the **Image**
*Purchasing Slaves on
the African Shore* on
myhistorylab.com

immigration alone ... America was an extension of Africa rather than Europe until late in the nineteenth century."

EUROPE ON THE EVE OF CONQUEST

What factors explain Spain's central role in New World exploration and colonization?

In the tenth century, Scandinavian seafarers known as Norsemen or Vikings established settlements in the New World, but almost 1,000 years passed before they received credit for their accomplishment. In 984, a band of Vikings led by Eric the Red sailed west from Iceland to a large island in the North Atlantic. Eric, who possessed a fine sense of public relations, named the island Greenland, reasoning that others would more willingly colonize the icebound region "if the country had a good name." A few years later, Eric's son Leif founded a small settlement he named Vinland at a location in northern Newfoundland now called L'Anse aux Meadows. At the time, the Norse voyages went unnoticed by other Europeans. The hostility of Native Americans, poor lines of communication, climatic cooling, and political upheavals in Scandinavia made it impossible to maintain these distant outposts.

L'Anse aux Meadows Located on Newfoundland, L'Anse aux Meadows was the site of a Norse settlement.

At the time of his first voyage in 1492, Christopher Columbus seems to have been unaware of these earlier exploits. His expeditions had to wait for a different political climate in Europe in which a newly united Spain took the lead in New World conquest.

Spanish Expansion

By 1500, centralization of political authority and advances in geographic knowledge were making Spain a world power. In the early fifteenth century, though, Spain consisted of several autonomous kingdoms. It lacked rich natural resources and possessed few good seaports. In fact, little about this land suggested its people would take the lead in conquering and colonizing the New World.

By the end of the 1400s, however, Spain suddenly came alive with creative energy. The marriage of Spain's two principal Christian rulers, King Ferdinand of Aragon and Queen Isabella of Castile, sparked a drive for political consolidation that, because of the monarchs' fervid Catholicism, took on the characteristics of a religious crusade. Spurred by the militant faith of their monarchs, the armies of Castile and Aragon waged holy war—known as the *Reconquista*—against the kingdom of Granada, the last independent Muslim state in Spain. In 1492, Granada fell, and, for the first time in seven centuries, the entire Iberian Peninsula was under Christian rulers. Spanish authorities showed no tolerance for people who rejected the Catholic faith.

During the *Reconquista*, thousands of Jews and Moors (Spanish Muslims) were driven from the country. Indeed, Columbus undoubtedly encountered such refugees as he was preparing for his famous voyage. From this volatile social and political environment came the *conquistadores*, men eager for personal glory and material gain, uncompromising in religion, and loyal to the crown. They were prepared to employ fire and sword in any cause sanctioned by God and king, and these adventurers carried European culture to the most populous regions of the New World.

Long before Spaniards ever reached the West Indies, they conquered the indigenous peoples of the Canary Islands, a strategically located archipelago in the eastern Atlantic. The harsh labor systems the Spanish developed in the Canaries served as models of subjugation in America. An early fifteenth-century Spanish chronicle described the Canary natives as "miscreants ... [who] do not acknowledge their creator and live in part like beasts." Many islanders died of disease; others were killed in battle or enslaved. The new Spanish landholders introduced sugar, a labor-intensive plantation crop. They forced slaves captured in Africa to provide the labor. Dreams of wealth drove this oppressive process. Through the centuries, European colonists would repeat it many times.

> **Quick Check**
> ✓ Who were the *conquistadores*, and what were their motivations in the New World?

The Strange Career of Christopher Columbus

If it had not been for Christopher Columbus (Cristoforo Colombo), Spain might never have gained an American empire. Little is known about his early life. Born in the Italian city of Genoa in 1451 of humble parentage, Columbus soon devoured the classical learning that had so recently been rediscovered and made available in print. He mastered geography, and—perhaps while sailing the coast of West Africa—he became obsessed with the idea of voyaging west across the Atlantic Ocean to reach Cathay, as China was then known to Europeans.

In 1484, Columbus presented his plan to the king of Portugal. However, while the Portuguese were just as interested as Columbus in reaching Cathay, they elected to voyage around the continent of Africa instead of following the route Columbus suggested. They suspected that Columbus had underestimated the circumference of the earth and that he would starve before reaching Asia. The Portuguese decision eventually paid off handsomely. In 1498, one of their captains, Vasco da Gama, returned from India with a fortune in spices and other luxury goods.

Undaunted by rejection, Columbus petitioned Isabella and Ferdinand for financial backing. They were initially no more interested in his grand design than the Portuguese had been. But time was on Columbus's side. Spain's aggressive new monarchs envied the success of their neighbor, Portugal. Columbus played on the rivalry between the countries, talking of wealth and empire. Indeed, for a person with little success or apparent support, he was supremely confident. One contemporary reported that when Columbus "made up his mind, he was as sure he would discover what he did discover, and find what he did find, as if he held it in a chamber under lock and key."

Columbus's stubborn lobbying for the "Enterprise of the Indies" wore down opposition in the Spanish court, and the two sovereigns provided him with a small

> **Watch** the **Video**
> *How Should We Think of Columbus?* on
> **myhistorylab.com**

fleet of three ships: the *Niña*, the *Pinta*, and the *Santa Maria*. The indomitable admiral set sail for Cathay in August 1492, the same year that Grenada fell.

Educated Europeans of the fifteenth century knew the world was round. No one seriously believed that Columbus and his crew would tumble off the edge of the earth. The concern was with size, not shape. Columbus estimated the distance to the mainland of Asia to be about 3,000 nautical miles, a voyage his small ships would have no difficulty completing. The actual distance is 10,600 nautical miles, however, and had the New World not been in his way, he and his crew would have run out of food and water long before they reached China, as the Portuguese had predicted.

After stopping in the Canary Islands to refit the ships, Columbus continued westward in early September. When the tiny Spanish fleet sighted an island in the Bahamas after only 33 days at sea, the admiral concluded he had reached Asia. Since his mathematical calculations had obviously been correct, he assumed he would soon encounter the Chinese. It never occurred to Columbus that he had stumbled upon a New World. He assured his men, his patrons, and perhaps himself that the islands were indeed part of the fabled "Indies." Or, if not the Indies themselves, then they were surely an extension of the great Asian landmass. He searched for the splendid cities Marco Polo had described in his accounts of China in the thirteenth century, but instead of wealthy Chinese, Columbus encountered Native Americans, whom he appropriately, if mistakenly, called "Indians."

After his first voyage of discovery, Columbus returned to the New World three more times. But despite his courage and ingenuity, he could never find the treasure his financial supporters in Spain demanded. Columbus died in 1506 a frustrated but wealthy entrepreneur, unaware that he had reached a previously unknown continent separating Asia from Europe. The final disgrace came in December 1500 when an ambitious falsifier, Amerigo Vespucci, published a sensational account of his travels across the Atlantic that convinced German mapmakers he had proved America was distinct from Asia. Before the misconception could be corrected, the name *America* gained general acceptance throughout Europe.

👁 **Watch** the **Video**
What is Columbus's Legacy? on
myhistorylab.com

Quick Check

✔ What did educated Europeans believe about the shape and size of the Earth prior to 1492?

SPAIN IN THE AMERICAS

How did Spanish conquest of Central and South America transform Native American cultures?

Only two years after Columbus's first voyage, Spain and Portugal almost went tlo war over the anticipated treasure of Asia. Pope Alexander VI negotiated a settlement that pleased both kingdoms. Portugal wanted to exclude the Spanish from the west coast of Africa and, what was more important, from Columbus's new route to "India." Spain insisted on maintaining complete control over lands discovered by Columbus, which were still regarded as extensions of China. The **Treaty of Tordesillas** (1494) divided the entire world along a line located 270 leagues west of the Azores. Any lands discovered west of the line belonged to Spain. At the time, no European had ever seen Brazil, which turned out to be on Portugal's side of the line. (Brazilians speak Portuguese.) The treaty failed to discourage future English, Dutch, and French adventurers from trying their luck in the New World.

The *Conquistadores*: Faith and Greed

Spain's new discoveries unleashed a horde of *conquistadores* on the Caribbean. These independent adventurers carved out small settlements on Cuba, Hispaniola, Jamaica, and Puerto Rico in the 1490s and early 1500s. They were not interested in creating a permanent society in the New World. Rather, they came for instant wealth, preferably in gold, and were not squeamish about the means they used to get it. Bernal Díaz, one of the first Spaniards to migrate to the region, explained he had traveled to America "to serve God and His Majesty, to give light to those who were in darkness, and to grow rich, as all men desire to do." In less than two decades, the Indians who had inhabited the Caribbean islands had been exterminated, victims of exploitation and disease.

For a quarter century, the *conquistadores* concentrated their energies on the major islands that Columbus had discovered. Rumors of fabulous wealth in Mexico, however, aroused the interest of many Spaniards, including Hernán Cortés, a minor government functionary in Cuba. Like so many members of his class, he dreamed of glory, military adventure, and riches that would transform him from an ambitious court clerk into an honored nobleman or *hidalgo*. On November 18, 1518, Cortés and a small army left Cuba to verify the stories of Mexico's treasure. Events soon demonstrated that Cortés was a leader of extraordinary ability.

His adversary was the legendary Aztec emperor Montezuma. The confrontation between the two powerful personalities is one of the more dramatic stories of early American history. A fear of competition from rival *conquistadores* coupled with a burning desire to conquer a new empire drove Cortés forward. Determined to push his men through any obstacle, he burned the ships that had carried them to Mexico to prevent them from retreating. Cortés led his 600 followers across rugged mountains and gathered allies from among the Tlaxcalans, a tributary people eager to free themselves from Aztec domination.

In war, Cortés possessed obvious technological superiority over the Aztec. The sound of gunfire initially frightened the Indians. Moreover, Aztec troops had never seen horses, much less armored horses carrying sword-wielding Spaniards. But these elements would have counted for little had Cortés not also gained a psychological advantage over his opponents. At first, Montezuma thought that the Spaniards were gods, representatives of the fearful plumed serpent, Quetzalcoatl. Instead of resisting, the emperor hesitated. When Montezuma's resolve hardened, it was too late. Cortés's victory in Mexico, coupled with other conquests in South America, transformed Spain, at least temporarily, into the wealthiest state in Europe (see Map 1.4).

View the **Closer Look**
An Early European Image of Native Americans on
myhistorylab.com

Quick Check

✓ How did Cortés and his small band of Spanish soldiers manage to conquer the Aztec empire?

From Plunder to Settlement

With the conquest of Mexico, renamed New Spain, the Spanish crown confronted a difficult problem. Ambitious *conquistadores*, interested chiefly in their own wealth and glory, had to be brought under royal authority. Adventurers like Cortés were

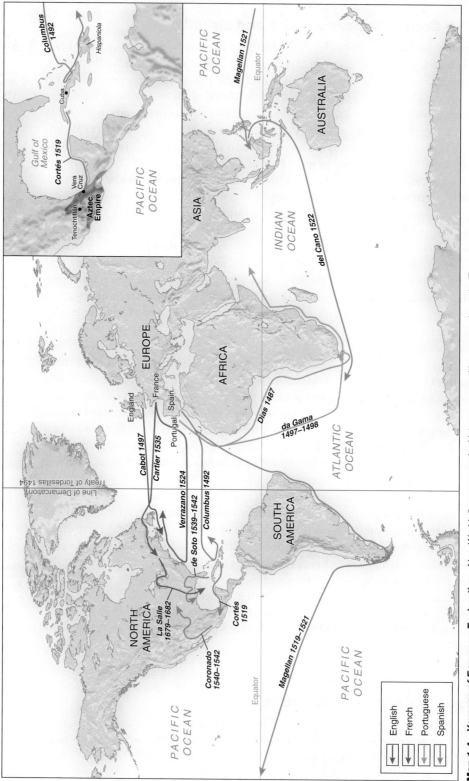

Map 1.4 Voyages of European Exploration New World discovery sparked intense competition among the major European states.

20

stubbornly independent, quick to take offense, and thousands of miles away from the seat of imperial government.

The crown found a partial solution in the *encomienda* system. The monarch rewarded the leaders of the conquest with Indian villages. The people who lived in the settlements provided the *encomenderos* with labor tribute in exchange for legal protection and religious guidance. The system, of course, cruelly exploited Indian laborers. One historian concluded, "The first encomenderos, without known exception, understood Spanish authority as provision for unlimited personal opportunism." Cortés alone was granted the services of more than 23,000 Indian workers. The *encomienda* system made the colonizers more dependent on the king, for it was he who legitimized their

Indian Slaves In 1595, Theodore de Bry depicted the harsh Spanish labor discipline on a sugar plantation on the Island of Hispaniola.

title. The new economic structure helped to transform "a frontier of plunder into a frontier of settlement."

Spain's rulers attempted to maintain tight control over their American possessions. The volume of correspondence between the two continents, much of it concerning mundane matters, was staggering. All documents were duplicated several times by hand. Because the trip to Madrid took months, a year often passed before a simple request was answered. But somehow the cumbersome system worked. In Mexico, officials appointed in Spain established a rigid hierarchical order, directing the affairs of the countryside from urban centers.

The Spanish also brought Catholicism to the New World. The Dominicans and Franciscans, the two largest religious orders, established Indian missions throughout New Spain. Some friars tried to protect the Native Americans from the worst exploitation. One courageous Dominican, Fra Bartolomé de las Casas, published an eloquent defense of Indian rights, *Historia de las Indias*, that questioned the legitimacy of European conquest of the New World. Las Casas's work provoked heated debate in Spain and initiated reforms designed to bring greater "love and moderation" to Spanish–Indian relations. It is impossible to ascertain how many converts the friars made. In 1531, however, a newly converted Christian Indian reported a vision of the Virgin Mary, a dark-skinned woman of obvious Indian ancestry, who became known throughout the region as the **Virgin of Guadalupe.** This figure—the result of a creative blending of Indian and European cultures—became a powerful symbol of Mexican nationalism in the wars for independence fought against Spain almost three centuries later.

Read the **Document**
Bartolome de las Casas, "Of the Islands of Hispaniola" on **myhistorylab.com**

View the **Image**
Cruel Conquistadors Torturing Native Americans on **myhistorylab.com**

The Virgin of Guadalupe The Virgin of Guadalupe, depicted here in a 1531 representation, is a popular religious symbol of Mexico. Like the Indian Juan Diego, to whom she is said to have appeared and offered comfort, the Virgin is dark-skinned.

Quick Check

✓ Describe the character of Spanish-Indian relations following the conquest of Mexico.

About 250,000 Spaniards migrated to the New World during the sixteenth century. Another 200,000 made the journey between 1600 and 1650. Most colonists were single males in their late twenties seeking economic opportunities. They generally came from the poorest agricultural regions of southern Spain—almost 40 percent migrating from Andalusia. Since so few Spanish women migrated, especially in the sixteenth century, the men often married Indians and blacks, unions that produced mixed-race descendents known as *mestizos* and *mulattos*. The frequency of interracial marriage indicated that the people of New Spain were more tolerant of racial differences than were the English who settled in North America. For the people of New Spain, economic worth affected social standing as much if not more than skin color did. Persons born in the New World, even those of Spanish parentage (*criollos*), were regarded as socially inferior to natives of the mother country (*peninsulares*).

Spain claimed far more of the New World than it could manage. Spain's rulers regarded the American colonies primarily as a source of precious metals, and between 1500 and 1650, an estimated 200 tons of gold and 16,000 tons of silver were shipped back to the Spanish treasury in Madrid. This great wealth, however, proved a mixed blessing. The sudden acquisition of so much money stimulated a horrendous inflation that hurt ordinary Spaniards. They were hurt further by long, debilitating European wars funded by American gold and silver. Moreover, instead of developing its own industry, Spain became dependent on the annual shipment of bullion from America. In 1603, one insightful Spaniard declared, "The New World conquered by you, has conquered you in its turn." This weakened, although still formidable, empire would eventually extend its territorial claims north to California and the Southwest (see Chapter 4).

THE FRENCH CLAIM CANADA

What was the character of the French empire in Canada?

French interest in the New World developed slowly. More than three decades after Columbus's discovery, King Francis I sponsored the unsuccessful efforts of Giovanni da Verrazzano to find a short water route to China via a northwest passage around or through North America. In 1534, the king sent Jacques Cartier on a similar quest. The rocky, barren coast of Labrador depressed the explorer. He grumbled, "I am rather inclined to believe that this is the land God gave to Cain."

Discovery of a large, promising waterway the following year raised Cartier's spirits. He reconnoitered the Gulf of Saint Lawrence, traveling up the magnificent river as far as modern Montreal. But Cartier got no closer to China, and, discouraged by the harsh winters, he headed home in 1542. Not until 65 years later did Samuel de Champlain resettle this region for France. He founded Quebec in 1608.

As with other colonial powers, the French declared they had migrated to the New World in search of wealth and to convert the Indians to Christianity. As it turned out, these economic and spiritual goals required full cooperation between the French and the Native Americans. In contrast to the English settlers, who established independent farms and regarded the Indians at best as obstacles to civilization, the French viewed the natives as necessary economic partners. Furs were Canada's most valuable export, and to obtain the pelts of beaver and other animals, the French were absolutely dependent on Indian hunters and trappers. French traders lived among the Indians, often taking native wives and studying local cultures.

Read the **Document** *Jacques Cartier, First Contact with the Indians (1534)* on **myhistorylab.com**

Frenchmen known as *coureurs de bois*, following Canada's great river networks, paddled deep into the heart of the continent for fresh sources of furs. Some intrepid traders penetrated beyond the Great Lakes into the Mississippi Valley. In 1673, Père Jacques Marquette journeyed down the Mississippi River, and nine years later, Sieur Robert de La Salle reached the Gulf of Mexico. In the early eighteenth century, the French established small settlements in Louisiana, the most important being New Orleans. The spreading French influence worried English colonists living along the Atlantic coast, for the French seemed to be cutting them off from the trans-Appalachian west.

Catholic missionaries also depended on Indian cooperation. Canadian priests were drawn from two orders, the Jesuits and the Recollects, and although measuring their success in the New World is difficult, it seems they converted more Indians than did their English Protestant counterparts to the south. Like the fur traders, the missionaries lived among the Indians and learned their languages.

The French dream of a vast American empire suffered from serious flaws. The crown remained largely indifferent to Canadian affairs. Royal officials in New France received limited and sporadic support from Paris. An even greater problem was the decision to settle what many peasants and artisans considered a cold, inhospitable land. Throughout the colonial period, Canada's European population remained small. A census of 1663 recorded only 3,035 French residents. By 1700, there were only 15,000. Men far outnumbered women, thus making it hard for settlers to form new families. Moreover, because of the colony's geography, all exports and imports had to go through Quebec. It was relatively easy, therefore, for crown officials to control that traffic, usually by awarding fur-trading monopolies to court favorites. Such practices created political tensions and hindered economic growth.

THE ENGLISH TAKE UP THE CHALLENGE

Why did England not participate in the early competition for New World colonies?

The first English visit to North America remains shrouded in mystery. Fishermen working out of Bristol and other western English ports may have landed in Nova Scotia and Newfoundland as early as the 1480s. The huge stock of codfish of the Grand Banks undoubtedly drew vessels of all nations, and during summers sailors probably dried and salted their catches on Canada's convenient shores. John Cabot (Giovanni Caboto), a Venetian sea captain, completed the first recorded transatlantic voyage by an English vessel in 1497, while attempting to find a northwest passage to Asia.

Cabot died during a second voyage in 1498. Although Sebastian Cabot continued his father's explorations in the Hudson Bay region in 1508–1509, England's interest in the New World waned. For the next three-quarters of a century, the English people were preoccupied with more pressing domestic and religious concerns. When curiosity about the New World revived, however, Cabot's voyages established England's belated claim to American territory.

Birth of English Protestantism

Read the **Document**
Henry VII, Letters of Patent Granted to John Cabot on **myhistorylab.com**

At the time of Cabot's death, England was not prepared to compete with Spain and Portugal for the riches of the Orient. Although Henry VII, the first Tudor monarch, brought peace to England in 1485 after a bitter civil war, the country still contained too many "over-mighty subjects," powerful local magnates who maintained armed retainers and often paid little attention to royal authority. Henry possessed no standing army; his small navy intimidated no one. The Tudors gave nominal allegiance to the pope in Rome, but unlike the rulers of Spain, they were not crusaders for Catholicism.

International diplomacy also worked against England's early entry into New World colonization. In 1509, to cement an alliance between Spain and England, the future Henry VIII married Catherine of Aragon, daughter of Ferdinand and Isabella. As a result of this marital arrangement, English merchants enjoyed limited rights to trade in Spain's American colonies, but any attempt by England at independent colonization would have threatened those rights and jeopardized the alliance.

By the end of the sixteenth century, however, conditions within England had changed dramatically, in part because of the Protestant Reformation. The English began to consider their former ally, Spain, to be the greatest threat to English aspirations. Tudor monarchs, especially Henry VIII (r. 1509–1547) and his daughter Elizabeth I (r. 1558–1603), developed a strong central administration, while England became increasingly Protestant. The merger of English Protestantism and English nationalism helped propel England into a central role in European affairs and was crucial in creating a powerful sense of an English identity among all classes of people.

Popular anticlericalism helped spark religious reformation in England. Although they observed traditional Catholic ritual, the English people had long resented paying monies to a pope who lived in far-off Rome. Early in the sixteenth century, criticism of the clergy grew increasingly vocal. Cardinal Thomas Wolsey, the most powerful prelate in England, flaunted his immense wealth and unwittingly became a symbol of spiritual corruption. Parish priests were objects of ridicule; they seemed theologically ignorant and eager to line their own pockets. Anticlericalism did not run as deep in England as it had in Martin Luther's Germany, but by the late 1520s, the Catholic Church could no longer take for granted the allegiance of the great mass of the population. The people's growing anger is central to understanding the English Reformation. Put simply, if ordinary English men and women had not accepted separation from Rome, then Henry VIII could not have forced them to leave the church.

The catalyst for Protestant Reformation in England was the king's desire to rid himself of his wife, Catherine of Aragon. Their marriage had produced a daughter,

Mary, but no son. The need for a male heir obsessed Henry. He and his counselors assumed a female ruler could not maintain domestic peace, and England would fall again into civil war. The answer seemed to be remarriage. Henry petitioned Pope Clement VII for a divorce (technically, an annulment), but the Spanish were unwilling to tolerate the public humiliation of Catherine. They forced the pope to procrastinate. In 1527, time ran out. The king fell in love with Anne Boleyn and moved to divorce Catherine with or without papal consent. Anne would become his second wife in 1533 and would later deliver a daughter, Elizabeth.

The final break with Rome came swiftly. Between 1529 and 1536, the king, acting through Parliament, severed all ties with the pope, seized church lands, and dissolved many of the monasteries. In March 1534, the Act of Supremacy announced, "The King's Majesty justly and rightfully is supreme head of the Church of England." The entire process, which one historian termed a "state reformation," was conducted with impressive efficiency. Land formerly owned by the Catholic Church passed quickly into private hands, and within a short period, property holders throughout England had acquired a vested interest in Protestantism. Beyond breaking with the papacy, Henry showed little enthusiasm for theological change. Many Catholic ceremonies survived.

The split with Rome, however, opened the door to increasingly radical religious ideas. In 1539, an English translation of the Bible first appeared in print. Before then, Scripture had been widely available only in Latin, the language of an educated elite. For the first time in English history, ordinary people could read the word of God in the vernacular. It was a liberating experience that persuaded some men and women that Henry had not sufficiently reformed the English church.

With Henry's death in 1547, England entered a period of political and religious instability. Edward VI, Henry's young son by his third wife, Jane Seymour, came to the throne, but he was a sickly child. Militant Protestants took control, insisting the Church of England remove every trace of its Catholic origins. When young Edward died in 1553, these ambitious efforts came to a sudden halt. Henry's eldest daughter, Mary I, ascended the throne. Fiercely loyal to the Catholic faith of her mother, Catherine of Aragon, Mary vowed to return England to the pope.

Hundreds of Protestants were executed; others scurried off to the safety of Geneva and Frankfurt, where they absorbed the most radical Calvinist doctrines of the day. When Mary died in 1558 and was succeeded by Elizabeth I, the "Marian exiles" flocked back to England, more eager than ever to rid the Tudor church of Catholicism. Queen Elizabeth governed the English people from 1558 to 1603, an intellectually exciting period during which some of her subjects took the first halting steps toward colonizing the New World. Elizabeth recognized that her most urgent duty as queen was to end the religious turmoil that had divided the country for a generation. She established a unique church, Catholic in much of its ceremony and government but clearly Protestant in doctrine. Under her so-called Elizabethan settlement, the queen assumed the title "Supreme Governor of the Church in England." Some churchmen urged her to abolish all Catholic rituals, but she ignored these strident reformers. The young queen understood that she could not rule effectively without the full support of her people, and that neither radical change nor widespread persecution would gain a monarch lasting popularity.

Quick Check

✓ What was the impact of the Protestant Reformation on English politics?

Religion, War, and Nationalism

Slowly, but steadily, English Protestantism and English national identity merged. A loyal English subject in the late sixteenth century loved the queen, supported the Church of England, and hated Catholics, especially those who lived in Spain. Elizabeth herself came to symbolize this militant new chauvinism. Her subjects adored the Virgin Queen and applauded when her famed "Sea Dogs"—dashing figures such as Sir Francis Drake and Sir John Hawkins—seized Spanish treasure ships in American waters. These raids were little more than piracy, but in this undeclared state of war, such harassment passed for national victories. There seemed to be no reason patriotic Elizabethans should not share in the wealth of the New World. With each engagement, each threat, each plot, English nationalism took deeper root. By the 1570s, it had become obvious that powerful ideological forces similar to those that had moved the Spanish subjects of Isabella and Ferdinand almost a century earlier were driving the English people.

In the mid-1580s, Philip II, who had united the empires of Spain and Portugal in 1580, decided that England's arrogantly Protestant queen could be tolerated no longer. He ordered the construction of a mighty fleet, hundreds of transport vessels designed to carry Spain's finest infantry across the English Channel. When one of Philip's lieutenants viewed the Armada at Lisbon in May 1588, he described it as la *felicissima armada*, the invincible fleet. The king believed that with the support of England's oppressed Catholics, Spanish troops would sweep Elizabeth from power.

The Spanish Armada was a grand scheme; it was an even grander failure. In 1588, a smaller, more maneuverable English navy dispersed Philip's Armada, and severe storms finished it off. Spanish hopes for Catholic England lay wrecked along the rocky coasts of Scotland and Ireland. English Protestants interpreted victory in providential terms: "God breathed and they were scattered."

Even as the Spanish military threat grew, Sir Walter Ralegh, one of the Queen's favorite courtiers, launched a settlement in North America. He diplomatically named his enterprise Virginia, in honor of his patron Elizabeth, the Virgin Queen. In 1587 Ralegh dispatched colonists under the command of John White to Roanoke, a site on the coast of present-day North Carolina, but poor planning, preparation for war with Spain, and hostilities with Native Americans doomed the experiment. When English vessels finally returned to Roanoke, the settlers had disappeared. No one has ever explained what happened to the "lost" colonists.

📖 **Read** the **Document**
John White, Letter to Richard Hakluyt (1590) on **myhistorylab.com**

Quick Check

✓ How did Protestantism and English national identity become merged under Queen Elizabeth I?

CONCLUSION: CAMPAIGN TO SELL AMERICA

Had it not been for Richard Hakluyt the Younger, who publicized explorers' accounts of the New World, the dream of American colonization might have died in England. Hakluyt never saw America. Nevertheless, his vision of the New World powerfully shaped English public opinion. He interviewed captains and sailors and collected their stories in a massive book titled *The Principall Navigations, Voyages, and Discoveries of the English Nation* (1589).

The work appeared to be a straightforward description of what these sailors had seen across the sea. That was its strength. In reality, Hakluyt edited each piece so it would drive home the book's central point: England needed American colonies. Indeed, they were essential to the nation's prosperity and independence. In Hakluyt's America, there were no losers. "The earth bringeth fourth all things in aboundance, as in the first creations without toil or labour," he wrote of Virginia. His blend of piety, patriotism, and self-interest proved popular, and his *Voyages* went through many editions.

Hakluyt's enthusiasm for the spread of English trade throughout the world may have blinded him to the aspirations of other peoples who actually inhabited those distant lands. He continued to collect testimony from adventurers and sailors who claimed to have visited Asia and America. In a popular new edition of his work published between 1598 and 1600 and entitled the *Voyages*, he catalogued in extraordinary detail the commercial opportunities awaiting courageous and ambitious English colonizers. Hakluyt's entrepreneurial perspective obscured other aspects of the European Conquest, which would soon transform the face of the New World. He paid little attention, for example, to the rich cultural diversity of the Native Americans; he said not a word about the pain of the Africans who traveled to North and South America as slaves. Instead, he and many other polemicists for English colonization led the ordinary men and women who crossed the Atlantic to expect a paradise on earth. By fanning such unrealistic expectations, Hakluyt persuaded European settlers that the New World was theirs for the taking, a self-serving view that invited ecological disaster and human suffering.

Indian Fishing Techniques John White depicted fishing techniques practiced by the Indians of the present-day Carolinas. In the canoe, Indians use dip nets and multipronged spears. In the background, they stab at fish with long spears. At left, a weir traps fish by taking advantage of the river current's natural force.

1 STUDY RESOURCES

((●—Listen to the **Chapter Audio** for Chapter 1 on **myhistorylab.com**

TIMELINE

24,000–17,000 B.C. Indians cross the Bering Strait into North America, p. 5

2000–1500 B.C. Agricultural Revolution transforms Native American life, p. 6

A.D. **1001** Norsemen establish a small settlement in Vinland (Newfoundland), p. 16

1469 Marriage of Isabella and Ferdinand unites Spain, p. 16

1492 Columbus lands at San Salvador, p. 5

1497 Cabot leads first English exploration of North America, p. 24

1498 Vasco da Gama of Portugal reaches India by sailing around Africa, p. 17

1506 Columbus dies in Spain after four voyages to America, p. 18

1521 Cortés defeats the Aztecs at Tenochtitlán, p. 19

1529–1536 Henry VIII begins English Reformation, p. 24

1534 Cartier claims Canada for France, p. 22

1558 Elizabeth I becomes queen of England, p. 25

1585 First Roanoke settlement established on coast of North Carolina, p. 26

1588 English defeat Spanish Armada, p. 26

1608 Champlain founds Quebec, p. 23

Chapter Review

NATIVE AMERICANS BEFORE THE CONQUEST

What explains cultural differences among Native American groups before European conquest?

Paleo-Indians crossed into North America from Asia 20,000 years ago. During the migrations, they divided into distinct groups, often speaking different languages. The Agricultural Revolution sparked population growth, allowing some groups, such as the Aztecs, to establish complex societies. The Eastern Woodland Indians, who lived along the Atlantic coast, had just begun to practice agriculture when the Europeans arrived. *(p. 5)*

CONDITIONS OF CONQUEST

How did Europeans and Native Americans interact during the period of first contact?

Native Americans initially welcomed the opportunity to trade with the Europeans. The newcomers insisted on "civilizing" the Indians. Neither Christianity nor European-style education held much appeal for Native Americans, and they resisted efforts to transform their cultures. Contagious Old World diseases, such as smallpox, decimated the Indians, leaving them vulnerable to cultural imperialism. *(p. 10)*

WEST AFRICA: ANCIENT AND COMPLEX SOCIETIES

What was the character of the West African societies European traders first encountered?

West Africans had learned of Islam long before European traders arrived looking for slaves. The earliest Europeans found powerful local rulers who knew how to profit from commercial exchange. Slaves who had been captured in distant wars were taken to so-called slave factories where they were sold to Europeans and then shipped to the New World. *(p. 13)*

EUROPE ON THE EVE OF CONQUEST

What factors explain Spain's central role in New World exploration and colonization?

The unification of Spain under Ferdinand and Isabella, and the experience of the *Reconquista*, provided Spain with advantages in its later conquest of the New World. The Spanish crown supported the explorations of Christopher Columbus, who thought he had discovered a new route to Asia. His voyages gave the Spanish a head start in claiming American lands. *(p. 16)*

SPAIN IN THE AMERICAS

How did Spanish conquest of Central and South America transform Native American cultures?

Spanish *conquistadores* conquered vast territories in the Caribbean, Mexico, and Central and South America during the sixteenth century. Catholic missionaries followed the *conquistadores* to convert the Indians to Christianity. Although the Spanish conquerors cruelly exploited the Indians as laborers, intermarriage between the groups created a new culture blending Spanish and Indian elements. *(p. 18)*

THE FRENCH CLAIM CANADA

What was the character of the French empire in Canada?

The French in Canada focused on building a trading empire rather than on settlement. The *coureurs de bois* and Catholic missionaries lived among the Indians, learning their languages and customs. French explorers followed the extensive river networks of North America and claimed vast stretches of land along the St. Lawrence and Mississippi Rivers. *(p. 22)*

THE ENGLISH TAKE UP THE CHALLENGE

Why did England not participate in the early competition for New World colonies?

During the early 1500s, religious turmoil preoccupied England's monarchs. After ascending the throne in 1558, Queen Elizabeth I ended internal religious struggle by establishing an English Church that was Protestant in doctrine but Catholic in ceremony. Under Elizabeth, English nationalism merged with anti-Catholicism to challenge Spanish control of the Americas. *(p. 23)*

KEY TERM QUESTIONS

1. How did environmental conditions lead to the formation of Beringia? (p. 5)

2. How did the Agricultural Revolution change Native American societies? (p. 6)

3. How did the Indians of the Eastern Woodland Cultures differ from Indians living in other regions? (p. 9)

4. How did the Columbian Exchange threaten the existence of Native Americans? (p. 12)

5. Who were the *conquistadores*, and what where their motivations in the New World? (p. 17)

6. What were the successes and failures of the Treaty of Tordesillas? (p. 18)

7. How did the *encomienda* system exploit Indian laborers? (p. 21)

8. Why was the Virgin of Guadalupe a significant symbol for Mexicans? (p. 21)

9. What were the *coureurs de bois* looking for while following Canada's river networks? (p. 23)

10. How did the Protestant Reformation change the relationship between England and Spain? (p. 24)

11. What was the significance of the failure of The Spanish Armada's invasion of England? (p. 26)

MyHistoryLab Connections

Visit **www.myhistorylab.com** for a customized Study Plan to build your knowledge of *New World Encounters*.

Question for Analysis

1. What were the challenges facing Pre-Columbian societies in the New World?

   View the **Map** *Pre-Columbian Societies of the Americas* p. 6

2. How does this image represent a European stereotype of Native Americans?

   View the **Closer Look** *An Early European Image of Native Americans* p. 19

3. How much of a factor did new technology play in Columbus's 1492 voyage?

   Watch the **Video** *How Should We Think of Columbus?* p. 17

4. How does Las Casas characterize the native peoples?

   Read the **Document** *Bartolome de las Casas, "Of the Island of Hispaniola"* p. 21

5. What motivated King Henry VII to grant the patent to John Cabot?

   Read the **Document** *Henry VII, Letters of Patent Granted to John Cabot* p. 24

Other Resources from this Chapter

View the **Image** *Clovis Points*

Read the **Document** *Thomas Hariot, The Algonquian Peoples*

View the **Image** *English Trade with Indians*

View the **Map** *Native American Population Loss, 1500–1700*

Read the **Document** *Ghana and its people in the Eleventh Century*

View the **Image** *Purchasing Slaves on the African Shore*

View the **Image** *Cruel Conquistadors Torturing Native Americans*

Read the **Document** *Jacques Cartier, First Contact with the Indians*

Read the **Document** *John White Letter to Richard Hakuyt*

Watch the **Video** *What is Columbus's Legacy?*

2 England's New World Experiments

1607–1732

Contents and Spotlight Questions

BREAKING AWAY: DECISIONS TO MOVE TO AMERICA PG. 32

Why did the Chesapeake colonies not prosper during the earliest years of their settlement?

A "NEW" ENGLAND IN AMERICA PG. 41

How did differences in religion affect the founding of the New England colonies?

DIVERSITY IN THE MIDDLE COLONIES PG. 48

How did ethnic diversity shape the development of the Middle Colonies?

PLANTING THE SOUTHERN COLONIES PG. 53

How was the founding of the Carolinas different from the founding of Georgia?

((•— Listen to the **Chapter Audio** for Chapter 2 on **myhistorylab.com**

PROFIT AND PIETY: COMPETING VISIONS FOR ENGLISH SETTLEMENT

In spring 1644, John Winthrop, governor of Massachusetts Bay, learned that Native Americans had overrun the scattered tobacco plantations of Virginia, killing some 500 colonists. Winthrop never thought much of the Chesapeake settlements. He regarded the people who had migrated to that part of America as grossly materialistic, and because Virginia had recently expelled several Puritan ministers, Winthrop decided the hostilities were God's way of punishing the tobacco planters for their worldliness: "It was observable that this massacre came upon them soon after they had driven out the godly ministers we had sent to them." When Virginians appealed to Massachusetts for military supplies, they received a cool reception. "We were weakly provided ourselves," Winthrop explained, "and so could not afford them any help of that kind."

Captain John Smith and Powhatan The story of Pocahontas rescuing Capt. John smith just as he was about to be executed by her father Powhatan is well-known. In all likelihood the ceremony, pictured here, was never intended to end in Smith's death. Instead, Powhatan symbolically spared Smith's life in order to emphasize the werowance's authority over Smith and the Jamestown settlers who had come to live in his lands.

31

In 1675, the tables turned. Native Americans declared all-out war against the New Englanders, and soon reports of the destruction of Puritan communities reached Virginia. "The Indians in New England have burned Considerable Villages," wrote one leading tobacco planter, "and have made them [the New Englanders] desert more than one hundred and fifty miles of those places they had formerly seated."

News of New England's adversity did not displease Sir William Berkeley, Virginia's royal governor. He and his friends held the Puritans in contempt. Indeed, the New Englanders reminded them of the religious fanatics who had provoked civil war in England and who in 1649 had executed King Charles I. Berkeley noted that he might have shown more pity for the New Englanders "had they deserved it of the King." The governor, sounding like a Puritan himself, described the Indians as the "Instruments" with which God intended "to destroy the King's Enemies." For good measure, Virginia outlawed the export of foodstuffs to its embattled northern neighbors.

Such extraordinary disunity in the colonies—not to mention lack of compassion—may surprise anyone searching for the roots of modern nationalism in this early period. English colonization in the seventeenth century did not spring from a desire to build a centralized empire in the New World similar to that of Spain or France. Instead, the English crown awarded colonial charters to a wide variety of entrepreneurs, religious idealists, and aristocratic adventurers who established separate and profoundly different colonies. Not only did New Englanders have little in common with the earliest Virginians and Carolinians, but they were often divided among themselves.

Migration itself helps to explain this striking competition and diversity. At different times, different colonies appealed to different sorts of people. Men and women moved to the New World for various reasons, and as economic, political, and religious conditions changed on both sides of the Atlantic during the seventeenth century, so too did patterns of English migration.

BREAKING AWAY: DECISIONS TO MOVE TO AMERICA

Why did the Chesapeake colonies not prosper during the earliest years of their settlement?

English colonists crossed the Atlantic for many reasons. Some wanted to institute a purer form of worship, more closely based on their interpretation of Scripture. Others dreamed of owning land and improving their social position. A few came to the New World to escape bad marriages, jail terms, or the dreary prospect of lifelong poverty. Since most seventeenth-century migrants, especially those who transferred to the Chesapeake colonies, left almost no records of their lives in England, it is futile to try to isolate a single cause or explanation for their decision to leave home.

In the absence of detailed personal information, historians usually have assumed that poverty, or the fear of soon falling into poverty, drove people across the Atlantic. No doubt economic considerations figured heavily in the final decision to leave England. But so did religion, and the poor of early modern England were often among those demanding the most radical ecclesiastical reform. As a recent historian of seventeenth-century migration concluded, "Individuals left for a variety of motives, some idealistic, others practical, some simple, others complex, many perhaps contradictory and imperfectly understood by the migrants themselves."

Whatever their reasons for crossing the ocean, English migrants to America in this period left a nation wracked by recurrent, often violent political and religious controversy. During the 1620s, autocratic Stuart monarchs—James I (r. 1603–1625) and his son Charles I (r. 1625–1649)—who succeeded Queen Elizabeth I on the English throne fought constantly with the members of Parliament over rival notions of constitutional and representative government.

Regardless of the exact timing of departure, English settlers brought with them ideas and assumptions that helped them make sense of their everyday experiences in an unfamiliar environment. Their values were tested and sometimes transformed in the New World, but they were seldom destroyed. Settlement involved a complex process of adjustment. The colonists developed different subcultures in America, and in each it is possible to trace the interaction between the settlers' values and the physical elements, such as the climate, crops, and soil, of their new surroundings. The Chesapeake, the New England colonies, the Middle Colonies, and the Southern Colonies formed distinct regional identities that have survived to the present day.

The Chesapeake: Dreams of Wealth

After the Roanoke debacle in 1590, English interest in American settlement declined, and only a few aging visionaries such as Richard Hakluyt kept alive the dream of colonies in the New World. These advocates argued that the North American mainland contained resources of incalculable value. An innovative group, they insisted, might reap great profits and supply England with raw materials that it would otherwise be forced to purchase from European rivals: Holland, France, and Spain.

Moreover, any enterprise that annoyed Catholic Spain or revealed its weakness in America seemed a desirable end in itself to patriotic English Protestants. Anti-Catholicism and hatred of Spain became an integral part of English national identity during this period, and unless one appreciates just how deeply those sentiments ran in the popular mind, one cannot fully understand why ordinary people who had no direct financial stake in the New World so generously supported English efforts to colonize America. Soon after James I ascended to the throne (1603), adventurers were given an opportunity to put their theories into practice in the colonies of Virginia and Maryland, an area known as the Chesapeake, or later, as the Tobacco Coast.

View the **Map**
The Colonies to 1740 on
myhistorylab.com

Quick Check
✓ Why did some people continue to advocate colonies in the New World?

Entrepreneurs in Virginia

During Elizabeth I's reign, the major obstacle to successful colonization of the New World had been raising money. No single person, no matter how rich or well connected, could underwrite the vast expenses a New World settlement required. The solution to this financial problem was the joint-stock company, a business organization in which many people could invest without fear of bankruptcy. A merchant or landowner could purchase a share of stock at a stated price, and at the end of several years, the investor could anticipate recovering the initial amount plus a portion of whatever profits the company had made. Joint-stock ventures sprang up like mushrooms. Affluent English citizens, and even some of more modest fortunes, rushed to invest in the companies, and, as a result, some projects amassed large amounts of capital, enough certainly to launch a new colony in Virginia.

On April 10, 1606, King James issued the first Virginia charter, which authorized the London Company to establish plantations in Virginia. The London Company was an ambitious business venture. Its leader, Sir Thomas Smith, was reputedly London's wealthiest merchant. Smith and his partners gained possession of the territory lying between present-day North Carolina and the Hudson River. These were generous but vague boundaries, to be sure, but the Virginia Company—as the London Company soon called itself—set out immediately to find the treasures Hakluyt had promised.

In December 1606, the *Susan Constant*, the *Godspeed*, and the *Discovery* sailed for America. The ships carried 104 men and boys who had been instructed to establish a fortified outpost some hundred miles up a large navigable river. The natural beauty and economic potential of the region were apparent to everyone. A voyager on the expedition reported seeing "faire meaddowes and goodly tall trees, with such fresh waters running through the woods, as almost ravished [us] at first sight."

The leaders of the colony selected—without consulting resident Native Americans—what the Europeans considered a promising location more than 30 miles from the mouth of the James River. A marshy peninsula jutting out into the river became the site for one of America's most unsuccessful villages, Jamestown. Modern historians have criticized the choice, for the low-lying ground proved to be a disease-ridden death trap; even the drinking water was contaminated with salt. But Jamestown seemed the ideal place to build a fort, since surprise attack by Spaniards or Native Americans rather than sickness appeared the more serious threat in the early months of settlement.

🔍 **View** the **Image**
Mural of Jamestown Settlement on
myhistorylab.com

However, avarice soon became an issue. Virginia's adventurers had traveled to the New World in search of the sort of instant wealth they imagined the Spaniards had found in Mexico and Peru. Tales of rubies and diamonds lying on the beach probably inflamed their expectations. Even when it must have been apparent that such expectations were unfounded, the first settlers often behaved in Virginia as if they expected to become rich. Instead of cooperating for the common good—guarding or farming, for example—individuals pursued personal interests. They searched for gold when they might have helped plant corn. No one would take orders, and those who were supposed to govern the colony looked after their private welfare while disease, war, and starvation ravaged the settlement.

Quick Check

✓ Why did Jamestown come so close to failing in its early years?

Threat of Anarchy

Virginia might have failed had it not been for Captain John Smith. Before coming to Jamestown, he had traveled throughout Europe and fought with the Hungarian army against the Turks—and, if Smith is to be believed, he was saved from certain death by various beautiful women. Because of his reputation for boasting, historians have discounted Smith's account of life in early Virginia. Recent scholarship, however, has affirmed the truthfulness of his curious story.

In Virginia, Smith brought order out of anarchy. While members of the council in Jamestown debated petty politics, he traded with the local Indians for food, mapped the Chesapeake Bay, and may even have been rescued from execution by a young Indian girl, Pocahontas. In the fall of 1608, he seized control of the ruling council and instituted tough military discipline. Under Smith, no one enjoyed special privilege. Those whom he forced to work came to hate him. But he managed to keep them alive, no small achievement in such a deadly environment.

Leaders of the Virginia Company in London recognized the need to reform the entire enterprise. After all, they had spent considerable sums and had received nothing in return. In 1609, the company directors obtained a new charter from the king, which completely reorganized the Virginia government. Henceforth all commercial and political decisions affecting the colonists rested with the company, a fact that had not been made sufficiently clear in the 1606 charter. Moreover, in an effort to raise scarce capital, the original partners opened the joint-stock company to the general public. For a little more than £12—approximately one year's wages for an unskilled English laborer—a person or group of persons could purchase a stake in Virginia. It was anticipated that in 1616 the profits from the colony would be distributed among the shareholders. The company sponsored a publicity campaign; pamphlets and sermons extolled the colony's potential and exhorted patriotic English citizens to invest in the enterprise.

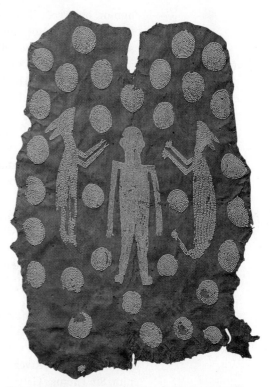

Powhatan Ceremonial Cloak In 1608, Powhatan, the father of Pocahontas, gave this shell-decorated ceremonial cloak to Captain Christopher Newport, commander of the fleet that brought the first English settlers to Jamestown. (*Source: Ashmolean Museum, Oxford, England, U.K.*)

The burst of energy came to nothing. Bad luck and poor planning plagued the Virginia Company. A vessel carrying additional settlers and supplies went aground in Bermuda, and while this misadventure did little to help the people at Jamestown, it provided Shakespeare with the idea for his play *The Tempest*.

Between 1609 and 1611, the remaining Virginia settlers lacked capable leadership, and, perhaps as a result, they lacked food. The terrible winter of 1609–1610 was termed the "starving time." A few desperate colonists were driven to cannibalism, an ironic situation since early explorers had assumed that only Native Americans would eat human flesh. In England, Smith heard that one colonist had killed his wife, powdered (salted) her, and "had eaten part of her before it was known; for which he was executed." The captain, who possessed a droll sense of

Read the **Document** *John Smith, "The Starving Time"* on **myhistorylab.com** humor, observed, "Now, whether she was better roasted, broiled, or carbonadoed [sliced], I know not, but such a dish as powdered wife I never heard of." Other settlers simply lost the will to live.

The presence of so many Native Americans was an additional threat to Virginia's survival. The first colonists found themselves living—or attempting to live—in territory controlled by what was probably the most powerful Indian confederation east of the Mississippi River. Under the leadership of their paramount chief or *werowance*, Powhatan, these Indians had by 1608 created a loose association of some 30 tribes. When Captain John Smith arrived to lead several hundred adventurers, the Powhatans (named for their king) numbered some 14,000 people, including 3,200 warriors. These people hoped to enlist the Europeans as allies against native enemies.

When it became clear that the two groups, holding such different notions about labor and property and about exploiting the natural environment, could not coexist in peace, the Powhatans tried to drive the invaders out of Virginia, once in 1622 and again in 1644. Their numbers sapped by losses from European diseases, the Powhatan failed both times. The failure of the second campaign destroyed the Powhatan empire.

In June 1610, the settlers who had survived despite starvation and conflicts with the Indians actually abandoned Virginia. Through a stroke of luck, however, a new governor and new colonists arrived from England just as they were sailing down the James River. The governor and the deputy governors who succeeded him, Sir Thomas Gates and Sir Thomas Dale, ruled by martial law. The new colonists, many of them male and female servants employed by the company, were marched to work by the beat of the drum. Such methods saved the colony but could not make it flourish. In 1616, company shareholders received no profits. Their only reward was the right to a piece of unsurveyed land located 3,000 miles from London.

View the **Image**
Powhatan in Longhouse on
myhistorylab.com

Quick Check

✓ Why did the first Virginia settlers not cooperate for the common good?

Tobacco Saves Virginia

The economic solution to Virginia's problems grew in the vacant lots of Jamestown. Only Indians bothered to cultivate tobacco until John Rolfe, a settler who achieved notoriety by marrying Pocahontas, realized this local weed might be a valuable export. Rolfe experimented with the crop, eventually growing in Virginia a milder variety that had been developed in the West Indies that was more appealing to European smokers.

Virginians suddenly possessed a means to make money. Tobacco proved relatively easy to grow, and settlers who had avoided work now threw themselves into its production with single-minded diligence. In 1617, one observer found that Jamestown's "streets and all other spare places [are] planted with tobacco … the Colony dispersed all about planting tobacco." Although King James I originally considered smoking immoral and unhealthy, he changed his mind when the duties he collected on tobacco imports began to mount.

The Virginia Company sponsored another ambitious effort to transform the colony into a profitable enterprise. In 1618, Sir Edwin Sandys (pronounced Sands) led a faction of stockholders that began to pump life into the dying organization by instituting sweeping reforms and eventually ousting Sir Thomas Smith and his friends. Sandys wanted private investors to develop their own estates in Virginia. Before 1618, there had been little incentive to do so, but by relaxing Dale's martial law and promising an elective representative assembly called the House of Burgesses, Sandys thought he could make the colony more attractive to wealthy speculators.

Even more important was Sandys's method for distributing land. Colonists who covered their own transportation cost to America were guaranteed a headright, a 50-acre lot for which they paid only a small annual rent. Adventurers were granted additional headrights for each servant they brought to the colony. This allowed prosperous planters to build up huge estates while they also acquired dependent laborers. This land system persisted long after the ompany's collapse. So too did the notion that the wealth of a few justified the exploitation of many others.

Sandys also urged the settlers to diversify their economy. Tobacco alone, he argued, was not a sufficient base. He envisioned colonists busily producing iron and tar, silk and glass, sugar and cotton. There was no end to his suggestions. He scoured Europe for skilled artisans and exotic plants. To finance such a huge project, Sandys relied on a lottery, a game of chance that promised a continuous flow of capital into the company's treasury. The final element in the grand scheme was people. Sandys sent English settlers by the thousand to Jamestown, ordinary men and women swept up by the same hopes that had carried the colonists of 1607 to the New World.

View the **Image**
First House of Burgesses Meeting in Jamestown on **myhistorylab.com**

Quick Check

✓ In what sense did tobacco save the Chesapeake colonies?

Time of Reckoning

Company records reveal that between 1619 and 1622, 3,570 individuals were sent to the colony. People seldom moved to Virginia as families. Although the first women arrived in Jamestown in 1608, most emigrants were single males in their teens or early twenties who came to the New World as indentured servants. In exchange for transportation across the Atlantic, they agreed to serve a master for a stated number of years. The length of service depended in part on the age of the servant. The younger the servant, the longer he or she served. In return, the master promised to give the laborers proper care and, at the conclusion of their contracts, provide them with tools and clothes according to "the custom of the country."

Powerful Virginians corrupted the system. Poor servants wanted to establish independent tobacco farms. As they discovered, however, headrights were awarded not to the newly freed servant, but to the great planter who had paid for the servant's transportation to the New World and for his or her food and clothing during the indenture. And even though indentured servants were promised land when they were freed, they were most often cheated, becoming members of a growing, disaffected landless class in seventeenth-century Virginia.

Life in the Chesapeake Shown here is a reconstruction of a free white planter's house from the late seventeenth-century Chesapeake.

Whenever possible, planters in Virginia purchased able-bodied workers, in other words, persons (preferably male) capable of hard agricultural labor. This preference skewed the colony's sex ratio. In the early decades, men outnumbered women by as much as six to one. Such gender imbalance meant that even if a male servant lived to the end of his indenture—an unlikely prospect—he could not realistically expect to start his own family. Moreover, despite apparent legal safeguards, masters could treat dependent workers as they pleased; after all, these people were legally considered property. Servants were sold, traded, even gambled away. It does not require much imagination to see that a society that tolerated such an exploitative labor system might later embrace slavery.

Most Virginians did not live long enough to worry about marriage. Death was omnipresent. Indeed, extraordinarily high mortality was a major reason the Chesapeake colonies developed so differently from those of New England. On the eve of the 1618 reforms, Virginia's population stood at approximately 700. The Virginia Company sent at least 3,500 more people, but by 1622 only 1,240 were still alive. "It Consequentilie followes," declared one angry shareholder, "that we had then lost 3000 persons within those 3 yeares." The major killers were contagious diseases. Salt in the water supply also took a toll. And on Good Friday, March 22, 1622, the Powhatan Indians slew 347 Europeans in a well-coordinated surprise attack.

No one knows for certain how such a horrendous mortality rate affected the survivors. At the least, it must have created a sense of impermanence, a desire to escape Virginia with a little money before sickness or violence ended the adventure. The settlers who drank to excess aboard the tavern ships anchored in the James River described the colony "not as a place of Habitacion but only of a short sojourninge."

On both sides of the Atlantic people wondered whom to blame. The burden of responsibility lay largely with the Virginia Company. In fact, its scandalous mismanagement embarrassed James I, and in 1624 he dissolved the bankrupt enterprise and transformed Virginia into a royal colony. The crown appointed a governor and a council. No provision was made, however, for continuing the House of Burgesses. While elections to the Burgesses were hardly democratic, it did provide wealthy planters a voice in government. Even without the king's authorization, the representatives gathered annually after 1629, and in 1639, King Charles I recognized the body's existence.

Read the **Document**
Wessell Webling, His Indenture (1622) on **myhistorylab.com**

Quick Check

✓ What explains the extraordinary death rate in early Virginia?

Maryland: A Catholic Refuge

By the end of the seventeenth century, Maryland society looked remarkably like that of its Chesapeake neighbor, Virginia. At the time of its first settlement in

1634, however, no one would have predicted that Maryland, a colony wholly owned by a Catholic nobleman, would have survived, much less become a flourishing tobacco colony (see Map 2.1).

The driving force behind the founding of Maryland was Sir George Calvert, later Lord Baltimore. Calvert, a talented and well-educated man, enjoyed the patronage of James I. He was awarded lucrative positions in the government, the most important being the king's secretary of state. In 1625, however, Calvert shocked almost everyone by publicly declaring his Catholicism; in this fiercely anti-Catholic society, persons who openly supported the Church of Rome were immediately stripped of civil office. Although forced to resign as secretary of state, Calvert retained the crown's favor.

Before resigning, Calvert sponsored a settlement on the coast of Newfoundland, but after visiting it, he concluded that no English person, whatever his or her religion, would transfer to a place where the "ayre [is] so intolerably cold." He turned his attention to the Chesapeake, and on June 30, 1632, Charles I granted George Calvert's son, Cecilius, a charter for a colony to be located north of Virginia. The boundaries of the settlement, named Maryland in honor of Charles's queen, were so vaguely defined that they generated legal controversies not fully resolved until the 1760s when Charles Mason and Jeremiah Dixon surveyed their famous boundary line between Pennsylvania and Maryland.

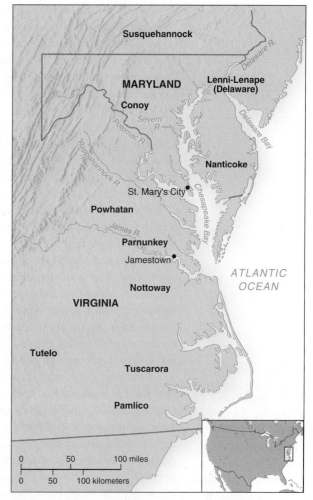

Map 2.1 *Chesapeake Colonies, 1640*   The many deep rivers flowing into the Chesapeake Bay provided English planters with a convenient transportation system, linking them directly by sea to European markets.

Cecilius, the second Lord Baltimore, wanted to create a sanctuary for England's persecuted Catholics. He also intended to make money. Without Protestant settlers, it seemed unlikely Maryland would prosper, and Cecilius instructed his brother Leonard, the colony's governor, to do nothing that might frighten off hypersensitive Protestants. The governor was ordered to "cause all Acts of the Roman Catholic Religion to be done as privately as may be and … [to] instruct all Roman Catholics to be silent upon all occasions of discourse concerning matters of Religion." On March 25, 1634, the *Ark* and *Dove*, carrying about 150 settlers, landed safely, and within days, the governor purchased from the Yaocomico Indians a village that became St. Mary's City, the first capital of Maryland.

Read the Document
George Alsop from "A Character of the Province of Maryland" on **myhistorylab.com**

The colony's charter was a throwback to an earlier feudal age. It transformed Lord Baltimore into a "palatine lord," a proprietor with almost royal powers. Settlers swore an oath of allegiance not to the king of England but to Lord Baltimore. In England, such practices had long ago been abandoned. As the proprietor, Lord Baltimore owned outright almost six million acres and had absolute authority over anyone living in his domain.

On paper, at least, everyone in Maryland was assigned a place in an elaborate social hierarchy. Members of a colonial ruling class, persons who purchased 6,000 acres from Baltimore, were called lords of the manor. These landed aristocrats were permitted to establish local courts of law. People holding less acreage enjoyed fewer privileges, particularly in government. Baltimore figured that land sales and rents would finance the entire venture.

Baltimore's feudal system never took root in Chesapeake soil. People refused to play the social roles the lord proprietor had assigned them. These tensions affected Maryland's government. Baltimore assumed that his brother, acting as his deputy in America, and a small appointed council of local aristocrats would pass laws and carry out routine administration. When an elected assembly first convened in 1635, Baltimore allowed the delegates to discuss only those acts he had prepared. The members of the assembly bridled at such restrictions, insisting on exercising traditional parliamentary privileges. Neither side gained a clear victory in the assembly, and for almost 25 years, legislative squabbling contributed to the political instability that almost destroyed Maryland.

The colony drew both Protestants and Catholics, and the two groups might have lived in harmony had civil war not broken out in England in the 1640s. When Oliver Cromwell and the Puritan faction executed King Charles I in 1649, transforming England briefly into a republic, it seemed Baltimore might lose his colony. To head this off and placate Maryland's restless Protestants, the proprietor drafted the famous "Act concerning Religion" in 1649, which extended toleration to everyone who accepted the divinity of Christ. At a time when European rulers regularly persecuted people for their religious beliefs, Baltimore championed liberty of conscience.

However laudable the act may have been, it did not heal religious divisions in Maryland, and when local Puritans seized the colony's government in 1650, they repealed the act. For almost two decades, vigilantes roamed the countryside, and one armed group temporarily drove Leonard Calvert out of Maryland. In 1655, civil war flared again, and the Calvert family did not regain control until 1658.

In this troubled sanctuary, ordinary planters and their workers cultivated tobacco on plantations dispersed along riverfronts. In 1678, Baltimore complained that he could not find 50 houses in a space of 30 miles. Tobacco affected almost every aspect of local culture. "In Virginia and Maryland," one member of the Calvert family explained, "Tobacco, as our Staple, is our all, and indeed leaves no room for anything Else." A steady stream of indentured servants supplied the plantations with dependent laborers—until African slaves replaced them at the end of the seventeenth century.

Europeans sacrificed much by coming to the Chesapeake. For most of the seventeenth century, their standard of living there was primitive compared with that of people of the same social class who had remained in England. Two-thirds of the planters, for example, lived in houses of only two rooms and of a type associated with the poorest classes in contemporary English society.

Quick Check

✓ What motives led Lord Baltimore to establish the colony of Maryland?

A "NEW" ENGLAND IN AMERICA

The Pilgrims enjoy almost mythic status in American history. These brave refugees crossed the cold Atlantic in search of religious liberty, signed a democratic compact aboard the *Mayflower*, landed at Plymouth Rock, and gave us our Thanksgiving Day. As with most legends, this one contains only a core of truth.

How did differences in religion affect the founding of the New England colonies?

The Pilgrims were not crusaders out to change the world. Rather, they were humble English farmers. Their story began in the early 1600s in Scrooby Manor, a small community located approximately 150 miles north of London. Many people in this area believed the Church of England, or Anglican Church, retained too many traces of its Catholic origin. Its very rituals compromised God's true believers. So, early in the reign of James I, the Scrooby congregation formally left the established state church. Like others who followed this logic, they were called Separatists. Since English law required citizens to attend Anglican services, the Scrooby Separatists moved to Holland in 1608–1609 rather than compromise their beliefs.

The Netherlands provided the Separatists with a good home—too good. The members of the little church feared they were losing their identity; their children were becoming Dutch. In 1617, therefore, some of the original Scrooby congregation vowed to sail to America. Included in this group was William Bradford, a wonderfully literate man who later wrote *Of Plymouth Plantation*, one of the first and certainly most poignant accounts of an early American settlement.

Poverty presented the major obstacle to the Pilgrims' plans. They petitioned for a land patent from the Virginia Company of London. They also looked for someone willing to underwrite the staggering costs of colonization. The negotiations went well, or so it seemed. After stopping in England to take on supplies and laborers, the Pilgrims set off for America in 1620 aboard the *Mayflower*, armed with a patent to settle in Virginia and indebted to English investors who were only marginally interested in religious reform.

Because of an error in navigation, the Pilgrims landed not in Virginia but in what is today Massachusetts in New England. The patent for which they had worked so diligently had no validity there. In fact, the crown had granted New England to another company. Without a patent, the colonists possessed no authorization to form a civil government, a serious matter since some sailors who were not Pilgrims threatened mutiny. To preserve the struggling community from anarchy, 41 men signed an agreement known as the Mayflower Compact to "covenant and combine our selves together into a civil body politick."

Read the **Document** *Mayflower Replica Plymouth, Massachusetts* on **myhistorylab.com**

Although later praised for its democratic character, the Mayflower Compact could not ward off disease and hunger. During the first months in Plymouth, death claimed approximately half of the 102 people who had initially set out from England. Moreover, debts contracted in England severely burdened the new colony. To their credit, the Pilgrims honored their financial obligations, but it took almost 20 years to satisfy the English investors. Without Bradford, whom they elected as governor, the settlers might have been overwhelmed. Through strength of will and self-sacrifice, however, Bradford persuaded frightened men and women that they could survive in America.

Bradford had help. Almost anyone who has heard of the Plymouth Colony knows of Squanto, a Patuxet Indian who welcomed the first Pilgrims in excellent English. In 1614 unscrupulous adventurers had kidnapped Squanto and sold him in Spain as a slave. Somehow he escaped bondage, making his way to London, where merchants who owned land in Newfoundland taught him to speak English. They apparently hoped that he would deliver moving public testimonials about immigrating to the New World. In any case, Squanto returned to the Plymouth area just before the Pilgrims arrived. Squanto joined Massasoit, a Native American leader, in teaching the Pilgrims much about hunting and agriculture, a debt that Bradford acknowledged. Although evidence for the so-called First Thanksgiving is sketchy, it is certain that without Native American support the Europeans would have starved.

European diseases had destroyed many of the Indian villages near Plymouth before the Pilgrims arrived. Now the Pilgrims were able to move onto cleared land left empty by the disappearance of the Indians. In time, the Pilgrims replicated the humble little farm communities they had known in England. They formed Separatist congregations to their liking, and the population slowly increased. But because Plymouth offered only limited economic prospects, it attracted few new settlers. In 1691, the colony was absorbed into its larger and more prosperous neighbor, Massachusetts Bay.

The Puritan Migration to Massachusetts

Read the
Document
*Reasons for the
Plantation in New
England* on
myhistorylab.com

In the early seventeenth century, an extraordinary spirit of religious reform burst forth in England, and before it burned itself out, Puritanism had transformed the face of England and America. Modern historians have difficulty comprehending this powerful spiritual movement. Some consider the Puritans neurotic individuals who condemned liquor and sex, dressed in drab clothes, and minded their neighbors' business.

This crude caricature is based on a profound misunderstanding of the actual nature of this broad popular movement. The seventeenth-century Puritans were more like today's radical political reformers, men and women committed to far-reaching institutional change, than like naive do-gooders or narrow fundamentalists. To their enemies, of course, the Puritans were irritants, always pointing out civil and ecclesiastical imperfections and urging everyone to try to fulfill the commands of Scripture. Many people, however, shared their vision, and their values remained a dominant element in American culture at least until the Civil War.

The Puritans were products of the Protestant Reformation. They accepted a notion advanced by the sixteenth-century French-Swiss theologian John Calvin that an omnipotent God predestined some people to salvation and condemned others to eternal damnation no matter how good or sinful their lives were. But instead of waiting passively for Judgment Day, the Puritans examined themselves for signs of grace, for hints that God had placed them among his "elect." A member of the elect, they argued, would try to live according to Scripture, to battle sin and eradicate corruption.

For the Puritans, the logic of everyday life was clear. If the Church of England contained unscriptural elements—clerical vestments associated with Catholic ritual, for example—then they must be eliminated. If the pope in Rome was in league with the Antichrist foretold in the Bible, then Protestant kings should not ally with Catholic states. If God condemned licentiousness and intoxication, then local officials should punish whores, adulterers, and drunks. There was nothing improper about an occasional beer or passionate physical love within marriage, but when sex and drink became ends in themselves, the Puritans thought England's ministers and magistrates should speak out. Persons of this temperament were more combative than the Pilgrims had been. They wanted to purify the Church of England from within, and before the 1630s at least, separatism held little appeal for them.

From the Puritan perspective, James I and Charles I seemed unconcerned about the spiritual state of the nation. James tolerated corruption within his court and condoned gross public extravagance. Charles I persecuted Puritan ministers, forcing them either to conform to his theology or lose their licenses to preach. As long as Parliament met, Puritan voters in the various boroughs and counties of England elected men sympathetic to their point of view. These outspoken representatives criticized royal policies. Because of their defiance, Charles decided in 1629 to rule England without Parliament and four years later named William Laud, who represented everything the Puritans detested, archbishop of Canterbury, the leading position within the Church of England. The doors of reform slammed shut. The corruption remained.

John Winthrop, the future governor of Massachusetts Bay, was caught up in these events. Little about his background suggested such an auspicious future. He owned a small manor in Suffolk, one that never produced sufficient income to support his growing family. He dabbled in law. But the core of Winthrop's life was a faith in God so intense that his contemporaries immediately identified him as a Puritan. The Lord, he concluded, was displeased with England. Time for reform was running out. In May 1629, he wrote to his wife, "I am verily perswaded God will bring some heavye Affliction upon this lande, and that speedylye." He was, however, confident that the Lord would "provide a shelter and a hidinge place for us."

Read the
Document
John Winthrop, "A Model of Christian Charity" (1630) on
myhistorylab.com

Quick Check

✓ Why did the Puritans choose to leave England?

"A City on a Hill"

A fleet bearing Puritan settlers, John Winthrop among them, departed England in March 1630. By the end of the Puritan colony's first year, almost 2,000 people had arrived in Massachusetts Bay, and before the "Great Migration" concluded in the early 1640s, more than 16,000 men and women had arrived there.

Historians know a lot about the background of these settlers. Many of them originated in an area northeast of London called East Anglia, where Puritan ideas had taken deep root. London, Kent, and the West Country also contributed to the stream of emigrants. In some instances, entire villages were reestablished across the Atlantic. Many Bay Colonists had been farmers in England, but a surprisingly large number came from industrial centers, such as Norwich, where cloth was manufactured for the export trade.

Whatever their backgrounds, they moved to Massachusetts as nuclear families—fathers, mothers, and their dependent children—a form of migration strikingly different from the one that peopled Virginia and Maryland. Moreover, because the settlers had already formed families in England, the colony's sex ratio was more balanced than that found in the Chesapeake colonies. Finally, and perhaps more significantly, once they had arrived in Massachusetts, these men and women survived. Indeed, their life expectancy compares favorably to that of modern Americans. Many factors help explain this phenomenon—clean drinking water and a healthy climate, for example. While the Puritans could not have planned to live longer than did colonists in other parts of the New World, this remarkable accident reduced the emotional shock of long-distance migration.

The first settlers possessed another source of strength and stability. They were bound together by a common sense of purpose. God, they insisted, had formed a special covenant with the people of Massachusetts Bay. The Lord expected them to live according to Scripture and reform the church—in other words, to create an Old Testament "City on a Hill" that would stand as a beacon of righteousness for the rest of the Christian world. If they fulfilled their side of the bargain, the settlers could anticipate peace and prosperity.

The Bay Colonists developed an innovative form of church government known as Congregationalism. Under this system, each village church was independent of outside

Old Ship Meetinghouse This early Puritan meetinghouse in Hingham, Massachusetts, was called the Old Ship Meetinghouse because its interior design resembled the hull of a ship. The oldest surviving wooden church in the United States, it could accommodate about 700 people.

interference. The American Puritans, of course, wanted nothing of bishops. The people were the church, and as a body, they pledged to uphold God's law. In the Salem Church, for example, the members covenanted "with the Lord and with one another and do bind ourselves in the presence of God to walk together in all his ways."

Simply because a person happened to live in a certain community did not mean he or she automatically belonged to church. The churches of Massachusetts were voluntary institutions. To join one a man or woman had to provide testimony—a confession of faith—before neighbors who had already been admitted as full members. It was a demanding process. But most men and women in early Massachusetts aspired to full membership, which entitled them to receive the sacraments and gave some of them responsibility for choosing ministers, disciplining sinners, and settling difficult questions of theology. Although women and blacks could not vote for ministers, they did become members of the Congregational churches.

The government of Massachusetts was neither a democracy nor a theocracy. The magistrates elected in Massachusetts did not believe they represented the voters, much less the whole populace. They ruled in the name of the electorate, but their responsibility was to God. In 1638, Winthrop warned against overly democratic forms, since "the best part [of the people] is always the least, and of that best part the wiser is always the lesser." The Congregational ministers possessed no formal political authority in Massachusetts Bay and could not even hold civil office. Voters often ignored the recommendations of their ministers.

In New England, the town became the center of public life. In other regions of British America, where the county was the focus of local government, people did not experience the same density of social and institutional interaction. In Massachusetts, groups of men and women voluntarily covenanted together to observe common goals. The community constructed a meetinghouse where religious services and town meetings were held. This powerful sense of shared purpose—something that later Americans have greatly admired—should not obscure the fact that the founders of New England towns also had a keen eye for personal profit. Seventeenth-century records reveal that speculators often made a good deal of money from selling "shares" in village lands. But acquisitiveness never got out of control, and recent studies have shown that entrepreneurial practices rarely disturbed the peace of the Puritan communities. Inhabitants generally received land sufficient to build a house and support a family. Although villagers escaped the kind of feudal dues collected in other parts of America, they were expected to contribute to the minister's salary, pay local and colony taxes, and serve in the militia.

> **Quick Check**
> ✓ What did the founders of Massachusetts mean when they referred to their colony as a "City on a Hill"?

Competing Truths in New England

The European settlers of Massachusetts Bay managed to live in peace—at least with each other. This was a remarkable achievement considering the chronic instability that plagued other colonies. The Bay Colonists disagreed over many issues, sometimes vociferously; towns disputed with neighboring villages over boundaries. But the people inevitably relied on the civil courts to mediate differences. They believed in a rule of law, and in 1648 the colonial legislature, called the General Court, drew up the *Lawes and Liberties*, the first alphabetized code of law printed in English. In clear prose, it explained to ordinary colonists their rights and responsibilities as citizens of the commonwealth. The code engendered public trust in government and discouraged magistrates from the arbitrary exercise of authority.

The Puritans never supported religious toleration. They transferred to the New World to preserve *their own* freedom of worship. They expressed little concern for the religious freedom of those they deemed heretics. The most serious challenges to Puritan orthodoxy in Massachusetts Bay came from two charismatic people. The first, Roger Williams, arrived in 1631 and immediately attracted loyal followers. Indeed, everyone seemed to have liked him as a person.

Williams's *religious ideas*, however, created controversy. He preached extreme separatism. The Bay Colonists, he exclaimed, were impure in the sight of the Lord so long as they remained even nominal members of the Church of England. More-over, he questioned the validity of the colony's charter, since the king had not first purchased the land from the Indians, a view that threatened the integrity of the entire colonial experiment. Williams also insisted that the civil rulers of Massachusetts had no business punishing settlers for their religious beliefs. Monitoring people's consciences was God's responsibility, not men's. The Bay magistrates were prepared neither to tolerate heresy nor to accede to Williams's other demands, and in 1636, after failing to reach a compromise with him, they banished him from the colony. Williams then worked out the logic of his ideas in Providence, a village he founded in what would become Rhode Island.

The Bay magistrates rightly concluded that Anne Hutchinson, posed an even graver threat to the peace of the commonwealth than Williams had. This intelligent woman, her husband William, and her children arrived in the New World in 1634. Even contemporaries found her religious ideas, which consisted of a highly personal form of spirituality, usually termed antinomianism, confusing.

Hutchinson shared her thoughts with other Bostonians, many of them women. Her outspoken views scandalized orthodox leaders of church and state. She suggested that all but two ministers in the colony had lost touch with the "Holy Spirit" and were preaching a doctrine in the Congregational churches that was little better than that of Archbishop Laud. When authorities demanded she explain her unusual opinions, she suggested that she experienced divine inspiration independently of either the Bible or the clergy. In other words, Hutchinson's teachings could not be tested by Scripture, a position that seemed dangerously subjective. Indeed, her theology threatened the very foundation of Massachusetts Bay. Without clear, external standards, one person's truth was as valid as anyone else's, and from Winthrop's perspective, Hutchinson's teachings invited civil and religious anarchy. But her challenge to authority was not simply theological. As a woman, her aggressive speech sparked a deeply misogynist response from the colony's male leaders.

When this woman described Congregational ministers—some of them the leading divines of Boston—as unconverted men, the General Court intervened. For two days in 1637, the ministers and magistrates of Massachusetts Bay cross-examined

Hutchinson. In this intense theological debate, she more than held her own. She knew as much about the Bible as did her inquisitors.

Hutchinson defied the ministers and magistrates to demonstrate exactly where she had gone wrong. Just when it appeared Hutchinson had outmaneuvered—indeed, embarrassed—her opponents, she let down her guard, declaring that what she knew of God came "by an immediate revelation.... By the voice of his own spirit to my soul." Here was what her accusers had suspected but could not prove. She had confessed in open court that the Spirit can live without the Moral Law. This antinomian statement fulfilled the worst fears of the Bay rulers, and they were relieved to exile Hutchinson and her followers to Rhode Island.

> **Quick Check**
> ✓ In what ways did Roger Williams and Anne Hutchinson pose a threat to the Massachusetts Bay Colony?

Mobility and Division

Massachusetts Bay spawned four new colonies, three of which survived to the American Revolution (see Map 2.2). New Hampshire became a separate colony in 1677. Its population grew slowly, and for much of the colonial period, New Hampshire remained economically dependent on Massachusetts, its commercial neighbor to the south.

Far more people were drawn to the fertile lands of the Connecticut River Valley. In 1636, settlers founded the villages of Hartford, Windsor, and Wethersfield. No one forced these men and women to leave Massachusetts, and in their new surroundings, they recreated a society that looked much like the one they had known in the Bay Colony. Through his writings, Thomas Hooker, Connecticut's most prominent minister, helped all New Englanders define Congregational church policy. Puritans on both sides of the Atlantic read Hooker's beautifully crafted works. In 1639, representatives from the Connecticut towns passed the Fundamental Orders, a blueprint for civil government, and in 1662, King Charles II awarded the colony its own charter.

In 1638, another group, led by Theophilus Eaton and the Reverend John Davenport, settled New Haven and several adjoining towns along Long Island Sound. These emigrants, many of whom had come from London, lived briefly in Massachusetts Bay but then insisted on forming a Puritan commonwealth of their own, one that established a closer relationship between church and state than the Bay

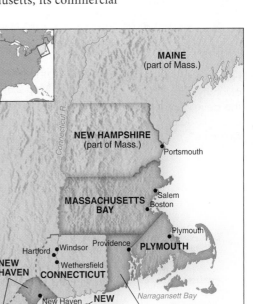

Map 2.2 *New England Colonies, 1650* The early settlers quickly carved up New England. New Haven briefly flourished as a separate colony before being taken over by Connecticut in 1662. Long Island later became part of New York; Massachusetts absorbed Plymouth; and in 1677, New Hampshire became a separate colony.

Colonists had allowed. The New Haven colony never prospered, and in 1662, it was absorbed into Connecticut.

Rhode Island experienced a different history. From the beginning, it drew people of an independent mind, and according to one Dutch visitor, Rhode Island was "the receptacle of all sorts of riff-raff people…. All the cranks of New-England retire thither." This, of course, was an exaggeration. Roger Williams founded Providence in 1636; two years later, Anne Hutchinson took her followers to Portsmouth. Other groups settled around Narragansett Bay. Not surprisingly, these men and women appreciated the need for toleration. No one was persecuted in Rhode Island for his or her religious beliefs.

One might have thought the separate Rhode Island communities would cooperate for the common good. They did not. Villagers fought over land and schemed with outside speculators to divide the tiny colony into even smaller pieces. In 1644, Parliament issued a patent for the "Providence Plantations," and in 1663, the Rhode Islanders obtained a royal charter. But for most of the seventeenth century, colony-wide government existed in name only. Despite their constant bickering, however, the settlers of Rhode Island built up a profitable commerce in agricultural goods.

Quick Check

✓ What religious and economic factors led to the settlement of other New England colonies beyond Masschusetts Bay?

DIVERSITY IN THE MIDDLE COLONIES

How did ethnic diversity shape the development of the Middle Colonies?

New York, New Jersey, Pennsylvania, and Delaware were settled for different reasons (see Map 2.3). William Penn, for example, envisioned a Quaker sanctuary; the Duke of York worried chiefly about his own income. Despite the founders' intentions, however, some common characteristics emerged. Both colonies developed a strikingly heterogeneous population, men and women of different ethnic and religious backgrounds. This cultural diversity influenced the economic, political, and ecclesiastical institutions of the Middle Colonies. The raucous, partisan public life of the Middle Colonies foreshadowed later American society.

Anglo-Dutch Rivalry on the Hudson

Read the **Document**
Father Isaac Jogues' Description of New York, 1640 on **myhistorylab.com**

By the early seventeenth century, the Dutch were Europe's most aggressive traders. The Netherlands—a small, loosely federated nation—possessed the world's largest merchant fleet. Its ships vied for the commerce of Asia, Africa, and the Americas. Dutch rivalry with Spain, a fading though still formidable power, was largely responsible for the settlement of New Netherland. While searching for the elusive Northwest Passage in 1609, Henry Hudson, an English explorer employed by a Dutch company, sailed up the river that now bears his name. Further voyages led to the establishment of trading posts in what became the colony of New Netherland, although permanent settlement did not occur until 1624. The area also seemed an excellent base from which to attack Spain's colonies in the New World.

The directors of the Dutch West India Company sponsored two small outposts, Fort Orange (Albany), located well up the Hudson River, and New Amsterdam (New York City) on Manhattan Island. The first Dutch settlers were salaried employees, not colonists, and their superiors in Europe expected them to spend most of their time gathering furs. They did not receive land for their troubles. Needless to say, this arrangement attracted few Dutch immigrants.

The colony's European population may have been small—only 270 in 1628—but its ethnic mix was extraordinary. One visitor to New Amsterdam in 1644 maintained he had heard "eighteen different languages" spoken there. Even if this report was exaggerated, there is no doubt the Dutch colony drew English, Finns, Germans, and Swedes. By the 1640s, a sizable community of free blacks (probably former slaves who had gained their freedom through self-purchase) had developed in New Amsterdam, adding African tongues to the cacophony of languages. New England Puritans who left Massachusetts and Connecticut to stake out farms on eastern Long Island further fragmented the colony's culture.

New Netherland lacked capable leadership. The company sent a number of director-generals to oversee judicial and political affairs. With-

Map 2.3 *Middle Colonies, 1685* New York and Philadelphia became colonial America's most important commercial ports.

out exception, these men were temperamentally unsuited to govern an American colony. They adopted autocratic procedures, lined their own pockets, and, in one case, blundered into a war that killed scores of Indians and settlers. The company made no provision for an elected assembly. As much as they could, the scattered inhabitants living along the Hudson River ignored company directives. They felt no loyalty to the trading company that had treated them so shabbily. Long Island Puritans complained bitterly about the absence of representative institutions. The Dutch system has been described as "unstable pluralism."

In August 1664, the Dutch lost their tenuous hold on New Netherland. The English crown, eager to score an easy victory over a commercial rival, dispatched a fleet of warships to New Amsterdam. The commander of this force, Colonel Richard Nicolls, ordered the colonists to surrender. The last director-general, a colorful character named Peter Stuyvesant, rushed wildly about the city urging the settlers to resist the English. But no one obeyed. Even the Dutch remained deaf to his appeals. Instead, they accepted the Articles of Capitulation, a generous agreement that allowed Dutch nationals to remain in the province and retain their property under English rule.

Charles II had already granted his brother James, the Duke of York, a charter for the newly captured territory and much else besides. The duke became absolute proprietor over Maine, Martha's Vineyard, Nantucket, Long Island, and the rest of New York all the way south to Delaware Bay. The king perhaps wanted to encircle New England's potentially disloyal Puritan population, but he also created a bureaucratic nightmare.

t' Fort nieuw Amsterdam op de Manhatans

New Amsterdam Dutch colonization in the first half of the seventeenth century extended from New Amsterdam (New York City) up the Hudson River to Fort Orange (Albany).

Quick Check

✓ Why were the Dutch unable to establish a permanent colony in what became New York?

The Duke of York had acquired a thorough aversion to representative government. He had no intention of letting such a participatory system take root in New York. "I cannot *but* suspect," he announced, that an assembly "would be of dangerous consequence." The Long Islanders felt betrayed. In part to appease these outspoken critics, Governor Nicolls—one of the few competent administrators to serve in the Middle Colonies—drew up in March 1665 a legal code known as the Duke's Laws. It guaranteed religious toleration and created local governments.

There was no provision, however, for an elected assembly or for democratic town meetings. The legal code disappointed the Puritan migrants on Long Island, and when the duke's officers attempted to collect taxes, these people protested that they were "inslav'd under an Arbitrary Power."

The Dutch kept silent. For decades they remained a large unassimilated ethnic group. They continued to speak their own language, worship in their own churches (Dutch Reformed Calvinist), and eye their English neighbors with suspicion. In fact, the colony seemed little different from what it had been under the Dutch West India Company: a loose collection of independent communities ruled by an ineffectual central government.

Confusion in New Jersey

Only three months after receiving a charter for New York, the Duke of York gifted its southernmost lands to two courtiers who had served Charles II during the English Civil War. The land between the Hudson and Delaware Rivers went to John, Lord Berkeley and Sir George Carteret to form a colony named New Jersey (in honor of Carteret's birthplace, the Isle of Jersey in the English Channel). But before learning of James's decision, the governor of the colony had allowed migrants from New England to take up farms west of the Hudson River. In exchange for small annual rents to the duke, these settlers were granted the rights to establish an elected assembly, a headright system, and liberty of conscience. Berkeley and Carteret recruited colonists on similar terms, assuming that that they would receive the rent money. Soon it was not clear who owned what in New Jersey.

The result was chaos. Some colonists insisted that the governor had authorized their assembly. Others, equally insistent, claimed that Berkeley and Carteret had done so. Both sides were wrong. Neither the proprietors nor the governor possessed any legal right to set up a colonial government. James could transfer land to favorite courtiers, but no matter how many times the land changed hands, the government remained his personal responsibility. Knowledge of the law failed to quiet the controversy. Through it all, the duke showed not the slightest interest in the peace and welfare of the people of New Jersey.

Berkeley grew tired of the venture. It generated headaches rather than income. In 1674, he sold his proprietary rights to a group of surprisingly quarrelsome Quakers. The sale necessitated the division of the colony into two separate governments known as East and West Jersey. Neither half prospered. Carteret and his heirs tried unsuccessfully to turn a profit in East Jersey. The Quaker proprietors fought among themselves with such intensity that not even William Penn could bring tranquility to their affairs. Penn wisely turned his attention to the unclaimed territory across the Delaware River. The West Jersey proprietors went bankrupt, and in 1702 the Crown reunited the two Jerseys into a single royal colony.

Quick Check

✓ What caused chaos during the settlement of New Jersey?

Quakers in America

The founding of Pennsylvania cannot be separated from the history of the Quaker movement. Believers in an extreme form of antinomianism, the Quakers saw no need for a learned ministry, since one person's interpretation of Scripture was as valid as anyone else's. This radical religious sect gained its name from the derogatory term that English authorities sometimes used to describe those who quake or "tremble at the word of the Lord." The name persisted even though the Quakers preferred being called Professors of the Light or, more commonly, Friends.

Quakers practiced humility in their daily lives. They wore simple clothes and employed old-fashioned forms of address that set them apart from their neighbors. Friends refused to honor worldly position and accomplishment or to swear oaths in courts of law. They were also pacifists. Quakers considered all persons equal in the sight of the Lord, a belief that generally annoyed people of rank and achievement.

Moreover, the Quakers never kept their thoughts to themselves. They preached conversion constantly, spreading the "Truth" throughout England, Ireland, and America. The Friends played important roles in the early history of New Jersey, Rhode Island, and North Carolina, as well as Pennsylvania. In some places, the "publishers of Truth" wore out their welcome. English authorities harassed the Quakers. Thousands were jailed, and in Massachusetts Bay between 1659 and 1661, Puritan magistrates ordered several Friends put to death. But persecution only inspired the persecuted Quakers to redouble their efforts.

Quick Check

✓ What explains Puritan hostility toward the Quakers?

Penn's "Holy Experiment"

William Penn, the founder of Pennsylvania, dedicated his life to the Quaker faith, a commitment that led to the founding of Pennsylvania. His personality was complex. He was an athletic person who threw himself into intellectual pursuits. He was a bold visionary capable of making pragmatic decisions. He came from an aristocratic family and yet spent his adult life involved with a religious movement associated with the lower class.

In 1688, Penn negotiated one of the more impressive land deals in the history of American real estate. Charles II awarded Penn a charter making him the sole proprietor of a vast area called Pennsylvania (literally, "Penn's woods"). The name embarrassed the modest Penn, but he knew better than to look the royal gift horse in the mouth. In 1682, the new proprietor purchased from the Duke of York the so-called Three Lower Counties that eventually became Delaware. Traders in Swedish employ had begun establishing trading posts along the river in the 1630s. In 1655, the Dutch took over full control of these New Sweden territories, but the Duke of York pushed them out in 1664. Penn's astute purchase of these Lower Counties guaranteed that Pennsylvania would have access to the Atlantic and determined even before Philadelphia had been established that it would become a commercial center.

Read the
Document
*William Penn, "Model
for Government"
(1681)* on
myhistorylab.com

Penn lost no time in launching his "Holy Experiment." In 1682, he set forth his ideas in an unusual document known as the Frame of Government. The royal charter gave Penn the right to create any form of government he desired, and his imagination ran wild. His plan blended traditional notions about the privileges of a landed aristocracy with daring concepts of personal liberty. Penn guaranteed that settlers would enjoy, among other things, liberty of conscience, freedom from persecution, no taxation without representation, and due process of law.

Penn promoted his colony aggressively throughout England, Ireland, and Germany. He had no choice. His only source of revenue was the sale of land and the collection of quitrents. Penn commissioned pamphlets in several languages extolling the quality of Pennsylvania's rich farmland. The response was overwhelming. People poured into Philadelphia, the new city Penn had laid out, and the surrounding area. In 1685 alone, 8,000 immigrants arrived. Most of the settlers were Irish, Welsh, and English Quakers, and they generally moved to America as families. But Penn opened the door to men and women of all nations. He asserted that the people of Pennsylvania "are a collection of divers nations in Europe, as French, Dutch, Germans, Swedes, Danes, Finns, Scotch, Irish, and English."

The settlers were by no means all Quakers. The founder of Germantown, Francis Daniel Pastorius, called the ship that brought him to the New World a "Noah's Ark" of religions, and within his own household, there were servants who subscribed "to the Roman [Catholic], to the Lutheran, to the Calvinistic, to the Anabaptist, and to the Anglican church, and only one Quaker." Ethnic and religious diversity was crucial in the development of Pennsylvania's public institutions, and its politics were more quarrelsome than those in more homogeneous colonies such as Virginia and Massachusetts.

In 1701, legal challenges in England forced Penn to depart for the mother country. Just before he sailed, Penn signed the Charter of Liberties, a new frame of government that established a unicameral or one-house legislature (the only one in colonial America) and gave the representatives the right to initiate bills. Penn also allowed the assembly to conduct its business without proprietary interference. The charter provided for the political separation of the Three Lower Counties (Delaware), whose settlers had never shown any enthusiasm for Penn's "Holy Experiment" and who had been demanding autonomy. This hastily drafted document served as Pennsylvania's constitution until the American Revolution.

Quick Check

✓ How did the Quaker religion influence the development of Pennsylvania?

PLANTING THE SOUTHERN COLONIES

In some ways, Carolina society looked much like the one that had developed in Virginia and Maryland. In both areas, white planters forced African slaves to produce staple crops for a world market. But such superficial similarities masked substantial regional differences. In fact, "the South"—certainly the fabled solid South of the early nineteenth century—did not exist during the colonial period. The Carolinas, joined much later by Georgia, stood apart from their northern neighbors (see Map 2.4). As a historian of colonial Carolina explained, "the southern colonies were never a cohesive section in the same way that New England was. The great diversity of population groups … discouraged southern sectionalism."

How was the founding of the Carolinas different from the founding of Georgia?

Founding the Carolinas

On March 24, 1663, Charles II granted a group of eight courtiers, styled the Proprietors of Carolina, a charter to the vast territory between Virginia and Spanish-ruled Florida running west as far as the "South Seas," even though no one knew where that was. After initial setbacks, the most energetic proprietor, Anthony Ashley Cooper, later Earl of Shaftesbury, realized that without an infusion of new money Carolina would fail. In 1669, he persuaded other Carolinian proprietors to invest their own capital in the colony. Once he received sufficient funds, he dispatched 300 English colonists to Port Royal under the command of Joseph West. The fleet put in briefly at the Caribbean island of Barbados to pick up additional recruits, and in March 1670, after being punished by Atlantic gales that destroyed one ship, the expedition arrived at its destination. Only 100 people were still alive. The unhappy settlers did not remain long at Port Royal, an unappealing, low-lying place badly exposed to Spanish attack. They moved northward, locating eventually along the more secure Ashley River. Later the colony's administrative center, Charles Town (it did not become Charleston until 1783) was established at the junction of the Ashley and Cooper rivers.

Before 1680, almost half the men and women who settled in the Port Royal area came from Barbados. This small Caribbean island, which produced an annual fortune in

Charles Town This engraving from 1671 of the fortified settlement at Charleston, South Carolina, shows the junction of the Ashley and Cooper rivers. Many of Charleston's settlers came from the sugar plantations of Barbados.

Map 2.4 *The Carolinas and Georgia* Caribbean sugar planters migrated to the Goose Creek area, where they eventually mastered rice cultivation. Poor harbors in North Carolina retarded the spread of European settlement there.

sugar, depended on slave labor. By the third quarter of the seventeenth century, Barbados had become overpopulated. Wealthy families could not provide their sons and daughters with sufficient land to maintain social status, and as the crisis intensified, Barbadians looked to Carolina for relief.

These migrants, many of whom were rich, traveled to Carolina both as individuals and as family groups. Some even brought gangs of slaves with them to the American mainland. The Barbadians carved out plantations on the tributaries of the Cooper River and established themselves immediately as the colony's most powerful political faction. "So it was," wrote historian Richard Dunn, "that these Caribbean pioneers helped to create on the North American coast a slave-based plantation society closer in temper to the islands they fled from than to any other mainland English settlement."

Much of the planters' time was taken up with the search for a profitable crop. The early settlers experimented with several plants: tobacco, cotton, mulberry trees for silk, and grapes. The most successful items turned out to be beef, animal skins, and naval stores (especially tar used to maintain ocean vessels). By the 1680s, some Carolinians had built up great herds of cattle—700 or 800 head in some cases. Traders who dealt with Indians brought back thousands of deerskins from the interior. They also often returned with Indian slaves. These commercial resources, together with tar and turpentine, enjoyed a good market. The planters did not fully appreciate the value of rice until the 1690s, but once they did, it quickly became the colony's main staple.

Proprietary Carolina was in a constant political uproar. Factions vied for special privilege. The Barbadian settlers, known locally as the Goose Creek Men, resisted the proprietors' policies at every turn. A large community of French Protestant Huguenots located in Craven County distrusted the Barbadians. The proprietors—an ineffectual group after Cooper died in 1683—appointed incompetent governors who only made things worse. One visitor observed that "the Inhabitants of Carolina should be as free from Oppression as any [people] in the Universe ... if their own Differences amongst themselves do not occasion the contrary." By the end of the seventeenth century, the Commons House of Assembly had assumed the right to initiate legislation. In 1719, the colonists overthrew the last proprietary governor. In 1729, the king created separate royal governments for North and South Carolina, hoping that splitting the colonies would help lead to more effective (and more peaceable) governance.

Quick Check

✓ How did the Barbadian background of the early settlers shape the economic development of the Carolinas?

Founding of Georgia

The early history of Georgia was strikingly different from that of Britain's other mainland colonies. Its settlement was really an act of aggression against Spain, which had as good a claim to this area as did the English. During the eighteenth century, the two nations were often at war (see Chapter 4), and South Carolinians worried that the Spaniards moving up from bases in Florida would occupy the disputed territory between Florida and the Carolina grant.

The colony owed its existence primarily to James Oglethorpe, a British general and member of Parliament who believed that he could thwart Spanish designs on the area south of Charles Town while providing a fresh start for London's worthy poor, saving them from debtors' prison. (Until the nineteenth century, debtors could be imprisoned if they could not repay what they owed.) Although Oglethorpe envisioned Georgia as an asylum as well as a garrison, the military aspects of his proposal appealed to the British government. In 1732, King George II granted Oglethorpe and a board of trustees a charter for a new colony named after him to be located between the Savannah and Altamaha rivers and from "sea to sea." The trustees living in the mother country were given complete control over Georgia politics, a condition the settlers soon found intolerable.

During the first years of colonization, Georgia fared no better than had earlier utopian experiments. The English poor showed little desire to move to an inclement frontier, and the trustees, in their turn, provided little incentive for emigration. Each colonist received only 50 acres. Another 50 acres could be added for each servant transported to Georgia, but no settler could amass more than 500 acres. Moreover, land could be passed only to an eldest son, and if a planter had no sons when he died, the holding reverted to the trustees. Slavery was prohibited. So was rum.

Almost as soon as they arrived in Georgia, the settlers complained. The colonists demanded slaves, pointing out to the trustees that without an unfree labor force they could not compete economically with their South Carolina neighbors. The settlers also wanted a voice in local government. In 1738, 121 people living in the new colony's capital, Savannah, petitioned for fundamental reforms in the colony's constitution. Oglethorpe responded angrily, "The idle ones are indeed for Negroes. If the petition is countenanced, the province is ruined." In 1741, the settlers again petitioned Oglethorpe, addressing him as "our Perpetual Dictator."

While the colonists grumbled about restrictions, Oglethorpe tried and failed to capture the Spanish fortress at St. Augustine in Florida (1740). This disappointment coupled with the growing popular unrest destroyed his interest in Georgia. The trustees were forced to compromise their principles. In 1738, they eliminated restrictions on the amount of land a man could own and allowed women to inherit land. In 1750, they permitted the settlers to import slaves. Soon Georgians could drink rum. In 1751, the trustees returned Georgia to the king, undoubtedly relieved to be free of what had become a hard-drinking, slave-owning plantation society much like that in South Carolina. The king authorized an assembly in 1751, but Georgia still attracted few new settlers.

Quick Check

✓ Why did Georgia settlers object to the government imposed upon them by James Oglethorpe?

TABLE 2.1   England's Principal Mainland Colonies

Name	Original Purpose	Date of Founding	Principal Founder	Major Export	Estimated Population ca. 1700
Virginia	Commercial venture	1607	Captain John Smith	Tobacco	64,560
New Amsterdam (New York)	Commercial venture	1613 (made English colony, 1664)	Peter Stuyvesant, Duke of York	Furs, grain	19,107
Plymouth	Refuge for English Separatists	1620 (absorbed by Massachusetts, 1691)	William Bradford	Grain	Included with Massachusetts
New Hampshire	Commercial venture	1623	John Mason	Wood, naval stores	4,958
Massachusetts	Refuge for English Puritans	1628	John Winthrop	Grain, wood	55,941
Maryland	Refuge for English Catholics	1634	Lord Baltimore (George Calvert)	Tobacco	34,100
Connecticut	Expansion of Massachusetts	1635	Thomas Hooker	Grain	25,970
Rhode Island	Refuge for dissenters from Massachusetts	1636	Roger Williams	Grain	5,894
Delaware	Commercial venture	1638 (included in Penn grant, 1681; given separate assembly, 1703)	William Penn	Grain	2,470
North Carolina	Commercial venture	1663	Anthony Ashley Cooper	Wood, naval stores, tobacco	10,720
South Carolina	Commercial venture	1663	Anthony Ashley Cooper	Naval stores, rice, indigo	5,720
New Jersey	Consolidation of new English territory, Quaker settlement	1664	Sir George Carteret	Grain	14,010
Pennsylvania	Refuge for English Quakers	1681	William Penn	Grain	18,950
Georgia	Discourage Spanish expansion; charity	1733	James Oglethorpe	Rice, wood, naval stores	5,200 (in 1750)

Sources: U.S. Bureau of the Census, *Historical Statistics of the United States: Colonial Times to 1970*, Washington, D.C., 1975; John J. McCusker and Russell R. Menard, *The Economy of British America, 1607–1789*, Chapel Hill, 1985.

CONCLUSION: LIVING WITH DIVERSITY

Long after he had returned from his adventures in Virginia, Captain John Smith reflected on the difficulty of establishing colonies in the New World. It was a task for which most people were not suited. "It requires," Smith counseled, "all the best parts of art, judgment, courage, honesty, constancy, diligence, and industry, [even] to do neere well." On another occasion, Charles I warned Lord Baltimore that new settlements "commonly have rugged and laborious beginnings."

In the seventeenth century, women and men had followed leaders such as Baltimore, Smith, Winthrop, Bradford, Penn, and Berkeley to the New World in anticipation of creating a successful new society. Some migrants were religious visionaries; others were hardheaded businessmen. The results of their efforts, their struggles to survive in an often hostile environment, and their interactions with various Native American groups yielded a spectrum of settlements along the Atlantic coast, from the quasi-feudalism of South Carolina to the Puritan commonwealth of Massachusetts Bay.

The diversity of early English colonization must be emphasized precisely because it is so easy to overlook (see Table 2.1). Even though the colonists eventually banded together and fought for independence, persistent differences separated New Englanders from Virginians, Pennsylvanians from Carolinians. The interpretive challenge, of course, is to comprehend how European colonists managed during the eighteenth century to overcome fragmentation and develop the capacity to imagine themselves a nation.

2 STUDY RESOURCES

((•—Listen to the **Chapter Audio** for Chapter 2 on **myhistorylab.com**

TIMELINE

1607 First English settlers arrive at Jamestown, p. 37

1608–1609 Scrooby congregation (Pilgrims) leaves England for Holland, p. 41

1609–1611 "Starving time" in Virginia threatens survival of the colonists, p. 35

1619 Virginia assembly, called House of Burgesses, meets for the first time, p. 37

1620 Pilgrims sign the Mayflower Compact, p. 41

1622 Indian attack devastates Virginia, p. 38

1624 Dutch investors create permanent settlements along Hudson River, p. 48
• James I, king of England, dissolves Virginia Company, p. 38

1625 Charles I ascends English throne, p. 33

1634 Colony of Maryland is founded, p. 39

1636 Puritan settlers found Hartford and other Connecticut Valley towns, p. 47

1638 Anne Hutchinson exiled to Rhode Island, p. 47
• Theophilus Eaton and John Davenport lead settlers to New Haven Colony, p. 47

1639 Connecticut towns accept Fundamental Orders, p. 47

1644 Second major Indian attack in Virginia, p. 36

1649 Charles I executed during English Civil War, p. 40

1663 Rhode Island obtains royal charter, p. 48
• Proprietors receive charter for Carolina, p. 53

1664 English conquer New Netherland, p. 49

1677 New Hampshire becomes a royal colony, p. 47

1681 William Penn granted patent for his "Holy Experiment," p. 52

1732 James Oglethorpe receives charter for Georgia, p. 55

CHAPTER REVIEW

BREAKING AWAY: DECISIONS TO MOVE TO AMERICA

Why did the Chesapeake colonies not prosper during the earliest years of settlement?

Poor governance in early Virginia, founded in 1607, led to starvation and hostilities with the Powhatan Indians. Founded in 1634 as a refuge for Catholics, Maryland's early politics were plagued by religious tensions that sometimes led to large-scale violence. Both colonies imported predominately young, male indentured servants as laborers and suffered high mortality rates from disease. This resulted in transient and unruly societies with few stable families. *(p. 32)*

A "NEW" ENGLAND IN AMERICA

What role did differences in religion play in the founding of the New England colonies?

Religious persecution drove thousands of Puritans to New England. John Winthrop hoped the settlers would reform English Protestantism and create a "City on a Hill." The Puritans did not welcome dissent. They exiled Roger Williams and Anne Hutchinson to Rhode Island for their religious beliefs. Stable nuclear families and good health helped Puritans avoid the social turmoil that plagued the Chesapeake colonies. *(p. 41)*

DIVERSITY IN THE MIDDLE COLONIES

How did ethnic diversity shape the development of the Middle Colonies?

After conquering the Dutch colony of New Netherland in 1664, the English renamed it New York. Despite the conquest, the Dutch remained an influential minority in the colony, and ethnic rivalries shaped the politics of New York for decades. In 1681, Charles II granted William Penn, a Quaker, a charter to establish Pennsylvania. Penn's guarantee to respect all Christian settlers' liberty of conscience drew immigrants from across Northern Europe. *(p. 48)*

PLANTING THE SOUTHERN COLONIES

How was the founding of the Carolinas different from that of Georgia?

Immigrants from Barbados began settling in the Carolinas in the 1670s. Barbadian immigrants to the Carolinas, many of whom were wealthy planters seeking new lands for plantations, brought slavery with them when they moved. Georgia was founded in 1732 as an alternative to debtors' prison for impoverished Englishmen and as a military outpost to guard against the Spanish in Florida. *(p. 53)*

KEY TERM QUESTIONS

1. How did the joint-stock company make possible the launching of a new colony in Virginia? (p. 33)

2. What was the purpose of creating the House of Burgesses in Virginia? (p. 37)

3. How did the headright system help to establish the colony in Virginia? (p. 37)

4. Why were most indentured servants unable to reap the benefits of coming to the New World? (p. 37)

5. What purpose did the Mayflower Compact serve when it was signed in 1620? (p. 41)

6. How did the Protestant Reformation influence the Puritans? (p. 42)

7. What were the backgrounds of the Puritans participating in the "Great Migration"? (p. 44)

8. Why did antinomianism threaten many in the Massachusetts Bay Colony? (p. 46)

9. How did the Quakers' religious beliefs differ from that of the Puritans? (p. 51)

MyHistoryLab Connections

Visit **www.myhistorylab.com** for a customized Study Plan to build your knowledge of *New World Experiments*.

Question for Analysis

1. How similar were the settlers that founded the first colonies in the New World?

   View the **Map** *The Colonies to 1740* p. 33

2. What stereotypes of Native Americans does John Smith evoke in *The Starving Time*?

   Read the **Document** *John Smith, The Starving Time* p. 35

3. How important was tobacco to the economy of Maryland?

   Read the **Document** *George Alsop, From a Character of the Province of Maryland* p. 39

4. How does Winthrop portray the Puritan purpose in America as a divine mandate?

   Read the **Document** *John Winthrop, A Model of Christian Charity* p. 43

Other Resources from this Chapter

View the **Image** *Mural of Jamestown Settlement*

View the **Image** *Powhattan in Longhouse*

View the **Image** *First House of Burgessess Meeting in Jamestown*

Read the **Document** *Wessell Webling, His Indenture*

View the **Image** *Mayflower Replica Plymouth, Massachusetts*

Read the **Document** *Reasons for the Plantation in New England*

Read the **Document** *Father Isaac Jogues Description of New York, 1640*

Read the **Document** *William Penn "Model for Government"*

Read the **Document** *James Oglethorpe to the Trustees*

3 PUTTING DOWN ROOTS

Opportunity and Oppression in
Colonial Society, 1619–1692

Contents and Spotlight Questions

SOCIAL STABILITY: NEW ENGLAND COLONIES OF THE SEVENTEENTH CENTURY PG. 63

What factors explain the remarkable social stability achieved in early New England?

THE CHALLENGE OF THE CHESAPEAKE ENVIRONMENT PG. 66

What factors contributed to political unrest in the Chesapeake region during this period?

RACE AND FREEDOM IN BRITISH AMERICA PG. 69

How did African American slaves preserve an independent cultural identity in the New World?

BLUEPRINT FOR EMPIRE PG. 73

Why did England discourage free and open trade in colonial America?

COLONIAL POLITICAL REVOLTS PG. 75

How did colonial revolts affect the political culture of Virginia and New England?

((•─ **Listen** to the **Chapter Audio** for Chapter 3 on **myhistorylab.com**

FAMILIES IN AN ATLANTIC EMPIRE

The Witherspoon family moved from Great Britain to the South Carolina backcountry early in the eighteenth century. Although otherwise indistinguishable from the thousands of other ordinary families that put down roots in English America, the Witherspoons were made historical figures by the candid account of pioneer life produced by their son, Robert, who was only a small child at the time of their arrival.

The Mason Children David, Joanna, and Abigail, c. 1670. An early portrait of three children from a wealthy Massachusetts Bay Colony family.
(*Source: The Freake-Gibbs Painter, American. "The Mason Children: Davis, Joanna and Abigail," 1670. Oil on canvas, 39-1/2" 42-11/16". The Fine Arts Museum of San Francisco, San Francisco, CA. Gift of Mr. and Mrs. John D. Rockefeller, III.*)

The Witherspoons' initial reaction to the New World—at least, that of the mother and children—was utter despondence. "My mother and us children were still in expectation that we were coming to an agreeable place," Robert confessed, "but when we arrived and saw nothing but a wilderness and instead of a fine timbered house, nothing but a very mean dirt house, our spirits quite sunk." For many years, the Witherspoons feared they would be killed by Indians, become lost in the woods, or be bitten by snakes.

Yet the Witherspoons managed to survive the early difficult years on the Black River. To be sure, the Carolina backcountry did not look much like the world they had left behind, but the difference apparently did not discourage Robert's father. He had a vision of what the Black River settlement might become. "My father," Robert recounted, "gave us all the comfort he [could] by telling us we would get all these trees cut down and in a short time [there] would be plenty of inhabitants, [and] that we could see from house to house."

Robert Witherspoon's account reminds us how the early history of colonial America was an intimate story of families, and not, as some commentators would have us believe, just of individuals. The peopling of the Atlantic frontier—the cutting down of the forests and the creation of new communities where one could see from "house to house"—was not a process that involved what we would today recognize as state policy. Family considerations influenced men and women as they made the important decisions that would shape their new lives in the colonies. It was within this primary social unit that most colonists earned their livelihoods, educated their children, defined gender, sustained religious tradition, and nursed each other in sickness. In short, the family was the source of their societal and cultural identities.

Early colonial families did not exist in isolation. They were part of larger societies. As we have already seen, the character of the first English settlements in the New World varied substantially (see Chapter 2). During much of the seventeenth century, these initial differences grew stronger as each region responded to different environmental conditions and developed its own traditions. The various local societies in which families like the Witherspoons put down roots reflected several critical elements: supply of labor, abundance of land, unusual demographic patterns, and commercial ties with European markets. In the Chesapeake, for example, an economy based almost entirely on a single staple—tobacco—created an insatiable demand for indentured servants and black slaves. In Massachusetts Bay, the extraordinary longevity of the founders generated a social and political stability that Virginians and Marylanders did not attain until the very end of the seventeenth century.

By 1660, it seemed regional differences had undermined the idea of a unified English empire in America. During the reign of Charles II (r. 1660–1685), however, a trend toward cultural convergence began. Although subcultures had evolved in strikingly different directions, countervailing forces such as common language and religion gradually pulled English American settlers together. Parliament took advantage of this trend and began to establish uniform rules for the expanding American empire. The process was slow and uneven, often sparking violent colonial resistance. By the end of the seventeenth century, however, England had made significant progress toward transforming the New World provinces into an empire that produced needed raw materials and purchased manufactured goods. If a person was black and enslaved, however, he or she was likely to experience oppression rather than opportunity in British America.

SOCIAL STABILITY: NEW ENGLAND COLONIES OF THE SEVENTEENTH CENTURY

Seventeenth-century New Englanders replicated a traditional social order they had known in England. The transfer of a familiar way of life to the New World seemed less difficult for these Puritan migrants than it did for the many English men and women who settled in the Chesapeake colonies. Their contrasting experiences, fundamental to understanding the development of both cultures, can be explained, at least in part, by the extraordinary strength and resilience of New England families.

What factors explain the remarkable social stability achieved in early New England?

Immigrant Families and New Social Order

Early New Englanders believed God ordained the family for human benefit. It was essential to the maintenance of social order, since outside the family, men and women succumbed to carnal temptation. Such people had no one to sustain them or remind them of Scripture. "Without Family care," declared the Reverend Benjamin Wadsworth, "the labour of Magistrates and Ministers for Reformation and Propagating Religion, is likely to be in great measure unsuccessful."

The godly family, at least in theory, was ruled by a patriarch, father to his children, husband to his wife, the source of authority and object of unquestioned obedience. The wife shared responsibility for raising children, but in important decisions, especially those about property, she was expected to defer to her spouse.

The New Englanders' concern about the character of the godly family is not surprising. This institution was central in shaping their society. In contrast to those who migrated to Virginia and Maryland, New Englanders crossed the Atlantic within nuclear families. That is, they moved within established units consisting of a father, mother, and their dependent children. People who migrated to America within families preserved local English customs more fully than did the youths who traveled to other parts of the continent as single men and women. The comforting presence of immediate family members reduced the shock of adjusting to a strange environment 3,000 miles from home. Even in the 1630s, the ratio of men to women in New England was fairly well balanced, about three males for every two females. Persons who had not already married in England before coming to the New World could expect to form nuclear families of their own.

Early New England marriage patterns did not differ substantially from those in seventeenth-century England. The average age for men at first marriage was the mid-twenties. Wives were slightly younger than their husbands, the average age being about 22. There is no evidence that New Englanders favored child brides. Nor, for that matter, were Puritan families unusually large by European standards of the period.

The explanation for the region's impressive growth turned out to be survival rather than fertility. Put simply, people who, under normal conditions, would have died in contemporary Europe lived in New England. Indeed, the life expectancy of seventeenth-century settlers was not much less than our own. Males who survived infancy might expect to see their seventieth birthday. Twenty percent of the men of the first generation reached age 80. The figures for women were only slightly lower. Why the early settlers lived so long is not entirely clear. No doubt, pure drinking water, a cool climate that retarded the spread of fatal contagious disease, and a dispersed population promoted good health.

Longer life altered family relations. New England males lived to see not only their own children reach adulthood but the birth of grandchildren. This may have been one of the first societies in recorded history in which a person could reasonably anticipate knowing his or her grandchildren, a demographic surprise that contributed to social stability. The traditions of particular families and communities literally remained alive in the memories of the colony's oldest citizens.

Quick Check

✓ How did families contribute to social order in seventeenth-century New England?

Puritan Women in New England

New England relied heavily on the work of women. They did not, however, necessarily do the same jobs that men performed. Women usually handled separate tasks, including cooking, washing, clothes making, dairying, and gardening. Their production of food was essential to the survival of most households. Sometimes wives—and the overwhelming majority of adult seventeenth-century women were married—raised poultry, and by selling surplus birds, they achieved some economic independence. When people in one New England community chided a man for allowing his wife to peddle her fowl, he responded, "I meddle not with the geese nor turkeys for they are hers." In fact, during this period women were often described as "deputy husbands," a label that drew attention both to their dependence on family patriarchs and to their roles as decision makers.

More women than men also joined churches. Within a few years of founding, many New England congregations contained two female members for every male, a process historians describe as the "feminization of colonial religion." Contemporaries offered different explanations for the gender shift. Cotton Mather, the leading Congregational minister of Massachusetts Bay, argued that God had created "far more *godly Women*" than men. Others thought that the life-threatening experience of childbirth gave women a deeper appreciation of religion.

In political and legal matters, society sharply curtailed the rights of colonial women. According to English common law, a wife exercised no control over property. She could not, for example, sell land, although her husband could dispose of their holdings without her permission. Divorce was extremely difficult to obtain in any colony before the American Revolution. Indeed, a person married to a cruel or irresponsible spouse had little recourse but to run away or accept the unhappy situation.

Yet most women were neither prosperous entrepreneurs nor abject slaves. Letters indicate that men and women generally accommodated themselves to the

Read the **Document**
Prenuptial Agreement, (1653) on
myhistorylab.com

gender roles they thought God had ordained. One of early America's most creative poets, Anne Bradstreet, wrote movingly of the fulfillment she had found with her husband. In "To my Dear and loving Husband," Bradstreet declared:

> If ever two were one, then surely we.
> If ever man were lovíd by wife, then thee;
> If ever wife was happy in a man,
> Compare with me ye woman if you can.

Although Puritan couples worried that the affection they felt for a spouse might turn their thoughts away from God's perfect love, this was a danger they were willing to risk.

Read the Document
"Anne Bradstreet, "Before the Birth of One of Her Children" on myhistorylab.com

Quick Check

✓ What was life like for women in seventeenth-century New England?

Establishing a New Social Order

During the seventeenth century, New England colonists gradually sorted themselves out into distinct social groupings. Persons who would never have been "natural rulers" in England became provincial gentry in the northern colonies. It helped, of course, to be wealthy and educated, but these attributes alone could not guarantee a newcomer's acceptance into the local ruling elite, at least not during the early decades of settlement. In Massachusetts and Connecticut, Puritan voters expected their leaders to join Congregational churches and defend orthodox religion.

While most New Englanders accepted a hierarchical view of society, they disagreed over their assigned places. Both Massachusetts Bay and Connecticut passed sumptuary laws—statutes that limited wearing fine apparel to the wealthy and prominent—to curb the pretensions of those of lower status. Yet such restraints could not prevent some people from rising and others from falling within the social order.

Most northern colonists were **yeomen** (independent farmers) who worked their own land. While few became rich, even fewer fell hopelessly into debt. Their daily lives, especially for those who settled New England, centered on scattered little communities where they participated in village meetings, church affairs, and militia training. Owning land gave agrarian families a sense of independence from external authority. As one man bragged to those who had stayed behind in England, "Here are no hard landlords to rack us with high rents or extorting fines. . . . Here every man may be master of his own labour and land . . . and if he have nothing but his hands he may set up his trade, and by industry grow rich."

Many northern colonists worked as servants at some point in their lives. This system of labor differed greatly from the pattern of servitude that developed in seventeenth-century Virginia and Maryland. New Englanders seldom recruited servants from the Old World. The forms of agriculture practiced in this region, mixed cereal and dairy farming, made employing large gangs of dependent workers uneconomic. Rather, New England families placed their adolescent children in nearby homes. These young persons contracted for four or five years and seemed more like apprentices than servants. Servitude was not simply a means by which one group exploited another. It was a form of vocational training in which the children of both the rich and the poor participated.

By the end of the seventeenth century, the New England Puritans had developed a compelling story about their own history in the New World. The founders had been extraordinarily godly men and women, and in a heroic effort to establish a purer form of religion, pious families had passed "over the vast ocean into this vast and howling wilderness." Although the children and grandchildren of the first generation sometimes questioned their own ability to please the Lord, they recognized the mission to the New World had been a success: They were "as Prosperous as ever, there is Peace & Plenty, & the Country flourisheth."

Quick Check

✓ What counted more in determining social status in early New England—piety or wealth?

THE CHALLENGE OF THE CHESAPEAKE ENVIRONMENT

What factors contributed to political unrest in the Chesapeake region during this period?

A different regional society developed in England's Chesapeake colonies, Virginia and Maryland. This contrast with New England seems puzzling. After all, the two areas were founded at roughly the same time by men and women from the same mother country. In both regions, settlers spoke English, accepted Protestantism, and gave allegiance to one crown. And yet, seventeenth-century Virginia looked nothing like Massachusetts Bay. To explain the difference, colonial historians have studied environmental conditions, labor systems, and agrarian economies. The most important reason for the distinctiveness of these early southern plantation societies, however, turned out to be the Chesapeake's death rate, a frighteningly high mortality that tore at the very fabric of traditional family life.

Families at Risk

Unlike New England's settlers, the men and women who emigrated to the Chesapeake region did not move in family units. They traveled to the New World as young unmarried servants, youths cut off from the security of traditional kin relations. Although these immigrants came from a cross section of English society, most had been poor to middling farmers. It is now estimated that 70 to 85 percent of the white colonists who went to Virginia and Maryland during the seventeenth century were not free; that is, they owed four or five years' labor in exchange for the cost of passage to America. If the servant was under age 15, he or she had to serve seven years. Most of these laborers were males between the ages of 18 and 22. In fact, before 1640, the ratio of males to females was 6 to 1. This figure dropped to about 2.5 to 1 by the end of the century, but the sex ratio in the Chesapeake was never as favorable as it had been in early Massachusetts.

Most immigrants to the Chesapeake region died soon after arriving. It is difficult to ascertain the exact cause of death in most cases, but malaria and other diseases took a frightful toll. Life expectancy for Chesapeake males was about 43, some ten to 20 years less than for men born in New England! For women, life was even shorter. Twenty-five percent of all children died in infancy; another 25 percent did not see their twentieth birthdays. The survivors were often weak or ill, unable to perform hard physical labor.

Because of the unbalanced sex ratio, many adult males could not find wives. Migration not only cut them off from their English families but also deprived them of an opportunity to form new ones. Without a constant flow of immigrants, the population of Virginia and Maryland would have actually declined.

High mortality compressed the family life cycle into a few years. One partner in a marriage usually died within seven years. Only one in three Chesapeake marriages survived for as long as a decade. Not only did children not meet grandparents—they often did not even know their own parents. Widows and widowers quickly remarried, bringing children by former unions into their new homes, and a child often grew up with persons to whom he or she bore no blood relation.

Women were in great demand in the early southern colonies. Some historians have argued that scarcity heightened the woman's bargaining power in the marriage market. An immigrant did not have to obtain parental consent to marry. She was on her own in the New World and could select whomever she pleased. If a woman lacked beauty or strength, or if she were of low moral standards, she could still be confident of finding an American husband. Such negotiations may have provided Chesapeake women with a means of improving their social status.

Nevertheless, liberation from traditional restraints on seventeenth-century women must not be exaggerated. Women servants were vulnerable to sexual exploitation by their masters. Moreover, in this unhealthy environment, childbearing was extremely dangerous, and women in the Chesapeake usually died 20 years earlier than their New England counterparts.

Quick Check
✓ How did the high mortality rates in the early Chesapeake colonies affect economic and family life?

The Structure of Planter Society

Colonists who managed to survive grew tobacco—as much tobacco as they could. This crop became the Chesapeake staple, and since it was relatively easy to cultivate, anyone with a few acres of cleared land could harvest leaves for export. Cultivation of tobacco did not, however, produce a society roughly equal in wealth and status. To the contrary, tobacco generated inequality. Some planters amassed fortunes; others barely subsisted. Labor made the difference, for to succeed in this staple economy, one had to control the labor of other men and women. More workers in the fields meant larger harvests and, of course, larger profits. Since free persons showed no interest in growing another man's tobacco, not even for wages, wealthy planters relied on white laborers who were not free and on slaves. The social structure that developed in the seventeenth-century Chesapeake reflected a wild, often unscrupulous scramble to bring men and women of three races—black, white, and Indian—into various degrees of dependence.

Great planters dominated Chesapeake society. The group was small, only a trifling portion of the population of Virginia and Maryland. During the early seventeenth century, the composition of Chesapeake gentry was continually in flux. Some gentlemen died before they could establish a secure claim to high social status; others returned to England, thankful to have survived. Not until the 1650s did the family names of those who would become famous eighteenth-century gentry appear in the records. The first gentlemen were not—as genealogists sometimes discover to their dismay—dashing cavaliers who had fought in the English Civil War for King Charles I. Rather, such Chesapeake gentry as the Burwells, Byrds, Carters, and Masons consisted originally of the younger sons of English merchants and artisans.

Freemen formed the largest class in Chesapeake society. Their origins were strikingly different from those of the gentry, or from those of New England's yeomen farmers. Chesapeake freemen traveled to the New World as indentured servants, signing contracts in which they sold their labor for a set number of years in exchange for passage from Europe. If they had dreamed of becoming great planters, they were disappointed. Most seventeenth-century freemen lived on the edge of poverty. Some freemen, of course, did better in America than they would have in England, but in both Virginia and Maryland, historians have found a sharp economic division separating the gentry from the rest of white society.

Read the
Document
*Virginia Law on
Indentured Servitude*
on
myhistorylab.com

Below the freemen came indentured servants. Membership in this group was not demeaning; after all, servitude was a temporary status. But servitude in the Chesapeake colonies was not the benign institution it was in New England. Great planters purchased servants to grow tobacco. No one seemed overly concerned whether these laborers received decent food and clothes, much less whether they acquired trade skills. Young people, thousands of them, cut off from family ties, sick often to the point of death, unable to obtain normal sexual release, regarded their servitude as a form of slavery. Not surprisingly, the gentry worried that unhappy servants and impoverished freemen, what the planters called the "giddy multitude," would rebel at the slightest provocation, a fear that turned out to be justified.

The character of social mobility—and this observation applies only to whites—changed during the seventeenth century. Until the 1680s, it was relatively easy for a newcomer who possessed capital to join the planter elite. No one paid much attention to the reputation or social standing of one's English family.

After the 1680s, however, a demographic shift occurred. Although infant mortality remained high, life expectancy for those who survived childhood in the Chesapeake improved significantly, and for the first time in the history of Virginia and Maryland, important leadership positions went to men who had been born in America. A political historian described this transition as the "emergence of a creole majority," in other words, as the rise of an indigenous ruling elite. Before this time, immigrant leaders had died without heirs or had returned as quickly as possible to England. The members of the new creole class took a greater interest in local government. Their activities helped give the tobacco colonies the political and cultural stability that had eluded earlier generations of planter adventurers.

The key to success in this creole society was ownership of slaves. Those planters who held more blacks could grow more tobacco and thus could acquire fresh capital to purchase even more laborers. Over time, the rich not only became richer; they formed a distinct ruling elite that newcomers found increasingly difficult to enter.

Opportunities for advancement also decreased for freemen in the region. Studies of mid-seventeenth-century Maryland reveal that some servants managed to become moderately prosperous farmers and small officeholders. But as the gentry consolidated its hold on political and economic institutions, ordinary people discovered it was much harder to rise in Chesapeake society. Those men and women with more ambitious dreams headed for Pennsylvania, North Carolina, or western Virginia.

Social institutions that figured importantly in the daily experience of New Englanders were either weak or nonexistent in the Chesapeake colonies. In part, the sluggish development resulted from the continuation of high infant mortality rates. There was little incentive to build elementary schools, for example, if half the children would die before reaching adulthood. The great planters sent their sons to England or Scotland for their education, and even after the founding of the College of William and Mary in Virginia in 1693, the gentry continued to patronize English schools. As a result, higher education in the South languished for much of the colonial period.

Tobacco influenced the spread of other institutions in the region. Planters were scattered along the rivers, often separated from their nearest neighbors by miles of poor roads. Since the major tobacco growers traded directly with English merchants, they had no need for towns.

Quick Check

✓ Why did the great planters purchase so many indentured servants during this period?

RACE AND FREEDOM IN BRITISH AMERICA

Many people who landed in the colonies had no desire to come to the New World. They were Africans taken as slaves to cultivate rice, sugar, and tobacco. As the Native Americans were exterminated and the supply of white indentured servants dried up, European planters demanded ever more African laborers.

How did African American slaves preserve an independent cultural identity in the New World?

Roots of Slavery

Much is known about the transfer of African peoples across the Atlantic. During the entire history of this human commerce, between the sixteenth and nineteenth centuries, slave traders carried almost 11 million blacks to the Americas. Most of these men and women were sold in Brazil or the Caribbean. A relatively small number of Africans reached British North America, and of this group, most arrived after 1700. Because slaves performed hard physical labor, planters preferred purchasing young males. In many early slave communities, men outnumbered women by a ratio of two to one.

English colonists did not hesitate to enslave black people or, for that matter, Native Americans. While the institution of slavery had long died out in England itself, New World settlers quickly discovered how well slave labor operated in the Spanish and Portuguese colonies. The decision to bring African slaves to the colonies, therefore, was primarily economic.

English masters, however, seldom justified the practice purely in terms of planter profits. Indeed, they adopted a different pattern of rhetoric. English writers associated blacks in Africa with heathen religion, barbarous behavior, sexual promiscuity—with evil itself. From such a racist perspective, the enslavement of Africans seemed unobjectionable. The planters argued that the Bible

Virginian Luxuries Undated, unsigned, and hidden on the back of another painting, the two-part painting *Virginian Luxuries* depicts a white man kissing a black woman and whipping a black man.

condoned slavery and maintained that if black slaves converted to Christianity, shedding their supposedly savage ways, they would actually benefit from their loss of freedom.

Africans first landed in Virginia in 1619 as a cargo of slaves a Dutch trader stole from a Spanish ship in the Caribbean. For the next 50 years, the status of the colony's black people remained unclear. English settlers classified some black laborers as slaves for life, as chattel to be bought and sold at the master's will. But other Africans became servants, presumably for stated periods of time, and a few blacks even purchased their freedom. Several seventeenth-century Africans became successful Virginia planters.

One reason Virginia lawmakers tolerated such confusion was that the black population remained small. By 1660, fewer than 1,500 people of African origin lived in the entire colony (compared to 26,000 whites), and it hardly seemed necessary for the legislature to draw up an elaborate slave code to control so few men and women. If the planters could have obtained more black laborers, they certainly would have. There is no evidence that the great planters preferred white indentured servants to black slaves. The problem was supply. During this period, slave traders sold their cargoes on Barbados or the other sugar islands of the West Indies, where they fetched higher prices than Virginians could afford to pay. In fact, before 1680, most blacks who reached England's colonies on the North American mainland came from Barbados or through New Netherland rather than directly from Africa. (See Map 3.1.)

By the end of the seventeenth century, the legal status of Virginia's black people was no longer in doubt. They were slaves for life, and so were their children after them. This transformation reflected changes in the supply of Africans to British North America. After 1672, the Royal African Company was chartered to meet the colonial planters' demands for black laborers. Historian K. G. Davies terms this organization "the strongest and most effective of all European companies formed exclusively for the African trade." Between 1695 and 1709, more than 11,000 Africans were sold in Virginia alone; many others went to Maryland and the Carolinas. Although American merchants—most of them based in Rhode Island—entered the trade during the eighteenth century, the British supplied the bulk of the slaves to the mainland market for the entire colonial period.

The expanding black population apparently frightened white colonists, for as the number of Africans increased, lawmakers drew up ever stricter slave codes. During

View the **Closer Look**
Plan and Sections of a Slave Ship and Illustration of a Slave Camp on
myhistorylab.com

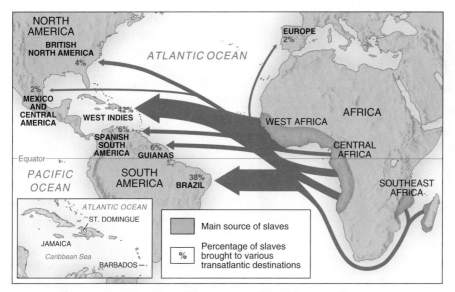

Map 3.1 *Origins and Destinations of African Slaves, 1619–1760*   Although many African slaves were carried to Britain's North American colonies, far more slaves were sold in the Caribbean sugar colonies and Brazil, where, because of horrific health conditions, the death rate far exceeded that of the British mainland colonies.

this period, racism, always latent in New World societies, was fully revealed. By 1700, slavery was unequivocally based on the color of a person's skin. Blacks fell into this status simply because they were black. A vicious pattern of discrimination had been set in motion. Even conversion to Christianity did not free the African from bondage. The white planter could deal with his black property as he alone saw fit, and one revolting Virginia statute excused masters who killed slaves, on the grounds that no rational person would purposely "destroy his own estate." Black women constantly had to fear sexual violation by a master or his sons. Children born to a slave woman became slaves regardless of the father's race. Unlike the Spanish and French colonies, where persons of lighter color enjoyed greater privileges in society, the English colonies tolerated no mixing of the races. Mulattoes and pure Africans received the same treatment.

Quick Check

✓ Why did the slave population in British North America remain relatively small for most of the seventeenth century?

Constructing African American Identities

The slave experience varied from colony to colony. The daily life of a black person in South Carolina, for example, was different from that of an African American who lived in Pennsylvania or Massachusetts Bay. The size and density of the slave population largely determined how successfully blacks could maintain a separate cultural identity. In the lowlands of South Carolina during the eighteenth century, 60 percent of the population was black. The men and women were placed on large, isolated rice plantations and had limited contact with whites. In these areas blacks developed creole languages that mixed basic English vocabulary with words from

Aboard a Slave Ship This watercolor, *Slave Deck of the Albanoz* (1846), by naval officer Lieutenant Godfrey Meynell, shows slaves packed with cargo in the hold of a ship after being taken captive in West Africa.

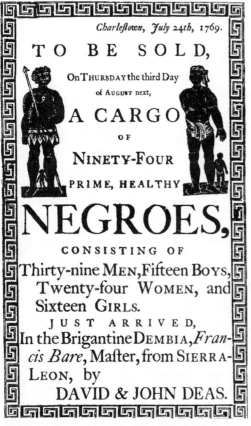

Slave Auctions This public notice announces a slave auction to be held at the Charles Town wharf (1769).

African languages. Until the end of the nineteenth century, one creole language, Gullah, was spoken on some of the Sea Islands along the Georgia–South Carolina coast. Slaves on the large rice plantations also established elaborate and enduring kinship networks that may have helped mitigate the more dehumanizing aspects of bondage.

In the New England and Middle Colonies, and even in Virginia, African Americans made up a smaller percentage of the population: 40 percent in Virginia, 8 percent in Pennsylvania, and 3 percent in Massachusetts. In such environments, contact between blacks and whites was more frequent than in South Carolina and Georgia. These population patterns profoundly affected northern and Chesapeake blacks, for while they escaped the physical drudgery of rice cultivation, they found it more difficult to preserve an independent African identity. In northern cities, slaves working as domestics and living in their masters' houses saw other blacks but had little opportunity to develop creole languages or reaffirm a common African past.

The process of establishing African American traditions involved reshaping African and European customs into something that was neither African nor European. It was African American. The slaves accepted Christianity but did so on their own terms—terms their masters seldom fully understood. Blacks transformed Christianity into an expression of religious feeling in which an African element remained vibrant. In music and folk art, they gave voice to a cultural identity that even the most degrading conditions could not eradicate.

A major turning point in the history of African Americans occurred during the early eighteenth century. The number of live births exceeded deaths, and from this time on, the expansion of the African American population owed more to natural increase than to the importation of new slaves. Thousands of new Africans arrived each year, but the creole population was always much larger than that of the immigrant blacks. This demographic shift did not occur in the Caribbean or South American colonies until much later. Historians believe that North American blacks enjoyed a healthier climate and better diet than did other New World slaves.

Although mainland blacks lived longer than those of Jamaica or Barbados, they were still slaves. They protested their debasement in many ways, some in individual acts of violence, others in organized revolt. The most serious slave rebellion of the colonial period was the Stono Uprising, when 150 South Carolina blacks seized guns and ammunition and murdered white planters in September 1739. "With Colours displayed, and two Drums beating," they marched toward Spanish Florida, where they had been promised freedom. The militia overtook the rebellious slaves and killed most of them. Although the uprising was short-lived, such incidents helped persuade whites everywhere that their own blacks might secretly be planning bloody revolt.

Read the **Document**
James Oglethorpe, The Stono Rebellion (1739) on **myhistorylab.com**

Quick Check

✓ How did African American slaves preserve cultural practices associated with West African societies?

BLUEPRINT FOR EMPIRE

Until the mid-seventeenth century, English political leaders largely ignored the American colonists. Private companies and aristocratic proprietors had created these societies, some for profit, others for religious sanctuary, but in no case did the crown provide financial or military assistance. After the Restoration of Charles II in 1660, Englishmen of various sorts—courtiers, merchants, parliamentarians—concluded that the colonists should be brought more tightly under the control of the mother country. The regulatory policies that evolved during this period formed a framework for an empire that survived with only minor adjustment until 1765.

Why did England discourage free and open trade in colonial America?

Response to Economic Competition

By the 1660s the dominant commercial powers of Europe adopted economic principles that later critics would term mercantilism. Mercantilists argued that since trading nations were competing for the world's resources—mostly for raw materials from dependent colonies—one nation's commercial success translated directly into a loss for its rivals. It seemed logical, therefore, that England would want to protect its own markets from France or Holland by passing mercantilist trade policies discouraging its colonies from trading with other European powers. For seventeenth-century planners, free markets made no sense. They argued that trade tightly regulated by the central government represented the only way to increase the nation's wealth at the expense of competitors.

National interest alone, however, did not shape public policy. Instead, the needs of powerful interest groups led to the rise of English commercial regulation. Each group looked to colonial commerce to solve a different problem. The king wanted money. English merchants were eager to exclude Dutch rivals from lucrative American

Wedding in the Slave Quarters *Old Plantation,* a watercolor by an unknown artist (about 1800), shows that African wedding customs survived plantation slavery.

markets and needed government assistance to compete with the Dutch, even in Virginia or Massachusetts Bay. For the landed gentry who sat in Parliament, England needed a stronger navy, and that in turn meant expanding the domestic shipbuilding industry. And almost everyone agreed England should establish a more favorable balance of trade, that is, increase exports, decrease imports, and grow richer at the expense of other European states. None of these ideas was particularly innovative, but taken together they provided a blueprint for England's first empire.

Quick Check

✓ Why did seventeenth-century English rulers support mercantilism?

Regulating Colonial Trade

Parliament passed a Navigation Act in 1660. The statute was the most important piece of imperial legislation drafted before the American Revolution. Colonists from New Hampshire to South Carolina and the Caribbean islands paid close attention to this statute, which stated (1) that no ship could trade in the colonies unless it had been constructed in either England or America and carried a crew that was at least 75 percent English (for these purposes, colonists counted as Englishmen), and (2) that certain enumerated goods of great value that were not produced in England—tobacco, sugar, cotton, indigo, etc.—could be transported from the colonies only to an English or another colonial port. In 1704, Parliament added rice and molasses to the enumerated list; in 1705, rosins, tars, and turpentine for shipbuilding were included.

The 1660 act was masterfully conceived. It encouraged the development of domestic shipbuilding and prohibited European rivals from obtaining enumerated goods anywhere except in England. Since the Americans had to pay import duties in England (for this purpose colonists did not count as Englishmen) on such items as sugar and tobacco, the legislation also gave the crown another source of income.

In 1663, Parliament passed a second Navigation Act known as the Staple Act, which stated that, with a few exceptions, nothing could be imported into the colonies unless it had first been transshipped through England, a process that greatly increased the price colonial consumers ultimately paid.

The Navigation Acts attempted to eliminate the Dutch, against whom the English fought three wars in this period (1652–1654, 1664–1667, and 1672–1674), as the intermediaries of American commerce. Just as English merchants were celebrating their victory, however, an unanticipated rival appeared: New England merchant ships sailed out of Boston, Salem, and Newport to become formidable competitors in maritime commerce.

During the 1660s, the colonists showed little enthusiasm for the new imperial regulations. Reaction to the Navigation Acts varied from region to region. Virginians bitterly protested them. The collection of English customs on tobacco reduced the planters' profits. Moreover, excluding the Dutch from the trade reduced competition and meant that growers often had to sell their crops at artificially low prices. The Navigation Acts hit the small planters especially hard, for they were least able to absorb increased production costs. Even though the governor of Virginia lobbied on the planters' behalf, the crown turned a deaf ear.

At first, New Englanders simply ignored the commercial regulations. Indeed, one Massachusetts merchant reported in 1664 that Boston entertained "near one hundred sail of ships, this year, of ours and strangers." The strangers, of course, were the Dutch, who had no intention of obeying the Navigation Acts so long as they could reach colonial ports. Some New England merchants found clever ways to circumvent the Navigation Acts. These crafty traders picked up cargoes of enumerated goods such as sugar or tobacco, sailed to another colonial port (thereby fulfilling the letter of the law), and then made directly for Holland or France. Along the way they paid no customs.

To plug the loophole, Parliament passed the Navigation Act of 1673. This statute established a plantation duty, a sum of money equal to normal English customs duties to be collected on enumerated products at the various colonial ports. New Englanders could now sail wherever they pleased within the empire, but they could not escape paying customs.

Parliament passed the last major piece of imperial legislation in 1696. It tightened enforcement procedures, putting pressure on the colonial governors to exclude England's competitors from American ports. It also expanded the American customs service and set up vice-admiralty courts in the colonies. Established to settle disputes that occurred at sea, vice-admiralty courts required neither juries nor oral cross-examination, both traditional elements of the common law. But they were effective and even popular for resolving maritime questions quickly enough to send ships to sea again with little delay. One other significant change in the imperial system occurred in 1696. King William III replaced the ineffective Lords of Trade with a body of advisers that came to be known as the Board of Trade. This group was expected to monitor colonial affairs closely and give government officials the best advice on commercial and other problems. For decades, it energetically carried out its responsibilities.

The members of Parliament believed these reforms would compel the colonists to accept the Navigation Acts, and they were largely correct. By 1700, American goods transshipped through the mother country accounted for a quarter of all English exports, an indication that the colonists found it profitable to obey the commercial regulations. In fact, during the eighteenth century, smuggling from Europe to America dried up almost completely.

Quick Check

✓ How did the Navigation Acts establish the foundation for a commercial empire?

COLONIAL POLITICAL REVOLTS

The Navigation Acts created an illusion of unity. English administrators superimposed a system of commercial regulation on different, often unstable American colonies and called it an empire. But these statutes did not remove long-standing differences. Within each colony's society, men and women struggled to bring order out of disorder, establish stable ruling elites, defuse ethnic and racial tensions, and cope with population pressures that imperial planners only dimly understood. During the late seventeenth century, these efforts sometimes sparked revolt.

How did colonial revolts affect the political culture of Virginia and New England?

First, the Virginians rebelled, and then a few years later, political violence swept through Maryland, New York, and Massachusetts Bay, England's most populous mainland colonies. Historians once interpreted these events as rehearsals for the American Revolution, or even for Jacksonian democracy in the 1830s. They perceived the rebels as frontier democrats, rising against an entrenched aristocracy.

Research suggests, however, that this view misconstrued these late-seventeenth-century rebellions. The uprisings were not confrontations between ordinary people and their rulers. Indeed, the events were not in any modern sense of the word ideological. In each colony, the local gentry split into factions, usually the "outs" versus the "ins," and each side proclaimed its political legitimacy.

Civil War in Virginia: Bacon's Rebellion

After 1660, the Virginia economy suffered a prolonged depression. Returns from tobacco had not been good for some time, and the Navigation Acts reduced profits even further. Indentured servants complained about lack of food and clothing. No wonder that Virginia's governor, Sir William Berkeley, despaired of ever ruling "a People where six parts of seven at least are Poor, Endebted, Discontented and Armed." In 1670, he and the House of Burgesses disfranchised all landless freemen, persons they regarded as troublemakers, but the threat of social violence remained.

Things changed when Nathaniel Bacon arrived in Virginia in 1674. This ambitious young man came from a respectable English family and set himself up immediately as a substantial planter. But he wanted more. Bacon envied the government patronage monopolized by Berkeley's cronies, a group known locally as the Green Spring faction. When Bacon attempted to obtain a license to engage in the fur trade, he was rebuffed. This lucrative commerce was reserved for the governor's friends. If Bacon had been willing to wait, he probably would have been accepted into the ruling clique, but as events would demonstrate, he was not a patient man.

Read the **Document** *Nathaniel Bacon's Declaration (July 30, 1676)* on **myhistorylab.com**

Events beyond Bacon's control thrust him suddenly into the center of Virginia politics. In 1675, Indians reacting to white encroachment attacked outlying plantations, killing colonists, and Virginians expected the governor to send an army to retaliate. Instead, early in 1676, Berkeley called for constructing a line of defensive forts, a plan that the settlers considered both expensive and ineffective. Indeed, the strategy raised embarrassing questions. Was Berkeley protecting his own fur monopoly? Was he planning to reward his friends with contracts to build useless forts?

While people speculated, Bacon offered to lead a volunteer army against the Indians at no cost to the hard-pressed Virginia taxpayers. All he demanded was an official commission from Berkeley giving him military command and the right to attack other Indians, not just the hostile Susquehannocks. The governor refused. With some justification, Berkeley regarded his upstart rival as a fanatic on the subject of Indians. The governor saw no reason to exterminate peaceful tribes simply to avenge the death of a few white settlers.

Read the **Document** *Declaration Against Nathaniel Bacon (1676)* on **myhistorylab.com**

What followed would have been comic had not so many people died. Bacon thundered against the governor's treachery; Berkeley labeled Bacon a traitor. Both men appealed to the populace for support. On several occasions, Bacon marched his followers to the frontier, but they either failed to find the enemy or, worse, massacred friendly Indians. At one point, Bacon burned Jamestown to the ground, forcing the governor to flee to the colony's Eastern Shore. Bacon's bumbling lieutenants chased Berkeley across Chesapeake Bay only to be captured themselves. Thereupon, the governor mounted a new campaign.

As Bacon's Rebellion dragged on, it became apparent that Bacon and his gentry supporters had only the vaguest notion of what they were trying to achieve. The members of the planter elite never seemed to appreciate that the rank-and-file soldiers, often black slaves and poor white servants, had legitimate grievances against Berkeley's corrupt government and were demanding reforms, not just a share in the governor's fur monopoly.

When Charles II learned of the fighting in Virginia, he dispatched 1,000 regular soldiers to Jamestown. By the time they arrived, Berkeley had regained control over the colony's government. In October 1676, Bacon died after a brief illness, and his followers soon dispersed.

Berkeley, now old and embittered, was recalled to England in 1677. His successors, especially Lord Culpeper (1680–1683) and Lord Howard of Effingham (1683–1689), seemed interested primarily in enriching themselves at the expense of the Virginia planters. Their self-serving policies, coupled with the memory of near anarchy, helped heal divisions within Virginia's ruling class. For almost a century, in fact, the local gentry formed a united front against greedy royal appointees.

Quick Check

✓ What were the underlying causes of Bacon's Rebellion?

The Glorious Revolution in the Bay Colony

During John Winthrop's lifetime (1588–1649), Massachusetts settlers developed an inflated sense of their independence from the mother country. After 1660, however, it became difficult even to pretend that the Puritan colony was a separate state. Royal officials demanded full compliance with the Navigation Acts. Moreover, the growth of commerce attracted new merchants to the Bay Colony, men who were Anglicans rather than Congregationalists and who maintained close business contacts in London. These persons complained loudly of Puritan intolerance. The Anglican faction was never large, but its presence divided Bay leaders. A few Puritan ministers and magistrates regarded compromise with England as treason, a breaking of the Lord's covenant. Other spokesmen, recognizing the changing political realities within the empire, urged a more moderate course.

In 1675, amid this ongoing political crisis, the Indians dealt the New Englanders a terrible setback. Metacomet, a Wampanoag chief the whites called King Philip, declared war against the colonists. The powerful Narragansett Indians, whose lands the settlers had long coveted, joined Metacomet, and in little more than a year of fighting the Indians destroyed scores of frontier villages, killed hundreds of colonists, and disrupted the entire regional economy. More than 1,000 Indians and New Englanders died in the conflict. The war left the people of Massachusetts deeply in debt and more than ever uncertain of their future. As in other parts of colonial America, the defeated Indians were forced off their lands, compelled by events to become either refugees or economically marginal figures in white society.

In 1684, the debate over the Bay Colony's relation to the mother country ended abruptly. The Court of Chancery, sitting in London and acting on a petition from the king, annulled the charter of the Massachusetts Bay Company. In one stroke of a pen, the patent that Winthrop had so lovingly carried to America in 1630, the foundation for a "City on a Hill," was gone. The decision forced the most stubborn Puritans to recognize they were part of an empire run by people who did not share their religious vision.

James II, who succeeded Charles II in 1685, disliked representative institutions. He decided to restructure the government of the entire region in the Dominion of New England. Between 1686 and 1689, the Dominion incorporated Massachusetts, Connecticut, Rhode Island, Plymouth, New York, New Jersey, and New Hampshire under a single appointed royal governor. For this demanding position, James selected Sir Edmund Andros (pronounced Andrews), a military veteran of tyrannical temperament. Andros arrived in Boston in 1686, and within months he had alienated everyone: Puritans, moderates, even Anglican merchants. Not only did Andros abolish elective assemblies, he also enforced the Navigation Acts with such rigor that he brought about a commercial depression. Andros declared normal town meetings illegal, collected taxes the people never approved, and packed the courts with supporters who detested the local population. Eighteenth-century historian and royal governor Thomas Hutchinson compared Andros unfavorably with the Roman tyrant Nero.

In late 1688, the ruling class of England deposed James II, an admitted Catholic, and placed his Protestant daughter, Mary, and her husband, William of Orange, on the throne as joint monarchs, who reigned as William III and Mary II. As part of the settlement, William and Mary accepted a Bill of Rights, stipulating the constitutional rights of all Englishmen. When news of this **Glorious Revolution** reached Boston, the Bay colonists overthrew the hated Andros regime. The New England version of the Glorious Revolution (April 18, 1689) was so popular that no one came to the governor's defense. Andros was jailed without a shot having been fired.

Thanks largely to the lobbying of Increase Mather, who pleaded the colonists' case in London, William III abandoned the Dominion of New England, and in 1691 granted Massachusetts a new royal charter. This document differed substantially from the company patent of 1629. The freemen no longer selected their governor. The choice now belonged to the king. Membership in the General Court was determined by annual election, and these representatives in turn chose the men who sat in the governor's council or upper house, subject always to the governor's veto. Moreover, the franchise, restricted here as in other colonies to adult males, was determined on the basis of personal property rather than church membership, a change that brought Massachusetts into conformity with general English practice. Town government remained much as it had been in Winthrop's time.

Quick Check

✓ Why did colonists overthrow the Dominion of New England in 1689?

Contagion of Witchcraft

The instability of the Massachusetts government following Andros's arrest—what Reverend Samuel Willard described as "the short Anarchy accompanying our late Revolution"—allowed what under normal political conditions would have been an isolated, though ugly, local incident to become a major crisis. Fearful men and women living in Salem Village, a small, unprosperous farming community, nearly overwhelmed the new rulers of Massachusetts Bay.

Accusations of witchcraft were not uncommon in seventeenth-century New England. Puritans believed that an individual might make a compact with the devil, but during the first decades of settlement, authorities had executed only about 15 alleged witches. Sometimes villagers simply ignored suspected witches. Never before had fears of witchcraft plunged an entire community into panic.

The terror in Salem Village began in late 1691, when several adolescent girls started to behave strangely. They cried out for no apparent reason; they twitched on the ground. When neighbors asked what caused their suffering, the girls said they were victims of witches, seemingly innocent persons who lived in the community. The arrest of several alleged witches did not relieve the girls' "fits," nor did prayer solve the problem. More accusations were made, and at least one person confessed, providing a frightening description of the devil as "a thing all over hairy, all the face hairy, and a long nose." In June 1692, a special court began to send men and women to the gallows. By the end of

Read the **Document**
Cotton Mather, Memorable Providences Relating to Witchcraft on **myhistorylab.com**

the summer, the court had hanged 19 people; another person was pressed to death with heavy rocks. Other suspects died in jail.

Then suddenly, the storm was over. Led by Increase Mather, prominent Congregational ministers belatedly urged leniency and restraint. Especially troubling to the clergymen was the court's decision to accept spectral evidence, that is, reports of dreams and visions in which the accused appeared as the devil's agent. Worried about convicting people on such dubious testimony, Mather declared, "It were better that ten suspected witches should escape, than that one innocent person should be condemned." The colonial government accepted the ministers' advice and convened a new court that acquitted, pardoned, or released the remaining suspects. After the Salem nightmare, witchcraft ceased to be a capital offense.

No one knows exactly what sparked the terror in Salem Village. The community had a history of religious discord, and during the 1680s the people split into angry factions over the choice of a minister. Economic tensions also played a part. Poorer, more traditional farmers accused members of prosperous, commercially oriented families of being witches. The underlying misogyny of the entire culture meant that more victims were women than men. Terror of attack by Native Americans may also have influenced this ugly affair. Indians in league with the French in Canada had recently raided nearby communities, killing people related to the bewitched Salem girls and, significantly, during the trials some victims described the Devil as a "tawny man."

Cotton Mather The publication of Cotton Mather's *Memorable Providences, Relating to Witchcrafts and Possessions* (1689) contributed to the hysteria that resulted in the Salem witchcraft trials. Mather is shown here surrounded by some of the forms a demon assumed in the "documented" case of an English family besieged by witches.

Quick Check

✓ Why were so many apparently innocent people convicted of witchcraft in Salem from 1691 to 1692?

CONCLUSION: FOUNDATIONS OF AN ATLANTIC EMPIRE

"It is no little Blessing of God," Cotton Mather announced proudly in 1700, "that we are part of the *English* nation." A half century earlier, John Winthrop would not have spoken these words, at least not with such enthusiasm. The two men were, of course, products of different political cultures. It was not so much that the character of Massachusetts society had changed. In fact, the Puritan families of 1700 were much like those of the founding generation. Rather, the difference was in England's attitude toward the colonies. Rulers living more than 3,000 miles away now made political and economic demands that Mather's contemporaries could not ignore.

The creation of a new imperial system did not, however, erase sectional differences. By 1700, for example, the Chesapeake colonies were more, not less, committed to cultivating tobacco and to slave labor. Although the separate regions were being pulled slowly into England's commercial orbit, they had little to do with each other. The elements that sparked a powerful sense of nationalism among colonists dispersed over a huge territory would not be evident for a long time. It would be a mistake, therefore, to anticipate the coming of the American Revolution.

3 STUDY RESOURCES

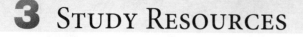 Listen to the **Chapter Audio** for Chapter 3 on **myhistorylab.com**

TIMELINE

1619 First blacks arrive in Virginia, p. 70

1660 Charles II is restored to the English throne, p. 73
  • Parliament passes the First Navigation Act, p. 75

1663 Second Navigation (Staple) Act passed, p. 74

1673 Plantation duty imposed to close loopholes in commercial regulations, p. 75

1675 King Philip's (Metacomet's) War devastates New England, p. 77

1676 Bacon's Rebellion threatens Governor Berkeley's government in Virginia, p. 77

1684 Charter of the Massachusetts Bay Company revoked, p. 77

1686 Dominion of New England established, p. 78

1688 James II driven into exile during Glorious Revolution, p. 78

1689 Rebellion in Massachusetts, p. 78

1692 Witch trials wrack Salem Village, p. 79

1696 Parliament establishes Board of Trade, p. 75

1739 Stono Uprising of South Carolina slaves terrifies white planters, p. 73

CHAPTER REVIEW

SOCIAL STABILITY: NEW ENGLAND COLONIES OF THE SEVENTEENTH CENTURY

What factors explain the remarkable social stability achieved in early New England?

Seventeenth-century New Englanders migrated to America in family groups, ensuring that the ratio of men to women remained roughly even, making it easier for young people to marry and start families. Stable marriage, together with New England's healthy climate, led to rapid population growth. While many young New Englanders served as servants, most seventeenth-century colonists eventually acquired property. (*p. 63*)

THE CHALLENGE OF THE CHESAPEAKE ENVIRONMENT

What factors contributed to political unrest in the Chesapeake region during this period?

Most immigrants to the early Chesapeake colonies were single young male indentured servants. Disease killed many of them shortly after arriving. Men outnumbered women, making it difficult for freemen to marry. Because of the short life expectancy, marriages did not last long. Economic inequality and family instability contributed to political unrest. (*p. 66*)

RACE AND FREEDOM IN BRITISH AMERICA

How did African American slaves preserve an independent cultural identity in the New World?

Slaves, especially those in the South, developed new creole languages that blended English with African languages. They established enduring kinship networks that helped mitigate the hardships of slavery. Enslaved Africans also developed new forms of music and folk art that drew upon African roots and adapted the Christianity taught them by their masters to include African religious elements. (*p. 69*)

BLUEPRINT FOR EMPIRE

Why did England discourage free and open trade in colonial America?

During the seventeenth century, Parliament passed mercantilist laws declaring that colonial raw materials and commerce would benefit only the mother country and not a European rival. These commercial regulations represented England's new blueprint for the empire. (*p. 73*)

COLONIAL POLITICAL REVOLTS

How did colonial revolts affect the political culture of Virginia and New England?

During Bacon's Rebellion, landless freemen rose up against the governor and demanded Indian lands.

Although the rebellion failed, it unified Virginia's ruling elite. In 1684, James II restructured the northern colonies to increase crown authority. New Englanders threw off the Dominion of New England in 1689 and negotiated for government charters that allowed significant local autonomy. (*p. 75*)

KEY TERM QUESTIONS

1. What was life like for a yeomen farmer in the northern colonies? (p. 65)

2. How did the life of an indentured servant differ from that of a member of the gentry? (p. 68)

3. How did the chartering of the Royal African Company solidify slavery in Virginia? (p. 70)

4. What argument did proponents of mercantilism employ? (p. 73)

5. Why did England seek to control the distribution of enumerated goods from the colonies? (p. 74)

6. Why did Parliament pass the Navigation Acts? (p. 74)

7. What were the underlying causes of Bacon's Rebellion? (p. 76)

8. Why did colonists overthrow the Dominion of New England in 1689? (p. 77)

9. How did the colonists respond to the Glorious Revolution? (p. 78)

10. Why would clergymen find the court's acceptance of spectral evidence troubling? (p. 79)

MYHISTORYLAB CONNECTIONS

Visit **www.myhistorylab.com** for a customized Study Plan to build your knowledge of *Putting Down Roots*.

Question for Analysis

1. Why was cruelty such an important element of the slave capturing process?

   View the **Closer Look** Plan and Sections of a Slave Ship and an Illustration of a Slave Camp p. 70

2. What happened to the Slaves who participated in the Stono Rebellion?

   Read the **Document** James Oglethorpe, The Stono Rebellion p. 73

3. What was the purpose of issuing a declaration against Nathaniel Bacon?

   Read the **Document** Declaration Against Nathaniel Bacon (1676) p. 76

4. Why would Mather include a description of the signs of witchcraft in his account?

   Read the **Document** Cotton Mather, Memorable Providences Relating to Witchcraft p. 78

Other Resources from This Chapter

Read the **Document** Prenuptial Agreement, 1653

Read the **Document** Anne Bradstreet Before the Birth of One of Her Children

Read the **Document** Nathaniel Bacon's Declaration

Read the **Document** Virginia Law on Indentured Servitude

Contents and Spotlight Questions

TENSIONS IN THE BACKCOUNTRY PG. 85

What difficulties did Native Americans face in maintaining their cultural independence on the frontier?

SPANISH BORDERLANDS OF THE EIGHTEENTH CENTURY PG. 89

Why was the Spanish empire unable to control its northern frontier?

THE IMPACT OF EUROPEAN IDEAS ON AMERICAN CULTURE PG. 91

How did European ideas affect eighteenth-century American life?

RELIGIOUS REVIVALS IN PROVINCIAL SOCIETIES PG. 96

How did the Great Awakening transform the religious culture of colonial America?

CLASH OF POLITICAL CULTURES PG. 98

Why were eighteenth-century colonial assemblies not fully democratic?

CENTURY OF IMPERIAL WAR PG. 101

Why did colonial Americans support Great Britain's wars against France?

(((•─[Listen to the **Chapter Audio** for Chapter 4 on **myhistorylab.com**

William Byrd III Byrd's *History of the Dividing Line Run in the Year 1728* contains a marvelously satirical account of the culture of poor country farmers in eighteenth-century North Carolina.

CONSTRUCTING AN ANGLO-AMERICAN IDENTITY: THE JOURNAL OF WILLIAM BYRD

William Byrd II (1674–1744) was a type of British American one would not have encountered during the earliest years of settlement. This successful Tidewater planter was a product of a new, more cosmopolitan environment, and as an adult, Byrd seemed as much at home in London as in his native Virginia. In 1728, at the height of his political influence in Williamsburg, the capital of colonial Virginia, Byrd accepted a commission to help survey a disputed boundary with North Carolina. During his long journey into the backcountry, Byrd kept a journal, a satiric, often bawdy chronicle of daily events that is now regarded as a classic of early American literature.

On his trip into the wilderness, Byrd met many different people. No sooner had he left the familiar world of tobacco plantations than he came across a self-styled "Hermit," an Englishman who apparently preferred the freedom of the woods to the constraints of society. "He has no other Habitation but a green Bower or Harbour," Byrd reported, "with a Female Domestick as wild & as dirty as himself."

As the boundary commissioners pushed farther into the backcountry, they encountered highly independent men and women of European descent, small frontier families that Byrd regarded as living no better than savages. He attributed their uncivilized behavior to a diet of too much pork. "The Truth of it is, these People live so much upon Swine's flesh … [that it] makes them … extremely hoggish in their Temper, & many of them seem to Grunt rather than Speak in their ordinary conversation." The wilderness journey also brought Byrd's party into contact with Native Americans, whom he properly distinguished as Catawba, Tuscarora, Usheree, and Sapponi Indians.

Byrd's journal invites us to view the rapidly developing eighteenth-century backcountry from a fresh perspective. It was not a vast empty territory awaiting the arrival of European settlers. Maps often sustain this false impression. Depicting cities and towns, farms and plantations clustered along the Atlantic coast, they suggest a "line of settlement" pushing outward into a huge blank area with no mark of civilization. The people Byrd met on his journey into the backcountry would not have understood such maps. The empty space on the maps was their home. They experienced the frontier as populous zones of many cultures stretching from the English and French settlements in the north all the way to the Spanish borderlands in the far southwest.

The point is not to discount the significance of the older Atlantic settlements. During the eighteenth century, Britain's 13 mainland colonies were transformed. Their population grew at unprecedented rates. German and Scots-Irish immigrants arrived in huge numbers. So, too, did African slaves.

Wherever they lived, colonial Americans of this period were less isolated from one another than colonists had been during the seventeenth century. Indeed, after 1690, men and women expanded their cultural horizons, becoming part of a larger Anglo-American empire. The change was striking. Colonists whose parents or grandparents had come to the New World to confront a "howling wilderness" now purchased European manufactures, read English journals, participated in imperial wars, and sought favors from a growing number of resident royal officials. No one—not even the inhabitants of the distant frontiers—could escape Britain's influence. The cultural, economic, and political links connecting the colonists to the imperial center in London grew stronger with time.

This surprising development raises a difficult question. If the eighteenth-century colonists were so powerfully attracted to Great Britain, why did they ever declare independence? The answer may be that as the colonists became more British, they also inevitably became more American. This helps explain the appearance after midcentury of genuine nationalist sentiment. Political, commercial, and military links that brought the colonists into more frequent contact with Britain also made them more aware of other colonists. It was within an expanding, prosperous empire that they first began seriously to consider what it meant to be American.

Read the **Document** *William Byrd—An American Gentleman* on **myhistorylab.com**

TENSIONS IN THE BACKCOUNTRY

Accurate population data from the colonial period are difficult to find. The first national census did not occur until 1790. Still, pre-Revolutionary sources indicate that the total white population of Britain's 13 mainland colonies rose from about 250,000 in 1700 to 2,150,000 in 1770, an annual growth rate of 3 percent.

What difficulties did Native Americans face in maintaining their cultural independence on the frontier?

Few societies in recorded history have expanded so rapidly. If the growth rate had not dropped during the nineteenth and twentieth centuries, the United States today would have more than one billion people. Natural reproduction was responsible for most of the growth. More families bore children who in turn lived long enough to have children of their own. Because of this sudden expansion, the colonial population was strikingly young; approximately one-half of the populace at any given time was under age 16.

Not only was the total population increasing rapidly; it also was becoming more dispersed and heterogeneous. Each year thousands of non-English Europeans arrived. Unlike those seventeenth-century English settlers in search of religious sanctuary or instant wealth (see Chapter 2), the newcomers generally hoped to obtain their own land and become independent farmers. These people often traveled to the backcountry, a region stretching approximately 800 miles from western Pennsylvania to Georgia. Although they planned to follow the customs they had known in Europe, they found it far more demanding than they had anticipated to survive on the British frontier. They plunged into a complex, fluid, often violent society that included Native Americans, African Americans, as well as other Europeans. (See Map 4.1.)

Map 4.1 *Distribution of European and African Immigrants in the Thirteen Colonies* A flood of non-English immigrants swept the British colonies between 1700 and 1775.

Quick Check

✓ Why did so many Scots-Irish migrate to America during the eighteenth century?

Scots-Irish Flee English Oppression

During the seventeenth century, English rulers thought they could dominate Catholic Ireland by transporting thousands of lowland Scottish Presbyterians to northern Ireland. These settlers became known as the Scots-Irish. The plan failed. Anglican English officials discriminated against the Presbyterians. They passed laws that placed the Scots-Irish at a disadvantage when they traded in England; they taxed them exorbitantly.

After several poor harvests in the 1720s, many Scots-Irish began to emigrate to America, where they hoped to find the freedom and prosperity that had been denied them in Ireland. Often entire Presbyterian congregations followed charismatic ministers to the New World, intent on replicating a distinctive, fiercely independent culture on the frontier. An estimated 150,000 Scots-Irish migrated to the colonies before the Revolution.

Most Scots-Irish immigrants landed in Philadelphia, but instead of remaining there, they carved out farms on Pennsylvania's western frontier. The colony's proprietors welcomed the new settlers, for it seemed they would form an ideal barrier between the Indians and the older, coastal communities. The Penn family soon had second thoughts, however. The Scots-Irish squatted on whatever land looked best. When colony officials pointed out that large tracts had already been reserved, the immigrants retorted that "it was against the laws of God and nature that so much land should be idle when so many Christians wanted it to labour on and to raise their bread." Wherever they located, the Scots-Irish challenged established authority.

Germans Search for a Better Life

A second large body of non-English settlers, more than 100,000 people, came from the upper Rhine Valley, the German Palatinate. Some of the migrants, especially those who relocated to America around 1700, belonged to small pietistic Protestant sects whose religious views were similar to those of the Quakers. These Germans moved to the New World primarily to find religious toleration. Under the guidance of Francis Daniel Pastorius (1651–1720), Mennonites established a prosperous community in Pennsylvania known as Germantown.

By midcentury, however, the characteristics of the German migration had begun to change. Many Lutherans transferred to the Middle Colonies. Unlike members of the pietistic sects, these men and women were not in search of religious freedom. Rather, they traveled to the New World to improve their material lives. The Lutheran Church in Germany initially tried to control the distant congregations, but although the migrants fiercely preserved much of traditional German culture, they were eventually forced to accommodate to new social conditions. Henry Melchior Mühlenberg (1711–1787), a tireless leader, helped German Lutherans through a difficult cultural adjustment. In 1748, Mühlenberg organized a meeting of local pastors and lay delegates that ordained ministers of their own choosing, an act of spiritual independence that has been called "the most important single event in American Lutheran history."

The German migrants—mistakenly called Pennsylvania Dutch because the English confused *deutsch* (meaning "German") with *Dutch* ("a person from Holland")—began reaching Philadelphia in large numbers after 1717. By 1766, persons of German stock accounted for more than one-third of Pennsylvania's population. Even their most vocal detractors admitted the Germans were the best farmers in the colony.

After 1730, Germans and Scots-Irish pushed south from western Pennsylvania into the Shenandoah Valley, thousands of them settling in the backcountry of Virginia and the Carolinas. The Germans usually remained wherever they found unclaimed fertile land. By contrast, the Scots-Irish often moved two or three times, acquiring a reputation as a rootless people.

Wherever the newcomers settled, they often found themselves living beyond the effective authority of colonial governments. To be sure, backcountry residents petitioned for assistance during wars against the Indians, but they preferred to be left alone. These conditions heightened the importance of religious institutions within the small ethnic communities. Although the stimulus for coming to America may have been a desire for economic independence and prosperity, backcountry families—especially the Scots-Irish—flocked to evangelical Protestant preachers, to Presbyterian and later Baptist and Methodist ministers, who not only fulfilled the settlers' spiritual needs but also gave these scattered communities a moral character that survived long after the colonial period.

Read the **Document**
Peter Kalm, a Swedish Visitor to Philadelphia 1748 on **myhistorylab.com**

Quick Check

✓ Why did the new German and Scots-Irish immigrants to America move west after they arrived in the colonies?

Native Americans Stake Out a Middle Ground

During much of the seventeenth century, various Indian groups who contested the English settlers for control of coastal lands suffered terribly, sometimes from war, but more often from contagious diseases such as smallpox. The two races found it difficult to live in close proximity. As one Indian informed the Maryland assembly in 1666, "Your hogs & Cattle injure Us, You come too near Us to live & drive Us from place to place. We can fly no farther; let us know where to live & how to be secured for the future from the Hogs & Cattle."

Against such odds the Indians managed to survive. By the eighteenth century, the site of the most intense and creative contact between the races had shifted to the huge territory between the Appalachian Mountains and the Mississippi River, where several hundred thousand Native Americans made their homes.

View the **Image**
*William Penn Making
a Treaty with the
Indians 1682* on
myhistorylab.com

Many Indians had only recently migrated to the area. The Delaware, for example, retreated to far western Pennsylvania and the Ohio Valley to escape almost continuous confrontation with advancing European invaders. Other Indians drifted west in less happy circumstances. They were refugees, the remnants of Native American groups who had lost so many people that they could no longer sustain an independent cultural identity. These survivors joined with other Indians to establish new multiethnic communities. Stronger groups of Indians, such as the Creek, Choctaw, Chickasaw, Cherokee, and Shawnee, generally welcomed the refugees. Strangers were formally adopted to replace relatives killed in battle or overcome by sickness.

The concept of a **middle ground**—a geographical area where two district cultures interacted with neither holding a clear upper hand—helps us understand how eighteenth-century Indians held their own in the backcountry beyond the Appalachian Mountains. The Native Americans never intended to isolate themselves completely from European contact. They relied on white traders, French and English, to provide essential metal goods and weapons. The goal of the Indian confederacies was rather to maintain a strong independent voice in these commercial exchanges, whenever possible playing the French against the British. So long as they had sufficient military strength they compelled everyone who came to negotiate in the "middle ground" to give them proper respect. Native Americans took advantage of rivals when possible; they compromised when necessary. It is best to imagine the Indians' middle ground as an open, dynamic process of creative interaction.

However desirable they may have appeared, European goods subtly eroded traditional Native American authority structures. During the period of earliest encounter with white men, Indian leaders reinforced their own power by controlling the character and flow of commercial exchange. If a trader wanted a rich supply of animal skins, for example, he soon learned that he had better negotiate directly with a chief or tribal elder. But as more European traders operated within the "middle ground," ordinary Indians began to bargain for themselves, obtaining colorful and durable manufactured items without first consulting a Native American leader. Independent commercial dealings of this sort weakened the Indians' ability to resist organized white aggression. As John Stuart, a superintendent of Indian affairs, explained in 1761, "A modern Indian cannot subsist without Europeans; And would handle a Flint Ax or any other rude utensil used by his ancestors very awkwardly; So that what was only convenience at first is now become Necessity."

The survival of the middle ground depended ultimately on factors over which the Native Americans had little control. Imperial competition between France and Great Britain enhanced the Indians' bargaining position. But after the British defeated the French in 1763, the Indians no longer received the same solicitous attention. Keeping old allies happy seemed to the British a needless expense. Moreover, contagious disease continued to take a fearful toll. In the southern backcountry between 1685 and 1790, the Indian population dropped an astounding 72 percent. In the Ohio Valley, the numbers suggest similar rates of decline.

Quick Check

✓ How did Native Americans manipulate the "middle ground" to their advantage?

SPANISH BORDERLANDS OF THE EIGHTEENTH CENTURY

The Spanish empire continued to shape borderlands societies into the eighteenth century. As anyone who visits the modern American Southwest discovers, Spanish administrators and priests—not to mention ordinary settlers—left a lasting imprint on its cultural landscape.

Until 1821, when Mexico declared independence from Madrid, Spanish authorities struggled to control a vast northern frontier. During the eighteenth century, the Spanish empire in North America included widely dispersed settlements such as San Francisco and San Diego in California; Santa Fe, New Mexico; San Antonio, Texas; and St. Augustine, Florida (see Map 4.2). In these borderland communities, European colonists mixed with peoples of other races and backgrounds, forming multicultural societies.

Why was the Spanish empire unable to control its northern frontier?

Conquering the Northern Frontier

In the late sixteenth century, Spanish settlers, led by Juan de Oñate, established European communities north of the Rio Grande. The Pueblo Indians resisted the invasion of colonists, soldiers, and missionaries, and in a major rebellion in 1680 led by El Popé, the native peoples drove the whites out of New Mexico. The Spanish did not reconquer this fiercely contested area until 1692. By then, Native American

Read the **Document** *Testimony of Pedro Naranjo to Spanish Authorities* on **myhistorylab.com**

Map 4.2 *The Spanish Borderlands, ca. 1770*   In the eighteenth century, Spain's North American empire extended across what is now the southern United States from Florida through Texas and New Mexico to California.

hostility coupled with the failure to find precious metal had cooled Spain's enthusiasm for the northern frontier.

Concern over French encroachment in the Southeast led Spain to colonize St. Augustine (Florida) in 1565. This was the first permanent European settlement in what would become the United States, predating the founding of Jamestown and Plymouth by decades. Pedro Menéndez de Avilés brought some 1,500 soldiers and settlers to St. Augustine, where they constructed an impressive fort, but the colony failed to attract additional Spanish migrants.

California also never figured prominently in Spain's plans for the New World. Early explorers reported finding only impoverished Indians along the Pacific coast. Adventurers saw no natural resources worth mentioning, and since the area was difficult to reach from Mexico City—the overland trip could take months—California received little attention. Fear that the Russians might seize the entire region belatedly sparked Spanish activity, however, and after 1769, two indomitable servants of empire, Fra Junípero Serra and Don Gaspar de Portolá, organized permanent missions and *presidios* (forts) at San Diego, Monterey, San Francisco, and Santa Barbara.

View the **Map**
Spanish America to 1610 on
myhistorylab.com

Quick Check

✓ Why did the Spanish not more aggressively develop California and the Southwest?

Spanish Mission Baroque-style eighteenth-century Spanish mission at San Xavier del Bac outside present-day Tucson, Arizona. Spanish missions dotted the frontier of northern New Spain from Florida to California.

Peoples of the Spanish Borderlands

In contrast to the English frontier settlements of the eighteenth century, the Spanish outposts in North America grew slowly. A few Catholic priests and imperial administrators traveled to the northern provinces, but the danger of Indian attack and a harsh physical environment discouraged ordinary colonists. Most European migrants were soldiers in the pay of the empire. Although some colonists came directly from Spain, most had been born in other Spanish colonies such as the Canaries or New Spain, and because European women rarely appeared on the frontier, Spanish males formed relationships with Indian women, fathering mestizos, children of mixed race.

As in other eighteenth-century frontiers, encounters with Spanish soldiers, priests, and traders altered Native American cultures. The experience here was quite different from that of the whites and Indians in the British backcountry. The Spanish exploited Native American labor, reducing entire Indian villages to servitude. Many Indians moved to the Spanish towns, and although they lived alongside the Europeans—something rare in British America—they were consigned to the lowest social class, objects of European contempt. However much their material conditions changed, the southwestern Indians resisted efforts to convert them to Catholicism. The Pueblo maintained their own religious forms—often at great personal risk—and they sometimes murdered priests who became too intrusive. Angry Pueblo Indians at Taos reportedly fed the hated Spanish friars corn tortillas containing urine and mouse meat.

The Spanish empire never had the resources necessary to secure the northern frontier. The small military posts were intended primarily to discourage other European powers such as France, Britain, and Russia from taking territory claimed by Spain. It would be misleading, however, to stress the fragility of Spanish colonization. The urban design and public architecture of many southwestern cities still reflect the vision of the early Spanish settlers, and the old borderlands largely remain Spanish speaking to this day.

View the **Image**
The Alamo on
myhistorylab.com

Quick Check
✓ How successful were the Spanish in assimilating the Pueblos to imperial rule?

THE IMPACT OF EUROPEAN IDEAS ON AMERICAN CULTURE

The character of the older, more established British colonies changed almost as rapidly as that of the backcountry. The rapid growth of an urban cosmopolitan culture impressed eighteenth-century commentators, and although most Americans still lived on scattered farms, they had begun to participate aggressively in an exciting consumer marketplace that expanded their imaginative horizons.

How did European ideas affect eighteenth-century American life?

American Enlightenment

European historians often refer to the eighteenth century as an Age of Reason. During this period, a body of new, often radical, ideas swept through the salons and universities, altering how educated Europeans thought about God, nature, and society. This intellectual revolution, called the Enlightenment, involved the work of Europe's greatest minds, men such as Newton and Locke, Voltaire and Hume. Their writings received a mixed reception in the colonies. On the whole, the American Enlightenment was tamer than its European counterpart, for while the colonists welcomed experimental science, they defended traditional Christianity.

Enlightenment thinkers shared basic assumptions. Philosophers of the Enlightenment replaced the concept of original sin with a much more optimistic view of human nature. A benevolent God, having set the universe in motion, gave human beings the power of reason to enable them to comprehend the orderly workings of His creation. Everything, even human society, operated according to these mechanical rules. The responsibility of right-thinking men and women, therefore, was to make certain that institutions such as church and state conformed to self-evident natural laws. It was possible to achieve perfection in this world. In fact, human suffering was the result of people's losing touch with the fundamental insights of reason.

For many Americans, the appeal of the Enlightenment was its focus on a search for useful knowledge, ideas, and inventions to improve the quality of human life. What mattered was practical experimentation. A speech delivered in 1767 before the members of the American Society in Philadelphia reflected the new utilitarian spirit: "Knowledge is of little Use when confined to mere Speculation, But when speculative Truths are reduced to Practice, when Theories grounded upon Experiments ... and the Arts of Living made more easy and comfortable ... Knowledge then becomes really useful."

The Enlightenment spawned scores of earnest scientific tinkerers, people who dutifully recorded changes in temperature, strange plants and animals, and astronomic phenomena. While these eighteenth-century Americans made few earth-shattering discoveries, they did encourage their countrymen, especially those who attended college, to apply reason to the solution of social and political problems.

Quick Check

✓ What were the basic intellectual assumptions of the American Enlightenment?

Benjamin Franklin

Benjamin Franklin (1706–1790) absorbed the new cosmopolitan culture. European thinkers regarded him as a fellow *philosophe*, a person of reason and science, a role that he self-consciously cultivated when he visited England and France in later life. Franklin had little formal education, but as a young man working in his brother's print shop, he kept up with the latest intellectual currents. In his *Autobiography*, Franklin described the excitement of discovering a new British journal. It was like a breath of fresh air to a boy growing up in Puritan New England: "I met with an odd volume of *The Spectator* ... I had never before seen any of them. I bought it, read it over and over, and was much delighted with it. I thought the writing excellent, and wished if possible to imitate it."

After he moved to Philadelphia in 1723, Franklin devoted himself to the pursuit of useful knowledge, ideas that would increase the happiness of his fellow Americans. Franklin never denied the existence of God. Rather, he pushed the Lord aside, making room for the free exercise of human reason. Franklin tinkered, experimented, and reformed. Almost everything aroused his curiosity. His investigation of electricity brought him world fame, but Franklin was never satisfied with his work in this field until it yielded practical application. In 1756, he invented the lightning rod. He also designed an efficient stove that is still used today. In modern America, Franklin has become exactly what he would have wanted to be, a symbol of material progress through human ingenuity.

Benjamin Franklin Franklin exemplified the scientific curiosity and search for practical knowledge characteristic of Enlightenment thinkers of the eighteenth century. His experiments on electricity became world famous and inspired others to study the effects of the strange force.

Franklin promoted the spread of reason. In Philadelphia, he organized groups that discussed the latest European literature, philosophy, and science. In 1727, for example, he "form'd most of my ingenious Acquaintances into a Club for mutual Improvement, which we call'd the Junto." Four years later Franklin helped found the Library Company, a voluntary association that for the first time allowed people like him to pursue "useful knowledge." The members of these societies communicated with Americans in other colonies, providing them not only with new information but also with models for their own clubs and associations. Such efforts broadened the intellectual horizons of many colonists, especially those who lived in cities.

Read the **Document**
Franklin, Observations Concerning the Increase of Mankind on **myhistorylab.com**

Quick Check

✓ What characteristics did Benjamin Franklin possess that made him an Enlightenment figure?

Economic Transformation

The colonial economy kept pace with the stunning growth in population. During the first three-quarters of the eighteenth century, the population increased at least eightfold. Yet even with so many additional people to feed and clothe, the per

Boston Harbor This engraving of a work by William Burgis depicts the port of Boston at mid-century.

capita income did not decline. Indeed, except for poor urban dwellers, such as sailors whose employment varied with the season, white Americans did well. Abundant land and the growth of agriculture accounted for their economic success. New farmers could not only provide for their families' well-being but could also sell their crops in European and West Indian markets. Each year, more Americans produced more tobacco, wheat, or rice—to cite just the major export crops—and thus maintained a high level of individual prosperity without developing an industrial base.

At midcentury, colonial exports flowed along well-established routes. More than half of American goods produced for export went to Britain. The Navigation Acts (see Chapter 3) were still in effect, and "enumerated" items such as tobacco had to be landed first at a British port. Furs were added to the restricted list in 1722. The White Pines Acts passed in 1711, 1722, and 1729 forbade Americans from cutting white pine trees without a license. The purpose of this legislation was to reserve the best trees for the Royal Navy. The Molasses Act of 1733—also called the Sugar Act—placed a heavy duty on molasses imported from foreign ports; the Hat and Felt Act of 1732 and the Iron Act of 1750 attempted to limit the production of colonial goods that competed with British exports.

These statutes might have created tensions between the colonists and the mother country had they been rigorously enforced. Crown officials, however, generally ignored the new laws. New England merchants imported molasses from French Caribbean islands without paying the full customs; iron masters in the Middle Colonies continued to produce iron. Even without the Navigation Acts, however, most colonial exports would have been sold on the English market. The emerging consumer society in Britain was creating a new generation of buyers who possessed enough income to purchase American goods, especially sugar and tobacco. This rising demand was the major market force shaping the colonial economy.

((•⫿Listen to the
Audio File
*The Connecti-
cut Peddler* on
myhistorylab.com

Quick Check

✓ Why did Americans in the first half of the eighteenth century not complain about the Navigation Acts?

Birth of a Consumer Society

After midcentury, Americans began buying more English goods than their parents or grandparents had done, giving birth to a **consumer revolution**. Between 1740 and 1770, English exports to the American colonies increased by an astounding 360 percent.

In part, this new American market shift reflected a transformation in the British economy. The pace of the British economy picked up dramatically after 1690. Small factories produced certain goods more efficiently and more cheaply than the colonists could. The availability of these products altered the lives of most Americans, even those with modest incomes. Staffordshire china replaced crude earthenware; imported cloth replaced homespun. Franklin noted in his *Autobiography* how changing consumer habits affected his life. For years, he had eaten his breakfast in an earthenware bowl with a pewter spoon, but one morning it was served "in a china bowl, with a spoon of silver." Franklin observed that "this was the first appearance of plate and china in our house which afterwards in the course of years, as our wealth increased, augmented gradually to several hundred pounds in value." In this manner, British industrialization undercut American handicraft and folk art.

To help Americans purchase manufactured goods, British merchants offered generous credit. Colonists deferred final payment by paying interest on their debts. The temptation to acquire English finery blinded many people to hard economic realities. They gambled on the future, hoping bumper crops would reduce their dependence on the large merchant houses of London and Glasgow. Some persons lived within their means, but the aggregate American debt continued to grow. Colonial leaders tried various expedients to remain solvent—issuing paper money, for example—and while these efforts delayed a crisis, the balance-of-payments problem was clearly very serious.

Intercoastal trade also increased in the eighteenth century. Southern planters sent tobacco and rice to New England and the Middle Colonies, where these staples were exchanged for meat, wheat, and goods imported from Britain. By 1760, approximately 30 percent of the colonists' total tonnage capacity was involved in this "coastwise" commerce. Backcountry farmers in western Pennsylvania and the Shenandoah Valley also carried their grain to market along an old Iroquois trail that became known

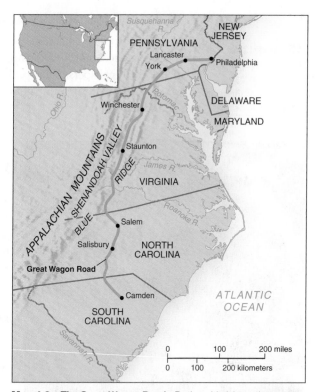

Map 4.3   *The Great Wagon Road*   By the mid-eighteenth century, the Great Wagon Road had become a major highway for the settlers in Virginia and the Carolina backcountry.

as the Great Wagon Road, a rough, hilly highway that by the time of the Revolution stretched 735 miles along the Blue Ridge Mountains to Camden, South Carolina (see Map 4.3). Long, graceful Conestoga wagons carried most of their produce. German immigrants in the Conestoga River Valley in Lancaster County, Pennsylvania, had invented these "wagons of empire."

The shifting patterns of trade had immense effects on the development of an American culture. First, the flood of British imports eroded local and regional identities. Commerce helped to "Anglicize" American culture by exposing colonial consumers to a common range of British manufactured goods. Deep sectional differences remained, but Americans from New Hampshire to Georgia were increasingly drawn into a sophisticated economic network centered in London. Second, the expanding coastal and overland trade brought colonists of different backgrounds into more frequent contact. Ships that sailed between New England and South Carolina, and between Virginia and Pennsylvania, provided dispersed Americans with a means to exchange ideas and experiences on a more regular basis. Mid-eighteenth-century printers, for example, established dozens of new journals. These weekly newspapers carried information not only about the mother country and world commerce but also about the colonies.

Quick Check

✓ How did Americans manage to pay for so many new consumer goods?

RELIGIOUS REVIVALS IN PROVINCIAL SOCIETIES

How did the Great Awakening transform the religious culture of colonial America?

A sudden, spontaneous series of Protestant revivals in the mid-eighteenth century, known as the Great Awakening, profoundly affected the lives of ordinary people. This new, highly personal appeal to a "new birth" in Christ caused men and women of all backgrounds to rethink basic assumptions about church and state, institutions and society.

The Great Awakening

Whatever their origins, the seeds of the Great Awakening were generally sown on fertile ground. In the early eighteenth century, many Americans—especially New Englanders—complained that organized religion had lost vitality. They looked back at Winthrop's generation with nostalgia, assuming that common people at that time must have possessed greater piety than did later, more worldly colonists. Congregational ministers seemed obsessed with dull, scholastic matters; they no longer touched the heart. And in the Southern Colonies, there were simply not enough ordained ministers to tend to the religious needs of the population.

George Whitefield The fervor of the Great Awakening was intensified by the eloquence of itinerant preachers such as George Whitefield, the most popular evangelical of the mid-eighteenth century. (*Source*: John Wollaston, "George Whitefield," ca. 1770. National Portrait Gallery, London.)

The Great Awakening arrived unexpectedly in Northampton, a small farm community in western Massachusetts. It was sparked by Jonathan Edwards, the local Congregational minister. Edwards accepted the traditional teachings of Calvinism, reminding his parishioners that an omnipotent God had determined their eternal fate. There was nothing they could do to save themselves. They were totally dependent on the Lord's will. He thought his fellow ministers had grown soft. They left men and women with the mistaken impression that sinners might somehow avoid damnation by performing good works.

Read the **Document** *Jonathan Edwards, "Sinners in the Hands of an Angry God"* on **myhistorylab.com**

Although Edwards was an outstanding theologian, he did not possess the dynamic personality to sustain the revival. That role fell to George Whitefield, a young, inspiring preacher from England who toured the colonies from New Hampshire to Georgia. While Whitefield was not an original thinker, he was an extraordinarily effective public speaker. And like his friend Benjamin Franklin, he symbolized the cultural forces that were transforming the Atlantic world.

Whitefield's audiences came from all groups of American society: rich and poor, young and old, rural and urban. While he described himself as a Calvinist, Whitefield welcomed all Protestants. He spoke from any available pulpit: "Don't tell me you are a Baptist, an Independent, a Presbyterian, a dissenter, tell me you are a Christian, that is all I want."

Whitefield was a brilliant entrepreneur. Like Franklin, with whom he published many popular volumes, the itinerant minister possessed an almost intuitive sense of how to turn this burgeoning consumer society to his own advantage, and he embraced the latest merchandising techniques. He appreciated, for example, the power of the press in selling the revival, and he regularly advertised his own work in British and American newspapers. The crowds flocked to hear Whitefield, while his critics grumbled about the commercialization of religion. One anonymous writer in Massachusetts noted that there was "a very wholesome law of the province to discourage Pedlars in Trade," and it seemed high time "to enact something for the discouragement of Pedlars in Divinity also."

Read the **Document**
Benjamin Franklin on George Whitefield (1771) on **myhistorylab.com**

Quick Check
✓ What explains the Reverend George Whitefield's extraordinary popularity among colonial Americans?

Evangelical Religion

Other American-born itinerant preachers, who traveled from settlement to settlement throughout the colonies to spread their message, followed Whitefield's example. The most famous was Gilbert Tennent, a Scots-Irish Presbyterian who had been educated in the Middle Colonies. His sermon "On the Danger of an Unconverted Ministry," printed in 1741, set off a storm of protest from established ministers who were insulted by assertions that they did not understand true religion. Lesser-known revivalists traveled from town to town, colony to colony, challenging local clergymen who seemed hostile to evangelical religion. Men and women who thronged to hear the itinerants were called "New Lights." During the 1740s and 1750s, many congregations split between defenders of the new emotional preaching and those who regarded the movement as dangerous nonsense.

Despite Whitefield's successes, many ministers remained suspicious of the itinerants and their methods. Some complaints may have just been sour grapes. One "Old Light" spokesman labeled Tennent "a monster! impudent and noisy." He claimed Tennent told anxious Christians that "they were damned! damned! damned! This charmed them; and, in the most dreadful winter I ever saw, people wallowed in snow, night and day, for the benefit of his beastly brayings; and many ended their days under these fatigues." Charles Chauncy, minister of the prestigious First Church of Boston, raised more troubling issues. How could the revivalists be certain God had sparked the Great Awakening? Perhaps the itinerants had relied too much on emotion? "Let us esteem those as friends of religion," Chauncy advised, "… who warn us of the danger of enthusiasm, and would put us on our guard, that we may not be led aside by it."

Despite occasional anti-intellectual outbursts, the New Lights founded several important centers of higher learning. They wanted to train young men to carry on the good works of Edwards, Whitefield, and Tennent. In 1746, New Light Presbyterians established the College of New Jersey, which later became Princeton University. Just before his death, Edwards was appointed its president. The evangelical minister Eleazar Wheelock launched Dartmouth (1769); other revivalists founded Brown (1764) and Rutgers (1766).

The Great Awakening also encouraged men and women who had been taught to remain silent before traditional authority figures to speak up, to take an active role in their salvation. They could no longer rely on ministers or institutions. The individual alone stood before God. Knowing this, New Lights shattered the old harmony among Protestant sects. In its place, they introduced a noisy, often bitter competition. As one New Jersey Presbyterian complained, "There are so many particular *sects* and *Parties* among professed Christians ... that we know not ... in which of these different *paths*, to steer our course for *Heaven*."

View the **Image**
*Richard Allen
Portrait* on
myhistorylab.com

Expressive evangelicalism struck a particularly responsive chord among African Americans. Itinerant ministers frequently preached to large, sympathetic audiences of slaves. Richard Allen (1760–1831), founder of the African Methodist Episcopal Church (AME), reported he owed his freedom in part to a traveling Methodist minister who persuaded Allen's master that slavery was sinful. Allen himself was converted, as were thousands of other black colonists. According to one historian, evangelical preaching "shared enough with traditional African styles and beliefs such as spirit possession and ecstatic expression ... to allow for an interpenetration of African and Christian religious beliefs."

With religious contention came an awareness of a larger community, a union of fellow believers that extended beyond the boundaries of town and colony. In fact, evangelical religion was one of several forces at work during the mid-eighteenth century that brought scattered colonists into contact with one another for the first time. In this sense, the Great Awakening was a "national" event long before a nation actually existed.

Quick Check

✓ What message did evangelical ministers bring to ordinary Americans?

People who had been touched by the Great Awakening shared an optimism about the future of America. With God's help, social and political progress was possible, and from this perspective, the New Lights did not sound much different than the mildly rationalist American spokesmen of the Enlightenment. Both groups prepared the way for the development of a revolutionary mentality in colonial America.

CLASH OF POLITICAL CULTURES

Why were the eighteenth-century colonial assemblies not fully democratic?

The political history of the eighteenth century illuminates a growing tension within the empire. Americans of all regions repeatedly stated their desire to replicate British political institutions. Parliament, they claimed, provided a model for the American assemblies. Although England has never had a formal written constitution, it did develop over the centuries a system of legal checks and balances that, in theory at least, kept the monarch from becoming a tyrant. The colonists claimed that this unwritten constitution preserved their rights and liberties. However, the more the colonists studied British political theory and practice—in other words, the more they attempted to become British—the more aware they became of major differences.

Governing the Colonies: The American Experience

The colonists assumed—perhaps naively—that their own governments were modeled on Britain's balanced constitution. They argued that within their political systems, the governor corresponded to the king and the governor's council to the House of Lords. They saw colonial assemblies as American reproductions of the House of Commons and expected them to preserve the people's interests against those of the monarch and aristocracy. As the colonists discovered, however, general theories about a mixed constitution were even less relevant in America than they were in Britain.

By midcentury, most of the mainland colonies had royal governors appointed by the crown. Many of these governors were career army officers who through luck, charm, or family connection had gained the ear of someone close to the king. These patronage posts did not generate enough income to interest the most powerful or talented personalities of the period, but they did draw mid-level bureaucrats who were ambitious, desperate, or both. It is perhaps not surprising that most governors decided simply not to "consider any Thing further than how to sit easy."

Whatever their demerits, royal governors possessed enormous powers. In fact, they could do things in America that a king could not do in eighteenth-century Britain, such as veto legislation and dismiss judges. The governors also served as military commanders in each province.

Political practice in America differed from the British model in another crucial respect. Royal governors were advised by a council, usually a body of about 12 wealthy colonists selected by the Board of Trade in London on the recommendation of the governor. During the seventeenth century, the council had played an important role in colonial government, but its ability to exercise independent authority declined during the eighteenth century. Its members did not represent a distinct aristocracy within American society the way the House of Lords did in Britain.

If royal governors did not look like kings, nor American councils look like the House of Lords, colonial assemblies bore little resemblance to the eighteenth-century House of Commons. The major difference was the size of the American franchise. In most colonies, adult white males who owned a little land could vote in colonywide elections. One historian estimates that 95 percent of this group in Massachusetts were eligible to vote. In Virginia it was about 85 percent. These figures—much higher than those in contemporary England—have led scholars to view the colonies as "middle-class democracies," societies run by moderately prosperous yeomen farmers who—in politics at least—exercised independent judgment. There were too many of them to bribe, no "rotten" boroughs with few or no voters as there were in Britain, and when these people moved west, colonial assemblies usually created new electoral districts to represent them.

Colonial governments were not democracies in the modern sense. Possessing the right to vote was one thing, exercising it another. Americans participated in elections when major issues were at stake—the formation of banks in mid-eighteenth-century Massachusetts, for example—but usually they were content to let members of the rural and urban gentry represent them in the assemblies. To be sure, unlike modern democracies, colonial politics excluded women and nonwhites from voting. The point to remember, however, is that American voters always had the power to expel legislative rascals. This political reality kept autocratic gentlemen from straying too far from the will of the people.

Quick Check

✓ What was the structure of royal government in eighteenth-century America?

Colonial Assemblies

Elected members of the colonial assemblies believed that they had an obligation to preserve colonial liberties. They perceived any attack on the legislature as an assault on the rights of Americans. The representatives brooked no criticism, and several colonial printers were jailed because they criticized actions taken by a lower house.

So aggressive were these bodies in seizing privileges, determining procedures, and controlling money bills that historians have described the political development of eighteenth-century America as "the rise of the assemblies." No doubt this is exaggerated, but the long series of imperial wars against the French, demanding large public expenditures, transformed the small, amateurish assemblies of the seventeenth century into the more professional, vigilant legislatures of the eighteenth.

This political system seemed designed to generate hostility. Colonial legislators had no reason to cooperate with appointed royal governors. Alexander Spotswood, Virginia's governor from 1710 to 1722, for example, attempted to institute a new land program backed by the crown. When persuasion and gifts failed, he tried chicanery. But the members of the House of Burgesses refused to support a plan that did not suit their own interests. Before leaving office, Spotswood gave up trying to carry out royal policy. Instead, he allied himself with the gentry who controlled the House and the Council and became a wealthy man because they rewarded their new friend with large tracts of land.

A few governors managed briefly to recreate in America the political culture of patronage, a system that eighteenth-century Englishmen took for granted. Most successful in this endeavor was William Shirley, who held office in Massachusetts from 1741 to 1757. The secret to his political successes in America was connection to people who held high office in Britain. But Shirley's practices—and those of men like him—clashed with the colonists' perception of politics. They really believed in the purity of the balanced constitution. They insisted on complete separation of executive and legislative authority.

A major source of shared political information was the weekly journal, a new and vigorous institution in American life. In New York and Massachusetts especially, weekly journals urged readers to preserve civic virtue and be vigilant against the spread of privileged power.

The rise of the assemblies also shaped American culture in subtler ways. During the century, the law became increasingly English in character. The Board of Trade, the Privy Council that advised the king in London and acted as a court of appeals for the colonies, and Parliament scrutinized court decisions and legislative actions from all 13 mainland colonies. As a result, local legal practices that had been widespread during the seventeenth century became standardized. Indeed, according to one historian, the colonial legal system by 1750 "was substantially that of the mother country." Not surprisingly, many men who served in colonial assemblies were either lawyers or had received legal training. When Americans from different regions met—as they frequently did before the Revolution—they discovered that they shared a commitment to preserving the English common law.

As political developments drew the colonists closer to the mother country, they also made Americans more aware of each other. As their horizons widened, they learned they operated within the same general imperial system. Like the revivalists and merchants—people who crossed old boundaries—colonial legislators laid the foundation for a larger cultural identity.

Quick Check

✓ Why were the plans of royal governors so often defeated by colonial assemblies?

CENTURY OF IMPERIAL WAR

Warfare in the colonies changed radically during the eighteenth century. The founders of England's mainland colonies had engaged in intense local conflicts with the Indians, such as King Philip's War (1675–1676) in New England. But after 1690, the colonists were increasingly involved in hostilities that originated on the other side of the Atlantic, in political and commercial rivalries between Britain and France. The external threat to security forced people in different colonies to devise unprecedented measures of military and political cooperation. (See Table 4.1.)

Why did colonial Americans support Great Britain's wars against France?

View the **Map** *European Claims in America, C. 1750* on **myhistorylab.com**

The French Threat

On paper, at least, the British colonies enjoyed military superiority over the settlements of New France. King Louis XIV of France (r. 1643–1715) had an army

TABLE 4.1   A Century of Conflict: Major Wars, 1689–1763

Dates	European Name	American Name	Major Allies	Issues	Major American Battle	Treaty
1689–1697	War of the League of Augsburg	King William's War	Britain, Holland, Spain, their colonies, and Native American allies against France, its colonies, and Native American allies	Opposition to French bid for control of Europe	New England troops assault Quebec under Sir William Phips (1690)	Treaty of Ryswick (1697)
1702–1713	War of the Spanish Succession	Queen Anne's War	Britain, Holland, their colonies, and Native American allies against France, Spain, their colonies, and Native American allies	Austria and France hold rival claims to Spanish throne	Attack on Deerfield (1704)	Treaty of Utrecht (1713)
1743–1748	War of the Austrian Succession (War of Jenkins' Ear)	King George's War	Britain, its colonies, and Native American allies, and Austria against France, Spain, their Native American allies, and Prussia	Struggle among Britain, Spain, and France for control of New World territory; among France, Prussia, and Austria for control of central Europe	New England forces capture Louisbourg under William Pepperell (1745)	Treaty of Aix-la-Chapelle (1748)
1756–1763	Seven Years' War	French and Indian War	Britain, its colonies, and Native American allies against France, its colonies, and Native American allies	Struggle among Britain, Spain, and France for worldwide control of colonial markets and raw materials	British and Continental forces capture Quebec under Major General James Wolfe (1759)	Peace of Paris (1763)

Theyanoguin Native Americans often depended on British trade goods and sometimes adopted British dress. Here the Mohawk chief Theyanoguin, called King Hendrick by the British, wears a cloak he received from Queen Anne of England during a visit to London in 1710. During the Seven Years' War, Theyanoguin mobilized Mohawk support for the British.

Quick Check

✓ Why during the eighteenth century did Britain's American colonists come to view the French as a serious threat?

of 100,000 well-armed troops, but he dispatched few of them to the New World. He left the defense of Canada and the Mississippi Valley to the companies engaged in the fur trade. Although France sent more troops to Canada in the mid-eighteenth century, meeting this defensive challenge seemed almost impossible for the French outposts strung out along the St. Lawrence River and the Great Lakes. In 1754, New France contained only 75,000 inhabitants compared to 1.2 million people in Britain's mainland colonies.

For most of the eighteenth century, the theoretical advantages the English colonists enjoyed did them little good. While the British settlements possessed a larger and more prosperous population, they were divided into separate governments that sometimes seemed more suspicious of each other than of the French. When war came, French officers and Indian allies skillfully exploited these jealousies. Moreover, although the population of New France was comparatively small, it was concentrated along the St. Lawrence, so that while the French found it difficult to mount effective offensives against the English, they could easily mass the forces to defend Montreal and Quebec.

During the early eighteenth century, English colonists came to believe that the French planned to "encircle" them, to confine the English to a narrow strip of land along the Atlantic coast. The English noted as early as 1682 that La Salle had claimed for the king of France a territory—Louisiana—that included all the people and resources located on "streams and Rivers" flowing into the Mississippi River. To make good on their claim, the French constructed forts on the Chicago and Illinois rivers. In 1717, they established a military post 200 miles up the Alabama River, within striking distance of the Carolina frontier. In 1718, they settled New Orleans. One New Yorker declared in 1715 that "it is impossible that we and the French can both inhabit this Continent in peace but that one nation must at last give way to the other."

On their part, the French suspected their rivals intended to seize all of North America. Land speculators and frontier traders pushed into territory claimed by the French and owned by the Native Americans. In 1716, one Frenchman urged his government to hasten the development of Louisiana, since "it is not difficult to guess that their [the British] purpose is to drive us entirely out ... of North America."

King George's War and Its Aftermath

In 1743, after many small frontier engagements, the Americans were dragged into King George's War (1743–1748), known in Europe as the War of the Austrian Succession, in which the colonists scored a magnificent victory over the French. Louisbourg, a gigantic fortress on Cape Breton Island, the easternmost promontory of Canada, guarded the approaches to the Gulf of St. Lawrence and Quebec. It was described as the Gibraltar of the New World. New England troops under William

Pepperell captured Louisbourg in June 1745, a feat that demonstrated the British colonists could fight and mount effective joint operations.

The French were not prepared to surrender an inch. But the English colonies were growing more populous, and the English possessed a seemingly inexhaustible supply of manufactured goods to trade with the Indians. The French decided in the early 1750s, therefore, to seize the Ohio Valley before the Virginians could do so. They established forts throughout the region, the most formidable being Fort Duquesne, located at a strategic fork in the Ohio River and later renamed Pittsburgh. (See Map 4.4.)

Although France and Britain had not officially declared war, British officials advised the governor of Virginia to "repell force by force." The Virginians needed little encouragement. They were eager to make good their claim to the Ohio Valley. In 1754, militia companies under a promising young officer, George Washington, constructed Fort Necessity not far from Fort Duquesne. The plan failed. The French and their Indian allies overran the exposed outpost (July 3, 1754). The humiliating setback revealed that a single colony could not defeat the French.

Benjamin Franklin, for one, appreciated the need for intercolonial cooperation. When British officials invited representatives from Virginia, Maryland, and the northern colonies to Albany (June 1754) to discuss relations with the Iroquois, Franklin used the occasion to present a blueprint for colonial union. His **Albany Plan** envisioned the formation of a Grand Council, made up of elected delegates from the colonies, to oversee matters of common defense, western expansion, and Indian affairs. A President General appointed by the king would preside.

First reaction to the Albany Plan was enthusiastic. To take effect, however, it required the support of the separate colonial assemblies and Parliament. It received

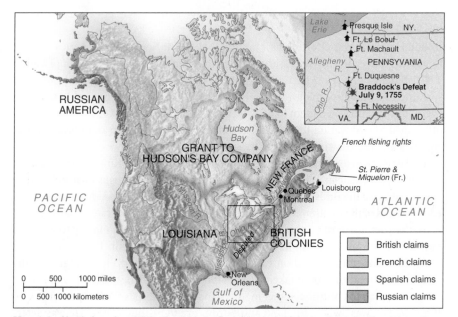

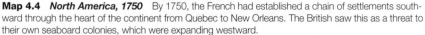

Map 4.4   *North America, 1750*   By 1750, the French had established a chain of settlements southward through the heart of the continent from Quebec to New Orleans. The British saw this as a threat to their own seaboard colonies, which were expanding westward.

The Albany Plan The first political cartoon to appear in an American newspaper was created by Benjamin Franklin in 1754 to emphasize the importance of the Albany Plan.

Quick Check

✓ Why did Benjamin Franklin's Albany Plan receive so little support?

neither. The assemblies were jealous of their fiscal authority, and the British thought the scheme undermined the crown's power over American affairs.

In 1755, the Ohio Valley again became the scene of fierce fighting. Even though there was still no formal declaration of war, the British resolved to destroy Fort Duquesne, and to that end, they dispatched units of the regular army to America. In command was Major General Edward Braddock, an obese, humorless veteran who inspired neither fear nor respect. One colonist described Braddock as "very indolent, Slave to his passions, women & wine, as great an Epicure as could be in his eating, tho a brave man."

On July 9, Braddock led 2,500 British redcoats and colonists to humiliating defeat. The French and Indians opened fire as Braddock's army waded across the Monongahela River, about eight miles from Fort Duquesne. Along a narrow road congested with wagons and confused men, Braddock ordered a counterattack, described by one of his officers as "without any form or order but that of a parcell of school boys coming out of s[c]hool." Nearly 70 percent of Braddock's troops were killed or wounded. The general himself died in battle. The French, who suffered only light casualties, remained in firm control of the Ohio Valley.

Seven Years' War

Britain's imperial war effort had hit bottom. No one in England or America seemed to possess the leadership necessary to drive the French from the Mississippi Valley. The cabinet of George II (r. 1727–1760) lacked the will to organize and finance a sustained military campaign in the New World, and colonial assemblies balked every time Britain asked them to raise men and money. On May 18, 1756, the British officially declared war on the French, a conflict called the French and Indian War in America and the Seven Years' War in Europe.

View the Map
The Seven Years' War on
myhistorylab.com

Had it not been for William Pitt, the most powerful minister in King George's cabinet, the military stalemate might have continued. This self-confident Englishman believed he alone could save the British empire, an opinion he publicly expressed. When he became effective head of the ministry in December 1756, Pitt could demonstrate his talents.

In the past, warfare on the European continent had worked mainly to France's advantage. Pitt saw no point in concentrating on Europe, and in 1757 he advanced a new imperial policy based on commercial assumptions. In Pitt's judgment, the critical confrontation would take place in North America, where Britain and France were struggling to control colonial markets and raw materials. Indeed, according to Pitt, America was "where England and Europe are to be fought for." He was determined to expel the French from the continent, however great the cost.

To direct the grand campaign, Pitt selected two relatively obscure officers, Jeffrey Amherst and James Wolfe. It was a masterful choice, one that a less self-assured man would never have risked. Both officers were young, talented, and ambitious. On July 26, 1758, forces under their direction recaptured Louisbourg, the same fortress the colonists had taken a decade earlier!

This victory cut the Canadians' main supply line with France. The small population of New France could no longer meet the military demands placed on it. As the situation became increasingly desperate, the French forts in the Ohio Valley and the Great Lakes began to fall. Duquesne was abandoned late in 1758 as French and Indian troops under the Marquis de Montcalm retreated toward Quebec and Montreal. During the summer of 1759, the French surrendered key forts at Ticonderoga, Crown Point, and Niagara. Quebec itself fell in September 1759. (See Map 4.5.)

The **Peace of Paris of 1763**, signed on February 10, almost fulfilled Pitt's grandiose dreams. Britain took possession of an empire that stretched around the globe. Only Guadeloupe and Martinique, the Caribbean sugar islands, were given back to the French. After a century-long struggle, the French had been driven from the mainland of North America. Even Louisiana passed out of France's control into Spanish hands. The treaty gave Britain title to Canada, Spanish Florida, and all the land east of the Mississippi River. Moreover, with the stroke of a diplomat's pen, 80,000 French-speaking Canadians, most of them Catholics, became the subjects of George III. (See Map 4.6.)

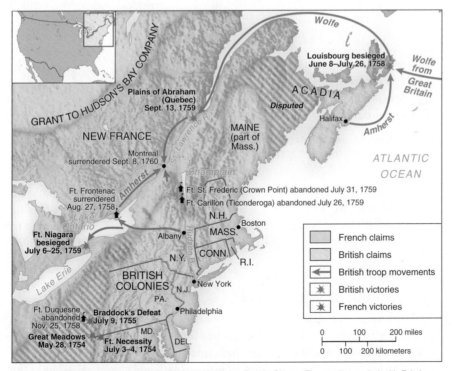

Map 4.5 *The Seven Years' War, 1756–1763 Major Battle Sites*   The conflict ended with Britain driving France from mainland North America.

Map 4.6 *North America After 1763*   The Peace of Paris of 1763 redrew the map of North America. Great Britain received all the French holdings except for a few islands in the Atlantic and some sugar-producing islands in the Caribbean.

Quick Check

✓ How did the Peace of Paris of 1763 transform North American politics?

The Americans were overjoyed. It was a time of good feelings and national pride. Together, the British and their colonial allies had thwarted the "Gallic peril." Samuel Davies, a Presbyterian who had brought the Great Awakening to Virginia, declared that the long-awaited victory would inaugurate "a new heaven and a new earth."

Perceptions of War

The Seven Years' War made a deep impression on American society. Even though Franklin's Albany Plan had failed, the war had forced the colonists to cooperate on an unprecedented scale. It also drew them into closer contact with Britain. They became aware of being part of a great empire, military and commercial, but in the process of waging war, they acquired a more intimate sense of an America that lay beyond the plantation and the village. Conflict had carried thousands of young men across colonial boundaries, exposing them to a vast territory full of opportunities for a booming population. Moreover, the war trained a corps of American officers, people like George Washington, who learned that the British were not invincible.

British officials later accused the Americans of ingratitude. Britain, they claimed, had sent troops and provided funds to liberate the colonists from the threat of French attack. The Americans cheered on the British but dragged their feet at every stage, refusing to pay the bills. These charges were later incorporated into a general argument justifying parliamentary taxation in America.

The British had a point. The colonists were, in fact, slow to provide the men and materials to fight the French. Nevertheless, they did contribute to the war effort, and it was reasonable for Americans to regard themselves as at least junior partners in the empire.

> **Quick Check**
> ✓ Why did victory over France not generate greater mutual respect between American colonists and the British?

CONCLUSION: RULE BRITANNIA?

James Thomson, an Englishman, understood the hold of empire on the popular imagination of the eighteenth century. In 1740, he composed words that British patriots have proudly sung for more than two centuries:

> Rule Britannia, Britannia rule the waves,
> Britons never will be slaves.

Colonial Americans—at least, those of British background—joined this chorus. By midcentury they took their political and cultural cues from Great Britain. They fought in its wars, purchased its consumer goods, flocked to hear its evangelical preachers, and read its publications. The empire gave the colonists a compelling source of identity.

An editor justified the establishment of New Hampshire's first newspaper in precisely these terms: "By this Means, the spirited *Englishman*, the mountainous *Welshman*, the brave *Scotchman*, and *Irishman*, and the loyal *American*, may be firmly united and mutually RESOLVED to guard the glorious Throne of BRITANNIA … as *British Brothers*, in defending the Common Cause." Even new immigrants, the Germans, Scots-Irish, and Africans, who felt no political loyalty to Britain and no affinity for its culture, had to assimilate to some degree to the dominant English culture of the colonies.

Americans hailed Britannia. In 1763, they were the victors, the conquerors of the backcountry. In their moment of glory, the colonists assumed that Britain's rulers saw the Americans as "Brothers," equal partners in the business of empire. Only slowly would they learn the British had a different perception. For them, "American" was a way of saying "not quite English."

4 STUDY RESOURCES

((•—[Listen to the **Chapter Audio** for Chapter 4 on **myhistorylab.com**

TIMELINE

1680 El Popé leads Pueblo Revolt against the Spanish in New Mexico, p. 89

1706 Birth of Benjamin Franklin, p. 92

1734–1736 First expression of the Great Awakening at Northampton, Massachusetts, p. 96

1740 George Whitefield electrifies listeners at Boston, p. 96

1745 Colonial troops capture Louisbourg, p. 103

1748 American Lutheran ministers ordained in Philadelphia, p. 87

1754 Albany Congress meets, p. 103

1755 French and Indians defeat Braddock in western Pennsylvania, p. 104

1756 Seven Years' War is formally declared, p. 104

1759 British conquer Quebec, p. 105

1763 Peace of Paris ends French and Indian War, p. 106

1769 Fra Junípero Serra begins to build missions in California, p. 90

1821 Mexico declares independence from Spain, p. 89

CHAPTER REVIEW

TENSIONS IN THE BACKCOUNTRY

What difficulties did Native Americans face in maintaining their cultural independence on the frontier?

Britain's American colonies experienced extraordinary growth during the eighteenth century. German and Scots-Irish migrants poured into the backcountry, where they clashed with Native Americans. The Indians played off French and British imperial ambitions in the "middle ground," but disease and encroachment by European settlers undermined the Indians' ability to resist. (p. 85)

SPANISH BORDERLANDS OF THE EIGHTEENTH CENTURY

Why was the Spanish empire unable to control its northern frontier?

During the late 1600s and early 1700s, the Spanish empire expanded its authority north of Mexico. New settlements were established in the Southwest and California. Although the Spanish constructed missions and forts, a lack of settlers and troops made it impossible for them to impose effective imperial authority. Much of the territory they claimed remained under the control of Indian peoples. (p. 89)

THE IMPACT OF EUROPEAN IDEAS ON AMERICAN CULTURE

How did European ideas affect eighteenth-century American life?

During the Enlightenment, educated Europeans and American colonists, like Benjamin Franklin, brought scientific reason to the study of religion, nature, and society. By midcentury, economic growth sparked a consumer revolution that introduced colonists to an unprecedented array of imported manufactured items. New ideas and goods helped integrate the American colonies into mainstream British culture. (p. 91)

RELIGIOUS REVIVALS IN PROVINCIAL SOCIETIES

How did the Great Awakening transform the religious culture of colonial America?

The Great Awakening brought a new form of evangelical religion to ordinary Americans. It emphasized personal salvation through a "New Birth" and membership in a large community of believers. Itinerant preachers such as George Whitefield drew huge crowds throughout the colonies. Other ministers followed Whitefield, inviting ordinary Americans to question traditional religious authorities. (p. 96)

CLASH OF POLITICAL CULTURES

Why were the eighteenth-century colonial assemblies not fully democratic?

Most eighteenth-century colonial governments were comprised of a royal governor, an appointed governor's council, and an elected assembly. Although these representative assemblies did not allow women, blacks, or the poor to vote, they did enfranchise most of the white adult male population. Assemblies guarded their privileges and powers, often conflicting with royal governors who tried to expand their authority. (p. 98)

CENTURY OF IMPERIAL WAR

Why did colonial Americans support Britain's wars against France?

France and Britain waged almost constant war in North America. By 1750, Britain's American colonists believed the French in Canada planned to encircle their settlements, cutting them off from the rich lands of the Ohio Valley. The Seven Years' War drove the French from Canada, a victory that generated unprecedented enthusiasm for the British Empire in the colonies. (p. 101)

KEY TERM QUESTIONS

1. Why did tensions arise in the backcountry? (p. 85)

2. How did the formation of a "middle ground" help Native Americans survive in the backcountry? (p. 88)

3. What were the basic beliefs of Enlightenment thinkers? (p. 91)

4. How did the consumer revolution affect the British economy? (p. 94)

5. How did the Great Awakening transform the religious culture of colonial America? (p. 96)

6. Why were many ministers suspicious of itinerant preachers? (p. 97)

7. Why did Benjamin Franklin's Albany Plan fail? (p. 103)

8. Why did it take so long for Britain to defeat the French in the Seven Years' War? (p. 104)

9. How did the Peace of Paris of 1763 transform North American politics? (p. 105)

MYHISTORYLAB CONNECTIONS

Visit **www.myhistorylab.com** for a customized Study Plan to build your knowledge of *Experience of Empire*.

Question for Analysis

1. How does Peter Kalm's description of Philadelphia give us a feel for what life was like in the 18th Century?

   Read the **Document** *Peter Kalm, A Swedish Visitor to Philadelphia, 1748* p. 87

2. According to Naranjo, what transpired on the first day of the uprising?

   Read the **Document** *Testimony of Pedro Naranjo to Spanish Authorities* p. 89

3. What was Franklin's assessment of the contributions the colonies made to the British Empire?

   Read the **Document** *Franklin, Observations Concerning the Increase of mankind* p. 93

4. Why did audiences respond so favorably to Jonathan Edwards' preaching?

   Read the **Document** *Jonathan Edwards, Sinners in the Hands of an Angry God* p. 96

5. What were the effects of The Seven Years War?

   View the **Map** *The Seven Years War* p. 104

Other Resources from this Chapter

Read the **Document** *William Byrd, Diary—An American Gentlemen*

View the **Image** *William Penn Making a Treaty with the Indians, 1682*

View the **Map** *Spanish America to 1610*

View the **Image** *The Alamo*

Listen to the **Audio File** *The Connecticut Peddler*

View the **Image** *Richard Allen Portrait*

View the **Image** *European Claims in America, c. 1750*

Read the **Document** *Benjamin Franklin on George Whitefield (1771)*

5 THE AMERICAN REVOLUTION
From Elite Protest to Popular Revolt, 1763–1783

Contents and Spotlight Questions

STRUCTURE OF COLONIAL SOCIETY   PG. 113

Why did Americans resist parliamentary taxation?

ERODING THE BONDS OF EMPIRE   PG. 117

What events eroded the bonds of empire during the 1760s?

STEPS TOWARD INDEPENDENCE   PG. 125

What events in 1775 and 1776 led to the colonists' decision to declare independence?

FIGHTING FOR INDEPENDENCE   PG. 128

Why did it take eight years of warfare for the Americans to gain independence?

((•—**Listen** to the **Chapter Audio** for Chapter 5 on **myhistorylab.com**

MOMENT OF DECISION: COMMITMENT AND SACRIFICE

Even as the British army poured into Boston in 1774, demanding obedience to king and Parliament, few Americans welcomed the possibility of revolutionary violence. For many colonial families, it would have been easier, certainly safer, to accede to imperial demands for taxes enacted without their representation. But they did not do so.

For the Patten family, the time of reckoning arrived in spring 1775. Matthew Patten had been born in Ulster, a Protestant Irishman, and with Scots-Irish friends and relatives, he migrated to New Hampshire, where they founded a settlement of 56 families known as Bedford. Matthew farmed the unpromising, rocky soil that he, his wife Elizabeth, and their children called home. In time, distant decisions about taxes and representation shattered the peace of Bedford. The Pattens found themselves drawn into a war not

The Patten family farmstead in Bedford, New Hampshire The Patten Family Farmstead in Bedford, New Hampshire. Scots-Irish immigrants and others on the colonial frontier in the 1770s, worked to keep their farms running and struggled to live normal lives even as Revolution engulfed the country.

of their own making but which, nevertheless, compelled them to sacrifice the security of everyday life for liberty.

On April 20, 1775, accounts of Lexington and Concord reached Bedford. Matthew noted in his diary, "I Received the Melancholy news in the morning that General Gage's troops had fired on our Countrymen at Concord yesterday." His son John marched with neighbors to support the Massachusetts soldiers. The departure was tense. "Our Girls sit up all night baking bread and fitting things for him," Matthew wrote.

The demands of war had only just begun. In late 1775 John volunteered for an American march on British Canada. On the long trek over impossible terrain, the boy died. The father recorded his emotions in the diary. John "was shot through his left arm at Bunker Hill fight and now was lead after suffering much fategue to the place where he now lyes in defending the just Rights of America to whose end he came in the prime of life by means of that wicked Tyrannical Brute (nea worse than Brute) of Great Britain [George III]. He was Twenty four years and 31 days old."

The initial stimulus for rebellion came from the gentry, from the rich and well-born, who resented Parliament's efforts to curtail their rights within the British empire. But as these influential planters, wealthy merchants, and prominent clergymen discovered, the revolutionary movement generated a momentum that they could not control. As relations with Britain deteriorated, particularly after 1765, the traditional leaders of colonial society encouraged ordinary folk to join the protest—as rioters, petitioners, and, finally, soldiers. Newspapers, sermons, and pamphlets helped transform what had begun as a squabble among the gentry into a mass movement. Once the people became involved in shaping the nation's destiny, they could never again be excluded.

Had it not been for ordinary militiamen like John Patten, the British would have easily crushed American resistance. Although some accounts of the Revolution downplay the military side of the story, leaving the impression that a few famous "Founding Fathers" effortlessly carried the nation to independence, a more persuasive explanation must recognize the centrality of armed violence in achieving nationhood.

The American Revolution involved a massive military commitment. If common American soldiers had not been willing to stand up to seasoned British troops, to face the terror of the bayonet charge, independence would have remained a dream of intellectuals. Proportionate to the population, a greater percentage of Americans died in military service during the Revolution than in any war in American history, except the Civil War.

The concept of liberty so magnificently expressed in revolutionary pamphlets was not, therefore, simply an abstraction, an exclusive concern of political theorists such as Thomas Jefferson and John Adams. It also motivated ordinary folk—the Patten family, for example—to fight and risk death. Those who survived the ordeal were never the same, for the experience of fighting, of assuming responsibility in battle and perhaps even of killing British officers, gave new meaning to the idea of social equality.

STRUCTURE OF COLONIAL SOCIETY

Colonists who were alive during the 1760s did not anticipate national independence. For many Americans, it was an era of optimism. The population grew. In 1776, approximately 2.5 million people, black and white, were living in Britain's 13 mainland colonies. The ethnic and racial diversity of these men and women amazed European visitors.

Why did Americans resist parliamentary taxation?

The American population on the eve of independence was also extraordinarily young, an important fact in understanding the development of political resistance. Nearly 60 percent of the American people were under age 21. At any given time, most people in this society were small children. Many of the young men who fought the British during the Revolution either had not been born or had been infants during the Stamp Act crisis. Any explanation for the coming of independence, therefore, must include the political mobilization of so many young people.

Americans also experienced prosperity after the Seven Years' War ended in 1763. To be sure, some ports went through a difficult period as colonists who had been employed during the war were thrown out of work. Sailors and ship workers were especially vulnerable to layoffs of this sort. In general, however, white Americans did very well. Their standard of living was not substantially lower than that of the English. A typical white family of five—a father, mother, and three dependent children—not only could have afforded decent food, clothing, and housing but would have had money left over with which to buy consumer goods. Even the poorest colonists seem to have benefited from a rising standard of living. Although they may not have done as well as their wealthier neighbors, they too wanted to preserve gains they had made.

Breakdown of Political Trust

Ultimate responsibility for preserving the empire fell to King George III (r. 1760–1820). When he became king, he was only age 22 but was determined to play an aggressive role in government. This dismayed England's political leaders. For decades, a powerful though loosely associated group of aristocrats who called themselves Whigs had set policy and controlled patronage. King George II (r. 1727–1760) had accepted their dominance. So long as the Whigs in Parliament did not meddle with his beloved army, he had let them run the nation.

George III destroyed this time-tested arrangement. He selected as his chief minister the Earl of Bute, a Scot whose chief qualification for office was his friendship with the young king. The Whigs who dominated Parliament were outraged. Bute had no ties with the members of the House of Commons; he owed them no favors.

By 1763 Bute, despairing of public life, left office. His departure, however, neither restored the Whigs to preeminence nor dampened the king's enthusiasm for domestic politics. Everyone agreed George could select whomever he desired for cabinet posts, but until 1770, no one seemed able to please him for long. Ministers came and went, often for no other reason than George's personal distaste. Because of this chronic instability, bureaucrats who directed routine colonial affairs did not know what was expected of them. In the absence of clear long-range policy, ministers made narrow decisions or did nothing. With such turbulence around him, the king showed little interest in the American colonies.

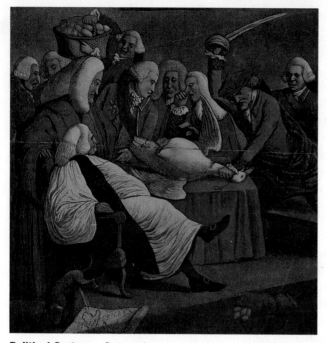

Political Cartoons Cartoons became a popular way of criticizing government during this period. Here, King George III watches as the kilted Lord Bute slaughters the goose America. A cabinet member holds a basket of golden eggs at rear. At front left, a dog urinates on a map of British America.

The king, however, does not bear the sole responsibility for Britain's loss of empire. The members of Parliament who actually drafted the statutes that gradually drove a wedge between the colonies and Britain must share the blame. They failed to resolve the explosive constitutional issues of the day.

The central element in the Anglo-American debate was a concept known as **parliamentary sovereignty**, the doctrine that Parliament enjoyed absolute legislative authority throughout Britain and its colonies. According to this theory, parliamentary decisions superceded any legislation passed by colonial assemblies. The British ruling classes had an historic view of the role of Parliament that most colonists never shared. They insisted that Parliament was the dominant element within the constitution. It protected rights and property from an arbitrary monarch. Under the Stuart monarchs, especially Charles I (r. 1625–1649), the authority of Parliament had been challenged. But the crown did not formally recognize Parliament's supreme authority in matters such as taxation until the Glorious Revolution of 1688. Almost no one, including George III, would have dissented from a speech made in 1766 before the House of Commons, in which a representative declared, "The parliament hath, and must have, from the nature and essence of the constitution, has had, and ever will have a sovereign supreme power and jurisdiction over every part of the dominions of the state, *to make laws in all cases whatsoever.*"

Quick Check

✓ Why were members of the British government adamant in their defense of parliamentary sovereignty?

Such a constitutional position did not leave much room for compromise. Most members of Parliament took a hard line on this issue. The notion of dividing or sharing sovereignty made no sense to the British ruling class. As Thomas Hutchinson, royal governor of Massachusetts, explained, no middle ground existed "between the supreme authority of Parliament and the total dependence of the colonies: it is impossible there should be two independent legislatures in one and the same state."

No Taxation Without Representation: The American Perspective

Americans did not see it in their "interest" to maintain the "supremacy of Parliament." The crisis in imperial relations forced the colonists first to define and then defend principles rooted in their own political culture. For more than a century, their ideas about the colonies' role within the British empire had remained a vague, untested bundle of assumptions about personal liberties, property rights, and representative institutions.

By 1763, however, certain fundamental American beliefs had become clear. From Massachusetts to Georgia, colonists defended the powers of the provincial assemblies. They drew on a rich legislative history of their own. In the eighteenth century, the American assemblies had expanded their authority over taxation and expenditure. Since no one in Britain bothered to clip their legislative wings, these provincial bodies assumed a major role in policymaking and routine administration. In other words, by midcentury the assemblies looked like American copies of Parliament. It seemed unreasonable, therefore, for the British suddenly to insist on the supremacy of Parliament. As the legislators of Massachusetts observed in 1770, "This house has the same inherent rights in this province as the house of commons in Great Britain."

The constitutional debate turned ultimately on the meaning of representation itself. In 1764, a British official informed the colonists that even though they had not elected members to Parliament—indeed, even though they had had no direct contact with the current members—they were nevertheless "virtually" represented by that august body. The members of Parliament, he declared, represented the political interests of everyone who lived in the British empire. It did not really matter whether everyone had cast a vote.

The colonists ridiculed this notion of virtual representation. The only representatives the Americans recognized as legitimate were those actually chosen by the people for whom they spoke. On this crucial point they would not compromise. As John Adams insisted, a representative assembly should mirror its constituents: "It should think, feel, reason, and act like them." Since the members of Parliament could not possibly "think" like Americans, it followed logically they could not represent them. And if they were not genuine representatives, the members of Parliament—pretensions to sovereignty notwithstanding—had no business taxing the American people. Thus, in 1764 the Connecticut Assembly declared in bold letters, "NO LAW CAN BE MADE OR ABROGATED WITHOUT THE CONSENT OF THE PEOPLE BY THEIR REPRESENTATIVES."

Quick Check

✔ How did Parliament and the American colonists differ in their ideas about representative government?

Justifying Resistance

The political ideology that had the greatest popular appeal among the colonists contained a strong moral component, one that British rulers and American Loyalists (people who sided with the king and Parliament during the Revolution) never fully understood. The precise origins of this highly religious perspective on civil government are difficult to locate, but the Great Awakening created a general awareness of an obligation to conduct public and private affairs according to Scripture (see Chapter 4).

Americans expressed their political beliefs in language borrowed from English writers. The person most frequently cited was John Locke, the influential seventeenth-century philosopher. His *Two Treatises of Government* (1690) seemed, to colonial readers at least, a brilliant description of what was in fact American political practice. Locke claimed that all people possessed natural and inalienable rights. To preserve these God-given rights—life, liberty, and property, for example—free men (the status of women in Locke's work was less clear) formed contracts. These agreements were the foundation of human society and civil government. They required the consent of the people who were actually governed. There could be no coercion. Locke justified rebellion against arbitrary government that was by its very nature unreasonable. Americans delighted in Locke's

Read the **Document**
James Otis, An American Colonist Opposes New Taxes on **myhistorylab.com**

ability to unite traditional Protestant religious values with a spirited defense of popular government. They seldom missed a chance to quote "the Great Mr. Locke."

Revolutionary Americans also endorsed ideas associated with the so-called Commonwealthmen. These radical eighteenth-century English writers helped persuade the colonists that *power* was dangerous, a force that would destroy liberty unless it was countered by *virtue*. Persons who shared this charged moral outlook regarded bad policy as not simply the result of human error. Rather, it indicated sin and corruption.

Insistence on public virtue—sacrifice of self-interest to the public good—became the dominant theme of revolutionary political writing. American pamphleteers seldom took a dispassionate, legalistic approach to their analysis of power and liberty. Instead, they exposed plots hatched by corrupt courtiers, such as the Earl of Bute. None of them—or their readers—doubted that Americans were more virtuous than the British.

During the 1760s, however, popular writers were not certain how long the colonists could hold out against arbitrary taxation, standing armies, and Anglican bishops—in other words, against a host of external threats designed to crush American liberty. In 1774, for example, the people of Farmington, Connecticut, declared that "the present ministry, being instigated by the devil and led by their wicked and corrupt hearts, have a design to take away our liberties and properties, and to enslave us forever." These Connecticut farmers described Britain's leaders as "pimps and parasites." This highly emotional, conspiratorial rhetoric sometimes shocks modern readers who assume that America's revolutionary leaders were products of the Enlightenment, persons who relied solely on reason to solve social and political problems. Whatever the origins of their ideas may have been, the colonial pamphleteers successfully roused ordinary men and women to resist Britain with force of arms.

Colonial newspapers spread these ideas through a large dispersed population. Most adult white males—especially those in the northern colonies—were literate, and the number of journals published in this country increased dramatically during the revolutionary period. For the first time in American history, persons throughout the colonies could follow events in distant American cities. The availability of newspapers meant that the details of Bostonians' confrontations with British authorities were known throughout the colonies. These shared political experiences drew Americans together, allowing—in the words of John Adams—"Thirteen clocks … to strike together—a perfection of mechanism which no artist had ever before effected."

Quick Check

✓ How did American colonists justify their resistance to parliamentary soverignty?

ERODING THE BONDS OF EMPIRE

What events eroded the bonds of empire during the 1760s?

The Seven Years' War saddled Britain with a national debt so huge that more than half the annual budget went to pay the interest on it. Almost everyone in government assumed that with the cessation of hostilities, most of the troops in America would be disbanded, thus saving money. George III, however, insisted on keeping the largest peacetime army in British history on active duty, supposedly to protect Indians from predatory American frontiersmen.

Colonists doubted the value of this expensive army. Britain did not leave enough troops in America to ensure peace on the frontier. The army's weakness was dramatically demonstrated in spring 1763.

The native peoples of the backcountry—the Seneca, Ottawa, Miami, Creek, and Cherokee—had begun discussing how to turn back the tide of white settlement. The powerful spiritual leader Neolin, known as the Delaware Prophet and claiming visions from the "Master of Life," urged the Indians to restore their cultures to the "original state that they were in before the white people found out their country." If moral regeneration required violence, so be it. Neolin converted Pontiac, an Ottawa warrior, to the cause. Pontiac, in turn, coordinated an uprising among the western Indians who had been French allies and hated the British—even those sent to protect them from land-grabbing colonists. This formidable Native American resistance was known as Pontiac's Rebellion. In May, Pontiac attacked Detroit; other Indians harassed the Pennsylvania and Virginia frontiers. In 1764, after his followers began deserting, Pontiac sued for peace. During even this brief outbreak, the British army could not defend exposed colonial settlements, and thousands were killed.

For the Native Americans who inhabited the Ohio Valley, this was a period of almost unmitigated disaster. In fact, more than any other group, the Indians suffered from imperial reorganization. The French defeat made it impossible for native peoples to play off one imperial power against European rivals in the middle ground (see Chapter 4). The British now regarded their former Indian allies as little more than a nuisance. Diplomatic gifts stopped; humiliating restrictions were placed on trade.

Even worse, Pontiac's rising unloosed vicious racism along the colonial frontier. American colonists often used any excuse to attack local Indians, peaceful or not. Late in 1763, vigilantes known as the Paxton Boys murdered Christian Indians, women and children, near Lancaster, Pennsylvania. White neighbors treated the killers as heroes, and the atrocity ended only after the Paxton Boys threatened to march on Philadelphia in search of administrators who dared to criticize such cold-blooded crimes. One of the administrators, Benjamin Franklin, observed sadly, "It grieves me to hear that our Frontier People are yet greater Barbarians than the Indians, and continue to murder them in time of Peace."

Whatever happened to the Indians, the colonists intended to settle the fertile region west of the Appalachian Mountains. After the British government issued the Proclamation of 1763, which prohibited governors from granting land beyond the headwaters of rivers flowing into the Atlantic, disappointed Americans viewed the army as an obstruction to legitimate economic development, an expensive domestic police force.

Paying Off the National Debt

The task of reducing England's debt fell to George Grenville, the rigid, unimaginative chancellor of the exchequer (finance minister) who replaced Bute in 1763 as the king's first minister. After reviewing Britain's finances, Grenville concluded that the colonists would have to contribute to the maintenance of the army. The first bill he steered through Parliament was the Revenue Act of 1764, known as the Sugar Act.

This legislation placed a new burden on the Navigation Acts that had governed the flow of colonial commerce for almost a century (see Chapter 3). Those acts had forced Americans to trade almost exclusively with Britain. They were not, however, primarily intended to raise money for the British government. The Sugar Act—and the acts that followed—redefined the relationship between America and Britain. Parliament now expected the colonies to generate revenue. The preamble of the Sugar Act proclaimed explicitly: "It is just and necessary that a revenue be raised … in America for defraying the expenses of defending, protecting, and securing the same."

The Americans immediately protested Grenville's scheme as unconstitutional. The Rhode Island Assembly said that the Sugar Act taxed the colonists in a manner "inconsistent with their rights and privileges as British subjects." James Otis, a fiery orator from Massachusetts, exclaimed the legislation deprived Americans of "the right of assessing their own taxes."

The act generated no violence, however. Ordinary men and women were only marginally involved in drafting formal petitions. The protest was still confined to the colonial assemblies, merchants, and the well-to-do who had personal interests in commerce.

Quick Check

✓ Why did Parliament think that the colonies should contribute to paying off Britain's national debt?

The Protest Spreads

The Stamp Act of 1765, which placed a tax on newspapers and printed matter produced in the colonies, transformed a debate among gentlemen into a mass political movement. Colonial agents had presented Grenville with alternative schemes for raising money in America, but he rejected them. The majority of the House of Commons assumed that Parliament possessed the right to tax the colonists. They responded with enthusiasm when the chancellor announced a plan to squeeze £60,000 annually out of the Americans by requiring them to purchase special seals or stamps to validate legal documents. The Stamp Act was scheduled to go into effect on November 1, 1765, and in anticipation of brisk sales, Grenville appointed stamp distributors for every colony.

Some members of Parliament warned that the act would raise a storm of protest in the colonies. Colonel Isaac Barré, a veteran of the Seven Years' War, warned his colleagues that the Americans would not surrender their rights without a fight. But Barré's appeal fell on deaf ears. Throughout the colonies, extra-legal, semi-secret groups known as the "Sons of Liberty" put political and economic pressure on neighbors who wanted to remain neutral in the contest with Britain.

Word of the Stamp Act reached America in May. It was soon clear that Barré had gauged the colonists' response correctly. The most dramatic reaction occurred in Virginia's House of Burgesses. Patrick Henry, young and eloquent, whose fervor contemporaries compared to evangelical preachers, introduced five resolutions protesting the Stamp Act on the floor of the assembly. He timed his move carefully. It was late in the session; many of the more conservative burgesses had departed for their plantations. Even then, Henry's resolves declaring that Virginians had the right to tax themselves as they alone saw fit passed by narrow margins. The fifth resolution, stricken almost immediately from the legislative records, announced that any attempt to collect stamp revenues in America was "illegal, unconstitutional, and unjust, and has a manifest tendency to destroy British as well as American liberty."

Henry's five resolutions, known popularly as the Virginia Resolves, might have remained a local matter had if not for the colonial press. Newspapers throughout America printed Henry's resolutions, but, perhaps because editors did not really know what had happened in Williamsburg, they reported that all five resolutions had received the burgesses' full support. Several journals even carried two resolves that Henry had not dared to introduce. A result of this misunderstanding was that the Virginians appeared to have taken a radical position on the supremacy of Parliament, one that other Americans now trumpeted before their own assemblies. No wonder Francis Bernard, royal governor of Massachusetts, called the Virginia Resolves an "alarm bell."

Not to be outdone, Massachusetts called a general meeting to protest Grenville's policy. Nine colonies sent representatives to the Stamp Act Congress in New York City in October 1765. It was the first intercolonial gathering since the abortive Albany Congress of 1754. The delegates drafted petitions to the king and Parliament that restated the colonists' belief "that no taxes should be imposed on them, but with their own consent, given personally, or by their representatives." The tone of the meeting was restrained, even conciliatory. The congress studiously avoided any mention of independence or disloyalty to the crown.

Resistance to the Stamp Act soon spread to the streets. By taxing deeds, marriage licenses, and playing cards, the act touched the lives of ordinary women and men. Anonymous artisans and seamen, angered by Parliament's insensitivity and fearful that the statute would increase unemployment and poverty, organized mass protests in the major ports.

By November 1, 1765, stamp distributors in almost every American port had publicly resigned. Without distributors, the hated revenue stamps could not be sold. The courts soon reopened; most newspapers were published. Daily life in the colonies was undisturbed, with one exception: The Sons of Liberty persuaded— some said coerced—colonial merchants to boycott British goods until Parliament repealed the Stamp Act. The merchants showed little enthusiasm for such tactics, but the threat of tar and feathers stimulated cooperation.

The boycott was a masterful political innovation. Never before had a resistance movement organized itself so centrally around ordinary consumers' market decisions. The colonists depended on British imports—cloth, metal goods, and ceramics. Each year they imported more consumer goods than they could afford. In this charged atmosphere, one in which ordinary people talked constantly of conspiracy and corruption, it is not surprising that Americans of different classes and backgrounds advocated a radical change in buying habits. Private acts suddenly became part of the public sphere. Personal excess threatened to contaminate the political community. This logic explains the power of an appeal made in a Boston newspaper: "Save your money and you can save your country." In 1765 the boycott had little effect on the sale of British goods in America. By 1773, however, it had seriously reduced the flow of British commerce, especially the trade for tea. (See Map 5.1.)

The boycotts mobilized colonial women. They could not vote or hold civil office, but such legal discrimination did not mean that women were not part of the broader political culture. Since wives and mothers spent their days involved with household chores, they assumed special responsibility to reform consumption, root out luxury, and promote frugality. Indeed, in this realm they possessed real power; they monitored the ideological commitment of the entire family. Throughout the colonies, women altered styles of dress, made homespun cloth, and shunned imported items on which Parliament had placed a tax.

Read the **Document**
Benjamin Franklin, Testimony Against the Stamp Act (1766) on **myhistorylab.com**

View the **Image**
1765 Stamp Act Protest on **myhistorylab.com**

View the **Image**
Women Signing an Anti-tea Agreement on **myhistorylab.com**

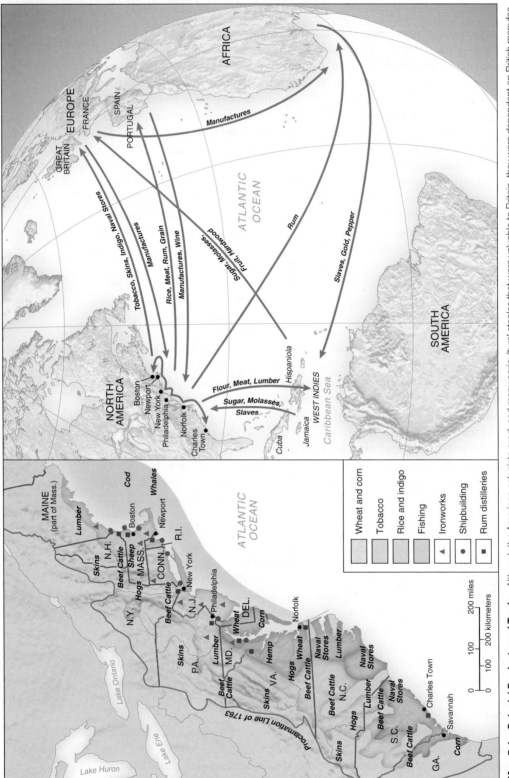

Map 5.1 Colonial Products and Trade Although the American colonists produced many agricultural staples that were valuable to Britain, they were dependent on British manufactures such as cloth, metal goods, and ceramics.

On March 18, 1766, the House of Commons voted 275 to 167 to rescind the Stamp Act. Lest this retreat be interpreted as weakness, Parliament simultaneously passed the Declaratory Act, a shrill defense of its supremacy over the Americans "in all cases whatsoever." The colonists' insistence on no taxation without representation failed to impress British rulers. British merchants, supposedly America's allies, claimed sole responsibility for the Stamp Act repeal. The colonists' behavior had only complicated the task, the merchants lectured. If the Americans knew what was good for them, they would keep quiet.

The Stamp Act crisis eroded the colonists' respect for imperial officeholders in America. Suddenly, these men—royal governors, customs collectors, soldiers—appeared alien, as if their interests were not those of the people over whom they exercised authority. One person who had been forced to resign as stamp distributor for South Carolina noted: "The Stamp Act had introduc'd so much Party Rage, Faction, and Debate that the ancient Harmony, Generosity, and Urbanity for which these People were celebrated is destroyed, and at an End."

Quick Check

✓ Was the repeal of the Stamp Act a victory for the American cause?

Fueling the Crisis

Charles Townshend, the new chancellor of the exchequer, claimed he could solve the American controversy. In January 1767, he surprised everyone by blithely announcing that he knew a way to obtain revenue from the Americans. The members of the House of Commons were so pleased with the news that they voted to lower taxes in Britain, an action that threatened fiscal chaos.

A budgetary crisis forced Townshend to make good on his boast. His scheme was a grab bag of duties on American imports of paper, glass, paint, lead, and tea, collectively known as the Townshend Revenue Acts (June–July 1767). He hoped to generate sufficient funds to pay the salaries of royal governors and other imperial officers, freeing them from dependence on the colonial assemblies.

The chancellor recognized that without tough enforcement his duties would not produce the promised revenues. Therefore, he created an American Board of Customs Commissioners, a body based in Boston, supported by reorganized vice-admiralty courts in Boston, Philadelphia, and Charles Town. For good measure, Townshend persuaded Parliament to order the governor of New York to veto all bills that colony's assembly passed until it supplied resident British troops in

Daughters of Liberty   The boycott movement drew many colonial women into popular politics. In this 1774 woodcut, a Daughter of Liberty stands ready to resist British oppression.

((•●⎯ **Listen** to the
Audio File
*The Liberty
Song* on
myhistorylab.com

Quick Check

✓ Why did Charles
Townshend so
badly misread the
American situation?

accordance with the Quarterly Act (May 1765). This law required the colonies to house soldiers in barracks, taverns, and vacant buildings and provide the army with firewood, candles, and beer, among other items. Many Americans regarded this as more taxation without representation, and in New York, at least, colonists refused to pay.

Americans showed no more willingness to pay Townshend's duties than they had to buy Grenville's stamps. The Sons of Liberty organized boycotts of British goods. Men and women took oaths before neighbors promising not to purchase certain goods until Parliament repealed their unconstitutional taxation.

Surge of Force

In October 1768, British rulers made another mistake, one that raised tensions almost to the pitch they had reached during the Stamp Act riots. The issue at the heart of the trouble was the army. To save money and intimidate troublemakers, the ministry transferred 4,000 regular troops (redcoats) from Nova Scotia and Ireland to Boston. To make relations with the Bostonians worse, redcoats—men who were ill treated and underpaid—competed in their spare time for jobs with dockworkers and artisans. Work was already in short supply in Boston, and the streets crackled with tension.

🔍⎯ **View** the **Image**
*"Bostonians Paying
the Excise Man"* on
myhistorylab.com

When colonists questioned why the army had been sent to a peaceful city, pamphleteers responded that it was there to further a conspiracy originally conceived by Bute to oppress Americans, take away their liberties, and collect illegal revenues. Such rhetoric may sound excessive, but to Americans who had absorbed the political theories of the Commonwealthmen, a pattern of tyranny seemed obvious.

Colonists had no difficulty interpreting the violence that erupted in Boston on March 5, 1770. In the gathering dusk of that afternoon, young boys and street toughs threw rocks and snowballs at a small, isolated patrol of soldiers outside the offices of the hated customs commissioners in King Street. The details are obscure, but it appears that as the mob became more threatening, the soldiers panicked and fired, killing five Americans.

Pamphleteers promptly labeled the incident the **Boston Massacre**. The victims were seen as martyrs and were memorialized in extravagant terms. In one eulogy, Joseph Warren addressed the dead men's widows and children, dramatically re-creating the gruesome scene in King Street: "Behold thy murdered husband gasping on the ground … take heed, ye orphan babes, lest, whilst your streaming eyes are fixed upon the ghastly corpse, your feet slide on the stones bespattered with your father's brains." To

The Boston Massacre This etching by Paul Revere shows British redcoats firing on ordinary citizens, an event know as the Boston Massacre. In subsequent editions, the blood spurting from the dying Americans became more conspicuous.

propagandists like Warren, it mattered little that the five civilians had been bachelors! Paul Revere's blood-splattered engraving of the massacre became an instant best-seller. Confronted with such intense reactions and the possibility of massive armed resistance, crown officials removed the army to an island in Boston Harbor.

At this critical moment, the king's new first minister restored a measure of tranquility. Lord North, congenial, well-meaning, but not very talented, became chancellor of the exchequer after Townshend's death in 1767. North was appointed the first minister in 1770, and for the next 12 years—indeed, throughout most of the American crisis—he retained his office. The secret to his success seems to have been an ability to get along with George III and build a majority in Parliament.

One of North's first recommendations to Parliament was to repeal the Town-shend duties. These ill-conceived duties had unnecessarily angered the colonists and hurt English manufacturers. By taxing British exports such as glass and paint, Parliament had only encouraged the Americans to develop their own industries. Without much prodding, Parliament dropped all the Townshend duties—except for tea. The tax on tea was retained, not for revenue purposes, North insisted, but as a reminder that Britain's rulers still subscribed to the principles of the Declaratory Act. They would not compromise the supremacy of Parliament.

Samuel Adams (1722–1803) refused to accept the notion that the repeal of the Townshend duties had secured American liberty. During the early 1770s, while colonial leaders turned to other matters, Adams kept the cause alive with a drum-fire of publicity. He reminded Bostonians that the tax on tea remained in force. He organized public anniversaries commemorating the repeal of the Stamp Act and the Boston Massacre. Adams was a revolutionary, an ideologue burning with indigna-tion at the real and alleged wrongs his countrymen suffered.

With each new attempt by Parliament to assert its supremacy over the colonists, more Bostonians listened to Adams. He observed ominously that the British intended to use the tea revenue to pay judicial salaries, thus freeing colonial judges from dependence on the assemblies. When in November 1772 Adams suggested forming a **committee of correspondence** to communicate grievances to villagers throughout Massachusetts, he received broad support. Americans in other colonies copied his idea. It was a brilliant stroke. Adams developed a structure of political cooperation independent of royal government.

Read the **Document** Boston Gazette *Description of the Boston Massacre* on **myhistorylab.com**

Quick Check

✓ Why was it a mistake for the British to station regular troops in Boston?

The Final Provocation: The Boston Tea Party

In May 1773, Parliament passed the Tea Act, legislation the Americans might have welcomed. After all, it lowered the price for their favorite beverage. Parliament wanted to save one of Britain's largest businesses, the East India Company, from bankruptcy. This commercial giant imported Asian tea into Britain, where it was resold to wholesalers. The tea was also subject to heavy duties. The company tried to pass these charges on to consumers, but American tea drinkers preferred cheaper leaves smuggled in from Holland.

The Tea Act changed the rules. Parliament not only allowed the company to sell directly to American retailers, thus cutting out intermediaries, but also eliminated the duties paid in Britain. If all had gone according to plan, the agents of the East India Company in America would have undersold their competitors, including the Dutch smugglers, and the new profits would have saved the company.

But Parliament's logic was flawed. First, since the tax on tea, collected in American ports, remained in effect, this new act seemed a devious scheme to win popular support for Parliament's right to tax the colonists without representation. Second, the act threatened to undercut powerful colonial merchants who sold smuggled Dutch tea. The British government might have been well advised to devise another plan to rescue the ailing company. In Philadelphia and New York City, colonists turned back the tea ships before they could unload.

Read the **Document** Hewes, "A Retrospect on the Boston Tea Party" on **myhistorylab.com**

In Boston, however, the issue was less easily resolved. Governor Hutchinson, a strong-willed man, would not let the vessels return to England. Patriots would not let them unload. So, crammed with tea, the ships sat in Boston Harbor waiting for the colonists to make up their minds. On the night of December 16, 1773, they did so. Men disguised as Mohawk Indians boarded the ships and pitched 340 chests of tea worth £10,000 over the side. John Adams sensed the event would have far-reaching significance. "This Destruction of the Tea," he scribbled in his diary, "is so bold, so daring, so firm, intrepid, and inflexible, and it must have so important consequences, and so lasting, that I can't but consider it as an epocha in history."

News of the **Boston Tea Party** stunned the North ministry. The Bostonians had treated parliamentary supremacy with contempt. British rulers saw no humor whatsoever in the destruction of private property by subjects of the crown dressed in costume. To quell such rebelliousness, Parliament passed the **Coercive Acts.** (In America, they were called the Intolerable Acts.) The legislation (1) closed the port of Boston until the city compensated the East India Company for the lost tea; (2) restructured the Massachusetts government by transforming the upper house of the legislature from an elective to an appointed body and restricting the number of town meetings to one a year; (3) allowed the royal governor to transfer British officials arrested for offenses committed in the line of duty to England, where there was little likelihood they would be convicted; and (4) authorized the army to quarter troops wherever they were needed, even if this required the compulsory requisition of uninhabited private buildings. George III enthusiastically supported this tough policy; he appointed General Thomas Gage as the colony's new royal governor. Gage apparently won the king's favor by announcing that in America, "Nothing can be done but by forcible means."

The sweeping denial of constitutional liberties confirmed the colonists' worst fears. To men like Samuel Adams, it seemed as if Britain intended to enslave the American people. Colonial moderates found their position shaken by the Coercive Acts' vindictiveness. Edmund Burke, one of America's last friends in Parliament, noted sadly in the Commons, that "this is the day, then, that you wish to go to war with all America, in order to conciliate that country to this."

If in 1774 Parliament thought it could isolate Boston from the rest of America, it was in for a rude surprise. Colonists in other parts of the continent recognized immediately that the principles at stake in Boston affected all Americans. Charity suddenly became a political act. People from Georgia to New Hampshire sent livestock, grain, and money to Boston. Ordinary colonists showed they were prepared to make a personal sacrifice for the cause of America.

The sticking point remained—as it had been in 1765—the sovereignty of Parliament. No one in Britain could think of a way around this constitutional impasse. In 1773, Benjamin Franklin had offered a suggestion: "The Parliament has no right to make any law whatever, binding on the colonies ... the king, and not the king, lords, and commons collectively, is their sovereign." But so long as it seemed possible to coerce the Americans into obedience, Britain's rulers had little incentive to accept such a humiliating compromise.

Quick Check

✓ Did the coercive acts represent an overreaction by Parliament to the Boston Tea Party?

STEPS TOWARD INDEPENDENCE

During the summer of 1774, committees of correspondence analyzed the perilous situation in which the colonists found themselves. The committees endorsed a call for a Continental Congress, a gathering of 55 elected delegates from 12 colonies (Georgia sent none but agreed to support the action taken). This First Continental Congress convened in Philadelphia on September 5. It included some of America's most articulate, respected leaders; John Adams, Samuel Adams, Patrick Henry, Richard Henry Lee, Christopher Gadsden, and George Washington.

What events in 1775 and 1776 led to the colonists' decision to declare independence?

Differences of opinion soon surfaced. Delegates from the Middle Colonies—Joseph Galloway of Pennsylvania, for example—wanted to proceed with caution, but Samuel Adams and other more radical members pushed the moderates toward confrontation. Boston's master politician engineered congressional acceptance of the Suffolk Resolves, a statement drawn up in Suffolk County, Massachusetts, that encouraged forcible resistance to the Coercive Acts.

This decision established the tone of the meeting. Moderates introduced conciliatory measures, which received polite discussion but failed to win a majority vote. Just before returning to their homes (September 1774), the delegates created the "Association," an inter-colonial agreement to halt commerce with Britain until Parliament repealed the Intolerable Acts. This was a brilliant revolutionary decision. The Association authorized a vast network of local committees to enforce nonimportation, a policy by which colonial consumers and shopkeepers promised not to buy British goods. Violators were denounced, shamed, forced either to apologize publicly or to be shunned by their patriot neighbors. In many of the communities, the committees were the government, distinguishing, in the words of James Madison, "Friends from Foes." George III sneered at these activities: "I am not sorry that the line of conduct seems now chalked out ... the New England Governments are in a state of Rebellion, blows must decide whether they are to be subject to this country or independent."

Shots Heard Around the World

The king was correct. Before Congress reconvened, "blows" fell at Lexington and Concord, two small villages in eastern Massachusetts. On the evening of April 18, 1775, General Gage dispatched troops from Boston to seize rebel supplies.

Read the
Document
*Joseph Warren,
'Account of the Battle
of Lexington'* on
myhistorylab.com

Paul Revere, a renowned silversmith and patriot, warned the colonists that the redcoats were coming. The Lexington militia, a collection of ill-trained farmers, boys, and old men, decided to stand on the village green on the following morning, April 19, as the British soldiers passed on the road to Concord. No one planned to fight, but in a moment of confusion, someone fired; the redcoats discharged a volley, and eight Americans lay dead.

Word of the incident spread rapidly. By the time the British force reached its destination, the countryside swarmed with "minutemen," special companies of Massachusetts militia prepared to respond instantly to military emergencies. The redcoats found nothing significant in Concord and left. Their long march back to Boston became a rout. Lord Percy, a British officer who brought up reinforcements, remarked more in surprise than bitterness that "whoever looks upon them [the American soldiers] as an irregular mob, will find himself much mistaken." On June 17, colonial militiamen again held their own against seasoned troops at the Battle of Bunker Hill near Boston. The British finally took the hill, but after this costly "victory" in which he suffered 40 percent casualties, Gage complained that the Americans had displayed "a conduct and spirit against us, they never showed against the French."

Quick Check

✓ Why did the British general Thomas Gage underestimate the Americans' military resolve?

BEGINNING "THE WORLD OVER AGAIN"

Members of the Second Continental Congress gathered in Philadelphia in May 1775. They faced an awesome responsibility. British government in the mainland colonies had almost ceased to function, and with Americans fighting redcoats, the country desperately needed strong central leadership. Slowly, often reluctantly, Congress took control of the war. The delegates formed a Continental Army and appointed George Washington its commander, in part because he seemed to have military experience than anyone else available and in part because he looked like he should be commander in chief. The delegates were also eager to select someone who was not from Massachusetts, a colony that seemed already to possess too much power in national councils. Congress purchased military supplies and, to pay for them, issued paper money. But while Congress was assuming the powers of a sovereign government, the congressmen refused to declare independence. They debated and fretted, listened to the moderates who played on the colonists' loyalty to Britain, and then did nothing.

Convinced that force could make up for earlier failures of policy, the British government found a way to transform colonial moderates into angry rebels. In December 1775, Parliament passed the Prohibitory Act, declaring war on American commerce. Until the colonists begged for pardon, they could not trade with the rest of the world. The British navy blockaded their ports and seized American ships on the high seas. (See Table 5.1.) Lord North also hired German mercenaries to help put down the rebellion. And in America, Virginia's royal governor Lord Dunmore further undermined the possibility of reconciliation by urging the colony's slaves to take up arms against their masters. Few did so, but the effort to stir up black rebellion infuriated the Virginia gentry.

Thomas Paine (1737–1809) pushed the colonists closer to forming an independent republic. In England, Paine had failed at various jobs, but while still in

TABLE 5.1 Chronicle of Colonial-British Tension

Legislation	Date	Provisions	Colonial Reaction
Sugar Act	April 5, 1764	Revised duties on sugar, coffee, tea, wine, other imports; expanded jurisdiction of vice-admiralty courts	Several assemblies protest taxation for revenue
Stamp Act	March 22, 1765; repealed March 18, 1766	Printed documents (deeds, newspapers, marriage licenses, etc.) issued only on special stamped paper purchased from stamp distributors	Riots in cities; collectors forced to resign; Stamp Act Congress (October 1765)
Quartering Act	May 1765	Colonists must supply British troops with housing, other items (candles, firewood, etc.)	Assemblies protest; New York Assembly punished for failure to comply, 1767
Declaratory Act	March 18, 1766	Parliament declares its sovereignty over the colonies "in all cases whatsoever"	Ignored in celebration over repeal of the Stamp Act
Townshend Revenue Acts	June 26, 29, July 2, 1767; all repealed— except duty on tea, March 1770	New duties on glass, lead, paper, paints, tea; customs collections tightened in America	Nonimportation of British goods; assemblies protest; newspapers attack British policy
Tea Act	May 10, 1773	Parliament gives East India Company right to sell tea directly to Americans; some duties on tea reduced	Protests against favoritism shown to monopolistic company; tea destroyed in Boston (December 16, 1773)
Coercive Acts (Intolerable Acts)	March–June 1774	Closes port of Boston; restructures Massachusetts government; restricts town meetings; troops quartered in Boston; British officials accused of crimes sent to England or Canada for trial	Boycott of British goods; First Continental Congress (September 1774)
Prohibitory Act	December 22, 1775	Declares British intention to coerce Americans into submission; embargo on American goods; American ships seized	Drives Continental Congress closer to decision for independence

England, Paine had the good fortune to meet Benjamin Franklin, who presented him with letters of introduction to the leading patriots of Pennsylvania. At the urging of his new American friends, Paine produced *Common Sense* in 1776, an essay that became an instant best-seller. In only three months, it sold more than 120,000 copies. Paine confirmed in forceful prose what the colonists had not yet been able to state coherently.

Common Sense stripped kingship of historical and theological justification. For centuries, the English had maintained the legal fiction that the monarch could do no wrong. When the government oppressed the people, the royal counselors were blamed. The crown was above suspicion. To this, Paine cried nonsense. Monarchs

Read the **Document**
Thomas Paine, A Freelance Writer Urges his Readers to use Common Sense on **myhistorylab.com**

Congress Voting Independence Oil painting by Robert Edge Pine and Edward Savage, 1785. The committee Congress appointed to draft a declaration on independence included (center, standing) John Adams, Roger Sherman, Robert Livingston, Thomas Jefferson, and (center fore-ground, seated) Benjamin Franklin. The committee members are shown submitting Jefferson's draft to the speaker.

ruled by force. George III was a "royal brute," who by his arbitrary behavior had surrendered his claim to the colonists' obedience. All power came from the people. *Common Sense* was a powerful democratic manifesto.

Paine's greatest contribution to the revolutionary cause was persuading ordinary folk to sever their ties with Britain. It was not reasonable, he argued, to regard England as the mother country: "Europe, and not England, is the parent country of America. This new world hath been the asylum for the persecuted lovers of civil and religious liberty from *every part* of Europe." No doubt that message impressed Pennsylvania's German population. The time had come for the colonists to form an independent republic: "We have it in our power to begin the world over again … the birthday of a new world is at hand."

On July 2, 1776, after a long and tedious debate, Congress finally voted for independence: 12 states for, none against (New York abstained). Thomas Jefferson, a young Virginia planter who enjoyed a reputation as a graceful writer, drafted a formal declaration that was accepted with alterations two days later. Much of the Declaration of Independence consisted of a list of specific grievances against George III and his government. Like a skilled lawyer, Jefferson presented the evidence for independence. But the document did not become famous for those passages. Long after the establishment of the new republic, the Declaration challenged Americans to make good on the principle that "all men are created equal." John Adams expressed the patriots' fervor when he wrote on July 3, "Yesterday the greatest question was decided, which ever was debated in America, and a greater perhaps, never was or will be decided among men."

Quick Check

✓ Why do you think Thomas Paine's *Common Sense* became an instant bestseller?

FIGHTING FOR INDEPENDENCE

Why did it take eight years of warfare for the Americans to gain independence?

Only fools and visionaries expressed optimism about America's prospects of winning independence in 1776. The Americans had taken on a formidable military power. Britain's population was perhaps four times that of its former colonies. Britain also possessed a strong manufacturing base, a well-trained regular army supplemented by thousands of German mercenaries (Hessians), and a navy that dominated the seas. Many British officers were battlefield veterans. They already knew what the Americans would slowly learn: Waging war requires discipline, money, and sacrifice.

The British government was confident that it could beat the Americans. In 1776, Lord North and his colleagues regarded the war as a police action. A mere show of force would intimidate the upstart colonists. As soon as the rebels in Boston had been humbled, the British argued, other colonies would desert the cause for independence. General Gage, for example, told the king that the colonists "will be Lions, whilst we are Lambs … if we take a resolute part they will undoubtedly prove very weak." Since this advice confirmed George's views, he called Gage "an honest determined man."

As later events demonstrated, of course, Britain had become involved in an impossible military situation. Three separate elements neutralized the larger power's advantages over its adversary. First, the British had to transport men and supplies across the Atlantic, a logistic challenge of unprecedented complexity. Unreliable lines of communication broke down under the strain of war.

Second, America was too vast to be conquered by conventional military methods. Redcoats might gain control over the major ports, but as long as the Continental Army remained intact, the rebellion continued. As Washington explained, "the possession of our Towns, while we have an Army in the field, will avail them little.… . It is our Arms, not defenceless Towns, they have to subdue." Even if Britain had recruited enough soldiers to occupy the entire country, it would still have lost the war. As one Loyalist instructed the king, "if all America becomes a garrison, she is not worth your attention." Britain could only win by crushing the American will to resist.

And third, British strategists never appreciated the depth of the Americans' commitment to a political ideology. In the wars of eighteenth-century Europe, such beliefs had seldom mattered. European troops before the French Revolution broke out in 1789 served because they were paid or because the military was a vocation, not because they hoped to advance a set of constitutional principles. Americans were different. To be sure, some young men were drawn to the military by bounty money or the desire to escape unhappy families. A few were drafted. But the American troops still had a remarkable commitment to republican ideals. One French officer reported from the United States, "It is incredible that soldiers composed of men of every age, even of children of fifteen, of whites and blacks, almost naked, unpaid, and rather poorly fed, can march so well and withstand fire so steadfastly."

Building a Professional Army

Washington insisted on organizing a regular well-trained field army. Some advisers urged the commander in chief to wage a guerrilla war in which small partisan bands would sap Britain's will to fight. But Washington recognized that the Continental Army was not just a fighting force but a symbol of the republican cause. Its very existence would sustain American hopes, and so long as the army survived, American agents could plausibly solicit foreign aid. This thinking shaped Washington's wartime strategy; he studiously avoided "general actions" in which the Continental Army might be destroyed. Critics complained about Washington's caution, but as they soon discovered, he understood better than they what independence required.

If the commander in chief was correct about the army, however, he failed to comprehend the political importance of the militia. These scattered, almost amateur, military units seldom altered the outcome of battle, but they did maintain control over large areas not directly occupied by the British army. Throughout the war, they compelled men and women who would rather have remained neutral to support the American effort.

For the half million African American colonists, most of them slaves, the fight for independence was poignant. After all, they wanted to achieve personal and political freedom. Many African Americans supported whichever side seemed most likely to deliver them from bondage. An estimated 5,000 African Americans took up arms to fight the British. The Continental Army included two all-black units, one from Massachusetts, the other from Rhode Island. In 1778, the Rhode Island legislature voted to free any slave who volunteered to serve. According to the lawmakers, history taught that "the wisest, the freest, and bravest nations … liberated their slaves, and enlisted them as soldiers to fight in defence of their country." In the South, especially in Georgia and South Carolina, more than 10,000 African Americans supported the British. After the patriots won the war, these men and women relocated to Nova Scotia, Florida, and Jamaica. Some eventually resettled in West Africa.

Quick Check

✓ Why did George Washington insist on organizing a regular field army?

"Times That Try Men's Souls"

View the **Map**
The American Revolution on
myhistorylab.com

After the embarrassing defeats in Massachusetts, Sir William Howe replaced the ill-fated Gage. British rulers now understood that a simple police action would not crush the American rebellion. Parliament authorized sending more than 50,000 troops to the mainland colonies. After evacuating Boston—an untenable position—British forces stormed ashore at Staten Island in New York Harbor on July 3, 1776. From this more central location, Howe believed he could cut the New Englanders off from the rest of America. (See Map 5.2.)

When Washington learned the British were planning to occupy New York City, he transferred many of his inexperienced soldiers to Long Island, where they suffered a major defeat (August 27, 1776). Howe then drove the Continental Army across the Hudson River into New Jersey.

These swift victories persuaded Howe that few Americans enthusiastically supported independence. He issued a general pardon to anyone who would swear allegiance to George III. More than 3,000 men and women who lived in areas occupied by the British took the oath. This group included one frightened signer of the Declaration of Independence. Howe perceived that a lasting peace in America would require his troops to treat "our enemies as if they might one day become our friends." A member of Lord North's cabinet grumbled that this was "a sentimental manner of making war." The pardon plan failed not because Howe lacked toughness, but because his soldiers and officers treated loyal Americans as inferior, an attitude that did little to promote good relations. In any case, as soon as the redcoats left a pardoned region, the rebel militia retaliated against those who had deserted the patriot cause.

In December 1776, Washington's bedraggled army retreated across the Delaware River into Pennsylvania. American prospects appeared bleaker than at any other time during the war. The Continental Army lacked basic supplies, and many men who had signed up for short-term enlistments prepared to go home. "These are the times that try men's souls," Paine wrote in a pamphlet titled *American Crisis*. "The summer soldier and the sunshine patriot will, in this crisis, shrink from the service of their country, but he that stands it *now* deserves … love and thanks… ." Washington determined to attempt a desperate stroke.

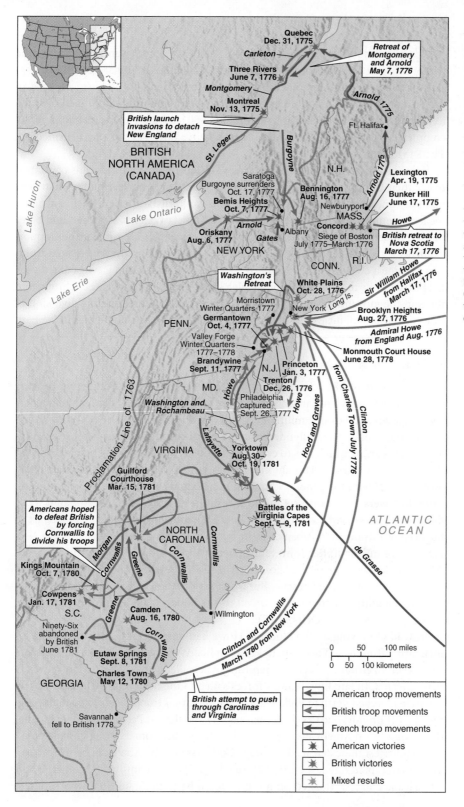

Map 5.2 *The American Revolution, 1775–1781* Battles were fought in the colonies, on the western frontier, and along the Gulf of Mexico. The major engagements of the first years of the war, from the spontaneous rising at Concord in 1775 to Washington's well-coordinated attack on Trenton in December 1776, were fought in the northern colonies. In the middle theater of war, Burgoyne's attempt in 1777 to cut New England off from the rest of the colonies failed when his army was defeated at Saratoga. Action in the final years of the war, from the battles at Camden, Kings Mountain, Cowpens, and Guilford Courthouse to the final victory at Yorktown, occurred in the South.

Howe played into Washington's hands. The British forces were dispersed for the winter in small garrisons across New Jersey. While the Americans could not possibly have defeated the combined British army, they could—with luck—capture an exposed post. On the night of December 25, Continental soldiers slipped over the ice-filled Delaware River and at Trenton took 900 sleeping Hessian mercenaries by complete surprise. In January, Washington gained another victory, at Princeton. The Patriot cause revived.

If this victory in the east served to cheer Patriots on, many Americans continued to eye their frontiers with trepidation. Many Indian nations, fearing the encroachment of American settlers, had cast their lots militarily with the British. All along the long frontier, warriors from the Cherokee, Choctaw, Creek, Shawnee, and other nations raided American settlements and garrisons from 1776 on. For the Iroquois Confederacy, a two-century-old alliance of six related nations, the American Revolution became a civil war as the Mohawk, Seneca, Onondaga, and Cayuga allied with the British, while the Tuscarora and Oneida supported to the rebel cause. Throughout the war, the movements of Native American forces would require the diversion of Continental and militia troops toward the frontier and away from the war in the East.

Quick Check

✓ Why did the first year of war go so badly for the Americans?

Victory in a Year of Defeat

In the summer of 1777, General John Burgoyne, a dashing though overbearing officer, descended from Canada with a force of British regulars, German mercenaries, Canadian and Loyalist militiamen, and Native American warriors—more than 7,000 troops total. They intended to clear the Hudson Valley of rebel resistance; join Howe's army, which was to come up to Albany; and cut New England off from the other states. Burgoyne fought in a grand style. Accompanied by a German band, 30 carts filled with the general's liquor and belongings, and 2,000 dependents and camp followers, the British set out to thrash the Americans. The campaign was a disaster. Military units, mostly from New England, cut the enemy force apart in the deep woods north of Albany. At the battle of Bennington (August 16), the New Hampshire militia under John Stark overwhelmed 1,000 German mercenaries. After this setback, Burgoyne's forces struggled forward, desperately hoping that Howe would rush to their rescue. But when his situation at Saratoga became hopeless, the haughty Burgoyne was forced to surrender 5,800 men to the American General Horatio Gates (October 17).

Instead of moving up the Hudson, Howe had unexpectedly decided to take his main army from New York City to Philadelphia. What he hoped to achieve was not clear, even to Britain's rulers. When Burgoyne called for assistance, Howe was in Pennsylvania. In late July, Howe's forces sailed to the head of the Chesapeake Bay and then marched north to Philadelphia. Washington's troops obstructed their progress, first at Brandywine Creek (September 11) and then at Paoli (September 20), but the outnumbered Americans could not stop the British from entering Philadelphia.

Anxious lest these defeats discourage Congress and the American people, Washington attempted one last battle before winter. At Germantown (October 4), the Americans counterattacked on a fog-covered battlefield, but just when success seemed assured, they broke off the fight. "When every thing gave the most flattering hopes of victory," Washington complained, "the troops began suddenly to retreat." Bad luck, confusion, and incompetence contributed to the failure. A discouraged Continental Army dug in at Valley Forge, 20 miles outside of Philadelphia, where diseases killed 2,500 Americans. Few of the soldiers realized their situation was not nearly as desperate as it had been in 1776.

Quick Check

✓ What role did poor British planning play in the American victory at Saratoga?

The French Alliance

Even before the Americans declared their independence, French agents began to explore ways to aid the colonists, not because the French monarchy favored the republican cause but because it hoped to embarrass the British. The French deeply resented their defeat during the Seven Years' War. During the early months of the Revolution, the French covertly sent tons of military supplies to the Americans. The negotiations for these arms involved secret agents and fictitious trading companies, a type of clandestine operation more typical of modern times than of the eighteenth century. But when American representatives, Benjamin Franklin for one, pleaded for official recognition of American independence or for outright military alliance, the French advised patience. The international stakes were too great for King Louis XVI openly to back a cause that had little chance of success.

Some adventurous French military men embraced the American cause despite their nation's official neutrality. The most famous of these men, the Marquis de Lafayette, set sail in spring 1777, despite being expressly forbidden to do so by King Louis XVI. Once in the United States, Lafayette became an aide-de-camp to George Washington, serving as a trusted advisor, able administrator, and effective diplomat.

It was the victory at Saratoga in 1778 that finally earned the Americans official support from France. It convinced the French that the rebels had formidable forces and were serious in their resolve. Franklin hinted to French officials in Paris that the Americans might accept a British peace initiative. If the French wanted the war to continue, if they really wanted to embarrass their old rival, then they had to do what the British refused to do: formally recognize the independence of the United States.

Map 5.3   Spain entered the Revolutionary War as an ally of France in 1779. By 1781, Spanish forces operating out of New Orleans and St. Louis had captured British forts in the Mississippi Valley and the Midwest from Baton Rouge and Natchez to as far north as the modern state of Michigan. On the Gulf Coast, Spanish amphibious forces led by Count Bernardo de Galvez had also overran British posts from what is now Mobile, Alabama to Pensacola in what was then the British colony of West Florida. Spain retained these Gulf Coast ports and regained all of Florida in the Treaty of Paris in 1783.

The stratagem paid off. On February 6, 1778, the French presented American representatives with two separate treaties. The Treaty of Amity and Commerce established commercial relations with the United States. It tacitly accepted the existence of a new, independent republic. The Treaty of Alliance was even more generous, considering America's obvious military and economic weaknesses. If France and Britain went to war (they did so on June 14, as everyone expected), the French agreed to reject "either Truce or Peace with Great Britain … until the independence of the United States shall have been formally or tacitly assured by the Treaty or Treaties that shall terminate the War." Even more amazing, France surrendered its claim to all British territories east of the Mississippi. The Americans pledged not to sign a separate peace with Britain without first informing their new ally. France also made no claim to recover Canada, asking only for British islands in the Caribbean. Never had Franklin worked his magic to greater effect.

French intervention instantly transformed British strategy. A colonial rebellion became a world conflict. British and French forces clashed in the Mediterranean, in India and the Indian Ocean, in the Caribbean, and on the coast of West Africa. To counter the French, Britain had to divert scarce military resources, especially newer warships, from the American theater to the English Channel. In fact, there was talk in London of a French invasion. French diplomacy also convinced the Spanish, eager to benefit from Britain's seeming weakness, to enter the world conflict in 1779. More British ships and troops had to be diverted to the West Indies and Florida to counter Spanish threats. The navies of its imperial rivals threatened the overextended British fleet. By concentrating their warships in a specific area, the French or Spanish could hold off or even defeat British squadrons, an advantage that figured significantly in the war's final victory at Yorktown.

Quick Check

✓ What role did French support play in the winning of the Revolutionary War?

The Final Campaign

Strategists calculated that Britain's last chance of winning the war lay in the southern colonies, a region largely untouched in the early fighting. Intelligence reports indicated that Georgia and South Carolina contained many Loyalists who would take up arms for the crown if only they received support from the regular army. The southern strategy British leaders devised in 1779 turned the war into a bitter guerrilla conflict. During the last months of battle, British officers worried that their search for an easy victory had inadvertently opened a Pandora's box of uncontrollable partisan furies.

The southern campaign opened in spring 1780. Savannah, Georgia had already fallen in 1779. General Sir Henry Clinton, who had replaced Howe after Saratoga, now reckoned that if the British could take Charles Town, they could control the entire South. A fleet carrying nearly 8,000 redcoats reached South Carolina in February. Complacent Americans had allowed the city's fortifications to decay. In a desperate effort to save the city, General Benjamin Lincoln's forces dug trenches and reinforced walls, but to no avail. Clinton and his second in command, Lord Cornwallis, encircled the city, and on May 12, Lincoln surrendered an American army of almost 6,000 men.

Despite this victory, partisan warfare weakened the British army. Tory raiders showed little interest in serving as regular soldiers. They preferred night riding, indiscriminate plundering, or murdering neighbors against whom they harbored ancient grudges. The British had unleashed a horde of bandits across South Carolina. Men who supported independence or who had fallen victim to Loyalist guerrillas bided their time. Their chance came on October 7 near Kings Mountain, North Carolina. In the most vicious fighting of the Revolution, the backwoodsmen annihilated a force of British regulars and Tory raiders that had strayed too far from base. One witness reported that when a British officer tried to surrender, at least seven Americans shot him down.

Battle of Yorktown French assistance on land and sea helped the Americans to defeat the British in the American Revolution. In this French print of the battle at Yorktown, French ships block the entrance of Chesapeake Bay, preventing British vessels from resupplying their troops on land. Yorktown, which was unknown to the French artist who made this print, is depicted as a European walled city.

Cornwallis, confused by the enemy's guerilla tactics and poorly supplied, squandered his strength chasing American forces across the Carolinas. He abandoned whatever military strategy had compelled him to leave Charles Town. In early 1781, Cornwallis informed Clinton, "Events alone can decide the future Steps." Events, however, did not run in the British favor. Congress sent General Nathanael Greene to the South with a new army. This young Rhode Islander was the most capable general on Washington's staff. Greene joined Daniel Morgan, leader of the famed Virginia Riflemen. In tactically brilliant engagements, they sapped the strength of Cornwallis's army, at Cowpens, South Carolina (January 17, 1781), and Guilford Courthouse, North Carolina (March 15). Clinton fumed that the inept Cornwallis had left "two valuable colonies behind him to be overrun and conquered by the very army which he boasts to have completely routed but a week or two before."

Cornwallis pushed north into Virginia, shadowed by about 4,500 American troops under the command of the Marquis de Lafayette. Planning, apparently, to establish a base on the coast, Cornwallis began to fortify Yorktown, a sleepy tobacco market on a peninsula bounded by the York and James rivers. Washington watched these maneuvers closely. The canny Virginia planter knew this territory intimately. He sensed that Cornwallis had made a blunder. When Washington learned the French fleet could gain temporary dominance in the Chesapeake Bay, he rushed south from New Jersey to join Lafayette, who was now maneuvering to contain the British forces. With Washington went thousands of well-trained French troops under the Comte de Rochambeau. All the pieces fell into place. The French admiral, the Comte de Grasse, cut Cornwallis off from the sea, while Washington and his lieutenants encircled the British on land. On October 19, 1781, Cornwallis surrendered his entire army of 6,000 men. When Lord North heard of the defeat at Yorktown, he moaned, "Oh God! It is all over." The British still controlled New York City, Charles Town, and Savannah but except for a few skirmishes,

View the Image
Surrender at Yorktown on
myhistorylab.com

Quick Check

✓ Why did the "Southern Campaign" not work out as British strategists had anticipated?

the fighting ended. The task of securing the independence of the United States was now in the hands of the diplomats. The preliminary agreement signed in Paris on September 3, 1783, not only guaranteed the independence of the United States; it also transferred all the territory east of the Mississippi River, except Florida, which Britain surrendered to Spain, to the new republic. The Treaty of Paris of 1783 established generous boundaries on the north and south (effectively ceding away the land of their erstwhile Indian allies) and gave the Americans important fishing rights in the North Atlantic.

The Loyalist Dilemma

No one knows how many Americans supported the crown during the Revolution. Some Loyalists undoubtedly avoided making a public commitment that might have led to banishment or loss of property. But for many, neutrality proved impossible. Almost 100,000 men and women permanently left America. While some of these exiles had been imperial officeholders—Thomas Hutchinson, for example—they came from all ranks and backgrounds. More than 30,000 farmers resettled in Canada. Others relocated to England, the West Indies, or Africa.

The political ideology of the Loyalists was not substantially different from that of their opponents. Like other Americans, they believed that men and women were entitled to life, liberty, and the pursuit of happiness. But the Loyalists were convinced that independence would destroy those values by promoting disorder. By turning their backs on Britain, a source of tradition and stability, the rebels seemed to have encouraged licentiousness, even anarchy in the streets. The Loyalists suspected that Patriot demands for freedom were self-serving, even hypocritical, for as Perserved Smith, a Loyalist from Ashfield, Massachusetts, observed, "Sons of liberty ... did not deserve the name, for it was evident all they wanted was liberty from oppression that they might have liberty to oppress!"

The Loyalists were caught in a bind. The British never trusted them. After all, they were Americans. During the early stages of the war, Loyalists organized militia companies and hoped to pacify large areas of the countryside with the support of the regular army. The British generals were unreliable partners, however, for no sooner had they called on loyal Americans to come forward than the redcoats marched away, exposing the Tories to rebel retaliation. And in Britain, they were treated as second-class citizens. While many received monetary compensation for their sacrifice, they were never regarded as the equals of native-born British citizens. The Loyalist community in London was gradually transformed into a collection of bitter men and women who felt unwelcome on both sides of the Atlantic.

Although many Loyalists eventually returned to their homes, a sizable number could not do so. For them, the sense of loss was a heavy emotional burden. Perhaps the most poignant testimony came from a young mother living in exile in Nova Scotia: "I climbed to the top of Chipman's Hill and watched the sails disappear in the distance, and such a feeling of loneliness came over me that though I had not shed a tear through all the war I sat down on the damp moss with my baby on my lap and cried bitterly."

Quick Check

✓ Why did so many loyalists decide to leave the United States during the Revolution?

CONCLUSION: PRESERVING INDEPENDENCE

Watch the **Video**
The American Revolution as Different Americans Saw It on **myhistorylab.com**

The American people had waged war against the most powerful nation in Europe and emerged victorious. The Treaty of Paris marked the conclusion of a colonial rebellion, but it remained for the men and women who had resisted taxation without representation to work out the full implications of republicanism. What would be the new government look like? What powers would be delegated to the people, the states, the federal authorities? How far would the wealthy, well-born leaders of the rebellion be willing to extend political, social, and economic rights?

For many Americans the challenge of nation building appeared more formidable than waging war against Britain. As Philadelphia physician Dr. Benjamin Rush explained, "There is nothing more common than to confound the terms of American Revolution with those of the late American war. The American war is over, but this is far from being the case with the American Revolution. On the contrary, nothing but the first act of the great drama is closed."

5 STUDY RESOURCES

Listen to the **Chapter Audio** for Chapter 5 on **myhistorylab.com**

TIMELINE

1764 Parliament passes Sugar Act to collect American revenue, p. 118

1765 Stamp Act receives support of House of Commons (March), p. 118
• Stamp Act Congress meets in New York City (October), p. 119

1766 Stamp Act repealed; Declaratory Act becomes law (March 18), p. 121

1767 Townshend Revenue Acts anger Americans (June–July), p. 121

1770 Parliament repeals Townshend duties except one on tea (March), p. 122
• British troops fire on civilians during "Boston Massacre" (March), p. 122

1772 Samuel Adams forms committee of correspondence, p. 123

1773 Lord North's government passes Tea Act (May), p. 123
• Bostonians hold Tea Party (December), p. 124

1774 Parliament punishes Boston with Coercive Acts (March–June), p. 124
• First Continental Congress convenes (September), p. 125

1775 Patriots take stand at Lexington and Concord (April), p. 125
• Second Continental Congress gathers (May), p. 126
• Americans hold their own at Bunker Hill (June), p. 126

1776 Declaration of Independence signed, p. 128
• British defeat Washington at Long Island (August), p. 130
• American victory at Trenton (December), p. 130

1777 Burgoyne surrenders at Saratoga (October), p. 132

1778 French treaties recognize independence of the United States (February), p. 133

1780 British take Charles Town (May), p. 134

1781 Cornwallis surrenders at Yorktown (October), p. 135

1783 Peace treaty signed (September), p. 136

CHAPTER REVIEW

STRUCTURE OF COLONIAL SOCIETY

Why did Americans resist parliamentary taxation?

During the 1760s British rulers claimed that Parliament could make laws for the colonists "in all cases whatsoever." Americans challenged this "parliamentary sovereignty." Drawing on the work of John Locke, the English philosopher, they insisted that God had given them certain natural and inalienable rights. By attempting to tax them without representation, Parliament threatened those rights. *(p. 113)*

ERODING THE BONDS OF EMPIRE

What events eroded the bonds of empire during the 1760s?

Wars in America were expensive. Parliament established the Proclamation Line of 1763 to reduce the costs of protecting the frontier, but this angered colonists seeking new lands in the west. Parliament also concluded that the colonists should help reduce the national debt, but when it passed the Stamp Act (1765), Americans protested. Colonists boycotted British manufactured goods. Taken aback, Parliament repealed the hated statute, while maintaining in the Declaratory Act (1766) its complete legislative authority over the Americans. *(p. 116)*

STEPS TOWARD INDEPENDENCE

What events in 1775 and 1776 led to the colonists' decision to declare independence?

In 1775, following battles at Lexington and Concord, militiamen from throughout New England descended upon Boston, besieging the British troops encamped there. In response, the Continental Congress formed the Continental Army and appointed George Washington commander. In 1776, Thomas Paine's *Common Sense* convinced colonists that a republic was a better form of government than monarchy, and Congress declared independence. *(p. 125)*

FIGHTING FOR INDEPENDENCE

Why did it take eight years of warfare for the Americans to gain independence?

To win their independence, the colonies first had to overcome the formidable military power of Great Britain. Britain had four times the population of the colonies, was the world's leading manufacturer, had a well-trained and experienced army and the world's best navy. The outgunned colonists had to rely on a war of attrition. It was only after the victory at Saratoga in 1777 convinced the French to enter into an alliance that the colonists were able to win conclusive battles and successfully end the war. *(p. 128)*

KEY TERM QUESTIONS

1. How did the confrontation between King George III and the Whigs lead to political turmoil (p. 113)

2. Why was the British government adamant in its defense of parliamentary sovereignty? (p. 114)

3. How would Loyalists have disputed the reasons Americans offered for resisting British authority? (p. 115)

4. Was the repeal of the Stamp Act of 1765 a victory for the American cause? (p. 118)

5. How did delegates to the Stamp Act Congress present their views to the King and Parliament? (p. 119)

6. How did the Boston Massacre affect colonial loyalty to Britain? (p. 122)

7. How did the committees of correspondence influence colonial resistance to Britain? (p. 123)

8. How did Parliament respond to the Boston Tea Party? (p. 124)

9. Were the Coercive Acts an overreaction by Parliament to the Boston Tea Party? (p. 124)

10. What differences of opinion arose during the First Continental Congress? (p. 125)

11. What did the Second Continental Congress accomplish? (p. 126)

12. Why was Thomas Paine's Common Sense so important? (p. 127)

13. Why was the French role at Yorktown so significant? (p. 135)

14. What was the significance of the Treaty of Paris of 1783? (p. 136)

MyHistoryLab Connections

Visit **www.myhistorylab.com** for a customized Study Plan to build your knowledge of *The American Revolution*.

Question for Analysis

1. What important details concerning the Boston Tea Party are mentioned in Hewes, "A Retrospect on the Boston Tea Party"?

   Read the **Document** *Hewes, A Retrospect on the Boston Tea Party* p. 124

2. According to Joseph Warren, who was the aggressor in the Battle of Lexington?

   Read the **Document** *Joseph Warren, Account of the Battle of Lexington* p. 126

3. Why did the British have such a difficult time fighting against the colonists?

   View the **Map** *The American Revolution* p. 130

4. Did the colonists fight the British as an entirely unified people?

   Watch the **Video** *The American Revolution as Different Americans Saw It* p. 137

Other Resources from this Chapter

Read the **Document** *James Otis, An American Colonist Opposes New Taxes*

Read the **Document** *Benjamin Franklin, Testimony Against the Stamp Act*

View the **Image** *1765 Stamp Act Protest*

View the **Image** *Women Signing Anti-Tea Agreement*

Listen to the **Audio File** *The Liberty Song*

Read the **Document** *Boston Gazette Description of the Boston Massacre*

View the **Image** *Bostonians Paying the Excise Man*

Read the **Document** *Thomas Paine, A Freelance Writer Urges His Readers*

View the **Image** *Surrender at Yorktown*

Contents and Spotlight Questions

DEFINING REPUBLICAN CULTURE PG. 142

What were the limits of equality in the "republican" society of the new United States?

STUMBLING TOWARD A NEW NATIONAL GOVERNMENT PG. 150

Why did many Americans regard the Articles of Confederation as inadequate?

"HAVE WE FOUGHT FOR THIS?" PG. 153

Why did Constitutional delegates compromise on representation and slavery?

WHOSE CONSTITUTION? STRUGGLE FOR RATIFICATION PG. 161

What issues separated Federalists from Antifederalists during debates over ratification?

((•—[**Listen** to the **Chapter Audio** for Chapter 6 on **myhistorylab.com**

A NEW POLITICAL MORALITY

I n 1788, Lewis Hallam and John Henry petitioned the General Assembly of Pennsylvania to open a theater in Philadelphia. Although a 1786 state law banned the performance of stage plays and "disorderly sports," many Philadelphia leaders favored the request to hold "dramatic representations" in their city. A committee appointed to study the issue concluded that a theater would contribute to "the general refinement of manners and the polish of society." Some supporters even argued that the sooner the United States had a professional theater the sooner it would escape the "foreign yoke" of British culture.

Quakers dismissed these claims: Such "seminaries of lewdness and irreligion" would quickly undermine "the virtue of the people.... [N]o sooner is a playhouse opened than it becomes surrounded with ... brothels." Since

Liberty Displaying the Arts and Sciences The Library Company of Philadelphia commissioned this painting by Samuel Jennings in 1792. The broken chain at the feet of the goddess Liberty is meant to demonstrate her opposition to slavery. (*Source: The Library Company of Philadelphia.*)

Pennsylvania was already suffering from a "stagnation of commerce [and] a scarcity of money"—unmistakable signs of God's displeasure—it seemed unwise to risk further divine punishment by encouraging new "hot-beds of vice."

Other citizens interpreted the revolutionary experience from an entirely different perspective. At issue, they insisted, was not popular morality, but state censorship. If the government silenced the stage, then "the same authority... may, with equal justice, dictate the shape and texture of our dress, or the modes and ceremonies of our worship." Depriving those who wanted to see plays of an opportunity to do so, they argued, "will abridge the natural right of every freeman, to dispose of his time and money, according to his own tastes and dispositions." The General Assembly apparently agreed. By 1789, Philadelphians were once again enjoying the liberty of attending the theater.

Throughout post-Revolutionary America everyday matters such as opening a new playhouse provoked passionate debate. The divisions were symptomatic of a new, uncertain political culture struggling to find the proper balance between public morality and private freedom. During the long fight against Britain, Americans had defended individual rights. But they also believed that a republic that compromised its virtue could not preserve liberty and independence.

In 1776, Thomas Paine had reminded ordinary men and women that "the sun never shined on a cause of greater worth....'Tis not the concern of a day, a year, or an age; posterity are virtually involved in the contest, and will be more or less affected, even to the end of time, by the proceedings now." During the 1780s Americans understood their responsibility not only to each other, but also to history. They worried, however, that they might not meet the challenge. Individual states seemed intent on looking out for local interests rather than the national welfare. Revolutionary leaders such as George Washington and James Madison concluded that the United States needed a strong central government to protect rights and property. Their quest for solutions brought forth a new and enduring constitution.

DEFINING REPUBLICAN CULTURE

What were the limits of equality in the "republican" society of the new United States?

Today, the term *republican* no longer possesses the evocative power it did for most eighteenth-century Americans. For them, it defined not a political party, but a political culture. Those Americans who read deeply in ancient and renaissance history knew that most republics had failed, often within a few years, replaced by tyrants who cared not at all what ordinary people thought about the public good. To preserve their republic from such a fate, victorious revolutionaries such as Samuel Adams recast fundamental political values. For them, republicanism represented more than a form of government. It was a way of life, a core ideology, an uncompromising commitment to maintain liberty and equality, while guarding against the corruptions of power and self-interest.

White Americans emerged from the Revolution with an almost euphoric sense of the nation's destiny. This expansive outlook, encountered among so many ordinary men and women, owed much to the spread of Protestant evangelicalism. However skeptical Jefferson, Franklin, and other leaders may have been about revealed religion, most Americans subscribed to an almost utopian vision of the country's future. To this new republic, God had promised progress and prosperity.

However, the celebration of liberty met with a mixed response. Some Americans—often the very men who had resisted British tyranny—worried that the citizens of the new nation were caught up in a wild, destructive scramble for material wealth. Democratic excesses seemed to threaten order and endanger property rights. Surely a republic could not survive unless its citizens showed greater self-control. For these people, the state assemblies appeared to be the greatest source of instability. Popularly elected representatives lacked what men of property defined as civic virtue, an ability to work for the common good rather than their private interests.

Working out the tensions between order and liberty, between property and equality, generated an outpouring of political genius. At other times in American history, persons of extraordinary talent have been drawn to theology, commerce, or science, but during the 1780s, the country's intellectual leaders—Thomas Jefferson, James Madison, Alexander Hamilton, and John Adams, among others—focused on the problem of how republicans ought to govern themselves.

Read the **Document** *George Washington, Manners and Etiquette* on **myhistorylab.com**

Social and Political Reform

Following the war, Americans aggressively ferreted out and, with republican fervor, denounced any traces of aristocratic pretense. As colonists, they had resented the claim that English aristocrats were privileged simply because of noble birth. Even so committed a republican as George Washington had to be reminded that artificial status was contrary to republican principles. In 1783, he and the officers who had served during the Revolution formed the Society of the Cincinnati, a hereditary organization in which membership passed from father to eldest son. The soldiers wanted to maintain old friendships, but anxious republicans throughout America let out a howl of protest. One South Carolina legislator, Aedanus Burke, warned that the Society intended to create "an hereditary peerage ... [which would] undermine the Constitution and destroy civil liberty." After an embarrassed Washington called for reforming the Society's bylaws, the Cincinnati

Questions of Equality in the New Republic In this illustration, which appeared as the frontispiece in the 1792 issue of *The Lady's Magazine and Repository of Entertaining Knowledge*, the "Genius of the Ladies Magazine" and the "Genius of Emulation" (holding in her hand a laurel crown) present to Liberty a petition for the rights of women. (*Source: The Library Company of Philadelphia.*)

crisis receded. The fear of privilege remained, however. Wealthy Americans dropped honorific titles such as "esquire." Lawyers of republican persuasion chided judges who had adopted the English custom of wearing great flowing wigs to court.

The appearance of equality was as important as its achievement. In fact, the distribution of wealth in postwar America was more uneven than it had been in the mid-eighteenth century. The sudden accumulation of large fortunes by new families made other Americans particularly sensitive to aristocratic display. It seemed intolerable that a revolution waged against a monarchy should produce a class of persons legally, or even visibly, distinguished from their fellow citizens.

To root out the notion of a privileged class, states abolished laws of primogeniture and entail. In colonial times, these laws allowed a landholder either to pass his entire estate to his eldest son or to declare that his property could never be divided, sold, or given away. Jefferson claimed that the repeal of these practices would eradicate "antient [sic] and future aristocracy; a foundation [has been] laid for a government truly republican." He may have exaggerated the social impact of this reform, but its symbolism counted as much as real social practice. Republican legislators wanted to cleanse traces of the former feudal order from the statute books.

Republican ferment also encouraged states to lower property requirements for voting. After the break with Britain, this seemed logical. As one group of farmers declared, no man can be "free & independent" unless he possesses "a voice ... in the choice of the most important Officers in the Legislature." Pennsylvania and Georgia allowed all white male taxpayers to vote. Other states were less democratic, but except for Massachusetts, they reduced property qualifications.

The most important changes in voting patterns were the result of western migration. As Americans moved to the frontier, they received full political representation in their state legislatures. Because new districts tended to be poorer than established coastal settlements, their representatives seemed less cultured, less well trained than those eastern voters elected. Moreover, western delegates resented traveling so far to attend legislative meetings. They lobbied to transfer state capitals to more convenient locations. During this period, Georgia moved the seat of its government from Savannah to Augusta, South Carolina from Charles Town to Columbia, North Carolina from New Bern to Raleigh, Virginia from Williamsburg to Richmond, New York from New York City to Albany, and New Hampshire from Portsmouth to Concord.

After gaining independence, Americans also reexamined the relation between church and state. Republican spokesmen such as Thomas Jefferson insisted that rulers had no right to interfere with the free expression of religious beliefs. As governor of Virginia, he advocated disestablishing the Anglican Church, which had received tax monies and other benefits during the colonial period. Jefferson and his allies regarded such privilege not only as a denial of religious freedom—rival denominations did not receive tax money—but also as a vestige of aristocratic society.

In 1786, Virginia cut the last ties between church and state. Other southern states also disestablished the Anglican Church, but in Massachusetts, Connecticut, and New Hampshire, Congregational churches continued to enjoy special status. Moreover, while Americans championed toleration, they seldom favored philosophies that radically challenged Christian values.

Quick Check

✓ During the 1780s, why were Americans so sensitive to the dangers of "aristocratic display"?

African Americans in the New Republic

Revolutionary fervor forced Americans to confront the most appalling contradiction to republican principles—slavery. The Quaker John Woolman (1720–1772) probably did more than any other white person of the era to remind people of the evils of this institution. A trip he took through the southern colonies as a young man impressed upon Woolman "the dark gloominess" of slavery. In a sermon, the outspoken humanitarian declared "that Men having Power too often misapplied it; that though we made Slaves of the Negroes, and the Turks made Slaves of the Christians, I believed that Liberty was the natural Right of all Men equally."

During the revolutionary period, abolitionist sentiment spread. Both in private and public, people began to criticize slavery in other than religious language. No doubt, the double standard of their own political rhetoric embarrassed many white Americans. They demanded liberation from parliamentary enslavement but held hundreds of thousands of blacks in bondage.

By keeping the issue of slavery before the public through writing and petitioning, African Americans undermined arguments in favor of human bondage. They demanded freedom, reminding white lawmakers that African American men and women had the same natural right to liberty as did other Americans. In 1779, for example, African Americans in Connecticut asked the state assembly "whether it is consistent with the present Claims, of the United States, to hold so many Thousands, of the Race of Adam, our Common Father, in perpetual Slavery." In New Hampshire, 19 persons who called themselves "natives of Africa" reminded legislators that "private or public tyranny and slavery are alike detestable to minds conscious of the equal dignity of human nature."

Read the **Document** *Slave Petition to the General Assembly in Connecticut (1779) on* **myhistorylab.com**

The scientific accomplishments of Benjamin Banneker (1731–1806), Maryland's African American astronomer and mathematician, and the international fame of Phillis Wheatley (1753–1784), Boston's celebrated "African muse," made it difficult for white Americans to maintain that African Americans could not hold their own in a free society. Wheatley's poems went through many editions. After reading her work, the great French philosopher Voltaire rebuked a friend who had claimed "there never would be Negro poets." As Voltaire discovered, Wheatley wrote "excellent verse in English." Banneker enjoyed a well-deserved reputation as a scientist. After receiving a copy of an almanac that Banneker had published in Philadelphia, Jefferson concluded "that nature has given to our black brethren, talents equal to those of the other colors of men."

In the northern states, there was no real economic justification for slavery. White laborers, often recent European immigrants, resented having to compete against slaves. This economic situation, combined with the acknowledgment of the double standard slavery represented, contributed to the establishment of antislavery societies. In 1775, Franklin helped organize in Philadelphia the Society for the Relief of Free Negroes, Unlawfully Held. John Jay, Alexander Hamilton, and other prominent New Yorkers founded a Manumission Society in 1785. By 1792, antislavery societies were meeting from Virginia to Massachusetts. In the northern states at least, these groups, working for the same ends as Christian evangelicals, put slaveholders on the intellectual defensive for the first time in American history.

Phillis Wheatley This engraving of Wheatley appeared in her volume of verse, *Poems on Various Subjects, Religious and Moral* (1773), the first book published by an African American.

Read the
Document
*Phillis Wheatley,
Religious and Moral
Poems* on
myhistorylab.com

Read the
Document
*Richard Allen,
"Address to the Free
People of Colour"* on
myhistorylab.com

In states north of Virginia, the abolition of slavery took different forms. Even before achieving statehood in 1791, Vermont drafted a constitution (1777) that prohibited slavery. In 1780, the Pennsylvania legislature passed a law for gradual emancipation. Although the Massachusetts assembly refused to address the issue directly, the state courts liberated its African Americans. A judge ruled slavery unconstitutional in Massachusetts because it conflicted with a clause in the state bill of rights declaring "all men … free and equal." According to one enthusiast, this decision freed "a Grate number of Blacks … who … are held in a state of slavery within the bowels of a free and christian Country." By 1800, slavery was on the road to extinction in the northern states.

These positive developments did not mean that white people accepted blacks as equals. In the very states that outlawed slavery, African Americans faced systematic discrimination. Free blacks were generally excluded from voting, juries, and militia duty—they were denied rights and responsibilities associated with full citizenship. They rarely enjoyed access to education. In cities such as Philadelphia and New York, where African Americans went to look for work, they ended up living in segregated wards or neighborhoods. Even in the churches—institutions that had often attacked slavery—free African Americans were denied equal standing with white worshippers. Humiliations of this sort persuaded African Americans to form their own churches. In Philadelphia, Richard Allen, a former slave, founded the Bethel Church for Negro Methodists (1793) and later organized the **African Methodist Episcopal Church** (1814), an institution of cultural and religious significance for nineteenth-century American blacks.

Even in the South, where African Americans made up much of the population, slavery disturbed thoughtful white republicans. Some planters simply freed their slaves. By 1790, 12,766 free blacks lived in Virginia. By 1800, there were 30,750. This trend reflected uneasiness among white masters. Richard Randolph, one of Virginia's wealthier planters, explained that he freed his slaves "to make restitution, as far as I am able, to an unfortunate race of bond-men, over whom my ancestors have usurped and exercised the most lawless and monstrous tyranny." George Washington also freed his slaves in his will after his death. But most southern slaveholders, especially in South Carolina and Georgia, rejected manumission. Their well-being depended on slave labor. Perhaps more significant, however, is that no southern leader during the era of republican experimentation defended slavery as a positive good. Such racist rhetoric did not become part of the public discourse until the nineteenth century.

Despite promising starts, the southern states did not abolish slavery. The economic incentives to maintain a servile labor force, especially after the invention of the cotton gin in 1793 and the opening up of the Alabama and Mississippi frontier, overwhelmed the initial abolitionist impulse. An opportunity to translate the principles of the American Revolution into social practice had been lost, at least temporarily. Jefferson reported in 1805, "I have long since given up the expectation of any early provision for the extinction of slavery among us." Unlike some contemporary Virginians, the man who wrote the Declaration of Independence condoned slavery on his own plantation, even fathering children by a woman who, since she was his slave, had little choice in her pregnancies.

Quick Check

✓ Why did the new republican governments not bring liberty and equality to African Americans living in the United States?

The Challenge of Women's Rights

The revolutionary experience accelerated changes in how ordinary people viewed the family. At the beginning of the eighteenth century, fathers claimed authority over their families simply because they were fathers. As patriarchs, they demanded obedience. Fathers could treat wives and children however they pleased. John Locke had powerfully undermined arguments of this sort. In *Some Thoughts Concerning Education* (1693), Locke insisted that the mind was not formed at birth. Children learned from experience. If the infant witnessed violent, arbitrary behavior, then the baby would become an abusive adult. As Locke warned parents, "If you punish him [the child] for what he sees you practice yourself, he will not think that Severity to proceed from Kindness in you careful to amend a Fault in him; but will be apt to interpret it, as Peevishness and Arbitrary Imperiousness of a Father." Enlightened eighteenth-century parents—especially fathers—condemned tyranny in the home.

In this changing intellectual environment, American women began making new demands not only on their husbands but on republican institutions. Abigail Adams, wife of future President John Adams and one of the era's most articulate women, instructed her husband, as he set off for the Second Continental Congress: "I desire you would Remember the Ladies, and be more generous and favourable to them than your ancestors. Do not put such unlimited power into the hands of the Husbands." John responded condescendingly. The "Ladies" would have to wait until the country achieved independence. In 1777, Lucy Knox took an even stronger line with her husband, General Henry Knox. When he was about to return home from the army, she warned him, "I hope you will not consider yourself as commander in chief in your own house—but be convinced … that there is such a thing as equal command."

Read the **Document** *John Adams to Abigail Adams, July 3, 1776* on **myhistorylab.com**

If Knox accepted Lucy's argument, he did so because she was a good republican wife and mother. In fact, women justified their assertiveness largely on the basis of political ideology. If survival of republics really depended on the virtue of their citizens, they argued, then it was the special responsibility of women as mothers to nurture the right values in their children and as wives to instruct their husbands in proper behavior. Contemporaries claimed that the woman who possessed "virtue and prudence" could easily "mold the taste, the manners, and the conduct of her admirers, according to her pleasure." In fact, "nothing short of a general reformation of manners would take place, were the ladies to use their power in discouraging our licentious manners."

Read the **Document** *Molly Wallace, Valedictory Address (1792)* on **myhistorylab.com**

Ill-educated women could not fulfill these expectations. Women required education that was at least comparable to what men received. Many female academies were established during this period to meet what many Americans, men as well as women, now regarded as a pressing social need. The schools may have received widespread encouragement precisely because they did not radically challenge traditional gender roles. The educated republican woman of the late eighteenth century did not pursue a career; she followed a familiar routine as wife and mother. The frustration of not being allowed to develop her talents may explain the bitterness of a graduation oration an otherwise obscure woman delivered in 1793: "Our high and mighty Lords … have denied us the means of knowledge, and then reproached us for want of it…. They doom'd the sex to servile or frivolous employments, on purpose to degrade their minds, that they themselves might hold unrivall'd, the power and pre-eminence they had usurped."

During this period, women began to petition for divorce on new grounds. One case reveals changing attitudes toward women and the family. In 1784, John Backus, an undistinguished Massachusetts silversmith, was hauled before a court and asked why he beat his wife. He responded that "it was Partly owing to his Education for his father treated his mother in the same manner." The difference between Backus's case and his father's was that Backus's wife refused to tolerate such abuse, and she sued successfully for divorce. Divorce patterns in Connecticut and Pennsylvania show that after 1773, women divorced on about the same terms as men.

The war itself presented some women with fresh opportunities. In 1780, Ester DeBerdt Reed founded a large volunteer women's organization in Philadelphia—the first of its kind in the United States—that raised more than $300,000 for Washington's army. Other women ran farms and businesses while their husbands fought the British. And in 1790, the New Jersey legislature allowed women who owned property to vote.

Despite these scattered gains, republican society still defined women's roles exclusively in terms of mother, wife, and homemaker. Other pursuits seemed unnatural, even threatening. It is perhaps not surprising, therefore, that in 1807, New Jersey lawmakers—angry that

Abigail Adams Benjamin Blyth painted this portrait of Abigail Adams, wife of the future President John Adams, c. 1766.

women voters had apparently determined the result of a close election—repealed female suffrage in the interests of "safety, quiet, and good order and dignity of the state." Even such an allegedly progressive thinker as Jefferson could not imagine allowing women to participate in serious politics. When in 1807 his secretary of the treasury, Albert Gallatin, called attention to the shortage of educated people to serve in government jobs and suggested recruiting women, Jefferson responded sharply: "The appointment of a woman to office is an innovation for which the public is not prepared, nor am I."

Quick Check

✓ What evidence argues that this was a period of significant progress for women in the United States?

The States: Experiments in Republicanism

In May 1776, the Second Continental Congress invited the states to adopt constitutions. The old colonial charters filled with references to king and Parliament were no longer adequate, and within a few years, most states had acted. Rhode Island and Connecticut already enjoyed republican government through their unique seventeenth-century charters that allowed the voters to select both governors and legislators. Eleven other states plus Vermont created new political structures. Their deliberations reveal how Americans in different regions and reacting to different social pressures defined fundamental republican principles.

Several constitutions were experimental, and states rewrote documents that had been drafted in the first flush of independence. These early constitutions nevertheless provided the framers of the federal Constitution of 1787 with insights into the strengths and weaknesses of government based on the will of the people.

Despite disagreements over details, Americans who wrote the various state constitutions shared two political assumptions. First, they insisted on *written* documents. This represented a major break with English practice. Political philosophers in the mother country had long boasted of Britain's unwritten constitution, a collection of judicial decisions and parliamentary statutes. But this vaunted system had not protected the colonists from oppression; hence, after declaring independence, Americans demanded that their state constitutions explicitly define the rights of the people and the power of their rulers.

Second, the authors of the state constitutions believed men and women possessed certain natural rights over which government exercised no control whatsoever. So that future rulers—potential tyrants—would know the exact limits of authority, these fundamental rights were carefully spelled out. Indeed, the people of Massachusetts rejected the proposed state constitution of 1778 largely because it lacked a full statement of their basic rights. They demanded a guarantee of "rights of conscience, and ... security of persons and property, which every member in the State hath a right to expect from the supreme power."

Eight state constitutions contained specific declarations of rights. The length and character of these lists varied, but, in general, they affirmed three fundamental freedoms: religion, speech, and press. They protected citizens from unlawful searches and seizures and upheld trial by jury.

Quick Check

✓ Following independence, why did the states insist on drafting *written* constitutions?

STUMBLING TOWARD A NEW NATIONAL GOVERNMENT

Why did many Americans regard the Articles of Confederation as inadequate?

When the Second Continental Congress convened in 1775, the delegates found themselves waging war in the name of a country that did not yet exist. As the military crisis deepened, Congress gradually—often reluctantly—assumed greater authority over national affairs. But everyone agreed such narrow measures were a poor substitute for a legally constituted government. The separate states could not deal with the range of issues that the American people now confronted. Indeed, if independence meant anything in a world of sovereign nations, it implied the creation of a central authority able to conduct war, borrow money, regulate trade, and negotiate treaties.

Articles of Confederation

Creating a viable central government proved more difficult than anyone anticipated. Congress appointed a committee to draw up a plan for confederation. John Dickinson, the lawyer who had written an important revolutionary pamphlet titled *Letters from a Farmer in Pennsylvania*, headed the committee. Dickinson envisioned a strong central government. The report his committee presented on July 12, 1776, shocked delegates who assumed that the constitution would authorize a loose confederation of states. Dickinson's plan placed the western territories, land the separate states claimed for themselves, under congressional control. His committee also called for equal state representation in Congress.

Since some states, such as Virginia and Massachusetts, were more populous than others, this fueled tensions between large and small states. Also unsettling was Dickinson's recommendation that taxes be paid to Congress on the basis of a state's total population, black as well as white, a formula that angered southerners who did not think slaves should be counted for purposes of taxation.

Read the **Document** *John Dickinson, from* Letters from a Farmer in Pennsylvania on **myhistorylab.com**

The Articles of Confederation that Congress finally approved in November 1777 bore little resemblance to Dickinson's original plan. The Articles jealously guarded the sovereignty of the states. The delegates who drafted the framework shared a republican conviction that power—especially power so far removed from the people—was dangerous. The only way to preserve liberty was to place as many constraints as possible on federal authority.

The result was a government that many people regarded as powerless. The Articles provided for a single legislative body consisting of representatives selected annually by the state legislatures. Each state had one vote in Congress. It could send as many as seven delegates, or as few as two, but if they divided evenly on an issue, the state lost its vote. There was no independent executive and no veto over legislative decisions. The Articles also denied Congress the power of taxation, a serious oversight in time of war. To obtain funds, the national government had to ask the states for contributions, called requisitions. If a state failed to cooperate—and many did—Congress limped along without financial support. All 13 states had to assent to amendments to this constitution. The authors expected the weak national government to handle foreign relations, military and Indian affairs, and interstate disputes. They did not award Congress ownership of the lands west of the Appalachians.

The new constitution sent to the states for ratification met apathy and hostility. Most Americans were far more interested in local affairs than in the acts of Congress. When a British army marched through a state, creating a need for immediate military aid, people spoke positively about central government, but as soon as the threat passed, they sang a different tune. During this period, even the slightest encroachment on state sovereignty rankled republicans who feared centralization would promote corruption.

Quick Check

✓ During the Revolution, why did Congress not create a stronger federal government?

Western Land: Key to the First Constitution

The major bone of contention with the Articles, however, was the disposition of the vast, unsurveyed territory west of the Appalachians. Although various states claimed the region, most of it actually belonged to Native Americans. In land grabs that federal negotiators called treaties, the United States government took much of modern Ohio, Indiana, Illinois, and Kentucky. Since the Indians had put their faith in the British during the war, they could do little to resist these humiliating agreements. As John Dickinson, then serving as the president of the Supreme Executive Council of Pennsylvania, told the Indians, since Britain has surrendered "the back country with all the forts … that they [the Indians] must now depend upon us for the preservation." If they dared to resist, "we will instantly turn upon them our armies … and extirpate them from the land where they were born and now live."

Some states, such as Virginia and Georgia, claimed land from the Atlantic Ocean to the elusive "South Seas," in effect extending their boundaries to the Pacific coast by virtue of royal charters. State legislators—their appetites whetted by aggressive land speculators—anticipated large revenues through land sales. Connecticut, New York, Pennsylvania, and North Carolina also announced intentions to seize western land.

Other states were not blessed with vague or ambiguous royal charters. The boundaries of Maryland, Delaware, and New Jersey had been established years earlier. It seemed as if people in these states would be cut off from the anticipated bounty. In protest, these "landless" states refused to ratify the Articles of Confederation. Marylanders were particularly vociferous. All the states had sacrificed for the common good during the Revolution, they complained. It appeared only fair that all states should profit from the fruits of victory, in this case, from the sale of western lands. Maryland's spokesmen feared that if Congress did not void Virginia's excessive claims to all of the Northwest Territory (the land west of Pennsylvania and north of the Ohio River) and to a large area south of the Ohio, beyond the Cumberland Gap, known as Kentucky, then Marylanders would desert their home state in search of cheap Virginia farms, leaving Maryland an underpopulated wasteland.

View the **Map**
*Western Land Claims
Ceded by the States* on
myhistorylab.com

The states resolved the controversy in 1781 as much by accident as by design. Virginia agreed to cede its holdings north of the Ohio River to the Confederation if Congress nullified land companies' purchases from the Indians. A practical consideration had softened Virginia's resolve. Republicans such as Jefferson worried about expanding their state beyond the mountains; with poor transportation links, it seemed impossible to govern such a large territory from Richmond.

Quick Check

✓ Why did the question of the western lands cause such conflict between the states under the Articles of Confederation?

The western settlers might even come to regard Virginia as a colonial power insensitive to their needs. Marylanders who dreamed of making fortunes on the land market grumbled, but when a British army appeared on their border, they accepted the Articles (March 1, 1781). Congress required another three years to work out the details of the Virginia cession. Other landed states followed Virginia's example. These transfers established an important principle. After 1781, it was agreed that the West belonged not to the separate states but to the United States. (See Map 6.1.)

Northwest Ordinance: The Confederation's Major Achievement

However weak Congress may have been, it did score one impressive triumph. Congressional action brought order to western settlement, especially in the Northwest Territory, and incorporated frontier Americans into an expanding federal system. In 1781, the prospects for success did not seem promising. For years, colonial authorities had ignored people who migrated far inland, sending neither money nor soldiers to protect them from Indian attack. Tensions between the seaboard colonies and the frontier regions sometimes flared into violence. Disorders occurred in South Carolina in 1767, in North Carolina in 1769, and in Vermont in 1777. With thousands of men and women, most of them squatters, pouring across the Appalachians, Congress had to act quickly to avoid the errors of royal and colonial authorities.

The initial attempt to deal with this explosive problem came in 1784. Jefferson, then serving as a member of Congress, drafted an ordinance that became the basis for more enduring legislation. He recommended carving ten new states out of the western lands north of the Ohio River that Virginia had recently ceded to the United States. He specified that each new state establish a republican form of government. When the population of a territory equaled that of the smallest state already in the Confederation, the region could apply for full statehood. In the meantime, free white males could participate in local government, a democratic guarantee that frightened some of Jefferson's more conservative colleagues.

The impoverished Congress was eager to sell off the western territory as quickly as possible. The frontier represented income that did not depend on the unreliable generosity of the states. In 1785, the Land Ordinance established an orderly process for laying out new townships and marketing public lands. Public response

Map 6.1   *Northwest Territory*   The U.S. government auctioned off the land in the Northwest Territory, the region defined by the Ohio River, the Great Lakes, and the Mississippi River. Proceeds from the sale of one section in each township were set aside for the construction of public schools.

disappointed Congress. Surveying the lands took longer than anticipated, and few persons possessed enough hard currency to make even the minimum purchase. Nevertheless, small homesteaders settled wherever they pleased, refusing to pay either government or speculators for the land.

Congress worried about the excess liberty on the frontier. In the 1780s, the West seemed to be filling up with people who by eastern standards were uncultured. Timothy Pickering, a New Englander, declared that "the emigrants to the frontier lands are the least worthy subjects in the United States. They are little less savage than the Indians; and when possessed of the most fertile spots, for want of industry, live miserably." The charge was as old as the frontier itself. Seventeenth-century Englishmen had said the same things of the earliest Virginians. The lawless image stuck, however. Even a sober observer such as Washington insisted that the West crawled with "banditti." The Ordinance of 1784 placed the government of the territories in the hands of people about whom congressmen and speculators had second thoughts.

These various currents shaped the Ordinance of 1787, one of the final acts passed under the Confederation. The bill, also called the Northwest Ordinance, provided a new structure for government of the Northwest Territory. It authorized creating between three and five territories, each to be ruled by a governor, a secretary, and three judges appointed by Congress. When the population of a territory reached 5,000, voters who owned property could elect an assembly, but its decisions were subject to the governor's absolute veto. Once 60,000 persons resided in a territory, they could write a constitution and petition for full statehood. While these procedures represented a retreat from Jefferson's original proposal, the Ordinance of 1787 contained several significant features. A bill of rights guaranteed the settlers the right to trial by jury, freedom of religion, and due process of law. The act also outlawed slavery, which freed the future states of Ohio, Indiana, Illinois, Michigan, and Wisconsin from the curse of human bondage. (See Map 6.2.)

By contrast, Congress paid less attention to settlement south of the Ohio River. Thousands of Americans had already streamed into a part of Virginia known as Kentucky. The most famous of these settlers was Daniel Boone. In 1775, the population of Kentucky was approximately 100; by 1784, it had jumped to 30,000.

Quick Check

✓ How did the Northwest Ordinance resolve the problem of the western lands?

"HAVE WE FOUGHT FOR THIS?"

By 1785, the country seemed to have lost direction. The optimism that sustained revolutionary patriots had dissolved into pessimism and doubt. Many Americans, especially those who had provided leadership during the Revolution, agreed something had to be done. In 1786, Washington observed, "What astonishing changes a few years are capable of producing. Have we fought for this? Was it with these expectations that we launched into a sea of trouble, and have bravely struggled through the most threatening dangers?"

Why did Constitutional delegates compromise on representation and slavery?

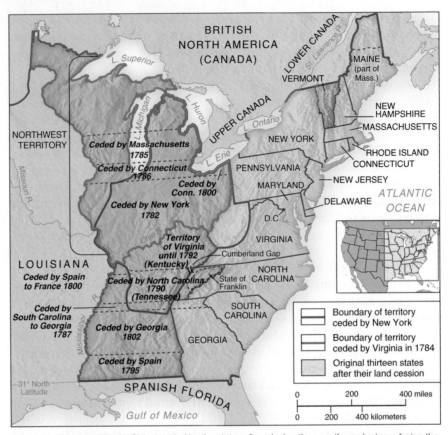

Map 6.2 *Western Land* Claims ceded by the states after winning the war, the major issue facing the Continental Congress under the Articles of Confederation was mediating conflicting states' claims to rich western land. By 1802, the states had ceded all rights to the federal government.

The Genius of James Madison

The conviction of people such as Washington that the nation was in crisis reflected tensions within republican thought. They supported open elections and the right of individuals to advance their own economic well-being. But when these elements seemed to undermine social and political order, they feared that liberty had been carried too far. The situation had changed rapidly. As recently as the 1770s, republicans had insisted that the greatest threat to the American people was concentration of power in the hands of unscrupulous rulers. They therefore transformed state governors into figureheads and weakened the Confederation.

By the mid-1780s, persons of property and standing saw the problem in a different light. Recent experience suggested that ordinary citizens did not possess sufficient virtue to sustain a republic. The states had been plagued not by executive tyranny but by an excess of democracy, by a failure of the majority to preserve the property rights of the minority, by an unrestrained individualism that promoted anarchy rather than order.

Many state leaders did not seem concerned about the fiscal health of the national government. Presses churned out worthless paper currency, and in some state assemblies impeded the collection of debt. In Rhode Island, legislators made it illegal for merchants to reject Rhode Island money even though everyone knew it had no value. No wonder Governor William Livingston of New Jersey declared in 1787, "We do not exhibit the virtue that is necessary to support a republican government."

As Americans tried to interpret these experiences within a republican framework, they were checked by the most accepted political wisdom of the age. Baron de Montesquieu (1689–1755), a French political philosopher of immense reputation and author of *The Spirit of the Laws* (1748), declared flatly that a republican government could not flourish in a large territory. The reasons were clear. If the people lost direct control over their representatives, they would fall prey to tyrants. Large distances allowed rulers to hide their corruption; physical separation presented aristocrats with opportunities to seize power.

In the United States, most learned men treated Montesquieu's theories as self-evident truths. His writings seemed to demonstrate the importance of preserving the sovereignty of the states. However much these small republics abused the rights of property and ignored minority interests, it was plainly unscientific to maintain that a republic of 13 states, millions of people, and vast territory could survive.

James Madison rejected Montesquieu's argument and helped Americans think of republican government in radical new ways. This soft-spoken, unprepossessing Virginian was the most brilliant American political thinker of his generation. One French official described Madison as "a man one must study a long time in order to make a fair appraisal." Those who listened carefully to what Madison said, however, soon recognized his genius for translating theory into practice.

View the Image
James Madison, Portrait on
myhistorylab.com

Madison delved into the writings of a group of Scottish philosophers, the most prominent being David Hume (1711–1776). From their works he concluded that Americans need not fear an expanded republic. Madison perceived that "inconveniences of popular States contrary to prevailing Theory, are in proportion not to the extent, but to the narrowness of their limits." Indeed, it was in small states such as Rhode Island that legislative majorities tyrannized the propertied minority. In a large territory, Madison explained, "the Society becomes broken into a greater variety of interest, of pursuits, of passions, which check each other, whilst those who may feel a common sentiment have less opportunity of communication and contact."

Quick Check

✓ How did James Madison respond to republican fears that a nation as large as the United States could never be successfully governed as a republic?

Constitutional Reform

A movement to overhaul the Articles of Confederation began in 1786, when Madison and his friends persuaded the Virginia assembly to recommend a convention to explore creating a unified system of "commercial regulations." Congress supported the idea. In September, delegates from five states arrived in Annapolis, Maryland, to discuss issues that extended far beyond commerce. The small turnout was disappointing, but nationalists hatched an even bolder plan. The delegates advised Congress to hold a second meeting in Philadelphia "to take into consideration the situation of the United States, to devise such further provisions as shall appear to them necessary to render the constitution of the Federal Government adequate to the exigencies of the Union." Staunch states' rights advocates in Congress may not have known what was afoot, but Congress authorized a grand convention to gather in May 1787.

Events played into Madison's hands. Soon after the Annapolis meeting, an uprising known as Shays's Rebellion, involving thousands of impoverished farmers, erupted in western Massachusetts. No matter how hard these men worked, they found themselves in debt to eastern creditors. They complained of high taxes and interest rates and, most of all, of a state government insensitive to their problems. In 1786, Daniel Shays, a veteran of the battle of Bunker Hill, and his armed neighbors closed a county courthouse where creditors were suing to foreclose farm mortgages. The insurgents threatened to seize the federal arsenal in Springfield. Congress did not have funds sufficient to support an army, and the arsenal might have fallen. But wealthy Bostonians raised 4,000 troops to suppress the insurrection. The victors were in for a surprise. At the next general election, Massachusetts voters selected representatives sympathetic to Shays's demands, and a new liberal assembly reformed debtor law.

Nationalists throughout the United States were less forgiving. Shays's Rebellion symbolized the breakdown of law and order that they had predicted. "Great commotions are prevailing in Massachusetts," Madison wrote. "An appeal to the

Read the **Document**
Military Reports of Shays's Rebellion on **myhistorylab.com**

Shays's Rebellion This 1787 woodcut portrays Daniel Shays with one of his chief officers, Jacob Shattucks. Shays led farmers in western Massachusetts in revolt against a state government that seemed insensitive to the needs of poor debtors. Their rebellion frightened conservative leaders, who demanded a strong new federal government.

sword is exceedingly dreaded." The time had come for sensible people to speak up for a strong national government. The unrest in Massachusetts persuaded persons who might have ignored the Philadelphia meeting to participate in drafting a new constitution.

Quick Check

✓ What role did Shays's Rebellion play in bringing about constitutional reform?

The Philadelphia Convention

In the spring of 1787, 55 men representing 12 states traveled to Philadelphia. Rhode Island refused to take part, which Madison attributed to its "wickedness and folly." Jefferson described the convention as an "assembly of demi-Gods," but this flattering depiction is misleading. However much modern Americans revere the Constitution, they should remember that its authors did not possess divine insight into the nature of government. They were practical people—lawyers, merchants, and planters—many of whom had fought in the Revolution and served in the Congress of the Confederation. Most were in their thirties or forties. The gathering included George Washington, James Madison, George Mason, Robert Morris, James Wilson, John Dickinson, Benjamin Franklin, and Alexander Hamilton, to name some of the more prominent participants. Absent were John Adams and Thomas Jefferson, who were conducting diplomacy in Europe; Patrick Henry, a localist suspicious of strong central government, "smelled a rat" and remained in Virginia.

As soon as the Constitutional Convention opened on May 25, the delegates made two important procedural decisions. First, they voted "that nothing spoken in the House be printed, or communicated without leave." The rule was stringently enforced. Sentries kept out uninvited visitors, windows stayed shut in the sweltering heat to prevent sound from either entering or leaving the chamber, and members were forbidden to copy the daily journal without official permission. As Madison explained, the secrecy rule saved "both the convention and the community from a thousand erroneous and perhaps mischievous reports." It also has made it difficult for modern lawyers and judges to determine what the delegates had in mind when they wrote the Constitution.

Second, the delegates decided to vote by state. But to avoid the problems that had plagued the Confederation, key proposals needed the support of only a majority of the states instead of the nine states the Articles required.

Quick Check

✓ Why were the men who drafted the consitution so concerned with secrecy?

Inventing a Federal Republic

Even before all the delegates had arrived, Madison drew up a framework for a new federal system known as the Virginia Plan. It envisioned a national legislature of two houses, one elected *directly* by the people, the other chosen by the first house from nominations made by the state assemblies. Representation in both houses was proportional to the state's population. The Virginia Plan also provided for an executive elected by Congress. Madison persuaded Edmund Randolph, Virginia's popular governor, to present this scheme to the convention on May 29. Randolph claimed that the Virginia Plan merely revised sections of the Articles, but everyone, including Madison, knew better. "My ideas," Madison confessed, "strike ... deeply at the old Confederation." He was determined to restrain the state assemblies, and in the original Virginia Plan, Madison gave the federal government power to veto state laws. Since most delegates at the Philadelphia convention sympathized with the nationalist position, Madison's blueprint for a strong federal government was referred for further study and debate. Men who allegedly had come together to reform the Confederation found themselves discussing the details of "a *national* Government ... consisting of a *supreme* Legislature, Executive, and Judiciary."

The Virginia Plan had been pushed through the convention so fast that opponents hardly had an opportunity to object. On June 15, they spoke up. William Paterson, a New Jersey lawyer, advanced the so-called New Jersey Plan, which retained the unicameral legislature in which each state possessed one vote but gave Congress new powers to tax and regulate trade. Paterson argued that these revisions, while more modest than Madison's plan, would have greater appeal for the American people: "I believe that a little practical virtue is to be preferred to the finest theoretical principles, which cannot be carried into effect." The delegates listened politely but only New Jersey, New York, and Delaware voted in favor of it.

Rejecting this framework did not resolve the most controversial issue before the convention. Paterson and others feared that under the Virginia Plan, small states would lose their separate identities. They maintained that unless each state possessed an equal vote in Congress, the small states would find themselves at the mercy of their larger neighbors.

This argument outraged delegates who favored a strong federal government. It awarded too much power to the states. "For whom [are we] forming a Government?" James Wilson of Pennsylvania cried. "Is it for men, or for the imaginary beings called States?" It seemed absurd that 68,000 Rhode Islanders should have the same voice in Congress as 747,000 Virginians.

Quick Check

✓ Did the New Jersey plan represent a significant retreat from the main points of the Virginia plan?

Compromise Saves the Convention

Mediation was the only way to overcome what Roger Sherman of Connecticut called "a full stop in proceedings." On July 2, the convention elected a "grand committee" of one person from each state to resolve differences between the large and small states. Franklin, at age 81 the oldest delegate, served as chair. The two fiercest supporters of proportional representation, Madison and Wilson, were left off the committee, a sign that the small states would salvage something from the compromise.

Watch the **Video**
Slavery and the Constitution on
myhistorylab.com

The committee recommended equal representation for the states in the upper house of Congress and proportionate representation in the lower house. Only the lower house could initiate money bills. One member of the lower house should be selected for every 30,000 inhabitants of a state. Southern delegates insisted that this number include slaves. In the so-called three-fifths rule, the committee agreed that to determine representation in the lower house, every five slaves in a congressional district would count as three free voters, This gave the South much greater power in the new government than it would have otherwise received. As with most compromises, the one Franklin's committee negotiated fully satisfied no one. It did, however, overcome a major impasse. After the small states gained an assured voice in the upper house, the Senate, they cooperated enthusiastically in creating a strong central government.

Despite these advances, in late August, a disturbing issue came before the convention. It was a harbinger of the great sectional crisis of the nineteenth century. Many northern representatives wanted to end the slave trade immediately. They despised the three-fifths rule that seemed to award slaveholders extra power simply because they owned slaves. "It seemed now to be pretty well understood," Madison jotted in his private notes, "that the real difference of interest lay, not between the large and small but between the N. and Southn. States. The institution of slavery and its consequences formed a line of discrimination."

Whenever northern delegates—and on this point they were not united—pushed too aggressively, southerners threatened to bolt the convention, thereby destroying any hope of establishing a strong national government. Curiously, even recalcitrant southerners avoided using the word *slavery*. They seemed embarrassed to call the institution by its true name. In the Constitution itself, slaves were described as "other persons," "such persons," "persons held to Service or Labour," as everything but slaves.

A few northern delegates such as Roger Sherman sought to mollify the southerners, especially the South Carolinians, who spoke passionately about preserving slavery. Gouverneur Morris, a Pennsylvania representative, would have none of it. He reminded the convention that "the inhabitant of Georgia and S.C. who goes to the Coast of Africa, and in defiance of the most sacred laws of humanity tears away his fellow creatures from their dearest connections and damns them to the most cruel bondage, shall have more votes in a Government instituted for the protection of the rights of mankind, than the Citizen of Pa. or N. Jersey."

Ignoring Morris's attacks, the delegates reached an uneasy compromise on the slave trade. Southerners feared that the new Congress would pass commercial regulations that hurt the planters—export taxes on rice and tobacco, for example. They demanded a two-thirds majority of the federal legislature be required to pass trade laws. They backed down on this point, however, in exchange for guarantees that Congress would not interfere with the slave trade until 1808 (see Chapter 8). The South even won a clause assuring the return of fugitive slaves. "We have obtained," Charles Cotesworth Pinckney told the planters of South Carolina, "a right to recover our slaves in whatever part of America they may take refuge, which is a right we had not before."

Although these deals disappointed many northerners, they conceded that establishing a strong national government was of greater immediate importance than ending the slave trade. "Great as the evil is," Madison wrote, "a dismemberment of the union would be worse."

Read the **Document** *The Debates in the Federal Convention of 1787* on **myhistorylab.com**

Quick Check

✓ Why did the delegates think a compromise on slavery and states' rights was necessary to achieve the ratification of a new constituion?

The Last Details

On July 26, the convention formed a Committee of Detail, a group that prepared a rough draft of the Constitution. After the committee completed its work—writing a document that still, after so much debate, preserved the fundamental points of the Virginia Plan— the delegates reconsidered each article. The task required the better part of a month.

During these sessions, the convention concluded that the president, as they now called the chief executive, should be selected by an electoral college, a body of prominent men in each state chosen by local voters. The number of "electoral" votes each state held equaled its number of representatives and senators. This awkward device guaranteed that the president would not be indebted to the Congress for his office. Whoever received the second most votes in the electoral college automatically became vice president. If no person received a majority of the votes, the lower house—the House of Representatives—would decide the election, with each state casting a single vote. Delegates also gave the president veto power over legislation and the right to nominate judges. Both privileges would have been unthinkable a decade earlier, but the state experiments revealed the importance of having an independent executive to maintain a balanced system of republican government.

As the meeting was concluding, delegates expressed concern about the absence of a bill of rights. Most state constitutions included such declarations. Virginians such as George Mason insisted that the states and their citizens needed explicit protection from excesses by the federal government. While many delegates sympathized with Mason's appeal, they noted that the hour was late and, in any case, that the proposed Constitution provided security for individual rights. During the hard battles over ratification, the delegates may have regretted passing over the issue so lightly.

Quick Check

✓ Why did the delegates to the Constitutional Convention fail to Include a formal Bill of Rights?

We the People

Now that many issues were settled, the delegates had to overcome the hurdle of ratifying the Constitution. They adopted an ingenious procedure. Instead of submitting the Constitution to the state legislatures, all of which had a vested interest in the status quo and most of which had two houses, either of which could block approval, they called for electing 13 state conventions to review the new federal government. Moreover, the Constitution would take effect after the assent of only nine states. There was no danger that the proposed system would fail simply because a single state like Rhode Island withheld approval.

The convention asked the urbane Gouverneur Morris to make final stylistic changes in the wording of the Constitution. When Morris examined the working draft, he discovered that it spoke of the collection of states forming a new government. This wording presented problems. Ratification required only nine states. No one knew whether all the states would accept the Constitution and, if not, which nine would. New England states, for example, might reject the document. Morris's brilliant phrase "We the People of the United States" eliminated this difficulty. The new nation was a republic of the people, not of the states.

Quick Check

✓ What was the "ingenious procedure for ratification" adopted by the Constitutional Convention delegates?

On September 17, 39 men signed the Constitution. A few delegates, like Mason, could not support it. Others had gone home. For more than three months, Madison had been the convention's driving intellectual force. He now generously summarized the experience: "There never was an assembly of men, charged with a great and arduous trust, who were more pure in their motives, or more exclusively or anxiously devoted to the object committed to them."

WHOSE CONSTITUTION? STRUGGLE FOR RATIFICATION

Supporters of the Constitution recognized that ratification would not be easy. After all, the convention had been authorized only to revise the Articles. Instead it produced a new plan that fundamentally altered relations between the states and the central government. (See Table 6.1.) The delegates dutifully dispatched copies of the Constitution to the Congress of Confederation, then meeting in New York City. That powerless body referred the document to the separate states without any recommendation. The fight for ratification had begun.

What issues separated Federalists from Antifederalists during debates over ratification?

Federalists and Antifederalists

Proponents of the Constitution enjoyed great advantages over the unorganized opposition. In the contest for ratification, they took no chances. Their most astute move was to adopt the label Federalist. The term cleverly suggested that they stood for a confederation of states rather than for a supreme national authority. In fact, they envisioned a strong centralized national government able to field a formidable army. Critics of the Constitution, who tended to be poorer, less urban, and less well educated than their opponents, cried foul, but they were stuck with the name Antifederalist, a misleading term that made their cause seem a rejection of the very notion of a federation of the states.

The Federalists recruited the most prominent public figures of the day. In every state convention, speakers favoring the Constitution were more polished and fully prepared than their opponents. In New York, the campaign to win ratification sparked publication of *The Federalist*, a brilliant series of essays written by Madison, Hamilton, and John Jay in 1787 and 1788. The nation's newspapers overwhelmingly supported the new government. Few journals even carried Antifederalist writings. In some states, the Federalists adopted questionable tactics to gain ratification. In Pennsylvania, for example, they achieved a quorum for a crucial vote by dragging opposition delegates into the meeting from the streets. In New York, Hamilton threatened upstate Antifederalists that New York City would secede from the state unless the state ratified the Constitution.

In these battles, the Antifederalists articulated a political philosophy that had popular appeal. Like the extreme republicans who drafted the first state constitutions, the Antifederalists were suspicious of political power. They warned that public officials, however selected, would scheme to expand their authority.

Preserving individual liberty required constant vigilance. The larger the republic, the greater the opportunity for political corruption. Local voters could not know what their representatives in a distant national capital were doing. The government the Constitution outlined invited precisely the kinds of problems that Montesquieu had described in *The Spirit of the Laws*: "In so extensive a republic," one Antifederalist declared, "the great officers of government would soon become above the control of the people, and abuse their power."

Read the **Document**
Publius James Madison Federalist Paper Number 10 on **myhistorylab.com**

Antifederalists demanded direct, personal contact with their representatives. Elected officials should reflect the character of their constituents as closely as possible. It seemed unlikely that in large congressional districts, the people could preserve such close ties with their representatives. According to the Antifederalists, the Constitution favored persons wealthy enough to have forged a reputation that extended

TABLE 6.1 Revolution or Reform? The Articles of Confederation and the Constitution Compared

Political Challenge	Articles of Confederation	Constitution
Mode of ratification or amendment	Require confirmation by every state legislature	Requires confirmation by three-fourths of state conventions or legislatures
Number of houses in legislature	One	Two
Mode of representation	Two to seven delegates represent each state; each state holds only one vote in Congress	Two senators represent each state in upper house; each senator holds one vote. One representative to lower house represents every 30,000 people (in 1788) in a state; each representative holds one vote
Mode of election and term of office	Delegates appointed annually by state legislatures	Senators chosen by state legislatures for six-year term (direct election after 1913); representatives chosen by vote of citizens for two-year term
Executive	No separate executive: Delegates annually elect one of their number as president, who possesses no veto, no power to appoint officers or conduct policy. Administrative functions of government theoretically carried out by Committee of States, practically by various single-headed departments	Separate executive branch: President elected by electoral college to four-year term; granted veto, power to conduct policy and appoint ambassadors, judges, and officers of executive departments established by legislation
Judiciary	Most adjudication left to state and local courts; Congress is final court of appeal in disputes between states	Separate branch consisting of Supreme Court and inferior courts established by Congress to enforce federal law
Taxation	States alone can levy taxes; Congress funds the Common Treasury by making requisitions for state contributions	Federal government granted powers of taxation
Regulation of commerce	Congress regulates foreign commerce by treaty but holds no check on conflicting state regulations	Congress regulates foreign commerce by treaty; all state regulations must obtain congressional consent

beyond a single community. Samuel Chase told the members of the Maryland ratifying convention that under the new system, "the distance between the people and their representatives will be so great that there is no probability of a farmer or planter being chosen … only the *gentry*, the *rich*, and the well-born will be elected."

Federalist speakers mocked their opponents' localist perspective. The Constitution deserved general support precisely because it ensured that future Americans would be represented by "natural aristocrats," individuals possessing greater insights, skills, and training than did the ordinary citizen. These talented leaders could discern the entire population's interests. They were not tied to the selfish needs of local communities. "The little demagogue of a petty parish or county will find his importance annihilated [under the Constitution] and his intrigues useless," predicted Charles Cotesworth Pinckney, a South Carolina Federalist.

Historians have generally accepted the Federalist critique. It would be a mistake, however, to see the Antifederalists as "losers" or as persons who could not comprehend social and economic change. Although their rhetoric echoed an older moral view of political culture, they accepted more easily than did many Federalists a liberal marketplace in which ordinary citizens competed as equals with the rich and well-born. They believed the public good was best served by allowing individuals like themselves to pursue their own private interests. They had been doing that on the local level during the 1780s and resented the imposition of elite controls over their affairs. Although the Antifederalists lost the battle over ratification, their ideas about political economy found many champions in the age of Andrew Jackson.

Many different types of people supported the Constitution. Historians have been unable to discover sharp correlations between wealth and occupation on the one hand and attitudes toward the proposed system of central government on the other. In general, Federalists lived in more commercialized areas than did their opponents. In the cities, artisans as well as merchants called for ratification. Farmers who were only marginally involved in commercial agriculture frequently voted Antifederalist.

Despite passionate pleas from Patrick Henry and other Antifederalists, most state conventions quickly adopted the Constitution. Delaware acted first (December 7, 1787). Within eight months of the Philadelphia meeting, eight of the nine states required to launch the government had ratified the document. The contests in Virginia (June 1788) and New York (July 1788) generated bitter debate, but they too joined the Union, leaving only North Carolina and Rhode Island outside the United States. Eventually (November 21, 1789, and May 29, 1790), even these states ratified the Constitution. Still, the vote had been close. The Constitution was ratified in New York by a tally of 30 to 27, in Massachusetts by 187 to 168, and in Virginia by 89 to 79. A few votes in key states could have defeated the new government. (See Map 6.3.)

While the state conventions sparked angry rhetoric, Americans soon closed ranks behind the Constitution. An Antifederalist who represented one Massachusetts village explained that "he had opposed the adoption of this Constitution; but that he had been overruled … by a majority of wise and understanding men [and that now] he should endeavor to sow the seeds of union and peace among the people he represented."

Read the **Document**
Patrick Henry, Against Ratification of the Constitution (1788) on **myhistorylab.com**

Quick Check
✓ What were the major political issues separating Federalists from Antifederalists?

Adding the Bill of Rights

The first ten amendments to the Constitution are the major legacy of the Antifederalist argument. In almost every state convention, opponents of the Constitution pointed to the need for greater protection of individual liberties, rights that people presumably had possessed in a state of nature. "It is necessary," wrote one Antifederalist, "that the sober and industrious part of the community should be defended from the rapacity and violence of the vicious and idle. A bill of rights, therefore, ought to set forth the purposes for which the compact is made, and serves to secure the minority against the usurpation and tyranny of the majority." The list of fundamental rights varied from state to state, but most Antifederalists demanded guarantees for jury trial and freedom of religion. They wanted prohibitions against cruel and unusual punishments. There was also considerable support for freedom of speech and of the press.

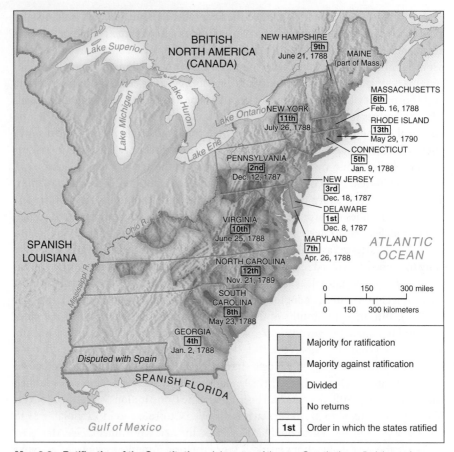

Map 6.3 *Ratification of the Constitution*   Advocates of the new Constitution called themselves Federalists, and those who opposed its ratification were known as Antifederalists.

Madison and others regarded the proposals with little enthusiasm. In *The Federalist* No. 84, Hamilton reminded the American people that "the constitution is itself … a BILL OF RIGHTS." But after the adoption of the Constitution had been assured, Madison moderated his stand. A bill of rights would appease able men such as George Mason and Edmund Randolph, who might otherwise remain alienated from the new federal system. "We have in this way something to gain," Madison concluded, "and if we proceed with caution, nothing to lose."

The crucial consideration was caution. People throughout the nation advocated a second constitutional convention to take Antifederalist criticism into account. Madison wanted to avoid such a meeting. He feared that members of the first Congress might use a bill of rights as an excuse to revise the entire Constitution.

Madison carefully reviewed these recommendations and the declarations of rights that had appeared in the early state constitutions. On June 8, 1789, he placed before the House of Representatives a set of amendments to protect individual rights from government interference. Madison told Congress that the greatest dangers to popular liberties came from "the majority [operating] against the minority."

A committee compressed his original ideas into ten amendments that were ratified and became known collectively as the Bill of Rights. For many modern Americans these amendments are the most important section of the Constitution. Madison had hoped that additions would be inserted into the text of the Constitution at the appropriate places, not tacked onto the end, but he was overruled.

The Bill of Rights protected the freedoms of assembly, speech, religion, and the press; guaranteed speedy trial by an impartial jury; preserved the people's right to bear arms; and prohibited unreasonable searches. Other amendments dealt with legal procedure. Some opponents of the Constitution urged Congress to provide greater safeguards for states' rights, but Madison had no intention of backing away from a strong central government. Only the Tenth Amendment addressed the states' relation to the federal system. To calm Antifederalist fears, this crucial article specified that those "powers not delegated to the United States by the Constitution, nor prohibited by it to the States, are reserved to the States respectively, or to the people."

On September 25, 1789, both houses of Congress passed the Bill of Rights. By December 15, 1791, three-fourths of the states had ratified the amendments. Madison was proud of his achievement. He had secured individual rights without undermining the Constitution. When he asked his friend Jefferson for his opinion of the Bill of Rights, Jefferson responded with typical republican candor: "I like [it] … as far as it goes; but I should have been for going further."

Read the **Document**
The Bill of Rights (1789) on **myhistorylab.com**

Quick Check

✓ Why did the men who originally drafted the Constitution not include a Bill of Rights?

CONCLUSION: SUCCESS DEPENDS ON THE PEOPLE

By 1789, one phase of American political experimentation had ended. The people gradually, often haltingly, had learned that in a republican society, they themselves were sovereign. They could no longer blame government failures on inept monarchs or greedy aristocrats. They bore a great responsibility. Americans had demanded a government of the people only to discover during the 1780s that in some situations, the people could not always be trusted with power, majorities could tyrannize minorities, and the best government could abuse individual rights.

Contemporaries had difficulty deciding just what had been accomplished. A writer in the *Pennsylvania Packet* thought the American people had preserved order: "The year 1776 is celebrated for a revolution in favor of liberty. The year 1787 … will be celebrated with equal joy, for a revolution in favor of Government." But aging Patriots grumbled that perhaps order had been achieved at too high a price. In 1788, Richard Henry Lee remarked, "'Tis really astonishing that the same people, who have just emerged from a long and cruel war in defense of liberty, should now agree to fix an elective despotism upon themselves and their posterity."

But most Americans probably would have accepted the optimistic assessment of Benjamin Franklin. As he watched the delegates to the Philadelphia convention sign the Constitution, he noted a sun carved on the back of George Washington's chair. "I have," the aged philosopher noted, "… often in the course of the session … looked at [the sun] behind the President without being able to tell whether it was rising or setting; but now at length I have the happiness to know that it is a rising and not a setting sun."

6 STUDY RESOURCES

((•—[**Listen** to the **Chapter Audio** for Chapter 6 on **myhistorylab.com**

TIMELINE

1776 Second Continental Congress authorizes colonies to create republican government (May), p. 149
- Eight states draft new constitutions; two others already enjoy republican government by virtue of former colonial charters, p. 149

1777 Congress accepts Articles of Confederation (November), p. 150

1781 States ratify Articles of Confederation following settlement of Virginia's western land claims, p. 151

1783 Society of the Cincinnati raises a storm of criticism, p. 143

1785 Congress passes Land Ordinance for Northwest Territory, p. 152

1786 Annapolis Convention suggests revising the Articles of Confederation (September), p. 155
- Shays's Rebellion frightens American leaders, p. 156

1787–1788 All states except North Carolina and Rhode Island ratify Constitution, p. 163

1791 Bill of Rights (first ten amendments to the Constitution) ratified, p. 165

CHAPTER REVIEW

DEFINING REPUBLICAN CULTURE

What were the limits of equality in the "republican" society of the new United States?

Some Americans worried that the scramble for material wealth would undermine republican values in the new nation. Disparities in wealth made some worry that a hereditary aristocracy might grow up to dominate government. Elites worried that democratic excesses would lead to men without property, and the personal independence and stability that came with it, rising to power. Enslaved African Americans and most women were denied the rights to property and the independence required to become full citizens of a republican society. *(p. 142)*

STUMBLING TOWARD A NEW NATIONAL GOVERNMENT

Why did many Americans regard the Articles of Confederation as inadequate?

During the Revolution, Americans showed little interest in establishing a strong national government. Under the Articles of Confederation (1777), an underfunded Congress limped along without direction, while the states competed over western lands. Only after Virginia ceded its claims could Congress draft the Northwest Ordinance, which provided an orderly plan for settling the Ohio Valley. The weak Congress was not even able to force the British to live up to their obligations under the Treaty of Paris of 1783. *(p. 150)*

"HAVE WE FOUGHT FOR THIS?"

Why did Constitutional delegates compromise on representation and slavery?

James Madison's Virginia Plan for the Constitution called for representation in both houses of Congress to be proportional to a state's population. Small states objected that this would put them at the mercy of larger states. Southern states feared that more populous northern states might vote to outlaw slavery. To prevent a breakdown, the delegates compromised. Each state would have an equal number of representatives in the Senate and slaves would be counted as three-fifths of a person when determining representation for the federal government. *(p. 153)*

WHOSE CONSTITUTION? STRUGGLE FOR RATIFICATION

What issues separated Federalists from Antifederalists during debates over ratification?

During the debates of 1787–88, Federalists, who favored stronger national government, defended the Constitution against Antifederalists, who opposed centralized authority. By the end of 1791, enough state conventions had endorsed the Constitution for ratification. To appease the Antifederalists, Congress in 1789 added a Bill of Rights to protect the freedoms of citizens against the power of the national government. *(p. 161)*

KEY TERM QUESTIONS

1. What did republicanism represent for most eighteenth-century Americans? (p. 142)

2. Why did African Americans form the African Methodist Episcopal Church? (p. 146)

3. Why were the authors of the state constitutions so concerned with natural rights? (p. 149)

4. Why did the Articles of Confederation favor the sovereignty of the states rather than that of the federal government? (p. 150)

5. How did the Northwest Ordinance resolve the problem of the western lands? (p. 153)

6. Did Shays's Rebellion betray or uphold the spirit of the American Revolution? (p. 156)

7. How did the New Jersey Plan differ from the Virginia Plan? (p. 157)

8. Why was the three-fifths rule necessary to achieve ratification of a new constitution? (p. 158)

9. What issues separated Federalists from Antifederalists during debates over ratification? (p. 161)

10. Why did Antifederalists oppose the Constitution? (p. 161)

11. Why did the men who originally drafted the Constitution not include a Bill of Rights? (p. 165)

MYHISTORYLAB CONNECTIONS

Visit **www.myhistorylab.com** for a customized Study Plan to build your knowledge of *The Republican Experiment*.

Question for Analysis

1. What drove Phillis Wheatley to write on the subjects discussed in her poetry?

   Read the Document *Phill is Wheatley, Religious and Moral Poems* p. 146

2. Why did the disposition of western lands cause an impasse in the ratification of the Articles of Confederation?

   View the Map *Western Land Claims Ceded by the States* p. 151

3. What motivated Daniel Shays to lead a rebellion?

   Read the Document *Military Reports of Shays's Rebellion* p. 156

4. Was slavery protected by the Constitution?

   Watch the Video *Slavery and the Constitution* p. 158

5. Why was Patrick Henry against ratification of the Constitution?

   Read the Document *Patrick Henry, Against Ratification of the Constitution?* p. 163

Other Resources from this Chapter

Read the Document *George Washington, Manners and Etiquette*

Read the Document *Slave Petition to the General Assembly in Connecticut*

Read the Document *Richard Allen, "Address to the Free People of Colour"*

Read the Document *John Adams to Abigail Adams, July 3, 1776*

Read the Document *Molly Wallace Valedictory Address, 1792*

Read the Document *John Dickinson, Letters from a Farmer in Pennsylvania*

View the Image *James Madison, Portrait*

Read the Document *The Debates in the Federal Convention of 1787*

Read the Document *Publius James Madison Federalist Paper Number 10*

Read the Document *The Bill of Rights*

7 Democracy and Dissent

The Violence of Party Politics, 1788–1800

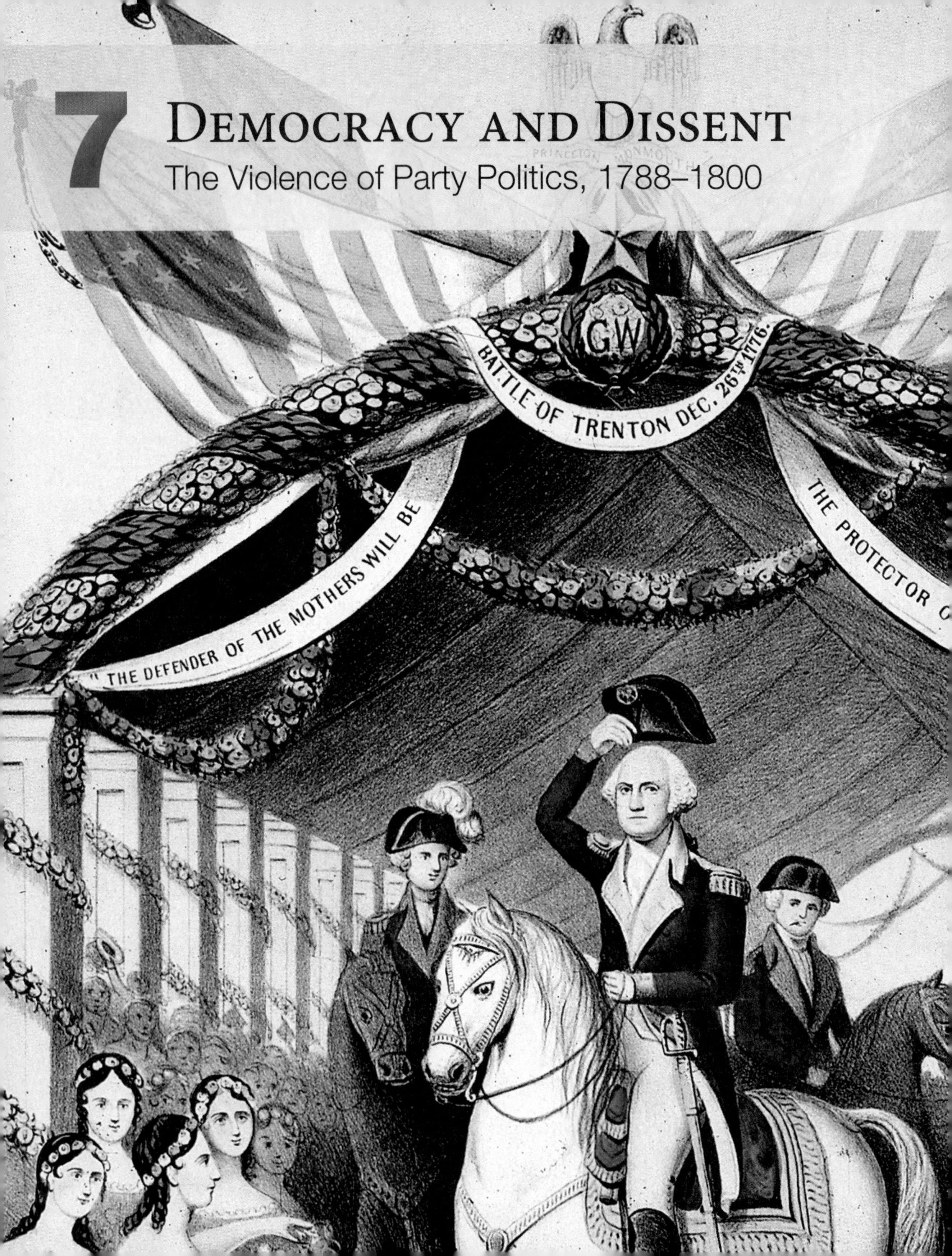

Contents and Spotlight Questions

PRINCIPLE AND PRAGMATISM: ESTABLISHING A NEW GOVERNMENT PG. 171

Why was George Washington unable to overcome division within the new government?

HAMILTON'S PLAN FOR PROSPERITY AND SECURITY PG. 173

Why did many Americans oppose Alexander Hamilton's blueprint for national prosperity?

CHARGES OF TREASON: THE BATTLE OVER FOREIGN AFFAIRS PG. 176

How did foreign affairs affect domestic politics during the 1790s?

POPULAR POLITICAL CULTURE PG. 181

Why was it hard for Americans to accept political dissent as a part of political activity?

THE ADAMS PRESIDENCY: POLITICS OF MISTRUST PG. 183

Why were some Federalists willing to sacrifice political freedoms for party advantage?

((•—[**Listen** to the **Chapter Audio** for Chapter 7 on **myhistorylab.com**

FORCE OF PUBLIC OPINION

While presiding over the first meeting of the U.S. Senate in 1789, Vice President John Adams called the senators' attention to a pressing procedural question: How would they address George Washington, the newly elected president? Adams insisted that Washington deserved an impressive title to lend dignity and weight to his office. The vice president warned the senators that if they called Washington simply "president of the United States," the "common people of foreign countries [as well

The Hero of Trenton Well-wishers spread flowers in front of George Washington as he rides through Trenton, New Jersey, on his way from Virginia to New York for his inauguration as the first president of the United States in 1789.

as] the sailors and soldiers [would] despise him to all eternity." Adams recommended "His Highness, the President of the United States, and Protector of their Liberties." Some senators favored "His Elective Majesty" or "His Excellency."

Adams's initiative caught many persons, including Washington, by surprise. They regarded the debate as ridiculous. James Madison, a member of the House of Representatives, announced that pretentious European titles were ill-suited to the "genius of the people" and "the nature of our Government." Thomas Jefferson, who was then working as a diplomat in Paris, could not comprehend what motivated the vice president. In private correspondence, he repeated Benjamin Franklin's judgment that Adams "means well for his Country, is always an honest Man, often a wise one, but sometimes, and in some things, absolutely out of his senses." When the senators learned that their efforts embarrassed Washington, they dropped the topic. The leader of the new republic would be called president of the United States. One wag, however, dubbed the portly Adams "His Rotundity."

The comic-opera quality of the debate about how to address Washington should not obscure the participants' concern about setting government policy. The members of the first Congress could not take the survival of republican government for granted. All of them, of course, wanted to secure the Revolution. The recently ratified Constitution transferred sovereignty from the states to the people, a bold and unprecedented decision that many Americans feared would generate chronic instability. Translating constitutional abstractions into practical legislation would have been difficult, even under the most favorable conditions. But these were trying times. Britain and France, rivals again in a century of war, put nearly unbearable pressures on the leaders of the new republic and, in the process, made foreign policy a bitterly divisive issue.

Although no one welcomed them, political parties gradually took shape. Neither the Jeffersonians (also called the Republicans) nor the Federalists—as the two major groups were called—doubted that the United States would one day become a great commercial power. They differed, however, on how best to manage the transition from an agrarian household economy to an international system of trade and industry. The Federalists encouraged rapid integration of the United States into a world economy, but however enthusiastic they were about capitalism, they did not trust the people or local government to do the job effectively. A modern economy, they insisted, required strong national institutions that would be directed by a social elite who understood the financial challenge and would work in the best interests of the people.

Such claims frightened persons who came to identify themselves as Jeffersonians. Strong financial institutions, they thought, had corrupted the government of Britain from which they had just separated themselves. They searched for alternative ways to accommodate the needs of commerce and industry. Unlike the Federalists, the Jeffersonians put their faith in the people, defined for the most part politically as white yeoman farmers. The Jeffersonians insisted that ordinary entrepreneurs, if they could be freed from intrusive government regulations, could be trusted to resist greed and crass materialism and to sustain the virtue of the republic.

During the 1790s, former allies were surprised to discover themselves at odds over such basic issues. One person—Hamilton, for example—would stake out a position. Another, such as Jefferson or Madison, would respond, perhaps speaking a little more extravagantly than a specific issue demanded, goaded by the rhetorical nature of public debate. The first would then rebut the new position passionately. By the mid-1790s, this dialectic had almost spun out of control, taking the young republic to the brink of political violence.

Leaders of every persuasion had to learn to live with "public opinion." The revolutionary elite had invited the people to participate in government, but the gentlemen assumed that ordinary voters would automatically defer to their social betters. Instead, the Founders discovered they had created a rough-and-tumble political culture, a robust public sphere of cheap newspapers and street demonstrations. The newly empowered "public" followed the great debates of the period through articles they read in hundreds of highly partisan journals and magazines.

PRINCIPLE AND PRAGMATISM: ESTABLISHING A NEW GOVERNMENT

In 1788, George Washington enjoyed great popularity. The people remembered him as the selfless leader of the Continental Army. Even before the states had ratified the Constitution, everyone assumed he would be chosen president of the United States. He received the unanimous support of the electoral college, an achievement that no subsequent president has duplicated. John Adams, a respected Massachusetts lawyer who had championed independence in 1776, was elected vice president.

Why was George Washington unable to overcome division within the new government?

Getting Started

Washington owed much of his success as the nation's first president to an instinctive feeling for the symbolic possibilities of political power. Although he possessed only modest speaking abilities and never matched the intellectual brilliance of some contemporaries, Washington sensed that he had come to embody the hopes and fears of the new republic. Without ever displaying the attributes necessary to achieve charisma—an instinctive ability that some leaders have to merge their own personality with the abstract goals of the government—he carefully monitored his official behavior. Washington knew that if he did not demonstrate the existence of a strong republic, people who championed the sovereignty of the individual states would attempt to weaken federal authority before it was ever established.

View the **Image**
Washington Taking the Oath of Office on **myhistorylab.com**

The first Congress quickly established executive departments. Some congressmen wanted to prohibit presidents from dismissing cabinet-level appointees without Senate approval, but James Madison—still a voice for a strong, independent executive—successfully resisted this restriction on presidential authority. The chief executive could not function unless he had confidence in the people with whom he worked. In 1789, Congress created the Departments of War, State, and the Treasury, and as secretaries, Washington nominated Henry Knox, Thomas Jefferson, and Alexander Hamilton, respectively. Edmund Randolph served as part-time attorney general, a position that ranked slightly lower than the head of a department.

To modern Americans accustomed to a huge federal bureaucracy, Washington's government seems amazingly small. When Jefferson arrived in New York, the first national capital, to take over the State Department, for example, he found two chief clerks, two assistants, and a part-time translator. With this tiny staff, he not only maintained contacts with the representatives of foreign governments, collected information about world affairs, and communicated with U.S. officials overseas, but also organized the first federal census in 1790.

Congress also provided for a federal court system. The Judiciary Act of 1789 created a Supreme Court staffed by a chief justice and five associate justices. It also set up 13 district courts authorized to review the decisions of the state courts. John Jay, a leading figure in New York politics, became chief justice. But since federal judges in the 1790s were expected to travel hundreds of miles over terrible roads to attend sessions of the inferior courts, few persons of outstanding talent and training joined Jay on the federal bench.

Remembering the financial insecurity of the old Confederation government, the new Congress passed the tariff of 1789, a tax of approximately 5 percent on imports. The new levy generated considerable revenue for the young republic. Even before it went into effect, however, the act sparked controversy. Southern planters, who relied heavily on European imports and the northern shippers who could control the flow of imports into the South, claimed that the tariff discriminated against southern interests in favor of those of northern merchants.

View the **Image**
*Washington's First
Cabinet* on
myhistorylab.com

Quick Check

✓ What was the structure of the federal government under President Washington?

Conflicting Visions: Jefferson and Hamilton

Washington's first cabinet included two extraordinary personalities, Alexander Hamilton and Thomas Jefferson. Both had served with distinction during the Revolution, were recognized by contemporaries as men of genius and ambition, and brought to public office a vision of how the American people could achieve greatness.

However much these two men had in common, serious differences emerged. Washington's secretaries disagreed on how the United States should fulfill its destiny. As head of the Treasury Department, Hamilton urged his fellow citizens to think in terms of bold commercial development, of farms and factories embedded within a complex financial network that would reduce the nation's reliance on foreign trade. Because Britain already had an elaborate banking and credit system, Hamilton looked to that country for economic models that might be reproduced on this side of the Atlantic.

Hamilton was also concerned about the people's role in public policy. His view of human nature caused him to fear democratic excess. He assumed that in a republican society, the gravest threat to political stability was anarchy rather than monarchy. The best hope for the survival of the republic, Hamilton believed, lay with the country's moneyed classes. If the wealthiest people could be persuaded that their economic self-interest could be advanced—or at least made less insecure—by the central government, then they would work to strengthen it, and thus bring more prosperity to the common people. Hamilton saw no conflict between private greed and public good; one was the source of the other.

On almost every detail, Jefferson challenged Hamilton's analysis. The secretary of state assumed that the strength of the American economy lay not in its industrial potential but in its agricultural productivity. The "immensity of land" represented the country's major economic resource. Contrary to the claims of some critics, Jefferson did not advocate agrarian self-sufficiency or look back nostalgically to a golden age dominated by simple yeomen. He recognized the necessity of change. While he thought that those who worked the soil were more responsible citizens than those who labored in factories for wages, he encouraged the nation's farmers to participate in an expanding international market. Americans could exchange raw materials "for finer manufactures than they are able to execute themselves."

Unlike Hamilton, Jefferson had faith in the American people's ability to shape policy. He instinctively trusted the people, feared that uncontrolled government power might destroy their liberties, and insisted that public officials follow the letter of the Constitution, a frame of government he described as "the wisest ever presented to men." The greatest threat to the young republic, he argued, came from the corrupt activities of pseudo-aristocrats, persons who placed the protection of "property" and "civil order" above the preservation of "liberty." To tie the nation's future to the selfish interests of a privileged class—bankers, manufacturers, and speculators—seemed cynical and dangerous. He despised speculators who encouraged "the rage of getting rich in a day." Such "gaming" promoted the kinds of vice that threatened republican government. To mortgage the future of the common people by creating a large national debt struck Jefferson as insane. But the responsibility for shaping the economy of the new nation fell mainly to Alexander Hamilton as the first secretary of the treasury.

Quick Check

✓ Why did Alexander Hamilton and Thomas Jefferson find it so difficult to cooperate as members of Washington's cabinet?

HAMILTON'S PLAN FOR PROSPERITY AND SECURITY

The unsettled state of the nation's finances was a staggering challenge for the new government. Hamilton threw himself into the task. He read deeply in economic literature. He developed a questionnaire to find out how the U.S. economy worked and sent it to commercial and political leaders throughout the country. But when Hamilton's three major reports—on public credit, banking, and manufacturers—were complete, they bore the stamp of his own creative genius. The secretary synthesized a vast amount of information into an economic blueprint so complex, so innovative that even his allies were baffled.

Hamilton presented his *Report on the Public Credit* to Congress on January 14, 1790. His research revealed that the nation's outstanding debt was approximately $54 million. This sum represented obligations that the U.S. government had incurred during the Revolutionary War. It included foreign loans and loan certificates the government had issued to its own citizens and soldiers. But that was not all.

Why did many Americans oppose Alexander Hamilton's blueprint for national prosperity?

The states owed creditors approximately $25 million. During the 1780s, Americans desperate for cash had sold government certificates to speculators at greatly discounted prices. Approximately $40 million of the nation's debt was owed to 20,000 people, only 20 percent of whom were the original creditors.

Debt as a Source of National Strength

Hamilton's *Report on the Public Credit* contained two major recommendations covering funding and assumption. First, under his plan, the United States promised to fund its foreign and domestic obligations at full face value. Current holders of loan certificates, whoever they were and no matter how they had obtained them, could exchange the old certificates for new government bonds bearing a moderate rate of interest. Second, the secretary urged the federal government to assume responsibility for paying the remaining state debts.

Hamilton reasoned that his credit system would accomplish several goals. It would reduce the power of the individual states in shaping national economic policy, something Hamilton regarded as essential in maintaining a strong federal government. Moreover, the creation of a fully funded national debt would signal to foreign and domestic investors that the United States was now solvent, that its bonds represented a good risk. Hamilton argued that investment capital, which might otherwise flow to Europe, would remain in this country, providing money for commercial and industrial investment. In short, he invited the country's wealthiest citizens to invest in the future of the United States. Critics claimed that the only people who stood to profit from the scheme were Hamilton's friends—some of whom sat in Congress and who had purchased many public securities at very low prices.

To Hamilton's surprise, Madison—his friend and collaborator in writing *The Federalist*—attacked the funding scheme in the House of Representatives. The Virginia congressman agreed that the United States should honor its debts. He worried, however, about the citizens and soldiers who, because of financial hardship, had been compelled to sell their certificates at prices far below face value. If the government treated the current holders of certificates less generously, Madison declared, then there might be sufficient funds to provide equitable treatment for the distressed Patriots. Whatever its moral justification, Madison's plan proved unworkable. Too many records had been lost since the Revolution for the Treasury Department to identify all the original holders. In February 1790, Congress defeated Madison's proposal.

The assumption portion of Hamilton's plan unleashed even greater criticism. Some states had already paid their revolutionary debts. Hamilton's program seemed designed to reward certain states—Massachusetts and South Carolina, for example—simply because they had failed to put their finances in order. The secretary's congressional opponents also became suspicious that assumption was merely a ploy to increase the power and wealth of Hamilton's friends.

On April 12, a rebellious House led by Madison defeated assumption. The victory was short-lived. Hamilton and his supporters resorted to legislative horse trading to pass his program. In exchange for locating the new federal capital on the Potomac River, a move that would stimulate the depressed economy of north-ern Virginia, key congressmen who shared Madison's political philosophy changed their votes on assumption. Hamilton may also have offered Virginia more federal money than it deserved. In August, Washington signed assumption and funding into law. The first element of Hamilton's design was now in place.

Quick Check

✓ What did Alexander Hamilton hope his new credit system would accomplish?

Interpreting the Constitution: The Bank Controversy

Hamilton submitted his second report to Congress in January 1791. He proposed that the government charter a national bank. This private institution would be funded in part by the federal government. Indeed, since the Bank of the United States would own millions of dollars of new U.S. bonds, its financial stability would be tied directly to the strength of the federal government and, of course, to the success of Hamilton's program. The secretary of the treasury argued that a growing financial community required a central bank to facilitate complex commercial transactions. The bank not only would serve as the main depository of the U.S. government but also would issue currency acceptable to pay federal taxes. Because of that guarantee, the money would maintain its value while in circulation.

Madison and others in Congress raised a howl of protest. While they were not oblivious to the services a national bank might provide for a growing country, they suspected that banks—especially those modeled on British institutions—might "perpetuate a large monied interest" in the United States. The Constitution said nothing about chartering financial corporations. Critics warned that if Hamilton and his supporters were allowed to stretch fundamental law on this occasion, they could not be held back in the future. Popular liberties would be at the mercy of whoever held office. "To take a single step," Jefferson warned, "beyond the bound-aries thus specifically drawn around the powers of Congress is to take possession of a boundless field of power, no longer susceptible to definition." On this issue, Hamilton refused to compromise: "This is the first symptom of a spirit which must either be killed or will kill the constitution of the United States."

Even though the bank bill passed Congress (February 8), Washington considered vetoing it on constitutional grounds. Before doing so, however, he requested written opinions from his cabinet. Jefferson's rambling, wholly predictable attack on the bank was not one of his more persuasive performances. By contrast, Hamilton wrote a mas-terful essay. He assured the president that Article I, Section 8 of the Constitution— "The Congress shall have Power ... To make all Laws which shall be necessary and proper for carrying into Execution the foregoing Powers"—justified issuing charters to national banks. The "foregoing Powers" on which Hamilton placed so much weight were taxation, regulation of commerce, and making war. He articulated a doctrine of implied powers that the Constitution did not explicitly grant to the fed-eral government, but which it could be interpreted to grant. His interpretation of the Constitution was something that neither Madison nor Jefferson had anticipated. Ham-ilton's "loose construction" carried the day. Washington signed the bank act into law.

Hamilton triumphed in Congress, but the general public reacted with fear and hostility. When news of his proposal to fund the national debt at full face value

Quick Check

✓ How did Hamilton justify the creation of the Bank of the United States?

leaked out, for example, speculators rushed to rural areas to buy loan certificates from unsuspecting citizens at bargain prices. To backcountry farmers, making money without physical labor appeared immoral, unrepublican, and un-American. When the greed of a former Treasury official led to several serious bankruptcies in 1792, ordinary citizens began to listen more closely to what Madison, Jefferson, and their associates were saying about corruption in high places.

Setback for Hamilton

In his third major report, *Report on Manufactures*, submitted to Congress in December 1791, Hamilton revealed the final details of his grand design for the economic future of the United States. This lengthy document suggested ways the federal government might stimulate manufacturing. To free itself from dependence on European imports, Hamilton observed, the country had to develop its own industry—textile mills, for example. Without government intervention, however, the process would take decades. Americans would continue to invest in agriculture. But protective tariffs and industrial bounties would accelerate the growth of a balanced economy. With proper planning, the United States would soon hold its own with Britain and France.

📖 **Read** the **Document** *Alexander Hamilton, Opposing Visions for the New Nation* on **myhistorylab.com**

In Congress, the battle lines were drawn. Hamilton's opponents—not yet a disciplined party but a loose coalition of men who shared Madison's and Jefferson's misgivings about the secretary's program—ignored his economic arguments. Instead, they engaged him on moral and political grounds. Madison railed against the dangers of "consolidation," which threatened to concentrate power in the federal government, leaving the states defenseless.

Jefferson attacked the *Report on Manufactures* from a different angle. He assumed—largely because Europe's urban poverty had horrified him—that cities breed vice. The government, Jefferson argued, should not promote their development. He believed that Hamilton's proposal guaranteed that American workers would leave the countryside and crowd into urban centers: "I think our government will remain virtuous for many centuries as long as they [the people] are chiefly agricultural … When they get piled upon one another in large cities, as in Europe, they will become corrupt as in Europe." Southern congressmen also saw tariffs and bounties as vehicles for enriching Hamilton's northern friends at the planters' expense. The recommendations in the *Report on Manufactures* were soundly defeated in the House of Representatives.

Quick Check

✓ Why did Congress reject Hamilton's *Report on Manufactures*?

CHARGES OF TREASON: THE BATTLE OVER FOREIGN AFFAIRS

How did foreign affairs affect domestic politics during the 1790s?

During Washington's second term (1793–1797), war in Europe thrust foreign affairs into the forefront of American life. The impact of this development on domestic politics was devastating. Officials who had disagreed on economic policy now began to identify their interests with either Britain or France, Europe's most powerful nations. Political differences, however trivial, were suddenly cited as evidence that one group or the other had entered into treasonous correspondence with external enemies eager to compromise the independence and prosperity of the United States.

Formal political organizations—the Federalists and Republicans—were born in this poisonous atmosphere. The clash between the groups developed over how best to preserve the new republic. The Republicans (Jeffersonians) advocated states' rights, strict interpretation of the Constitution, friendship with France, and vigilance against "the avaricious, monopolizing Spirit of Commerce and Commercial Men." The Federalists urged a strong national government, central economic planning, closer ties with Britain, and maintenance of public order, even if that meant calling out federal troops.

The Peril of Neutrality

Britain treated the United States arrogantly. The young republic could not even compel its old adversary to comply with the Treaty of 1783, in which the British had agreed to vacate military posts in the Northwest Territory. In 1794, approximately 1,000 British soldiers still occupied American land, an obstruction that Governor George Clinton of New York claimed had excluded U.S. citizens "from a very valuable trade to which their situation would naturally have invited them." Moreover, even though 75 percent of American imports came from Britain, that country refused to grant the United States full commercial reciprocity. Among other provocations, it barred American shipping from the lucrative West Indian trade.

France presented a different challenge. In May 1789, Louis XVI, desperate for revenue, authorized a meeting of a representative assembly known as the

Execution of Louis XVI The execution of the king by French revolutionaries deepened the growing political division in America. Although they deplored the excesses of the Reign of Terror, Jeffersonian Republicans continued to support the French people. Federalists feared that the violence and lawlessness would spread to the United States.

Estates General. By so doing, the king unleashed revolutionary forces that eventually toppled the monarchy and cost him his life (January 1793). The men who seized power—and they came and went rapidly—were militant republicans, ideologues eager to liberate all Europe from feudal institutions. In the early years of the French Revolution, France drew on the American experience. Thomas Paine and the Marquis de Lafayette enjoyed great popularity. But the French could not stop the revolutionary violence. Constitutional reform turned into bloody purges. One radical group, the Jacobins, guillotined thousands of its opponents and suspected monarchists during the so-called Reign of Terror (October 1793–July 1794). These horrific events left Americans confused. While those who shared Jefferson's views cheered the spread of republicanism, others who sided with Hamilton condemned French expansionism and political excess.

Read the **Document** *Proclamation of Neutrality* on **myhistorylab.com**

In the face of growing international tension, neutrality seemed the most prudent course for the United States. But that policy was easier for a weak country to proclaim than defend. In February 1793, France declared war on Britain—what the leaders of revolutionary France called the "war of all peoples against all kings." These powerful European rivals immediately challenged the official American position on shipping: "free ships make free goods," meaning that belligerents should not interfere with the shipping of neutral carriers. To make matters worse, no one was certain whether the Franco-American treaties of 1778 (see Chapter 5) legally bound the United States to support its old ally against Britain.

Both Hamilton and Jefferson wanted to avoid war. The secretary of state, however, believed that nations desiring American goods should be forced to honor American neutrality. If Britain treated the United States as a colonial possession, if the Royal Navy stopped American ships on the high seas and forced seamen to serve the king—in other words, if it impressed American sailors—then the United States should award France special commercial advantages. Hamilton thought Jefferson's scheme insane. He pointed out that Britain had the largest navy in the world and was not likely to be coerced by American threats. The United States, he counseled, should appease the former mother country even if that meant swallowing national pride.

Quick Check

✓ Why could America's political leaders not ignore the French Revolution?

Jay's Treaty Sparks Domestic Unrest

Britain's refusal to abandon its forts in the Northwest Territory remained a source of tension. In June 1793, a new element was added. The London government blockaded French ports to neutral shipping. In November, the Royal Navy captured hundreds of American vessels trading in the French West Indies. The British had not even given the United States advance warning of a change in policy. Outraged members of Congress, especially those who identified with Jefferson and Madison, demanded retaliation: an embargo, stopping debt payment, even war.

Before this rhetoric produced armed struggle, Washington made an effort to preserve peace. In May 1794, he sent Chief Justice John Jay to London to negotiate a formidable list of grievances. Jay's main objectives were removal of the British forts on U.S. territory, payment for ships taken in the West Indies, improved commercial relations, and acceptance of the American definition of neutral rights.

Jefferson's supporters—by now called the Republican interest—anticipated a treaty favorable to the United States. After all, they explained, the war with France had not gone well for Britain, and the British people were surely desperate for American foodstuffs. Even before Jay departed, however, his mission stood little chance of success. Hamilton, anxious as ever to placate the British, had secretly informed British officials that the United States would compromise on most issues.

When Jay reached London, he encountered polite but firm resistance. His efforts resulted in a political humiliation known as **Jay's Treaty**. The chief justice did persuade the British to abandon their frontier posts and allow small American ships to trade in the British West Indies, but the British rejected outright the U.S. position on neutral rights. The Royal Navy would continue to search American vessels for contraband and impress sailors suspected of being British citizens. There would be no compensation for the ships seized in 1793 until the Americans paid British merchants for debts contracted before the Revolution. And to the annoyance of southerners, not a word was said about the slaves the British had carried off at the conclusion of the war. While Jay salvaged peace, he appeared to have betrayed the national interest.

Read the
Document
The Jay Treaty on
myhistorylab.com

News of Jay's Treaty produced an outcry. Even Washington was apprehensive. He submitted the document to the Senate without recommending ratification, a sign that the president was not happy with the results of Jay's mission. After a bitter debate, the Senate, controlled by Federalists, accepted a revised version of the treaty. The vote was 20 to 10, the bare two-thirds majority the Constitution required.

The details of the Jay agreement soon leaked to the press. The popular journals sparked a firestorm of objection. Throughout the country, people who had formerly been apathetic about national politics were swept up in a wave of protest. Urban mobs condemned Jay's alleged sellout; rural settlers burned him in effigy. Jay jokingly told friends he could find his way across the country simply by following the light of those fires. Southerners announced they would not pay prerevolutionary debts to British merchants. The Virginia legislature proposed a constitutional amendment reducing the Senate's role in treaty-making.

In the House, Republican congressmen, led by Madison, thought they could stop Jay's Treaty by refusing to appropriate funds to implement it. They demanded that Washington show the House state papers relating to Jay's mission. The challenge raised complex constitutional issues. The House was claiming a voice in treaty ratification, a power explicitly reserved to the Senate. There was also the question of executive secrecy in the interest of national security. Washington told the rebellious representatives that "the nature of foreign negotiations requires caution; and their success must often depend on secrecy."

The president played a trump card. He raised the possibility that the House was contemplating his impeachment. This, of course, was unthinkable. Even criticizing Washington in public was politically dangerous. As soon as he redefined the issue before Congress, petitions supporting the president flooded into the nation's capital. The Maryland legislature, for example, declared its "unabated reliance on the integrity, judgment, and patriotism of the President of the United States," a statement that called into question the patriotism of certain Republican congressmen. The Federalists won a stunning tactical victory over the opposition. Had a less popular man than Washington occupied the presidency, however, they would not have fared so well. The division between the two parties was now beyond repair. The Republicans labeled the Federalists "the British party"; Federalists believed that the Republicans were in league with the French.

By the time Jay's Treaty became law (June 14, 1795), the two giants of Washington's first cabinet had retired. Late in 1793, Jefferson returned to his Virginia plantation, Monticello. Despite his separation from day-to-day political affairs, he remained the chief spokesman for the Republican party. His rival, Hamilton, left the Treasury in January 1795 to practice law in New York City. He maintained close ties with important Federalists. Even more than Jefferson, Hamilton concerned himself with the details of party organization.

Quick Check

✓ Why did Jay's Treaty spark such hostility throughout the nation?

Pushing the Native Americans Aside

Before Britain finally withdrew its troops from the Great Lakes and Northwest Territory, British officers encouraged local Indian groups—the Shawnee, Chippewa, and Miami—to attack American settlers and traders. The Indians, who even without British encouragement knew that the newcomers intended to seize their land, won several impressive victories over federal troops in the area that would become western Ohio and Indiana. In 1790, General Josiah Harmar led his soldiers into an ambush. The following year, an army under General Arthur St. Clair suffered more than 900 casualties near the Wabash River. But the Indians were militarily more vulnerable than they realized. When confronted with a U.S. army under General Anthony Wayne, they received no support from the British. At the Battle of Fallen Timbers (August 20, 1794), Wayne's forces crushed Indian resistance in the Northwest Territory. The native peoples were compelled to sign the Treaty of Greenville, formally ceding to the U.S. government the land that became Ohio. In 1796, the last British soldiers departed for Canada.

Shrewd negotiations mixed with pure luck helped secure the nation's southwestern frontier with Spain. For complex reasons involving European diplomacy, Spanish officials in 1795 encouraged the U.S. representative in Madrid, Thomas Pinckney, to discuss the navigation of the Mississippi River. Before this initiative, the Spanish government not only had closed the river to American commerce but had incited the Indians to harass American settlers. Relations between the two countries probably would have deteriorated further had the United States not signed Jay's Treaty. The Spanish assumed—erroneously—that Britain and the United States had formed an alliance to strip Spain of its North American possessions.

To avoid this imagined disaster, officials in Madrid offered Pinckney extraordinary concessions: the opening of the Mississippi, the right to deposit goods in New Orleans without paying duties, a secure southern boundary on the 31st parallel (a line roughly parallel to the northern boundary of Florida and running west to the Mississippi), and a promise to stay out of Indian affairs. An amazed Pinckney signed the Treaty of San Lorenzo (Pinckney's Treaty) on October 27, 1795. In March 1796, the Senate ratified it without a single dissenting vote. Pinckney, who came from a prominent South Carolina family, became the hero of the Federalist party. (See Map 7.1.)

Quick Check

✓ Why did "The opening of the Mississippi" figure so prominently in American Politics during the 1790s?

POPULAR POLITICAL CULTURE

More than any other event during Washington's administration, ratification of Jay's Treaty generated intense political strife. Even as members of Congress voted as Republicans or Federalists, they condemned the rising partisan spirit as a threat to the stability of the United States. Popular writers equated "party" with "faction" and "faction" with "conspiracy to overthrow legitimate authority." Party conflict

Why was it hard for Americans to accept political dissent as a part of political activity?

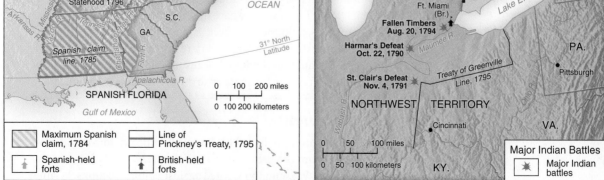

Map 7.1 *Conquest of the West*   Withdrawal of the British, defeat of Native Americans, and negotiations with Spain secured the nation's frontiers.

also suggested that Americans had lost the common purpose that had united them during the Revolution. Contemporaries did not appreciate the beneficial role that parties could play in presenting alternative solutions to foreign and domestic problems. Organized opposition smacked of disloyalty and therefore had to be eliminated by any means—fair or foul.

Whiskey Rebellion: Charges of Republican Conspiracy

Political tensions became explosive in 1794. The Federalists convinced themselves that the Republicans were actually prepared to employ violence against the U.S. government. Although the charge was baseless, it took on plausibility in the context of growing party strife.

The crisis developed when farmers in western Pennsylvania protested a federal excise tax on distilled whiskey that Congress had passed in 1791. They did not relish paying any taxes, but this tax struck them as particularly unfair. They made a good deal of money distilling their grain into whiskey, and the excise threatened to put them out of business.

Largely because the Republican governor of Pennsylvania refused to suppress the angry farmers, Washington and other leading Federalists assumed that the insurrection represented a direct political challenge. The president called out 15,000 militiamen and, accompanied by Hamilton, he marched against the rebels. The expedition was a fiasco. The distillers disappeared. Predictably, no one in the Pittsburgh region seemed to know where the troublemakers had gone. Two supposed rebels were convicted of high crimes against the United States; one was reportedly a "simpleton" and the other insane. Washington pardoned both men. As peace returned to the frontier, Republicans gained electoral support from voters the Federalists had alienated.

In the national political forum, however, the Whiskey Rebellion had just begun. Spokesmen for both parties offered sinister explanations for the seemingly innocuous affair. Washington blamed the Republican clubs for promoting civil unrest. He apparently believed that the opposition party had dispatched French agents to western Pennsylvania to undermine the federal government. In November 1794, Washington informed Congress that these "self-created societies"—the Republican political clubs—had inspired "a spirit inimical to all order." Indeed, the Whiskey Rebellion had been "fomented by combinations of men who ... have disseminated, from an ignorance or perversion of facts, suspicions, jealousies, and accusations of the whole Government."

The president's interpretation of this rural tax revolt was no more charitable than the conspiratorial explanation the Republicans offered. Jefferson labeled the entire episode a Hamiltonian device to create an army to intimidate Republicans.

Read the
Document
*George Washington,
Whiskey Rebellion
Address to the Congress (1794)* on
myhistorylab.com

Quick Check

✓ Why did Washington and his supporters see the Whiskey Rebellion as something more sinister than just an "embarassing fiasco"?

Washington's Farewell

In September 1796, Washington published his Farewell Address, formally declaring his intention to retire from the presidency. In the address, printed in newspapers throughout the country, Washington warned against political factions. Written largely by Hamilton, who drew on a draft Madison had prepared years earlier, the

The Whiskey Rebellion Tarring and feathering federal officials was one way western Pennsylvanians protested the tax on whiskey in 1794. Washington's call for troops to put down the insurrection drew more volunteers than he had been able to raise during most of the Revolution. (*Source: Whiskey Rebellion, c. 1790s, hand-colored woodcut/North Wind Picture Archives.*)

address served narrowly partisan ends. The product of growing political strife, it sought to advance the Federalist cause in the forthcoming election. By waiting until September to announce his retirement, Washington denied the Republicans time to organize an effective campaign. There was an element of irony in this initiative. Washington had always maintained he stood above party. While he may have done so early in his presidency, events such as Jay's Treaty and the suppression of the Whiskey Rebellion transformed him in the eyes of many Americans into a spokesman solely for Hamilton's Federalist party.

Washington also spoke about foreign policy in the address. He counseled the United States to avoid permanent alliances with distant nations that had no real interest in American security. This statement guided foreign relations for years and became the credo of American isolationists, who argued that the United States should steer clear of foreign entanglements.

> **Quick Check**
> ✓ In what ways was Washington's Farewell Address in 1796 a piece of party propaganda?

THE ADAMS PRESIDENCY: POLITICS OF MISTRUST

The election of 1796 took place in an atmosphere of mutual distrust. Jefferson, soon to be the vice president, informed a friend that "an Anglican and aristocratic party has sprung up, whose avowed object is to draw over us the substance, as they have already done the forms, of British government." The Federalists were convinced their Republican opponents wanted to hand the government over to French radicals.

During the campaign, the Federalists sowed the seeds of their eventual destruction. Party stalwarts agreed that John Adams should stand against the Republican candidate, Thomas Jefferson. Hamilton, however, schemed to deprive Adams of the

> **Why** were some Federalists willing to sacrifice political freedoms for party advantage?

presidency. He apparently feared that an independent-minded Adams would be difficult to manipulate. He was correct.

Hamilton exploited an awkward feature of the electoral college. In accord with the Constitution, each elector cast two ballots. The person who gained the most votes became president. The runner-up, regardless of party affiliation, became vice president. Ordinarily the Federalist electors would have cast one vote for Adams and one for Thomas Pinckney, the hero of the negotiations with Spain and the party's choice for vice president. Everyone hoped, of course, there would be no tie. Hamilton secretly urged southern Federalists to support only Pinckney, even if that meant throwing away an elector's second vote. If everything had gone according to plan, Pinckney would have received more votes than Adams. But when New Englanders loyal to Adams heard of Hamilton's maneuvering, they dropped Pinckney. When the votes were counted, Adams had 71, Jefferson 68, and Pinckney 59. (See Table 7.1.) Hamilton's treachery angered the new president and heightened tensions within the Federalist party.

The XYZ Affair and Domestic Politics

Foreign affairs immediately occupied Adams's attention. The French regarded Jay's Treaty as an affront. By allowing Britain to define the conditions for neutrality, the United States had in effect sided with that nation against France.

Relations between France and the United States had deteriorated. The French refused to receive Charles Cotesworth Pinckney, the U.S. representative in Paris. Pierre Adet, the French minister in Philadelphia, openly tried to influence the 1796 election in favor of the Republicans. His meddling not only embarrassed Jefferson, it offended the American people. The situation then took a violent turn. In 1797, French privateers began seizing American ships. Since neither the United States nor France declared war, the hostilities came to be known as the Quasi-War.

Hamilton and his friends welcomed an outpouring of anti-French sentiment. The High Federalists—Hamilton's wing of the party—counseled the president to prepare for all-out war, hoping that war would purge the United States of French influence. Adams would not escalate the conflict. He dispatched a special

TABLE 7.1 The Election of 1796		
Candidate	**Electoral Vote**	**Party**
J. Adams	Federalist	71
Jefferson	Republican	68
T. Pinckney	Federalist	59
Burr	Republican	30

commission to Paris in an attempt to remove the sources of antagonism. This famous negotiating team consisted of Charles Pinckney, John Marshall, and Elbridge Gerry. They were instructed to obtain compensation for the ships French privateers had seized and release from the treaties of 1778. Federalists still worried that this old agreement might oblige the United States to defend French colonies in the Caribbean against British attack, which they were reluctant to do. In exchange, the commission offered France the same commercial privileges Jay's Treaty granted to Britain. While the diplomats negotiated, Adams talked of strengthening American defenses, rhetoric that pleased militant Federalists.

The outrageous treatment it received in France shocked the commission. Instead of dealing directly with Talleyrand, the French foreign minister, they met with obscure intermediaries who demanded a huge bribe. The commission reported that Talleyrand would not open negotiations unless he was given $250,000. The French government also expected a "loan" of millions of dollars. The Americans refused to play this insulting

President Adams John Adams in the suit and sword he wore for his 1797 inauguration. The portrait is by English artist William Winstanley, 1798.

game. Pinckney replied, "No, no, not a sixpence," and with Marshall he returned to the United States. When they arrived home, Marshall offered his much-quoted toast: "Millions for defense, but not one cent for tribute."

Diplomatic humiliation set off a political explosion. When Adams presented the commission's official correspondence to Congress—the names of Talleyrand's lackeys were labeled X, Y, and Z—the Federalists burst out with a war cry. At last, they would be able to even old scores with the Republicans. In April 1798, a Federalist newspaper in New York City announced that any American who refused to censure France "must have a soul black enough to be *fit for treasons, strategems, and spoils.*" Rumors of conspiracy, referring to the incident as the XYZ Affair, spread through the country. Friendships between Republicans and Federalists were shattered. Jefferson described the tense political atmosphere in a letter to an old colleague: "You and I have formerly seen warm debates and high political passions. But gentlemen of different politics would then speak to each other, and separate the business of the Senate from that of society. It is not so now. Men who have been intimate all their lives, cross the streets to avoid meeting, and turn their heads another way, lest they should be obliged to touch their hats."

Quick Check

✓ During the XYZ affair, why did representatives of the French Government treat American diplomats with such disrespect?

Crushing Political Dissent

In spring 1798, High Federalists assumed that Adams would ask Congress for a declaration of war. In the meantime, they pushed for rearmament, new warships, harbor fortifications, and, most important, an expanded U.S. Army. About the need for land forces, Adams remained skeptical. He saw no likelihood of French invasion.

The president missed the political point. The Federalists wanted the army not to thwart French aggression but to stifle internal opposition. Indeed, militant Federalists used the XYZ Affair to institute what Jefferson termed the "reign of witches." The threat to the Republicans was not simply a figment of the vice president's overwrought imagination. When Theodore Sedgwick, a Federalist senator from Massachusetts, learned of the commission's failure, he observed in words that capture the High Federalists' vindictiveness, "It will afford a glorious opportunity to destroy faction. Improve it."

During summer 1798, a provisional army gradually came into existence. Washington agreed to lead the troops, but only if Adams appointed Hamilton second in command. This demand placed the president in a dilemma. Several revolutionary veterans—Henry Knox, for example—outranked Hamilton. Moreover, the former secretary of the treasury had consistently undermined Adams's authority. To give Hamilton a powerful position seemed awkward at best. When Washington insisted, however, Adams was forced to appoint Hamilton.

The chief of the High Federalists threw himself into recruiting and supplying the troops. No detail escaped his attention. He and Secretary of War James McHenry made certain that in this political army, only loyal Federalists received commissions. They even denied Adams's son-in-law a post. The entire enterprise took on an air of unreality. Hamilton longed for military glory. He may have contemplated attacking Spain's Latin American colonies. His obsession, however, was to restore political order. No doubt he agreed with a Federalist senator from Connecticut who predicted that the Republicans "never will yield till violence is introduced; we must have a partial civil war … and the bayonet must convince some, who are beyond the reach of other arguments."

Hamilton should not have treated Adams with such open contempt. Adams was still the president. Without presidential cooperation, Hamilton could not fulfill his grand military ambitions. Yet whenever pressing questions concerning the army arose, Adams was nowhere to be found. He let commissions lie on his desk unsigned; he took overlong vacations to New England. He made it clear his first love was the navy. In May 1798, the president persuaded Congress to establish the Navy Department. For this new cabinet position, he selected Benjamin Stoddert, who did not take orders from Hamilton. Moreover, Adams further infuriated the High Federalists by refusing to ask Congress for a declaration of war. When they pressed him, Adams threatened to resign, making Jefferson president. As the weeks passed, the American people increasingly regarded the idle army as an expensive extravagance.

Quick Check

✓ Why were the high Federalists willing to place party advantage over the welfare of the entire nation?

Silencing Political Opposition: The Alien and Sedition Acts

The Federalists did not rely solely on the army to crush dissent. During the summer of 1798, Congress passed four bills known collectively as the **Alien and Sedition Acts**. This legislation authorized using federal courts and the powers of the presidency to silence the Republicans. The acts were born of fear and vindictiveness. To punish Jefferson's followers, the Federalists created the nation's first major crisis over civil liberties.

Congress drew up three Alien Acts. The first, the Alien Enemies Law, vested the president with extraordinary wartime powers. On his own authority, he could detain or deport citizens of nations with which the United States was at war and who behaved in a manner he thought suspicious. Since Adams refused to ask for a declaration of war, this legislation never went into effect. A second act, the Alien Law, empowered the president to expel any foreigner from the United States by executive decree. Congress limited the acts to two years. While Adams did not attempt to enforce them, the mere threat of arrest caused Frenchmen to flee the country. The third act, the Naturalization Law, was the most flagrantly political. It established a 14-year probationary period before foreigners could apply for U.S. citizenship. Recent immigrants, especially the Irish, tended to vote Republican. The Naturalization Law, therefore, was designed to keep "hordes of wild Irishmen" away from the polls for as long as possible.

The Sedition Law struck at the heart of free political exchange. It defined criticism of the U.S. government as criminal libel; citizens found guilty by a jury were

Party Conflict In the early years of the republic, political dissent sometimes escalated to physical violence. This fistfight took place on the floor of Congress, February 15, 1798. The combatants are Republican Matthew Lyon and Federalist Roger Griswold.

Read the
Document
*The Alien and Sedi-
tion Acts (1798)* on
myhistorylab.com

Quick Check

✓ Why did leaders of
the Federalist party
not appreciate that
the Alien and Sedi-
tion Acts undermined
the Constitution of
the United States?

subject to fines and imprisonment. Congress entrusted enforcement of the act to the federal courts. Republicans justly worried that the Sedition Law undermined rights guaranteed by the First Amendment. The High Federalists dismissed their complaints: The Constitution, they declared, did not condone "the most ground-less and malignant lies, striking at the safety and existence of the nation." They were determined to shut down the opposition press and were willing to give the government almost dictatorial powers to do so. The Jeffersonians also expressed concern over the federal judiciary's expanded role in punishing sedition. They believed such matters were best left to state officials.

The Federalists' enforcement of the Sedition Law did not silence opposition—indeed, it sparked even greater criticism and created martyrs. The administration's actions persuaded Republicans that the survival of free government was at stake. Time was running out. "There is no event," Jefferson warned, "… however atrocious, which may not be expected."

Kentucky and Virginia Resolutions

By the fall of 1798, Jefferson and Madison were convinced that the Federalists envisioned the creation of a police state. According to Madison, the Sedition Law "ought to produce universal alarm." It threatened the free communication of ideas that he "deemed the only effectual guardian of every other right." Extreme Republicans such as John Taylor of Virginia recommended secession from the Union; others advocated armed resistance. But Jefferson counseled against such strategies. "This is not the kind of opposition the American people will permit," he reminded his desperate supporters. The last best hope for American freedom lay in the state legislatures.

Read the
Document
*The Kentucky and
Virginia Resolutions
(1798, 1799)* on
myhistorylab.com

As the crisis deepened, Jefferson and Madison drafted separate protests known as the **Kentucky and Virginia Resolutions**. Both statements defended the right of individual state assemblies to interpret the constitutionality of federal law. Jefferson wrote the Kentucky Resolutions in November 1798. In an outburst of partisan anger, he flirted with a doctrine of nullification that was as dangerous to the survival of the United States as anything Hamilton and his High Federalist friends advanced.

In the Kentucky Resolutions, Jefferson described the federal union as a compact. The states transferred certain explicit powers to the national government, but they retained full authority over all matters the Constitution did not specifically mention. Jefferson rejected Hamilton's broad interpretation of the "general welfare" clause.

When Madison drafted the Virginia Resolutions in December, he took a more temperate stand. Madison urged the states to defend the rights of the American people, but he resisted the notion that a single state legislature could or should overthrow federal law.

The Virginia and Kentucky Resolutions were not intended as statements of abstract principles and most certainly not as a justification for southern secession. They were pure political party propaganda. Jefferson and Madison reminded

American voters during a period of severe domestic tension that the Republicans offered an alternative to Federalist rule. No other state legislatures passed the Resolutions. Even in Virginia, where the Republicans enjoyed broad support, important figures such as John Marshall and George Washington criticized the states' rights argument.

Quick Check

✓ How did the Kentucky and Virginia Resolutions propose to protect American freedoms?

Adams's Finest Hour

In February 1799, President Adams belatedly declared his independence from the Hamiltonian wing of the Federalist party. Throughout the confrontation with France, Adams had shown little enthusiasm for war. Following the XYZ debacle, he began to receive reports that Talleyrand had changed his tune. The French foreign minister told Elbridge Gerry and other Americans that the bribery episode had been an unfortunate misunderstanding. If the United States sent new representatives, he would negotiate in good faith. The High Federalists ridiculed this report. But Adams threw his waning prestige behind peace. In February, he asked the Senate to confirm William Vans Murray as U.S. representative to France.

When the new negotiators—Oliver Ellsworth and William Davie joined Murray—arrived in France in November 1799, they discovered that yet another group had come to power there. This government, headed by Napoleon Bonaparte, cooperated in drawing up an agreement known as the Convention of Mortefontaine. The French refused to compensate the Americans for vessels taken during the Quasi-War, but they declared the treaties of 1778 null and void. Moreover, the convention removed annoying French restrictions on U.S. commerce. Not only had Adams avoided war, he had created an atmosphere of mutual trust that paved the way for the purchase of the Louisiana Territory.

Quick Check

✓ Was the Convention of Mortefontaine a victory for American diplomacy?

The Peaceful Revolution: The Election of 1800

On the eve of the election of 1800, the Federalists were fatally divided. Adams enjoyed wide popularity among the rank and file, especially in New England, but articulate party leaders such as Hamilton vowed to punish the president for betraying their militant policies. The former secretary of the treasury attempted to rig the voting in the electoral college, so that the party's vice presidential candidate, Charles Cotesworth Pinckney, would receive more ballots than Adams and America would be saved from "the fangs of Jefferson." As in 1796, the conspiracy backfired. The Republicans gained 73 votes while the Federalists trailed with 65.

However, the election was not resolved in the electoral college. When the ballots were counted, Jefferson and his running mate, Aaron Burr, had tied. This accident—a Republican elector should have thrown away his second vote—sent the selection of the next president to the House of Representatives, a lame-duck body that the Federalist party still controlled. (See Table 7.2.)

As the House began its work on February 27, 1801, excitement ran high. Each state delegation cast a single vote, with nine votes needed for election. On the first

((•—[Listen to the **Audio File** *Jefferson and Liberty* on **myhistorylab.com**

TABLE 7.2   The Election of 1800

Candidate	Electoral Vote	Party
Jefferson	Republican	73
Burr	Republican	73
J. Adams	Federalist	65
C. Pinckney	Federalist	64

ballot, Jefferson received the support of eight states, Burr six, and two states divided evenly. People predicted a quick victory for Jefferson, but after dozens of ballots, the House had still not selected a president. The drama dragged on for six days. To add to the confusion, Burr refused to withdraw. Contemporaries thought his ambition had overcome his good sense.

The logjam finally broke when leading Federalists decided that Jefferson, whatever his faults, would make a more responsible president than would the shifty Burr. Even Hamilton labeled Burr "the most dangerous man of the community." On the thirty-sixth ballot, Representative James A. Bayard of Delaware announced he no longer supported Burr. This decision, coupled with Burr's inaction, gave Jefferson the presidency, ten states to four.

The Twelfth Amendment, ratified in 1804, saved the American people from repeating this potentially dangerous turn of events. Henceforth, the electoral college cast separate ballots for president and vice president.

During the final days of his presidency, Adams appointed as many Federalists as possible to the federal bench. Jefferson protested the hasty manner in which these "midnight judges" were selected. One of them, John Marshall, became chief justice of the United States, a post he held with distinction for 34 years. But behind the last-minute flurry of activity lay bitterness and disappointment. Adams never forgave Hamilton. The Federalist party was left splintered and dispirited. On the morning of Jefferson's inauguration, Adams slipped away from the capital—now located in Washington, D.C.—unnoticed and unappreciated.

In the address that Adams missed, Jefferson attempted to quiet partisan fears. "We are all republicans; we are all federalists," the new president declared. By this statement, he did not mean to suggest that party differences were no longer important. Jefferson reminded his audience that whatever the politicians might say, the people shared a deep commitment to a federal union based on republican ideals set forth during the American Revolution. Indeed, the president interpreted the election of 1800 as revolutionary, the fulfillment of the principles of 1776.

Recent battles, of course, colored Jefferson's judgment. The contests of the 1790s had been hard fought, the outcome often in doubt. Jefferson looked back at this period as a confrontation between the "advocates of republican and those of kingly government." He believed that only his own party's vigilance had saved the country from Federalist "liberticide."

Read the **Document**
Jefferson's First Inaugural Address (1801) on **myhistorylab.com**

Quick Check

✓ What did Jefferson mean when he claimed in his first inaugural address that "We are all Republicans; we are all Federalists"?

CONCLUSION: DANGER OF POLITICAL EXTREMISM

From a broader historical perspective, the election of 1800 seems noteworthy for what did not occur. There were no riots, no attempted coup, no secession from the Union, only the peaceful transfer of government from the leaders of one political party to those of the opposition.

Americans had weathered the Alien and Sedition Acts, the meddling by predatory foreign powers in domestic affairs, the shrill partisan rhetoric of hack journalists, and now, at the start of a new century, they were impressed with their own achievement. As one woman who attended Jefferson's inauguration noted, "The changes of administration which in every government and in every age have most generally been epochs of confusion, villainy and bloodshed, in this our happy country take place without any species of distraction, or disorder." But as she understood—indeed, as modern Americans must constantly relearn—extremism in the name of partisan political truth can easily unravel the delicate fabric of representative democracy and leave the republic at the mercy of those who would manipulate the public for private benefit.

7 STUDY RESOURCES

((•●—|Listen to the **Chapter Audio** for Chapter 7 on **myhistorylab.com**

TIMELINE

1789 George Washington inaugurated (April), p. 169
- Louis XVI of France calls meeting of the Estates General (May), p. 177

1790 Congress approves Hamilton's plan for funding and assumption of states' debts (July), p. 173

1791 Bank of the United States chartered (February), p. 175
- Congress rejects Hamilton's *Report on Manufactures* (December), p. 176

1793 France's revolutionary government announces a "war of all people against all kings" (February), p. 178
- Jefferson resigns as secretary of state (December), p. 180

1794 U.S. Army puts down Whiskey Rebellion (July–November), p. 182
- General Anthony Wayne defeats Indians at Battle of Fallen Timbers (August), p. 180

1795 Hamilton resigns as secretary of the treasury (January), p. 180
- Jay's Treaty divides the nation (June), p. 180
- Pinckney's Treaty with Spain is a welcome surprise (October), p. 181

1796 Washington's Farewell Address (September), p. 182
- John Adams elected president (December), p. 184

1797 XYZ Affair poisons U.S. relations with France (October), p. 185

1798–1800 Quasi-War with France, p. 184

1798 Congress passes the Alien and Sedition Acts (June and July), p. 187
- Virginia and Kentucky Resolutions protest the Alien and Sedition Acts (November and December), p. 188

1800 Convention of Mortefontaine ends Quasi-War with France (September), p. 189

1801 House of Representatives elects Thomas Jefferson president (February), p. 190

CHAPTER REVIEW

PRINCIPLE AND PRAGMATISM: ESTABLISHING A NEW GOVERNMENT

Why was George Washington unable to overcome division within the new government?

Despite his huge popularity among all segments of the American population, President Washington was unable to bridge the differences between the two most brilliant and strong-willed members of his cabinet: Thomas Jefferson and Alexander Hamilton. These two men fought throughout Washington's presidency over their different visions for the future of the republic. Hamilton imagined an urban commercial nation with a strong central government; Jefferson championed a simple agrarian republic. *(p. 171)*

HAMILTON'S PLAN FOR PROSPERITY AND SECURITY

Why did many Americans oppose Alexander Hamilton's blueprint for national prosperity?

Many citizens – especially farmers and former soldiers felt resented that Hamilton's plan to fund state loan certificates at full value would reward the immoral, unrepublican and un-American actions of speculators by allowing them to make money without physical labor. Many also complained that this plan rewarded the financial irresponsibility of states like Massachusetts and South Carolina. Supporters of Jefferson rejected Hamilton's vision of the United States as a commercial and manufacturing nation, feared that his plan for a Bank of the United States would "perpetuate a large monied interest," and protested that his doctrine of implied powers would lead to the steady growth of governmental power. *(p. 173)*

CHARGES OF TREASON: THE BATTLE OVER FOREIGN AFFAIRS

How did foreign affairs affect domestic politics during the 1790s?

The French Revolution split American opinion. Republicans cheered it; Federalists condemned it. When France declared war on Britain (1793), The French Revolution split American opinion. Republicans cheered it; Federalists condemned it. The extremely unpopular Jay's Treaty (1794) with

Britain provoked heated political debate between its Federalist supporters and Republican opponents. Disagreements over how to deal with French aggression and insults during the Quasi-War and the XYZ Affair drove a wedge between the peace-seeking President John Adams and the High Federalists who called for war and military expansion. This divide helped Jefferson win the election of 1800. *(p. 176)*

POPULAR POLITICAL CULTURE

Why was it hard for Americans to accept political dissent as a part of political activity?

In the 1790s, many Americans equated political dissent with disloyalty. During the Whiskey Rebellion (1794), both Federalists and Republicans feared the other party planned to use violence to crush political opposition. In the 1790s, many Americans lamented the loss of unity that had tied them together during the struggle for independence. Moreover, because equated political dissent with disloyalty, they feared that partisan politics might lead to a conspiracy to overthrow the legitimately elected government. During the Whiskey Rebellion (1794), both Federalists and Republicans feared the other party planned to use violence to crush political opposition. *(p. 181)*

THE ADAMS PRESIDENCY: POLITICS OF MISTRUST

Why were some Federalists willing to sacrifice political freedoms for party advantage?

Many Republicans believed that the support of Jeffersonian Republicans for France had compromised American sovereignty. Hamilton and the High Federalists believed that a standing army was necessary to defend against invasion and to silence domestic dissent so that it could not split the republic apart. They rationalized that the sacrifice of political liberties entailed in the Alien and Sedition Acts were necessary to protect the Republic from corrupting foreign (particularly French influences). This was especially important since they anticipated the onset of a war with France. They used the rationale of national security to justify their pursuit of party power. *(p. 183)*

KEY TERM QUESTIONS

1. How did Hamilton justify the creation of the Bank of the United States? (p. 175)

2. Why did Hamilton articulate a doctrine of implied powers? (p. 175)

3. Why could America's leaders not ignore the French Revolution? (p. 178)

4. Why did Jay's Treaty spark such hostility? (p. 179)

5. Why did Washington and his supporters see the Whiskey Rebellion as more sinister than just an "embarrassing fiasco"? (p. 182)

6. Why was Washington's Farewell Address in 1796 a piece of party propaganda? (p. 182)

7. Why did the United States and France fight a Quasi-War rather than a declared war in 1797? (p. 184)

8. During the XYZ Affair, why did representatives of the French government treat American diplomats with such disrespect? (p. 185)

9. Why did Federalist leaders not understand that the Alien and Sedition Acts undermined the Constitution? (p. 187)

10. How did the Kentucky and Virginia Resolutions propose to protect American freedoms? (p. 188)

MyHISTORYLAB CONNECTIONS

Visit **www.myhistorylab.com** for a customized Study Plan to build your knowledge of *Democracy and Dissent.*

Question for Analysis

1. How did Hamilton's vision for the nation differ from Jefferson?

   Read the **Document** *Alexander Hamilton, Opposing Visions for the New Nation* p. 176

2. What was the significance of the Jay Treaty?

   Read the **Document** *The Jay Treaty* p. 179

3. What did Washington seek to accomplish with address to Congress regarding the Whiskey Rebellion?

   Read the **Document** *George Washington, Whiskey Rebellion Address to Congress (1794)* p. 181

4. What were the Alien and Sedition Acts designed to do?

   Read the **Document** *The Alien and Sedition Acts (1798)* p. 188

5. How did the Kentucky and Virginia Resolutions propose to protect American freedoms?

   Read the **Document** *The Kentucky and Virginia Resolutions (1798, 1799)* p. 188

Other Resources from this Chapter

View the **Image** *Washington Taking the Oath of Office*

View the **Image** *Washington's First Cabinet*

Read the **Document** *Proclamation of Neutrality*

Listen to the **Audio File** *Jefferson and Liberty*

Read the **Document** *Jefferson's First Inaugural Address*

8 REPUBLICAN ASCENDANCY
The Jeffersonian Vision, 1800–1814

Contents and Spotlight Questions

THE REPUBLIC EXPANDS   PG. 196

How did the Republic's growth shape the market economy and relations with Native Americans?

JEFFERSON AS PRESIDENT   PG. 200

How did practical politics challenge Jefferson's political principles?

RACE AND DISSENT UNDER JEFFERSON   PG. 203

How did Jeffersonians deal with the difficult problems of party politics and slavery?

EMBARRASSMENTS OVERSEAS   PG. 208

Why did the United States find it difficult to avoid military conflict during this period?

THE STRANGE WAR OF 1812   PG. 213

Why is the War of 1812 sometimes thought of as a "second war of independence"?

((•—|**Listen** to the **Chapter Audio** for Chapter 8 on **myhistorylab.com**

LIMITS OF EQUALITY

British visitors often expressed contempt for Jeffersonian society. Wherever they traveled in the young republic, they met ill-mannered people inspired with a passion for liberty and equality. Charles William Janson, an Englishman who lived in the United States for 13 years, recounted an exchange he found particularly unsettling that had occurred at the home of an American acquaintance: "On knocking at the door, it was opened by a servant maid, whom I had never before seen." The woman's behavior astonished Janson: "The following is the dialogue, word for word, which took place on this occasion:—'Is your master at home?'—'I have no

President Jefferson In 1800, Thomas Jefferson and Aaron Burr each received 73 electoral votes. The election was finally decided in February 1801 when the House of Representatives, on the thirty-sixth ballot, chose Jefferson by a vote of 10 to 4. This flag commemorates Jefferson's victory in the election.

master.'—'Don't you live here?'—'I stay here.'—'And who are you then?'—'Why, I am Mr.—'s *help*. I'd have you know, *man*, that I am no *sarvant* [sic]; none but *negers* [sic] are *sarvants*.'"

In this exchange, Janson encountered the authentic voice of Jeffersonian republicanism—self-confident, assertive, racist, and status conscious. The maid believed she was her employer's equal, perhaps not in wealth but surely in character. She may have even dreamed of owning a house staffed with "*help*." American society fostered such ambition. In the early nineteenth century, thousands of settlers poured across the Appalachians or moved to cities in search of opportunity. Thomas Jefferson and men who stood for public office under the banner of the Republican party claimed to speak for these people.

The limits of the Jeffersonian vision were obvious even to contemporaries. The people who spoke most eloquently about equal opportunity often owned slaves. As early as the 1770s, the famed English essayist Samuel Johnson had chided Americans for their hypocrisy: "How is it that we hear the loudest yelps for liberty from the drivers of Negroes?" Little had changed since the Revolution. African Americans, who represented one-fifth of the population of the United States, were excluded from the new opportunities opening up in the cities and the West. Indeed, the maid Janson encountered insisted—with no apparent sense of inconsistency—that her position was superior to that of blacks, who were brought involuntarily to lifelong servitude.

It is not surprising that in this highly charged racial climate Federalists accused the Republicans, especially those who lived in the South, of hypocrisy. In 1804, a Massachusetts Federalist sarcastically defined "Jeffersonian" as "an Indian word, signifying '*a great tobacco planter, who had herds of black slaves.*'" Race was always just beneath the surface of political maneuvering. Indeed, the acquisition of the Louisiana Territory and the War of 1812 fanned fundamental disagreement about the spread of slavery to the western territories.

In other areas, the Jeffersonians did not fulfill even their own high expectations. As members of an opposition party during the presidency of John Adams, they insisted on a strict interpretation of the Constitution, peaceful foreign relations, and reducing the federal government's role in the lives of average citizens. But once in power after the election of 1800, Jefferson and his supporters discovered that unanticipated pressures, foreign and domestic, forced them to moderate these goals. Before he retired from office in 1809, Jefferson interpreted the Constitution in a way that permitted the government to purchase the Louisiana Territory when the opportunity arose; he regulated the national economy with a rigor that would have surprised Alexander Hamilton; and he led the country to the brink of war.

How did the Republic's growth shape the market economy and relations with Native Americans?

THE REPUBLIC EXPANDS

During the early nineteenth century, the population of the United States grew substantially. The 1810 census counted 7,240,000 Americans, a jump of almost 2 million in ten years. Of this total, approximately 20 percent were black slaves, most of whom lived in the South. The large population increase was the result primarily of natural reproduction. During Jefferson's presidency few immigrants moved to the New World. The largest single group in this society was children under the age of 16, boys and girls who were born after Washington's election and who defined their own futures at a time when the nation's boundaries were rapidly expanding. For white Americans, it was a time of optimism. Many people with entrepreneurial skills or engineering capabilities aggressively advanced in a society that seemed to rate personal merit higher than family background.

Even as Americans defended the rights of individual states, they were forming strong regional identifications. In commerce and politics, they perceived themselves as representatives of distinct subcultures—southerners, New Englanders, or westerners. These broadening geographic horizons reflected improved transportation links that enabled people to travel more easily. But the growing regional mentality was also the product of defensiveness. While local writers celebrated New England's cultural distinctiveness, for example, they were uneasy about the region's rejection of the democratic values that were sweeping the rest of the nation. Moreover, people living south of the Potomac River began describing themselves as southerners, not as citizens of the Chesapeake or the Carolinas as they had done in colonial times.

This shifting focus of attention resulted not only from an awareness of shared economic interests but also from a sensitivity to outside attacks on slavery. Several times during the first 15 years of the nineteenth century, conspirators advocated secession. Though the schemes failed, they revealed powerful sectional loyalties that threatened national unity.

Westward the Course of Empire

The most striking changes occurred in the West. Before the end of the American Revolution, only Indian traders and a few hardy settlers had ventured across the Appalachians. After 1790, however, a flood of people rushed west to stake out farms on the rich soil. Many settlers followed the so-called northern route across Pennsylvania or New York into the old Northwest Territory. Pittsburgh and Cincinnati, both strategically located on the Ohio River, became important commercial ports. In 1803, Ohio joined the Union. Territorial governments were formed in Indiana (1800), Louisiana (1805), Michigan (1805), Illinois (1809), and Missouri (1812).

Pittsburgh *View of the City of Pittsburgh in 1817,* painted by a Mrs. Gibson while on her honeymoon. As the frontier moved west, Pittsburgh became an important commercial center.

Southerners poured into the new states of Kentucky (1792) and Tennessee (1796). Wherever they located, Westerners depended on water transportation. Because of the extraordinarily high cost of hauling goods overland, riverboats represented the only economical means of carrying agricultural products to distant markets. The Mississippi River was the crucial commercial link for the entire region. Westerners did not feel secure so long as Spain controlled New Orleans, the southern gate of the Mississippi.

Families that moved west attempted to transplant familiar eastern customs to the frontier. In areas such as the Western Reserve, a narrow strip of land along Lake Erie in northern Ohio, the influence of New England remained strong. In general, however, a creative mixing of peoples of different backgrounds in a strange environment generated distinctive folkways. Westerners developed their own heroes, such as Mike Fink, the legendary keelboatman of the Mississippi River; Daniel Boone, the famed trapper and Indian fighter; and the eye-gouging "alligatormen" of Kentucky and Tennessee. Americans who crossed the mountains were ambitious and self-confident, excited by the challenge of almost unlimited geographic mobility.

Quick Check

✓ What was the appeal of the West for so many Americans after 1790?

Tenskwatawa Tenskwatawa, known as the Prophet, provided spiritual leadership for the union of the native peoples he and his brother Tecumseh organized to resist white encroachment on Native American lands.

Native American Resistance

At the beginning of the nineteenth century, a substantial number of Native Americans lived in the greater Ohio Valley; the land belonged to them. The tragedy was that the Indians, many dependent on trade with the white people and ravaged by disease, lacked unity. Small groups of Native Americans, allegedly representing the interests of an entire tribe, sold off huge pieces of land, often for whiskey and trinkets.

Such fraudulent transactions disgusted the Shawnee leaders Tenskwatawa (known as the Prophet) and his brother Tecumseh. Tecumseh rejected classification as a Shawnee and may have been the first native leader to identify himself self-consciously as "Indian." These men attempted to revitalize native cultures. Against overwhelming odds, they briefly persuaded Native Americans living in the Indiana Territory to avoid contact with whites, resist alcohol, and, most important, hold on to their land. White intruders saw Tecumseh as a threat to progress. During the War of 1812, they shattered the Indians' dream of cultural renaissance. The populous Creek nation, located in the modern states of Alabama and Mississippi, also resisted the settlers' advance, but its warriors were crushed by Andrew Jackson's Tennessee militia at the Battle of Horseshoe Bend (March 1814).

Well-meaning Jeffersonians disclaimed any intention to destroy the Indians. The president talked of creating a vast reservation beyond the Mississippi River, just as the British had talked before the Revolution of a sanctuary beyond the Appalachians. He sent federal agents to "civilize" the Indians, to transform them into yeoman farmers. But even the most enlightened white thinkers did not believe Indians cultures were worth preserving. In fact, in 1835, the Democratic national convention selected a vice presidential candidate, Richard Johnson of Kentucky, whose major qualification for high office seemed to be that he had killed Tecumseh. And as early as 1780, Jefferson himself—then serving as the governor of Virginia—instructed a military leader on the frontier, "If we are to wage a campaign against these Indians the end proposed should be their extermination, or their removal beyond the lakes of the Illinois river. The same world will scarcely do for them and us."

Read the **Document** *Pennsylvania Gazette Indian Hostilities* on **myhistorylab.com**

Quick Check

✓ What would Tecumseh have thought of Federal attempts to "civilize" the Indians?

Commercial Life in the Cities

Before 1820, the prosperity of the United States depended primarily on agriculture and trade. Jeffersonian America was by no stretch of the imagination an industrial economy. Most of the population—84 percent in 1810—was directly involved in agriculture. Southerners concentrated on the staple crops of tobacco, rice, and cotton, which they sold on the European market. In the North, people generally produced livestock and grain.

The cities of Jeffersonian America functioned chiefly as depots for international trade. Only about 7 percent of the nation's population lived in urban centers. Most of these people owed their livelihoods either directly or indirectly to the carrying trade. Major port cities of the early republic—New York, Philadelphia, and Baltimore, for example—had some of the highest population densities ever recorded in this country's history. In 1800, more than 40,000 New Yorkers crowded into only 1.5 square miles; in Philadelphia, some 46,000 people were packed into less than one square mile. As is common today, many city dwellers rented living space. Since the demand for housing exceeded the supply, the rents were high.

American cities exercised only a marginal influence on the nation's vast hinterland. Because of the high cost of land

Spinning Mill Although cotton was an important trade in the early nineteenth century, technological advances in textile production were slow to take hold. Some spinning mills, such as the one pictured here, were built in New England, but what historians call the "Industrial Revolution" did not begin for several more decades.

transportation, urban merchants seldom purchased goods for export—flour, for example—from a distance of more than 150 miles. The separation between rural and urban Americans was far more pronounced during Jefferson's presidency than it was after the development of canals and railroads a few decades later (see Chapter 9).

There was some technological advancement. Samuel Slater, an English-born designer of textile machinery, established cotton-spinning mills in New England, but until the 1820s, these plants employed few workers. In fact, during this period households produced far more cloth than factories did. Another far-sighted inventor, Robert Fulton, sailed the first American steamship up the Hudson River in 1807. In time, this marvelous innovation opened new markets for domestic manufacturers, especially in the West. At the end of the War of 1812, however, few people anticipated how power generated by fossil fuel would transform the American economy.

Ordinary workers often felt threatened by the new machines. Skilled artisans who had spent years mastering a trade and took pride in producing an object that expressed their own personalities found the industrial workplace alienating. Moreover, they rightly feared that innovative technology designed to improve efficiency might throw traditional craftspeople out of work or transform independent entrepreneurs into dependent wage laborers.

Quick Check

✓ What was the character of cities in an expanding Republican economy?

JEFFERSON AS PRESIDENT

How did practical politics challenge Jefferson's political principles?

The District of Columbia seemed an appropriate capital for a Republican president. At the time of Jefferson's first inauguration in 1801, Washington was still an isolated rural village, a far cry from crowded Philadelphia and New York. Jefferson fit comfortably into Washington society. He despised ceremony and shocked foreign dignitaries by meeting them in his slippers or a threadbare jacket. He spent as much time as his duties allowed in reading and reflection.

But Jefferson was also a politician to the core. He ran for the presidency to achieve specific goals: reduce the size and cost of federal government, repeal obnoxious Federalist legislation such as the Alien Acts, and maintain international peace. To accomplish his program, Jefferson needed the full cooperation of congressional Republicans, some of whom were fiercely independent. Over such figures Jefferson exercised political mastery. He established close ties with the leaders of Congress. While he seldom announced his plans in public, his legislative lieutenants knew exactly what he desired. Contemporaries who described Jefferson as a weak president—and some Federalists did just that—did not read the scores of memoranda he sent to political friends or witness the meetings he held with important Republicans. In two terms as president, Jefferson never had to veto an act of Congress.

Jefferson carefully selected the members of his cabinet. During Washington's administration, he had witnessed—even provoked—severe infighting; as president, he nominated only those who enthusiastically supported his programs. James Madison, the leading figure at the Constitutional Convention, became secretary of state. For the Treasury, Jefferson chose Albert Gallatin, a Swiss-born financier who understood the complexities of the federal budget. "If I had the universe to choose from," the president announced, "I could not change one of my associates to my better satisfaction."

Political Reforms

A top priority of the new government was cutting the national debt. Throughout American history, presidents have advocated such reductions, but their rhetoric has seldom yielded tangible results. Jefferson succeeded. He and Gallatin regarded a large federal deficit as dangerous. Both men associated debt with Alexander Hamilton's Federalist financial programs, measures they considered harmful to republicanism. Jefferson claimed that legislators elected by the current generation did not have the right to mortgage the future of unborn Americans.

Jefferson also wanted to diminish the activities of the federal government. He urged Congress to repeal all direct taxes, including the tax that had sparked the Whiskey Rebellion in 1794. Secretary Gallatin calculated that customs receipts could fund the entire cost of national government. As long as commerce flourished, revenues were sufficient. When war closed foreign markets, however, the funds dried up.

To help pay the debt inherited from the Adams administration, Jefferson cut the national budget. He closed several American diplomatic missions in Europe and slashed military spending. In his first term, Jefferson reduced the size of the U.S. Army by 50 percent. Only 3,000 soldiers were left to guard the entire frontier. He also retired most of the navy's warships. When New Englanders claimed these cuts left the country defenseless, Jefferson countered with a glib argument. As ships of the U.S. Navy sailed the oceans, he claimed, they were liable to provoke hostilities, even war; by reducing the size of the fleet, he promoted peace.

More than budgetary considerations prompted Jefferson's military reductions. He was suspicious of standing armies. The militia could defend the republic if it were attacked. No doubt, his experiences during the Revolution influenced his thinking on military affairs, for in 1776, an aroused populace had taken up arms against the British. To ensure that the citizen soldiers would receive professional leadership, Jefferson created the Army Corps of Engineers and the military academy at West Point in 1802.

Political patronage was a burden for the new president. Republicans had worked hard for Jefferson's victory. As soon as he took office, they stormed the executive mansion seeking federal jobs. While the president controlled several hundred jobs, he refused to dismiss all the Federalists. To be sure, he acted quickly to remove the so-called midnight appointees, partisan selections that Adams had made after Jefferson's election. But to transform federal hiring into an undisciplined spoils system, especially at the highest levels of the federal bureaucracy, seemed to Jefferson to be shortsighted. Moderate Federalists might be converted to the Republican party. In any case, the government needed their expertise. At the end of his first term, half of the people holding federal office were appointees of Washington and Adams.

Jefferson's political moderation hastened the demise of the Federalist party. This loose organization had nearly destroyed itself during the election of 1800. After Adams's defeat, prominent Federalists such as Fisher Ames and John Jay withdrew from national affairs. They refused to adopt the popular forms of campaigning that the Republicans had developed so successfully during the late 1790s. The mere prospect of flattering the common people was odious enough to drive Federalists into political retirement.

Many of them also sensed that national expansion worked against their interests. The creation of new states and congressional reapportionment increased

Republican representatives in Washington. By 1805, the Federalists retained only a few seats in New England and Delaware. "The power of the [Jefferson] Administration," confessed John Quincy Adams in 1802, "rests upon the support of a much stronger majority of the people throughout the Union than the former administrations ever possessed since the first establishment of the Constitution."

After 1804, younger Federalists attempted to pump life into the dying party. They experimented with popular election techniques. In some states, they tightened party organization, held nominating conventions, and campaigned energetically for office. These were essential reforms, but except for a brief Federalist revival in the Northeast between 1807 and 1814, the results were disappointing. Even the younger Federalists thought it demeaning to appeal for votes. Diehards such as Timothy Pickering promoted wild secessionist schemes in New England. The most promising moderates—John Quincy Adams, for example—joined the Republicans.

Quick Check

✓ Why did Jefferson find it so difficult to reduce the size of the federal government?

The Louisiana Purchase

When Jefferson took office, he was confident that Louisiana and Florida would eventually become part of the United States. Spain owned these territories, and Jefferson assumed he could persuade the rulers of that notoriously weak nation to sell their colonies. If that peaceful strategy failed, the president was prepared to threaten forcible occupation.

In May 1801, however, prospects for the easy or inevitable acquisition of Louisiana darkened. Jefferson learned that Spain had transferred title to the entire region to France, its powerful northern neighbor. To make matters worse, the French leader Napoleon seemed intent on reestablishing an empire in North America. Even as Jefferson sought more information about the transfer, Napoleon was dispatching an army to suppress a rebellion in France's sugar-rich Caribbean colony, Haiti. From that island stronghold, French troops could occupy New Orleans and close the Mississippi River to American trade.

A sense of crisis enveloped Washington. Congressmen urged Jefferson to prepare for war against France. Tensions increased when the Spanish officials who still governed New Orleans announced the closing of that port to American commerce (October 1802). Jefferson assumed that the Spanish had acted on orders from France. Despite this provocation, the president preferred negotiations to war. In January 1803, he asked James Monroe, a loyal Republican from Virginia, to join the American minister, Robert Livingston, in Paris and explore the possibility of purchasing New Orleans.

By the time Monroe joined Livingston in France, Napoleon had lost interest in an American empire. The army he sent to Haiti succumbed to tropical diseases. By the end of 1802, more than 30,000 veteran troops had died there. The diplomats from the United States knew nothing of these developments. They were surprised, therefore, in April 1803 when Talleyrand, the French foreign minister, offered to sell the entire Louisiana Territory for only $15 million. The Louisiana Purchase doubled the size of the United States.

The American people responded enthusiastically to the news. Only a few disgruntled New England Federalists thought the United States was already too large. Jefferson was relieved. The nation had avoided war with France. Nevertheless, he

View the **Closer Look**
Map of the Louisiana Purchase of 1803 on **myhistorylab.com**

Watch the **Video**
Lewis and Clark: What Were They Trying to Accomplish? on **myhistorylab.com**

 Read the **Document**
Constitutionality of the Louisiana Purchase (1803) on **myhistorylab.com**

worried that the purchase might be unconstitutional. The president pointed out that the Constitution did not specifically authorize acquiring vast new territories and thousands of foreign citizens. To escape this apparent legal dilemma, Jefferson proposed amending the Constitution. Few persons, even his closest advisers, shared the president's scruples. Events in France soon forced Jefferson to adopt a more pragmatic course. When he heard that Napoleon had become impatient for his money, Jefferson rushed the treaty to a Senate eager to ratify it. Nothing more was said about amending the Constitution.

Quick Check

✓ Did the Louisiana Purchase represent a compromise by Jefferson in his interpretation of the constitution? Why or why not?

The Lewis and Clark Expedition

In the midst of the Louisiana controversy, Jefferson dispatched a secret message to Congress requesting $2,500 to explore the Far West (January 1803). How closely this decision was connected to the Paris negotiations is not clear. Whatever the case, the president asked his private secretary, Meriwether Lewis, to discover whether the Missouri River "may offer the most direct & practicable water communication across this continent for the purposes of commerce." The president also regarded the expedition as an opportunity to collect data about plants and animals. He personally instructed Lewis in the latest techniques of scientific observation. While preparing for this adventure, Lewis's second in command, William Clark, assumed such a prominent role that it became known as the Lewis and Clark Expedition. The effort owed much of its success to a young Shoshoni woman known as Sacagawea. She served as a translator and helped persuade suspicious Native Americans that the explorers meant no harm. As Clark explained, "A woman with a party of men is a token of peace."

The expedition set out from St. Louis up the Missouri River in May 1804. They barely survived crossing the snow-covered Rocky Mountains and then proceeded down the Columbia River. With their food supply running low, the Americans reached the Pacific Ocean in November 1805. The group returned safely the following September. The expedition fulfilled Jefferson's scientific expectations and reaffirmed his faith in the future prosperity of the United States. (See Map 8.1.)

Read the **Document** *Sacagawea Interprets for Lewis and Clark* on **myhistorylab.com**

Quick Check

✓ How did the Lewis and Clark expedition reinforce Jefferson's faith in the future of the New Republic?

RACE AND DISSENT UNDER JEFFERSON

Jefferson concluded his first term on a wave of popularity. He had maintained the peace, reduced taxes, and expanded the United States. He overwhelmed his Federalist opponent Charles Cotesworth Pinckney in the presidential election of 1804 (see Table 8.1). Republicans also controlled Congress. John Randolph, the most articulate member of the House of Representatives, exclaimed, "Never was there an administration more brilliant than that of Mr. Jefferson up to this period. We were indeed in the full tide of successful experiment!"

But a perceptive observer might have seen signs of serious division within the Republican party and the country. The president's heavy-handed attempts to reform the federal courts stirred deep animosities. Republicans had begun sniping at other Republicans. Congressional debates over the slave trade revealed powerful sectional loyalties and profound disagreement.

How did Jeffersonians deal with the difficult problems of party politics and slavery?

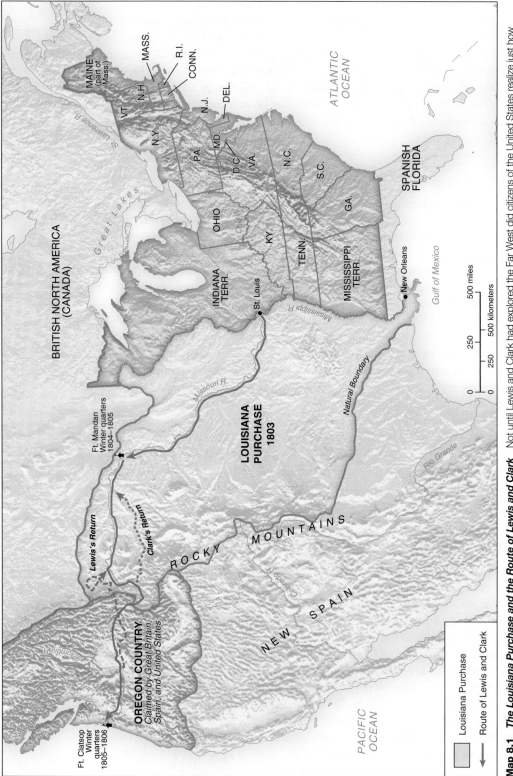

Map 8.1 The Louisiana Purchase and the Route of Lewis and Clark Not until Lewis and Clark had explored the Far West did citizens of the United States realize just how much territory Jefferson had acquired through the Louisiana Purchase.

TABLE 8.1 The Election of 1804

Candidate	Party	Electoral Vote
Jefferson	Republican	162
C. Pinckney	Federalist	14

Attack on the Judges

Jefferson's controversy with the federal bench commenced the moment he became president. The Federalists, realizing they would soon lose control over the executive branch, had passed the Judiciary Act of 1801. This law created circuit courts and 16 new judgeships. Through his "midnight" appointments, Adams had filled these positions with Federalist stalwarts. Such blatant partisan behavior angered Jefferson. In the courts, he explained, the Federalists hoped to preserve their political influence, and "from that battery all the works of Republicanism are to be beaten down and erased." Even more infuriating was Adams's appointment of John Marshall as the new chief justice. This shrewd, largely self-educated Virginian of Federalist background could hold his own against the new president.

In January 1802, Jefferson's congressional allies called for repeal of the Judiciary Act. In public debate, they studiously avoided the obvious political issue. The new circuit courts should be closed not only because they were staffed by Federalists but also because they were needlessly expensive. The judges did not hear enough cases to warrant continuance. The Federalists mounted an able defense. The Constitution provided for removing federal judges only when they were found guilty of high crimes and misdemeanors. By repealing the Judiciary Act, the legislative branch would in effect be dismissing judges without a trial, a violation of their constitutional rights. This argument made little impression on the Republicans. In March, the House, following the Senate, voted for repeal.

While Congress debated the Judiciary Act, another battle erupted. One of Adams's "midnight" appointees, William Marbury, complained that the new administration would not give him his commission for the office of justice of the peace for the District of Columbia. He sought redress before the Supreme Court, demanding that the justices compel James Madison, the secretary of state, to deliver the necessary papers. The Republicans were furious when Marshall agreed to hear the case. Apparently the chief justice wanted to provoke a confrontation with the executive branch.

Marshall was too clever to jeopardize the independence of the Supreme Court over such a relatively minor issue. In his celebrated *Marbury v. Madison* decision (February 1803), Marshall berated the secretary of state for withholding Marbury's commission. Nevertheless, he concluded that the Supreme Court did not possess jurisdiction over such matters. Marbury was out of luck. The Republicans were so pleased with the outcome that they failed to examine the logic of Marshall's decision. He had ruled that part of the earlier act of Congress, the one on which Marbury based his appeal, was unconstitutional. This was the first time the Supreme Court asserted its right to judge the constitutionality of congressional acts. While contemporaries did not fully appreciate the significance of Marshall's doctrine, *Marbury v. Madison* later served as an important precedent for judicial review, the Supreme Court's authority to determine the constitutionality of federal statutes.

Neither Marbury's defeat nor repeal of the Judiciary Act placated extreme Republicans. They insisted that federal judges be made more responsive to the will of the people. One solution, short of electing federal judges, was impeachment. This clumsy device enabled the legislature to remove particularly offensive officeholders. In 1803, John Pickering, an incompetent judge from New Hampshire, presented the Republicans with a curious test case. This Federalist appointee was an insane alcoholic. While his outrageous behavior on the bench embarrassed everyone, Pickering had not committed any high crimes against the U.S. government. Ignoring such legal niceties, Jefferson's congressional allies pushed for impeachment. Although the Senate convicted Pickering (March 1804), many senators refused to compromise the letter of the Constitution and were conspicuously absent for the final vote.

Jefferson was apparently so eager to purge the courts of Federalists that he failed to heed these warnings. By the spring of 1803, he had set his sights on a target far more important than John Pickering. In a Baltimore newspaper, the president stumbled on the transcript of a speech allegedly delivered before a federal grand jury. The words seemed almost treasonous. The speaker was Samuel Chase, a justice of the Supreme Court, who had frequently attacked Republican policies. Jefferson leapt at the chance to remove Chase from office. The moment he learned of Chase's actions, the president asked a leading Republican congressman, "Ought the seditious and official attack on the principles of our Constitution ... go unpunished?" The congressman took the hint. Within weeks, the Republican-controlled House of Representatives indicted Chase.

Even at this early stage of the impeachment, members of Congress expressed uneasiness. The charges against Chase were purely political. There was no doubt that his speech had been indiscreet. He had told the Baltimore jurors that "our late reformers"—in other words, the Republicans—threatened "peace and order, freedom and property." But while Chase lacked judgment, his attack on the administration hardly seemed criminal. If the Senate convicted Chase, every member of the Supreme Court, including Marshall, might also be dismissed.

Chase's trial before the Senate was one of the most dramatic events in American legal history. Chase and his lawyers conducted a masterful defense. By contrast, John Randolph, the congressman who served as chief prosecutor, behaved erratically, betraying repeatedly his ignorance of the law. While most Republican senators disliked the arrogant Chase, they refused to expand the constitutional definition of impeachable offenses to suit Randolph's argument. On March 1, 1805, the Senate acquitted the justice of all charges. The experience apparently convinced Chase of the need for greater moderation. After returning to the Court, he refrained from attacking Republican policies. His Jeffersonian opponents also learned something important. American politicians did not like tampering with the Constitution to get rid of judges, even an imprudent one like Chase.

Read the **Document**
Opinion for the Supreme Court for Marbury v. Madison on **myhistorylab.com**

Quick Check

✔ Why did the federal courts become the focus of party controversy under Jefferson?

The Slave Trade

Slavery sparked angry debate at the Constitutional Convention of 1787 (se Chapter 6). If delegates from the northern states had refused to compromise on the issue, southerners would not have supported the new government. The slave sta demanded much in return for cooperation. According to an agreement that determined the size of a state's congressional delegation, a slave counted as three-fifths of a free white male. This formula meant that while blacks did not vote, they increased the number of southern representatives. The South in turn agreed only that after 1808 Congress *might consider* banning the importation of slaves into the United States. Slaves even influenced the outcome of national elections. Without the three-fifths rule, for example, Adams would have had the electoral votes to defeat Jefferson in 1800.

In December 1806, Jefferson urged Congress to prepare legislation outlawing the slave trade. In early 1807, legislators debated how to end the embarrassing commerce. The issue cut across party lines. Northern representatives generally favored a strong bill; some even wanted to make smuggling slaves into the country a capital offense. But the northerners could not figure out what to do with black people captured by the customs agents who would enforce the legislation. To sell these Africans would involve the federal government in slavery, which many northerners found morally repugnant. Nor was there much sympathy for freeing them. Ignorant of the English language and lacking personal possessions, these blacks seemed unlikely to long survive free in the South.

The Internal Slave Trade Although the external slave trade was officially outlawed in 1808, the commerce in humans persisted. An estimated 250,000 African slaves were brought illicitly to the United States between 1808 and 1860. The internal slave trade also continued. Folk artist Lewis Miller sketched this slave coffle marching from Virginia to new owners in Tennessee under the watchful eyes of mounted white overseers.

the
ument
ngress Prohibits
mportation of
Slaves on
myhistorylab.com

Southern congressmen responded with threats and ridicule. They told their northern colleagues that no one in the South regarded slavery as evil. It was naive, therefore, to expect planters to enforce a ban on the slave trade or inform federal agents when they spotted a smuggler. The notion that these culprits deserved capital punishment seemed viciously inappropriate.

The bill that Jefferson finally signed in March 1807 probably pleased no one. The law prohibited importing slaves into the United States after January 1, 1808. When customs officials captured a smuggler, the slaves were to be turned over to state authorities and disposed of according to local custom. Southerners did not cooperate. African slaves continued to pour into southern ports. Even more blacks would have been imported had Britain not also outlawed the slave trade in 1807. The Royal Navy then captured American slave smugglers off the coast of Africa. When anyone complained, the British explained that they were merely enforcing the laws of the United States.

Quick Check

✓ Why did the United States government not outlaw slavery altogether in 1807?

EMBARRASSMENTS OVERSEAS

Why did the United States find it difficult to avoid military conflict during this period?

During Jefferson's second term (1805–1809), the United States found itself in the midst of a world at war. A brief peace in Europe ended abruptly in 1803. The two military giants of the age, France and Great Britain, then fought for supremacy on land and sea. This was a kind of total war unknown in the eighteenth century. Napoleon's armies carried the ideology of the French Revolution across the Continent. The emperor—as Napoleon Bonaparte called himself after December 1804—transformed conquered nations into French satellites. Only Britain offered effective resistance.

At first, the United States profited from European adversity. As "neutral carriers," American ships transported goods to any port in the world where they could find a buyer. American merchants grew wealthy serving Britain and France. Since the Royal Navy did not allow direct trade between France and its colonies, American captains conducted "broken voyages," during which American vessels sailing out of French ports in the Caribbean would put in briefly to an American port, pay nominal customs, and then sail to France. For years, the British did little to halt this obvious subterfuge.

Napoleon's success on the battlefield, however, strained Britain's resources. In July 1805, a British admiralty court announced in the *Essex* decision that "broken voyages" were illegal. The Royal Navy began seizing American ships in record number. Moreover, as the war continued, the British stepped up the impressment of sailors on ships flying the U.S. flag. Estimates of the number of men impressed ranged as high as 9,000.

Beginning in 1806, the British government issued trade regulations known as the Orders in Council. These forbade neutral commerce with the Continent and threatened seizure of any ship that violated the orders. The declarations created what were in effect "paper blockades"; on paper commerce was prohibited. In reality the rival powers lacked the resources to enforce those blockades. Even the powerful British navy could not monitor every Continental port.

Napoleon responded with his own paper blockade called the Continental System. In the Berlin Decree of November 1806 and the Milan Decree of December 1807, he closed all Continental ports to British trade. Neutral vessels carrying British goods were liable to seizure. The Americans were caught between two conflicting systems.

This unhappy turn of international events baffled Jefferson. He had assumed that justice obliged civilized countries to respect neutral rights. Appeals to reason, however, made little impression on states at war. "As for France and England," the president growled, "... the one is a den of robbers, the other of pirates." In a desperate attempt to avoid hostilities for which the United States was ill prepared, Jefferson ordered James Monroe and William Pinckney to negotiate a commercial treaty with Britain. But the document they signed on December 31, 1806, said nothing about impressment. An angry president refused to submit the treaty to the Senate for ratification.

The United States soon suffered an even greater humiliation. A ship of the Royal Navy, the *Leopard*, sailing off the coast of Virginia, commanded an American warship to submit to a search for deserters (June 22, 1807). When the captain of the *Chesapeake* refused to cooperate, the *Leopard* opened fire, killing three men and wounding 18. The attack violated American sovereignty. Official protests received only a perfunctory apology from the British government, and the American people demanded revenge.

Embargo Divides the Nation

Jefferson found what he regarded as a satisfactory way to deal with European predators with a policy he called "peaceable coercion." If Britain and France refused to respect the rights of neutral carriers, then the United States would keep its ships at home. This protected them from seizure and deprived the European powers of needed American goods, especially food. The president predicted that a total embargo of American commerce would soon force Britain and France to negotiate with the United States in good faith: "Our commerce is so valuable to them that they will be glad to purchase it when the only price we ask is to do us justice." The Embargo Act became law on December 22, 1807.

But "peaceable coercion" became a Jeffersonian nightmare. The president naively believed the American people would enthusiastically support the embargo. Instead, compliance required enforcement acts that became increasingly harsh.

By mid-1808, Jefferson and Gallatin were regulating the smallest details of American economic life. The federal government supervised the coastal trade, lest a ship sailing between two states slip away to Europe or the West Indies. Overland trade with Canada was proscribed. When violations still occurred, Congress gave customs collectors the right to seize a vessel merely on suspicion of wrongdoing. A final desperate act in January 1809 prohibited the loading of any U.S. vessel,

The Embargo Act The Ograbme (embargo spelled backward) snapping turtle, created by cartoonist Alexander Anderson, is shown here biting an American tobacco smuggler who is breaking the embargo.

regardless of size, without authorization from a customs officer who was supported by the army, navy, and local militia.

Northerners hated the embargo. Persons near Lake Champlain in upper New York State simply ignored the regulations and roughed up customs officers who interfered with the Canadian trade. The administration was determined to stop the smugglers. Jefferson urged the governor of New York to call out the militia and sent federal troops to overawe the citizens of New York.

New Englanders considered the embargo lunacy. New England merchants were willing to take their chances on the high seas, but for reasons that few people understood, the president insisted that it was better to preserve ships from possible seizure than to make profits. Sailors and artisans were thrown out of work. The popular press maintained a constant howl of protest. Not surprisingly, the Federalist party revived in New England. Extremists suggested that state assemblies nullify federal law.

By 1809, Jefferson's foreign policy was bankrupt. The embargo never seriously damaged the British economy. In fact, British merchants took over lucrative markets that the Americans had been forced to abandon. Napoleon liked the embargo, since it seemed to harm Britain more than France. Faced with growing opposition, the Republicans in Congress panicked. One representative declared that "peaceful coercion" was a "miserable and mischievous failure" and joined his colleagues in repealing the embargo a few days before James Madison's inauguration. Relations between the United States and the great European powers were worse in 1809 than they had been in 1805. During his second term, the pressures of office weighed heavily on Jefferson. After so many years of public service, he welcomed retirement to Monticello.

Quick Check

✓ Why was Jefferson's embargo policy such a failure?

A New Administration Goes to War

In the election of 1808, the former secretary of state, James Madison, defeated the Federalist Charles Cotesworth Pinckney. The margin of victory was substantially lower than Jefferson's had been in 1804, a warning of political troubles ahead. (See Table 8.2.) The Federalists also doubled their seats in the House, from 24 to 48.

The new president confronted the same foreign policy problems that Jefferson had. Neither Britain nor France showed the slightest interest in respecting American neutral rights. Threats against either nation rang hollow so long as

TABLE 8.2   The Election of 1808

Candidate	Party	Electoral Vote
Madison	Republican	122
C. Pinckney	Federalist	47

the United States failed to develop its military strength. In May 1810, Congress passed Macon's Bill Number Two, sponsored by Nathaniel Macon of North Carolina. In a complete reversal of strategy, this poorly drafted legislation reestablished trade with *both* Britain and France. It also contained a curious carrot-and-stick provision. As soon as either of these states repealed restrictions on neutral shipping, the U.S. government promised to halt all commerce with the other.

Napoleon spotted a rare opportunity. He informed the U.S. minister in Paris that France would no longer enforce the hated Berlin and Milan Decrees. Madison reacted impulsively. Without waiting for further information from Paris, he announced that unless Britain repealed the Orders in Council by November, the United States would cut off commercial relations. Only later did the president learn that Napoleon had no intention of living up to his side of the bargain; his agents continued to seize American ships. Madison decided to ignore the French provocations, to pretend the emperor was behaving honestly. The British could not understand why the United States tolerated such obvious deception. No one in London would have suspected that the president really had no other options left.

Events unrelated to international commerce fueled anti-British sentiment in the western United States. Westerners believed—incorrectly—that British agents from Canada had persuaded Tecumseh's warriors to resist American settlement. According to rumors that ran through the region, the British dreamed of monopolizing the fur trade. In any case, General William Henry Harrison, governor of the Indiana Territory, marched an army to the edge of a large Shawnee village at the mouth of Tippecanoe Creek near the banks of the Wabash River. On November 7, 1811, the American troops routed the Indians at the Battle of Tippecanoe. Harrison became a national hero. In 1840 the American people would elect "Tippecanoe" president. This incident forced Tecumseh to seek British military assistance against the Americans, something he probably would not have done had Harrison left him alone.

Quick Check

✓ Why did the American government find it so hard to avoid entanglements in European affairs?

Fumbling Toward Conflict

In 1811, the anti-British mood of Congress intensified. Militant representatives, some elected to Congress for the first time in 1810, announced they would no longer tolerate national humiliation. They called for action, for resistance to Britain, for any course that promised to achieve respect for the United States and security

TABLE 8.3 The Election of 1812

Candidate	Party	Electoral Vote
Madison	Republican	128
Clinton	Republican* (antiwar faction)	89

*Clinton was nominated by a convention of antiwar Republicans and endorsed by the Federalists.

for its republican institutions. These aggressive nationalists, many of them from the South and West, have sometimes been labeled the **War Hawks**. They included Henry Clay, an earthy Kentucky congressman who served as speaker of the House, and John C. Calhoun, a brilliant South Carolinian. These fiery orators spoke of honor and pride, as if foreign relations were a sort of duel between gentlemen. While the War Hawks were Republicans, they repudiated Jefferson's policy of peaceful coercion.

Madison surrendered to the War Hawks. On June 1, 1812, he sent Congress a declaration of war against Britain. The timing was peculiar. Over the preceding months, tensions between the two nations had relaxed. No new attacks had occurred. Indeed, at the very moment Madison called for war, the British government was suspending the Orders in Council, a conciliatory gesture that probably would have preserved the peace.

View the **Image**
*British Impressment,
1812* on
myhistorylab.com

However inadequately Madison communicated his goals, he does seem to have had a plan. His major aim was to force the British to respect American maritime rights, especially in Caribbean waters. The president's problem was to figure out how a small, militarily weak nation like the United States could bring effective pressure on Britain. Madison's answer seemed to be Canada. This colony supplied Britain's Caribbean possessions with foodstuffs. The president reasoned, therefore, that by threatening to seize Canada, the Americans might compel the British to make concessions on maritime issues.

Congressional War Hawks may have had other goals. Some expansionists were probably more concerned about conquering Canada than they were about the impressment of American seamen. For others, the whole affair may have truly been about national pride. Andrew Jackson wrote, "For what are we going to fight? … [W]e are going to fight for the reestablishment of our national character, misunderstood and vilified at home and abroad." New Englanders in whose commercial interests the war would supposedly be waged ridiculed such chauvinism. The vote for war in Congress was close, 79 to 49 in the House, 19 to 13 in the Senate. With this doubtful mandate, the country marched to war against the most powerful maritime nation in Europe. The election of 1812 reflected division over the war. Antiwar Republicans nominated De Witt Clinton of New York, who was endorsed by the Federalists. Nevertheless, Madison won narrowly (see Table 8.3).

Quick Check

✓ Why were the War Hawks so intent on pushing the New Republic into a war with Great Britain?

THE STRANGE WAR OF 1812

Optimism for the War of 1812 ran high. The War Hawks apparently believed that even though the United States possessed only a small army and navy, it could sweep the British out of Canada. Such predictions flew in the face of reality. Not only did the Republicans fail to appreciate how unprepared the country was for war, but they also refused to mobilize needed resources. The House rejected direct taxes and authorized naval appropriations only with reluctance. Indeed, even as they planned for battle, the consequences of their political and economic convictions haunted the Republicans in Congress. They did not seem to understand that a weak, decentralized government—the one that Jeffersonians championed—was incapable of waging an expensive war against the world's greatest sea power. (See Map 8.2.)

Why is the War of 1812 sometimes thought of as a "second war of independence"?

View the **Map**
The War of 1812 on
myhistorylab.com

Fighting the British

American military operations focused initially on the western forts. The results were discouraging. On August 16, 1812, General William Hull surrendered an army to a smaller British force at Detroit. Michilimackinac was also lost. Marches against Niagara and Montreal achieved nothing. The militia, led by aging officers with little military aptitude, no matter how enthusiastic, was no match for well-trained European veterans. On the sea, the United States did better. In August, Captain Isaac Hull's *Constitution* defeated the *Guerrière* in a fierce battle, and American privateers destroyed or captured British merchant ships. These successes were deceptive, however. So long as Napoleon threatened the Continent, Britain could spare few warships for service in America. But when peace returned to Europe in 1814, Britain redeployed its fleet and easily blockaded the tiny U.S. Navy.

The campaigns of 1813 revealed that conquering Canada would be more difficult than the War Hawks ever imagined. Both sides recognized that whoever controlled the Great Lakes controlled the West. On Lake Erie, the Americans won the race for naval superiority. On September 10, 1813, Oliver Hazard Perry destroyed a British fleet at

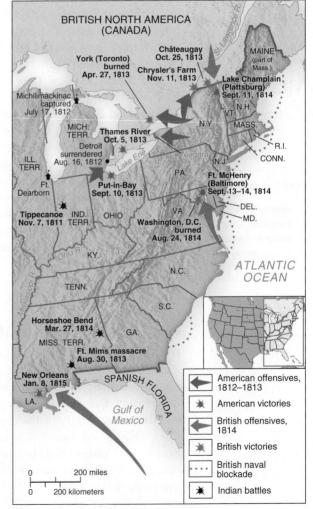

Map 8.2 *The War of 1812* The major battles of the War of 1812 brought few lasting gains to either the British or the Americans.

Put-in-Bay. In a much-quoted letter written after the battle, Perry exclaimed, "We have met the enemy; and they are ours." On October 5, General Harrison overran British troops and Indian warriors at the Battle of Thames River. During this engagement, Tecumseh was killed. On the other fronts, however, the war went badly for the Americans. General Wilkinson suffered an embarrassing defeat near Montreal (Battle of Chrysler's Farm, November 11), and the British navy held its own on Lake Ontario.

((•─ **Listen** to the
Audio File
*Star Spangled
Banner* on
myhistorylab.com

Throughout 1814, British warships harassed the Chesapeake coast. To their surprise, the British found the region almost totally undefended. On August 24, 1814, in retaliation for the Americans' destruction of the capital of Upper Canada (York, Ontario), a small British force burned the American capital, a victory more symbolic than strategic. Encouraged by their easy success and contemptuous of America's ragtag soldiers, the British launched a full-scale attack on Baltimore (September 13–14). To everyone's surprise, the fort guarding the harbor held out against a heavy naval bombardment, and the British gave up the operation. The survival of Fort McHenry inspired Francis Scott Key to write "The Star-Spangled Banner."

View the **Image**
*Burning of the White
House, 1814* on
myhistorylab.com

The **Battle of New Orleans** should never have occurred. The British landed a large assault force under General Edward Pakenham just when diplomats in Europe were preparing the final drafts of a peace treaty. The combatants, of course, knew nothing of these distant developments. On January 8, 1815, Pakenham ordered a frontal attack against General Andrew Jackson's well-defended positions. Pakenham was killed, and the British lost over 2,000 killed and wounded. The Americans suffered only light casualties. The victory not only made Jackson a national folk hero, but it also gave the people of the United States a much needed source of pride. Even in military terms, the battle was significant. If the British had managed to occupy New Orleans, the key to the trade of the Mississippi River Valley, they would have been difficult to dislodge regardless of the peace treaty.

Quick Check

✓ How well did the
Americans fare
militarily against the
British during the
War of 1812?

Hartford Convention: The Demise of the Federalists

In late 1814, leading New England politicians, most of them moderate Federalists, gathered in Hartford, Connecticut, to discuss relations between their region and the federal government in what became known as the Hartford Convention. Delegates were angry and hurt by the Madison administration's seeming insensitivity to the economic interests of the New England states. The embargo had soured New Englanders on Republican foreign policy. The War of 1812 added insult to injury. When British troops occupied the coastal villages of Maine, then part of Massachusetts, the president did nothing to drive them out.

The men who met at Hartford on December 15 did not advocate secession. Although people in other sections of the country cried treason, the delegates only recommended changing the Constitution. They drafted amendments that reflected the New Englanders' growing frustration. One proposal suggested that congressional representation be calculated on the basis of the number of white males living in a state. New England congressmen were tired of the three-fifths rule that gave southern slaveholders a disproportionately large voice in the House. The convention also wanted to limit each president to a single term, which New Englanders hoped might end Virginia's monopoly of the presidency. And finally, the delegates insisted that a two-thirds majority be necessary before Congress could declare war, pass commercial regulations, or admit new states to the Union. The moderate Federalists of New England were confident these changes would protect their region from the tyranny of southern Republicans.

The Battle of New Orleans This engraving by Joseph Yeager (c. 1815) depicts the Battle of New Orleans and the death of British Major General Edward Pakenham. The death of the British commander was a turning point in the battle, in which more than 2,000 British soldiers were killed or wounded at the hands of General Andrew Jackson and the American army.

Quick Check

✓ What factors led to the calling of the Hartford Convention and the drafting of the Hartford resolutions?

The convention dispatched its resolutions to Washington, but soon after an official delegation reached the federal capital, the situation became awkward. Everyone was celebrating the victory of New Orleans and the announcement of peace. Republicans in Congress accused the hapless New Englanders of disloyalty. People throughout the country were persuaded that wild secessionists had attempted to destroy the Union. The Hartford Convention accelerated the demise of the Federalist party.

CONCLUSION: THE "SECOND WAR OF INDEPENDENCE"

In August 1814, the United States dispatched a distinguished negotiating team to Ghent, a Belgian city, to open peace talks. At first, the British made impossible demands. They insisted on territorial concessions from the United States, the right to navigate the Mississippi River, and the creation of an Indian buffer state in the Northwest Territory. The Americans rejected the entire package. In turn, they lectured the British about maritime rights and impressment. Fatigue finally broke the deadlock. The British government realized that military force could not significantly alter the outcome of the war. Weary negotiators signed the Treaty of Ghent on Christmas Eve 1814. The document dealt with virtually none of the topics in Madison's war message to Congress. Neither side surrendered territory; Britain refused even to discuss impressment. The adversaries merely agreed to stop fighting, postponing the vexing issues of neutral rights until a later date. The Senate apparently concluded that stalemate was preferable to continued conflict and ratified the treaty 35 to 0.

Still, most Americans viewed the War of 1812 as a success. The country's military accomplishments had been unimpressive, but the people of the United States had been swept up in a contagion of nationalism. "The war," reflected Gallatin, had made Americans "feel and act more as a nation; and I hope that the permanency of the Union is thereby better secured."

8 STUDY RESOURCES

((•—⎸**Listen** to the **Chapter Audio** for Chapter 8 on **myhistorylab.com**

TIMELINE

1801 President Adams makes "midnight" appointments of federal judges, p. 201

1802 Judiciary Act repealed (March), p. 205

1803 Chief Justice John Marshall sets precedent for judicial review in *Marbury v. Madison* (February), p. 205
• Louisiana Purchase concluded with France (May), p. 202

1803–1806 Lewis and Clark explore the West, p. 203

1804 Jefferson elected to second term, p. 205

1805 Senate acquits Justice Samuel Chase (March), p. 206

1807 Embargo Act passed (December), p. 209

1808 Slave trade is ended (January), p. 208
  • Madison elected president, p. 210

1809 Embargo repealed, p. 210

1811 Harrison defeats Indians at Tippecanoe (November), p. 211

1812 Declaration of war against Britain (June), p. 212
  • Madison elected to second term p. 212

1813 Perry destroys British fleet at Battle of Put-in-Bay (September), p. 213

1814 Jackson crushes Creek Indians at Horseshoe Bend (March), p. 199
  • British troops burn Washington, D.C. (August), p. 214
  • Hartford Convention recommends constitutional changes (December), p. 214
  • Treaty of Ghent ends War of 1812 (December), p. 216

1815 Jackson routs British at Battle of New Orleans (January), p. 214

CHAPTER REVIEW

THE REPUBLIC EXPANDS

How did the Republic's growth shape the market economy and relations with Native Americans?

During Jefferson's administration, a rapidly growing population flooded into the Ohio and Mississippi valleys. Family farms produced crops for a robust international market. Cities served as centers, not of industry, but of commerce. When Native Americans such as Tecumseh resisted expansion, the United States government and ordinary white settlers pushed them aside. *(p. 196)*

JEFFERSON AS PRESIDENT

How did practical politics challenge Jefferson's political principles?

Jefferson brought to the presidency a commitment to a small, less expensive federal government. In office, however, he discovered that practical politics demanded compromises with Republican principles. He needed a government capable of responding to unexpected challenges and opportunities throughout the world. Although he worried that the Louisiana Purchase (1803) might exceed his authority under the Constitution, Jefferson accepted the French offer and sent Lewis and Clark to explore this vast territory. *(p. 200)*

RACE AND DISSENT UNDER JEFFERSON

How did Jeffersonians deal with the difficult problems of party politics and slavery?

To end Federalist control of the judiciary, Jefferson denied commissions to judges appointed at the end of the Adams administration and attempted to remove others from office. That failed, and the impeachment of Supreme Court Justice Samuel Chase embarrassed the administration. In 1807, after considerable debate and compromise, Jefferson signed into law a bill outlawing the international slave trade. *(p. 203)*

EMBARRASSMENTS OVERSEAS

Why did the United States find it difficult to avoid military conflict during this period?

During Jefferson's second term, Britain and France waged a world war. Both nations tried to manipulate the United States into taking sides. Recognizing that his country possessed only a weak navy and small army, Jefferson supported the Embargo Act (1807), which closed American ports to foreign commerce. This angered New Englanders who regarded open trade as the key to their region's prosperity. *(p. 208)*

THE STRANGE WAR OF 1812

Why is the War of 1812 sometimes thought of as a "second war of independence"?

Prior to the war, Britain treated the United States as though it were still a colonial possession and regularly seized sailors on American ships. In 1813, American troops failed to conquer Canada. In 1814, British troops burned Washington, D.C., in retaliation. In 1815, General Andrew Jackson won a stunning victory in the Battle of New Orleans. The resolutions of the Hartford Convention, criticizing the war and the Constitution, proved an embarrassment for the Federalists and accelerated their demise as a political party. *(p. 213)*

KEY TERM QUESTIONS

1. What would Tecumseh have thought of federal attempts to "civilize" the Indians? (p. 198)

2. Did the Louisiana Purchase represent a compromise by Jefferson in his interpretation of the Constitution? (p. 202)

3. How did the Lewis and Clark Expedition reinforce Jefferson's faith in the future of the new Republic? (p. 203)

4. What role did the Supreme Court's *Marbury v. Madison* decision play in the party controversy under Jefferson? (p. 205)

5. How did the *Marbury v. Madison* decision establish the principle of judicial review? (p. 206)

6. Why was the Embargo Act such a failure? (p. 209)

7. Why were the War Hawks so intent on pushing the new Republic into a war with Great Britain? (p. 212)

8. How well did the Americans fare militarily against the British during the War of 1812? (p. 213)

9. Why was the Battle of New Orleans fought after the War of 1812 had officially ended? (p. 214)

10. What factors led to the calling of the Hartford Convention and the drafting of the Hartford resolutions? (p. 214)

MyHistoryLab CONNECTIONS

Visit **www.myhistorylab.com** for a customized Study Plan to build your knowledge of *Republican Ascendancy*.

Question for Analysis

1. Why was the Louisiana Purchase so crucial for the United States?

   View the **Closer Look** *Map of the Louisiana Purchase of 1803* p. 202

2. How did the Lewis and Clark expedition fit into the idea that expansion was essential to liberty?

   Watch the **Video** *Lewis and Clark: What Were They Trying to Accomplish?* p. 202

Other Resources from this Chapter

Read the **Document** *Pennsylvania Gazette Indian Hostilities*

Read the **Document** *Constitutionality of the Louisiana Purchase*

Read the **Document** *Sacagawea Interprets for Lewis and Clark*

View the **Image** *British Impressment*

3. Why was the Supreme Court's ruling for Marbury v. Madison so significant?

Read the **Document** *Opinion of the Supreme Court for* Marbury v. Madison p. 205

4. Why did the United States government not outlaw slavery altogether in 1807?

Read the **Document** *Congress Prohibits the Importation of Slaves* p. 208

5. Why did the battles of the War of 1812 bring little lasting gain to either the British or the Americans?

View the **Map** *The War of 1812* p. 212

View the **Image** *Burning of the White House, 1814*

Listen to the **Audio File** *Star Spangled Banner*

9 NATION BUILDING AND NATIONALISM

1815–1825

Contents and Spotlight Questions

EXPANSION AND MIGRATION PG. 222

What key forces drove American expansion westward during this period?

TRANSPORTATION AND THE MARKET ECONOMY PG. 228

How did developments in transportation support the growth of agriculture and manufacturing?

THE POLITICS OF NATION BUILDING AFTER THE WAR OF 1812 PG. 234

What decisions did the federal government face as the country expanded?

(((•—Listen to the **Chapter Audio** for Chapter 9 on **myhistorylab.com**

A REVOLUTIONARY WAR HERO REVISITS AMERICA IN 1824

When the Marquis de Lafayette returned to the United States in 1824 he found a peaceful and prosperous nation. For more than a year, the great French hero of the American Revolution toured the country that he had helped to create and marveled at how much had changed since he had fought beside George Washington more than 40 years before. Lafayette hailed "the immense improvements" and "admirable communications" and was moved by "all the grandeur and prosperity of these happy United States, which ... reflect on every part of the world the light of a far superior political civilization."

Americans had good reasons to make Lafayette's return the occasion for patriotic celebration and reaffirmation. Since the War of 1812, the nation had been free from serious foreign threats to its independence and way of life. Its population, size, and wealth were growing rapidly. Its republican

Election Day in Philadelphia (1815) An exuberant crowd celebrates in the square outside Independence Hall in this painting by German American artist John Lewis Krimmel.

form of government, which many had considered a risky experiment, was apparently working well. James Monroe, the current president, had proclaimed in his first inaugural address that "the United States have flourished beyond example. Their citizens individually have been happy and the nation prosperous." Expansion "to the Great Lakes and beyond the sources of the great rivers which communicate through our whole interior" meant that "no country was ever happier with respect to its domain." As for the government, it was so near to perfection that "in respect to it we have no essential improvement to make."

Beneath the optimism and self-confidence, however, lay undercurrents of doubt and anxiety. The visit of the aged Lafayette signified the passing of the Founders. Less than a year after his departure, Thomas Jefferson and John Adams—who along with James Madison were the last of the great Founders still living—died within hours of each other on the fiftieth anniversary of the Declaration of Independence. Most Americans saw the coincidence as a good omen for the nation. But some asked if their republican virtue and self-sacrifice could be maintained in an increasingly prosperous and materialistic society. And what about the place of black slavery in a "perfect" democratic republic? Lafayette himself was disappointed that the United States had not freed the southern slaves.

But the peace following the War of 1812 did open the way for a surge of nation building. As new lands were acquired or opened up for settlement, hordes of pioneers often rushed in. Improved transportation soon gave many of them access to distant markets, and advances in processing raw materials led to the first stirrings of industrialization. Politicians looked for ways to encourage growth and expansion, and an active judiciary promoted economic development and asserted the priority of national over state and local interests. To guarantee the peace and security essential for internal progress, statesmen proclaimed a foreign policy designed to insulate America from external involvements. A new nation of great potential wealth and power was emerging.

EXPANSION AND MIGRATION

What key forces drive American expansion westward during this period?

Peace with Great Britain in 1815 allowed Americans to shift their attention from Europe and the Atlantic to the vast interior of North America.

Between the Appalachians and the Mississippi, settlement had already begun, especially in the new states of Ohio, Kentucky, and Tennessee. In the lower Mississippi Valley, the former French colony of Louisiana had been admitted as a state in 1812, and a thriving settlement existed around Natchez in the Mississippi Territory. Elsewhere in the trans-Appalachian west, white settlement was sparse, and much land remained in Indian hands. U.S. citizens, eager to expand into lands held by Indian nations and Spain, used diplomacy, military action, force, and fraud to "open" lands for settlement and westward migration.

Extending the Boundaries

Postwar expansionists turned their attention first to Spanish holdings, which included Florida and much of the present-day American West. The Spanish claimed possession of land extending along the Gulf Coast from Florida to the Mississippi. Between 1810 and 1812, however, the United States had annexed the area between the Mississippi and the Perdido River in what became Alabama, claiming that it was part of the Louisiana Purchase. The remainder, known as East Florida, became a prime object of territorial ambition for President James Monroe and his energetic secretary of state, John Quincy Adams. Adams had a grand design for continental expansion that required nullifying or reducing Spanish claims west and east of the Mississippi; he eagerly awaited an opportunity to apply pressure for that purpose.

General Andrew Jackson provided that opportunity. In 1816, U.S. troops crossed into East Florida in pursuit of hostile Seminole Indians. This raid touched off a wider conflict, and after taking command in late 1817, Jackson went beyond his official orders and occupied East Florida in April and May 1818. This operation became known as the First Seminole War.

In November 1818, Secretary Adams informed Spain that the United States had acted in self-defense and that further conflict would be avoided only if it ceded East Florida to the United States. The Madrid government, weakened by Latin American revolutions and the breaking up of its empire, was in no position to resist American bullying. As part of the Adams–Onís Treaty, signed on February 22, 1819, Spain relinquished Florida. In return, the United States assumed $5 million of the financial claims of American citizens against Spain.

A strong believer that the United States had a continental destiny, Adams also made Spain give up its claim to the Pacific coast north of California, thus opening a path for future American expansion. Taking advantage of Spain's desire to keep its title to Texas—part of which the United States had claimed as part of the Louisiana Purchase—Adams induced the Spanish minister Luis de Onís to agree to a new boundary between American and Spanish territory that ran north of Texas but extended to the Pacific. Great Britain and Russia still had competing claims to the Pacific Northwest, but the United States was now in a better position to acquire a Pacific coastline.

Interest in exploiting the Far West grew during the second and third decades of the nineteenth century. In 1811, a New York merchant, John Jacob Astor, founded the fur-trading post of Astoria at the mouth of the Columbia River in the Oregon Country. Astor's American Fur Company operated out of St. Louis in the 1820s and 1830s, with fur traders working their way up the Missouri River to the northern Rockies and beyond. First they limited themselves to trading for furs with the Indians, but later, businesses such as the Rocky Mountain Fur Company, founded in 1822, relied on trappers or "mountain men" who went after game on their own and sold the furs to company agents at an annual meeting or "rendezvous."

However, the area beyond the Mississippi did not draw substantial immigration during this period. The focus of attention between 1815 and the 1840s was the nearer west, the rich agricultural lands between the Appalachians and the

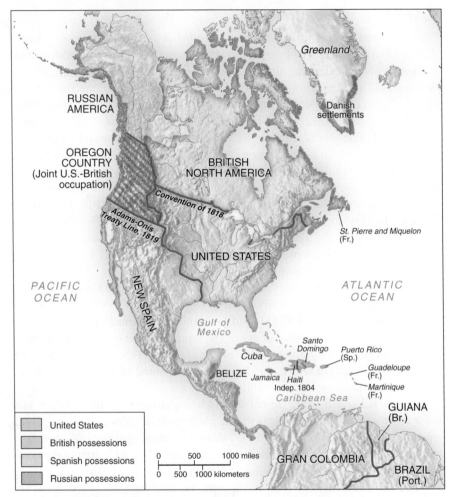

North America, 1819 Treaties with Britain following the War of 1812 setting the border between the United States and Canada (British North America) made this border the longest unfortified boundary line in the world.

Mississippi that were inhabited by numerous Indian tribes. Settlers poured across the Appalachians and filled the agricultural heartland of the United States. In 1810, only about one-seventh of the American population lived beyond the Appalachians; by 1840, more than one-third did. During that period, Illinois grew from a territory with 12,282 inhabitants to a state with 476,183; Mississippi's population of about 40,000 increased tenfold; and Michigan grew from a remote frontier area with fewer than 5,000 people into a state with more than 200,000. Eight new western states joined the Union during this period.

While some of the original buyers were land speculators, most of the new land did find its way into the hands of actual cultivators. In some areas, squatters arrived before the official survey and formed claims associations that policed land auctions to prevent "outsiders" from bidding up the price and buying their farms out from under them. Squatters also agitated for formal right of first purchase or preemption from the government. Between 1799 and 1830, Congress granted squatters in specific areas the right to purchase at the minimum price the land that they had already improved. In 1841, Congress formally acknowledged the right to farm on public lands with the assurance of a *future* preemption right.

Quick Check

✓ What territories did the United States acquire under secretary Adams, and how did it obtain them?

Native American Societies Under Pressure

Five Indian nations, with a combined population of nearly 60,000, occupied much of what later became Mississippi, Alabama, Georgia, and Florida. These nations—the Cherokee, Chickasaw, Choctaw, Creek, and Seminole—became known as the "Five Civilized Tribes" because by 1815 they had adopted many of the features of the surrounding white southern society: an agricultural economy, a republican government, and slavery. Indeed, the cultural transformation of the southeastern Indians was part of a conscious strategy to respond to Jeffersonian exhortations toward "civilization" and the promise of citizenship that came with it. But between 1815 and 1833, it became increasingly clear that however "civilized" Indians had become, most white Americans were not interested in incorporating them into U.S. society, whether as nations or as individuals.

The five nations varied in their responses to white encroachment on their lands. So-called mixed-blood leaders such as John Ross convinced the Cherokee to adopt a strategy of accommodation to increase their chances of survival; the Creek and Seminole, by contrast, forcibly resisted.

The Cherokee were the largest of the five nations. Traditional Cherokee society had combined hunting by men and subsistence farming by women. In the early nineteenth century, the shift to a more agrarian, market-based economy eroded the traditional matrilineal kinship system, in which a person belonged to his or her mother's clan. The new order replaced matrilineal inheritance with the U.S. system of patriarchy in which fathers headed the household and property passed from father to son. Emphasis on the nuclear family with the husband as producer and the wife as domestic caretaker diminished the clan's role.

Read the **Document**
The Cherokee Treaty of 1817 on **myhistorylab.com**

The shift toward agriculture also helped introduce American-style slavery to Cherokee society. As the Cherokee adopted plantation-style agriculture, they also began to adopt white attitudes toward blacks. By the time of Indian Removal in the 1830s and 1840s, a few Cherokee owned plantations with hundreds of slaves, and there were more than 1,500 slaves in the Cherokee Nation. Discrimination against Africans in all five nations grew under pressure of contact with whites. Beginning in the 1820s, the Cherokee Council adopted rules regulating slaves. Whereas a few Africans in the eighteenth century had been adopted into the tribe and become citizens, under the new laws, slaves could not intermarry with Cherokee citizens, engage in trade or barter, or hold property.

To head off encroachments by southern states, the Cherokee also attempted to centralize power in a republican government. As Cherokee historian William McLoughlin has described, "A series of eleven laws passed between 1820

Cherokee Literacy Sequoyah's invention of the Cherokee alphabet enabled thousands of Cherokees to read and write primers and newspapers in their own language.

and 1823 … constituted a political revolution in the structure of Cherokee government. Under these laws the National Council created a bicameral legislature, a district and superior court system, an elective system of representation by geographical district rather than by town, and a salaried government bureaucracy." This process culminated in the 1827 adoption of a formal written constitution modeled on the U.S. Constitution.

Sequoyah's invention of a written Cherokee language in 1821–1822 spurred a renaissance of Cherokee culture. He used a phonetic system, representing each syllable in the Cherokee language with symbols, eventually comprising 86 letters. While this alphabet was complicated and lacked punctuation marks, "Sequoyan" gave the Cherokee a new means of self-expression and a reinvigorated sense of their identity. The first American Indian newspaper, the *Cherokee Phoenix*, was published in Sequoyan in 1828. By the time of Indian Removal, Cherokee leaders like John Ross and Elias Boudinot could point with pride to high levels of Cherokee acculturation, education, and economic success at American-style "civilization."

The Seminole, the smallest of the five nations, present perhaps the starkest cultural contrast to the Cherokee, both because the Seminole reacted to pressure from white settlers with armed resistance rather than accommodation, and because their multicultural history gave them a different relationship to slavery.

The Seminole Nation in Florida, which formed after the European conquest of America, was an amalgam of many different peoples with roots in Africa and the New World. Disparate groups of Creek Indians migrating from Georgia and Alabama in the wake of war and disease mingled with the remnants of native Floridians to form the new tribe known as the Seminole. Spain had also granted asylum to runaway African American slaves from the Carolinas, who created autonomous "maroon communities" in Florida, allying with the Seminole to ward off slave-catchers. African Americans and Native Americans intermingled, and by the late eighteenth century, some African Americans were already known as "Seminole Negroes" or *estelusti*. The word *Seminole* itself meant "wild" or "runaway" in the Creek language.

Although the Seminoles adopted African slavery in the early nineteenth century, it was different from slavery as it existed among whites, or even among the Cherokee and Creek. Seminole "slaves" lived in separate towns, planted and cultivated fields in common, owned large herds of livestock, and paid their "owners" only an annual tribute, similar to what Seminole towns paid to the *micco*, or chief.

During the 1820s and 1830s, the estelusti and the Seminoles were allies in
wars against the Americans; however,
their alliance came under increasing
strain. In 1823, six Seminole leaders,
including one of some African ancestry known as "Mulatto King," signed
the Treaty of Moultrie Creek, removing the tribe from their fertile lands in
northern Florida to swampland south
of Tampa. The signers took bribes and
believed unfulfilled promises that they
would be allowed to stay on their lands.
The treaty also required the Seminoles
to return runaway slaves and turn away
future runaways. During the 1830s,
black Seminoles were some of the
staunchest opponents of Indian Re-

Competing Land Claims *View of the Great Treaty Held at Prairie du Chien
(1825).* Representatives of eight Native American tribes met with government agents
at Prairie du Chien, Wisconsin, in 1825 to define the boundaries of their respective
land claims. The United States claimed the right to make "an amicable and final
adjustment" of the claims. Within 25 years, most of the tribes present at Prairie du
Chien had ceded their land to the government.

moval, and they played a major role in the Second Seminole War, which was fought
to resist removal from 1835 to 1842. General Thomas W. Jesup, the leader of the U.S.
Army, claimed, "This, you may be assured is a negro and not an Indian war."

Treaties like the one signed at Moultrie Creek in 1823 reduced tribal holdings; the federal government used deception, bribery, and threats to induce land
cessions. When this did not yield results fast enough to suit southern whites who
coveted Indian land for mining, speculation, and cotton production, state governments began to act on their own, proclaiming state jurisdiction over lands federal
treaties still allotted to Indians within the state's borders. The stage was thus set for
the forced removal of the Five Civilized Tribes to the trans-Mississippi West during
the administration of President Andrew Jackson in the 1830s (see Chapter 10).

Farther north, in the Ohio Valley and the Northwest Territory, Native Americans
had already suffered military defeat in the conflict between Britain and the United
States, leaving them only a minor obstacle to white settlers and land speculators.
When the British withdrew from the Old Northwest in 1815, they left their former
Indian allies virtually defenseless before the tide of whites who rushed into the
region. Consigned by treaty to reservations outside the main lines of white advance,
most of the tribes were eventually forced west of the Mississippi.

The last stand of the Indians in this region occurred in 1831–1832, when a faction
of the confederated Sac and Fox under Chief Black Hawk refused to abandon their
lands east of the Mississippi. Federal troops and Illinois militia drove the Indians
back to the river, where they were almost exterminated while attempting to cross to
the western bank.

Uprooting Indian communities of the Old Northwest was part of a national
program for removing Indians of the eastern part of the country to an area
beyond the Mississippi. Many whites viewed Indian society and culture as radically inferior to their own and doomed by "progress." Furthermore, Indians based

Read the
Document
*Black Hawk, from
"The Life of Black
Hawk" (1833)* on
myhistorylab.com

property rights to land on use rather than absolute ownership. Whites saw this as an insuperable obstacle to economic development. Moving Indians west helped many Americans reap fortunes through land speculation. Andrew Jackson got rich speculating on lands he bought from the Chickasaws after negotiating a treaty with them and opening an area along the Mississippi to white settlement in 1814. Land he bought for $100, he later sold for $5,000. Jackson made his name fighting the Creeks in the 1810s. After victory in that conflict, he wrote to General Thomas Pinckney, "I must destroy these deluded victims doomed to distruction by their own restless and savage conduct," and added that he had "on all occasions preserved the scalps of my killed."

As originally conceived by Thomas Jefferson, removal would have allowed those Indians who became "civilized" to remain behind on individually owned farms and qualify for American citizenship. This policy would reduce Indian holdings without appearing to violate American standards of justice. Not everyone agreed with Jefferson's belief that Indians, unlike blacks, had the natural ability to adopt white ways and become useful citizens. People living on the frontier who coveted Indian land and risked violent retaliation for trying to take it were more likely to think of Native Americans as irredeemable savages or vermin to be exterminated if necessary. During the Monroe era (1817–1825), it became clear that white settlers wanted to remove all Indians, "civilized" or not. As president, Andrew Jackson presided over a far more aggressive Indian removal policy.

Quick Check

✓ In what ways did the Cherokee attempt to Increase their chances of survival in the face of American settlement, and how did they differ from the Seminoles?

TRANSPORTATION AND THE MARKET ECONOMY

How did developments in transportation support the growth of agriculture and manufacturing?

It took more than the spread of settlements to bring prosperity to new areas and ensure that the inhabitants would identify with older regions or with the country as a whole. Land transportation was so primitive that in 1813 it took 75 days for one wagon of goods drawn by four horses to travel about 1,000 miles from Worcester, Massachusetts, to Charleston, South Carolina. Coastal shipping eased the problem to some extent in the East and stimulated the growth of port cities. Traveling west over the mountains, however, meant months on the trail.

After the War of 1812, political leaders realized that national security, economic progress, and political unity more or less depended on an improved transportation network. Accordingly, President Madison called for a federally supported program of "internal improvements" in 1815. In the ensuing decades, the nationalists realized their vision of a transportation revolution to a considerable extent, although the direct role of the federal government proved to be less important than anticipated.

Roads and Steamboats

The first great federal transportation project was building the National Road between Cumberland, Maryland, on the Potomac and Wheeling, Virginia, on the Ohio (1811–1818). This impressive gravel-surfaced toll road was extended to Vandalia, Illinois, in 1838. By about 1825, thousands of miles of turnpikes—privately owned toll roads chartered by the states—crisscrossed southern New England, upstate New York, Pennsylvania, and northern New Jersey.

The toll roads, however, failed to meet the demand for low-cost transportation over long distances. Travelers benefited more than transporters of bulky freight, for whom the turnpikes proved expensive.

Even the National Road could not offer the low freight costs required for the long-distance hauling of wheat, flour, and the other bulky agricultural products of the Ohio Valley. These commodities needed water transportation.

The United States' natural system of river transportation was one of the most significant reasons for its rapid economic development. The Ohio–Mississippi system in particular provided ready access to the rich agricultural interior and a natural outlet for its products. By 1815, flatboats loaded with wheat, flour, and salt pork were making part of the 2,000-mile trip from Pittsburgh to New Orleans. Even after the coming of the steamboat, flatboats still carried much of the downriver trade.

The flatboat trade, however, was necessarily one-way. A farmer from Ohio or Illinois, or someone hired to do the job, could float down to New Orleans easily enough, but to get back, he usually had to walk overland through rough country. Until the problem of upriver navigation was solved, the Ohio–Mississippi could not carry the manufactured goods that farmers desired in exchange for their crops.

Fortunately, a solution was readily at hand: steam power. Late in the eighteenth century, American inventors had experimented with steam-driven riverboats. John Fitch even exhibited an early model to delegates at the Constitutional Convention in 1788. But making a commercially successful craft required further refinement. In 1807, Robert Fulton, backed by Robert R. Livingston—a prominent wealthy New Yorker—demonstrated the potential of the steamboat by propelling the *Clermont* 150 miles from New York City up the Hudson River. The first steamboat launched in the West was the *New Orleans*, which made the long trip from Pittsburgh to New Orleans in 1811–1812. Besides becoming a principal means of passenger travel on the inland waterways of the East, the river steamboat revolutionized western commerce. In 1815, the *Enterprise* made the first return trip from New Orleans to Pittsburgh. By 1820, 69 steamboats with a total capacity of 13,890 tons were plying western waters.

Steam transport reduced costs, moved goods and people faster, and allowed a two-way commerce on the Mississippi and Ohio rivers. The steamboat captured the American imagination. Great paddle wheelers became luxurious floating hotels, the natural habitats of gamblers, confidence men, and mysterious women. For the pleasure of passengers and

View the **Map**
Expanding America and Internal Improvements on
myhistorylab.com

River Transport *The Clermont on the Hudson (1830–1835)* by Charles Pensee. Although some called his *Clermont* "Fulton's Folly," Robert Fulton reduced the cost and increased the speed of river transport.

onlookers, steamboats sometimes raced against each other, and their more skillful pilots became folk heroes. But the boats also had a lamentable safety record, frequently running aground, colliding, or blowing up. The most publicized disasters of antebellum America were spectacular boiler explosions that killed hundreds of passengers. As a result, the federal government began in 1838 to attempt to regulate steamboats and monitor their construction and operation. The legislation, which failed to create an agency capable of enforcing minimum safety standards, was virtually the only federal effort before the Civil War to regulate domestic transportation.

A transportation system based solely on rivers and roads had one enormous gap—it did not provide an economical way to ship western farm produce directly east to ports engaged in transatlantic trade or to the growing urban market of the seaboard states. The solution the politicians and merchants of the Middle Atlantic and midwestern states offered was to build a system of canals that linked seaboard cities directly to the Great Lakes, the Ohio, and ultimately the Mississippi.

At 364 miles long, 40 feet wide, and 4 feet deep, and containing 84 locks, the Erie Canal, which opened in 1825 and linked Lake Erie to Buffalo, New York, was the most spectacular engineering achievement of the young republic. Furthermore, it was a great economic success and inspired numerous other canal projects in other states.

The canal boom ended when it became apparent that most of the waterways were unprofitable. State credit had been overextended, and the panic and depression of the late 1830s and early 1840s forced retrenchment. Moreover, railroads were competing for the same traffic, and a new phase in the transportation revolution was beginning. However, canals, while they failed to turn a profit for most investors, provided a vital service to those who used them and contributed to the new nation's economic development.

((•—[**Listen** to the
Audio File
The Erie Canal on
myhistorylab.com

Quick Check

✓ How did water transportation affect economic development, and how did this influence expansion westward?

The Canal Boom Illustration of a lock on the Erie Canal at Lockport, New York, 1838. The canal facilitated trade by linking the Great Lakes regions to the eastern seaports.

Emergence of a Market Economy

The desire to reduce the cost and increase the speed of shipping heavy freight over great distances laid the groundwork for a new economic system. Canals made it less expensive and more profitable for western farmers to ship wheat and flour to New York and Philadelphia and also gave manufacturers in the East ready access to an interior market. Steamboats reduced shipping costs on the Ohio and Mississippi and put farmers in the enviable position of receiving more for their crops and paying less for the goods they needed to import. Hence improved transport increased farm income and stimulated commercial agriculture.

At the beginning of the nineteenth century, the typical farming household consumed most of what it produced and sold only a small surplus in nearby markets. Most manufactured articles were produced at home. Easier and cheaper access to distant markets decisively changed this pattern. Between 1800 and 1840, agricultural output increased at an annual rate of approximately 3 percent, and a rapidly growing portion of this production consisted of commodities grown for sale rather than for home consumption. The rise in productivity was partly due to technological advances. Iron or steel plows proved better than wooden ones; the grain cradle displaced the scythe for harvesting; and better varieties or strains of crops, grasses, and livestock were introduced. But the availability of good land and the revolution in marketing were the most important spurs to profitable commercial farming. Good land made for high yields, at least for a time, and when excessive planting wore out the soil, a farmer could migrate to more fertile lands farther west. Transportation facilities made distant markets available and plugged farmers into a commercial network that provided credit and relieved them of the need to do their own selling.

The emerging exchange network encouraged movement away from diversified farming and toward regional concentration on staple crops. Wheat was the main cash crop of the North, and the center of its cultivation moved westward as soil depletion, pests, and plant diseases lowered yields in older regions. In 1815, the heart of the wheat belt was New York and Pennsylvania. By 1839, Ohio was the leading producer, and Indiana and Illinois were beginning to come into their own. On the rocky hillsides of New England, sheep raising was displacing mixed farming. But the prime examples of successful staple production in this era were in the South. Tobacco remained a major cash crop of the upper South (despite declining fertility and a shift to wheat in some areas); rice was important in coastal South Carolina; and sugar was a staple of southern Louisiana. Cotton, however, was the "king" crop in the lower South. It became the nation's principal export commodity and brought wealth and prosperity from South Carolina to Louisiana.

Five factors made the Deep South the world's greatest producer of cotton. First was the great demand generated by the rise of textile manufacturing in England and, to a lesser extent, in New England. Second was the cotton gin. Invented by Eli Whitney in 1793, this simple device cut the labor costs involved in cleaning the seeds from short-staple cotton, thus making it an easily marketable commodity.

A third reason for the rise of cotton was the availability of good land in the Southeast. As yields fell in the original areas of cultivation—mainly South Carolina and Georgia—the opening of the rich and fertile plantation areas or "black belts" of Alabama, Mississippi, and Louisiana shifted the Cotton Kingdom westward and vastly increased total production. In 1816, New Orleans, the great marketing center for western crops, received 37,000 bales of cotton (a bale of cotton weighs 480 pounds); in 1830, 428,000 arrived; in 1840, the annual number had reached 923,000. Between 1817 and 1840, the amount of cotton the South produced tripled from 461,000 to 1,350,000 bales.

View the **Image**
A Patent Drawing of Eli Whitney's Cotton Gin on
myhistorylab.com

A fourth factor—slavery, which provided a flexible system of forced labor—permitted operations on a scale impossible for the family labor system of the agricultural North. Finally, the cotton economy benefited from the South's splendid natural transportation system—its great network of navigable rivers extending deep into the interior from the cotton ports of Charleston, Savannah, Mobile, and, of course, New Orleans. The South had less need than other agricultural regions for artificial internal improvements such as canals and good roads. Planters could simply establish themselves on or near a river and ship their crops to market via natural waterways.

Quick Check

✓ What was the main agricultural crop of the South, and what factors made it so successful?

Early Industrialism

The growth of a market economy also created new opportunities for industrialists. In 1815, most manufacturing in the United States was carried on in households, in the workshops of skilled artisans, or in small mills that used waterpower to turn wheat into flour or timber into boards. The factory form of production, in which supervised workers tended or operated machines under one roof, was rare. It was found mainly in southern New England, where small spinning mills, relying heavily on the labor of women and children, accomplished one step in the manufacture of cotton textiles. But women working at home still spun most thread and wove, cut, and sewed most cloth.

As late as 1820, about two-thirds of the clothing Americans wore was made entirely in households by female family members—wives and daughters. However, they were producing a growing proportion of it for market rather than direct home consumption. Under the "putting-out" system of manufacturing, merchant capitalists provided raw material to people in their own homes, picked up finished or semifinished products, paid the workers, and took charge of distribution. Items such as simple shoes and hats were also made under the putting-out system. Home manufacturing of this type was centered in the Northeast, often done by farm families making profitable use of their slack seasons. It did not usually challenge the economic preeminence of agriculture or seriously disrupt rural life.

Artisans in small shops in towns made most articles that required greater skill—such as high-quality shoes and boots, carriages or wagons, mill wheels, and barrels or kegs. But after 1815, shops grew bigger; masters tended to become entrepreneurs rather than working artisans; and journeymen often became wage earners rather than aspiring masters. The growing market for low-priced goods also emphasized speed, quantity, and standardization in production. Even where no substantial mechanization was involved, shops dealing in handmade goods for a local clientele tended to become small factories turning out cheaper items for a wider public.

A fully developed factory system emerged first in textile manufacturing. The first cotton mills utilizing the power loom and spinning machinery—thus making it possible to turn fiber into cloth in a single factory—resulted from the efforts of three Boston merchants: Francis Cabot Lowell, Nathan Appleton, and Patrick Tracy Jackson. On a visit to England in 1810–1811, Lowell memorized the closely guarded industrial secret of how to construct a power loom. In Boston, he joined with Appleton and Jackson to acquire a site with water power at nearby Waltham and obtain a corporate charter for textile manufacturing on a new and expanded scale.

Under the name of the Boston Manufacturing Company, the associates began their Waltham operation in 1813. Its phenomenal success led to the erection of a larger and even more profitable mill at Lowell, Massachusetts, in 1822 and another at Chicopee in 1823. Lowell became the great showplace for early American industrialization. Its large and seemingly contented workforce of unmarried young women residing in supervised dormitories, its unprecedented scale of operation, its successful mechanization of almost every stage of the production process—all captured the American middle-class imagination in the 1820s and 1830s. But in the late 1830s and 1840s, conditions in the mills changed for the worse as the owners began to require more work for lower pay, and some of the mill women became militant labor activists. One of them, Sarah Bagley, helped found the Lowell Female Labor Reform Association in 1844. She led protests against long hours and changes that required more work from each operative. Other mills using similar labor systems sprang up throughout New England, which became the first important manufacturing area in the United States.

Read the **Document** *The Harbinger, "Female Workers at Lowell" (1836)* on **myhistorylab.com**

The shift in textile manufacture from domestic to factory production also shifted the locus of women's economic activity. As the New England textile industry grew, the putting-out system declined. Between 1824 and 1832, household production of textiles dropped from 90 to 50 percent in most parts of New England. The shift to factory production changed capitalist activity in the region. Before the 1820s, New England merchants concentrated mainly on international trade, and Boston mercantile houses made great profits. A major source of capital was the lucrative China trade carried on by fast, well-built New England vessels. When the success of Waltham and Lowell became clear, many merchants shifted their capital from oceanic trade to manufacturing. This had important political consequences, as leading politicians such as Daniel Webster no longer advocated a low tariff that favored importers over exporters. Many politicians now supported a high duty to protect manufacturers from foreign competition.

Early Industrialism Lowell, Massachusetts, became America's model industrial town in the first half of the nineteenth century. In this painting of the town in 1814 (when it was still called East Chelmsford), a multistory brick mill is prominent on the river. Textile mills sprang up throughout Lowell in the 1820s and 1830s, employing thousands of workers, mostly women. Below, a photograph from c. 1848 shows a Lowell mill worker operating a loom.

The development of other "infant industries" after the War of 1812 was less dramatic and would not come to fruition until the 1840s and 1850s. Technology to improve rolling and refining iron was imported from England; it gradually encouraged a domestic iron industry centered in Pennsylvania. The use of interchangeable parts in manufacturing small arms, pioneered by Eli Whitney and Simeon North, helped modernize the weapons industry and contribute to the growth of new forms of mass production.

One should not assume, however, that America had already experienced an industrial revolution by 1840. In that year, 63.4 percent of the nation's labor force was still employed in agriculture. Only 8.8 percent of workers were directly involved in factory production (others worked in trade, transportation, and the professions). Although this represented a significant shift since 1810, when the figures were 83.7 and 3.2 percent, the numbers would have to change much more before it could be said that industrialization had really arrived. The revolution that did occur during these years was essentially one of distribution rather than production. The growth of a market economy of national scope—still based mainly on agriculture but involving a rapid flow of capital, commodities, and services from region to region—was the major economic development of this period. And it had vast repercussions for American life.

For those who benefited from it most directly, the market economy provided firm evidence of progress and improvement. But many of those who suffered from its periodic panics and depressions regretted the loss of the individual independence and security that a localized economy of small producers had provided. These victims of boom and bust were receptive to politicians and reformers who attacked corporations and "the money power."

Quick Check

✓ Which manufacturing sector first fully adopted industrial production, and where was it centered?

THE POLITICS OF NATION BUILDING AFTER THE WAR OF 1812

What decisions did the federal government face as the country expanded?

Geographic expansion, economic growth, and the changes in American life that accompanied them were bound to generate political controversy. Farmers, merchants, manufacturers, and laborers were affected by the changes in different ways. So were northerners, southerners, and westerners. Federal and state policies that were meant to encourage or control growth and expansion did not benefit all these groups or sections equally, and unavoidable conflicts of interest and ideology occurred.

But, for a time, the national political arena did not prominently reflect these conflicts. A myth of national harmony prevailed, culminating in the Era of Good Feeling during James Monroe's two terms as president. Behind this facade, individuals and groups fought for advantage, as always, but without the public accountability and need for broad popular approval that a party system would have required. As a result, popular interest in national politics fell.

The absence of party discipline and programs did not immobilize the federal government. The president took important initiatives in foreign policy; Congress legislated on matters of national concern; and the Supreme Court made far-reaching decisions. The common theme of the public policies that emerged between the War of 1812 and the age of Andrew Jackson, which began in 1829, was an awakening nationalism—a sense of American pride and purpose that reflected the expansionism and material progress of the period.

The Missouri Compromise

In 1817, the Missouri territorial assembly applied for statehood. Since there were 2,000–3,000 slaves in the territory and the petition made no provision for emancipating them or for curbing slave imports, Missouri would enter the Union as a slave state unless Congress blocked it. Missouri was the first state, other than Louisiana, to be carved out of the Louisiana Purchase, and resolving the status of slavery there would have implications for the rest of the trans-Mississippi West.

When the question came before Congress in early 1819, sectional fears and anxieties bubbled to the surface. Many northerners resented southern control of the presidency and the fact that the three-fifths clause of the Constitution, by which every five slaves were counted as three persons in figuring the state's population, gave the South's free population added weight in the House of Representatives and the electoral college. The South, on the other hand, feared for the future of what it regarded as a necessary balance of power between the sections. Until 1819, a strict equality had been maintained by alternately admitting slave and free states; in that year, there were eleven of each. But the northern population was growing more rapidly than the southern, and the North had a decisive majority in the House. Hence the South saw its equal vote in the Senate as essential for preserving the balance.

In February 1819, Congressman James Tallmadge of New York introduced an amendment to the statehood bill, banning further introduction of slaves into Missouri and requiring the gradual elimination of slavery within the state. The House approved his amendment by a narrow margin. The Senate, however, voted it down. The issue remained unresolved until a new Congress convened in December. In the great debate that ensued in the Senate, Federalist leader Rufus King of New York argued that Congress was within its rights to require restricting slavery before Missouri could become a state. Southern senators protested that denying Missouri's freedom in this matter attacked the principle of equality among the states and showed that northerners were conspiring to upset the balance of power between the sections. They were also concerned about the future of African American slavery and the white racial privilege that went with it.

A statehood petition from the people of Maine, who were seeking to separate from Massachusetts, suggested a way out of the impasse. In February 1820, the Senate passed the Missouri Compromise, voting to couple the admission of Missouri as a slave state with the admission of Maine as a free state. An amendment

View the Map
The Missouri Compromise on
myhistorylab.com

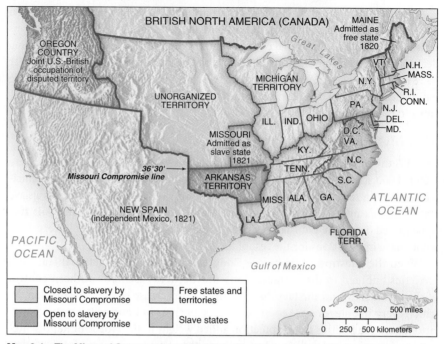

Map 9.1 *The Missouri Compromise, 1820–1821*   The Missouri Compromise kept the balance of power in the Senate by admitting Missouri as a slave state and Maine as a free state. The agreement temporarily settled the argument over slavery in the territories.

prohibited slavery in the rest of the Louisiana Purchase north of the southern border of Missouri, or above the latitude of 36°30', but allowed it below that line. The Senate's compromise then went to the House, where it was initially rejected. Through the adroit maneuvering of Henry Clay—who broke the proposal into three separate bills—it won House approval. The measure authorizing Missouri to frame a constitution and apply for admission as a slave state passed by the razor-thin margin of 90 to 87, with most northern representatives opposed (see Map 9.1).

A major sectional crisis had been resolved. But the Missouri affair was ominous for the future of North–South relations. Jefferson described the controversy as "a fire bell in the night," threatening the Union. In 1821, he wrote prophetically: "All, I fear, do not see the speck on our horizon which is to burst on us as a tornado, sooner or later. The line of division lately marked out between the different portions of our confederacy is such as will never, I fear, be obliterated." The congressional furor had shown that when slavery or its extension came directly before the people's representatives, regional loyalties took precedence over party or other considerations. Both sides used an emotional rhetoric of morality and fundamental rights, and votes followed sectional lines much more closely than on any other issue. If the United States were to acquire any new territories in which Congress had to determine the status of slavery, renewed sectional strife would be unavoidable.

Read the Document
Thomas Jefferson Reacts to The Missouri Compromise on **myhistorylab.com**

Quick Check

✓ What was the Missouri Compromise, and what problems did it resolve?

Postwar Nationalism and the Supreme Court

While the Monroe administration was proclaiming national harmony and congressional leaders were struggling to reconcile sectional differences, the third branch of government—the Supreme Court—was making a more substantial and enduring contribution to the growth of nationalism and a strong federal government. Much of this achievement was due to the firm leadership and fine legal mind of the chief justice of the United States, John Marshall.

A Virginian, a Federalist, and the devoted disciple and biographer of George Washington, Marshall served as chief justice from 1801 to 1835, and during that entire period, he dominated the Court as no other chief justice has ever done. Discouraging dissent and seeking to hammer out a single opinion on almost every case that came before the Court, he has been compared to a symphony conductor who was also composer of the music and principal soloist.

As the author of most of the major opinions the Court issued during its formative period, Marshall gave shape to the Constitution and clarified the crucial role of the Court in the American system of government. He placed the protection of individual liberty, especially the right to acquire property, above the attainment of political, social, or economic equality. Ultimately he was a nationalist, believing that the strength, security, and happiness of the American people depended mainly on economic growth and the creation of new wealth.

The role of the Supreme Court, in Marshall's view, was to interpret and enforce the Constitution in a way that encouraged economic development, especially against state legislatures' efforts to interfere with the constitutionally protected rights of individuals or combinations of individuals to acquire property through productive activity. To limit state action, he cited the contract clause of the Constitution, which prohibited a state from passing a law "impairing the obligation of contracts." As the legal watchdog of an enterprising, capitalist society, the Court could also approve a liberal grant of power for the federal government, so that the latter could fulfill its constitutional responsibility to promote the general welfare by encouraging economic growth and prosperity.

In major decisions between 1819 and 1824, the Marshall Court enhanced judicial power and used the contract clause of the Constitution to limit the power of state legislatures. It also strengthened the federal government by sanctioning a broad or loose construction of its constitutional powers and by affirming its supremacy over the states.

In Dartmouth College v. Woodward (1819), the Court was asked to rule whether the New Hampshire legislature could meddle in the governance of Dartmouth College, a private institution. Daniel Webster, arguing for the college and against the state, contended that Dartmouth's original charter of 1769 was a valid and irrevocable contract between the state and the trustees of the college. The Court accepted his argument. Speaking for all the justices, Marshall made the far-reaching

Read the **Document** *Dartmouth College V. Woodward* on **myhistorylab.com** determination that the Constitution's contracts clause fully protected any charter a state granted to a private corporation.

In practical terms, the Court's ruling in the Dartmouth case meant that the kinds of business enterprises state governments were incorporating—such as turnpike or canal companies and textile manufacturers—could hold on indefinitely to any privileges or favors that their original charters had granted. The decision therefore increased the power and independence of business corporations by weakening states' ability to regulate them or withdraw their privileges. The ruling fostered the growth of the modern corporation as a profit-making enterprise with only limited public responsibilities.

About a month after the Dartmouth ruling, in March 1819, the Marshall Court handed down its most important decision. The case of McCulloch v. Maryland arose because the state of Maryland had levied a tax on the Baltimore branch of the Bank of the United States, which had been rechartered for 25 years in 1816. The unanimous opinion of the Court, delivered by Marshall, was that the Maryland tax was unconstitutional. The two main issues were whether Congress had the right to establish a national bank and whether a state had the power to tax or regulate an agency or institution Congress created.

In response to the first question, Marshall set forth his doctrine of "implied powers." Conceding that the Constitution contained no specific authorization to charter a bank, the chief justice argued that such a right could be deduced from more general powers and from an understanding of the "great objects" for which the federal government had been founded. Marshall thus struck a blow for a loose construction of the Constitution and a broad grant of power to the federal government to encourage economic growth and stability.

In answer to the second question—the right of a state to tax or regulate a federal agency—Marshall held that the bank was indeed such an agency and that giving a state the power to tax it would also give the state the power to destroy it. In an important assertion of the supremacy of the national government, Marshall argued that the American people "did not design to make their government dependent on the states." This opinion ran counter to the view of many Americans, particularly in the South, that the Constitution did not take away sovereignty from the states. The debate over federal–state relations was not resolved until the northern victory in the Civil War decisively affirmed the dominance of federal authority. But Marshall's decision gave great new weight to a nationalist constitutional philosophy.

The *Gibbons v. Ogden* decision of 1824 bolstered Congress's power to regulate interstate commerce. A competing ferry service operating between New York and New Jersey challenged a steamboat monopoly granted by the state of New York. The Court declared the New York grant unconstitutional because it amounted to state interference with Congress's exclusive right to regulate interstate commerce. The Court's ruling went a long way toward freeing private interests engaged in furthering the transportation revolution from state interference.

This case showed the dual effect of Marshall's decision making. It broadened the power of the federal government at the expense of the states and encouraged the growth of a national market economy. The Court's actions provide the clearest and most consistent example of the main nationalistic trends of the period—the acknowledgment of the federal government's role in promoting a powerful and prosperous America and the rise of a nationwide capitalist economy.

Quick Check

✓ What did John Marshall believe the Supreme Court's role should be, and how did he help to create It?

Nationalism in Foreign Policy: The Monroe Doctrine

Foreign affairs also reflected the new spirit of nationalism. The main diplomatic challenge facing Monroe after his reelection in 1820 was how to respond to the successful revolt of most of Spain's and Portugal's Latin American colonies after the Napoleonic wars. In Congress, Henry Clay called for immediate recognition of the new states. In doing so, he expressed the belief of many Americans that their neighbors to the south were simply following the example of the United States in its own struggle for independence.

Before 1822, the administration stuck to a policy of neutrality. Monroe and Secretary of State Adams feared that recognizing the revolutionary governments would antagonize Spain and impede negotiations to acquire Florida. But pressure for recognition grew in Congress; in 1821, the House of Representatives, responding to Clay's impassioned oratory, passed a resolution of sympathy for Latin American revolutionaries and made it clear that the president would have the support of Congress if and when he decided to accord recognition. After the Adams–Onís Treaty ceding Florida to the United States had been formally ratified in 1821, Monroe agreed to recognition and diplomatic ties with the Latin American states. The U.S. recognized Mexico and Colombia in 1822, Chile and Argentina in 1823, Brazil (which had separated from Portugal) and the Federation of Central American States in 1824, and Peru in 1826.

Recognizing the Latin American states put the United States on a possible collision course with the major European powers. Austria, Russia, and Prussia were committed to rolling back the tides of liberalism, self-government, and national self-determination that had arisen during the French Revolution and its Napoleonic aftermath. After Napoleon's first defeat in 1814, the monarchs of Europe had joined in a "Grand Alliance" to protect "legitimate" authoritarian governments from democratic challenges. Great Britain was originally a member of this concert of nations but withdrew when its own interests conflicted with those of the other members. In 1822, the remaining alliance members, joined now by the restored French monarchy, authorized France to invade Spain and restore a Bourbon regime that might be disposed to reconquer the empire. This prospect alarmed both Great Britain and the United States.

Particularly troubling to American policymakers was the role of Czar Alexander I of Russia. Not only was the czar an outspoken and active opponent of Latin

American independence, but he was attempting to extend Russian claims on the Pacific coast of North America south to the 51st parallel—into the Oregon Country, which the United States wanted for itself.

The threat from the Grand Alliance pointed to a need for American cooperation with Great Britain, which had its own reasons for wanting to prevent a restoration of Spanish, Portuguese, or French power in the New World. Independent nations offered better and more open markets for British manufactured goods than the colonies of other nations, and the spokesmen for burgeoning British industrial capitalism anticipated a profitable economic dominance over Latin America. In early 1823, the British foreign secretary, George Canning, tried to exact from the French a pledge that they would not try to acquire territories in Spanish America. When that venture failed, he sought to involve the United States in a policy to prevent the Grand Alliance from intervening in Latin America.

In August 1823, Canning broached the possibility of joint Anglo-American action against the Alliance to Richard Rush, U.S. minister to Great Britain. Rush referred the suggestion to the president. Monroe welcomed the British initiative because he believed the United States should take an active role in transatlantic affairs by playing one European power against another. However, Secretary of State Adams favored a different approach. Adams distrusted the British and believed that avoiding entanglements in European politics while also discouraging European intervention in the Americas would best serve the national interest.

Read the
Document
*The Monroe Doctrine
(1823)* on
myhistorylab.com

Political ambition also predisposed Adams against joint action with Great Britain; he hoped to be the next president and did not want to give his rivals the chance to label him as pro-British. He therefore advocated unilateral action by the United States rather than a joint declaration with the British. As he told the cabinet in November, "It would be more candid, as well as more dignified, to avow our principles explicitly to Russia and France, than to come in as a cock-boat of the British man-of-war."

Adams managed to swing Monroe and the cabinet around to his viewpoint. In his annual message to Congress on December 2, 1823, Monroe included a far-reaching statement on foreign policy that was actually written mainly by Adams, who did become president in 1824. What came to be known as the Monroe Doctrine solemnly declared that the United States opposed further colonization in the Americas or any effort by European nations to extend their political systems outside their own hemisphere.

In return, the United States pledged not to involve itself in the internal affairs of Europe or to take part in European wars. The statement envisioned a North and South America composed entirely of independent states—with the United States preeminent among them.

Quick Check

✔ How and why did America's recognition of the Latin American republics change its relationship with the European Powers?

Although the Monroe Doctrine made little impression on the great powers of Europe when it was proclaimed, it signified the rise of a new sense of independence and self-confidence in American attitudes toward the Old World. The United States would now go its own way free of involvement in European conflicts and would protect its own sphere of influence from European interference.

CONCLUSION: THE END OF THE ERA OF GOOD FEELING

The consensus on national goals and leadership that Monroe had represented could not sustain itself. The Era of Good Feeling turned out to be a passing phase and something of an illusion. Although the pursuit of national greatness would continue, there would be sharp divisions over how to achieve it. A general commitment to the settlement of the West and the development of agriculture, commerce, and industry would endure despite differences over what role government should play in the process; but the idea that an elite of nonpartisan statesmen could define common purposes and harmonize competing elements—the concept of leadership that Monroe and Adams had advanced—would no longer be viable in the more contentious and democratic America of the Jacksonian era.

9 STUDY RESOURCES

((•—[Listen to the **Chapter Audio** for Chapter 9 on **myhistorylab.com**

TIMELINE

1813 Boston Manufacturing Company founds cotton mill at Waltham, Massachusetts, p. 223

1815 War of 1812 ends, p. 222

1818 Andrew Jackson invades Spanish Florida, p. 223

1819 Supreme Court hands down far-reaching decisions in Dartmouth College case and in *McCulloch v. Maryland,* p. 238
  • Adams–Onís Treaty cedes Spanish territory to the United States, p. 238

1820 Missouri Compromise resolves nation's first sectional crisis, p. 235
  • Monroe reelected president almost unanimously, p. 239

1823 Monroe Doctrine proclaimed, p. 240

1824 Lafayette revisits the United States, p. 221
  • Supreme Court decides *Gibbons v. Ogden,* p. 238
  • John Quincy Adams elected president, p. 240

1825 Erie Canal completed; canal era begins, p. 230

CHAPTER REVIEW

EXPANSION AND MIGRATION

What key forces drove American expansion westward during this period?

Westward expansion was fueled by the ambition to expand American territory and to economically exploit and develop the Far West. The First Seminole War gave Monroe and Adams a chance to push Spain from the southeast under the Adams–Onís Treaty, while entrepreneurs established a fur trade in the North and an aggressive "removal" policy forced Indian tribes from the South. *(p. 222)*

TRANSPORTATION AND THE MARKET ECONOMY

How did developments in transportation support the growth of agriculture and manufacturing?

New turnpikes, canals, steamboats, and eventually railroads expanded the access of farmers and small manufacturers to a regional and even national market. Farmers began to produce staple crops to sell rather than subsistence crops for their own families. Textile factories developed to turn southern cotton into clothing. In the North, industrialization increased efficiency but crowded workers into factories for long hours. *(p. 222)*

THE POLITICS OF NATION BUILDING AFTER THE WAR OF 1812

What decisions did the federal government face as the country expanded?

The government decided whether new states would allow slavery, how the Supreme Court would function, and how the United States would deal with the European powers. The Missouri Compromise established the 36°30' line dividing slave from free states, while the Court became the supreme constitutional interpreter. The Monroe Doctrine held that the United States and European powers should each control their respective hemispheres. *(p. 228)*

KEY TERM QUESTIONS

1. Why did Spain agree to the Adams–Onís Treaty in 1819? (p. 223)

2. Why did squatters push for formal preemption rights from the government? (p. 225)

3. Is the Era of Good Feeling an appropriate name for James Monroe's years as President of the United States? (p. 234)

4. What issues did the Missouri Compromise resolve? (p. 235)

5. What principle did Chief Justice John Marshall establish in his ruling in *Dartmouth College v. Woodward*? (p. 237)

6. What principle did Chief Justice John Marshall establish in his ruling in *McCulloch v. Maryland*? (p. 238)

7. What principle did Chief Justice John Marshall establish in his ruling in *Gibbons v. Ogden*? (p. 238)

8. What were the short- and long-term effects of the Monroe Doctrine? (p. 240)

MyHISTORYLAB CONNECTIONS

Visit **www.myhistorylab.com** for a customized Study Plan to build your knowledge of *Nation Building and Nationalism*.

Question for Analysis

1. What were some of the disadvantages of using rivers to transport products?

View the **Map** *Expanding America and Internal Improvements* p. 229

2. What was a typical day like for female factory workers?

Read the **Document** *The Harbinger, Female Workers at Lowell (1836)* p. 233

Other Resources from this Chapter

Read the **Document** *The Cherokee Treaty of 1817*

Read the **Document** *Black Hawk, from "The Life of Black Hawk"*

Listen to the **Audio File** *The Erie Canal*

View the **Image** *A Patent Drawing of Eli Whitney's Cotton Gin*

3. What was the most significant outcome of the Missouri Compromise?

🔍 **View** the **Map** *The Missouri Compromise* p. 235

4. What influence did the Monroe Doctrine have on the great powers of Europe?

📖 **Read** the **Document** *The Monroe Doctrine* p. 240

📖 **Read** the **Document** *Thomas Jefferson Reacts to Missouri*

📖 **Read** the **Document** *Dartmouth College v. Woodward*

10

THE TRIUMPH OF WHITE MEN'S DEMOCRACY

1824–1840

Contents and Spotlight Questions

DEMOCRACY IN THEORY AND PRACTICE PG. 247

How did the relationship between the government and the people change during this time?

JACKSON AND THE POLITICS OF DEMOCRACY PG. 251

What political conflicts did President Andrew Jackson face and how did he resolve them?

THE BANK WAR AND THE SECOND-PARTY SYSTEM PG. 259

What were the arguments for and against the Bank of the United States?

HEYDAY OF THE SECOND-PARTY SYSTEM PG. 263

What was the two-party system, and how were the parties different?

((•—[**Listen** to the **Chapter Audio** for Chapter 10 on **myhistorylab.com**

DEMOCRATIC SPACE: THE NEW HOTELS

During the 1820s and 1830s, the United States became a more democratic country for at least some of its population. The emerging spirit of popular democracy found expression in a new institution—the large hotel with several stories and hundreds of rooms. President-elect Andrew Jackson, the political figure who best represented the spirit of the age, stayed in the new National Hotel when he arrived in Washington in 1829 to prepare for his administration. After a horde of well-wishers made a shambles of the White House during his inaugural reception in March 1829, Jackson retreated to the hotel again for a little peace and a chance to consult with his advisers. The National was only one of several large "first-class"

Fine Accommodations New York's Astor House, completed in 1836, was one of the grandest of the new American hotels, offering fine accommodations to travelers who could afford to pay for them.

245

hotels that opened immediately before or during Jackson's presidency. Among the others were the Tremont House in Boston, the Baltimore City Hotel, and New York's Astor House.

The hotel boom responded to Americans' increasing tendency to move about the country. Entrepreneurs built these large places of accommodation to service the rising tide of travelers, transients, and new arrivals. The hotels provided lodging, food, and drink on an unprecedented scale and were as different from the inns of the eighteenth century as the steamboat was from the flatboat.

According to historian Doris Elizabeth King, "the new hotels were so obviously 'public' and 'democratic' in their character that foreigners were often to describe them as a true reflection of American society." Their very existence showed that many people, white males in particular, were on the move geographically and socially. Among the hotels' patrons were traveling salesmen, ambitious young men seeking to establish themselves in a new city, and restless pursuers of "the main chance" (unexpected economic opportunities) who were not ready to put down roots. Hotel managers shocked European visitors by failing to enforce traditional social distinctions among their clientele. Under the "American plan," guests were required to pay for their meals and eat at a common "table d'hôte" with anyone who happened to be there, including servants traveling with their employers. Ability to pay was the only requirement for admission (unless one was an unescorted woman or dark-skinned). Every white male patron, regardless of social background and occupation, enjoyed the personal service previously available only to a privileged class.

The hotel culture also revealed the limitations of the new democratic era. African Americans, Native Americans, and women were excluded or discriminated against, just as they were denied suffrage. The poor—of whom there were more than most European visitors recognized—could not afford the hotels and were consigned to squalid rooming houses. If the social equality *within* the hotel reflected a decline in traditional status distinctions, the broad gulf between potential patrons and those who could not pay what the hotels charged signaled growing inequality based on wealth rather than inherited status.

Hotel life also reflected the emergence of democratic politics. A new breed of professional politicians spent much of their time in hotels as they traveled about. Congressmen or state legislators often stayed in hotels during sessions, making deals and bargains. The hotel was thus a symbol for the democratic spirit of the age, one that shows its shortcomings and its strengths. The new democracy was first of all political. Amost all white males now had the right to vote, and modern political parties arose appealing to a mass electorate. It was also social. Democracy undermined the habit of deferring to people because of their birth or ancestry. People born in relatively humble circumstances increasingly hoped to climb the ladder of success. But the ideals of equal citizenship and opportunity did not extend across the lines of race and gender, which actually hardened during this period.

DEMOCRACY IN THEORY AND PRACTICE

During the 1820s and 1830s, *democracy* first became a generally accepted term to describe how American institutions were supposed to work. Although the Founders had defined democracy as direct rule by the people, most of them rejected this approach to government because it conflicted with their concept of a well-balanced republic led by a "natural aristocracy." For champions of popular government in the Jacksonian period, however, the people were sovereign and could do no wrong: "The voice of the people is the voice of God." Conservatives were less certain of the wisdom of the common folk. But even they were recognizing that they had to win over public opinion before making major decisions.

Besides evoking "popular sovereignty," the democratic impulse seemed to stimulate social leveling. Earlier Americans had usually assumed that the rich and wellborn were the natural leaders of the community and guardians of its culture and values. But by the 1830s, the disappearance of inherited social ranks and clearly defined aristocracies or privileged groups struck European visitors such as Alexis de Tocqueville as the most radical feature of democracy in America. Historians have described this development as a decline of the spirit of "deference."

The decline of deference meant that "self-made men" of lowly origins could more readily acquire power and influence and that exclusiveness and aristocratic pretensions were likely to provoke hostility or scorn. But economic equality— an equitable sharing of wealth—was not part of the mainstream agenda of the Jacksonian period. This was a competitive capitalist society. The watchword was equality of *opportunity*, not equality of *reward*. Life was a race. So long as all white males appeared to have an equal start, there could be no reason for complaint if some were winners and others losers. Historians now generally agree that economic inequality—the gap between rich and poor—actually increased during this period.

How did the relationship between the government and the people change during this time?

Democratic Culture

Although some types of inequality persisted or even grew during the age of democracy, they did so despite a growing belief that equality was the governing principle of American society.

One example of this was the decline of distinctive modes of dress for upper and lower classes. The elaborate periwigs and knee breeches of eighteenth-century gentlemen gave way to short hair and pantaloons for men of all classes. Fashionable dress among women also ceased to be a sure index of gentility; serving girls on their day off wore the same kind of finery as the wives and daughters of the wealthy—or at least reasonable imitations.

Yet in the cities, the rise of industrialization was also creating a permanent class of low-paid, unorganized wage earners. In rural areas, there was a significant division between successful commercial farmers and small holders, or tenants who subsisted on marginal land, as well as enormous inequality of status between southern planters and their black slaves.

Changes in the organization and status of the learned professions also showed that traditional forms of privilege and elitism were under attack. Under Jacksonian pressure, state legislatures abolished the licensing requirements for physicians that local medical societies had administered. As a result, quacks and folk healers could compete freely with established medical doctors.

The democratic tide also struck the legal profession. Local bar associations continued to set the qualifications for practicing attorneys, but in many places, they admitted persons with little or no formal training and the most rudimentary knowledge of the law. The clergy responded to the new democratic spirit by developing a more popular and emotional style of preaching to please their public.

In this atmosphere of democratic leveling, the popular press was increasingly important as a source of information and opinion. Written and read by common folk, hundreds of newspapers and magazines ushered the mass of white Americans into the political arena. New political views—which those in power might once have silenced—could now find an audience. Reformers of all kinds could easily publicize their causes, and the press became the venue for the great national debates on issues such as the government's role in banking and the status of slavery in new states and territories. As a profession, journalism was open to those who were literate and thought they had something to say. The editors of newspapers with a large circulation were the most influential opinion makers of the age.

The democratic spirit also found expression in new forms of literature and art for a mass audience. The intentions of individual artists and writers varied considerably. Some pandered to popular taste in defiance of traditional standards of high culture. Others tried to capture the spirit of the age by portraying the everyday life of ordinary Americans rather than the traditional subjects of "aristocratic" art. A few hoped to use literature and art to improve popular taste and instill deeper moral and spiritual values. But all of them were aware that their audience was the broad citizenry of a democratic nation rather than a refined elite.

A rise in literacy and a revolution in printing technology made a mass market for popular literature possible. More potential readers and lower publishing costs led to a flood of lurid and sentimental novels, some of which became the first American best-sellers. By the 1840s and 1850s, writers such as George Lippard, Mrs. E. D. E. N. Southworth, and Augusta Jane Evans had perfected the formulas that led to commercial success. Gothic horror and the perils of virtuous heroines threatened by dastardly villains were among the ingredients that readers came to expect from popular fiction.

Many of the new sentimental novels were written by and for women. Some women writers implicitly protested their situation by portraying men as tyrannical, unreliable, or vicious and the women they abandoned or failed to support as resourceful individualists able to make their own way in a man's world. But the standard happy endings sustained the convention that a woman's place was in the home: A virtuous and protective man usually turned up and saved the heroine from independence.

In the theater, melodrama became the dominant genre. Despite religious objections, theater-going was popular in the cities during the Jacksonian era. The standard fare involved the inevitable trio of beleaguered heroine, mustachioed villain, and a hero who asserted himself in the nick of time. Patriotic comedies extolling the common sense of the rustic Yankee who foiled the foppish European aristocrat were also popular and aroused the audience's democratic sympathies. Men and women of all classes went to the theater, and those in the cheap seats often became raucous and even violent when they did not like what they saw. Unpopular actors or plays could provoke riots. In 1849, in New York, 23 people were killed in disorders over an English actor who was the rival of Edwin Forrest, the era's most popular American thespian.

"Popular sovereignty" expressed itself less dramatically in the visual arts, but its influence was still felt. Beginning in the 1830s, painters turned from portraying great events and famous people to depicting everyday life. Democratic genre painters such as William Sidney Mount and George Caleb Bingham captured the lives of plain folk with skill and understanding. Mount, who painted lively rural scenes, expressed the credo of the democratic artist: "Paint pictures that will take with the public—never paint for the few but the many." Bingham was noted for his graphic images of Americans voting, carrying goods on riverboats, and engaging in other everyday activities.

Exponents of a higher culture and a more refined sensibility sought to enlighten or uplift the new public. The "Brahmin poets" of New England—Henry Wadsworth Longfellow, James Russell Lowell, and Oliver Wendell Holmes—offered lofty sentiments and moral messages to a receptive middle class. Ralph Waldo Emerson carried his philosophy of spiritual self-reliance to lyceums and lecture halls across the country. Great novelists such as Nathaniel Hawthorne and Herman Melville experimented with popular romantic genres. But Hawthorne and Melville failed to gain a large readership. Their ironic and pessimistic view of life clashed with the optimism of the age. For later generations of American critics, however, the works of Melville and Hawthorne became centerpieces of the American literary "renaissance" of the mid-nineteenth century. Hawthorne's *The Scarlet Letter* (1850) and Melville's *Moby-Dick* (1851) are now regarded as masterworks of fiction.

Read the **Document** *Ralph Waldo Emerson, "Self-Reliance"* on **myhistorylab.com**

Quick Check

✓ How did American culture reflect a growing spirit of "popular sovereignty"?

Democratic Political Institutions

The supremacy of democracy was most obvious in the new politics of universal white manhood suffrage and mass political parties. By the 1820s, most states had removed the last barriers to voting for all white males. This change was not as radical or controversial as it would be later in nineteenth-century Europe; so many Americans owned land that most voters were still men of property.

The proportion of public officials who were elected rather than appointed also increased. "The people" increasingly chose judges, as well as legislators and executive officers. A new style of politicking developed. Politicians had to get out and campaign, demonstrating in their speeches on the stump that they could mirror voters' fears and concerns. Electoral politics became more festive and dramatic.

Skillful and farsighted politicians—such as Martin Van Buren in New York—began in the 1820s to build stable statewide political organizations out of what had been loosely organized factions. Before the rise of effective national parties,

Stump Speeches Political candidates of the Jacksonian era traveled from town to town giving stump speeches. The political gatherings at which they spoke provided entertainment and were an excellent source of political news. This painting, *Stump Speaking* (1853/1854), is by George Caleb Bingham, one of the most prolific democratic genre painters.

politicians created true party organizations on the state level by dispensing government jobs to friends and supporters and attacking rivals as enemies of popular aspirations. Earlier politicians had regarded parties as a threat to republican virtue and had embraced them only as a temporary expedient, but Van Buren regarded a permanent two-party system as essential to democratic government. In his opinion, parties restricted the temptation to abuse power, a tendency deeply planted in the human heart. The major breakthrough in American political thought during the 1820s and 1830s was the idea of a "loyal opposition," ready to capitalize politically on the mistakes or excesses of the "ins" without denying the ins' right to act the same way when they became the "outs."

Changes in the method of nominating and electing a president fostered the growth of a national two-party system. By 1828, voters rather than state legislatures were choosing presidential electors in all but two of the 24 states. The new need to mobilize grassroots voters behind particular candidates required national organization. Coalitions of state parties that could agree on a single standard-bearer evolved into the great national parties of the Jacksonian era—the Democrats and the Whigs. When national nominating conventions appeared in 1831, representative party assemblies, not congressional caucuses or ad hoc political alliances, selected presidential candidates.

New political institutions and practices encouraged popular interest and participation. In the presidential election of 1824, less than 27 percent of adult white males voted. From 1828 to 1836, 55 percent did. Then it shot up to 78 percent in 1840—the first election in which two fully organized national parties each nominated a single candidate and campaigned in every state in the Union.

Quick Check

✓ What changed during the 1820s and 1830s in the way politicians were elected to public office?

Economic Issues

Economic questions dominated politics in the 1820s and 1830s. The Panic of 1819 and the subsequent depression heightened popular interest in government economic policy. No one really knew how to solve the problems of a market economy that went through cycles of boom and bust, but many still thought they had the answer. Some, especially small farmers, favored a return to a simpler and more "honest" economy without banks, paper money, and the easy credit that encouraged speculation. Others, particularly emerging entrepreneurs, saw salvation in government aid and protection for venture capital. Entrepreneurs appealed to state governments for charters that granted special privileges to banks, transportation enterprises, and manufacturing corporations. The economic distress of the early 1820s fostered the rapid growth of state-level political activity and organizations that foreshadowed the rise of national parties organized around economic programs.

Party disputes involved more than the direct economic concerns of particular interest groups. They also reflected the republican ideology that feared conspiracy against American liberty and equality. Whenever any group appeared to be exerting decisive influence over public policy, its opponents were quick to charge its members with corruption and the unscrupulous pursuit of power.

The notion that the American experiment was fragile, constantly threatened by power-hungry conspirators, took two principal forms. Jacksonians believed that "the money power" endangered the survival of republicanism; their opponents feared that populist politicians like Jackson himself—"rabble-rousers"—would gull the electorate into ratifying high-handed and tyrannical actions contrary to the nation's true interests.

The role of the federal government concerned both sides. Should it foster economic growth, as the National Republicans and later the Whigs contended, or should it simply attempt to destroy what Jacksonians decried as "special privilege" or "corporate monopoly"? Almost everyone favored equality of opportunity. The question was whether the government should actively support commerce and industry or stay out of the economy in the name of laissez-faire (the idea that the government should keep its hands off the economy) and free competition.

> **Quick Check**
>
> ✓ How did the Jacksonians differ from their opponents in their opinions about the New American Experiment?

JACKSON AND THE POLITICS OF DEMOCRACY

The public figure who symbolized the triumph of democracy was Andrew Jackson of Tennessee. Jackson lost the presidential election of 1824, but his victory four years later, his actions as president, and the great political party that formed around him refashioned national politics in a more democratic mold.

> **What** political conflicts did President Andrew Jackson face and how did he resolve them?

Jackson Comes to Power

In the election of 1824, Jackson won a plurality of the electoral votes, but not a majority. (See Table 10.1) The contest was thrown into the House of Representatives, where the legislators were to choose from among the three top candidates: John Quincy Adams of Massachusetts, Jackson, and William Crawford, a Georgian who favored limited government. Adams won when Henry Clay of Kentucky, who had come in fourth, threw his support behind Adams. When Adams appointed Clay secretary of state, Jacksonians charged that a "corrupt bargain" had cost their favorite the presidency. Although there was no evidence that Clay had bartered votes for the promise of a high office, many believed the charge. Adams assumed office under a cloud of suspicion.

TABLE 10.1 The Election of 1824

Candidate	Party	Popular Vote	Electoral Vote*
J. Q. Adams	No party designations	108,740	84
Jackson		153,544	99
Clay		47,136	37
Crawford		46,618	41

*No candidate received a majority of the electoral votes. The House of Representatives elected Adams.

Adams had a frustrating presidency. The political winds were blowing against nationalistic programs, partly because the country was just recovering from a depression that many thought federal banking and tariff policies had caused or made worse. But Adams refused to bow to public opinion and called for expanding federal activity. He had a special interest in government support for science and wanted a national university in Washington. Advocates of states' rights and a strict construction of the Constitution were aghast, and congressional opponents turned the administration's domestic program into a pipe dream.

Men hostile to the administration and favorable to Jackson controlled the Congress elected in 1826. The tariff issue was the main business on their agenda. Pressure for greater protection from foreign imports came not only from manufacturers but also from farmers, especially wool and hemp growers, who would supply critical votes in the presidential election of 1828. The cotton-growing South—the only section where tariffs of all kinds were unpopular—was assumed to be safely in Jackson's camp regardless of his stand on the tariff. Therefore, his supporters felt safe in promoting a high tariff to swing critical votes his way. Jackson himself had never categorically opposed protective tariffs so long as they were "judicious."

As it turned out, the resulting tariff law was anything but judicious. Congress tried to provide something for everybody. Those favoring protection for farmers agreed to protect manufacturers and vice versa. This across-the-board increase in duties, however, angered southern free traders and became known as the tariff of abominations.

The campaign of 1828 actually began with Adams's election in 1824. Rallying around the charge of a corrupt bargain between Adams and Clay, Jackson's supporters began to organize on the state and local level with an eye to reversing the outcome of the election. By late 1827, virtually every county and important town or city in the nation had a Jackson committee. Influential state or regional leaders who had supported other candidates in 1824 now created a formidable coalition behind the Tennessean.

The most significant of these were Vice President John Calhoun of South Carolina, who spoke for the militant states' rights sentiment of the South;

Senator Martin Van Buren, who dominated New York politics through the political machine known as the Albany Regency; and two Kentucky editors, Francis P. Blair and Amos Kendall, who mobilized opposition in the West to Henry Clay and his "American System," which advocated government encouragement of economic development through protective tariffs and federally funded internal improvements. As they prepared for 1828, these leaders and their local followers laid the foundations for the first modern American political party—the Democrats. That the Democratic party was founded to promote the cause of a particular presidential candidate revealed a central characteristic of the emerging two-party system. From this time on, according to historian Richard P. McCormick, national parties existed primarily "to engage in a contest for the presidency." Without this great prize, there would have been less incentive to create national organizations out of the parties and factions developing in the several states.

The election of 1828 saw the birth of a new era of mass democracy. The mighty effort for Jackson featured such electioneering techniques as huge public rallies, torchlight parades, and lavish barbecues or picnics that the candidate's supporters paid for. Many historians believe that the massive turnout at such events during much of the rest of the nineteenth century revealed a deeper popular engagement with politics than at other times in American history. But others have argued that it may merely have showed that politicians had learned that entertainment and treats could lure people to the polls.

Personalities and mudslinging dominated the campaign. The Democratic press and a legion of pamphleteers viciously attacked Adams and praised "Old Hickory," as Jackson was called. Adams' supporters responded in kind; they even accused Jackson's wife, Rachel, of bigamy and adultery because she had unwittingly married Jackson before being officially divorced from her first husband. The Democrats then came up with the utterly false charge that Adams's wife was born out of wedlock.

What gave Jacksonians the edge was their portrayal of Jackson as an authentic man of the people, despite his wealth in land and slaves. His backwoods upbringing, record as a military hero and Indian fighter, and even lack of education were touted as evidence that he was a true representative of the common people, especially the plain folk of the South and the West. Adams, according to Democrats, was the exact opposite—an overeducated aristocrat, more at home in the salon and the study than among plain people. Nature's nobleman was pitted against the aloof New England intellectual. Adams never had a chance.

Jackson won by a popular vote margin of 150,000 and by more than 2 to 1 in the electoral college. But outside the Deep South, voters divided fairly evenly. Adams, in fact, won a majority of the electoral vote in the North. (See Map 10.1) Furthermore, Jackson's mandate was unclear. Most of the politicians in his camp favored states' rights and limited government against the nationalism of Adams and Clay, but Jackson himself had never taken a clear public stand on such issues as banks, tariffs, and internal improvements. He did, however, support removing Indians from the Gulf states, a key to his immense popularity in that region.

View the **Image**
Andrew Jackson's Inauguration Lithograph on **myhistorylab.com**

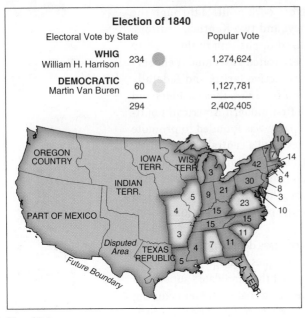

Election of 1840

	Electoral Vote by State		Popular Vote
WHIG William H. Harrison	234		1,274,624
DEMOCRATIC Martin Van Buren	60		1,127,781
	294		2,402,405

Map 10.1

Jackson was one of the most forceful and domineering American presidents. His most striking traits were an indomitable will, an intolerance of opposition, and a prickly pride that would not permit him to forgive or forget an insult or supposed act of betrayal. It is sometimes hard to determine whether principle or personal spite motivated his political actions. As a young man on the frontier, he had learned to fight his own battles. Violent in temper and action, he fought duels and battled the British, Spanish, and Indians with a zeal his critics found excessive. He was tough and resourceful, but he lacked the flexibility successful politicians usually show. Yet he generally got what he wanted.

Jackson's presidency commenced with his open endorsement of the rotation of officeholders, or what critics called "the spoils system." Although he did not actually replace many more federal officeholders with his supporters than his predecessors had, he was the first president to defend this practice openly as a legitimate democratic doctrine.

Midway through his first administration, however, Jackson did replace almost all of his original cabinet appointees. At the root of this upheaval was a feud between Jackson and Vice President Calhoun, but the Peggy Eaton affair in 1831 brought it to a head. Peggy O'Neale Eaton, the daughter of a Washington tavern owner, married Secretary of War John Eaton in 1829. Because of gossip about her moral character, other cabinet wives, led by Mrs. Calhoun, refused to receive her socially. Jackson became her fervent champion, partly because he found the charges against her reminiscent of the slanders against his late wife, who had died in 1828. When he raised the issue of Mrs. Eaton's social status at a cabinet meeting, only Secretary of State Van Buren, a widower, supported his stand. This seemingly trivial incident led to the resignation of all but one of the cabinet members (including Eaton), so the president could begin again with a fresh slate. Although Van Buren resigned with the rest to allow a thorough reorganization, Jackson rewarded his loyalty by appointing him minister to Britain and then choosing him as his vice president in 1832.

Quick Check

✔ What lessons do his sweeping electoral victory and his handling of The Peggy Eaton affair teach us about Andrew Jackson? What other political developments of the era helped him win election?

Indian Removal

View the **Closer Look**
Indian Removals on
myhistorylab.com

The first major policy question facing the Jackson administration concerned the fate of Native Americans. Jackson had long favored removing eastern Indians to lands beyond the Mississippi. In his military service on the southern frontier, he had already persuaded and coerced tribal groups to emigrate. Jackson's support of removal was no different from the policy of previous administrations. The only real issues were how rapidly and thoroughly it should be carried out and by what means. Georgia, Alabama, and Mississippi were clamoring for action.

Immediately after Jackson's election, Georgia extended its state laws over the Cherokee within its borders. Georgia declared that all Cherokee laws and customs were null and void, made all white people living in the Cherokee Nation subject to Georgia's laws, declared the Cherokee mere tenants at will on their land, and made it a crime for any Cherokee to try to influence another Cherokee to stay in Georgia. State officials also authorized the Georgia militia to use violence against the Cherokee to pressure them to give up their land and move west. Before Jackson's inauguration, Alabama and Mississippi also abolished the sovereignty of the Creeks and Choctaw, and declared state control of the tribes.

This legislation defied both the constitutional provisions giving the federal government exclusive jurisdiction over Indian affairs and specific treaties. But Jackson endorsed the state actions. He regarded Indians as children when they did the white man's bidding and savage beasts when they resisted. He was also aware of his political debt to the land-hungry states of the South. Consequently, in December 1829, he advocated a new and more coercive removal policy. Denying Cherokee autonomy, he asserted the primacy of states' rights over Indian rights and called for the speedy and thorough removal of all eastern Indians to designated areas beyond the Mississippi. Chief John Ross warned his people that "the object of the President is ... to create divisions among ourselves." President Jackson rejected Ross's appeal against Georgia's violation of federal treaty, and in 1830, the president's congressional supporters introduced a bill to implement the removal policy. Despite heated debate, the Indian Removal Act passed with strong support from the South and western border states.

Jackson then concluded the necessary treaties, using the threat of unilateral state action to bludgeon the tribes into submission. The treaty for Cherokee removal

A Falling House? Jackson's resigning cabinet members were, according to this cartoon, rats deserting a falling house. Jackson is seated on a collapsing chair, while the "altar of reform" and "public confidence in the stability of this administration" pillars topple to his left, and "resignations" flutter behind him. The president's foot is on the tail of the Secretary of State Martin Van Buren rat.

View the **Map**
Native American Land Cessions to 1829 on
myhistorylab.com

Trail of Tears Robert Lindneux, *The Trail of Tears* (1942). Cherokee Indians, carrying their few possessions, are prodded along by U.S. soldiers on the Trail of Tears. Thousands of Native Americans died on the ruthless forced march from their homelands in the East to the new Indian Territory in Oklahoma. (*Source: Robert Lindneux, American. "Trail of Tears." Courtesy of the Newberry Library, Chicago/Woolaroc Museum, Bartlesville, Oklahoma.*)

was negotiated with 75 out of 17,000 Cherokees, and none of the tribal officers was present. By 1833, all the southeastern tribes except the Cherokee had agreed to evacuate their ancestral homelands. Choctaw Chief David Folsom wrote, "We are exceedingly tired. We have just heard of the ratification of the Choctaw Treaty. Our doom is sealed. There is no course for us but to turn our faces to our new homes in the setting sun." Alexis de Tocqueville, the French author of *Democracy in America*, watched the troops driving the Choctaws across the Mississippi River in the winter of 1831. He wrote that Americans had deprived Indians of their rights "with singular felicity, tranquilly, legally, philanthropically…. It is impossible to destroy men with more respect for the laws of humanity."

Yet President Jackson was not always concerned with respect for the law. In 1832, he condoned Georgia's defiance of a Supreme Court decision (*Worcester v. Georgia*) that denied a state's right to jurisdiction over tribal lands. Georgia had arrested and sentenced to four years' hard labor a missionary who violated state law by going on tribal land without Georgia's permission. The Supreme Court declared the law unconstitutional. Jackson's legendary declaration that Chief Justice Marshall had "made his decision, now let him enforce it" is almost certainly apocryphal, as there was nothing for either Jackson or Marshall to "enforce"; the decision only required Georgia to release Worcester from custody, which it eventually did. But the story reflects Jackson's general attitude toward the Court's decisions on federal jurisdiction. He would not protect Indians from state action, no matter how violent or coercive, and he put the weight of the federal government behind removal policy.

The Cherokee held out until 1838, when military pressure forced them to march to the territory that is now Oklahoma. This trek—known as the Trail of Tears— was made under such harsh conditions that almost 4,000 of approximately 16,000 marchers died on the way. (See Map 10.2) The final chapter of Indian Removal was the Second Seminole War, which lasted from 1834 to 1841. Although the government had convinced a few Seminoles to sign a treaty in 1834 agreeing to removal, most Seminoles renounced it and resisted for years, making the bloody conflict the most expensive Indian war in U.S. history. The removal of the southeastern Indians exposed the prejudiced and greedy side of Jacksonian democracy.

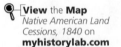

View the **Map**
Native American Land Cessions, 1840 on
myhistorylab.com

Quick Check

✔ What did the Indian Removal policy demonstrate about Jacksonian democracy?

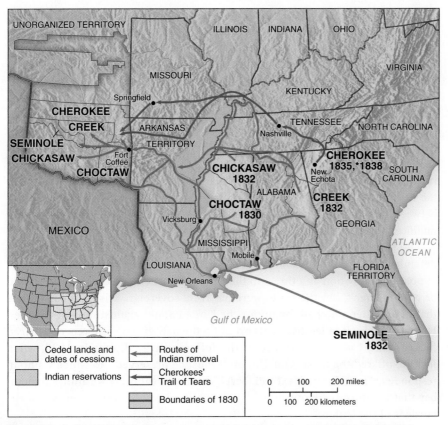

Map 10.2 *Indian Removal*   Because so many Native Americans, uprooted from their lands in the East, died on the forced march to Oklahoma, the route they followed became known as the Trail of Tears.

The Nullification Crisis

During the 1820s, southerners became increasingly fearful of federal encroachment on states' rights. Behind this concern, in South Carolina at least, was a strengthened commitment to slavery and anxiety about the use of federal power to strike at the "peculiar institution." Hoping to keep slavery itself out of the political limelight, South Carolinians seized on another grievance—the protective tariff—as the issue on which to take their stand in favor of a state veto power over federal actions they viewed as contrary to their interests. Tariffs that increased the prices that southern agriculturists paid for manufactured goods and that threatened to undermine their foreign markets by inciting other countries to erect their own protective tariffs hurt the staple-producing and exporting South.

Vice President Calhoun emerged as the leader of the states' rights insurgency in South Carolina, abandoning his earlier support of nationalism and the American System. After the tariff of abominations passed in 1828, the South

Carolina legislature declared the new duties unconstitutional and endorsed a lengthy affirmation—written anonymously by Calhoun—of nullification, or an individual state's right to set aside federal laws. Calhoun supported Jackson in 1828 and planned to serve amicably as his vice president, expecting Jackson to support his native region on the tariff and states' rights. He also hoped to succeed Jackson as president.

In the meantime, however, a bitter personal feud developed between Jackson and Calhoun. The vice president and his wife were prime movers in ostracizing Peggy Eaton. Evidence also came to light that Calhoun, as secretary of war in Monroe's cabinet in 1818, had advocated punishing Jackson for his incursion into Spanish-ruled Florida. As Calhoun lost favor, it became clear that Van Buren rather than the vice president would be Jackson's designated successor. The personal breach between Jackson and Calhoun colored and intensified their confrontation over nullification and the tariff.

The two men also differed on matters of principle. Although generally a defender of states' rights and strict construction of the Constitution, Jackson opposed nullification as a threat to the Union. In his view, federal power should be held in check, but the states were not truly sovereign. His nationalism was that of a soldier who had fought for the United States against foreign enemies. He was not about to let dissidents break up the nation. The differences between Jackson and Calhoun surfaced at the Jefferson Day dinner in 1830, when Jackson offered the toast "Our Union: It must be preserved," to which Calhoun responded, "The Union. Next to Liberty, the most dear. May we always remember that it can only be preserved by distributing equally the benefits and the burdens of the Union."

Read the **Document** *South Carolina Refuses the Tariff* on **myhistorylab.com**

In 1830 and 1831, the movement against the tariff grew in South Carolina. Calhoun openly took the lead, arguing that states could set aside federal laws. In 1832, a new tariff lowered the rates slightly but retained the principle of protection. Supporters of nullification argued that the new law simply demonstrated that they could expect no relief from Washington. The South Carolina legislature then called a special convention. In November 1832, its members voted to nullify the tariffs of 1828 and 1832 and forbid the collection of customs duties within the state.

Jackson reacted with characteristic decisiveness. He alerted the secretary of war to prepare for military action, denounced nullification as treasonous, and asked Congress for authority to use the army to enforce the tariff. He also sought to pacify the nullifiers by recommending a lower tariff. Congress responded by enacting the Force Bill—which gave the president the military powers he sought—and the compromise tariff of 1833. The latter was primarily the work of Jackson's enemy Henry Clay, but the president signed it anyway. Faced with Jackson's intention to use force and appeased by the lower tariff, South Carolina suspended the nullification ordinance in January 1833 and rescinded it in March, after the new tariff had been enacted. To demonstrate that they had not conceded their constitutional position, however, the convention delegates also nullified the Force Bill.

The nullification crisis revealed that South Carolinians would not tolerate federal acts that seemed contrary to their interests or interfered with slavery. The nullifiers' philosophy implied the right of secession and the right to declare laws of Congress null and void. As events would show, a fear of northern meddling with slavery was the main spur to the growth of a militant doctrine of state sovereignty in the South. At the time of the nullification crisis, the other slave states were less anxious about the future of the "peculiar institution" and did not embrace South Carolina's radical conception of state sovereignty. Jackson was himself a southerner, a slaveholder, and in general, a proslavery president.

But the Unionist doctrines that Jackson propounded in his proclamation against nullification alarmed farsighted southern loyalists. More strongly than any previous president, Jackson had asserted that the federal government was supreme over the states and that the Union was indivisible. He had also justified using force against states that denied federal authority.

Quick Check

✓ What was nullification, and why did it emerge in the south? How did Jackson respond to that crisis?

THE BANK WAR AND THE SECOND-PARTY SYSTEM

Jackson's most controversial use of executive power was his successful attack on the Bank of the United States. After it failed to recharter the original Bank of the United States in 1811, Congress chartered a second Bank of the United States in 1816, which became the object of Jackson's antagonism. The Bank War revealed some of the deepest concerns of Jackson and his supporters and expressed their concept of democracy. It also aroused intense opposition, which crystallized in a new national party—the Whigs. The destruction of the Bank and the ensuing economic disruption highlighted the issue of the government's relationship to the nation's financial system. Differences on this question strengthened the new two-party system.

What were the arguments for and against the Bank of the United States?

The Bank Veto and the Election of 1832

Jackson had strong reservations about banking and paper money in general—in part because of his own brushes with bankruptcy after accepting promissory notes

TABLE 10.2 The Election of 1832

Candidate	Party	Popular Vote	Electoral Vote
Jackson	Democratic	688,242	219
Clay	National Republican	473,462	49
Wirt	Anti-Masonic	101,051	7
Floyd	Independent Democratic	*	11

*Electors chosen by South Carolina legislature.

that depreciated in value. He also harbored suspicions that branches of the Bank of the United States had illicitly supported Adams in 1828. In 1829 and 1830, Jackson called on Congress to curb the Bank's power.

📖 **Read** the **Document**
Andrew Jackson, Veto of the Bank Bill on **myhistorylab.com**

Nicholas Biddle, the president of the Bank, began to worry about its charter, which was to come for up for renewal in 1836. Jackson was also listening to his "Kitchen Cabinet," especially Amos Kendall and Francis P. Blair, who thought an attack on the Bank would be a good party issue for the election of 1832. Biddle then made a fateful blunder. He sought recharter by Congress in 1832, four years ahead of schedule. Senator Henry Clay, leader of the anti-administration forces on Capitol Hill, encouraged this move because he was convinced that Jackson had chosen the unpopular side of the issue and that a congressional endorsement of the Bank would embarrass or even discredit the president. The bill to recharter was introduced in early 1832. Despite Jackson's opposition, it easily passed.

Bur Jackson vetoed the bill with ringing statements of principle. After repeating his opinion that the Bank was unconstitutional, notwithstanding a ruling by the Supreme Court, he argued that it violated the fundamental rights of the people in a democratic society.

Jackson thus called on the common people to fight the "monster" corporation. His veto message was the first to use more than strictly constitutional arguments and deal directly with social and economic issues. Attempts to override the veto failed, and Jackson resolved to take the issue to the people in the upcoming presidential election.

Quick Check

✓ What were Jackson's reasons for opposing the bank, and to whom did he turn for support in that effort?

The 1832 election, the first in which national nominating conventions chose the candidates, pitted Jackson against Henry Clay, standard-bearer of the National Republicans. Although the Democrats did not adopt a formal platform, the party firmly opposed rechartering the Bank. Clay and the National Republicans attempted to marshal the pro-Bank sentiment that was strong in many parts of the country. But Jackson won a personal triumph over Clay (see Table 10.2). His share of the popular vote was not as high as in 1828, but he still interpreted it as a mandate for continuing the war against the Bank.

Killing the Bank

Jackson now resolved to attack the Bank directly by removing federal deposits from Biddle's vaults. The Bank had used all the political influence it could muster to prevent Jackson's reelection, and Old Hickory regarded Biddle as a personal enemy.

To remove the deposits from the Bank, Jackson had to overcome resistance in his own cabinet. When one secretary of the treasury refused to support the policy, he was shifted to another cabinet post. When a second also balked, Roger B. Taney, a Jackson loyalist and opponent of the Bank, replaced him. In September 1833, Taney, as acting secretary of the treasury, ceased depositing government money in the Bank and began to withdraw the funds already there. Although Jackson had suggested that the government keep its money in some kind of public bank, he had never worked out the details or made a specific proposal to Congress. Instead, the funds were placed in 23 state banks. Opponents charged that these banks had been selected for political rather than fiscal reasons and dubbed them Jackson's "pet banks." Since Congress refused to regulate the credit policies of these banks, the way the state banks used the new deposits nullified Jackson's efforts to shift to a hard-money economy. They extended credit recklessly and increased the paper money in circulation.

The Bank of the United States counterattacked by calling in outstanding loans and instituting a policy of credit contraction that helped bring on a recession. Biddle hoped to show that weakening the Bank would hurt the economy. With justification, Jacksonians accused Biddle of deliberately and unnecessarily causing distress out of personal resentment and a desire to maintain his unchecked powers and privileges. The Bank never regained its charter.

Opposition to Jackson's fiscal policies grew in Congress. Clay and his supporters contended that the president had violated the Bank's charter and exceeded his constitutional authority when he removed the deposits. The Senate approved a motion of censure. Jacksonians in the House blocked similar action, but the president was further humiliated when the Senate refused to confirm Taney as secretary of the treasury. (Jackson later named him chief justice of the Supreme Court.) Congressmen who had defended Jackson's veto now thought he had abused the powers of his office.

A Hydra-Headed Bank Aided by Van Buren (center), Jackson wields his veto rod against the Bank of the United States, whose heads represent the directors of the state branches. Bank president Nicholas Biddle is wearing the top hat. In ancient mythology the Hydra was a snake with many heads; each time one was cut another would sprout up and it would not die.

(*Source: Collection of The New-York Historical Society. Negative number 42459.*)

View the **Image**
Jackson's Bank Crisis on
myhistorylab.com

Quick Check

✔ What did Jackson do to "kill the bank"?

The Emergence of the Whigs

The coalition that passed the censure resolution in the Senate provided the nucleus for a new national party—the Whigs. Its leadership and most of its support came from National Republicans associated with Clay and New England ex-Federalists led by Senator Daniel Webster of Massachusetts. Southern proponents of states' rights who had been upset by Jackson's stand on nullification and saw his withdrawal of federal deposits from the Bank as an unconstitutional abuse of power also supported the Whigs. Even Calhoun and his nullifiers occasionally cooperated with the Whig camp. The rallying cry for this diverse anti-Jackson coalition was "executive usurpation." The Whig label was chosen because of its associations with British and American revolutionary opposition to royal power and prerogatives. In their propaganda, the Whigs attacked the tyrannical designs of "King Andrew" and his court.

The Whigs also gradually absorbed the Anti-Masonic party, a surprisingly strong political movement that had arisen in the Northeast in the late 1820s and early 1830s. Capitalizing on the hysteria aroused by the 1826 disappearance and apparent murder of a New Yorker who had threatened to reveal the secrets of the Masonic order, the Anti-Masons exploited traditional American fears of secret societies and conspiracies. They also appealed to the moral concerns of the northern middle class under the sway of an emerging evangelical Protestantism. Anti-Masons detested Jacksonianism mainly because it tolerated diverse lifestyles. They believed that the government should restrict such "sinful" behavior as drinking, gambling, and breaking the Sabbath. But this diverse Whig coalition could not agree on a single candidate and lost the 1836 presidential election to Jackson's designated successor, Martin Van Buren. Nevertheless, the Whigs ran even with the Democrats in the South. (See Table 10.3)

President Van Buren immediately faced a catastrophic depression, known as the Panic of 1837. This was not exclusively, or even primarily, the result of government policies. It was international and reflected complex changes in the world economy that American policymakers could not control. But the Whigs blamed the state of the economy on Jacksonian finance, and the administration had to respond. Since Van Buren and his party were committed to a policy of laissez-faire on the federal level, they could do little or nothing to relieve economic distress through subsidies or relief measures. But Van Buren could try to salvage the federal funds deposited in shaky state banks and devise a new system of public finance that would not contribute to future panics by fueling speculation and credit expansion.

The economy doomed Van Buren's chances for reelection in 1840. The Whigs had the chance to offer alternative policies that promised to restore prosperity.

((•—|Listen to the
Audio File
Van Buren on
myhistorylab.com

|View the **Image**
1840 Campaign Ad on
myhistorylab.com

TABLE 10.3   The Election of 1836

Candidate	Party	Popular Vote	Electoral Vote
Van Buren	Democratic	764,198	170
Harrison	Whig	549,508	73
White	Whig	145,342	26
Webster	Whig	41,287	14
Mangum	Independent Democratic	*	11

*Electors chosen by South Carolina legislature.

They passed over the true leader of their party, Henry Clay, and nominated William Henry Harrison, an old military hero who was associated in the public mind with the Battle of Tippecanoe and the winning of the West. To increase the ticket's appeal in the South, they chose John Tyler of Virginia, a states' rights Democrat, as Harrison's running mate.

Using the slogan "Tippecanoe and Tyler, too," the Whigs pulled out all the stops. They organized rallies and parades, complete with posters, placards, campaign hats and emblems, special songs, and even log cabins filled with coonskin caps and barrels of cider for the faithful. Imitating the Jacksonian propaganda against Adams in 1828, they portrayed Van Buren as a luxury-loving aristocrat and compared him with their own homespun candidate. There was an enormous turnout on election day—78 percent of those eligible to vote. When it was over, Harrison had parlayed a narrow edge in the popular vote into a landslide in the electoral college. (See Map 10.3) The Whigs also won control of both houses of Congress.

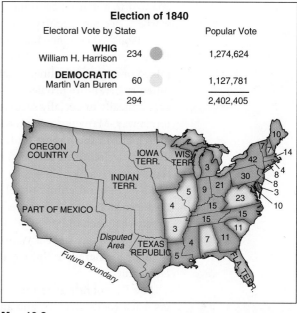

Election of 1840

Electoral Vote by State		Popular Vote
WHIG William H. Harrison	234	1,274,624
DEMOCRATIC Martin Van Buren	60	1,127,781
	294	2,402,405

Map 10.3

Quick Check

✓ Who came together to form the Whig Party, and how did they gain power in 1840?

HEYDAY OF THE SECOND-PARTY SYSTEM

America's second-party system came of age in the election of 1840. Unlike the earlier competition between Federalists and Jeffersonian Republicans, the rivalry between Democrats and Whigs made the two-party pattern a normal feature of electoral politics. During the 1840s, the two national parties competed on fairly equal terms for the support of the electorate. Allegiance to one party or the other became a source of personal identity for many Americans and increased their interest and participation in politics.

The parties offered voters a real choice of programs and ideologies. Whigs stood for a "positive liberal state"—which meant government had the right and duty to subsidize or protect enterprises that could contribute to general prosperity and economic growth. Democrats normally advocated a "negative liberal state" in which government kept its hands off the economy.

Economic issues helped determine each party's base of support. In the Whig camp were industrialists who wanted tariff protection, merchants who favored internal improvements to stimulate commerce, and farmers and planters who had

What was the two-party system, and how were the parties different?

adapted to a market economy. Democrats appealed mainly to smaller farmers, workers, declining gentry, and emerging entrepreneurs who were excluded from the established commercial groups that would benefit most from Whig programs. Democratic rhetoric about monopoly and privilege appealed to those who had mixed or negative feelings about a national market economy. This division also pitted richer, more privileged Americans against those who were poorer and less economically or socially secure. But it did not follow class lines in any simple or direct way. Many businessmen were Democrats; many wage earners voted Whig. Merchants in the import trade hated Whiggish high tariffs, whereas workers in industries clamoring for protection often concluded that such duties protected their jobs.

Lifestyles and ethnic or religious identity influenced party loyalties. In the northern states, one way to tell the typical Whig from the typical Democrat was to see what each did on Sunday. A person who went to an evangelical Protestant church was likely to be a Whig. The person who attended a ritualized service—Catholic, Lutheran, or Episcopalian—or did not go to church at all was probably a Democrat.

The Democrats were the favored party of immigrants, Catholics, freethinkers, backwoods farmers, and all those who enjoyed traditional amusements that the new breed of moral reformers condemned. One thing all these groups had in common was a desire to be left alone, free to think and behave as they liked. The Whigs enjoyed strong support among old-stock Protestants in smaller cities, towns, and prosperous rural areas devoted to market farming. In general, the Whigs welcomed a market economy but wanted to restrain the individualism and disorder it created by enforcing cultural and moral values derived from the Puritan tradition.

Nevertheless, party conflict in Congress centered on national economic policy. Whigs stood for a loose construction of the Constitution and federal support for business and economic development. Democrats defended strict construction, states' rights, and laissez-faire. Debates over tariffs, banking, and internal improvements remained vital during the 1840s.

True believers in both parties saw deep ideological or moral meaning in the clash over economic issues. Whigs and Democrats had conflicting views of the good society, and their policies reflected these differences. The Democrats were the party of white male equality and personal liberty. They perceived the American people as a collection of independent and self-sufficient white men. Government's job was to ensure that the individual was not interfered with—in his economic activity, his personal habits, or his religion (or lack of it). Democrats were ambivalent about the market economy because it threatened individual independence. The Whigs, on the other hand, were the party of orderly progress under the guidance of an enlightened elite. They believed that the propertied, the well-educated, and the pious should guide the masses toward the common good. Believing that a market economy would benefit everyone in the long run, they had no qualms about the rise of a commercial and industrial capitalism.

CONCLUSION: TOCQUEVILLE'S WISDOM

The French traveler Alexis de Tocqueville, author of the most influential account ever written of the emergence of American democracy, visited the United States in 1831 and 1832. He left before the presidential election and had little to say about national politics and political parties. For him, the essence of American democracy was local self-government, such as he observed in New England town meetings. The participation of ordinary citizens in the affairs of their communities impressed him. He praised Americans for not conceding their liberties to a centralized state, as he believed the French had done.

Yet Tocqueville was acutely aware of the limitations of American democracy. He knew that the kind of democracy men were practicing was not meant for women. Observing how women were strictly assigned to a separate domestic sphere, he concluded that Americans had never supposed "that democratic principles should undermine the husband's authority and make it doubtful who is in charge of the family." He also believed the nullification crisis foreshadowed destruction of the Union and predicted that slavery would lead to civil war and racial conflict. He noted the power of white supremacy, providing an unforgettable firsthand description of the sufferings of an Indian community during forced migration to the West, and a graphic account of how free blacks were segregated and driven from the polls in northern cities such as Philadelphia. White Americans, he believed, were deeply prejudiced against people of color, and he doubted it was possible "for a whole people to rise … above itself." A despot might force the equality and mingling of the races, but "while American democracy remains at the head of affairs, no one would dare attempt any such thing, and it is possible to foresee that the freer the whites in America are, the more they will seek to isolate themselves." Tocqueville clearly saw that Jacksonian democracy and equality were meant for only some of the people. His belief that slavery would endanger the union was prophetic.

10 STUDY RESOURCES

((•—[Listen to the **Chapter Audio** for Chapter 10 on **myhistorylab.com**

TIMELINE

1824 House of Representatives elects John Quincy Adams president, p. 251

1828 Congress passes "tariff of abominations," p. 252
• Andrew Jackson elected president, p. 254

1830 Congress passes Indian Removal Act, p. 255

1831 Jackson reorganizes his cabinet, p. 254
• First national nominating conventions meet, p. 250

1832 Jackson vetoes the bill rechartering the Bank of the United States, p. 260
• Jackson reelected, p. 259

1832–1833 Nullification crisis, p. 259

1833 Jackson removes federal deposits from the Bank of the United States, p. 260

1834 Whig party formed, p. 261

1836 Martin Van Buren elected president, p. 262

1837 Financial panic triggers depression, p. 262

1840 William Henry Harrison elected president, p. 263

Chapter Review

DEMOCRACY IN THEORY AND PRACTICE

How did the relationship between the government and the people change during this time?

The federal government grew more accountable to the people it represented. "Popular sovereignty" meant that men of modest backgrounds could attain new social status, while cultural expression reflected this "decline in deference." More public officials now had to seek popular election, but public opinion divided over the role of government in the economy. (*p. 247*)

JACKSON AND THE POLITICS OF DEMOCRACY

What political conflicts did Jackson face and how did he resolve them?

Jackson resolved political conflicts with iron-fisted authority. During the Peggy Eaton affair, he sacked his entire cabinet, and he handled the Indian dilemma by evicting Native Americans from their homeland. During the nullification crisis, he threatened South Carolina with military force. (*p. 251*)

THE BANK WAR AND THE SECOND-PARTY SYSTEM

What were the arguments for and against the Bank of the United States?

Nicholas Biddle believed that the Bank of the United States was essential to American economic stability. Jackson believed the federal bank to be unconstitutional and saw it as a personal enemy and "monster corporation." Bank proponents believed that Jackson's "Bank War" exceeded his constitutional authority, and the Whig party emerged in opposition to his policies. (*p. 259*)

HEYDAY OF THE SECOND-PARTY SYSTEM

What was the two-party system, and how were the parties different?

The "second-party system" was the rivalry between Whigs and Democrats. The Whigs included industrialists, merchants, and farmers who favored stimulus to commerce. Democrats included smaller farmers, wage workers, and declining gentry—individuals the new market economy had left behind. The division also marked cultural differences in religion, ethnicity, and lifestyle. (*p. 263*)

Key Term Questions

1. Why did Congress pass the tariff of abominations in 1828? (p. 252)

2. What does the Trail of Tears and Indian Removal policy in general tell us about Jacksonian democracy? (p. 256)

3. Why did nullification emerge in the South and how did Jackson respond to it? (p. 258)

4. Why was Jackson so intent on waging a Bank War? (p. 259)

5. What were the causes of the Panic of 1837? (p. 262)

6. How did America's second-party system arise? (p. 263)

MyHistoryLab Connections

Visit **www.myhistorylab.com** for a customized Study Plan to build your knowledge of *The Triumph of White Men's Democracy.*

Question for Analysis

1. What political, economic, and cultural forces contributed to the forced migration of Indians in the 1830s?

   View the **Closer Look** *Indian Removals* p. 254

2. In what areas of the country were Native Americans forced to give up their land?

   View the **Map** *Native American Land Cessions, 1840* p. 255

3. What was the central reason for which South Carolina rejected the tariff?

   Read the **Document** *South Carolina Refuses the Tariff* p. 258

4. What were Jackson's major objections to the national bank?

   Read the **Document** *Andrew Jackson, Veto of the Bank Bill* p. 260

Other Resources from this Chapter

Read the **Document** *Ralph Waldo Emerson, Self-Reliance*

View the **Image** *Andrew Jackson's Inauguration Lithograph*

View the **Map** *Native American Land Cessions to 1829*

View the **Image** *Jackson's Bank Crisis*

Listen to the **Audio File** *Van Buren*

View the **Image** *1840 Campaign Ad*

Contents and Spotlight Questions

THE WORLD OF SOUTHERN BLACKS   PG. 270

What factors made living conditions for southern blacks more or less difficult?

WHITE SOCIETY IN THE ANTEBELLUM SOUTH   PG. 276

What divided and united white southern society?

SLAVERY AND THE SOUTHERN ECONOMY   PG. 284

How was slavery related to economic success in the South?

((•—[Listen to the **Chapter Audio** for Chapter 11 on **myhistorylab.com**

NAT TURNER'S REBELLION: A TURNING POINT IN THE SLAVE SOUTH

On August 22, 1831, the worst nightmare of southern slaveholders became reality. Slaves in Southampton County, Virginia, rose in bloody rebellion. Their leader was Nat Turner, a preacher and prophet who believed God had given him a sign that the time was ripe to strike for freedom; a vision of black and white angels wrestling in the sky had convinced him that divine wrath was about to be visited upon the white oppressor.

Rallying followers as he went along, Turner led his band from plantation to plantation, killing of nearly 60 whites. The rebellion was short-lived; after only 48 hours, white forces dispersed the rampaging slaves. The rebels were then rounded up and executed, along with dozens of other slaves who were suspected of complicity. Turner was the last to be captured. He went to the gallows unrepentant, convinced he had acted in accordance with God's will.

Horrid Massacre in Virginia **(1831)** A composite of scenes of Nat Turner's Rebellion, an illustration from a book entitled "Authentic and impartial narrative of the tragical scene which was witnessed in Southampton County [New York, 1831].

After the initial panic and rumors of a wider insurrection had passed, white southerners went about the grim business of ensuring such an incident would never happen
again. The emergence of a more militant northern abolitionism strengthened their anxiety and determination. Just two years after African American abolitionist David Walker
published his *Appeal to the Colored Citizens of the World* in 1829, calling for blacks
to take up arms against slavery, William Lloyd Garrison put out the first issue of his
newspaper, *The Liberator*, the first publication by a white author to demand immediate abolition of slavery rather than gradual emancipation. Southerners saw Turner and
Garrison as two prongs of a revolutionary attack on the southern way of life. Although
no evidence came to light that abolitionist propaganda had directly influenced Turner,
many whites believed that it must have or that future rebels might be. Consequently,
they launched a massive campaign to quarantine the slaves from exposure to antislavery ideas and attitudes.

New laws restricted the ability of slaves to move about, assemble without white
supervision, or learn to read and write. The repression did not stop at the color line;
laws and the threat of mob action prevented white dissenters from publicly criticizing
or even questioning slavery. The South became a closed society with a closed mind.
Loyalty to the region was identified with defense of it, and proslavery agitators sought
to create a mood of crisis and danger requiring absolute unity and single-mindedness
among the white population. This embattled attitude fostered a more militant sectionalism and inspired threats to secede from the Union unless the South's peculiar institution could be made safe from northern or abolitionist attack.

The repression after the Nat Turner rebellion succeeded. Between 1831 and the
Civil War, no further uprisings resulted in the mass killing of whites. This once
led some historians to conclude that African American slaves were brainwashed
into docility. But resistance to slavery simply took less dangerous forms than open
revolt. The brute force employed to suppress the Turner rebellion and the elaborate
precautions taken against its recurrence showed slaves that it was futile to confront
white power directly. Instead, they asserted their humanity and maintained their
self-esteem in other ways. The heroic effort to endure slavery without surrendering
to it gave rise to an African American culture of lasting value.

THE WORLD OF SOUTHERN BLACKS

Most African Americans of the early to mid-nineteenth century experienced slavery on plantations, estates owned by planters who had 20 or more slaves. To ensure their personal safety and the profitability of their enterprises, the masters of
these agrarian communities used all the means—physical and psychological—
at their command to make slaves docile and obedient. Despite these pressures,
most African Americans managed to retain an inner sense of their own worth
and dignity. When conditions were right, they asserted their desire for freedom
and equality and showed their disdain for white claims that slavery was a positive
good. Although slave culture did not normally provoke violent resistance to the

---

Read the
Document
*The Confessions of
Nat Turner (1831)* on
myhistorylab.com

What factors
made living cond-
itions for southern
blacks more or
less difficult?

slaveholders' regime, the inner world that slaves made for themselves gave them the spiritual strength to thwart the masters' efforts to dominate their hearts and minds. Much of what we know about the world of Southern slaves comes from interviews ex-slaves gave in the 1930s, decades after slavery ended. While the transcriptions of these interviews often reflect the prejudices of the white interviewers, and are colored by the circumstances in which they were given, they remain an invaluable window into the lives of slaves.

View the **Map**
Slavery in the South on
myhistorylab.com

Slaves' Daily Life and Labor

Slaves' daily life varied with the region in which they lived and the type of plantation or farm on which they worked. On large plantations in the Cotton Belt, most slaves worked in "gangs" under an overseer. White overseers, sometimes helped by black "drivers," enforced a workday from sunup to sundown, six days a week. There was never a slack season under "King Cotton." Cultivation required year-round labor. Enslaved women and children also worked in the fields. Parents often brought babies and young children to the fields, where older children could care for them and mothers could nurse them during brief breaks. Older children worked in "trash gangs," weeding and yard cleaning. Life on the sugar plantations of Louisiana was much harsher: Slaves had to work into the night during harvest season, and mortality rates were high.

View the **Image**
*Slave Quarters, Hermit-
age Plantation* on
myhistorylab.com

Not all slaves in agriculture worked in gangs. In the low country of South Carolina and Georgia, slaves who cultivated rice worked under a "task system" that gave them more control over the pace of labor. With less supervision, they could complete their tasks within an eight-hour day. Slaves on small farms often worked side by side with their masters rather than in slave gangs, although such intimacy did not necessarily affect power relationships. While about three-quarters of slaves were field workers, slaves performed many other kinds of labor. They dug ditches, built houses, worked on boats and in mills (often hired out by their masters for a year), and were house servants, cooking, cleaning, and gardening. Some slaves, especially women, also worked within the slave community as preachers, caretakers of children, and healers. A few slaves, about 5 percent, worked in industry in the South, including mills, iron works, and railroad building. Slaves in cities did a wider range of jobs than plantation slaves, and in general enjoyed more autonomy. They worked in restaurants and saloons, in hotels, and as skilled tradesmen. Some urban slaves even lived apart from their masters and hired out their own time, returning part of their wages to their owners.

Picking Cotton Although cotton cultivation required constant attention, many of the tasks involved were relatively simple. On a cotton plantation most slaves, including women and children, were field hands who performed the same tasks. Here a slave family stands behind baskets of picked cotton in a Georgia cotton field.

Quick Check

✓ What were the differences between "gang" and "task" labor?

Most slaves also kept gardens or small farm plots for themselves to supplement their diets. They fished, hunted, and trapped animals. Many slaves also worked "overtime" for their own masters on Sundays or holidays in exchange for money or goods, or hired out their overtime hours to others. This "underground economy" suggests slaves' overpowering desire to provide for their families, sometimes even earning enough to purchase their freedom.

Slave Families, Kinship, and Community

More than any other institution, the African American family prevented slavery from becoming utterly demoralizing. Slaves had a strong and abiding sense of family and kinship. But the nature of the families or households that predominated on plantations or farms varied with circumstances. On large plantations with relatively stable slave populations, most slave children lived in two-parent households, and many marriages lasted for 20 to 30 years. The death or sale of one of the partners broke up more marriages than voluntary dissolutions did. Here mothers, fathers, and children were bonded closely, and parents shared child-rearing responsibilities (within the limits masters allowed). Masters and churches encouraged marital fidelity: Stable unions produced more offspring, and adultery and divorce were sinful.

But in areas where most slaves lived on farms or small plantations, and especially in the upper South where slaves were often sold or hired out, a different pattern seems to have prevailed. Under these circumstances, slaves' spouses frequently resided on other plantations or farms, often some distance away, and ties between husbands and wives were looser and more fragile. Female-headed families were the norm, and mothers, assisted in most cases by female relatives and friends, took responsibility for child rearing. Mother-centered families with weak conjugal ties were a natural response to the absence of fathers and the prospect of their being moved or sold beyond visiting distance. Where sale or relocation could break up unions at any time, it did not pay to invest all of one's emotions in a conjugal relationship. But whether the basic family form was nuclear or matrifocal (female-headed), it created infinitely precious ties for its members. The threat of breaking up a family through sale was a disciplinary tool that gave masters great power over their slaves.

The anguish that accompanied the breakup of families through sale showed the depth of kinship feelings. The first place that masters looked for a fugitive was near a family member who had been sold away. Indeed, many slaves tried to be sold with family members or to the same neighborhood. After emancipation, thousands of freed slaves wandered about looking for spouses, children, or parents from whom they had been forcibly separated years before. The famous spiritual "Sometimes I Feel Like a Motherless Child" expressed far more than religious need; it reflected slaves' family anxieties and personal tragedies.

Kinship and mutual obligation extended beyond the primary family. Slaves often knew their grandparents, uncles, aunts, and even cousins through direct contact or family lore. The names that slaves gave to their children or took for themselves revealed a sense of family continuity over three or four generations. Infants were

Read the **Document**
Poem, The Slave Auction on **myhistorylab.com**

View the **Image**
Slave Dealers on **myhistorylab.com**

frequently named after grandparents, and those slaves who took surnames often chose that of an ancestor's owner rather than the family name of a current master.

Kinship ties were not limited to blood relations. When sales broke up families, individuals who found themselves on plantations far from home were likely to be "adopted" into new kinship networks. New families quickly absorbed orphans or children without responsible parents. Soon after the Civil War, one Reconstruction official faced an elderly ex-slave named Roger, who demanded land "to raise crop on" for his "family of sixty 'parents,' that is, relations, children included." A family with 60 parents made no sense to this official, but it did in a community in which ties of affection and cooperation rather than "blood" relation often defined families.

Kinship provided a model for personal relationships and the basis for a sense of community. Everyone addressed elderly slaves as "uncle" and "aunty," and younger unrelated

A Slave Family Though death or sale broke up many slave families, some families, especially those on large, stable plantations, managed to stay together. This 1862 photograph by Timothy H. O'Sullivan shows five generations of a slave family, all born on the plantation of J. J. Smith in Beaufort, South Carolina.

slaves commonly called each other "brother" or "sister." Slave culture was a family culture, which was one of its greatest sources of strength and cohesion. Strong kinship ties, whether real or fictive, meant slaves could depend on one another in times of trouble. The kinship network also helped transmit African American folk traditions from one generation to the next. Together with slave religion, kinship gave African Americans a sense that they were members of a community, not just a collection of oppressed individuals.

Quick Check

✓ How did slave communities maintain kinship ties?

Resistance and Rebellion

Open rebellion, bearing arms against the oppressors by organized groups of slaves, was the most dramatic and clear-cut form of slave resistance. Between 1800 and 1831, slaves participated in revolts that showed their willingness to risk their lives in a desperate bid for liberation. In 1800, a Virginia slave named Gabriel Prosser mobilized a large band to march on Richmond. But a violent storm dispersed "Gabriel's army," and the uprising was suppressed without any loss of white life.

In 1811, hundreds of Louisiana slaves marched on New Orleans brandishing guns, waving flags, and beating drums. It took 300 soldiers of the U.S. Army, aided by armed planters and militiamen, to stop the advance and end the rebellion. In 1822, whites in Charleston, South Carolina, uncovered an extensive and well-planned conspiracy that a free black man named Denmark Vesey had organized to seize armories, arm the slaves, and burn the city. Although the Vesey conspiracy was nipped in the bud, it convinced South Carolinians that blacks were "the Jacobins of the country [a reference to the militants of the French Revolution] against whom we should always be on guard."

As we have already seen, the most bloody and terrifying slave revolt was the Nat Turner insurrection of 1831. Although it was the last slave rebellion of this kind before the Civil War, armed resistance had not ended. Indeed, the most sustained and successful effort of slaves to win their freedom by force took place in Florida between 1835 and 1842, when hundreds of black fugitives fought the U.S. Army in the Second Seminole War alongside the Indians who had given them a haven. The Seminoles were resisting removal to Oklahoma, but for the blacks who took part in it, the war was a struggle for their own freedom. When it ended, most of them were allowed to accompany their Indian allies to the trans-Mississippi West.

Few slaves ever took part in organized acts of violent resistance against white power. Most realized that the odds against a successful revolt were high. Bitter experience had shown them that the usual outcome was death to the rebels. As a consequence, they resisted white dominance in safer, more ingenious ways.

Watch the **Video**
Underground Railroad
on
myhistorylab.com

One way was to run away, and thousands of slaves did so. Most fugitives never got beyond the neighborhood of the plantation; after "lying out" for a time, they would return, often after negotiating immunity from punishment. But many escapees remained free for years, hiding in swamps or other remote areas. Others escaped to freedom in the North or Mexico. Fugitives stowed away aboard ships heading to northern ports or traveled over land for hundreds of miles, avoiding patrols and inquisitive whites by staying off the roads and moving only at night. Light-skinned blacks sometimes made it to freedom by passing for white. Some escaped with the help of the Underground Railroad, an informal network of sympathetic free blacks (and a few whites) who helped fugitives make their way North. The Underground Railroad had an estimated 3,200 active workers. It is estimated that 130,000 refugees (out of 4 million slaves) escaped the slave South between 1815 and 1860. By the 1850s, substantial numbers of Northerners had been in open violation of federal law by hiding runaways for a night. One resourceful slave even had himself packed in a box and shipped to the North. Henry "Box" Brown, like other successful fugitives, published an account of his life in slavery and his daring escape, and fashioned his story as a plea to support the antislavery cause. Such narratives by fugitive slaves are an important source of information about life under slavery.

The typical fugitive was a young, unmarried male from the upper South. For most slaves, however, flight was not an option. Either they lived too deep in the South to reach free soil, or they were reluctant to leave family and friends behind. Slaves who did not or could not leave the plantation had to oppose the masters' regime while remaining under the yoke of bondage.

The normal way of expressing discontent was through indirect or passive resistance. Many slaves worked slowly and inefficiently, not because they were naturally lazy (as whites supposed) but as a gesture of protest or alienation. As the words of a popular slave song said, "You may think I'm working/But I ain't." Others feigned illness or injury. Stealing provisions—a common activity—was another way to flout authority. According to the code of ethics prevailing in the slave quarters, theft from the master simply enabled slaves to get a larger share of the fruits of their own labors.

Many slaves committed acts of sabotage. Tools and agricultural implements were deliberately broken, animals were willfully neglected or mistreated, and barns or other outbuildings were set afire. Often masters could not identify the culprits because slaves did not readily inform on one another. The ultimate act of clandestine resistance was poisoning the master's food. Some slaves, especially the "conjure" men and women who practiced a combination of folk medicine and witchcraft, knew how to mix rare, virtually untraceable poisons, and many plantation whites became suddenly and mysteriously ill. Whole families died from obscure "diseases" that did not infect the slave quarters.

The folktales that slaves passed from generation to generation revealed the attitude behind such actions. The famous Br'er Rabbit stories showed how a small, apparently defenseless animal could outwit a bigger and stronger one through cunning and deceit. Although these tales often had an African origin, they also served as an allegory for the black view of the master–slave relationship. Other stories— which were not told in front of whites—openly portrayed the slave as a clever trickster outwitting the master.

Finally, slave religion, often practiced secretly at night and led by black preachers, gave African Americans a chance to create their own world. Religion seldom inspired slaves to open rebellion, but it encouraged community, solidarity, and self-esteem by giving them something infinitely precious of their own. Many religious songs referred to the promise of freedom, or demanded that an oppressor "let my people go." Nat Turner was a free black preacher.

Quick Check

✓ How successful were the Vesey Conspiracy and Nat Turner Insurrection?

Free Blacks in the Old South

Free blacks occupied an increasingly precarious position in the antebellum South. White southerners' fears of free blacks (like Turner) inciting slave revolts, and their reaction to abolitionists' attacks, led slaveholders after 1830 to defend slavery as a positive good rather than a necessary evil. This defense was racist, emphasizing a dual image of the black person: Under the "domesticating" influence of a white master, the slave was a happy child; outside of this influence, he was a savage beast. As whites strove to convince themselves and northerners that blacks were happy in slavery, they more frequently portrayed free blacks as savages who needed to be reined in.

Beginning in the 1830s, all the southern states cracked down on free blacks. Laws forced free people of color to register or have white guardians who were responsible for their behavior. Free blacks had to carry papers proving their status. In some states, they needed permission to move from one county to another. Licensing laws excluded blacks from several occupations, and the authorities often prevented blacks from holding meetings or forming organizations. Vagrancy and apprenticeship laws forced free blacks into economic dependency barely distinguishable from outright slavery.

Although beset by special problems of their own, most free blacks identified with the suffering of the slaves; when they could, they protested against the peculiar institution and worked for its abolition. Many of them had once been slaves themselves or were the children of slaves; often their relatives were still in bondage. They knew that the discrimination from which they suffered was rooted in slavery and the racial attitudes that accompanied it. So long as slavery existed, their own rights were likely to be denied. Even their freedom was at risk; former slaves who could not prove they had been legally freed could be reenslaved. This threat existed even in the North: Under federal fugitive slave laws, escaped slaves had to be returned to bondage. Even blacks who were born free were not safe. Kidnapping or fraudulent seizure by slave-catchers was always a risk.

Because of the elaborate system of control and surveillance, free blacks in the South could do little to work against slavery. Most found that survival depended on creating the impression of loyalty to the planter regime. In the Deep South, relatively privileged free people of color, mostly of racially mixed origin, were sometimes persuaded that it was to their advantage to preserve the status quo. As skilled artisans and small-business owners dependent on white favors and patronage, they had little incentive to risk everything by taking the side of the slaves. In southern Louisiana, a few mulatto planters even lived in luxury, supported by the labor of other African Americans.

However, although some free blacks created niches of relative freedom, their position in southern society became increasingly precarious. Beginning in the 1830s, southern whites sought to make the line between free and unfree a line between black and white. Free blacks were an anomaly in this system; increasingly, the southern answer was to exclude, degrade, and even enslave those free people of color who remained within their borders. Just before the Civil War, a campaign developed to carry the repression and discrimination to its logical conclusion: State legislatures proposed forcing free people of color to choose between leaving the state or being enslaved.

Quick Check

✓ What was life like for freed slaves in the South?

WHITE SOCIETY IN THE ANTEBELLUM SOUTH

What divided and united white southern society?

Those who know the Old South only from novels, films, and television are likely to imagine a land filled with majestic plantations. Pillared mansions behind oak-lined carriageways are portrayed as scenes of aristocratic splendor, where courtly gentlemen and elegant ladies, attended by hordes of uniformed black servants, lived in refined luxury. Such images suggest that the typical white southerner was an aristocrat whose family owned many slaves.

The great houses existed—many of them can still be seen in Virginia, the low country of South Carolina, and the lower Mississippi Valley—and some wealthy slaveholders' lifestyle was as aristocratic as any ever seen in the United States. But census returns indicate that this was the world of only a tiny percentage of slave-owners and of the total white population. In 1860, only one-quarter of all white southerners belonged to slave-owning families. Even in the Cotton Belt, only about

40 percent of whites were slaveholders on the eve of the Civil War. Planters were the minority of a minority, just 4 percent of the total white population of the South in 1860. Large planters who could build great houses and entertain lavishly, those who owned at least 50 slaves, comprised less than 1 percent of all whites.

Most southern whites, three-fourths of the white population, were non-slaveholding yeoman farmers or artisans. Yet even those who owned no slaves depended on slavery, whether economically, because they hired slaves, or psychologically, because having a degraded class of blacks below them made them feel better about their own place in society. However, the class divisions between slaveholders and non-slaveholders did contribute to the political rifts that became increasingly apparent on the eve of the Civil War.

The Planters' World

The great planters, although few in number, had a disproportionate influence on southern life. They set the tone and values for much of the rest of society, especially for the less wealthy slaveowners who sought to imitate the planters' style of living to the extent their resources allowed. Although many wealthy planters were too busy tending to their plantations to become openly involved in politics, they held more than their share of high offices and often exerted a decisive influence on public policy. In regions where plantation agriculture predominated, they were a ruling class in every sense of the term. Contrary to legend, most of the great planters of the pre–Civil War period were self-made rather than descendants of the old colonial gentry. Some were ambitious young men who married planters' daughters. Others started as lawyers and used their fees and connections to acquire plantations.

As the Cotton Kingdom spread west from South Carolina and Georgia to Alabama, Mississippi, Louisiana, and Texas, the men who became the largest slaveholders were less and less likely to have come from old, well-established planter families. Many of them began as hard-driving businessmen who built up capital from commerce, land speculation, banking, and even slave trading. They then used their profits to buy plantations. Sharp dealing and business skills were more important than genealogy in the competitive, boom-or-bust economy of the western Gulf states.

To succeed, a planter had to be a shrewd entrepreneur who kept a careful eye on the market, the prices of slaves and land, and his debts. Few planters could be men of leisure.

Likewise, the responsibility of running an extended household that produced much of its own food and clothing kept plantation

Plantation Mansion Painting by Adrien Persac depicting the back of a plantation house in Louisiana as seen from the bayou. Persac was commissioned to paint some of the great houses in the region, and in 1858 he published a map showing the plantations along the Mississippi River from Natchez to New Orleans.

mistresses from being the idle ladies of legend. Not only were plantation mistresses a tiny minority of the women who lived and worked in the slave states before the Civil War, but even women from the planter elite rarely lived lives of leisure.

A few of the richest and most secure plantation families did aspire to live like a traditional landed aristocracy, and visiting English nobility accepted them as equals. Big houses, elegant carriages, fancy-dress balls, and multitudes of house servants all reflected aristocratic aspirations. Dueling, despite efforts to repress it, remained the standard way to settle "affairs of honor" among gentlemen. Another sign of gentility was the tendency of planters' sons to avoid "trade" as a primary or secondary career in favor of law or the military. Planters' daughters were trained from girlhood to play the piano, speak French, dress in the latest fashions, and sparkle in the drawing room or on the dance floor. The aristocratic style originated among the older gentry of the seaboard slave states, but by the 1840s and 1850s, it had spread southwest as a second generation of wealthy planters began to displace the rough-hewn pioneers of the Cotton Kingdom.

Quick Check

✓ In what ways did members of the planter society shape themselves as an aristocracy?

Planters, Racism, and Paternalism

No assessment of the planters' outlook or "worldview" can be made without considering their relations with their slaves. Planters owned more than half of all the slaves in the South and set standards for treatment and management. Most planters liked to think of themselves as benevolent masters and often referred to their slaves as if they were members of an extended patriarchal family—a favorite phrase was "our people." According to this paternalistic ideology, blacks were a race of perpetual children requiring constant care and supervision by superior whites. Paternalistic rhetoric increased after abolitionists began to charge that slaveholders were sadistic monsters.

Paternalism went hand in hand with racism. In a typical proslavery apology, Georgia lawyer Thomas Reade Cobb wrote that "a state of bondage, so far from doing violence to the law of [the African's] nature, develops and perfects it; and that, in that state, he enjoys the greatest amount of happiness, and arrives at the greatest degree of perfection of which his nature is capable." The supposed mental and moral inferiority of Africans justified slavery. While some Europeans had drawn negative associations with blackness for centuries, a full-blown modern racism only developed on both sides of the Atlantic in the 1830s and 1840s. Racial "scientists" related skull size to mental ability, and some proslavery apologists even developed religious theories of "polygenesis," arguing that blacks were not descended from Adam and Eve. This racial ideology helped slaveholders believe that a benevolent Christian could justly enslave another human being.

While some historians have argued that paternalism was part of a social system that was organized like a family hierarchy rather than a brutal, profit-making arrangement, there was no inconsistency between planters' paternalism and capitalism. Slaves were a form of capital; that is, they were both the main tools of production for a booming economy and an asset in themselves, valuable for their rising prices, like shares in the stock market today. The ban on the transatlantic slave trade in 1808 was effective enough to make it economically necessary for the slave population to reproduce itself if slavery were to continue. Rising slave prices also inhibited extreme physical abuse and deprivation. It was in masters' self-interest to see that their slave property remained in good enough condition to work hard and produce children. Furthermore, a good return on their investment enabled southern planters to spend more on slave maintenance than masters in less prosperous plantation economies like the Caribbean or Brazil could.

Much of the slaveholders' "paternalist" writing discussed "the coincidence of humanity and interest," by which they meant that treating slaves well (including firm discipline) was in their best economic interest. There was a grain of truth in the planters' claim that their slaves were relatively well provided for. Comparative studies have suggested that pre–Civil War North American slaves enjoyed a higher standard of living than those in other New World slave societies, such as Brazil and Cuba. Their food, clothing, and shelter were normally sufficient to sustain life and labor at slightly above a bare subsistence level, and the rapid increase of the slave population in the Old South stands in sharp contrast to the usual failure of slave populations to reproduce themselves.

But some planters did not behave rationally. They lost their temper or tried to work more slaves than they could afford to maintain. Consequently, there were more cases of physical abuse and undernourishment than a purely economic calculation would lead us to expect.

The testimony of slaves themselves and of independent white observers suggests that masters of large plantations generally did not have close and intimate relationships with the mass of field slaves. The affection and concern associated with a father figure appears to have been limited mainly to relationships with a few favored house servants or other elite slaves, such as coachmen and skilled artisans. The field hands on large estates dealt mostly with overseers who were hired or fired because of their ability to meet production quotas.

The slave market revealed the limits of paternalism. Planters who looked down on slave traders as less than respectable gentlemen nevertheless broke apart families by selling slaves "down river" when they needed money. Even slaveholders who claimed not to participate in the slave market themselves often mortgaged slaves to secure debts; one-third of all slave sales in the South were court-ordered sheriff's auctions when masters defaulted on their debts.

While paternalism may have moderated planters' behavior, especially when economic self-interest reinforced "humanity," most departures from unremitting labor and harsh conditions were concessions that slaves' defiance and resistance wrested from owners at great personal risk.

Furthermore, when they were being realistic, planters conceded that the ultimate basis of their authority was fear, rather than the natural obedience of a loving parent–child relationship. Scattered among their statements are admissions that they relied on the "principle of fear," "more and more on the power of fear," or—most graphically—that it was necessary "to make them stand in fear." Devices for inspiring fear included whipping—a common practice on most plantations—and the threat of sale away from family and friends. Planters' manuals and instructions

Watch the **Video**
Moonlight and Magnolias: Creating the Old South on
myhistorylab.com

to overseers reveal that certain and swift punishment for any infraction of the rules or even for a surly attitude was the preferred method for maintaining order and productivity.

Slaves had little recourse against masters' abuse. They lacked legal protection because courts would not accept their testimony. Abolitionists were correct in condemning slavery on principle because it gave one human being nearly absolute power over another. This system was bound to result in atrocities and violence. Even Harriet Beecher Stowe acknowledged in *Uncle Tom's Cabin*, her celebrated antislavery novel of 1852, that most slaveholders were not as sadistic and brutish as Simon Legree. But—and this was her real point—an institution that made a Simon Legree possible was wrong in and of itself.

Quick Check

✓ How did whites see themselves in relation to their slaves?

Small Slaveholders

In 1860, 88 percent of all slaveholders owned fewer than 20 slaves and thus were not truly planters. Of these, most had fewer than ten. Some small slaveholders were urban merchants or professional men whose slaves were domestic servants, but more typical were farmers who used one or two slave families to ease the burden of their own labor. We know relatively little about life on these small slaveholding farms; unlike the planters, the owners left few records. But we do know that life was Spartan. Masters lived in log cabins or small frame cottages. Slaves lived in lofts or sheds that were not usually up to plantation housing standards.

For better or worse, relations between such owners and their slaves were more intimate than on larger estates. Unlike planters, these farmers often worked in the fields alongside their slaves and sometimes ate at the same table or slept under the same roof. But such closeness did not necessarily result in better treatment. Slave testimony reveals that both the best and the worst of slavery could be found on these farms, depending on the character and disposition of the master. Given a choice, most slaves preferred to live on plantations because they offered the sociability, culture, and kinship of the slave quarters and better food, clothing, and shelter.

Quick Check

✓ Why would most slaves prefer plantation life to small farms given the choice?

Yeoman Farmers

Just below the small slaveholders on the social scale was a substantial class of yeoman farmers who owned land they worked themselves. Contrary to another myth about the Old South, most of these people were not degraded, shiftless poor whites. Poor whites did exist, mainly as squatters on barren or sandy soil that no one else wanted. In parts of the South, many of those working the land were tenants; some of these were "shiftless poor whites," but others were ambitious young men seeking to accumulate the capital to become landowners. Most of the non-slaveholding rural population were proud, self-reliant farmers whose way of life did not differ markedly from that of family farmers in the Midwest during the early stages of settlement. If they were disadvantaged compared with farmers elsewhere in the United States, it was because the lack of economic development and urban

growth perpetuated frontier conditions and prevented them from producing a substantial surplus for market.

The yeomen were mostly concentrated in the backcountry, where slaves and
plantations were rare. Every southern state had hilly sections unsuitable for plantation agriculture. The foothills or interior valleys of the Appalachians and Ozarks offered reasonably good soils for mixed farming, and long stretches of piney barrens
along the Gulf Coast were suitable for raising livestock. In such regions slaveless
farmers concentrated, giving rise to the "white counties" that complicated southern
politics. A distinct group was the genuine mountaineers, who lived too high up for
farming and relied on hunting, lumbering, and distilling whiskey.

Yeoman women, much more than their wealthy counterparts, participated in
every dimension of household labor. They grew vegetables and chickens, made
handicrafts and clothing, and even labored in the fields. The poorest women even
worked for wages in small businesses or on nearby farms. They also raised much
larger families than their wealthier neighbors because children were a valuable
labor pool for the family farm.

More lower-class women also lived outside of male-headed households. Despite the pressures of respectability, there was more acceptance and sympathy
in less affluent communities for women who bore illegitimate children or were
abandoned by their husbands. Working women created a broader definition of
"proper households" and held families together in precarious conditions. The
lack of transportation, more than a failure of energy or character, limited the
prosperity of the yeomen. They mostly grew subsistence crops, mainly corn.
They did raise some of the South's cotton and tobacco, but the difficulty of marketing severely limited their production. Their main source of cash was livestock, especially hogs. Hogs could be walked to market over long distances, and
massive droves from the backcountry to urban markets were commonplace.
But southern livestock was of poor quality and did not bring high prices or big
profits.

Although they did not benefit directly from the peculiar institution, most yeomen and other non-slaveholders fiercely opposed abolitionism. A few antislavery
southerners, most notably Hinton R. Helper of North Carolina, tried to convince
the yeomen that they were victimized by planter dominance and should work for
its overthrow. These dissenters pointed out that slavery and the plantation system created a privileged class and limited the economic opportunities of the non-
slaveholding white majority.

Most yeomen were staunch Jacksonians who resented aristocratic pretensions
and feared concentrations of power and wealth in the hands of the few. They dis-
dained "cotton snobs" and rich planters. In state and local politics, they sometimes
voted against planter interests on issues involving representation, banking, and internal improvements. Why, then, did they fail to respond to antislavery appeals that
called on them to strike at the real source of planter power and privilege?

One reason was that some non-slaveholders hoped to get ahead, and in the
South this meant acquiring slaves. Just enough more prosperous yeomen broke into
the slaveholding classes to make this dream seem believable. Planters, anxious to

Read the
Document
Hinton Helper, A
White Southerner
Speaks on
myhistorylab.com

Yeoman Household Carl G. Von Iwonski, *Block House, New Braunfels*. Most slaveholders in the South were not large plantation owners but small farmers of modest means who lived not in pillared mansions but in small, rough log cabins. Many others were yeoman farmers who owned no slaves.

ensure the loyalty of non-slaveholders, encouraged the notion that every white man was a potential master.

Even if they did not aspire to own slaves, white farmers often viewed black servitude as providing a guarantee of their own liberty and independence. A society that gave them the right to vote and the chance to be self-sufficient on their own land encouraged the feeling that they were fundamentally equal to the largest slaveholders. Although they had no natural love of planters and slavery, they believed—or could be induced to believe—that abolition would threaten their liberty and independence. In part, their anxieties were economic; freed slaves would compete with them for land or jobs. But racism deepened their fears and made their opposition to black freedom implacable.

Emancipation was unthinkable because it would remove the pride and status that automatically went with a white skin in this acutely race-conscious society. Slavery, despite its drawbacks, kept blacks "in their place" and made all whites, however poor and uneducated they might be, feel they were free and equal members of a master race.

Quick Check

✓ What was the yeoman's attitude toward slavery?

A Closed Mind and a Closed Society

Despite the tacit assent of most non-slaveholders, the dominant planters never lost their fear that lower-class whites would turn against slavery. They felt threatened from two sides: from the slave quarters where a new Nat Turner might arise, and from the backcountry where yeomen and poor whites might heed the abolitionists' call and overthrow planter domination. Beginning in the 1830s, the ruling element tightened the screws of slavery and used their control of government and communications to create a mood of impending catastrophe to ensure that all southern whites were of one mind on the slavery issue.

Before the 1830s, the rights or wrongs of slavery had been openly discussed in much of the South. Apologists commonly described the institution as "a necessary evil." In the upper South, as late as the 1820s, there had been significant support for the American Colonization Society, with its program of gradual voluntary emancipation accompanied by deportation of the freedmen. In 1831 and 1832—in the wake of the Nat Turner uprising—the Virginia legislature debated gradual emancipation. Representatives of the yeoman farmers living west of the Blue Ridge Mountains supported getting rid of both slavery and blacks to ensure white safety. But the argument that slavery was "a positive good"—rather than an evil slated for gradual elimination—won the day, and emancipation was defeated.

The "positive good" defense of slavery was an answer to the abolitionist charge that the institution was inherently sinful. A host of books, pamphlets, and newspaper editorials published between the 1830s and the Civil War carried the message. Who was it meant to persuade? Partly, the argument was aimed at the North, to bolster anti-abolitionist sentiment. But the message was also clearly calculated to resolve the doubts and misgivings that southerners themselves had freely expressed before the 1830s. Much of the message may have been over the heads of non-slaveholders, many of whom were semiliterate, but some of the arguments, in popularized form, were used to arouse racial anxieties that tended to neutralize antislavery sentiment among the lower classes.

The proslavery argument had three main propositions. The first and foremost was that enslavement was the natural and proper status for people of African descent. Blacks were innately inferior to whites and suited only for slavery. Biased scientific and historical evidence supported this claim. Second, the Bible and Christianity were said to sanction slavery—a position made necessary by the abolitionist appeal to Christian ethics. Ancient Hebrew slavery was held up as a divinely sanctioned model. Saint Paul was quoted endlessly on the duty of servants to obey their masters. Third, efforts were made to show that slavery was consistent with the humanitarian spirit of the nineteenth century. The premise that blacks were naturally dependent led to the notion that they needed "family government" or a special regime equivalent to the asylums for the few whites who were also incapable of caring for themselves. The plantation allegedly provided such an environment, as benevolent masters guided and ruled this race of "perpetual children."

By the 1850s, the proslavery argument had gone beyond mere apology for the South and its peculiar institution to attack the free-labor system of the North. According to Virginian George Fitzhugh, the master–slave relationship was more humane than the one between northern employers and wage laborers. Slaves had security against unemployment and a guarantee of care in old age, whereas free workers might face destitution and even starvation at any time. Worker insecurity in free societies led inevitably to strikes, class conflicts, and socialism; slave societies, on the other hand, could better protect property rights and maintain other traditional values because their laboring class was better treated and more firmly controlled.

Proslavery southerners also attempted to seal off their region from antislavery ideas and influences. Whites who criticized slavery publicly were mobbed or persecuted. One of the last and bravest of the southern abolitionists, Cassius M. Clay of Kentucky, armed himself with a brace of pistols when he gave speeches, until the threat of mob violence finally forced him across the Ohio River. In 1856, a University of North Carolina professor was fired because he admitted he would vote for the moderately antislavery Republican party if he had a chance. Clergymen who questioned the morality of slavery were driven from their pulpits. Northern travelers suspected of being abolitionist agents were tarred and feathered. When abolitionists tried to send their literature through the mails during the 1830s, it was seized in southern post offices and publicly burned.

Read the
Document
*George Fitzhugh,
"The Blessings of
Slavery" (1857)* on
myhistorylab.com

Fears that non-slaveholding whites and slaves would get subversive ideas about slavery partly explain such flagrant denials of free speech and civil liberties. Hinton R. Helper's book *The Impending Crisis of the South*, an 1857 appeal to non-slaveholders to resist the planter regime, was suppressed with particular vigor; those found with copies were beaten up or even lynched. But the deepest fear was that abolitionist talk or antislavery literature would incite slaves to rebel. The Nat Turner rebellion raised such anxieties to panic pitch. Laws made it a crime to teach slaves to read and write. Other repressive legislation banned meetings unless a white man was present, restricted the activities of black preachers, and suppressed independent black churches. Free blacks thought to be potential instigators of slave revolt were watched and harassed.

But repression did not allay planters' fears of abolitionist subversion, lower-class white dissent, and, above all, slave revolt. Proslavery propaganda and national events in the 1850s created panic and desperation. More southerners became convinced that safety from abolitionism and its terrors required a formal withdrawal from the Union—secession.

Quick Check

✓ What were some of the strategies used by southern whites to fight antislavery efforts?

SLAVERY AND THE SOUTHERN ECONOMY

How was slavery related to economic success in the South?

Despite their internal divisions, white southerners from all regions and classes came to perceive that their interests were tied up with slavery, whether because they owned slaves themselves or because they believed slavery was essential to the "southern way of life" or "white men's democracy." The expansion of slavery can largely be attributed to the rise of "King Cotton"—the number of slaves in the South more than tripled between 1810 and 1860 to nearly 4 million. The cotton-growing areas of the South were becoming more dependent on slavery, while agriculture in the upper South was moving away from the institution. Yet slavery remained important to the economy of the upper South through the slave trade. To understand southern thought and behavior, it is necessary to bear in mind this major regional difference between a slave plantation society and a farming and slave-trading region.

The Internal Slave Trade

Tobacco, the original plantation crop of the colonial period, remained the principal slave-cultivated commodity of the upper tier of southern states. But markets were often depressed, and profitable tobacco cultivation was hard to sustain for long in one place because the crop depleted the soil. As slave prices rose (because of high demand in the lower South) and demand for slaves in the upper South fell, the "internal" slave trade took off. Economic historians have

Sales Lewis Miller, *Slave Sale, Virginia*, probably 1853. Slave auctions, such as the one depicted in Lewis Miller's sketchbook, were an abomination and embarrassment to many Americans.

concluded that the most important crop the tobacco kingdom produced was not the "stinking weed" but human beings cultivated for the auction block. The most profitable business for slaveholders in Virginia, Kentucky, Maryland, and the Carolinas was selling "surplus" slaves from the upper South to the Deep South, where staple crop production was more profitable. This interstate slave trade sent 600,000–700,000 slaves in a southwesterly direction between 1815 and 1860. (See Table 11.1.) A slave child born in the upper South in the 1820s had a 30 percent chance of being "sold downriver" by 1860. Such sales not only split families, but made it unlikely that the slaves sold would ever see friends or family again.

The slave trade provided crucial capital in a period of transition and innovation in the upper South. Nevertheless, the declining importance of slave labor in that region meant the peculiar institution had a weaker hold on public loyalty there than in the cotton states. More rapid urban and industrial development than elsewhere in the South accompanied this diversification of agriculture. As a result, Virginians, Marylanders, and Kentuckians were divided on whether their future lay with the Deep South's plantation economy or with the industrializing free-labor system that was flourishing north of their borders.

View the **Closer Look**
Slave Auction in Richmond, Virginia on
myhistorylab.com

Quick Check

✓ In what region did "internal" slave trading become the most profitable industry? why?

The Rise of the Cotton Kingdom

The warmer climate and good soils of the lower tier of southern states made it possible to raise crops more suited than tobacco or cereals to plantation agriculture and slave labor. Since the colonial or revolutionary periods, rice and long-staple fine cotton had been grown profitably on vast estates along the coast of South Carolina and Georgia. In Louisiana, between New Orleans and Baton Rouge, sugar was the cash crop. As in the West Indies, sugar production required heavy investment and backbreaking labor—in other words, large, well-financed plantations and small armies of slaves. But cultivation of rice, long-staple cotton, and sugar was limited to peripheral, semitropical areas. It was the rise of short-staple cotton as the South's major crop that strengthened the hold of slavery and the plantation on the southern economy.

Short-staple cotton differed from the long-staple variety in two important ways: Its bolls contained seeds that were much more difficult to extract by hand, and it could be grown almost anywhere south of Virginia and Kentucky—the main requirement was a guarantee of 200 frost-free days. Before the 1790s, the seed extraction problem had prevented short-staple cotton from becoming a major market crop. Eli Whitney's invention of the cotton gin, a machine that separates the seeds from raw cotton fibers, in 1793 resolved that difficulty, however, and the subsequent westward expansion opened vast areas for cotton cultivation. Unlike rice and sugar, cotton could be grown on small farms and plantations. But large planters enjoyed advantages that made them the main producers. Only relatively large operators could afford their own gins or possessed the capital to acquire the fertile bottomlands that brought the highest cotton yields. They also had lower transportation costs because they could monopolize land along rivers and streams that were the South's natural transportation arteries.

The first major cotton-producing regions were inland areas of Georgia and South Carolina, but the center of production shifted rapidly west. By the 1830s,

View the **Image**
Cotton Gin on a Plantation in Louisiana on
myhistorylab.com

TABLE 11.1   U.S. Slave Population, 1820 and 1860

	1820	1860
United States	1,538,125	3,953,760
North	19,108	64
South	1,519,017	3,953,696
Upper South	965,514	1,530,229
Delaware	4,509	1,798
Kentucky	127,732	225,483
Maryland	107,397	87,189
Missouri	10,222	114,931
North Carolina	205,017	331,059
Tennessee	80,107	275,719
Virginia	425,153	490,865
Washington, D.C.	6,377	3,185
Lower South	553,503	2,423,467
Alabama	41,879	435,080
Arkansas	1,617	111,115
Florida	*	61,745
Georgia	149,654	462,198
Louisiana	69,064	331,726
Mississippi	32,814	436,631
South Carolina	258,475	402,406
Texas	*	182,566

*Florida and Texas were not states in 1820.
Figure originally appeared in SLAVES WITHOUT MASTERS: THE FREE NEGRO IN THE ANTEBELLUM SOUTH
Copyright (c) 1974, 2007 by Ira Berlin. Reprinted by permission of The New Press. www.thenewpress.com.

Alabama and Mississippi had surpassed Georgia and South Carolina as cotton-growing states. By the 1850s, Arkansas, northwest Louisiana, and east Texas were the most prosperous and growing plantation regions. The rise in production that accompanied this expansion was phenomenal. Between 1792 and 1817, the South's output of cotton rose from about 13,000 bales to 461,000; by 1840, it was 1.35

million. In 1860, it peaked at a colossal 4.8 million bales. (Each bale weighed 480 pounds.) Most of the cotton was exported to the booming British textile industry. (See Figure 11.1.)

But the rise of the Cotton Kingdom did not bring uniform or steady prosperity to the lower South. Many planters worked the land until it was exhausted and then took their slaves west to richer soils, leaving depressed and ravaged areas behind them. Fluctuations in markets and prices also ruined planters. Depressions, including a wave of bankruptcies, followed boom periods. But during the rising output and high prices of the 1850s, the planters began to imagine they were immune to economic disasters.

Despite the insecurities, cotton production represented the Old South's best chance for profitable investment. Hence planters had little incentive to seek alternatives to slavery, the plantation, and dependence on a single cash crop. Slavery was an economically sound institution in 1860 and showed no signs of imminent decline. In the 1850s, planters could normally expect an annual return of 8 to 10 percent on capital invested. This was roughly equivalent to what could be obtained from the most lucrative sectors of northern industry and commerce.

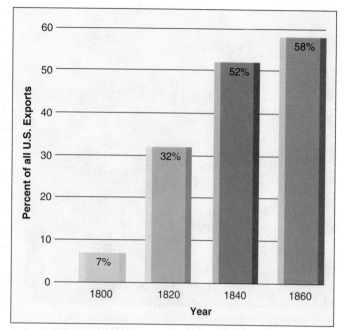

Cotton as a Percentage of All U.S. Exports, 1800–1860
Hine, Darlene, Clark, Hine, William, C., Harrold, Stanley, C. AFRICAN-AMERICAN ODYSSEY: THE COMBINED VOLUME, 4/E (c) 2008 Printed and Electronically reproduced by permission of Pearson Education, Inc., Upper Saddle River, New Jersey.

Yet just because the system made slaveholders wealthy does not mean that the benefits trickled down to the rest of the population—to the majority of whites who owned no slaves and to the slaves themselves—nor that it promoted efficiency and progressive change. Large plantation owners were the only segment of the population to enjoy the full benefits of the slave economy. Small slaveholders and non-slaveholders shared only to a limited extent in the bonanza profits of the cotton economy. The South's economic development was skewed in favor of a single route to wealth, open only to the minority with white skin and access to capital. Concentrating capital and business energies on cotton production foreclosed the diversified industrial and commercial growth that would have provided wider opportunities. Thus, compared to the industrializing North, the South was an underdeveloped region in which much of the population had little incentive to work hard.

Quick Check

✓ Why was the cotton gin so useful, and what effect did it have on southern agriculture?

CONCLUSION: WORLDS IN CONFLICT

If slaves lived in a distinct world of their own, so did planters, less affluent whites, and free blacks. The Old South was a divided society. The observations of northern traveler Frederick Law Olmsted in the 1850s bear this out. On a great plantation, he watched the

King Cotton Steamboats in New Orleans await bales of cotton for shipment. By 1860 production of "King Cotton" in the South peaked at 4.8 million bales.

slaves stop working when the overseer turned away; on a small farm, he saw a slave and his owner working in the fields together. Olmsted heard non-slaveholding whites damn the planters as "cotton snobs" but also call blacks "niggars" and express fear of interracial marriages if slaves were freed. He received hospitality from poor whites living in crowded one-room cabins and from wealthy planters in pillared mansions; life in the backcountry was radically different from that in the plantation belts.

The South was a kaleidoscope of groups divided by class, race, culture, and geography. What held it together and provided some unity were a booming plantation economy and a web of customary relationships and loyalties that could obscure the underlying cleavages and antagonisms. The fractured and fragile nature of this society would soon become apparent under the pressures of civil war.

11 STUDY RESOURCES

((•—Listen to the **Chapter Audio** for Chapter 11 on **myhistorylab.com**

TIMELINE

1793 Eli Whitney invents the cotton gin, p. 282

1800 Gabriel Prosser leads abortive slave rebellion in Virginia, p. 273

1822 Denmark Vesey conspiracy uncovered in Charleston, South Carolina, p. 274

1829 David Walker's *Appeal* calls for blacks to take up arms against slavery, p. 270

1831 Slaves under Nat Turner kill almost 60 whites in Virginia, p. 270

1832 Virginia legislature rejects gradual emancipation, p. 282

1835–1842 Blacks fight alongside Indians in the Second Seminole War, p. 274

1849 Cotton prices give rise to a sustained boom, p. 285

1857 Hinton R. Helper attacks slavery on economic grounds in *The Impending Crisis of the South*; the book is suppressed in the southern states, p. 284

1860 Cotton prices and production peak, p. 287

CHAPTER REVIEW

THE WORLD OF SOUTHERN BLACKS

What factors made living conditions for southern blacks more or less difficult?

Living conditions were difficult because slaves performed many types of labor. Some worked from sunup to sundown in gangs; others maintained more work control through the "task system"; urban slaves and free blacks had more autonomy. Family and community helped ease slave life, while some slaves resisted oppression by running away, sabotage, and even armed rebellion. *(p. 270)*

WHITE SOCIETY IN THE ANTEBELLUM SOUTH

What were the divisions and unities in white southern society?

While great planters were a tiny minority of the population, they set the tone for white southern society, propagating the ideology of "paternalism," that slaves were children who required a stern but loving parent. Most whites owned few or no slaves, but a political system of "white man's democracy" and the ideology of

white supremacy united them with large slaveholders. *(p. 276)*

SLAVERY AND THE SOUTHERN ECONOMY

How was slavery related to economic success in the South?

Slavery dominated the economy of the South: Tobacco gave way to the internal slave trade as the biggest business in the upper South, while the cotton gin made large-scale staple agriculture a booming economic machine in the Deep South, fueling the growth of a world textile industry and enriching the planter class. *(p. 284)*

KEY TERM QUESTIONS

1. Why did the Vesey conspiracy fail? (p. 274)

2. Who operated the Underground Railroad? (p. 274)

3. What was the yeoman's attitude toward slavery? (p. 280)

4. Why did the American Colonization Society transport so few slaves to Africa? (p. 282)

5. Why did the cotton gin transform southern agriculture? (p. 285)

MYHISTORYLAB CONNECTIONS

Visit **www.myhistorylab.com** for a customized Study Plan to build your knowledge of *Slaves and Masters*.

Question for Analysis

1. What caused Nat Turner to lead the slave revolt?

   Read the **Document** *Confessions of Nat Turner* p. 270

2. What impact did large concentrations of slaves have on white Southerners?

   View the **Map** *Slavery in the South* p. 271

3. What was the Underground Railroad?

   Watch the **Video** *Underground Railroad* p. 274

4. What factors might have influenced George Fitzhugh's position on slavery?

   Read the **Document** *George Fitzhugh, The Blessings of Slavery* p. 283

5. How did the economy of the internal slave trade contribute to the Civil War?

   View the **Closer Look** *Slave Auction in Richmond, Virginia* p. 285

Other Resources from this Chapter

View the **Image** *Slave Quarters, Hermitage Plantation*

Read the **Document** *Poem, The Slave Auction*

View the **Image** *Slave Dealers*

Read the **Document** *Runaway Slave Advertisements*

Watch the **Video** *Moonlight and Magnolias*

Read the **Document** *Hinton Helper, A White Southerner Speaks*

View the **Image** *Cotton Gin on a Plantation in Louisiana*

12 The Pursuit of Perfection

1800–1861

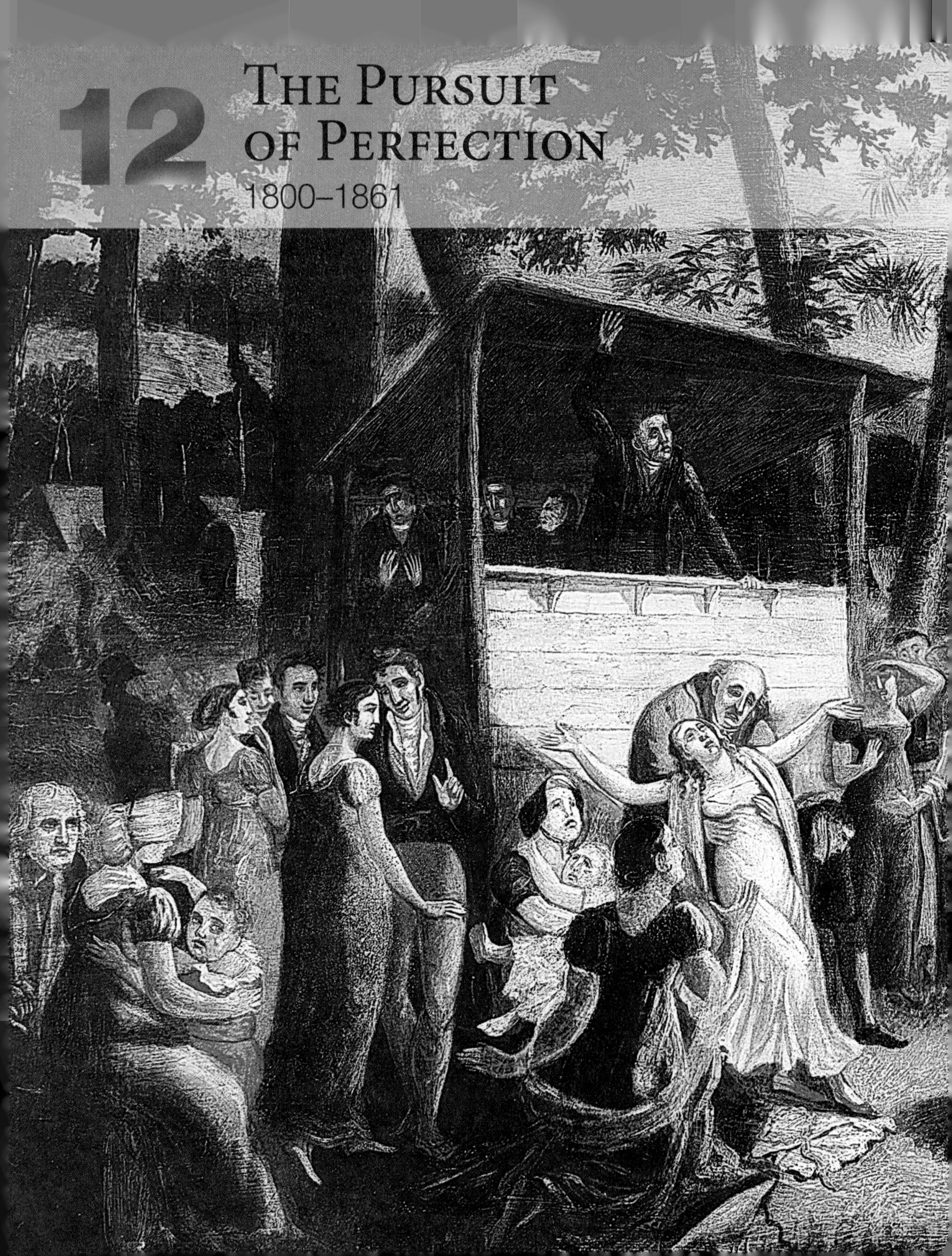

Contents and Spotlight Questions

THE RISE OF EVANGELICALISM PG. 292

How did the evangelical revivalism of the early nineteenth century spur reform movements?

DOMESTICITY AND CHANGES IN THE AMERICAN FAMILY PG. 297

What was the doctrine of "separate spheres," and how did it change family life?

REFORM TURNS RADICAL PG. 302

What were some of the major antebellum reform movements?

((•—[**Listen** to the **Chapter Audio** for Chapter 12 on **myhistorylab.com**

REDEEMING THE MIDDLE CLASS

In the winter of 1830–1831, a wave of religious revivals swept the northern states. The most dramatic and successful took place in Rochester, New York. For six months, Presbyterian evangelist Charles G. Finney preached almost daily, emphasizing that every man and woman had the power to choose Christ and a godly life.

Finney broke with his church's traditional belief that God's inscrutable will decided who would be saved when he preached that "sinners ought to be made to feel that they have something to do, and that something is to repent. That is something that no other being can do for them, neither God nor man, and something they can do and do now." Finney converted hundreds, and church membership doubled during his stay. The awakened Christians of Rochester were urged to convert relatives, neighbors, and employees. If enough people enlisted in the evangelical crusade, Finney proclaimed, the millennium would be achieved within months.

Finney's call for religious and moral renewal fell on fertile ground in Rochester. The bustling boomtown on the Erie Canal was suffering from

Revival Meeting, **1850** Christians respond emotionally at an open-air revival meeting. Oil on panel by Jeremiah Paul, c1850. The Granger Collection, NYC.

growing pains and tensions arising from rapid economic development. Leading families were divided into quarreling factions. Workers were threatening to break free from the control their employers had exerted over their lives. Most of the early converts were from the middle class. Businessmen who had been heavy drinkers and irregular churchgoers now abstained from alcohol and went to church at least twice a week. They pressured the employees in their workshops, mills, and stores to do likewise. More rigorous standards of proper behavior and religious conformity unified Rochester's elite and increased its ability to control the rest of the community. As in other cities the revival swept, evangelical Protestantism gave the middle class a stronger sense of identity and purpose.

But the war on sin was not always so unifying. Among those converted in Rochester and elsewhere were some who could not rest easy until the whole nation conformed to the pure Christianity of Christ's Sermon on the Mount. Finney expressed such a hope himself, but he concentrated on individual religious conversion and moral uplift, trusting that the purification of American society and politics would automatically follow. Other religious and moral reformers, however, were inspired to crusade against those social and political institutions that failed to achieve Christian perfection. These reformers attacked such collective "sins" as whiskey, war, slavery, and even government.

Religiously inspired reformism cut two ways. On the one hand, it imposed a new order and cultural unity on divided and troubled communities like Rochester. But it also inspired more radical movements or experiments that threatened to undermine established institutions that failed to live up to the more idealistic reformers' principles. One of these movements—abolitionism—challenged the central social and economic institution of the southern states and helped trigger political upheaval and civil war.

THE RISE OF EVANGELICALISM

How did the evangelical revivalism of the early nineteenth century spur reform movements?

American Protestantism was in ferment during the early nineteenth century. Denominations turned to revivalism to strengthen religious values and increase church membership. Mobilization of the faithful into associations to spread the gospel and reform American morals often followed spiritual renewals.

The Second Great Awakening

The Second Great Awakening, a wave of religious revivals, began in earnest on the southern frontier around 1800. In 1801, nearly 50,000 people gathered at Cane Ridge, Kentucky. According to a contemporary observer:

The noise was like the roar of Niagara. The vast sea of human beings seemed to be agitated as if by a storm. I counted seven ministers all preaching at once… . Some of the people were singing, others praying, some crying for mercy … while others were shouting most vociferously… . At one time I saw at least five hundred swept down in a moment, as if a battery of a thousand guns had been opened upon them, and then followed immediately shrieks and shouts that rent the heavens.

Emotional camp meetings, spontaneous religious gatherings organized usually by Methodists or Baptists but sometimes by Presbyterians, became a regular feature of religious life in the South and lower Midwest. On the frontier, the camp meeting met social and religious needs. In the sparsely settled southern backcountry, it was difficult to sustain local churches with regular ministers. Methodists sent out circuit riders. Baptists licensed uneducated farmers to preach to their neighbors. But for many people, the only way to get baptized or married or to have a communal religious experience was to attend a camp meeting.

Read the Document
Reverand Peter Cartwright, Cane Ridge on **myhistorylab.com**

In the South, Baptists and Presbyterians eventually deemphasized camp meetings in favor of "protracted meetings" in local churches that featured guest preachers holding forth day after day for up to two weeks. Southern evangelical churches, especially Baptist and Methodist, grew rapidly in membership and influence during the first half of the nineteenth century and became the focus of rural life. Although they fostered societies to improve morals—to encourage temperance and discourage dueling, for example—they generally shied away from social reform. The conservatism of a slaveholding society discouraged radical efforts to change the world.

Reformist tendencies were more evident in the distinctive revivalism that originated in New England and western New York. Northern evangelists were mostly Congregationalists and Presbyterians, influenced by New England Puritan traditions. Their greatest successes were not in rural or frontier areas but in small- to medium-sized towns and cities. Their revivals could be stirring affairs but were less extravagantly emotional than the camp meetings of the South. The northern brand of evangelism led to the formation of societies devoted to redeeming the human race in general and American society in particular.

The reform movement in New England began as an effort to defend Calvinism against the liberal views of religion fostered by the Enlightenment. The younger generation's growing acceptance of the belief that the Deity was the benevolent master architect of a rational universe, rather than an all-powerful, mysterious God, alarmed the Reverend Timothy Dwight, who became president of Yale College in 1795. Those religious liberals whose rationalism reached the point of denying the divinity of Jesus and the doctrine of the Trinity, and who therefore proclaimed themselves to be "Unitarians," particularly disturbed him.

To Dwight's horror, Unitarians captured fashionable and sophisticated New England congregations and even won control of the Harvard Divinity School. He fought back by preaching to Yale undergraduates that they were "dead in sin" and provoked campus revivals. But the harsh pessimism of orthodox Calvinist doctrine, with its stress on original sin and predestination, had limited appeal in a republic committed to freedom and progress.

Younger Congregational ministers reshaped New England Puritanism to increase its appeal to people who shared the prevailing optimism about human capabilities. The first great practitioner of the new evangelical Calvinism was Lyman Beecher, one of Dwight's pupils. Just before and after the War of 1812, Beecher promoted revivals in the Congregational churches of New England. He induced thousands—in his home church in Litchfield, Connecticut, and in other churches that offered him their pulpits—to acknowledge their sinfulness and surrender to God.

During the late 1820s, Beecher was forced to confront the new and more radical form of revivalism Charles G. Finney was practicing in western New York. Upstate New York was a hotbed of religious enthusiasms. Most its population consisted of transplanted New Englanders who had left behind their close-knit villages and ancestral churches but not their Puritan consciences. Troubled by rapid economic changes and the social dislocations that went with them, they were ripe for a new faith and fresh moral direction.

View the **Image**
*Methodist Camp
Meeting, 1819* on
myhistorylab.com

Although he worked within Congregational and Presbyterian churches (which were cooperating under a plan of union established in 1804), Finney was relatively indifferent to theological issues. His appeal was to emotion or the heart rather than to doctrine or reason. He wanted converts to feel the power of Christ and become new men and women. He eventually adopted the extreme view that redeemed Christians could be free of sin—as perfect as their Father in Heaven. This perfectionism led many evangelicals into moral reform movements.

Beginning in 1823, Finney conducted successful revivals in towns and cities of western New York, culminating in his triumph in Rochester in 1830–1831. Even more controversial than his freewheeling approach to theology was how he won converts. Finney sought instantaneous conversions. He held meetings that lasted all night or for days in a row, placing an "anxious bench" in front of the congregation where those who were repenting could receive special attention, and encouraged women to pray publicly for male relatives.

Finney's new methods and the emotionalism that accompanied them disturbed Beecher and eastern evangelicals. Finney also violated Christian tradition by allowing women to pray aloud in church. An evangelical summit meeting between Beecher and Finney, in New Lebanon, New York, in 1827, failed to resolve these and other issues. Beecher threatened to stand on the state line if Finney tried to bring his crusade to Connecticut. But it soon became clear that Finney was not merely stirring people up; he was leaving strong, active churches behind him. Opposition weakened. Finney eventually founded a tabernacle in New York City that became a rallying point for evangelical efforts to reach the urban masses.

Quick Check

✓ What made Revivalism such an effective means to win converts to religion?

From Revivalism to Reform

The northern wing of the Second Great Awakening, unlike the southern, inspired a great movement for social reform. Converts were organized into voluntary associations that sought to stamp out sin and social evil and win the world for Christ. Most of the converts of northern revivalism were middle-class citizens already active in their communities. They were seeking to adjust to the bustling world of the market revolution in ways that would not violate their traditional moral and social values. Their generally optimistic and forward-looking attitudes led to hopes that a wave of conversions would save the nation and the world.

In New England, Beecher and his evangelical associates established a network of missionary and benevolent societies. In 1810, Presbyterians and Congregationalists founded a Board of Commissioners for Foreign Missions and soon sent two missionaries to India. In 1816, the Reverend Samuel John Mills organized the American Bible Society. By 1821, it had distributed 140,000 Bibles, mostly in the West where churches and clergymen were scarce.

Another major effort went into publishing and distributing religious tracts, mainly by the American Tract Society, founded in 1825. Special societies targeted groups beyond the reach of regular churches, such as seamen, Native Americans, and the urban poor. In 1816–1817, middle-class women in New York, Philadelphia, Charleston, and Boston formed societies to spread the gospel in lower-class wards—where, as one of their missionaries put it, there was "a great mass of people beyond the restraints of religion."

Evangelicals also founded moral reform societies. Some of these aimed at curbing irreligious activity on the Sabbath; others sought to stamp out dueling, gambling, and prostitution. In New York in 1831, a zealous young clergyman claimed there were 10,000 prostitutes in the city laying their snares for innocent young men. As a result of this expose, an asylum was established to redeem "abandoned women." Middle-class women shifted the focus of this crusade to the men who patronized prostitutes and proposed that observers record and publish the names of men seen entering brothels. The plan was abandoned because it offended those who thought that suppressing public discussion and investigation of sexual vices would better serve the cause of virtue.

Beecher was especially influential in the temperance movement, the most successful reform crusade; his sermons against drink were the most important and widely distributed of the early tracts calling for total abstinence from "demon rum." The temperance movement was directed at a real social evil. Since the Revolution, whiskey had become the most popular American beverage. Made from corn by farmers or, by the 1820s, in commercial distilleries, it was cheaper than milk or beer and safer than water (which was often contaminated). In some areas, rum and brandy were also popular. Hard liquor was frequently consumed with food as a table beverage, even at breakfast, and children sometimes imbibed along with adults. Per capita annual consumption of distilled beverages in the 1820s was almost triple what it is today, and alcoholism had reached epidemic proportions.

The temperance reformers viewed drinking as a threat to public morality. Drunkenness was seen as a loss of self-control and moral responsibility that spawned crime, vice, and disorder. Above all, it threatened the family. Drinking was mainly a male vice, and the main target of temperance propaganda was the husband and father who abused, neglected, or abandoned his wife and children because he

THE DRUNKARD'S PROGRESS.

Temperance Propaganda warned that the drinker who began with "a glass with a friend" would inevitably follow the direct path to poverty, despair, and death. (*Source: "The Drunkard's Progress," Fruitlands Museum, Harvard, Massachusetts.*)

Read the **Document**
Lyman Beecher, "Six Sermons on Intemperance" (1828) on **myhistorylab.com**

View the **Image**
Temperance Pledge on **myhistorylab.com**

Quick Check

✔ What was the temperance movement, and why did it attract so many followers in this period?

was a slave to the bottle. Women played a vital role in the movement and in making it a crusade for protecting the home. The drinking habits of the poor or laboring classes also aroused concern. Particularly in urban areas, "respectable" and propertied people lived in fear that drunken mobs would attack private property and create chaos.

Many evangelical reformers regarded intemperance as the greatest obstacle to a republic of God-fearing, self-disciplined citizens. In 1826, clergymen active in mission work organized the American Temperance Society to coordinate and extend the work local churches and moral reform societies had begun. The original aim was to encourage abstinence from "ardent spirits" or hard liquor; there was no agreement on the evils of beer and wine. The society sent out lecturers, issued a flood of literature, and sponsored essay contests. Its agents organized revival meetings and called on attendees to pledge to abstain from spirits. The campaign was effective. By 1834, its 5,000 local branches had more than a million members, many of them women.

Some workingmen defiantly insisted on their right to drink, and built their own autonomous social life in grog halls and taverns, with heavy drinking an important part of it. But others joined temperance societies of their own. The Washingtonian Society, born in 1840, sought out the confirmed drunkard and offered him salvation. The Washingtonians held weekly experience meetings to testify to their own struggles with "Demon Drink" and tried to recreate the enjoyable community aspects of tavern life with temperance songs, poems, and theatre. Washingtonian Societies spread like wildfire among young men, women, and children, including African Americans.

Although it may be doubted whether many confirmed drunkards were cured, the movement did alter the drinking habits of middle-class American males by making temperance a mark of respectability. Per capita consumption of hard liquor declined more than 50 percent during the 1830s, and by 1850 it was down to one-third of what it had been in 1830.

Cooperating missionary and reform societies—collectively known as the "benevolent empire"—were a major force in American culture by the early 1830s. Efforts to modify American attitudes and institutions seemed to be bearing fruit. The middle class was embracing self-control and self-discipline, equipping individuals to confront a new world of economic growth and social mobility without losing their cultural and moral bearings.

DOMESTICITY AND CHANGES IN THE AMERICAN FAMILY

The evangelical culture of the 1820s and 1830s influenced the family as an institution and inspired new conceptions of its role in American society. Women—regarded as particularly susceptible to religious and moral influences—were increasingly confined to the domestic circle, but they became more important within it. Many parents viewed rearing children as essential preparation for a self-disciplined Christian life, and they did it with serious self-consciousness.

What was the doctrine of "separate spheres," and how did it change family life?

The Cult of Domesticity

The notion that women belonged in the home while the public sphere belonged to men has been called the ideology of "separate spheres." In particular, the view that women had a special role to play in the domestic sphere as guardians of virtue and spiritual heads of the home has been described as the Cult of Domesticity, or the "Cult of True Womanhood." For most men, a woman's place was in the home and on a pedestal. The ideal wife and mother was "an angel in the house," a model of piety and virtue who exerted a wholesome moral and religious influence over men and children. An 1846 poem expressed a masculine view of the true woman:

View the **Image**
Marriage Certificate, 1848 on **myhistorylab.com**

Read the **Document**
Matthew Carey, Rules for Husbands and Wives on **myhistorylab.com**

> I would have her as pure as the snow on the mount—
>
> As true as the smile that to infancy's given—
>
> As pure as the wave of the crystalline fount,
>
> Yet as warm in the heart as the sunlight of heaven.

The sociological reality behind the Cult of True Womanhood was a growing division between the working lives of middle-class men and women. In the eighteenth century and earlier, most economic activity had been centered in and near the home, and husbands and wives often worked together in a common enterprise. By the mid-nineteenth century, however, this way of life was declining, especially in the Northeast. In towns and cities, factories and counting-houses severed the home from the workplace. Men went forth every morning to their places of labor, leaving their wives at home to tend the house and the children. Married women were increasingly deprived of a productive economic role. The cult of domesticity made a virtue of the fact that men were solely responsible for running the world and building the economy.

A new conception of gender roles justified and glorified this pattern. The doctrine of "separate spheres"—set forth in novels, advice literature, and the new women's magazines—sentimentalized the woman who kept a spotless house, nurtured her children, and offered her husband a refuge from the heartless world of commerce and industry. From a modern point of view, it is easy to condemn the Cult of Domesticity as a rationalization for male dominance, and it largely was. Yet confinement to the home did not necessarily imply that women were inferior. By the standards of evangelical culture, women in the domestic sphere could be viewed as superior to men, since women could cultivate the "feminine" virtues of love and self-sacrifice and thus act as official guardians of religious and moral values.

Furthermore, many women used domestic ideology to fashion a role for themselves in the public sphere. The evangelical movement encouraged women's roles as the keepers of moral virtue. The revivals not only gave women a role in converting men but endowed Christ with stereotypical feminine characteristics. A nurturing, loving, merciful savior, mediating between a stern father and his erring children, provided the model for woman's new role as spiritual head of the home. Membership in evangelical church associations prepared women for new roles as civilizers of men and guardians of domestic culture and morality. Female reform societies taught women the strict ethical code they were to instill in other family members; mothers' groups showed them how to build character and encourage piety in children.

🔍 **View** the **Image**
Woman's Sphere on
myhistorylab.com

While many working-class women aspired to the ideal of True Womanhood, domestic ideology only affected the daily lives of relatively affluent women. Working-class wives were not usually employed outside the home during this period, but they labored long and hard within it. Besides cleaning, cooking, and taking care of many children, they often took in washing or piecework to supplement a meager family income. Their endless domestic drudgery made a sham of the notion that women had the time and energy for the "higher things of life." Life was especially hard for African American women. Most of those who were "free Negroes" rather than slaves did not have husbands who made enough to support them. They had to serve in white households or work at home doing other people's washing and sewing.

In urban areas, unmarried working-class women often lived on their own and toiled as household servants, in the sweatshops of the garment industry, and in factories. Barely able to support themselves and at the mercy of male sexual predators, they were in no position to identify with the middle-class ideal of elevated, protected womanhood. For some, the relatively well-paid and gregarious life of the successful prostitute seemed an attractive alternative to loneliness and privation.

For middle-class women whose husbands or fathers earned a good income, freedom from industrial or farm labor offered tangible benefits. They had the leisure to read the new literature directed primarily at housewives, participate in female-dominated charities, and cultivate deep friendships with other women. The result was a feminine subculture emphasizing "sisterhood" or "sorority." This growing sense of solidarity with other women and of the importance of sexual identity could transcend the private home and even the barriers of social class. Beginning in the 1820s, urban middle- and upper-class women organized societies for the relief and rehabilitation of poor or "fallen" women. Their aim was not economic and political equality with men but the elevation of all women to true womanhood.

For some women, the domestic ideal even sanctioned efforts to extend their sphere until it conquered the masculine world outside the home. This domestic feminism was reflected in crusades to stamp out such masculine sins as intemperance, gambling, and sexual vice.

In the benevolent societies and reform movements of the Jacksonian era, especially those designated as women's organizations, women handled money, organized meetings and public appeals, made contracts, and even gave orders to male subordinates. The desire to extend the feminine sphere motivated Catharine Beecher's campaign to make school teaching a woman's occupation. A prolific and influential writer on the theory and practice of domesticity, this unmarried daughter of Lyman Beecher saw the spinster-teacher as equivalent to a mother. By instilling in young males the virtues that only women could teach, the schoolmarm could help liberate America from corruption and materialism.

But the main focus of Beecher and other domestic feminists remained the role of married women who stayed home and did their part simply by being wives and mothers. Reforming husbands was difficult: They were away much of the time and tended to be preoccupied with business. But this very fact gave women primary responsibility for rearing children—to which nineteenth-century Americans attached almost cosmic significance. Since women were considered particularly well qualified to transmit piety and morality to future citizens of the republic, the Cult of Domesticity exalted motherhood and encouraged a new concern with childhood as the time when "character" was formed.

> **Quick Check**
>
> ✓ What was the doctrine of "separate spheres," and How did women extend the reach of the domestic sphere to encompass activities of public concern?

The Discovery of Childhood

The nineteenth century has been called "the century of the child." More than ever, childhood was seen as a distinct stage of life requiring the special and sustained attention of adults at least until the age of 13 or 14. The middle-class family now became "child-centered": The care, nurture, and rearing of children was viewed as the family's main function. Earlier, adults had treated children more casually, often sending them away from home for education or for apprenticeship at a young age. Among the well-to-do, children spent more time with servants or tutors than with their parents.

By the early nineteenth century, however, children were staying at home longer and receiving more attention from parents, especially mothers. The colonial custom of naming a child after a sibling who had died in infancy became much less common. Each child was now seen as a unique, irreplaceable individual.

New customs and fashions heralded the "discovery" of childhood. Books were published specifically for juveniles. Parents became more self-conscious about their responsibilities and sought help from experts on child rearing.

The new concern for children resulted in more intimate relations between parents and children. In advice manuals and sentimental literature, affection, not authority, bound the ideal family together. Discipline remained at the core of "family government," but the preferred method of enforcing good behavior changed. Shaming or withholding affection partially displaced corporal punishment. Disobedient middle-class children were now more likely to be confined to their rooms to reflect on their sins than to receive a thrashing. Discipline could no longer be justified as the constant application of physical force over naturally wayward beings. In an age of moral perfectionism, the role of discipline was to induce repentance and change basic attitudes. The goal was often described as "self-government"; to achieve it, parents used guilt, rather than fear, as their main source of leverage. A mother's sorrow or a father's stern silence was deemed more effective in forming character than blows or angry words.

Shared realities of childhood cut across class and ethnic lines. For example, mortality for infants and young children was high throughout the nineteenth century. Even wealthy families could expect to lose one child out of five or six before age five. But class and region made a big difference in children's lives. Farm children tended livestock, milked cows, churned butter, scrubbed laundry, harvested crops, and hauled water; working-class urban children did "outwork" in textiles, worked in street markets, and scavenged.

One important explanation for the growing focus on childhood is the smaller size of families. If nineteenth-century families had remained as large as those of earlier times, parents could not have lavished so much care and attention on individual offspring. For reasons not completely understood, the average number of children born to each woman during her fertile years dropped from 7.04 in 1800 to 5.42 in 1850. As a result, the average number of children per family declined about 25 percent, beginning a trend lasting to the present day.

Birth control contributed to this demographic revolution. Ancestors of the modern condom and diaphragm were openly advertised and sold during the pre–Civil War period, but most couples probably controlled family size by practicing the withdrawal method or having intercourse less often. Abortion was also common and on the rise. By 1850, there may have been one abortion for every five or six live births.

Parents seemed to understand that having fewer children meant they could provide their offspring with a better start in life. This was appropriate in a society that was shifting from agriculture to commerce and industry. For rural households short of labor, large families were an economic asset. For urban couples who hoped to send their children into a competitive world that demanded special talents and training, large families were a financial liability.

Quick Check

✓ How did notions of childhood change during the nineteenth century, and what difference did that make for family life?

The Extension of Education

Another change affecting children was the growing belief that the family could not carry the whole burden of socializing and reforming individuals, *and* that children needed schooling as well as parental nurturing. To extend the advantages of "family government" beyond the domestic circle, reformers established or improved public institutions that were designed to shape character and instill self-discipline. Between 1820 and 1850, the number of free public schools grew enormously. The new resolve to put more children in school for longer periods reflected many of the same values that exalted the child-centered family. Up to a certain age, children could be effectively nurtured and educated in the home. But after that they needed formal training at a character-molding institution that would prepare them to make a living and bear the burdens of republican citizenship. Intellectual training at school was regarded as less important than moral indoctrination.

Sometimes the school was a substitute for the family, since many children were thought to lack a proper home environment. The masses of poor and immigrant children who allegedly failed to get proper nurturing at home alarmed educational reformers. Schools had to make up for this disadvantage. Otherwise, people "incapable of self-government" would endanger the republic.

Before the 1820s, schooling in the United States was a haphazard affair. The wealthy sent their children to private schools, while some of the poor sent their children to charity or "pauper" schools that local governments financed. Public education was most highly developed in New England, where towns were required by law to support elementary schools. It was weakest in the South, where almost all education was private.

Demand for more public education began in the 1820s and early 1830s as a central focus of the workingmen's movements in eastern cities. These hard-pressed artisans viewed free schools open to all as a way to counter the growing gap between rich and poor. Affluent taxpayers, who did not see why they should pay to educate other people's children, opposed the demands. But middle-class reformers seized the initiative, shaped educational reform to fit their own end of social discipline, and provided the momentum for legislative success.

The most influential supporter of the common school movement was Horace Mann of Massachusetts. As a lawyer and state legislator, Mann worked tirelessly to establish a state board of education and tax support for local schools. In 1837, he persuaded the legislature to enact his proposals and subsequently became the first secretary of the new board, an office he held with distinction until 1848. He believed teachers and school officials could mold children like clay to a state of perfection. Like advocates of child rearing through moral influence rather than physical force, he discouraged corporal punishment except as a last resort. His position on this issue led to a bitter controversy with Boston schoolmasters who retained a Calvinist sense of original sin and favored a freer use of the rod.

Watch the **Video**
Who was Horace Mann and Why are so many schools Named after him? on **myhistorylab.com**

Against those who argued that school taxes violated property rights, Mann contended that private property was actually held in trust for the good of the community: "The property of this commonwealth is pledged for the education of all its youth up to such a point as will save them from poverty and vice, and prepare them for the adequate performance of their social and civil duties." Mann's conception of public education as a means of social discipline converted the middle and upper classes to the cause. By teaching middle-class morality and respect for order, the schools could turn potential rowdies and

Read the **Document**
Horace Mann, Report of the Massachusetts Board of Education on **myhistorylab.com**

revolutionaries into law-abiding citizens. Schools could also encourage social mobility by opening doors for lower-class children who were determined to do better than their parents.

In practice, new or improved public schools often alienated working-class pupils and their families rather than reforming them. Compulsory attendance laws deprived poor families of needed wage earners without guaranteeing jobs for those with an elementary education. As the laboring class became increasingly immigrant and Catholic in the 1840s and 1850s, dissatisfaction arose over the evangelical Protestant tone of "moral instruction" in the schools. Mann and his disciples were deliberately trying to impose a uniform culture on people who valued differing traditions.

In addition to the "three Rs" ("reading, 'riting, and 'rithmetic"), mid-nineteenth-century public schools taught the "Protestant ethic"—industry, punctuality, sobriety, and frugality. These were the virtues the famous *McGuffey's Eclectic Readers*, which first appeared in 1836, stressed. Millions of children learned to read by digesting McGuffey's parables about the terrible fate of those who gave in to sloth, drunkenness, or wastefulness. Such moral indoctrination helped produce generations of Americans with personalities and beliefs adapted to the needs of an industrializing society—people who could be depended on to adjust to the precise and regular routines of the factory or the office. But as an education for self-government—in the sense of learning to think for oneself—it left much to be desired.

Fortunately, however, education was neither limited to the schools nor devoted solely to children. Every city and almost every town or village had a lyceum, a debating society, or a mechanics' institute where adults of all social classes could broaden their intellectual horizons. Lyceums featured lectures on such subjects as "self-reliance" and "the conduct of life" by creative thinkers such as Ralph Waldo Emerson; explanations and demonstrations of the latest scientific discoveries; and debates on controversial issues.

Young Abraham Lincoln, who had received less than two years of formal schooling as a child in backwoods Indiana, sharpened his intellect in the early 1830s as a member of the New Salem, Illinois, debating society. In 1838, after moving to Springfield, he set forth his political principles when he spoke at the local lyceum on "The Perpetuation of Our Political Institutions." More than the public schools, the lyceums and debating societies fostered independent thought and encouraged new ideas.

Quick Check

✓ How did Horace Mann change ideas about public schooling in America?

REFORM TURNS RADICAL

What were some of the major antebellum reform movements?

During the 1830s, dissension split the great reform movement spawned by the Second Great Awakening. Efforts to promote evangelical piety, improve personal and public morality, and shape character through familial or institutional discipline continued and even flourished. But bolder spirits set their sights on the total liberation and perfection of the individual.

The Rise of Radical Abolitionism

The new perfectionism had its most important success within the antislavery movement. Before the 1830s, most people who expressed religious and moral concern over slavery were affiliated with the American Colonization Society. Most colonizationists admitted that slavery was an evil, but they also viewed it as a deeply rooted social and economic institution that could be eliminated only gradually and with the cooperation of slaveholders. Reflecting racial prejudice, they proposed to provide transportation to Africa for free blacks who chose to go, or were emancipated for that purpose, to relieve southern fears that a race war would erupt if freed slaves remained in America. In 1821, the society established the colony of Liberia in West Africa, and in the 1830s, a few thousand African Americans were settled there.

Colonization proved to be grossly inadequate as a step toward eliminating slavery. Many of the blacks transported to Africa were already free, and those liberated by masters whom the colonization movement influenced represented only a tiny percentage of the natural increase of the southern slave population. Northern blacks denounced the enterprise because it denied the prospect of racial equality in America. Black opposition to colonizationism helped persuade William Lloyd Garrison and other white abolitionists to repudiate the Colonization Society and support immediate emancipation without emigration. Garrison launched a more radical antislavery movement in 1831 in Boston, when he began to publish a journal called *The Liberator*. Besides calling for immediate and unconditional emancipation, Garrison denounced colonization as a slaveholder's plot to remove troublesome free blacks and an ignoble surrender to un-Christian prejudices. His rhetoric was as severe as his proposals were radical. As he wrote in the first issue of *The Liberator*, "I will be as harsh as truth and as uncompromising as justice…. I am in earnest—I will not equivocate—I will not excuse—I will not retreat a single inch—And I WILL BE HEARD!" Heard he was. In 1833, Garrison and other abolitionists founded the American Anti-Slavery Society. "We shall send forth agents to lift up the voice of remonstrance, of warning, of entreaty, and of rebuke," its Declaration of Sentiments proclaimed. The colonization movement was placed on the defensive, and many of its most active northern supporters became abolitionists.

The abolitionist movement, like the temperance crusade, was a direct outgrowth of the Second Great Awakening. Leading abolitionists had undergone conversion experiences in the 1820s and were already committed to Christian activism before they dedicated themselves to freeing the slaves. Several were ministers or divinity students seeking a mission that would fulfill spiritual and professional ambitions.

Theodore Dwight Weld personified the connection between revivalism and abolitionism. Weld came from a long line of New England ministers. After dropping out of divinity school because of physical and spiritual ailments, he migrated to western New York. There he fell under the influence of Charles G. Finney and, after a long struggle, underwent a conversion experience in 1826. He then became an itinerant lecturer for reform causes. By the early 1830s, he

Read the **Document** *Abolitionist Demands Immediate End* on **myhistorylab.com**

focused his attention on the moral issues raised by the institution of slavery. After a flirtation with colonization, Weld was converted to abolitionism in 1832, recognizing that colonizationists did not accept blacks as equals or "brothers-in-Christ." In 1834, he instigated what amounted to abolitionist revivals at Lane Theological Seminary in Cincinnati. When the seminary's trustees attempted to suppress discussion of immediate emancipation, Weld led most students in a walkout. The "Lane rebels" subsequently founded Oberlin College as a center for abolitionist activity.

In 1835 and 1836, Weld toured Ohio and western New York preaching abolitionism. He also supervised and trained other agents and orators to convert the region to immediate emancipation. The tried-and-true methods of the revival—fervent preaching, protracted meetings, and the call for individuals to come forth and announce their redemption—were put at the service of the antislavery movement. Weld and his associates often had to face angry mobs, but they left behind them tens of thousands of new abolitionists and hundreds of antislavery societies. Northern Ohio and western New York became hotbeds of abolitionist sentiment.

Antislavery orators and organizers tended to have their greatest successes in the small- to medium-sized towns of the upper North. The typical convert came from an upwardly mobile family engaged in small business, the skilled trades, or market farming. In larger towns and cities, or when they ventured close to the Mason–Dixon Line, abolitionists were more likely to encounter fierce and effective opposition. In 1835, Garrison was almost lynched in Boston. In New York City, the Tappan brothers—Lewis and Arthur—were frequently threatened and attacked. These two successful merchants used their wealth to finance antislavery activities. In 1835–1836, they supported a massive effort to distribute antislavery pamphlets through the U.S. mails. But most New Yorkers regarded them as dangerous radicals.

Abolitionists who thought of taking their message to the fringes of the South had reason to pause, given the fate of the antislavery editor Elijah Lovejoy. In 1837, while defending himself and his printing press from a mob in Alton, Illinois, just across the Mississippi River from slaveholding Missouri, Lovejoy was shot and killed.

Racism was a major cause of anti-abolitionist violence in the North. Rumors that abolitionists advocated or practiced interracial marriage could easily incite an urban crowd. If it could not find white abolitionists, the mob was likely to turn on local blacks. Working-class whites tended to fear that economic and social competition with blacks would increase if abolitionists freed the slaves and made them citizens. But "gentlemen of property and standing" dominated many of the mobs. Solid citizens resorted to violence, it would appear, because abolitionism threatened their conservative notions of social order and hierarchy.

By the end of the 1830s, the abolitionist movement was under stress. Besides the burden of external repression, there was internal dissension. Becoming an abolitionist required an exacting conscience and an unwillingness to compromise. These traits also made it difficult for abolitionists to work together and maintain a united

Read the **Document**
New England Writer Portrays Slavery, 1852 on **myhistorylab.com**

front. During the late 1830s, Garrison, the most visible abolitionist, began to adopt positions that other abolitionists found extreme and divisive. He embraced the nonresistant or "no-government" philosophy of Henry C. Wright and urged abolitionists to abstain from voting or participating in a corrupt political system. He attacked the clergy and the churches for refusing to take an antislavery stand and encouraged his followers to "come out" of the established denominations rather than work within them.

These positions alienated members of the Anti-Slavery Society who hoped that abolitionists could influence or take over organized religion and the political system. But Garrison's stand on women's rights led to an open break at the national convention of the American Anti-Slavery Society in 1840. Following their leader's principle that women should be equal partners in the crusade, a Garrison-led majority elected a woman to the society's executive committee. A minority, led by Lewis Tappan, then formed a competing organization—the American and Foreign Anti-Slavery Society.

The new organization never amounted to much, but the schism weakened Garrison's influence. When he repudiated the Constitution as a proslavery document and called for northern secession from the Union, few antislavery people in the Middle Atlantic or Midwestern states went along. Outside New England, most abolitionists worked within the churches and avoided controversial side issues such as women's rights and nonresistant pacifism. Some antislavery advocates became political activists. The Liberty party, organized in 1840, was their first attempt to enter the electoral arena under their own banner; it signaled a new effort to turn antislavery sentiment into political power.

Quick Check

✓ Who were the leading opponents of slavery, and What different approaches did they take to politics as they put forward demands for slavery's immediate abolition?

Black Abolitionists

From the beginning the abolitionist movement depended on the northern free black community. Most of the early subscribers to Garrison's *Liberator* were African Americans. Black orators, especially escaped slaves such as Frederick Douglass, brought home the realities of bondage to northern audiences. But relations between white and black abolitionists were often tense. Blacks protested that they did not have their fair share of leadership positions or influence over policy. Eventually a black antislavery movement emerged that was largely independent of the white-led crusade. In addition to Douglass, prominent black male abolitionists were Charles Remond, William Wells Brown, Robert Purvis, and Henry Highland Garnet. Outspoken women such as Sojourner Truth, Maria Stewart, and Frances Harper also played a significant role in black antislavery activity. The Negro Convention movement, which sponsored national meetings of black leaders beginning in 1830, provided an important forum for independent black expression. Their most eloquent statement came in 1854, when black leaders met in Cleveland to declare their faith in a separate identity, proclaiming, "We pledge our integrity to use all honorable means, to unite us, as one people, on this continent."

Read the **Document** *Maria Stewart, "The Miseries We Tasted"* on **myhistorylab.com**

Black newspapers, such as *Freedom's Journal,* first published in 1827, and the *North Star,* founded by Douglass in 1847, enabled black writers to preach liberation to black readers. African American authors also wrote books and pamphlets attacking slavery, refuting racism, and advocating resistance. One of the most influential publications was David Walker's *Appeal ... to the Colored Citizens of the World,* which appeared in 1829. Walker denounced slavery in the most vigorous language and called for a black revolt against white tyranny.

Free blacks in the North were also the main conductors on the fabled Underground Railroad, which opened a path for fugitives from slavery. Ex-slaves such as Harriet Tubman and Josiah Henson made regular forays into the slave states to lead other blacks to freedom, and free blacks ran many of the "stations" along the way. In northern towns and cities, free blacks organized "vigilance committees" to protect fugitives and thwart the slave-catchers. Blacks even used force to rescue recaptured fugitives from the authorities. In Boston in 1851, one such group seized a slave named Shadrack from a U.S. marshal who was returning him to bondage. In deeds and words, free blacks showed unyielding hostility to slavery and racism.

Historians have debated whether the abolitionist movement of the 1830s and early 1840s was a failure. It failed to convince most Americans that slavery was a sinful institution that should be abolished immediately. This position, which implied that blacks should be granted equality as American citizens, ran up against a commitment to white supremacy in all parts of the country. In the South, abolitionism helped inspire a more militant defense of slavery. The belief that peaceful agitation, or what abolitionists called "moral suasion," would convert slaveholders and their northern sympathizers to abolition was unrealistic.

But in another sense the crusade was successful. It made the public conscious of the slavery issue and convinced many northerners that the South's peculiar institution was morally wrong and dangerous to the American way of life. The South helped the antislavery cause in the North by responding hysterically and repressively to abolitionist agitation. In 1836, southern congressmen forced adoption of a "gag rule" requiring that abolitionist petitions be tabled without being read; the post office

Abolitionist Frederick Douglass, who escaped from slavery in 1838, became one of the most effective voices in the crusade against slavery.

Freedom Calling Harriet Tubman, far left, is shown here with some of the slaves she helped escape on the Underground Railroad. Born a slave in Maryland, she escaped to Philadelphia in 1849. She is said to have helped 300 African Americans flee slavery. She led many of them all the way to Canada, where they would be beyond the reach of the Fugitive Slave Law. (*Source: Smith College, Sophia Smith Collection, Northampton, Massachusetts.*)

refused to deliver antislavery literature in the slave states. Prominent northerners who had been unmoved by abolitionist depictions of slave suffering became more responsive when their own civil liberties were threatened. The politicians who later mobilized the North against the expansion of slavery into the territories drew strength from the antislavery and anti-southern sentiments that abolitionists had already called forth.

> **Quick Check**
>
> ✓ What was the Underground Railroad, and who were its main operators?

From Abolitionism to Women's Rights

Abolitionism also was a catalyst for the women's rights movement. From the beginning, women participated actively in the abolitionist crusade. Between 1835 and 1838, the American Anti-Slavery Society bombarded Congress with petitions, mostly calling for abolition of slavery in the District of Columbia. More than half of the thousands of these petitions included women's signatures.

Some antislavery women defied conventional ideas of their proper sphere by becoming public speakers and demanding an equal role in the leadership of antislavery societies. The most famous of these were the Grimké sisters, Sarah and Angelina, who attracted enormous attention as the rebellious daughters of a South Carolina slaveholder. When male abolitionists objected to their speaking in public to mixed audiences of men and women, Garrison defended them and helped forge a link between blacks' and women's struggles for equality.

A Mother's Movement Elizabeth Cady Stanton, a leader of the women's rights movement, reared seven children. In addition to her pioneering work, especially for woman suffrage, she also lectured on family life and child care.

Watch the **Video**
The Women's Rights Movement in the nineteenth Century on **myhistorylab.com**

Quick Check

✔ What goals did The Seneca Falls Convention seek to accomplish?

The battle to participate equally in the antislavery crusade made women abolitionists acutely aware of male dominance and oppression. For them, the same principles that justified the liberation of the slaves also applied to emancipating women from restrictions on their rights as citizens. In 1840, Garrison's American followers withdrew from the first World's Anti-Slavery Convention in London because the sponsors refused to seat the women in their delegation. Among the women excluded were Lucretia Mott and Elizabeth Cady Stanton.

Wounded by men's reluctance to extend the cause of emancipation to include women, Stanton and Mott began discussing plans for a women's rights convention. They returned to New York, where a campaign was already under way to reform the state's laws limiting the rights of married women. Ernestine Rose, a young Jewish activist, and Judge Thomas Herttell, a political radical and freethinker who had introduced the first bill to reform the state's marriage laws to the New York legislature, spearheaded this campaign. It came to a head at the famous Seneca Falls Convention, which Stanton and Mott organized in upstate New York in 1848. These early feminists, in their first national gathering, issued a Declaration of Sentiments, modeled on the Declaration of Independence, charging that "the history of mankind is a history of repeated injuries and usurpations on the part of man toward woman, having in direct object the establishment of an absolute tyranny over her." They demanded that all women be given the right to vote and that married women be freed from unjust laws giving husbands control of their property, persons, and children. Rejecting the Cult of Domesticity with its doctrine of separate spheres, these women and their male supporters launched the modern movement for gender equality.

CONCLUSION: COUNTERPOINT ON REFORM

Nathaniel Hawthorne was a great American writer who observed the perfectionist ferment of the age but suggested in his novels and tales that pursuit of the ideal led to a distorted view of human nature and possibilities.

He illustrated the dangers of pursuing perfection too avidly in his tale of a father who kills his beautiful daughter by trying to remove her one blemish, a birthmark. His greatest novels, *The Scarlet Letter* (1850) and *The House of the Seven Gables* (1851), probed New England's Puritan past and the shadows it cast on Hawthorne's own age. By dwelling on original sin as a psychological reality, Hawthorne told his contemporaries that they could never escape from guilt and evil. One had to accept the world as an imperfect place. Although he did not openly attack humanitarian reformers and cosmic optimists, Hawthorne's parables and allegories implicitly questioned the assumptions of pre–Civil War reform.

One does not have to agree with Hawthorne's pessimistic view of the human condition to acknowledge that perfectionist reformers promised more than they could deliver. Revivals could not make all men like Christ; temperance could not solve all social problems; and abolitionist agitation could not end slavery peacefully. The consequences of perfectionist efforts were often far different from what their proponents expected. In defense of the reformers, however, one could argue that Hawthorne's skepticism and fatalism were a prescription for doing nothing about intolerable evils. If the reform impulse was long on inspirational rhetoric but short on durable, practical achievements, it did at least disturb the complacent and opportunistic surface of American life and open the way to necessary changes. Nothing would improve unless people were willing to dream of improvements.

12 STUDY RESOURCES

((•—[Listen to the **Chapter Audio** for Chapter 12 on **myhistorylab.com**

TIMELINE

1801 Massive revival held at Cane Ridge, Kentucky, p. 292

1826 American Temperance Society organized, p. 296

1830–1831 Charles G. Finney evangelizes Rochester, New York, p. 294

1831 William Lloyd Garrison publishes first issue of *The Liberator*, p. 303

1833 Abolitionists found American Anti-Slavery Society, p. 303

1835–1836 Theodore Weld advocates abolition in Ohio and upstate New York, p. 304

1837 Massachusetts establishes a state board of education, p. 301

1840 American Anti-Slavery Society splits over women's rights and other issues, p. 305

1848 Feminists found the women's rights movement at Seneca Falls, New York, p. 308

CHAPTER REVIEW

THE RISE OF EVANGELICALISM

How did the evangelical revivalism of the early nineteenth century spur reform movements?

Evangelical revivalists preached the perfectibility of individual moral agents, encouraging each person to choose his or her own moral and political destiny. This perfectionism led evangelical Christians to organize voluntary associations and benevolent societies that would teach people moral and social values. The most important of these reform efforts was the temperance movement. *(p. 292)*

DOMESTICITY AND CHANGES IN THE AMERICAN FAMILY

What was the doctrine of "separate spheres," and how did it change family life?

The doctrine of "separate spheres" glorified women's role in caring for the home and family, guarding religious and moral values while men went into the public sphere to earn money and participate in politics. Smaller families and more leisure time for middle-class families also emphasized children's development, including new public schools open to all. *(p. 297)*

REFORM TURNS RADICAL

What were the major antebellum reform movements?

Religious revivalism inspired movements for temperance, abolition of slavery, and women's rights. These movements grew more radical over time, turning to the political sphere in the 1840s as they lost confidence that changing men's hearts could transform society. The abolitionists organized the Liberty party in 1840, and feminists held their first convention at Seneca Falls in 1848. *(p. 302)*

KEY TERM QUESTIONS

1. What was the Second Great Awakening? (p. 292)

2. Why did the temperance movement attract so many followers in the early nineteenth century? (p. 295)

3. What was the Cult of Domesticity? (p. 297)

4. How did Charles G. Finney's belief in perfectionism influence American Protestantism? (p. 294)

5. How did the "benevolent empire" affect American society? (p. 296)

6. What took place at the Seneca Falls Convention and why was it significant? (p. 308)

7. How did the Second Great Awakening help to bring about the abolitionist movement? (p. 303)

MYHISTORYLAB CONNECTIONS

Visit **www.myhistorylab.com** for a customized Study Plan to build your knowledge of *The Pursuit of Perfection*

Question for Analysis

1. Why did Beecher view alcohol consumption as such a threat to the nation?

   Read the **Document** *Lyman Beecher, Six Sermons on Intemperance* p. 296

Other Resources from this Chapter

Read the **Document** *Reverend Peter Cartwright, Cane Ridge*

View the **Image** *Methodist Camp Meeting, 1819*

2. Why was Horace Mann so important?

   👁—Watch the Video *Who Was Horace Mann and Why are So Many Schools Named After Him?* p. 301

3. How does Simon Legree treat Uncle Tom during the trip to the plantation?

   📖—Read the Document *New England Writer Portrays Slavery, 1852* p. 304

4. What is the tone of David Walker's Appeal?

   📖—Read the Document *David Walker, A Black Abolitionist Speaks Out (1829)* p. 306

5. How was the Women's Rights Movement of the Nineteenth Century connected to the abolitionist movement of the same period?

   👁—Watch the Video *The Women's Rights Movement in Nineteenth Century America* p. 308

🔍—View the Image *Marriage Certificate, 1848*

📖—Read the Document *Matthew Carey, Rules for Husbands and Wives* p. 297

🔍—View the Image *Woman's Sphere*

📖—Read the Document *Horace Mann Report on the Massachusetts Board of Education*

📖—Read the Document *Abolitionist Demands Immediate End to Slavery*

📖—Read the Document *Maria Stewart, The Miseries We Tasted*

Contents and Spotlight Questions

**TEXAS, MANIFEST DESTINY, AND
THE MEXICAN-AMERICAN WAR PG. 315**

Why did the U.S. annex Texas and the Southwest?

**INTERNAL EXPANSIONISM AND THE INDUSTRIAL
REVOLUTION PG. 324**

How did developments in transportation foster
industrialization and encourage immigration?

((•—Listen to the **Chapter Audio** for Chapter 13
on **myhistorylab.com**

THE SPIRIT OF YOUNG AMERICA

In the 1840s and early 1850s, politicians, writers, and entrepreneurs frequently proclaimed themselves champions of **Young America**. One of the first to use the phrase was the famous author and lecturer Ralph Waldo Emerson, who told an audience in 1844 that the nation was entering a new era of commercial development, technological progress, and territorial expansion. Emerson suggested that a progressive new generation—the Young Americans—would lead this surge of physical development. More than a slogan but less than an organized movement, Young America favored the market economy and industrial growth, a more aggressive foreign policy, and a celebration of America's unique strengths and virtues.

Young Americans favored enlarging the national market by acquiring new territory. They called for the annexation of Texas, claimed all of Oregon, and urged the seizure of vast territories from Mexico. They also celebrated the technological advances that would knit this new empire together, especially the telegraph and the railroad.

Young America was both a cultural and intellectual movement and an economic and political one. In 1845, a Washington journal hailed the

Ambition and Ambivalence Herman Melville, shown here in an 1870 portrait by Joseph Oriel Eaton, shaped the knowledge he gained as a merchant sailor into *Moby-Dick*, a cautionary saga about the dark side of human ambition.

49-year-old James K. Polk, the youngest man to have been elected president, as a sign that youth will "dare to take antiquity by the beard, and tear the cloak from hoary-headed hypocrisy. Too young to be corrupt … it is Young America, awakened to a sense of her own intellectual greatness by her soaring spirit. It stands in strength, the voice of the majority." During the Polk administration, Young American writers and critics—mostly based in New York City—called for a distinctive national literature, free of subservience to European themes or models and expressive of the democratic spirit. Their organ was the *Literary World*, a magazine founded in 1847. Its ideals influenced two of the greatest writers America has produced: Walt Whitman and Herman Melville.

Whitman captured the exuberance and expansionism of Young America in his "Song of the Open Road":

> From this hour I ordain myself loos'd of limits and imaginary lines,
> Going where I list, my own master total and absolute,
> ....
> I inhale great draughts of space,
> The east and the west are mine, and the north and the south are mine.
> I am larger, better than I thought.

Songs of Ourselves Walt Whitman in the "carpenter portrait" that appeared in the first edition of his great work, *Leaves of Grass*, in 1855. The poet's rough clothes and slouch hat signify his identification with the common people.

In *Moby-Dick*, Herman Melville produced a novel original enough in form and concept to more than fulfill the demand of Young Americans for "a New Literature to fit the New Man in the New Age." But Melville was too deep a thinker not to see the perils behind the soaring ambition and aggressiveness of the new age. The whaling captain Ahab, whose relentless pursuit of the white whale destroys himself and his ship, symbolized—among other things—the dangers facing a nation that was overreaching itself by indulging its pride and exalted sense of destiny with too little concern for the moral and practical consequences.

The Young American ideal—the idea of a young country led by young men into new paths of prosperity and greatness—appealed to many people and found support across party lines. But it came to be identified primarily with young Democrats who wanted to move their party away from its traditional fear of commerce and industry. Unlike old-line Jeffersonians and Jacksonians, Young Americans had no qualms about the market economy and the speculative, materialistic spirit it called forth.

Before 1848, the Young American impulse focused mainly on the great expanse of western lands that lay just beyond the nation's borders. After the Mexican-American War, when territorial gains extended the nation's boundaries from the Atlantic to the Pacific, attention shifted to internal development. Discoveries of gold in the nation's western territories fostered economic growth, technological advances spurred industrialization, and increased immigration brought more people to populate the lands newly acquired—by agreement or by force.

TEXAS, MANIFEST DESTINY, AND THE MEXICAN-AMERICAN WAR

The rush of settlers beyond the nation's borders in the 1830s and 1840s inspired politicians and propagandists to call for annexing those areas. Some proclaimed it was the Manifest Destiny of the United States to absorb all of North America, including Canada and Mexico. Such ambitions—and the policies they inspired—led to a diplomatic confrontation with Britain over claims to Oregon and a war with Mexico. (See Map 13.1)

Why did the U.S. annex Texas and the Southwest?

The Texas Revolution

While U.S. expansionists also clashed with Britain over territory in the Pacific Northwest, the major terrain of conflict was between the United States and Mexico in the Southwest. In 1821, Mexico, which then included areas that currently make up the states of Texas, New Mexico, Arizona, California, Nevada, Utah, and much of Colorado, declared its independence from Spain.

View the **Map**
Texas Revolution, 1836 on
myhistorylab.com

Map 13.1 *Territorial Expansion by the Mid-Nineteenth Century* Fervent nationalists promoted the growth of America through territorial expansion as the divinely ordained "Manifest Destiny" of a chosen people.

Newly independent Mexico encouraged trade with the United States and wooed American settlers to Texas, which was sparsely populated. It granted Stephen F. Austin, son of a one-time Spanish citizen, a huge piece of land there in hopes he would help attract and settle new colonists from the United States. Some 15 other Anglo-American *empresarios* received similar land grants in the 1820s. In 1823, 300 families from the United States were settled on the Austin grant. Within a year, the colony's population was 2,021. The offer of fertile and inexpensive land attracted many American immigrants.

But friction soon developed between the Mexican government and the Anglo-American colonists over slavery and the authority of the Catholic Church. Anglo-American settlers were not willing to become Mexicans. Yet under the terms of settlement, all people living in Texas had to become Mexican citizens and Roman Catholics. Slavery presented another problem. In 1829, Mexico freed all slaves under its jurisdiction. The Mexican government gave slaveholders in Texas an exemption that allowed them to emancipate their slaves and then force them to sign lifelong contracts as indentured servants, but many Texans refused to limit their ownership rights in any way. Settlers either converted to Catholicism in name only or ignored the requirement.

A Mexican commission reported in 1829 that Americans in Texas were flagrantly violating Mexican law—refusing to emancipate their slaves, evading import duties on goods from the United States, and not converting to Catholicism. In 1830, the Mexican Congress prohibited further American immigration and importation of slaves to Texas.

But the new law was feebly enforced, and the flow of settlers, slaves, and smuggled goods continued. Texans complained about the lack of local self-government. Under the Mexican federal constitution, Texas was part of the state of Coahuila, and Texan representatives were outnumbered three to one in the state legislature. In 1832, the colonists showed their displeasure by rioting in protest against the arrest of Anglo-Americans by a Mexican commander.

The Texans' status as "tolerated guests" was threatened in 1834 when General Antonio López de Santa Anna made himself dictator of Mexico and abolished its federal system. News of these developments reached Texas late in the year, along with rumors that the American immigrants were going to be disenfranchised or even expelled. The Texans, already aroused by earlier restrictive policies, prepared to resist Santa Anna's effort to enforce tariff regulations.

Santa Anna sent reinforcements. On June 30, 1835, before they arrived, settlers led by William B. Travis captured the Mexican garrison at Anahuac without firing a shot. The Texans first fought Mexican troops at Gonzales in October and forced a cavalry detachment to retreat. Shortly thereafter, Austin captured San Antonio along with most of the Mexican troops then in Texas.

Quick Check

✓ Why were Austin and the settlers so dissatisfied with Mexican rule over Texas?

The Republic of Texas

While this early fighting was going on, delegates from the American communities in Texas declared their independence on March 2, 1836. A constitution, based on that of the United States, was adopted for the new Republic of Texas, and a temporary government was installed to carry on the struggle. Although the ensuing conflict largely pitted Americans against Mexicans, some Texas Mexicans, or *Tejanos*, sided with the Anglo rebels. They too wanted to be free of Santa Anna's heavy-handed rule.

Within days after Texas declared itself a republic, rebels and Mexican troops in San Antonio fought the famous battle of the Alamo. Myths about this battle have magnified the Anglo rebels' valor at the Mexicans' expense. The folklore is based on fact—only 187 rebels fought off a far larger number of Mexican soldiers for more than a week before capitulating—but not all rebels fought to the death. The folk hero Davy Crockett and seven other survivors were captured and executed. Nevertheless, a tale that combined actual and mythical bravery inside the Alamo gave the insurrection inspiration, moral sanction, outside support, and the rallying cry "Remember the Alamo."

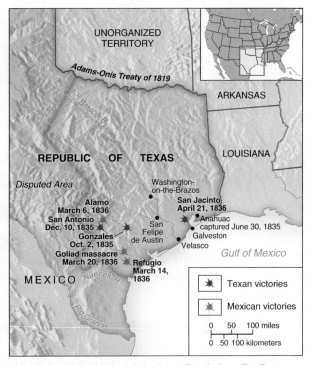

Map 13.2 *Major Battles of the Texas Revolution* The Texans suffered severe losses at the Alamo and Goliad, but they scored a stunning victory at San Jacinto.

The revolt ended with an exchange of slaughters. A few days after the Alamo battle, another Texas detachment was captured near the San Antonio River and marched to the town of Goliad, where most of its 350 members were executed. The next month, on April 21, 1836, the main Texas army, under Sam Houston, assaulted Santa Anna's troops at an encampment near the San Jacinto River during the siesta hour. The final count showed that 630 Mexicans and only a handful of Texans had been killed. Santa Anna was captured and forced to sign treaties recognizing the independence of Texas and its claim to territory all the way to the Rio Grande. (See Map 13.2)

Houston became the first president of Texas. He immediately sent an emissary to Washington to test the waters for annexation. Houston's agent found sympathy for Texas's independence, but Andrew Jackson and others told him that domestic politics and fear of a war with Mexico made immediate annexation impossible. The most that he could win from Congress and the Jackson administration was formal recognition of Texas sovereignty.

In its ten-year existence as the Lone Star Republic, Texas drew settlers from the United States. The Panic of 1837 impelled many debt-ridden and land-hungry farmers to take advantage of the free grants of 1,280 acres that Texas offered immigrating heads of white families. By 1844, Texas's population had soared from 30,000 to 142,000. Both newcomers and old settlers assumed that they would soon be annexed and restored to American citizenship.

View the **Image**
The Alamo on
myhistorylab.com

Quick Check

✓ What aspects of the Alamo folklore are true, and which are fictionalized?

Battle of San Jacinto In this panorama of the Texas Revolution's decisive battle at San Jacinto by H. A. McArdle, Sam Houston leads the charge against Santa Anna's forces.

The Annexation of Texas

⊙ **Watch** the **Video**
*The Annexation of
Texas* on
myhistorylab.com

President John Tyler initiated the politics of Manifest Destiny by making Texas annexation a major issue. As an "accidental president," a vice president who became president in 1841 when William Henry Harrison died after scarcely a month in office, Tyler needed an issue people could rally around. In 1843, he put the full weight of his administration behind the annexation of Texas, which he thought would solidify his support in the South. Secretary of State John C. Calhoun negotiated an annexation treaty that was brought before the Senate in 1844.

The strategy of linking annexation explicitly to the interests of the South and slavery led northern antislavery Whigs to charge that the whole scheme was a pro-slavery plot to advance the interests of one section of the nation against the other. The Senate rejected the annexation treaty by a decisive vote of 35 to 16 in June 1844. Tyler then attempted to admit Texas as a state through a joint resolution of both houses of Congress, but Congress adjourned before the issue came to a vote. The whole question was deferred in anticipation of the election of 1844.

Texas became the central issue in the 1844 campaign. But party lines held firm, and Tyler himself could not capitalize on the issue because neither party supported his stand. He tried to run as an independent but could not gain significant support and withdrew.

If the Democratic convention had been held in 1843—as originally scheduled—ex-President Martin Van Buren would have won the nomination. But postponing the conclave until May 1844 weakened his chances. The annexation question came to the fore, and Van Buren had to take a stand. He persisted in the view he had held as president—incorporating Texas would risk war with Mexico, arouse sectional strife, and destroy the unity of the Democratic party. These fears seemed

TABLE 13.1   The Liberty Party Swings an Election

Candidate	Party	Actual Vote in New York	National Electoral Vote	If Liberty Voters Had Voted Whig	Projected Electoral Vote
Polk	Democratic	237,588	170	237,588	134
Clay	Whig	232,482	105	248,294	141
Birney	Liberty	15,812	0	—	—

confirmed in 1844 when the dominant party faction in Van Buren's home state of New York opposed Tyler's Texas policy. To keep the issue out of the campaign, Van Buren struck a gentleman's agreement with Henry Clay, the overwhelming favorite for the Whig nomination, that both of them would publicly oppose immediate annexation.

Van Buren's opposition to annexation cost him the nomination. Southern delegates, who secured a rule requiring approval by a two-thirds vote, blocked Van Buren's nomination. After eight ballots, a dark horse candidate—James K. Polk of Tennessee—emerged triumphant. Polk, a protégé of Andrew Jackson, had been speaker of the House and governor of Tennessee.

An expansionist, Polk ran on a platform calling for the simultaneous annexation of Texas and assertion of American claims to all of Oregon. He identified himself and his party with the popular cause of turning the United States into a continental nation, an aspiration that attracted support from all parts of the country.

Polk won the election by a relatively narrow popular margin. He secured his triumph in the electoral college by winning New York and Michigan, where the Liberty party candidate, James G. Birney, took enough Whig antislavery votes away from Clay to affect the outcome. (See Tables 13.1 and 13.2) The close election did not prevent the Democrats from claiming that the people had backed an aggressive campaign to extend the borders of the United States.

After Polk's victory, Congress reconsidered the annexation of Texas. The mood had changed, and leading senators from both parties who had opposed Tyler's scheme for annexation by joint resolution changed their position. Congress approved annexation a few days before Polk took office. By contrast, the expansionist claim to all of the Oregon Country, jointly occupied by the U.S. and Britain, was

Read the
Document
James K. Polk, First
Inaugural Address on
myhistorylab.com

TABLE 13.2   The Election of 1844

Candidate	Party	Popular Vote	Electoral Vote
Polk	Democratic	1,338,464	170
Clay	Whig	1,300,097	105
Birney	Liberty	62,300	—

Quick Check

✓ Why and how did Texas cost Van Buren his party's nomination?

abandoned. Polk settled the Oregon question in 1846 with a treaty that garnered the U.S. its first deepwater port on the Pacific in Puget Sound, but ceded to Britain all of the Oregon territory above the 49th parallel. To northerners, who had hoped for more free states to balance the admission of Texas as a slave state, this concession demonstrated that Polk would be a southern president.

The Doctrine of Manifest Destiny

The expansionist mood that accompanied Polk's election and the annexation of Texas was given a name and a rationale in 1845. John L. O'Sullivan, a proponent of the Young America movement and editor of the influential *United States Magazine and Democratic Review*, charged that foreign governments were conspiring to block the annexation of Texas to thwart "the fulfillment of our manifest destiny to over-spread the continent allotted by providence for the free development of our yearly multiplying millions."

Besides coining the phrase *Manifest Destiny*, O'Sullivan pointed to the three main ideas that lay behind it. One was that God favored American expansionism. This notion came naturally out of the long tradition, going back to the New England Puritans, that identified the growth of America with the divinely ordained success of a chosen people. Second, the phrase "free development" implied that the spread of American rule meant "extending the area of freedom." Democratic institutions and local self-government would follow the flag if the United States annexed areas claimed by autocratic foreign governments. O'Sullivan's third premise was that population growth required territorial acquisitions.

Quick Check

✓ What was America's "Manifest Destiny," and what were the origins of this concept?

In its most extreme form, Manifest Destiny meant that the United States would occupy the entire North American continent. Nothing less would appease its land-hungry population.

War with Mexico

Although Mexico had offered to recognize Texas independence in 1845 to forestall annexation to the United States, it rejected the Lone Star Republic's dubious claim to the unsettled territory between the Nueces River and the Rio Grande. When the United States annexed Texas and assumed its claim to the disputed area, Mexico broke off diplomatic relations and prepared for war.

View the **Map**
Mexican-American War, 1846–1848 on
myhistorylab.com

Polk responded by placing troops in Louisiana on alert and dispatching John Slidell to Mexico City to resolve the boundary dispute and persuade the Mexicans to sell New Mexico and California to the United States. The Mexican government refused to receive Slidell because his appointment ignored the break in regular diplomatic relations. While Slidell was cooling his heels in Mexico City, in January 1846, Polk ordered General Zachary Taylor to advance beyond the Nueces and proceed toward the Rio Grande, thus encroaching on territory both sides claimed.

By April, Taylor was near Matamoros on the Rio Grande. On the opposite bank of the river, Mexican forces had erected a fort. On April 24, 1,600 Mexican soldiers crossed the river and the following day attacked a small American detachment, killing 16 and capturing the rest. Taylor told the president: "Hostilities may now be considered as commenced."

The news was neither unexpected nor unwelcome. Polk was already preparing his war message to Congress when he learned of the fighting on the Rio Grande. A short and decisive war would force the cession of California and New Mexico.

The Mexican-American War lasted much longer than expected because the Mexicans refused to make peace despite military defeats. In the first major campaign of the conflict, Taylor took Matamoros and overcame fierce resistance to capture the city of Monterrey.

Taylor's decision to allow the Mexican garrison there to go free and his unwillingness or inability to advance farther into Mexico angered Polk and led him to adopt a new strategy to win the war and a new commander to implement it. He ordered General Winfield Scott to attack Veracruz and place an American army within striking distance of Mexico City. With half his forces detached for this invasion, Taylor was left in northern Mexico. But this did not deprive him of a final moment of glory. At Buena Vista, in February 1847, he claimed victory over a sizable Mexican army sent to dislodge him. Despite his unpopularity with the administration, Taylor became a national hero and the Whig candidate for president in 1848.

Meanwhile, an expedition led by Stephen Kearny captured Santa Fe, proclaimed the annexation of New Mexico, and set off for California. There they found that American settlers, in cooperation with an exploring expedition under John C. Frémont, had declared independence as the Bear Flag Republic. The U.S. Navy had also captured Monterey on the California coast. With the addition of Kearny's troops, a relatively few Americans took possession of California by 1847 against weak Mexican opposition.

View the Image
Santa Anna Proclamation on **myhistorylab.com**

The decisive Veracruz campaign required massive and careful preparations. But in March 1847, the city fell after a 20-day siege. Then Scott began his advance on Mexico City. In the most important battle of the war, he defeated Santa Anna at Cerro Gordo on April 17 and 18. The Mexicans occupied an apparently impregnable position on high ground blocking the way to Mexico City. A daring flank attack that required soldiers to scramble up mountainsides enabled Scott to win a decisive victory. By August, American troops were in front of Mexico City. After a temporary armistice, which the Mexicans used to improve their defenses, Scott captured the city on September 14.

Quick Check

✓ How did the United States obtain New Mexico and California?

Settlement of the Mexican-American War

Accompanying Scott's army was a diplomat, Nicholas P. Trist, who was authorized to negotiate a peace treaty whenever the Mexicans decided they had had enough. But despite the unbroken American victories, no Mexican leader was willing to invite the wrath of a proud and patriotic citizenry by agreeing to the terms that Polk wanted to impose. Even after the capture of Mexico City, Trist found it difficult to exact an acceptable treaty from the Mexican government. In November, Polk ordered Trist to return to Washington.

Trist ignored Polk's instructions and lingered in Mexico City. On February 2, 1848, he finally signed a treaty that gained all the territory he had been commissioned to obtain. The Treaty of Guadalupe Hidalgo ceded New Mexico and California to the United States for $15 million, established the Rio Grande as the border between Texas and Mexico, and promised that the U.S. government would assume the financial claims of American citizens against Mexico. The 80,000 Mexican residents of the new territories would become U.S. citizens. When the agreement reached Washington, Polk censured Trist for disobeying orders but still sent the treaty to the Senate, which ratified it by a vote of 38 to 14 on March 10.

The United States gained 500,000 square miles of territory from the Mexican-American War. The size of the nation expanded by about 20 percent, adding the present states of California, Utah, New Mexico, Nevada, Arizona, and parts of Colorado and Wyoming. Those interested in a southern route for a transcontinental railroad pressed for even more territory. That pressure led in 1853 to the Gadsden Purchase, through which the United States acquired the southernmost parts of present-day Arizona and New Mexico. (See Map 13.3)

But why, given the expansionist spirit of the age, did the U.S. not just annex *all* of Mexico? According to historian Frederick Merk, a peculiar combination of racism and anti-colonialism dominated American opinion. It was one thing to acquire thinly populated areas where "Anglo-Saxon" pioneers could settle. It was something else to incorporate millions of mixed Spanish and Indian people. These "mongrels," charged racist opponents of the "All Mexico" movement, could never be fit citizens of a self-governing republic. They would have to be ruled the way the British governed India, and the possession of colonial dependencies was contrary to American ideals and traditions.

Merk's thesis sheds light on why the general public had little appetite for swallowing all of Mexico, but those actually making policy had more mundane and practical reasons for being satisfied with what Guadalupe Hidalgo obtained. What they had really wanted all along, historian Norman Graebner contends, were the great California harbors of San Francisco and San Diego. From these ports, Americans could trade directly with Asia and dominate the commerce of the Pacific. Once California had been acquired, policymakers had little incentive to press for more Mexican territory.

The war with Mexico provoked political dissension. Most of the Whig party opposed the war in principle, arguing that the United States had no valid claims to the area south of the Nueces. Whig congressmen voted for military appropriations while the conflict was going on, but they criticized the president for starting it. More ominous, northerners from both parties charged that the real purpose of the war was to spread slavery and increase the power of the southern states. While battles were being fought in Mexico, Congress was debating the Wilmot Proviso, a proposal to prohibit slavery in any territories acquired from Mexico. A bitter sectional quarrel over slavery was a legacy of the Mexican-American War (see Chapter 14).

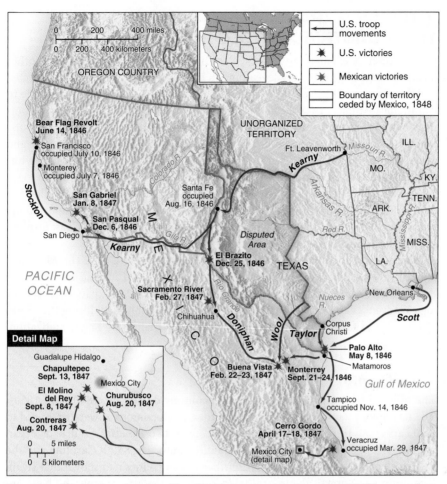

Map 13.3 *The Mexican-American War*   The Mexican-American War added 500,000 square miles of territory to the United States, but the cost was high: $100 million and 13,000 lives.

The domestic controversies the war aroused and the propaganda of Manifest Destiny revealed the limits of mid-nineteenth-century American expansionism and put a damper on efforts to extend the nation's boundaries further. Concerns about slavery and race impeded acquisition of new territory in Latin America and the Caribbean. Resolution of the Oregon dispute clearly indicated that the United States was not willing to fight a powerful adversary to obtain large chunks of British North America, and the old ambition of incorporating Canada faded. From 1848 until expansionism revived in the late nineteenth century, American growth usually took the form of populating and developing the vast territory already acquired. Although the treaty guaranteed the rights of the former inhabitants of Mexico, they in effect became second-class citizens of the United States.

Read the **Document**
Thomas Corwin, "Against the Mexican War" (1847) on **myhistorylab.com**

Quick Check

✓ Why, given the expanisonist spirit, did the United States not annex Mexico in its entirety?

INTERNAL EXPANSIONISM AND THE INDUSTRIAL REVOLUTION

How did developments in transportation foster industrialization and encourage immigration?

Young America expansionists saw a clear link between new territory and other forms of material growth and development. In 1844, Samuel F. B. Morse perfected and demonstrated his electric telegraph, a device that would make it possible to communicate rapidly over the continent. Simultaneously, the railroad was becoming a more important means of moving people and goods over the same great distances. Improvements in manufacturing and agriculture increased the volume and range of internal trade. The beginnings of mass immigration were providing human resources for exploiting new areas and economic opportunities.

The discovery of gold in newly acquired California in 1848 attracted a flood of emigrants from the East and foreign nations. The gold they unearthed spurred the national economy, and the rapid growth of population on the Pacific Coast inspired projects for transcontinental telegraph lines and railroad tracks.

Manifest Destiny and the thirst for new territory waned after the Mexican-American War. The expansionist impulse was channeled instead into internal development. Although the boundaries of the nation ceased to expand, the technological advances and population increase of the 1840s continued during the 1850s. The result was faster economic growth, more industrialization and urbanization, and a new American working class.

The Triumph of the Railroad

The railroad transformed the American economy during the 1840s and 1850s. The technology came from England, where steam locomotives were first used to haul cars along tracks in 1804. In 1830 and 1831, two American railroads began commercial operation—the Charleston and Hamburg in South Carolina and the Baltimore and Ohio in Maryland. After these pioneer lines had shown that steam locomotion was practical and profitable, other railroads were built and began to carry passengers and freight during the 1830s. But this early success was limited, because canals were strong competitors, especially for the freight business. Passengers might prefer the speed of trains, but the lower unit cost of transporting freight on the canal boats prevented most shippers from changing their habits. Furthermore, states such as New York and Pennsylvania had invested heavily in canals and resisted chartering a competitive form of transportation.

During the 1840s, rails extended beyond the northeastern and Middle Atlantic states, and mileage increased more than threefold, totaling more than 9,000 miles by 1850. By 1860, all the states east of the Mississippi had rail service. (See Map 13.4) In the 1840s and 1850s, railroads drove many of the canals out of business. Better tracks and more powerful locomotives that could haul more cars decreased the cost of hauling goods. Railroads had an enormous effect on the economy. Although English imports originally met the demand for iron rails, it eventually spurred development of the domestic iron industry. Since railroads required an enormous capital outlay, their promoters pioneered new methods for financing business enterprise. At a time when families or partnerships still owned most manufacturing and mercantile concerns, the railroad companies sold stock to the public and helped set the pattern for separating ownership from control that characterizes the modern corporation. They also developed new types of securities, such as "preferred stock" (with no voting rights but the assurance of a fixed rate of return) and long-term bonds at a set rate of interest.

Private capital did not fully meet the needs of the early railroad barons. State and local governments, convinced that railroads were the key to their prosperity, loaned them money, bought their stock, and guaranteed their bonds. Despite the dominant philosophy of laissez-faire, the federal government surveyed the routes of projected lines and provided land grants. In 1850, for example, the Illinois Central was granted millions of acres of public land. Forty companies received such aid before 1860, setting a precedent for the massive post–Civil War land grants to the railroads.

Read the **Document** *Senate Report on the Railroads (1852)* on **myhistorylab.com**

Quick Check

✓ What new political and financial arrangements emerged to encourage the growth of the railroads?

The Industrial Revolution Takes Off

While railroads were revolutionizing transportation, American industry was growing rapidly. The factory mode of production, which had originated before 1840 in the cotton mills of New England, was extended to other products (see Chapter 9). Instead of being done in different locations, wool was woven and processed in single production units beginning in the 1830s. By 1860, some of the largest textile mills in the country were producing wool cloth. In eastern Pennsylvania, iron was being forged and rolled in factories by 1850. The industries producing firearms, clocks, and sewing machines also adopted the factory system during this period.

The essential features of the emerging mode of production were gathering a supervised workforce in a single place, paying cash wages to workers, using interchangeable parts, and manufacturing by "continuous process." Within a factory setting, a sequence of continuous operations could rapidly and efficiently assemble standardized parts, manufactured separately and in bulk, into a final product. Mass production, which involved the division of labor into a series of relatively simple and repetitive tasks, contrasted sharply with the traditional craft mode of production, in which a single worker produced the entire product out of raw materials.

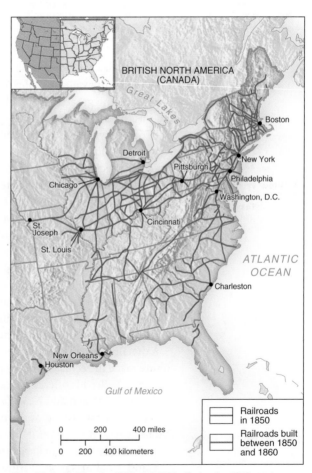

Map 13.4 *Railroads, 1850 and 1860*   During the 1840s and 1850s, railroad lines moved rapidly westward. By 1860, more than 30,000 miles of track had been laid.

Labor Advancements A revolution in farming followed the introduction of new farm implements such as Cyrus McCormick's reaper, which could do ten times the work of a single person. The lithograph, by an anonymous artist, is titled *The Testing of the First Reaping Machine near Steele's Tavern, Virginia, 1831.*

The transition to mass production often depended on new technology. Just as power looms and spinning machinery had made textile mills possible, new and more reliable machines or industrial techniques revolutionized other industries. Elias Howe's invention of the sewing machine in 1846 laid the basis for the ready-to-wear clothing industry and contributed to the mechanization of shoemaking. During the 1840s, iron manufacturers adopted the British practice of using coal rather than charcoal for smelting and thus produced a metal better suited to industrial needs. Charles Goodyear's discovery in 1839 of the process for vulcanizing rubber made new manufactured items available to the American consumer, most notably the overshoe.

Perhaps the greatest triumph of mid-nineteenth-century American technology was the development of the world's most sophisticated and reliable machine tools. Such inventions as the extraordinarily accurate measuring device known as the vernier caliper in 1851 and turret lathes in 1854 were signs of an American aptitude for precision toolmaking that was essential for efficient industrialization.

But progress in industrial technology and organization did not mean the United States had become an industrial society by 1860. Factory workers remained a small fraction of the workforce, and agriculture retained first place both as a source of livelihood for individuals and as a contributor to the gross national product. But farming itself, at least in the North, was undergoing its own technological revolution. John Deere's steel plow, invented in 1837 and mass produced by the 1850s, enabled midwestern farmers to cultivate the tough prairie soils that had resisted cast-iron implements. The mechanical reaper, patented by Cyrus McCormick in 1834, made harvesting grain much easier. Seed drills, cultivators, and threshing machines also came into widespread use before 1860. (See Table 13.3)

A dynamic interaction between advances in transportation, industry, and agriculture made the economy of the northern states stronger and more resilient during the 1850s. Railroads offered western farmers better access to eastern markets. After rails linked Chicago and New York in 1853, most midwestern farm commodities flowed east–west instead of the north–south direction based on riverborne traffic that had predominated until then.

The mechanization of agriculture also gave additional impetus to industrialization, and its labor-saving features released workers for other economic activities. The growth of industry and the modernization of agriculture were thus mutually reinforcing aspects of a single process of economic growth.

View the **Image**
Calico Factory, 1854 on
myhistorylab.com

Quick Check

✓ What technological developments contributed to the new "mass production"?

TABLE 13.3   The Age of Practical Invention

Year*	Inventor	Contribution	Importance/Description
1787	John Fitch	Steamboat	First successful American steamboat
1793	Eli Whitney	Cotton gin	Simplified process of separating fiber from seeds; helped make cotton a profitable staple of southern agriculture
1798	Eli Whitney	Jig for guiding tools	Facilitated manufacture of interchangeable parts
1802	Oliver Evans	Steam engine	First American steam engine; led to manufacture of high-pressure engines used throughout eastern United States
1813	Richard B. Chenaworth	Cast-iron plow	First iron plow to be made in three separate pieces, thus making possible replacement of parts
1830	Peter Cooper	Railroad locomotive	First steam locomotive built in America
1831	Cyrus McCormick	Reaper	Mechanized harvesting; early model could cut six acres of grain a day
1836	Samuel Colt	Revolver	First successful repeating pistol
1837	John Deere	Steel plow	Steel surface kept soil from sticking; farming thus made easier on rich prairies of Midwest
1839	Charles Goodyear	Vulcanization of rubber	Made rubber much more useful by preventing it from sticking and melting in hot weather
1842	Crawford W. Long	First administered ether	Reduced pain and risk of shock during operations in surgery
1844	Samuel F. B. Morse	Telegraph	Made long-distance communication almost instantaneous
1846	Elias Howe	Sewing machine	First practical machine for automatic sewing
1846	Norbert Rillieux	Vacuum evaporator	Improved method of removing water from sugar cane; revolutionized sugar industry and was later applied to many other products
1847	Richard M. Hoe	Rotary printing press	Printed an entire sheet in one motion; vastly speeded up printing process
1851	William Kelly	"Air-boiling process"	Improved method of converting iron into steel (usually known as Bessemer process because English inventor Bessemer had more advantageous patent and financial arrangements)
1853	Elisha G. Otis	Passenger elevator	Improved movement in buildings; when later electrified, stimulated development of skyscrapers
1859	Edwin L. Drake	First American oil well	Initiated oil industry in the United States
1859	George M. Pullman	Pullman passenger car	First railroad sleeping car suitable for long-distance travel

*Dates refer to patent or first successful use.

Source: Allan Weinstein and Frank Gatell, one table, "The Age of Practical Invention" in FREEDOM AND CRISIS, 3/E Copyright (c) 1983. Reprinted with permission of The McGrawHill Companies, Inc.

Mass Immigration Begins

The incentive to mechanize northern industry and agriculture came in part from a shortage of cheap labor. Compared to the industrializing nations of Europe, the economy of the United States in the early nineteenth century was labor-scarce. Since it was difficult to attract able-bodied men to work for low wages in factories or on farms, women and children were used extensively in the early textile mills, and commercial farmers had to rely on the labor of their family members. Labor-saving machinery eased but did not solve the labor shortage. Factories required more operatives. Railroad builders needed construction gangs. The growth of industrial work attracted many European immigrants during the two decades before the Civil War.

Between 1820 and 1840, an estimated 700,000 immigrants arrived in the United States, mainly from the British Isles and German-speaking areas of continental Europe. During the 1840s, this substantial flow became a flood. No fewer than 4.2 million people crossed the Atlantic between 1840 and 1860, and about 3 million of these arrived between 1845 and 1855. This was the greatest influx in proportion to total population—about 20 million—that the nation has ever experienced. (See Figure 13.1) The largest single source of the new mass immigration was Ireland, but Germany was not far behind. Smaller contingents came from Switzerland, Norway, Sweden, and the Netherlands.

The massive transatlantic movement had many causes; some people were "pushed" out of their homes; others were "pulled" toward America. The push factor that caused 1.5 million Irish to forsake the Emerald Isle between 1845 and 1854 was the great potato blight, which brought famine to a population that subsisted on this single crop. The low fares then prevailing on sailing ships bound from England to North America made escape to America possible. Ships involved in the timber trade carried their bulky cargoes from Boston or Halifax to Liverpool; as an alternative to returning to America partly in ballast, they packed Irish immigrants into their holds. The squalor and misery in these steerage accommodations were almost beyond belief.

Because of the ports involved in the lumber trade—Boston, Halifax, Saint John's, and Saint Andrews—the Irish usually arrived in Canada or the Northeast. Immobilized by poverty and a lack of the skills required for pioneering in the West, most of them remained in the Northeast. By the 1850s, they constituted much of the total population of Boston, New York, Philadelphia, and many smaller New England and

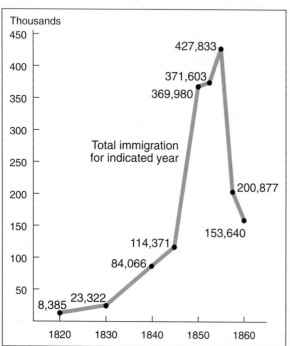

Figure 13.1 Immigration to the United States, 1820–1860

Middle Atlantic cities. Forced into low-paid menial labor and crowded into festering urban slums, they were looked down on by most native-born Americans. Their devotion to Catholicism aroused Protestant resentment and mob violence. Racists even doubted that the Irish were "white" like other northern Europeans. (See Chapter 14 for a discussion of nativism and anti-Catholicism.)

The million or so Germans who also came in the late 1840s and early 1850s were more fortunate. Most of them were also peasants, but unlike the Irish, they had fled hard times rather than outright catastrophe. Changes in German landholding patterns and a fluctuating market for grain squeezed small farmers. Those whose mortgages were foreclosed—or who could no longer make the regular payments to landlords that were the price of emancipation from feudal obligations—frequently immigrated to America. Again unlike the Irish, they often escaped with a little capital to make a fresh start in the New World.

Many German immigrants were artisans and sought to ply their trades in cities such as New York, St. Louis, Cincinnati, and Milwaukee—all of which became German American centers. But many peasants went back to the land. Their diversified agricultural skills and small amounts of capital enabled them to become successful midwestern farmers. In general, Germans encountered less prejudice and discrimination than the Irish. For Germans who were Protestant, religious affinity with their American neighbors made for relative tolerance. But even Catholic Germans normally escaped the scorn heaped on the Irish, perhaps because they were less poverty-stricken and were not members of an ethnic group Anglo-Americans had learned to despise from their English ancestors and cousins.

Economic opportunity attracted most of the Irish, German, and other European immigrants to America. A minority, like some German revolutionaries of 1848, chose the United States because they admired its democratic political system. But most immigrants were more interested in making a decent living than in voting or running for office. Peak periods of immigration—1845 to 1854 is a prime example—coincided closely with times of domestic prosperity and high demand for labor. During depressed periods, immigration dropped off.

The immigrants exacerbated the problems of America's rapidly growing cities. The old "walking city" in which rich and poor lived in close proximity near the center of town was giving way to a more segregated environment. Railroads and horse-drawn streetcars enabled the affluent to move to the first American suburbs, while areas nearer commercial and industrial centers became the congested abode of newcomers from Europe. Slums such as the notorious Five Points district in New York City were characterized by overcrowding, poverty, disease, and crime. Recognizing that these conditions created potential dangers for the entire urban population, middle-class reformers worked to professionalize police forces, introduce sanitary water and sewage disposal systems, and upgrade housing. They made some progress before the Civil War, but the lot of the urban poor, mainly immigrants, was not dramatically improved. Most urban immigrants' lives remained unsafe, unhealthy, and unpleasant.

Read the **Document**
Samuel Morse, Foreign Immigration (1835) on **myhistorylab.com**

Quick Check

✓ What were the new immigrants' reasons for migrating, and what conditions did they face on arrival?

The New Working Class

Most immigrants ended up as wage workers in factories, mines, and construction camps or as casual day laborers doing the many unskilled tasks urban and commercial growth required. By providing a vast pool of cheap labor, they fueled and accelerated the Industrial Revolution. During the 1850s, factory production in Boston and other port cities previously devoted to commerce grew—partly because thousands of recent Irish immigrants worked for the kind of low wages that almost guaranteed large profits for entrepreneurs.

In established industries and older mill towns of the Northeast, immigrants added to, or displaced, the native-born workers who had predominated in the 1830s and 1840s. The changing workforce of the textile mills in Lowell, Massachusetts, provided a striking example of this process. In 1836, only 3.7 percent of the workers in one Lowell mill were foreign born; most were young unmarried women from New England farms. By 1860, immigrants constituted 61.7 percent of the workforce. This trend reveals much about the changing character of the American working class. In the 1830s, most male workers were artisans. Factory work was still largely the province of women and children. Both groups were predominantly of American stock. In the 1840s, more men worked in factories, although women predominated in the textile industry. During that decade, conditions in many mills deteriorated. Relations between management and labor became more impersonal, and workers were pushed to increase their output. Workdays of 12–14 hours were common.

The result was an upsurge of labor militancy involving female and male factory workers. Mill girls in Lowell, for example, formed a union—the Female Labor Reform Association—and agitated for shorter working hours. On a broader front, workers' organizations petitioned state legislatures for laws limiting the workday to ten hours. Some such laws were actually passed, but they were ineffective because employers could still require a prospective worker to sign a contract agreeing to longer hours.

The increasing employment of immigrants between the mid-1840s and the late 1850s made it more difficult to organize industrial workers. Impoverished fugitives from the Irish potato famine tended to have lower economic expectations and more conservative social attitudes than did native-born workers. Consequently, the Irish

Greater Fortunes This 1854 cartoon, titled "The Old World and the New," shows a shabbily dressed man in Ireland examining posters for trips to New York (left). At right, he is shown later, in America, wearing finer clothes and looking at posters advertising trips for emigrants returning to Dublin. As was the case for many immigrants seeking economic opportunities in the "New World," his situation has apparently changed for the better.

immigrants were initially willing to work for less and were less prone to protest working conditions.

However, the new working class of former rural folk did not make the transition to industrial wage labor easily or without subtle and indirect protests. Tardiness, absenteeism, drunkenness, loafing, and other resistance to factory discipline reflected hostility to the unaccustomed and seemingly unnatural routines of industrial production. The adjustment to new styles and rhythms of work was painful and slow.

> **Quick Check**
> ✓ How did the constitution and behavior of the working class change in this period?

CONCLUSION: THE COSTS OF EXPANSION

By 1860, industrial expansion and immigration had created a working class of men and women who seemed destined for a life of low-paid wage labor. This reality stood in contrast to America's self-image as a land of opportunity and upward mobility. This ideal still had some validity in rapidly developing regions of the western states, but it was mostly myth for the increasingly foreign-born industrial workers of the Northeast.

Internal and external expansion had come at a heavy cost. Tensions associated with class and ethnic rivalries were only part of the price of rapid economic development. The acquisition of new territories was politically divisive and soon led to a catastrophic sectional controversy. In the late 1840s and early 1850s, Democratic Senator Stephen A. Douglas of Illinois (called the Little Giant because of his small stature and large presence) sought political power for himself and his party by combining an expansionist foreign policy with the economic development of the territories already acquired. Recognizing that the slavery question was the main obstacle to his program, he sought to neutralize it through compromise and evasion (see Chapter 14). His failure to win the presidency or even the Democratic nomination before 1860 showed that Young America's dream of a patriotic consensus for headlong expansion and economic development could not withstand the tensions and divisions that expansionist policies created and brought to light.

13 STUDY RESOURCES

((•—[Listen to the **Chapter Audio** for Chapter 13 on **myhistorylab.com**

TIMELINE

1823 American settlers arrive in Texas, p. 316

1830 Mexico attempts to halt American migration to Texas, p. 316

1831 American railroads begin commercial operation, p. 324

1834 Cyrus McCormick patents mechanical reaper, p. 326

1835 Revolution in Texas, p. 316

1836 Texas becomes independent republic, p. 316

1837 John Deere invents steel plow, p. 326

1841 President John Tyler inaugurated, p. 318

1844 Samuel F. B. Morse demonstrates electric telegraph, p. 324
- James K. Polk elected president on platform of expansionism, p. 319

1845 Mass immigration from Europe begins, p. 328
- United States annexes Texas, p. 320
- John L. O'Sullivan coins slogan "Manifest Destiny," p. 320

1846 War with Mexico, p. 320

1847 American conquest of California, p. 321
- Zachary Taylor defeats Mexicans at Buena Vista, p. 321
- Winfield Scott captures Veracruz and defeats Mexicans at Cerro Gordo, p. 321
- Mexico City falls to Americans, p. 321

1848 Treaty of Guadalupe Hidalgo consigns California and New Mexico to United States, p. 322
- Gold discovered in California, p. 324

1849 "Forty-niners" rush to California, p. 324

CHAPTER REVIEW

TEXAS, MANIFEST DESTINY, AND THE MEXICAN-AMERICAN WAR

Why did the U.S. annex Texas and the Southwest?

The annexation of Texas and the Southwest had several causes. Early settlers of Texas grew dissatisfied with the Catholic, antislavery Mexican administration. Many Americans believed that it was America's "Manifest Destiny" to expand across the continent. This ideology was a useful rallying cry for politicians willing to go to war with Mexico to gain new territory. *(p. 315)*

INTERNAL EXPANSIONISM AND THE INDUSTRIAL REVOLUTION

How did developments in transportation foster industrialization and encourage immigration?

Rail transportation allowed the swift movement of people and goods. Other advances in technology permitted the new "mass production." The new industries drew many immigrants from Ireland and Germany, who were fleeing famine and persecution. Immigration made labor more plentiful and thus cheaper, so working conditions declined. *(p. 324)*

KEY TERM QUESTIONS

1. Why were politicians, writers, and entrepreneurs so interested in championing Young America? (p. 313)

2. What was Manifest Destiny? (p. 315)

3. What elements of the Alamo folklore are true, and which are fictionalized? (p. 317)

4. What were the causes of the Mexican-American War? (p. 321)

5. What were the results of the Treaty of Guadalupe Hidalgo? (p. 322)

MyHistoryLab Connections

Visit **www.myhistorylab.com** for a customized Study Plan to build your knowledge of *An Age of Expansionism*

Question for Analysis

1. How did Texas join the Union?

👁 **Watch** the **Video** *The Annexation of Texas* p. 318

2. Where did the U.S. win battles in the Mexican-American War?

🔍 **View** the **Map** *Mexican-American War, 1846-1848* p. 320

3. What were the main reasons for increasing railroad construction?

📖 **Read** the **Document** *Senate Report on Railroads, 1852* p. 325

4. Why was Samuel Morse so fervently against immigration?

📖 **Read** the **Document** *Samuel Morse, Foreign Immigration* p. 329

Other Resources from this Chapter

🔍 **View** the **Map** *Texas Revolution, 1836*

🔍 **View** the **Image** *The Alamo*

📖 **Read** the **Document** *James K. Polk, First Inaugural Address*

🔍 **View** the **Image** *Santa Anna Proclamation*

📖 **Read** the **Document** *Thomas Corwin, Against the Mexican War*

🔍 **View** the **Image** *Calico Factory, 1854*

14 The Sectional Crisis
1846–1861

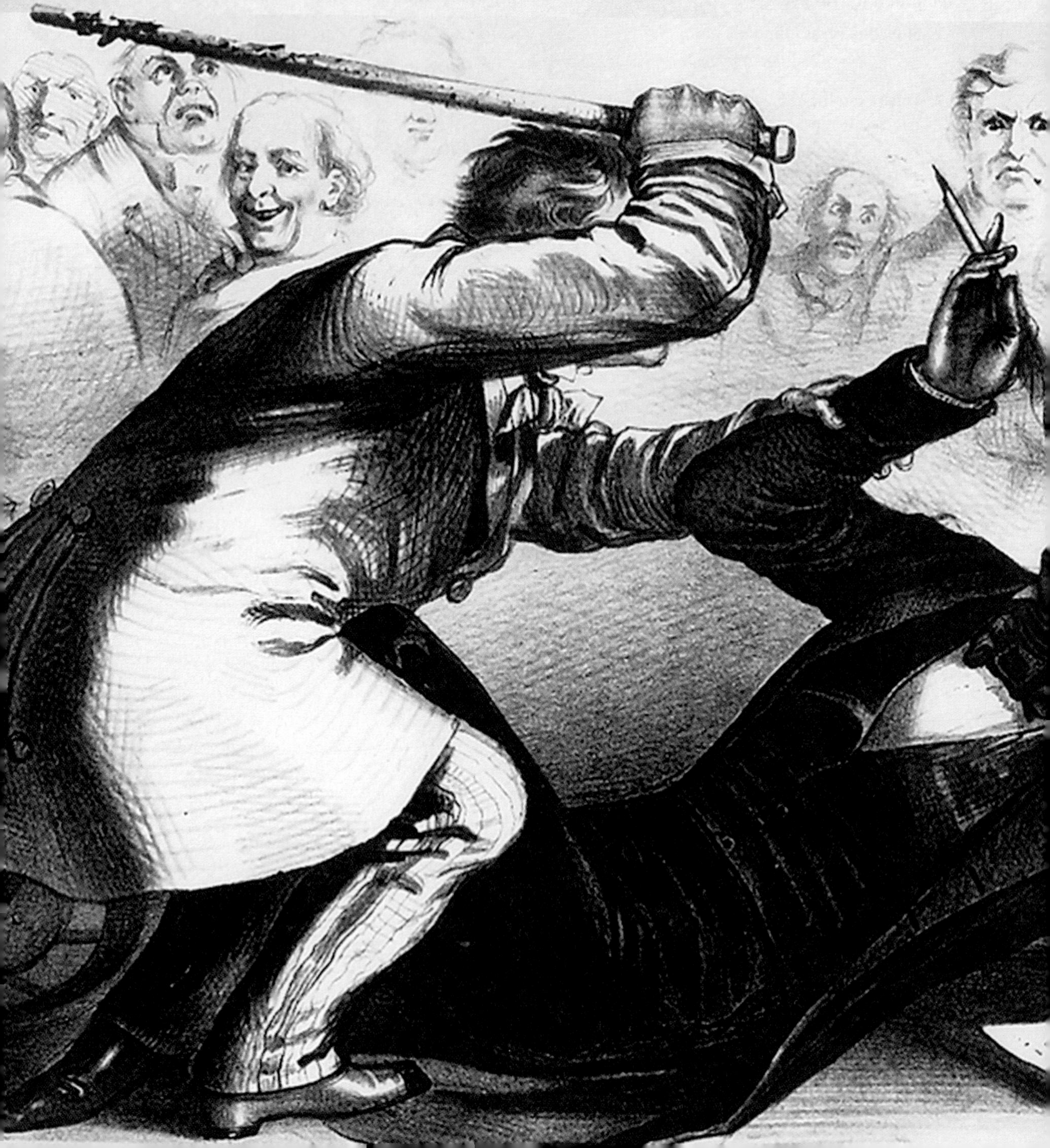

Contents and Spotlight Questions

THE COMPROMISE OF 1850 PG. 336

How did territorial expansion intensify the conflict over slavery?

POLITICAL UPHEAVAL, 1852–1856 PG. 341

How did the two-party system change during this period?

THE HOUSE DIVIDED, 1857–1860 PG. 347

How did the institution of slavery go beyond political and economic debates?

((•—Listen to the **Chapter Audio** for Chapter 14 on **myhistorylab.com**

BROOKS ASSAULTS SUMNER IN CONGRESS

On May 22, 1856, Representative Preston Brooks of South Carolina walked onto the floor of the Senate with a rattan cane in his hand. Charles Sumner, the antislavery senator from Massachusetts who had recently given a fiery oration condemning the South for plotting to extend slavery to the Kansas Territory, was seated at his desk. What was worse, the speech had insulted Senator Andrew Butler of South Carolina, Brooks' kinsman. When he reached Sumner, Brooks beat him over the head with the cane. Stunned, Sumner made a desperate effort to rise and ripped his bolted desk from the floor. He then collapsed under a torrent of blows as the cane shattered in Brooks' hand.

Sumner was so badly injured that he did not return to the Senate for three years. But Massachusetts reelected him in 1857 and kept his seat vacant as a reproach to southern brutality and "barbarism." In parts of the North, Sumner was hailed as a martyr to the cause of "free soil," and Brooks was denounced as a bully. But his fellow southerners lionized Brooks. When he

Dubious Support After his constituents learned of Preston Brooks's caning of Senator Sumner, they sent Brooks a gold-handled cowhide whip to use on other antislavery advocates.

resigned from the House after southern congressmen blocked a vote of censure, his constituents reelected him unanimously.

These contrasting reactions show how bitter sectional antagonism had become by 1856. Sumner spoke for the radical wing of the new Republican party, which was making a bid for national power by mobilizing the North against the alleged aggressions of "the slave power." Southerners viewed the very existence of this party as an insult to the South and a threat to its interests. Sumner came closer to being an abolitionist than any other member of Congress. Nothing created greater fear and anxiety among southerners than their belief that antislavery forces were plotting against their way of life. To many northerners, "bully Brooks" stood for all the arrogant and violent slaveholders who were allegedly conspiring to extend their barbaric labor system. By 1856, therefore, the sectional cleavage that would lead to the Civil War had already undermined national unity.

The crisis of the mid-1850s came only a few years after the elaborate compromise of 1850 had seemingly resolved the dispute over the future of slavery in the territories acquired in the Mexican War. The Kansas-Nebraska Act of 1854 renewed the agitation over the extension of slavery, revived sectional conflict, and led to the emergence of the Republican Party. From that point on, sectional confrontation increased and destroyed the prospects for a new compromise. Violence on the Senate floor foreshadowed violence on the battlefield.

THE COMPROMISE OF 1850

How did territorial expansion intensify the conflict over slavery

The conflict over slavery in the territories began in the late 1840s. During the early phase of the sectional controversy, the leaders of two strong national parties, each with substantial followings in both the North and the South, had a vested interest in resolving the crisis. Furthermore, the less tangible features of sectionalism—emotion and ideology—were less divisive than they later became. Hence, in 1850, a kind of give-and-take achieved a fragile compromise that would not be possible in the changed environment of the mid-1850s.

The Problem of Slavery in the Mexican Cession

As the price of union between states committed to slavery and those in the process of abolishing it, the Founders had attempted to limit the role of the slavery issue in national politics. The Constitution gave the federal government the right to abolish the international slave trade but no authority to regulate or destroy the institution where it existed under state law. It was easy to condemn slavery in principle but difficult to develop a practical program to eliminate it without defying the Constitution.

Radical abolitionists acknowledged this problem and resolved it by rejecting the law of the land in favor of a "higher law" prohibiting human bondage. In 1844, William Lloyd Garrison publicly burned the Constitution, condemning it as "a Covenant with Death, an Agreement with Hell." But Garrison spoke for a small minority dedicated to freeing the North, at whatever cost, from the sin of condoning slavery.

During the 1840s, most northerners showed that while they disliked slavery, they also detested abolitionism. They were inclined to view slavery as a backward and unwholesome institution, much inferior to their own free-labor system, and could be persuaded that slaveholders were power-hungry aristocrats seeking more than their share of national political influence. But they regarded the Constitution as a binding contract between slave and free states and were likely to be prejudiced against blacks and reluctant to accept them as free citizens. They saw no legal or desirable way to bring about emancipation within the southern states.

But the Constitution had not predetermined the status of slavery in *future* states. Since Congress could admit new states to the Union under any conditions it wished to impose, the price of admission could include the abolition of slavery. This had led to the Missouri crisis of 1819–1820 (see Chapter 9). The resulting compromise was designed to decide whether new states would be admitted as slave states or free by drawing a line between slave and free states and extending it westward through the unsettled portions of what was then American soil. When specific territories were settled, organized, and prepared for statehood, slavery would be permitted south of the line of 36°30' and prohibited north of it.

The tradition of providing both the free North and the slave South with opportunities to expand and create new states broke down when new territories were wrested from Mexico in the 1840s. The acquisition of Texas, California, and New Mexico—all south of the Missouri Compromise line—threatened to upset the parity between slave and free states. Since it was generally assumed in the North that Congress could prohibit slavery in new territories, a movement developed in Congress to do just that.

Quick Check

✓ What role did the Constitution play in the debates over slavery in existing states as well as in newly acquired territories?

The Wilmot Proviso Launches the Free-Soil Movement

The Free-Soil crusade began in August 1846, only three months after the start of the Mexican-American War, when Representative David Wilmot, a Pennsylvania Democrat, proposed an amendment to the military appropriations bill that would ban slavery in any territory acquired from Mexico. Wilmot spoke for the many northern Democrats who felt neglected and betrayed by the party's choice of Polk over Van Buren in 1844 and by Polk's "prosouthern" policies. Wilmot also proposed prohibiting free African Americans from settling in the new territories. This would enhance the economic opportunities of the North's common folk by preventing competition from slaves and free blacks. By thus linking racism with resistance to the spread of slavery, Wilmot appealed to a broad spectrum of northern opinion.

Northern Whigs shared Wilmot's concern about unregulated competition between slave and free labor in the territories. Voting for the measure also provided an outlet for their frustration at being unable to halt the annexation of Texas and the Mexican-American War. Whig leaders preferred that there be no expansion at all, but when expansion could not be avoided, northern Whigs endorsed the view that territory acquired from Mexico should not be used to increase the power of the slave states.

In the first House vote on the Wilmot Proviso, a sectional cleavage replaced party lines. Every northern congressman except for two Democrats voted for the

Read the **Document**
John C. Calhoun's Proposal to Preserve the Union on **myhistorylab.com**

Quick Check

✓ What was the
Wilmot Proviso, and
what effect did it have
on existing party lines?

amendment, and every southerner except two Whigs voted against it. After passing the House, the Proviso was blocked in the Senate by a combination of southern influence and Democratic loyalty to the administration. When the appropriations bill went back to the House without the Proviso, the administration's arm-twisting changed enough northern Democratic votes to pass the bill and thus defeat the Proviso.

Forging a Compromise

One early compromise reached on the Mexican cession was a formula known as "squatter sovereignty" that would enable the actual settlers to determine the status of slavery in a territory. The North and the South interpreted this proposal differently. For northern Democrats, squatter sovereignty—or popular sovereignty, as it was later called—meant the settlers could vote slavery up or down at the first meeting of a territorial legislature. For the southern wing of the party, it meant a decision would be made only when a convention drew up a constitution and applied for statehood. The chief proponent of squatter sovereignty was Senator Lewis Cass of Michigan, the Democratic nominee for president in 1848. Cass lost to General Zachary Taylor, who ran as a Whig war hero without a platform. (See Table 14.1) Taylor refused to commit himself on the status of slavery in the territories, although he promised not to veto any congressional legislation on the subject. Northern supporters of the Wilmot Proviso backed former President Van Buren, who ran under the new Free-Soil Party, the first broad, sectional, antislavery party. After Taylor won, he sought to bypass congressional debate by admitting California and New Mexico immediately as states, skipping the territorial stage; this triggered such strong southern opposition that others stepped in to seek a compromise.

Hoping again to play the role of "great pacificator" as he had in the Missouri Compromise of 1820, Senator Henry Clay of Kentucky tried to reduce sectional tension by providing mutual concessions on a range of divisive issues. On the critical territorial question, his solution was to admit California as a free state and organize the rest of the Mexican cession with no explicit prohibition of slavery—in other words, without the Wilmot Proviso. Noting that Mexican law had already abolished slavery in New Mexico, he also pointed out that its arid climate made it unsuitable for cotton culture and slavery. He also sought to resolve a boundary dispute between New Mexico and Texas by granting the disputed region to New Mexico while compensating Texas by having the federal government take over its state debt. As another concession to the North, he recommended prohibiting slave sales at auction in the District of Columbia and permitting the District's white inhabitants to abolish slavery if they saw fit. To appease the South, he called for a more effective Fugitive Slave Law.

TABLE 14.1   The Election of 1848

Candidate	Party	Popular Vote	Electoral Vote
Taylor	Whig	1,360,967	163
Cass	Democratic	1,222,342	127
Van Buren	Free-Soil	291,263	—

A Fragile Compromise Henry Clay, shown here addressing the Senate, helped negotiate the Compromise of 1850 to settle the dispute over the extension of slavery in territories acquired in the Mexican-American War. Daniel Webster, seated at left resting his head on his hand, supported Clay's proposed compromise. Ardent states' rightist John C. Calhoun, standing third from right, led the opposition.

These proposals provided the basis for the Compromise of 1850. Proposed in February 1850, it took months to get through Congress. One obstacle was President Taylor's resistance; although a southerner slaveholder, Taylor opposed extending slavery into the new western territories. Another obstacle was getting congressmen to vote for the compromise as a single package or "omnibus bill." Few politicians from either section were willing to go on record as supporting the key concessions to the *other* section. In July, two developments broke the logjam: President Taylor died and was succeeded by Millard Fillmore, who favored the compromise; and the omnibus strategy was abandoned in favor of a series of measures that could be voted on separately. After the breakup of the omnibus bill, some of Clay's proposals were modified to make them more acceptable to the South and the Democrats. Senator Stephen A. Douglas maneuvered the separate provisions through Congress.

As the price of Democratic support, the bills organizing New Mexico and Utah as territories included the popular sovereignty principle. Territorial legislatures in the Mexican cession were explicitly granted power over "all rightful subjects of legislation," which might include slavery. Half of the compensation to Texas for giving up its claims to New Mexico was paid directly to holders of Texas bonds. (See Map 14.1)

Read the
Document
*The Fugitive Slave Act
(1850)* on
myhistorylab.com

Abolition of the slave trade—but not slavery itself—in the District of Columbia and a new Fugitive Slave Law were also enacted. The latter was an outrageous piece of legislation. As the result of southern pressures and amendments, suspected fugitives were now denied a jury trial, the right to testify in their own behalf, and other basic constitutional protections. This removed any effective safeguards against accusers making false claims that a black person was an escaped slave—or even kidnapping free blacks.

The compromise passed because northern Democrats, southern Whigs, and representatives of both parties from the border states supported its key measures. A majority of congressmen from both sections did not support any single bill, and few senators or representatives actually voted for the entire package. Many northern Whigs and southern Democrats thought the end result conceded too much to the other section. Doubts lingered over the value or workability of a "compromise" that was more like an armistice or a cease-fire.

Yet the Compromise of 1850 did temporarily restore sectional peace. In southern state elections during 1850–1851, moderate coalitions defeated the radicals who viewed the compromise as a sellout to the North. But this emerging "unionism" was conditional. Southerners demanded strict northern adherence to the compromise, especially to the Fugitive Slave Law, as the price for suppressing threats of secession. In the North, the compromise received greater support. The Fugitive Slave Law was unpopular in areas where abolitionism was strong because it required northerners to enforce slavery, and there were sensational rescues or attempted rescues of

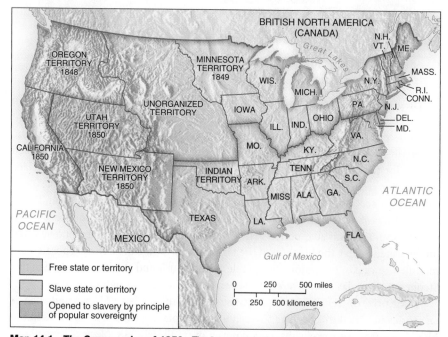

Map 14.1 *The Compromise of 1850* The "compromise" was actually a series of resolutions granting some concessions to the North—especially admission of California as a free state—and some to the South, such as a stricter Fugitive Slave Law.

escaped slaves. But the northern states largely adhered to the law during the next few years. When the Democrats and Whigs approved or condoned the compromise in their 1852 platforms, it seemed that sharp differences on the slavery issue had been banished from national politics again.

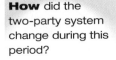

Quick Check

✓ What were the key provisions of the Compromise of 1850?

POLITICAL UPHEAVAL, 1852–1856

The second-party system—Democrats versus Whigs—survived the crisis over slavery in the Mexican cession, but the Compromise of 1850 may have fatally weakened it. Although both national parties had been careful during the 1840s not to alienate

How did the two-party system change during this period?

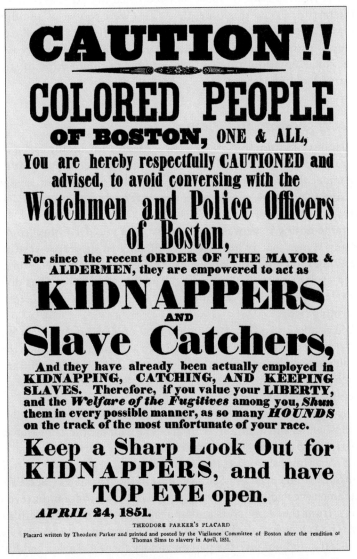

Caution! This abolitionist broadside was printed in response to a ruling that fugitive slave Thomas Sims must be returned to his master in Georgia.

their supporters in either section of the country, they had in fact offered voters alternative ways of dealing with slavery. Democrats had endorsed headlong territorial expansion with the promise of a fair division of the spoils between slave and free states. Whigs had generally opposed annexations or acquisitions, because they were likely to raise the slavery question and threaten sectional harmony. Each strategy could be presented to southern voters as a good way to protect slavery and to northerners as a good way to contain it.

The consensus meant the two major parties had to find other issues on which to base their distinctive appeals. Their failure to do so encouraged voter apathy and disenchantment with them. When the Democrats sought to revive the Manifest Destiny issue in 1854, they reopened the explosive issue of slavery in the territories. By this time, the Whigs were too weak and divided to respond with a policy of their own, and a purely sectional Free-Soil party—the Republicans—gained prominence. The collapse of the second-party system released sectional agitation from the constraints the competition of strong national parties had imposed.

The Party System in Crisis

The presidential campaign of 1852 was devoid of major issues. Whigs tried to revive interest in nationalistic economic policies, but with business thriving under the Democratic program of limited government involvement, a protective tariff, a national bank, and internal improvements got little support.

Another tempting issue was immigration. The massive influx from Europe upset many Whigs, partly because most of the new arrivals were Catholics, and the Whig following was largely evangelical Protestant. The immigrants also voted overwhelmingly Democratic. The Whig leadership was divided on whether to compete with the Democrats for the immigrant vote or restrict immigrant voting rights.

The Whigs nominated General Winfield Scott of Mexican-American War fame, who supported the faction that resisted nativism and sought to broaden the party's appeal. But Scott and his supporters could not sway Catholic immigrants from their Democratic allegiance, and nativist Whigs sat out the election to protest their party's disregard of their cultural prejudices.

But the main cause for Scott's crushing defeat was the support he lost in the South when he allied himself with the dominant northern antislavery wing of the party, led by Senator William Seward of New York. Democrat Franklin Pierce of New Hampshire, a colorless nonentity compared to his rival, swept the Deep South and edged out Scott in most of the free states. (See Table 14.2) The outcome revealed that the Whig party lacked a program that would distinguish it from the Democrats and appeal to voters in both sections of the country. The Whigs had declined to such an extent that even a war hero like General Scott could not give the party a victory the way Taylor had four years earlier.

TABLE 14.2 The Election of 1852

Candidate	Party	Popular Vote	Electoral Vote
Pierce	Democratic	1,601,117	254
Scott	Whig	1,385,453	42
Hale	Free-Soil	155,825	—

Despite their overwhelming victory in 1852, the Democrats had reasons for anxiety about their supporters' loyalty. Because the major parties had ceased to offer clear-cut alternatives to the electorate, voter apathy or alienation was growing. The Democrats won majorities in both North and South in 1852 primarily because the public viewed them as the most reliable supporters of the Compromise of 1850, not because of firm party allegiance.

Quick Check

✓ Why did the democrats win the election of 1852, and why were they uneasy despite this victory?

The Kansas-Nebraska Act Raises a Storm

In January 1854, Senator Stephen A. Douglas of Illinois proposed a bill to organize the territory west of Missouri and Iowa. Since this region fell within the area where the Missouri Compromise had banned slavery, Douglas hoped to head off southern opposition and keep the Democratic party united by disregarding the compromise line and setting up the territorial government in Kansas and Nebraska on the basis of popular sovereignty.

Douglas wanted to organize the Kansas-Nebraska area quickly because he supported the expansion of settlement and commerce. He hoped a railroad would soon be built to the Pacific with Chicago (or another midwestern city) as its eastern terminus. A controversy over slavery in the new territory would slow down the process of organization and settlement and hinder building the railroad. As a leader of the Democrats, Douglas also hoped his Kansas-Nebraska bill would revive the spirit of Manifest Destiny that had given the party cohesion and electoral success in the mid-1840s (see Chapter 13). As the main advocate for a new expansionism, he expected to win the Democratic nomination and the presidency in 1856.

The price of southern support, Douglas soon discovered, was an amendment explicitly repealing the Missouri Compromise. Although he realized this would "raise a hell of a storm," he agreed. In this more provocative form, the bill passed the Senate by a large margin and the House by a narrow one. Douglas had split his party: Half of the northern Democrats in the House voted against the legislation. (See Map 14.2)

The Democrats who broke ranks created the storm that Douglas had predicted but underestimated. "Independent Democrats" denounced the bill as "a gross violation of a sacred pledge." A memorial from 3,000 New England ministers described it as a craven and sinful surrender to the slave power. For many northerners, probably most, the Kansas-Nebraska Act was an abomination because it permitted the possibility of slavery in an area where it had been prohibited. Except for an aggressive minority, southerners had not pushed for such legislation or even shown much interest in it, but now they felt obliged to support it. Their support provided

View the **Image**
Stephen Douglas on **myhistorylab.com**

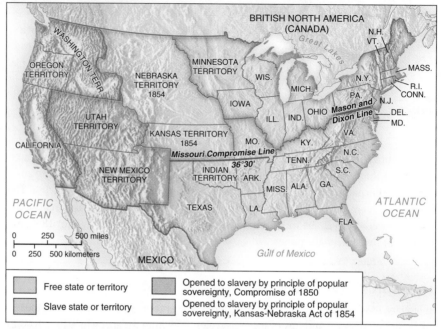

Map 14.2 *The Kansas-Nebraska Act of 1854*   The Kansas-Nebraska Act applied the principle of popular sovereignty to voters in the Kansas and Nebraska territories, allowing them to decide for themselves whether to permit slavery in their territories. The act repudiated the Missouri Compromise of 1820, which had prohibited slavery in the territory of the Louisiana Purchase north of 36°30' latitude.

ammunition to those who were seeking to convince the northern public of a conspiracy to extend slavery.

Douglas's bill was a catastrophe for sectional harmony. It repudiated a compromise that many in the North regarded as a binding sectional compact, almost as sacred and necessary to the survival of the Union as the Constitution itself. In defiance of the whole compromise tradition, it made a concession to the South over extending slavery without an equivalent concession to the North. It also shattered the fragile sectional accommodation of 1850 and made future compromises less likely. From then on, northern sectionalists would be fighting to regain what they had lost, while southerners would battle to maintain rights already conceded.

The act also destroyed what was left of the second-party system. The weakened and tottering Whig party disintegrated when its congressional representation split along sectional lines on the Kansas-Nebraska issue. The Democratic party survived, but its ability to act as a unifying national force was impaired. Northern desertions and southern gains (resulting from the recruitment of proslavery Whigs) destroyed the sectional balance within the party, placing it under southern control.

The Kansas-Nebraska furor also doomed the Pierce administration's efforts to revive an expansionist foreign policy. Pierce and Secretary of State William Marcy wanted to acquire Cuba from Spain. But northerners interpreted the administration's plan, made public in a memorandum known as the Ostend Manifesto, as an attempt to create a "Caribbean slave empire." The resulting storm of protest forced Pierce and his cohorts to abandon their scheme.

Quick Check

✓ Why did the Kansas-Nebraska Act divide the Democratic party along sectional lines and lead to the demise of the Whig party?

Kansas and the Rise of the Republicans

The new Republican party was an outgrowth of the anti-Nebraska coalition of 1854. A new political label was required because Free-Soil Democrats—who were important in the Midwest—refused to march under the Whig banner or support any candidate for high office who called himself a Whig.

In 1854–1855, some ex-Whigs had joined the short-lived nativist party known as the "Know-Nothings." The Know-Nothing party was founded in 1849 as an anti-immigrant vehicle. Massive immigration of Irish and Germans, most of whom were Catholic, led to increasing tension among ethnic groups during the 1840s and early 1850s. Native-born and even immigrant Protestants viewed the newcomers as bearers of alien cultures. Political nativism first emerged in the form of local "American" parties protesting immigrant influence in cities such as New York and Philadelphia. The Know-Nothings sought to extend the period of naturalization to undercut immigrant voting strength and keep aliens in their place.

When the Know-Nothing party split over the Kansas-Nebraska issue in 1856, most northern nativists became Republicans. The Republican argument that the "slave-power conspiracy" was a greater threat to American liberty and equality than an alleged "popish plot" proved persuasive. But Republican nativists did not have to abandon their ethnic and religious prejudices; the party showed a clear commitment to the values of native-born evangelical Protestants. On the local level, Republicans generally supported causes that reflected an anti-immigrant or anti-Catholic bias—such as banning the sale of alcoholic beverages, observance of the Sabbath, defense of Protestant Bible-reading in schools, and opposition to state aid for parochial education.

The Republican leaders were seasoned professional politicians, men who had earlier been prominent Whigs or Democrats. Adept at organizing the grass roots, building coalitions, and employing the techniques of popular campaigning, they built up an effective party apparatus in an amazingly short time. By 1856, the new party was well established throughout the North and was preparing to make a serious bid for the presidency.

The Republicans' position on slavery in the territories explains their rapid and growing appeal. Republicans viewed the unsettled West as a land of opportunities, a place to which the ambitious and hardworking could migrate to improve their social and economic position. But if slavery was permitted to expand, it would deny the rights of "free labor." Slaveholders would monopolize the best land, use their slaves to compete unfairly with free white workers, and block commercial and industrial development. They could also use their control of new western states to dominate the federal government in the interest of the "slave power." Republicans also pandered to racial prejudice: They presented their policy as a way to keep African Americans out of the territories, thus preserving the new lands for whites.

Although the Kansas-Nebraska Act raised the territorial issue and gave birth to the Republican party, the turmoil associated with attempts to implement popular sovereignty in Kansas enabled the Republicans to increase their following

View the **Closer Look**
The Compromise of 1850 on
myhistorylab.com

throughout the North. When Kansas was organized in 1854, a bitter contest began to control the territorial government between militant Free-Soilers from New England and the Midwest and slaveholding settlers from Missouri. In the first territorial elections, thousands of Missouri residents crossed the border to vote illegally. The result was a decisive victory for the slave-state forces. The legislature not only legalized slavery but made it a crime to speak or act against it.

Free-Soilers were already a majority of the actual residents of the territory when this legislature denied them the right to agitate against slavery. To defend themselves and their convictions, they took up arms and established a rival territorial government under a constitution that outlawed slavery.

A small-scale civil war then broke out between the rival regimes, culminating in May 1856 when proslavery adherents raided the free-state capital at Lawrence. Portrayed in Republican propaganda as "the sack of Lawrence," this incursion resulted in substantial property damage but no loss of life. More bloody was the reprisal by the antislavery zealot John Brown. After the attack on Lawrence, Brown and a few followers murdered five proslavery settlers in cold blood, in what became known as the Pottawatomie Massacre. During the next few months—until an effective territorial governor arranged a truce in 1856—a hit-and-run guerrilla war raged between free-state and slave-state factions.

Read the
Document
*John Gihon, Kansas
Begins to Bleed* on
myhistorylab.com

Quick Check

✓ What positions did the new Republican party take regarding immigration, western expansion, and slavery?

The Republican press had a field day with the events in Kansas, exaggerating the violence but correctly pointing out that the federal government was favoring a proslavery minority over a Free-Soil majority. Since the "sack of Lawrence" occurred about the same time that Preston Brooks assaulted Charles Sumner on the Senate floor, the Republicans launched their 1856 campaign under twin slogans: "Bleeding Kansas" and "Bleeding Sumner." The image of an evil and aggressive "slave power," using violence to deny constitutional rights to its opponents, aroused northern sympathies and won votes.

Sectional Division in the Election of 1856

The Republican nominating convention revealed the strictly sectional nature of the new party. Only a handful of delegates from the slave states attended, all from the upper South. The platform called for liberating Kansas from the slave power and congressional prohibition of slavery in all territories. The nominee was John C. Frémont, explorer of the West and one of the conquerors of California during the Mexican-American War.

The Democratic convention dumped Pierce, passed over Stephen A. Douglas, and nominated James Buchanan of Pennsylvania, who had a long career in public service. The platform endorsed popular sovereignty in the territories. The American party, a Know-Nothing remnant that survived mainly as the rallying point for anti-Democratic conservatives in the border states and the South, chose ex-President Millard Fillmore as its standard-bearer and received the backing of those northern Whigs who refused to become Republicans and hoped to revive the tradition of sectional compromise.

TABLE 14.3 The Election of 1856			
Candidate	Party	Popular Vote	Electoral Vote
Buchanan	Democratic	1,832,955	174
Frémont	Republican	1,339,932	114
Fillmore	American (Know-Nothing)	871,731	8

The election was really two separate races—one in the North, where the main contest was between Frémont and Buchanan; the other in the South, between Fillmore and Buchanan. Buchanan won, outpolling Fillmore in every slave state except Maryland and edging out Frémont in five northern states—Pennsylvania, New Jersey, Indiana, Illinois, and California. But Frémont won 11 of the 16 free states, sweeping the upper North with substantial majorities and winning more northern popular votes than either of his opponents. (See Table 14.3) Since the free states had a majority in the electoral college, a future Republican candidate could win the presidency by overcoming a slim Democratic edge in the lower North.

In the South, where the possibility of a Frémont victory had revived talk of secession, the results of the election brought relief tinged with anxiety. The very existence of a sectional party committed to restricting the expansion of slavery constituted an insult to the southerners' way of life. That such a party was popular in the North raised doubts about the security of slavery within the Union. The continued success of a unified Democratic party under southern control was widely viewed as the last hope for maintaining sectional balance and "southern rights."

Quick Check

✓ How was the election of 1860 really "two separate races"?

THE HOUSE DIVIDED, 1857–1860

The sectional quarrel became virtually irreconcilable between Buchanan's election in 1856 and Lincoln's victory in 1860. A series of incidents provoked one side or the other, heightened the tension, and ultimately brought the crisis to a head. Behind the panicky reaction to public events lay a growing sense that North and South were so different in culture and so opposed in basic interests that they could no longer coexist in the same nation.

How did the institution of slavery go beyond political and economic debates?

Cultural Sectionalism

Signs of cultural and intellectual cleavage had appeared well before the triumph of sectional politics. In the mid-1840s, the Methodist and Baptist churches split into northern and southern denominations because of differing attitudes toward slaveholding. Presbyterians and Episcopalians remained formally united but had informal northern and southern factions that went their separate ways on the slavery issue. Instead of unifying Americans around a common Protestant faith, the churches became nurseries of sectional discord. Northern preachers and congregations denounced slaveholding as a sin, while most southern churchmen rallied to a biblical defense of the peculiar institution and became apologists for the southern way of life. Prominent religious leaders—such as Henry Ward Beecher, George B. Cheever, and Theodore Parker in the North, and James H. Thornwell and Bishops Leonidas Polk and Stephen Elliott in the South—were in the forefront of sectional mobilization. As men of God, they helped to turn political questions into moral issues and reduced the prospects for a compromise.

Watch the **Video**
Harriet Beecher Stowe and the Making Of Uncle Tom's Cabin on **myhistorylab.com**

American literature also became sectionalized during the 1840s and 1850s. Southern men of letters, including such notable figures as novelist William Gilmore Simms and Edgar Allan Poe, wrote proslavery polemics. Popular novelists produced a flood of "plantation romances" that glorified southern civilization and sneered at that of the North. The notion that planter "cavaliers" were superior to money-grubbing Yankees was the message that most southerners derived from the homegrown literature they read. In the North, prominent men of letters—Emerson, Thoreau, James Russell Lowell, and Herman Melville—expressed antislavery sentiments in prose and poetry, particularly after the outbreak of the Mexican-American War.

Literary abolitionism climaxed in 1852 when Harriet Beecher Stowe published *Uncle Tom's Cabin*, an enormously successful novel (it sold more than 300,000 copies in one year) that fixed in the northern mind the image of the slaveholder as a brutal Simon Legree. Much of its emotional impact came from its portrayal of slavery as a threat to the family and the Cult of Domesticity. When the saintly Uncle Tom was sold away from his adoring wife and children, northerners shuddered with horror, and some southerners felt a twinge of conscience.

Southern defensiveness gradually hardened into cultural and economic nationalism. Southern schools banished northern textbooks in favor of those with a pro-southern slant; young men of the planter class were induced to stay in the South for higher education rather than go North to universities (as had been the custom); and a movement developed to encourage southern industry and commerce to reduce dependence on the North. Almost without exception, prominent southern educators and intellectuals of the late 1850s rallied behind southern sectionalism, and many even endorsed the idea of an independent southern nation.

Quick Check

✓ What aspects of American culture became sectionalized in the 1850s?

The Dred Scott Case

When James Buchanan was inaugurated on March 4, 1857, the dispute over the legal status of slavery in the territories was an open door through which sectional fears and hatreds could enter the political arena. Buchanan hoped to close that door by encouraging the Supreme Court to resolve the constitutional issue once and for all.

The Court was about to render its decision in the case of *Dred Scott v. Sandford*. Dred Scott was a Missouri slave who sued for his freedom on the grounds that he had lived for years in an area where the Missouri Compromise had outlawed slavery. The Court could have decided the issue on the narrow ground that a slave was not a citizen and therefore had no right to sue in federal courts. But President-elect Buchanan encouraged the Court to render a broader decision.

On March 6, Chief Justice Roger B. Taney announced that the majority had ruled against Scott. Taney argued that no African American—slave or free—could be a citizen of the United States. But the real bombshell was the ruling that Dred Scott would not have won his case even if he had been a legal plaintiff. His residence in the Wisconsin Territory established no right to freedom because Congress had no power to prohibit slavery there. The Missouri Compromise was thus unconstitutional and so, implicitly, was the plank in the Republican platform that called for excluding slavery from all federal territories.

In the North, and especially among Republicans, the Court's verdict was viewed as the latest diabolical act of the "slave-power conspiracy." Circumstantial evidence supported the charge that the decision was a political maneuver. Five of the six judges who voted in the majority were proslavery southerners. Their resolution of the territorial issue was close to the extreme southern-rights position John C. Calhoun had advocated in 1850.

Republicans denounced the decision as "a wicked and false judgment," "the greatest crime in the annals of the republic." But they stopped short of openly defying the Court's authority. Instead, they argued on narrow technical grounds that the decision as written was not binding on Congress, which could still enact a ban on slavery in the territories. The decision actually helped the Republicans build support; it lent credence to their claim that an aggressive slave power was dominating all branches of the federal government and attempting to use the Constitution to achieve its own ends.

Watch the **Video**
Dred Scott and the Crises that Led to the Civil War on **myhistorylab.com**

Quick Check

✓ What did chief justice Taney argue in his opinion, and what impact did this have on American sectionalism?

Debating the Morality of Slavery

In the aftermath of the Dred Scott decision, Stephen Douglas faced a tough reelection campaign to the Senate from Illinois in 1858. His opponent was the former Whig Congressman Abraham Lincoln. Their battle became a forum for the debate over slavery in the territories.

In the famous speech that opened his campaign, Lincoln tried to distance himself from his opponent by taking a more radical position: "A house divided against itself cannot stand. I believe this government cannot endure, permanently half *slave* and half *free*." Lincoln then described the chain of events between the Kansas-Nebraska Act and the Dred Scott decision as evidence of a plot to extend and nationalize slavery and tried to link Douglas to this proslavery conspiracy by pointing

Read the **Document**
Abraham Lincoln, Charleston Debate, 1858 on **myhistorylab.com**

Little Giant Stephen Douglas, the "Little Giant" from Illinois, won election to Congress when he was just 30 „years old. Four years later, he was elected to the Senate.

to his rival's unwillingness to take a stand on the morality of slavery, to his professed indifference about whether slavery was voted up or down in the territories. For Lincoln, the only security against the triumph of slavery and the slave power was moral opposition to human bondage.

In the series of debates that focused national attention on the Illinois contest, Lincoln hammered away at the theme that Douglas was a covert defender of slavery because he was not a principled opponent of it. Douglas accused Lincoln of endangering the Union by his talk of putting slavery on the path to extinction. Denying that he was an abolitionist, Lincoln distinguished between tolerating slavery in the South, where the Constitution protected it, and allowing it to expand to places where it could legally be prohibited. The Founders had restricted slavery, he argued. Douglas and the Democrats had departed from the great tradition of containing an evil that could not be immediately eliminated.

In the debate at Freeport, Illinois, Lincoln questioned Douglas on how he could reconcile popular sovereignty with the Dred Scott decision. The Little Giant responded that slavery could not exist without supportive legislation to sustain it and that territorial legislatures could simply not pass a slave code if they wanted to keep it out. Historians formerly believed that Douglas's "Freeport doctrine" alienated his southern supporters. In truth, Douglas had already undermined his popularity in the slave states. But the Freeport speech hardened southern opposition to his presidential ambitions.

Douglas's most effective debating point was to charge that Lincoln's moral opposition to slavery implied a belief in racial equality. Lincoln, facing a racist electorate, affirmed his commitment to white supremacy. He would grant blacks the right to the fruits of their own labor while denying them the "privileges" of full citizenship. Douglas made the most of this inherently contradictory position.

Although Republican candidates for the state legislature won a majority of the popular vote, the Democrats carried more counties and thus were able to reelect Douglas. Lincoln lost an office, but he won respect in Republican circles throughout the country. By stressing the moral dimension of the slavery question and undercutting any possibility of fusion between Republicans and Douglas Democrats, he had sharpened his party's ideological focus and stiffened its resolve not to compromise its Free-Soil position.

Slavery remained an emotional and symbolic issue. Events in late 1859 and early 1860 turned southern anxiety about northern attitudes and policies into a "crisis of fear." The most significant event was John Brown's raid on Harpers Ferry, Virginia, in October 1859. Brown led 18 men, including five free blacks, in seizing the federal arsenal and armory in Harpers Ferry, hoping to start an uprising against slavery. While he failed at that, and was hanged for treason, the sympathy and admiration he aroused in the North stunned southerners. Within the South, the raid and its aftermath touched off a frenzy of fear, repression, and mobilization.

Read the **Document** *Garrison on John Brown's Raid* on **myhistorylab.com**

Quick Check

✓ What was the basis of Lincoln's opposition to slavery?

The Election of 1860

The Republicans, sniffing victory and insensitive to the depth of southern feeling against them, met in Chicago on May 16 to nominate a presidential candidate. The initial front-runner, Senator William H. Seward of New York, had two strikes against him: He had a reputation for radicalism and a record of opposition to nativism. Most of the delegates wanted a less controversial nominee who could win two or three of the northern states that the Democratic had carried in 1856. Lincoln met their specifications: He was from Illinois, a state the Republicans needed to win; he seemed more moderate than Seward; and he had kept his distaste for Know-Nothingism to himself. He was also a self-made man, whose rise from frontier poverty to legal and political prominence embodied the Republican ideal of equal opportunity for all.

The Republican platform, like the nominee, was meant to broaden the party's appeal in the North. Although the platform retained a commitment to halt the expansion of slavery, it gave economic matters more attention than in 1856. It called for a high protective tariff, endorsed free homesteads, and supported federal aid for internal improvements, especially a transcontinental railroad. The platform was designed to attract enough ex-Whigs and renegade Democrats to give the Republicans a solid majority in the North.

The Democrats failed to present a united front against this formidable challenge. When the party first met in the sweltering heat of Charleston in late April, Douglas commanded a majority of the delegates but not the two-thirds required for nomination because of southern opposition. The convention did endorse popular sovereignty, but the price was a walkout by Deep South delegates who favored a federal slave code for the territories.

Unable to agree on a nominee, the convention reconvened in Baltimore in June. There, the pro-Douglas forces won a fight over whether to seat newly selected pro-Douglas delegations from some Deep South states in place of the

A Rising Star Abraham Lincoln, shown here in his first full-length portrait. Although Lincoln lost the contest for the Senate seat in 1858, the Lincoln–Douglas debates established his reputation as a rising star of the Republican party.

bolters from the first convention. But that led to another and more massive southern walk-out. The Democratic party fractured. The delegates who remained nominated Douglas and reaffirmed the party's commitment to popular sovereignty. The bolters nominated John Breckinridge of Kentucky on a plat-form of federal protection for slavery in the territories.

By the time the campaign was under way, four parties were running presidential candidates. In addition to the Republicans, the Douglas Democrats, and the "Southern Rights" Democrats, John Bell of Tennessee ran under the banner of the Constitutional Union party, a remnant of conservative Whigs and Know-Nothings. Taking no ex-plicit stand on slavery in the territories, the Constitutional Unionists tried to represent the spirit of sectional accommodation that had led to compromise in 1820 and 1850. In effect, the race became two separate two-party contests: In the North, the real choice was between Lincoln and Douglas; in the South, it was between Breckinridge and Bell.

The result was a stunning Republi-cans victory. By gaining the electoral votes of all the free states, except those from three districts of New Jersey that voted for Douglas, Lincoln won a decisive ma-jority over his combined opponents. In the North, his 54 percent of the popular vote annihilated Douglas. In the South, where Lincoln was not even on the ballot, Breckinridge triumphed everywhere ex-cept in Virginia, Kentucky, and Tennessee, which went for Bell. (See Map 14.3) The Republican strategy of seeking power by winning decisively in the majority section had succeeded. Although less than 40 per-cent of those who went to the polls through-out the nation voted for Lincoln, his support in the North was so solid that he would have won in the electoral college even if he had faced a single opponent.

Most southerners saw the election as a catastrophe. A candidate and a party with no support in their own section had won the presidency on a platform viewed as insulting to southern honor and hostile to southern interests. Since the birth of the republic, southerners had either sat in the White House or influenced those who did. Those days might now be gone forever. Rather than accept permanent minority status in American politics and face the resulting dangers to black slavery and white "liberty," the political leaders of the lower South launched a movement for immediate secession from the Union.

CONCLUSION: EXPLAINING THE CRISIS

Generations of historians have searched for the underlying causes of the crisis leading to disruption of the Union but have failed to agree on what these causes were. Some have stressed the clash of economic interests between agrarian and industrializing regions. But this interpretation does not reflect the way people at the time expressed their concerns. The main issues in the sectional debates of the 1850s were whether slavery was right or wrong and whether it should be extended or contained. Disagreements over protective tariffs and other economic measures benefiting one section or the other were secondary.

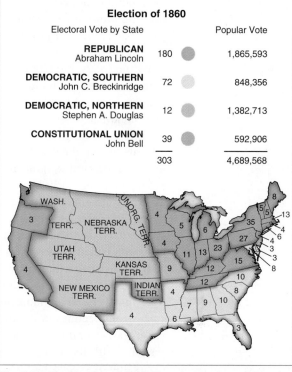

Map 14.3 *The Election of 1860* Many observers have said that the election of 1860 was really two elections: one in the North and one in the South. From this map, can you see why the candidate who won the northern election became president?

Another group of historians blame the crisis on "irresponsible" politicians and agitators on both sides of the Mason–Dixon Line. Public opinion was whipped into a frenzy over issues that competent statesmen could have resolved. But this viewpoint fails to acknowledge the depths of feeling that the slavery question aroused and underestimates the obstacles to a peaceful solution.

The dominant modern view is that the crisis was rooted in profound ideological differences over the morality and utility of slavery as an institution. Most interpreters agree that the roots of the conflict lay in the fact that the South was a slave society and determined to stay one, while the North was equally committed to a free-labor system. No other differences divided the regions in this decisive way. It is hard to imagine that secessionism would have developed if the South like the North had abolished slavery after the Revolution.

Nevertheless, the existence or nonexistence of slavery will not explain why the crisis came when and how it did. Why did the conflict become irreconcilable in the 1850s and not earlier? Why did it take the form of a political struggle over the future of slavery in the territories? Answers to both questions require an understanding of political developments that tensions over slavery did not directly cause.

By the 1850s, the established Whig and Democratic parties were in trouble, partly because they no longer offered the voters clear-cut alternatives on economic issues that had been the bread and butter of politics during the heyday of the second-party system. This created an opening for new parties and issues. After the Know-Nothings failed to make hostility to immigrants the basis for a political realignment, the Republicans used the issue of slavery in the territories to build the first successful sectional party in American history. They called for "free soil," not freedom for blacks because abolitionism conflicted with the northern majority's commitment to white supremacy and its respect for the original constitutional compromise that established a hands-off policy toward slavery in the South. For southerners, the Republican party now became the main issue, and they fought it from within the Democratic party.

If politicians seeking new ways to mobilize an apathetic electorate are seen as the main instigators of sectional crisis, we still have to ask why certain appeals were more effective than others. Why did the slavery extension issue arouse such strong feelings in the two sections during the 1850s? The same issue had arisen earlier and had proved adjustable, even in 1820 when the second-party system—with its vested interest in compromise—had not yet emerged. If the expansion of slavery had been as vital and emotional a question in 1820 as it was in the 1850s, the moribund Federalist party presumably would have revived in the form of a northern sectional party adamantly opposed to admitting slave states to the Union.

Ultimately, therefore, we must recognize that the crisis of the 1850s had both a deep social and cultural dimension and a purely political one. Beliefs and values had diverged significantly in the North and the South between the 1820s and the 1850s. Both sections continued to profess allegiance to the traditional "republican" ideals of individual liberty and independence, and both were influenced by evangelical religion. But differences in the economic and social development of each region transformed a common culture into two conflicting cultures. In the North, a rising middle class adapted to the new market economy with the help of an evangelical Christianity that sanctioned self-discipline and social reform (see Chapter 12). The South, on the other hand, embraced slavery as a foundation for white liberty and independence. Its evangelicalism encouraged personal piety but not social reform and gave only limited attention to building the kind of personal character that made for commercial success. The notion that white liberty and equality depended on resisting social and economic change and—to get to the heart of the matter—continuing to have enslaved blacks to do menial labor became more entrenched.

When politicians appealed to sectionalism during the 1850s, therefore, they could evoke conflicting views of what constituted the good society. The South—with its allegedly idle masters, degraded unfree workers, and shiftless poor whites—seemed to most northerners to be in flagrant violation of the Protestant work ethic and the ideal of open competition in "the race of life." From the dominant southern point of view, the North was a land of hypocritical money-grubbers who denied the obvious fact that the virtue, independence, and liberty of free citizens was possible only when dependent laboring classes—especially racially inferior ones—were kept under the kind of rigid control that only slavery could provide. Once these contrary views of the world had become the main themes of political discourse, sectional compromise was no longer possible.

14 STUDY RESOURCES

((•— Listen to the **Chapter Audio** for Chapter 14 on **myhistorylab.com**

TIMELINE

1846 Rep. David Wilmot introduces Proviso banning slavery in the Mexican cession, p. 337

1848 Free-Soil party founded, p. 338
- Zachary Taylor elected president, p. 338

1849 California seeks admission to the Union as a free state, p. 338

1850 Congress enacts Compromise of 1850, p. 339

1852 Harriet Beecher Stowe publishes *Uncle Tom's Cabin*, p. 348
- Franklin Pierce elected president, p. 343

1854 Kansas-Nebraska Act repeals Missouri Compromise, p. 343
- Republican party founded, p. 336

1854–1856 Civil war in Kansas Territory, p. 345

1856 Preston Brooks assaults Charles Sumner on Senate floor, p. 346
- James Buchanan elected president, p. 347

1857 Dred Scott decision legalizes slavery in all territories, p. 348

1858 Lincoln and Douglas debate slavery in Illinois, p. 349

1860 Democratic party splits into northern and southern factions with separate candidates and platforms (June), p. 351
- Abraham Lincoln elected president, p. 351

CHAPTER REVIEW

THE COMPROMISE OF 1850

How did territorial expansion intensify the conflict over slave ownership?

Manifest Destiny raised questions about states' rights. The Constitution did not permit the federal government to override state slavery laws, but the Wilmot Proviso attempted and failed to ban slavery in the Mexican cession. Despite that defeat, California was admitted as a free state under the Compromise of 1850, while the Fugitive Slave Law appeased the South. *(p. 336)*

POLITICAL UPHEAVAL, 1852–1856

How did the two-party system change during this period?

The Whig candidate lost in 1852 for supporting the antislavery cause, while the Kansas-Nebraska Act sought to repeal the Missouri Compromise— a move most northerners and some southerners considered abominable. This gave rise to Republicanism, which adhered to native Protestant values while supporting development in the West and opposing slavery. The 1856 election was largely a choice between rivals, one northern and one southern. *(p. 341)*

THE HOUSE DIVIDED, 1857–1860

How did the institution of slavery go beyond political and economic debates?

Slavery divided American society culturally, legally, and morally. Religious congregations broke up, while literature expressed increasingly the sentiments surrounding slaveholding. The Dred Scott decision stripped American blacks—free and slave alike—of most legal rights. Finally, Lincoln chose to oppose slavery on moral grounds, making freedom a human (and not simply legal) right. *(p. 347)*

KEY TERM QUESTIONS

1. How did the Wilmot Proviso blur party lines in Congress? (p. 337)

2. How did popular sovereignty try to resolve the slavery question? (p. 338)

3. What did the South and the North each gain from the Compromise of 1850? (p. 339)

4. Why were northerners so angry about the Fugitive Slave Law? (p. 340)

5. Why did the Kansas-Nebraska Act divide the Democratic Party along sectional lines and lead to the demise of the Whig Party? (p. 343)

6. Why was the Ostend Manifesto so controversial? (p. 344)

MyHistoryLab Connections

Visit **www.myhistorylab.com** for a customized Study Plan to build your knowledge of *The Sectional Crisis*

Question for Analysis

1. Why is the Fugitive Slave Act significant?

   Read the **Document** *The Fugitive Slave Act* p. 339

2. Was the Compromise of 1850 truly a compromise?

   View the **Closer Look** *The Compromise of 1850* p. 345

Other Resources from this Chapter

 Read the **Document** *John C. Calhoun's Proposal to Preserve the Union*

View the **Image** *Stephen Douglas*

3. Why did *Uncle Tom's Cabin* become a bestseller?

   Watch the **Video** *Harriet Beecher Stowe and the Making of Uncle Tom's Cabin* p. 348

4. What was decided in the Dred Scott Supreme Court case?

   Watch the **Video** *Dred Scott and the Crises that Led to the Civil War* p. 349

5. How do you think the audience reacted to Lincoln's introductory speech in Charleston?

   Read the **Document** *Abraham Lincoln, Charleston Debate in 1858* p. 349

Read the **Document** *John Gihon, Kansas Begins to Bleed*

Read the **Document** *Garrison on John Brown's Raid*

Contents and Spotlight Questions

THE STORM GATHERS PG. 361

What developments and events drew the Union toward Civil War?

ADJUSTING TO TOTAL WAR PG. 367

What challenges did "total war" bring for each side?

FIGHT TO THE FINISH PG. 371

How did the Union finally attain victory, and what role did emancipation play in it?

EFFECTS OF THE WAR PG. 380

How did the outcome of the war affect America socially and politically?

((•—|**Listen** to the **Chapter Audio** for Chapter 15 on **myhistorylab.com**

THE EMERGENCE OF LINCOLN

The man elected to the White House in 1860 was 6 feet, 4 inches tall and seemed even taller because of his disproportionately long legs and his habit of wearing a high silk "stovepipe" hat. But Abraham Lincoln's previous career provided no guarantee he would tower over most of the other presidents in more than height. When Lincoln sketched the events of his life for a campaign biographer in June 1860, he was modest almost to the point of self-deprecation. Regretting his "want of education," he assured the biographer that "he does what he can to supply the want."

Born to poor and illiterate parents on the Kentucky frontier in 1809, Lincoln received only two years of formal schooling in Indiana after the family moved there in 1816. But mostly he educated himself, reading and rereading treasured books by firelight. In 1831, when the

Matthew Brady's Lincoln On February 27, 1860, Abraham Lincoln gave a campaign speech at Cooper Union in front of 1500 people that helped him win the Presidency. In this forceful, hour-long speech, he proved that the Founders intended to regulate slavery. On his way there, he stopped at photographer Matthew Brady's studio. Brady's "Cooper Union Portrait" became the iconic image of President Lincoln. (Portrait of Abraham Lincoln, Matthew Brady, Library of Congress) family migrated to Illinois, he left home to make a living in the struggling settlement of New Salem, where he worked as a surveyor, shopkeeper, and postmaster. His brief career as a merchant was disastrous: He went bankrupt and was saddled with debt for years. But he found success in law and politics. While studying law on his own in New Salem, he was elected to the state legislature. In 1837, he moved to Springfield, a growing town that offered bright prospects for a young lawyer-politician. Lincoln combined exceptional political and legal skills with a down-to-earth, humorous way of addressing jurors and voters. He became a leader of the Whig party in Illinois and one of the most sought after lawyers in the central Illinois judicial circuit.

The high point of his political career as a Whig was one term in Congress (1847–1849). Lincoln did not seek reelection, but he would have faced certain defeat if he had. His opposition to the Mexican-American War alienated his constituency, and the voters elected a Democrat to succeed him in 1848. In 1849, President Zachary Taylor, for whom Lincoln had campaigned vigorously, did not give him a patronage job he coveted. Having been repudiated by the electorate and ignored by the national leadership of a party he had served loyally and well, Lincoln built his law practice.

The Kansas-Nebraska Act of 1854, with its advocacy of popular sovereignty, provided Lincoln with a heaven-sent opportunity to return to politics with a stronger base of support. For the first time, his ambition for political success and convictions about what was best for the country were easy to reconcile. Lincoln had long believed slavery was unjust and should be tolerated only to the extent the Constitution and the tradition of sectional compromise required. He attacked Douglas's plan of popular sovereignty because it broke with precedents for federal containment or control of the growth of slavery. After trying to rally Free-Soilers around the Whig standard, Lincoln threw in his lot with the Republicans, became leader of the new party in Illinois, attracted national attention in his bid for Douglas's Senate seat in 1858, and had the right qualifications when the Republicans chose a presidential nominee in 1860. That he had split rails with an axe as a young man was used in the campaign to show that he was a man of the people.

After Lincoln's election provoked southern secession and plunged the nation into the greatest crisis in its history, many people were skeptical of his abilities: Was he up to the responsibilities he faced? Lincoln had less experience relevant to a wartime presidency than any previous or future chief executive; he had never been a governor, senator, cabinet officer, vice president, or high-ranking military officer. But his training as a prairie politician would prove useful in the years ahead.

Lincoln was also an effective war leader because he identified wholeheartedly with the northern cause and could inspire others to make sacrifices for it. In his view, the issue in the conflict was nothing less than the survival of the kind of political system that gave men like himself a chance for high office.

The Civil War put on trial the very principle of democracy at a time when most European nations had rejected political liberalism and accepted the conservative view that popular government would inevitably collapse into anarchy. It also showed the shortcomings of a purely white man's democracy and brought the first hesitant steps toward black citizenship. As Lincoln put it in the Gettysburg Address in 1863, the only cause great enough to justify the enormous sacrifice of life on the battlefields was the struggle to preserve and extend the democratic ideal, to ensure that "government of the people, by the people, for the people, shall not perish from the earth."

THE STORM GATHERS

Lincoln's election provoked the secession of seven states of the Deep South but did not lead immediately to armed conflict. Before the sectional quarrel would turn from a cold war into a hot one, two things had to happen: A final effort to defuse the conflict by compromise and conciliation had to fail, and the North needed to develop a firm resolve to maintain the Union by military action.

What developments and events drew the Union toward Civil War?

The Deep South Secedes

South Carolina, which had long been in the forefront of southern rights and proslavery agitation, was the first state to secede. On December 20, 1860, a convention in Charleston declared unanimously that "the union now subsisting between South Carolina and other states, under the name of the 'United States of America,' is hereby dissolved." The constitutional theory behind secession was that the Union was a "compact" among sovereign states, each of which could withdraw from it by the vote of a convention similar to the one that had ratified the Constitution in the first place. The South Carolinians justified secession by charging that "a sectional party" had elected a president "whose opinions and purposes are hostile to slavery."

Watch the **Video** *What caused the Civil War?* on **myhistorylab.com**

Other states of the Cotton Kingdom felt similar outrage at Lincoln's election but less certainty about how to respond to it. Cooperationists, who believed the slave states should act as a unit, opposed those who advocated immediate secession by each state individually. If the cooperationists had triumphed, secession would have been delayed until a southern convention had agreed on it. Some of these moderates hoped to extort major concessions from the North and thus remove the need for dissolving the Union. But South Carolina's unilateral action weakened their cause.

Read the **Document** *South Carolina Declaration of the Causes of Secession* on **myhistorylab.com**

Elections for delegates to secession conventions in six other Deep South states were hotly contested. Cooperationists did well in Georgia, Louisiana, and Texas. But secessionists won a majority in every state. By February 1, six other states had left the Union—Alabama, Mississippi, Florida, Georgia, Louisiana, and Texas. In the upper South, however, calls for immediate secession failed; majority opinion in Virginia, North Carolina, Tennessee, and Arkansas did not think that Lincoln's election was a sufficient reason for breaking up the Union. These states had stronger ties to the northern economy, and moderate leaders were more willing to seek a sectional compromise.

Delegates from the Deep South met in Montgomery, Alabama, on February 4 to establish the Confederate States of America. The convention acted as a provisional government while drafting a constitution. Relatively moderate leaders, most of whom had not supported secession until *after* Lincoln's election, dominated the proceedings and defeated or modified the pet schemes of extreme southern nationalists. Voted down were proposals to reopen the Atlantic slave trade, abolish the three-fifths clause (in favor of counting all slaves in determining congressional representation), and prohibit admitting free states to the new Confederacy.

Read the
Document
Confederate Consti-
tution, 1861 on
myhistorylab.com

The resulting constitution was surprisingly similar to that of the United States. Most of the differences merely spelled out traditional southern interpretations of the federal charter: The central government was denied the authority to impose protective tariffs, subsidize internal improvements, or interfere with slavery in the states and was required to protect slavery in the territories. As president and vice president, the convention chose Jefferson Davis of Mississippi and Alexander Stephens of Georgia, men who had resisted secessionist agitation.

The moderation shown in Montgomery resulted in part from a desire to win support in the upper South. But it also revealed that proslavery reactionaries had never won a majority. Most southerners had opposed dissolving the Union so long as slavery seemed safe from northern interference.

Lincoln's election destroyed that sense of security. But the Montgomery convention made it clear that the new converts to secessionism did not want to establish a slaveholder's reactionary utopia. They wanted to re-create the Union as it had been before the rise of the Republican party. They opted for secession only when it seemed the only way to achieve their aim. The decision to allow free states to join the Confederacy reflected a hope that the old Union could be reconstituted under southern direction. Some optimists even predicted that all of the North except New England would transfer its loyalty to the new government.

Men of Moderation Jefferson Davis, inaugurated as president of the Confederacy on February 18, 1861, was a West Point graduate and had served as secretary of war under President Franklin Pierce and as a U.S. senator.

Secession and the formation of the Confederacy thus amounted to a conservative and defensive kind of "revolution." The only justification for southern independence on which a majority could agree was the need for greater security for the "peculiar institution." Vice President Stephens spoke for all the founders of the Confederacy when he described the cornerstone of the new government as "the great truth that the negro is not equal to the white man—that slavery—subordination to the superior race—is his natural condition."

Quick Check

✓ How did secessionists conceive of the U.S. constitution, and how did their new constitution differ?

The Failure of Compromise

While the Deep South was opting for independence, moderates in the North and border slave states were trying to devise a compromise that would stem the secessionist tide. In December 1860, Senator John Crittenden of Kentucky presented the Crittenden compromise, which advocated extending the Missouri Compromise line to the Pacific to protect slavery in the southwestern territories. The federal government would compensate the owners of escaped slaves, and a constitutional amendment would forever prohibit the federal government from abolishing or regulating slavery in the states.

Congressional Republicans seemed willing take the proposals seriously. However, their support evaporated when President-elect Lincoln adamantly opposed extending the compromise line. In the words of a fellow Republican, he stood "firm as an oak."

Lincoln's resounding "no" to the central provision of the Crittenden plan and similar proposals stiffened the backbone of congressional Republicans, and they voted against compromise as members of the committees both houses set up to avert war. Also voting against the Crittenden plan, and thereby ensuring its defeat, were the remaining senators and congressmen of the seceding states, who had vowed to support no compromise unless the majority of Republicans also endorsed it. Their purpose in taking this stand was to obtain guarantees that the northern sectional party would end its attacks on "southern rights." The Republicans did agree to support Crittenden's "un-amendable" amendment guaranteeing that slavery would be immune from federal interference. But this was not really a concession to the South, because Republicans had always acknowledged that the federal government had no constitutional authority to meddle with slavery in the states.

Lincoln and those who took his advice had what they considered good reasons for not making territorial concessions. They mistakenly believed that the secession movement was a conspiracy that reflected only a minority opinion in the South and that a strong stand would rally southern Unionists and moderates. However, Lincoln and the dedicated Free-Soilers for whom he spoke would probably not have given ground even if they had realized the secession movement was genuinely popular in the Deep South. In their view, extending the Missouri Compromise line of 36°30′ to the Pacific would not halt agitation for extending slavery. South of the line were Cuba and Central America, where southern expansionists dreamed of a Caribbean slave empire. The only way to resolve the crisis over the future of slavery and reunite the "house divided" was to remove any chance that slaveholders could enlarge their domain.

Lincoln was also convinced that backing down in the face of secessionist threats would undermine the democratic principle of majority rule. In his inaugural address of March 4, 1861, he recalled that during the winter, "patriotic men" had urged him to accept a compromise that would "shift the ground" on which he had been elected. But that would have signified that a victorious presidential candidate "cannot be inaugurated till he betrays those who elected him by breaking his pledges, and surrendering to those who tried and failed to defeat him at the polls." Such a concession would mean that "this government and all popular government is already at an end."

Quick Check

✓ What was the Crittenden compromise, and why was it rejected?

And the War Came

By the time of Lincoln's inauguration, the Confederacy had seized most federal in-stallations in the Deep South without firing a shot. President James Buchanan had denied the right of secession but had also refused to use "coercion" to maintain federal authority. Many in the North shared his doubts about whether a Union held together by force was worth preserving. The business community feared breaking commercial links with the cotton-producing South, and some antislavery Republi-cans and abolitionists thought the nation might be better off if "the erring sisters" were allowed "to depart in peace."

The collapse of compromise efforts eliminated the option of maintaining the Union peacefully and narrowed the choices to separation between the sections with or without war. By early March, public opinion was beginning to shift in favor of action to preserve the Union. Once the business community realized conciliation would not keep the cotton states in the Union, it put its weight behind coercion, reasoning that a temporary disruption of commerce was better than the permanent loss of the South as a market and source of raw materials.

In his inaugural address, Lincoln called for a cautious use of force. He would de-fend federal forts not yet in Confederate hands but would not attempt to recapture the ones already taken. He thus tried to shift the burden for beginning hostilities to the Confederacy, which would have to attack before it would be attacked.

As Lincoln spoke, U.S. forces held only four military installations within the se-ceded states. Two in the remote Florida Keys attracted little attention. The others were Fort Pickens on an island outside Pensacola in northwest Florida and Fort Sumter inside Charleston Harbor. Attention focused on Sumter because the Con-federacy, egged on by South Carolina, was demanding the surrender of a garrison that was within easy reach of shore batteries and running low on supplies. Shortly after taking office, Lincoln was informed that Sumter could not hold out much lon-ger and that he would have to decide whether to reinforce it or let it fall.

Initially, Lincoln's cabinet opposed reinforcing or provisioning Sumter, on the grounds that it was indefensible. Secretary of State Seward was so certain this would be the decision that he so advised Confederate representatives. But on April 4, Lincoln or-dered that the beleaguered troops in Charleston Harbor be resupplied. Two days later, he notified the governor of South Carolina that a relief expedition was being sent.

The expedition sailed on April 8 and 9, but before it arrived, Confederate au-thorities decided that sending supplies was a hostile act and attacked the fort. On the morning of April 12, shore batteries opened fire; the bombardment continued for 40 hours without loss of life but with heavy damage to the fort. Finally, on April 13, the Union forces under Major Robert Anderson surrendered, and the Confederate flag was raised over Fort Sumter. The South had won a victory but had also as-sumed responsibility for firing the first shot.

On April 15, Lincoln proclaimed that an insurrection against federal author-ity existed in the Deep South and called on the militia of the loyal states to pro-vide 75,000 troops for short-term service to put it down. Two days later, a Virginia

◉ **View** the **Image**
Fort Sumter on
myhistorylab.com

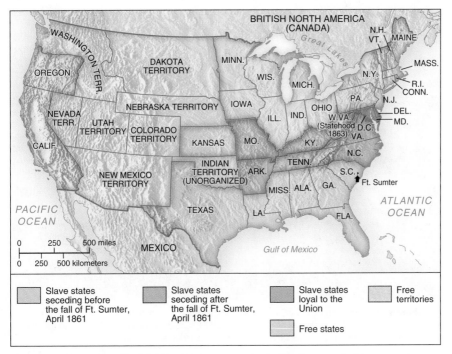

Map 15.1 *Secession*   The fall of Fort Sumter was a watershed for the secessionist movement.

convention that had rejected secession in February voted to join the Confederacy. Within five weeks, Arkansas, Tennessee, and North Carolina followed suit. These slave states of the upper South had been unwilling to secede just because Lincoln was elected, but when he called on them to provide troops to "coerce" other southern states, they had to choose sides. Believing that secession was a constitutional right, they cut their ties with a government that opted to use force to maintain the Union and asked them to join the effort. (See Map 15.1)

In the North, the firing on Sumter evoked an outpouring of patriotism and dedication to the Union. "It seems as if we were never alive till now; never had a country till now," wrote a New Yorker; and a Bostonian noted, "I never before knew what a popular excitement can be." Stephen A. Douglas, Lincoln's former political rival, pledged his full support for the crusade against secession and literally worked himself to death rallying midwestern Democrats behind the government. By firing on the flag, the Confederacy united the North. Everyone assumed the war would be short and not very bloody. Whether Unionist fervor could be sustained through a long and costly struggle remained to be seen.

The Confederacy, which now moved its capital to Richmond, Virginia, contained only 11 of the 15 states in which slavery was lawful. In the border slave states of Maryland, Delaware, Kentucky, and Missouri, local Unionism and federal intervention thwarted secession. Kentucky, the most crucial of these states, proclaimed

Bombardment This contemporary Currier and Ives lithograph depicts the bombardment of Fort Sumter on April 12–13, 1861. The soldiers are firing from Fort Moultrie in Charleston Harbor, which the Union garrison had evacuated the previous December in order to strengthen Fort Sumter.

its neutrality. It eventually sided with the Union, mainly because Lincoln, who was careful to respect this tenuous neutrality, provoked the South into violating it first by invading the state. Maryland surrounded the nation's capital and provided it with access to the free states. More ruthless methods, which included martial law to suppress Confederate sympathizers, kept it in the Union. In Missouri, regular troops, aided by a staunchly pro-Union German immigrant population, stymied the secession movement. But pro-Union forces failed to establish order in this deeply divided frontier state. Guerrilla fighting made wartime Missouri an unsafe and bloody place.

Hence the Civil War was not, strictly speaking, a struggle between slave and free states. Nor did it simply pit states that could not tolerate Lincoln's election against those that could. More than anything else, conflicting views on secession determined the division of states and the choices individuals made in areas where sentiment was divided. General Robert E. Lee, for example, was neither a defender of slavery nor a southern nationalist. But he followed Virginia out of the Union because he was the loyal son of a "sovereign state." General George Thomas, another Virginian, chose the Union because he believed it was indissoluble. Although concern about the future of slavery had driven the Deep South to secede in the first place, the actual lineup of states and supporters meant the two sides would initially define the war less as a struggle over slavery than as a contest to determine whether the Union was indivisible.

Quick Check

✓ What was Lincoln's attitude toward the use of force, and why did he want the south to initiate any hostilities that might occur?

ADJUSTING TO TOTAL WAR

The Civil War was a "total war" involving every aspect of society because the North could restore the Union only by defeating the South so thoroughly that its separatist government would collapse. It was a long war because the Confederacy put up "a hell of a fight" before it would agree to be put to death. Total war is a test of societies, economies, and political systems, as well as a battle of wits between generals and military strategists—and the Civil War was no exception.

What challenges did "total war" bring for each side?

Mobilizing the Home Fronts

North and South faced similar problems in trying to create the vast support systems armies in the field needed. (See Figure 15.1) At the beginning of the conflict, both sides had more volunteers than they could arm and outfit. But as hopes for a short and easy war faded, the pool of volunteers began to dry up. Many of the early recruits, who had been enrolled for short terms, were reluctant to reenlist. To resolve this problem, the Confederacy passed a conscription law in April 1862, and in July, Congress gave Lincoln the power to assign manpower quotas to each state and resort to conscription if they were not met.

To produce the materials of war, both governments relied mainly on private industry. In the North, especially, the system of contracting with private firms and individuals to supply the army resulted in corruption and inefficiency. The government bought shoddy uniforms that disintegrated in heavy rain, defective rifles, and

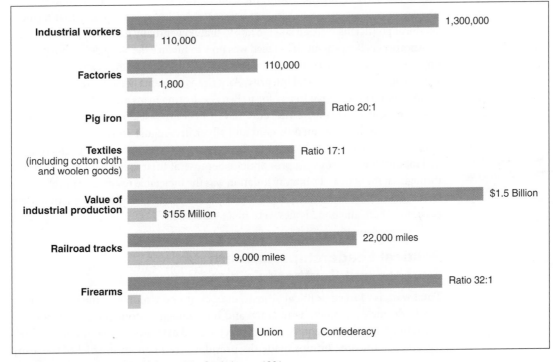

Figure 15.1 Resources of the Union and the Confederacy, 1861

horses unfit for service. But the North's economy was strong at the core. By 1863, its factories and farms were producing more than enough to provision the troops without lowering the living standards of the civilian population.

The southern economy was less adaptable to the needs of a total war. The South of 1861 imported most of its manufactured goods. As the Union blockade became more effective, the Confederacy had to rely on a government-sponsored crash program to produce war materials. The government encouraged and promoted private initiatives and built its own munitions plants. Astonishingly, the Confederate Ordnance Bureau, under the able direction of General Josiah Gorgas, produced or procured sufficient armaments to keep southern armies well supplied throughout the conflict.

Southern agriculture, however, failed to meet the challenge. Planters were reluctant to shift from staples that could no longer be readily exported to urgently needed foodstuffs. But more significant was the South's inadequate internal transportation system. Its limited rail network was designed to link plantation regions to port cities rather than to connect food-producing areas with centers of population, the way the North's was. Railroad construction during the war did not resolve the problem; most of the new lines facilitated the movement of troops, not the distribution of food.

Read the **Document**
Diary Of Joseph Addison Waddell on **myhistorylab.com**

When northern forces penetrated the South, they created new gaps in the system. As a result, much of the corn or livestock that was raised could not reach the people who needed it. Although well armed, Confederate soldiers were increasingly undernourished, and by 1863, civilians in urban areas were rioting to protest shortages of food. To supply the troops, the Confederate commissary resorted to the impressment of agricultural produce at below the market price, a policy that farmers and local politicians resisted so vigorously that it eventually had to be abandoned.

Another challenge both sides faced was how to finance the struggle. Although they imposed special war taxes, neither side was willing to resort to the heavy taxation that was needed to maintain fiscal integrity. Americans, it seems, were more willing to die for their government than to pay for it. Besides floating loans and selling bonds, both treasuries deliberately inflated the currency by printing vast amounts of paper money that could not be redeemed in gold and silver. In August 1861, the Confederacy issued $100 million of such currency. In early 1862, the Union printed $150 million in Treasury notes, known as greenbacks because of their color. The presses rolled throughout the war, and runaway inflation was the inevitable result. The problem was less severe in the North because its economy was stronger, war taxes on income were easier to collect, and bond issues were more successful.

Quick Check
✓ Which side was better suited economically for "total war," and why?

Political Leadership: Northern Success and Southern Failure

Total war also forced political adjustments. Both the Union and the Confederacy had to decide how much democracy and individual freedom could be permitted when military success required an unprecedented exercise of government authority. Since both constitutions made the president commander in chief of the army and navy, Lincoln and Jefferson Davis took actions that would have been regarded as arbitrary or even tyrannical in peacetime.

Lincoln was especially bold in assuming new executive powers. After the fighting started at Fort Sumter, he expanded the regular army and advanced public money to private individuals without congressional authorization. On April 27, 1861, he declared martial law, which enabled the military to arrest civilians suspected of aiding the enemy, and suspended the writ of habeas corpus in the area between Philadelphia and Washington, because of mob attacks on Union troops in Baltimore. Suspending the writ enabled the government to arrest Confederate sympathizers and hold them without trial. In September 1862, Lincoln extended this authority to all parts of the United States where "disloyal" elements were active. Such willingness to interfere with civil liberties was unprecedented and possibly unconstitutional, but Lincoln argued that "necessity" justified a flexible interpretation of his war powers. For critics of suspension, he had a question: "Are all the laws, *but one*, to go unexecuted, and the government itself to go to pieces, lest that one be violated?" In fact, however, most of the thousands of civilians military authorities arrested were not exercising their right to criticize the government but were suspected deserters and draft dodgers, refugees, smugglers, or people simply found wandering in areas under military control.

For the most part, the Lincoln administration tolerated a broad spectrum of political dissent. Although the government briefly closed down a few newspapers when they allegedly published false information or military secrets, anti-administration journals were allowed to criticize the president and his party at will. A few politicians were arrested for pro-Confederate activity, but many "Peace Democrats"—who called for restoring the Union by negotiation rather than force—ran for office and sat in Congress and state legislatures. They had ample opportunity to present their views to the public. In fact, vigorous two-party competition in the North during the Civil War strengthened Lincoln's hand. Since his war policies were also the platform of his party, he could usually rely on unified partisan backing for his most controversial decisions.

Lincoln was singularly adept at the art of party leadership; he accommodated factions and defined party issues and principles in a way that would encourage unity and dedication to the cause. Since the Republican party was the main vehicle for mobilizing and maintaining devotion to the Union effort, these political skills were crucial. When a majority of the party came around to the view that freeing the slaves was necessary to the war effort, Lincoln complied with their wishes while minimizing the disenchantment of the conservative minority. Lincoln held the party together by persuasion, patronage, and flexible policymaking; this cohesiveness was essential to Lincoln's success in unifying the nation by force.

Jefferson Davis, most historians agree, was a less effective war leader. He defined his powers as commander in chief narrowly and literally, which meant he personally directed the armed forces but left policymaking for mobilizing and controlling the civilian population primarily to the Confederate Congress. Unfortunately, he overestimated his capacities as a strategist and lacked the tact to handle field commanders who were as proud and testy as he was.

View the **Map**
The Civil War Part I: 1861–1862 on **myhistorylab.com**

Davis's greatest failing, however, was his lack of initiative and leadership in dealing with the home front. He devoted little attention to a deteriorating economic situation that caused great hardship and sapped Confederate morale. Although division and disloyalty were more serious in the South than in the North, he was extremely cautious in his use of martial law.

As the war dragged on, Davis's support eroded. State governors who resisted conscription and other policies that violated the tradition of states' rights opposed and obstructed him. Southern newspapers and the Confederate Congress attacked Davis's conduct of the war. His authority was further undermined because he did not have an organized party behind him, for the Confederacy never developed a two-party system. As a result, it was difficult to mobilize the support hard decisions and controversial policies required.

Quick Check

✓ In what ways did Lincoln assume stronger executive powers than a peacetime president, and was he justified in doing so?

Early Campaigns and Battles

The war's first major battle was a disaster for northern arms. Against his better judgment, General Winfield Scott, the aged army commander, responded to the "On to Richmond" clamor and ordered poorly trained Union troops under General Irvin McDowell to advance against the Confederate forces gathered at Manassas Junction, Virginia. They attacked the enemy position near Bull Run Creek on July 21, 1861. Confederate General Thomas J. Jackson earned the nickname "Stonewall" for holding the line against the northern assault until reinforcements routed the invading force. The raw Union troops stampeded back to safety in Washington.

This humiliating defeat led to a shake-up of the northern high command. George McClellan replaced McDowell as commander of troops in the Washington area and then became general in chief when Scott was eased into retirement. In the West, however, Union forces won important victories. In February 1862, a joint military–naval operation, under General Ulysses S. Grant, captured Fort Henry on the Tennessee River and Fort Donelson on the Cumberland along with 14,000 prisoners. The Confederate army withdrew from Kentucky and middle Tennessee. Southern forces in the West then massed at Corinth, Mississippi, just across the border from Tennessee. When a slow-moving Union army arrived just north of the Mississippi state line, the South attacked on April 6. In the battle of Shiloh, one of the bloodiest of the war, only the arrival of reinforcements prevented the annihilation of Union troops backed up against the Tennessee River. After a second day of fierce fighting, the Confederates retreated to Corinth, leaving the enemy battered and exhausted.

Although Shiloh halted the Union's effort to seize the Mississippi Valley, on April 26, a Union fleet from the Gulf captured New Orleans. The occupation of New Orleans, besides securing the mouth of the Mississippi and the largest city in the South, climaxed a series of naval and amphibious operations around the edges of the Confederacy. Bases were now available to enforce a blockade of the southern coast.

But Union forces made little headway on the eastern front. In May, Robert E. Lee took command of the Confederate Army of Northern Virginia, and in June

Casualties of War Alexander Gardner took this photograph of dead Confederate soldiers lined up for burial at Antietam, in Maryland, after the deadliest one-day battle of the war. Photographers working with Mathew Brady accompanied Union troops in battle. Their visual records of the campaigns and casualties stand as a testament to the hardships and horrors of war.

he began an all-out effort to expel Union forces from the outskirts of Richmond. All summer, Lee's forces battled McClellan's up and down the peninsula southeast of the city until McClellan withdrew. In September, Lee invaded Maryland, hoping to isolate Washington from the rest of the North. The bloodiest one-day battle of the war ensued. When the smoke cleared at Antietam on September 17, almost 5,000 men had been killed on the two sides and more than 18,000 wounded. The result was a draw, but Lee was forced to fall back south of the Potomac to protect his supply lines. McClellan was slow in pursuit, and Lincoln blamed him for letting the enemy escape. He replaced McClellan with General Ambrose E. Burnside, who was responsible for a disastrous assault on Confederate forces at the Battle of Fredericksburg, Virginia in December 1862. This Union defeat ended a year of bitter failure for the North in the East.

Quick Check

✓ What strategic choices did Union generals make in the early fighting that led to severe losses and heavy casualties?

FIGHT TO THE FINISH

The last two and a half years of the struggle saw the implementation of more radical war measures. The most dramatic and important of these was Lincoln's decision to free the slaves and bring the black population into the war on the Union side. The tide of battle turned decisively in the summer of 1863, but the South resisted valiantly for two more years until the sheer weight of the North's advantages in manpower and resources finally overcame it.

How did the Union finally attain victory, and what role did emancipation play in it?

The Road to Liberty In this allegorical painting, President Lincoln extends a copy of his proclamation to the goddess of liberty, who is driving her chariot, Emancipation.

The Coming of Emancipation

At the beginning of the war, when the North still hoped for a quick and easy victory, only dedicated abolitionists favored turning the struggle for the Union into a crusade against slavery. In summer 1861, Congress almost unanimously affirmed that the war was being fought only to preserve the Union, not to change the domestic institutions of any state. But as it became clear how hard subduing the "rebels" was going to be, sentiment developed for striking at the South's economic and social system by freeing its slaves. In July 1862, Congress authorized the confiscation of slaves whose masters supported the Confederacy. By this time, the slaves themselves were voting for freedom with their feet by deserting plantations in areas where the Union forces were close enough to offer a haven. They thus put pressure on the government to determine their status and, in effect, offered themselves as a source of manpower to the Union on the condition that they be made free.

Although Lincoln favored freedom for blacks as an ultimate goal, he was reluctant to commit his administration to immediate emancipation. In the fall of 1861 and spring of 1862, he had reversed the orders of field commanders who sought to free slaves in areas their forces occupied, thus angering abolitionists and the strongly antislavery Republicans known as Radicals. Lincoln's caution stemmed from fear of alienating Unionists in the border slave states and from his own preference for a gradual, compensated form of emancipation.

Lincoln was also aware that the racial prejudice of most whites in the North and the South was an obstacle to any program leading to emancipation. Although personally more tolerant than most white Americans, Lincoln was pessimistic about equality for blacks in the United States. He therefore coupled a proposal for gradual emancipation with a plea for government subsidies to support the voluntary "colonization" of freed blacks outside of the United States, and he sought places that would accept them.

But the slaveholding states that remained loyal to the Union refused to endorse Lincoln's gradual plan, and the failure of Union arms in the 1862 increased the clamor for striking directly at the South's peculiar institution. The Lincoln administration also realized that emancipation would win sympathy for the Union cause in Britain and France and might counter the threat that they would come to the aid of the Confederacy. In July, Lincoln read an emancipation proclamation to his cabinet, but Secretary of State Seward persuaded him not to issue it until the North had won a victory and could not be accused of acting out of desperation.

Finally, on September 22, 1862, Lincoln issued his preliminary Emancipation Proclamation. McClellan's success at Antietam provided the occasion, but the president was also responding to political pressures. Most Republican politicians were now committed to emancipation, and many were on the verge of repudiating the administration for its inaction. Had Lincoln failed to act, his party would have split, and he would have been in the minority faction. The proclamation gave the Confederate states 100 days to give up the struggle without losing their slaves. In December, Lincoln proposed that Congress approve constitutional amendments providing for gradual, compensated emancipation and subsidized colonization.

Since there was no response from the South and little enthusiasm in Congress for Lincoln's gradual plan, the president went ahead on January 1, 1863, and declared that all slaves in those areas under Confederate control "shall be ... thenceforward, and forever free." He justified the final proclamation as an act of "military necessity" sanctioned by the war powers of the president, and he authorized the enlistment of freed slaves in the Union army. The language and tone of the document—one historian has described it as having "all the moral grandeur of a bill of lading"—made it clear that blacks were being freed for reasons of state and not out of humanitarian conviction.

Despite its uninspiring origin and limited application—it did not extend to slave states loyal to the Union or to occupied areas and thus did not immediately free a single slave—the proclamation did commit the Union to abolishing slavery as a war aim. It also accelerated the breakdown of slavery as a labor system, a process that was already under way by early 1863. The blacks who had remained in captured areas or deserted their masters to cross Union lines before 1863 had been kept in a kind of way station between slavery and freedom, in accordance with the theory that they were "contraband of war." As word spread among the slaves that emancipation was now official policy, more of them were inspired to run off and seek the protection of northern armies. One slave who crossed the Union lines summed up their motives: "I wants to

Read the Document
The Emancipation Proclamation (1863) on
myhistorylab.com

Quick Check

✓ Why was Lincoln skeptical of immediate emancipation, and what changed his mind?

be free. I came in from the plantation and don't want to go back; … I don't want to be a slave again." Approximately one-quarter of the slave population gained freedom during the war under the terms of the Emancipation Proclamation and thus deprived the South of an important part of its agricultural workforce.

African Americans and the War

Almost 200,000 African Americans, most of them newly freed slaves, eventually served in the Union forces and made a vital contribution to the North's victory. Without them it is doubtful that the Union could have been preserved. Although enrolled in segregated units under white officers, initially paid less than their white counterparts, and used disproportionately for garrison duty or heavy labor behind the lines, "blacks in blue" fought heroically in major battles during the last two years of the war.

Those freed during the war who did not serve in the military were often conscripted as contract wage laborers on cotton plantations that "loyal" white planters owned or leased within occupied areas of the Deep South. Abolitionists protested that the coercion military authorities used to get blacks back into the cotton fields amounted to slavery in a new form, but those in power argued that the necessities of war and the northern economy required such "temporary" arrangements. Regimentation of the freedmen within the South also assured racist northerners, especially in the Midwest, that emancipation would not result in a massive migration of black refugees to their region of the country.

Read the **Document**
H. Ford Douglas to Frederick Douglass's Monthly (1863) on **myhistorylab.com**

The heroic performance of African American troops and the easing of northern fears of being swamped by black migrants deepened the commitment to permanent and comprehensive emancipation. Realizing that his

Black Soldiers This 1890 lithograph by Kurz and Allison commemorates the 54th Massachusetts Colored Regiment charging Fort Wagner, South Carolina, in July 1863. The 54th was the first African-American unit recruited during the war. Charles and Lewis Douglass, sons of Frederick Douglass, served with this regiment.

proclamation had a shaky constitutional foundation and might apply only to slaves actually freed while the war was going on, Lincoln sought to organize and recognize loyal state governments in southern areas under Union control on condition that their constitutions abolished slavery.

Finally, Lincoln pressed for an amendment to the Constitution outlawing involuntary servitude. After supporting its inclusion as a central plank in the Republican platform of 1864, Lincoln won congressional approval for the Thirteenth Amendment, which was passed by Congress in January 1865 and ratified in December. The cause of freedom for blacks and the cause of the Union had at last become one and the same. Lincoln, despite his earlier hesitations and misgivings, had earned the right to be called the Great Emancipator.

Quick Check

✓ What effect did African American troops have on the war in battle and on the homefront?

The Tide Turns

By 1863, the Confederate economy was in shambles. The social order of the South was also buckling. Masters were losing control of their slaves, and non-slaveholding whites were becoming disillusioned with the hardships of what some described as "a rich man's war and a poor man's fight." Yet the North had its own morale problems. The long series of eastern defeats had engendered war weariness, and the new policies that "military necessity" forced the government to adopt encountered fierce opposition.

The Enrollment Act of March 1863, which provided for outright conscription of white males but permitted men to hire substitutes or pay a fee to avoid military service, provoked a violent response from those unable to buy their way out of

Read the **Document** *If it were Not For My Trust In Christ, I do Not* on **myhistorylab.com**

THE RIOTS IN NEW YORK: THE MOB LYNCHING A NEGRO IN CLARKSON-STREET.—SEE PAGE 142.

An 1863 draft call in New York provoked violence against African Americans, viewed by the rioters as the cause of an unnecessary war, and rage against the rich men who had been able to buy exemptions from the draft. This 1863 illustration from *Harper's Weekly* depicts a mob lynching a black man on Clarkson Street in New York City.

service and unwilling to fight for blacks. Antidraft riots broke out, culminating in one of the bloodiest domestic disorders in American history—the New York Riot of July 1863. The New York mob, composed mainly of Irish-American laborers, burned the draft offices, the homes of Republicans, and a black orphanage. They also lynched more than a dozen defenseless blacks. At least 120 people died before federal troops restored order. Besides racial prejudice, the draft riots also reflected working-class anger at the wartime privileges and prosperity of the middle and upper classes; they exposed deep divisions on the administration's conduct of the war.

To fight dissension and "disloyalty," the government used martial law to arrest a few alleged ringleaders, including Democratic Congressman Clement Vallandigham of Ohio. Private organizations also issued propaganda attacking what they believed was a vast secret conspiracy to undermine the northern war effort. Historians disagree about the extent of covert and illegal antiwar activity. No vast conspiracy existed, but militant advocates of "peace at any price"— popularly known as Copperheads—were active in some areas, especially among the immigrant working classes of large cities and in southern Ohio, Indiana, and Illinois.

The only effective way to overcome the disillusionment that fed the peace movement was to win battles and convince the northern public that victory was assured. Before this could happen, the North suffered another humiliating defeat in the East. In May 1863, a Confederate army less than half their size routed Union forces under General Joseph Hooker at Chancellorsville, Virginia. Again, Lee demonstrated his superior generalship, this time by dividing his forces and sending Stonewall Jackson to make a surprise attack on the Union right. The Confederacy prevailed, but Jackson himself died from wounds received in the battle.

In the West, however, a major Union triumph was taking shape. For more than a year, General Ulysses S. Grant had been trying to capture Vicksburg, Mississippi, the almost inaccessible Confederate bastion that stood between the North and control of the Mississippi River. Finally, in late March 1863, he crossed to the west bank north of the city and moved his forces to south of it, where he joined up with naval forces that had run the Confederate batteries mounted on Vicksburg's high bluffs. In one of the boldest campaigns of the war, Grant crossed the river, deliberately cutting himself off from his sources of supply, and marched into the interior of Mississippi. Living off the land and out of communication with an anxious and perplexed Lincoln, his troops defeated two Confederate armies and advanced on Vicksburg from the east. After unsuccessfully assaulting the city, Grant settled down for a siege on May 22.

Meanwhile, President Davis approved Lee's plan to invade the Northeast. Although this would not relieve Vicksburg, it might win a victory that would more than compensate for the probable loss of the Mississippi stronghold. Lee's army crossed the Potomac in June and kept going until it reached Gettysburg, Pennsylvania. There Lee confronted a Union army that had taken up defensive positions on Cemetery Ridge and Culp's Hill.

On July 2, Confederate attacks failed to dislodge Union troops from the high ground they occupied. The following day, Lee decided to attack the strongest part of the Union line. The resulting charge on Cemetery Ridge was disastrous; Confederate soldiers dropped like flies under Union fire. The few who made it to the Union lines were killed or captured. Lee withdrew his battered troops, but because the Union army did not pursue him vigorously, he escaped again. Vicksburg fell to Grant on July 4, the same day Lee began his retreat. Northerners rejoiced that on Independence Day, the Union had secured control of the Mississippi and had finally won a major battle in the East. But Lincoln's joy turned to frustration when he learned his generals had missed the chance to end to the war.

View the **Image**
Confederate Captives Gettysburg, Matthew Brady on **myhistorylab.com**

Quick Check

✓ How did the tide turn against the Confederate army in the middle of 1863?

Last Stages of the Conflict

In 1863, the North also finally gained control of the middle South, where indecisive fighting had been going on since the conflict began. The main Union target was Chattanooga, "the gateway to the Southeast." In September, Union troops managed to maneuver the Confederates out of the city but were in turn surrounded and besieged there by southern forces. Grant arrived from Vicksburg to break the encirclement with assaults on the Confederate positions on Lookout Mountain and Missionary Ridge. The North was now poised to invade Georgia.

Grant's victories in the West earned him promotion to general in chief of the Union armies. In March 1864, he ordered a multipronged offensive to finish off the Confederacy. Its main movements were a thrust on Richmond under Grant's personal command and another by the western armies, under General William Tecumseh Sherman, toward Atlanta and the heart of Georgia.

View the **Map**
The Civil War Part II: 1863–1865 on **myhistorylab.com**

In May and June, Grant and Lee fought a series of bloody battles in northern Virginia that tended to follow a set pattern. Lee would take up an entrenched position in the path of the invading force, and Grant would attack it, sustaining heavy losses but also inflicting casualties the Confederate army could ill afford. When his direct assault had failed, Grant would move to his left, hoping in vain to maneuver Lee into a less defensible position. In the battles of the Wilderness, Spotsylvania, and Cold Harbor, the Union lost about 60,000 men—more than twice the number of Confederate casualties—without opening the road to Richmond. After losing thousands of soldiers in three days at Cold Harbor, Grant moved his army south of Richmond. There he drew up before Petersburg, a rail center that linked Richmond to the rest of the Confederacy; after failing to take it by assault, he settled down for another siege.

The siege of Petersburg was a drawn-out affair, and northern morale plummeted during the summer of 1864. Lincoln was facing reelection, and his failure to end the war dimmed his prospects. Although nominated with ease in June—with Andrew Johnson, a pro-administration Democrat from Tennessee, as his running mate—Lincoln confronted growing opposition within his own party, especially from Radicals who disagreed with his lenient approach to restoring seceded states to the Union (see Chapter 16).

TABLE 15.1	The Election of 1864		
Candidate	**Party**	**Popular Vote**	**Electoral Vote***
Lincoln	Republican	2,213,655	212
McClellan	Democratic	1,805,237	21

*Out of a total of 233 electoral votes. The 11 secessionist states—Alabama, Arkansas, Florida, Georgia, Louisiana, Mississippi, North Carolina, South Carolina, Tennessee, Texas, and Virginia—did not vote.

The Democrats made a strong bid for the White House. Their platform appealed to war weariness by calling for a cease-fire followed by negotiations to reestablish the Union. The party's nominee, General George McClellan, announced he would not be bound by the peace plank and would pursue the war. But he promised to end the conflict sooner than Lincoln could because he would not insist on emancipation as a condition for reunion. By late summer, Lincoln thought that he would lose.

But northern victories changed the political outlook. Sherman's invasion of Georgia went well. On September 2, Atlanta fell, and northern forces occupied the hub of the Deep South. The news unified the Republican party behind Lincoln. The election itself was almost an anticlimax: Lincoln won 212 of a possible 233 electoral votes and 55 percent of the popular vote. The Republican cause of "liberty and Union" was secure. (See Table 15.1)

The concluding military operations revealed the futility of further southern resistance. Sherman marched unopposed through Georgia to the sea, destroying almost everything of military or economic value in a corridor 300 miles long and 60 miles wide. The Confederate army that had opposed him at Atlanta moved into Tennessee, where Union forces almost destroyed it at Nashville in mid-December. Sherman captured Savannah on December 25. He then carried his scorched-earth policy into South Carolina with the aim of continuing through North Carolina and joining up with Grant at Petersburg.

While Sherman was invading the Carolinas, Grant finally forced the starving and exhausted Confederates to abandon Petersburg and Richmond on April 2, 1865. Grant then pursued them west for 100 miles, and cut off their line of retreat to the south. Recognizing the hopelessness of further resistance, Lee surrendered his army at Appomattox Courthouse on April 9. (See Map 15.2)

But the joy of the victorious North turned to sorrow and anger when John Wilkes Booth, a pro-Confederate actor, assassinated Abraham Lincoln as the president watched a play at Ford's Theater in Washington on April 14. Although Booth had a few accomplices, popular theories that the assassination was the result of a vast conspiracy involving Confederate leaders or Radical Republicans have never been substantiated.

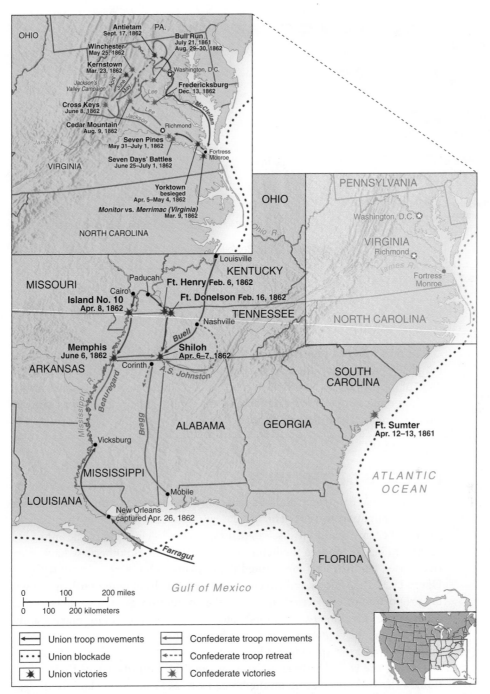

Map 15.2 Civil War, 1861–1865 In the western theater of war, Grant's victories at Port Gibson, Jackson, and Champion's Hill cleared the way for his siege of Vicksburg. In the east, after the hard-won Union victory at Gettysburg, the South never again invaded the North. In 1864 and 1865, Union armies gradually closed in on Lee's Confederate forces in Virginia. Leaving Atlanta in flames, Sherman marched to the Georgia coast, took Savannah, then moved his troops north through the Carolinas. Grant's army, though suffering enormous losses, moved on toward Richmond, marching into the Confederate capital on April 3, 1865, and forcing surrender.

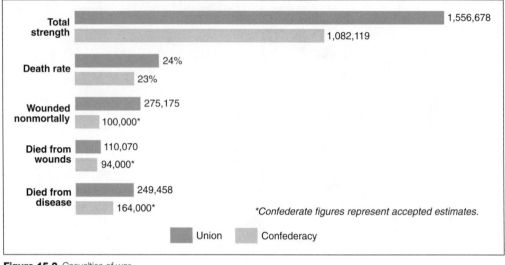

Figure 15.2 Casualties of war

Quick Check

✓ How did Generals
Grant and Sherman
affect the election of
1864?

The man who had spoken of the need to sacrifice for the Union cause at Gettysburg had himself given "the last full measure of devotion" to the cause of "government of the people, by the people, for the people." Four days after Lincoln's death, the only remaining Confederate force of any significance laid down its arms in North Carolina. The Union was saved.

EFFECTS OF THE WAR

How did the
outcome of the
war affect America
socially and
politically?

The nation that emerged from four years of total war was not the same America that had split apart in 1861. The 618,000 young men who were in their graves, victims of enemy fire or the diseases that spread rapidly in military encampments in this era before modern medicine and sanitation, would otherwise have married, raised families, and contributed their talents to building the country. (See Figure 15.2) The widows and sweethearts they left behind temporarily increased the proportion of unmarried women in the population. Some members of this generation of involuntary "spinsters" sought new opportunities for making a living or serving the community that went beyond the purely domestic roles previously prescribed for women.

During the war, northern women pushed the boundaries of their traditional roles by participating on the home front as fund-raisers and in the rear lines as army nurses and members of the Sanitary Commission. The Sanitary Commission promoted health in the northern army's camps through attention to cleanliness, nutrition, and medical care. Northern women simultaneously utilized their traditional position as nurturers to participate in the war effort while they advanced new ideas about their role in society. The many who had served as nurses or volunteer workers during the war were especially responsive to calls for broadening "the woman's sphere." Some northern women who were prominent in wartime service organizations led postwar philanthropic and reform movements. The war did not destroy the traditional barriers to sexual equality in American society, but women's efforts during the Civil War broadened beliefs about what women could accomplish outside of the home.

The war had a different effect on white women in the Confederacy. Southern women had always been involved in administering farms and plantations, but the war forced them to shoulder even greater burdens. Wealthy plantation mistresses had to run huge plantations without the benefit of extensive training or the assistance of male relatives. Farmers' wives found it hard to survive at all, especially at harvest time when they often had to do all the work themselves. The loss of fathers and brothers, the advance of Union troops, and the difficulty of controlling a slave labor force destroyed many southern women's allegiance to the Confederate cause. As in the North, the Civil War changed the situation of women in society. The devastation of the southern economy forced many women to play a more conspicuous public and economic role. They formed associations to assist returning soldiers, became teachers, and established benevolent and reform societies or temperance organizations. Although these changes created a more visible presence for southern women in public, the South remained more conservative in its views about women's "proper place" than did the North.

At enormous human and economic cost, the nation had emancipated four million African Americans from slavery, but it had not yet resolved that they would be equal citizens. At the time of Lincoln's assassination, most northern states still denied blacks equality under the law and the right to vote. Whether the North would extend more rights to southern freedmen than it had granted to "free Negroes" was an open question.

The impact of the war on white working people was also unclear. Those in the industrializing parts of the North had suffered and lost ground economically because prices had risen faster than wages during the conflict. But Republican rhetoric stressing "equal opportunity" and the "dignity of labor" raised hopes that the crusade against slavery could be broadened into a movement to improve the lot of working people in general. Foreign-born workers had additional reason to be optimistic; that so many immigrants had fought and died for the Union cause had—for the moment—weakened nativist sentiment and encouraged tolerance.

What the war definitely decided was that the federal government was supreme over the states and had broad constitutional authority to act for "the general welfare." The southern principle of state sovereignty and strict construction died at Appomattox. The United States was becoming a true nation-state with an effective central government. States still had primary responsibility for most government functions, and the Constitution limited what the national government could do; questions would continue to arise about where federal authority

Watch the **Video**
The Lives Of Southern Women on
myhistorylab.com

ended and states' rights began. Still, the war had determined where ultimate authority rested.

A broadened definition of federal powers had its greatest impact in economic policy. During the war, the Republican-dominated Congresses passed legislation to stimulate and direct the nation's economic development. Taking advantage of the absence of southern opposition, Republicans rejected the pre–Civil War tradition of virtual laissez-faire and enacted a Whiggish program of active support for business and agriculture. In 1862, Congress passed a high protective tariff, approved a homestead act to encourage settlement of the West by providing free land to settlers, granted huge tracts of public land to railroads to support building a transcontinental railroad, and gave the states land for agricultural colleges. In 1863, Congress set up a national banking system that required member banks to keep adequate reserves and invest one-third of their capital in government securities. The notes the national banks issued became the country's first standardized and reliable circulating paper currency.

These wartime achievements decisively shifted the relationship between the federal government and private enterprise. The Republicans changed a limited government that sought to do little more than protect the marketplace from the threat of monopoly into an activist state that promoted and subsidized the ambitious and industrious.

CONCLUSION: AN ORGANIZATIONAL REVOLUTION

The most pervasive effect of the war on northern society was to encourage an "organizational revolution." Aided by government policies, venturesome businessmen took advantage of the new national market military procurement created to build larger firms that could operate across state lines; some of the huge corporate enterprises of the postwar era began to take shape. Philanthropists also developed more effective national associations; the most notable of these were the Sanitary and Christian Commissions that ministered to the physical and spiritual needs of the troops. Efforts to care for the wounded influenced the development of the modern hospital and the rise of nursing as a female profession. Both the men who served in the army and those men and women who supported them behind the lines became accustomed to working in large, bureaucratic organizations that had scarcely existed before the war.

The North won the war mainly because it had shown a greater capacity than the South to organize, innovate, and "modernize." Its victory meant the nation as a whole would now embrace the concept of progress that the North had affirmed in its war effort—its advances in science and technology and its success in bringing together and managing large numbers of men and women for economic and social goals. The Civil War was thus a catalyst for the transformation of American society from an individualistic society of small producers into the more highly organized and "incorporated" America of the late nineteenth century.

15 STUDY RESOURCES

((•—Listen to the **Chapter Audio** for Chapter 15 on **myhistorylab.com**

TIMELINE

1860 South Carolina secedes from the Union (December), p. 361

1861 Rest of Deep South secedes, p. 361
- Confederacy founded (January–February), p. 361
- Confederate forces fire on Fort Sumter (April), p. 364
- Upper South secedes (April–May), p. 365
- South wins first Battle of Bull Run (July), p. 370

1862 Grant captures forts Henry and Donelson (February), p. 370
- Union navy captures New Orleans (April), p. 370
- McClellan leads unsuccessful campaign on the peninsula (March–July), p. 371
- McClellan stops Lee at Battle of Antietam (September), p. 371
- Lee defeats Union army at Fredericksburg (December), p. 371

1863 Lincoln issues Emancipation Proclamation (January), p. 373
- North gains major victories at Gettysburg and Vicksburg (July), p. 377
- Grant defeats Confederate forces at Chattanooga (November), p. 377

1864 Grant and Lee battle in northern Virginia (May–June), p. 377
- Atlanta falls to Sherman (September), p. 378
- Lincoln reelected president (November), p. 378
- Sherman marches through Georgia (November–December), p. 378

1865 Grant captures Petersburg and Richmond; Lee surrenders at Appomattox (April), p. 378

- Lincoln assassinated by John Wilkes Booth (April), p. 378

CHAPTER REVIEW

THE STORM GATHERS

What developments and events drew the Union toward Civil War?

Lincoln's election prompted the secession of seven states. In South Carolina, "cooperationism" was defeated, sparking other states to follow. Republicans rejected compromise on the question of slavery in new states, and Lincoln resolved to use force should the South strike first. At Fort Sumter in 1861 it did. *(p. 361)*

ADJUSTING TO TOTAL WAR

What challenges did "total war" bring for each side?

Total war meant no cease-fire until the southern separatists were defeated. The North, with its large population, heavy industry, and agriculture, was better suited for the long conflict. The South struggled to feed itself and lacked wealth, yet put up a strong fight. Meanwhile, Lincoln maintained northern unity. *(p. 367)*

FIGHT TO THE FINISH

How did the Union finally attain victory, and what role did emancipation play in it?

Lincoln was skeptical of emancipation, although he favored it morally. Later he saw the strategic benefit of opposing slavery, so he declared the freedom of slaves in unoccupied areas in the January 1863 Emancipation Proclamation. Many African Americans escaped slavery and joined the Union Army, helping to turn the tide of the war. Union victories helped reelect Lincoln in 1864. *(p. 371)*

EFFECTS OF THE WAR

How did the outcome of the war affect America socially and politically?

The Civil War changed the status of many social groups, including women, who took on new social roles after the death of male family members, and blacks, who were adjusting to free status in a white society. New national institutions, including benevolent organizations and banks, contributed to an "organizational revolution." The federal government grew stronger than ever. *(p. 380)*

KEY TERM QUESTIONS

1. Why did the cooperationists lose out to those who advocated immediate secession? (p. 361)

2. Why was the Crittenden compromise rejected? (p. 363)

3. Why did the Union issue greenbacks beginning in 1862? (p. 368)

4. Why did Lincoln issue the Emancipation Proclamation? (p. 373)

5. How did the government deal with Copperheads and others indifferent or hostile to the Union in the Civil War? (p. 376)

6. What was the Sanitary Commission during the Civil War? (p. 380)

MyHistoryLab Connections

Visit **www.myhistorylab.com** for a customized Study Plan to build your knowledge of *Secession and the Civil War*

Question for Analysis

1. Did the South's idea of what caused the Civil War change after the war?

    Watch the **Video** *What Caused the Civil War?* p. 361

2. How did the Emancipation Proclamation alter the wartime objectives of the Union?

   Read the **Document** *Emancipation Proclamation* p. 373

3. What were the key battles of the Civil War from 1863 to 1865?

   View the **Map** *The Civil War Part II, 1863-1865* p. 377

Other Resources from this Chapter

Read the **Document** *South Carolina Declaration of the Causes*

Read the **Document** *Confederate Constitution, 1861*

View the **Image** *Ft. Sumter*

Read the **Document** *Diary of Joseph Addison Waddell*

View the **Map** *The Civil War, 1861-1862*

Read the **Document** *H. Ford Douglas to Fredrick Douglass*

4. What factors impacted the lives of southern women in the period leading up to the Civil War?

👁 **Watch** the **Video** *The Lives of Southern Women* p. 382

📖 **Read** the **Document** *"If It Were Not For My Trust in Christ I Do Not Know How I Could Have Endured It"*

🔍 **View** the **Image** *Confederate Captives, Gettysburg, Matthew Brady*

16 The Agony of Reconstruction

1863–1877

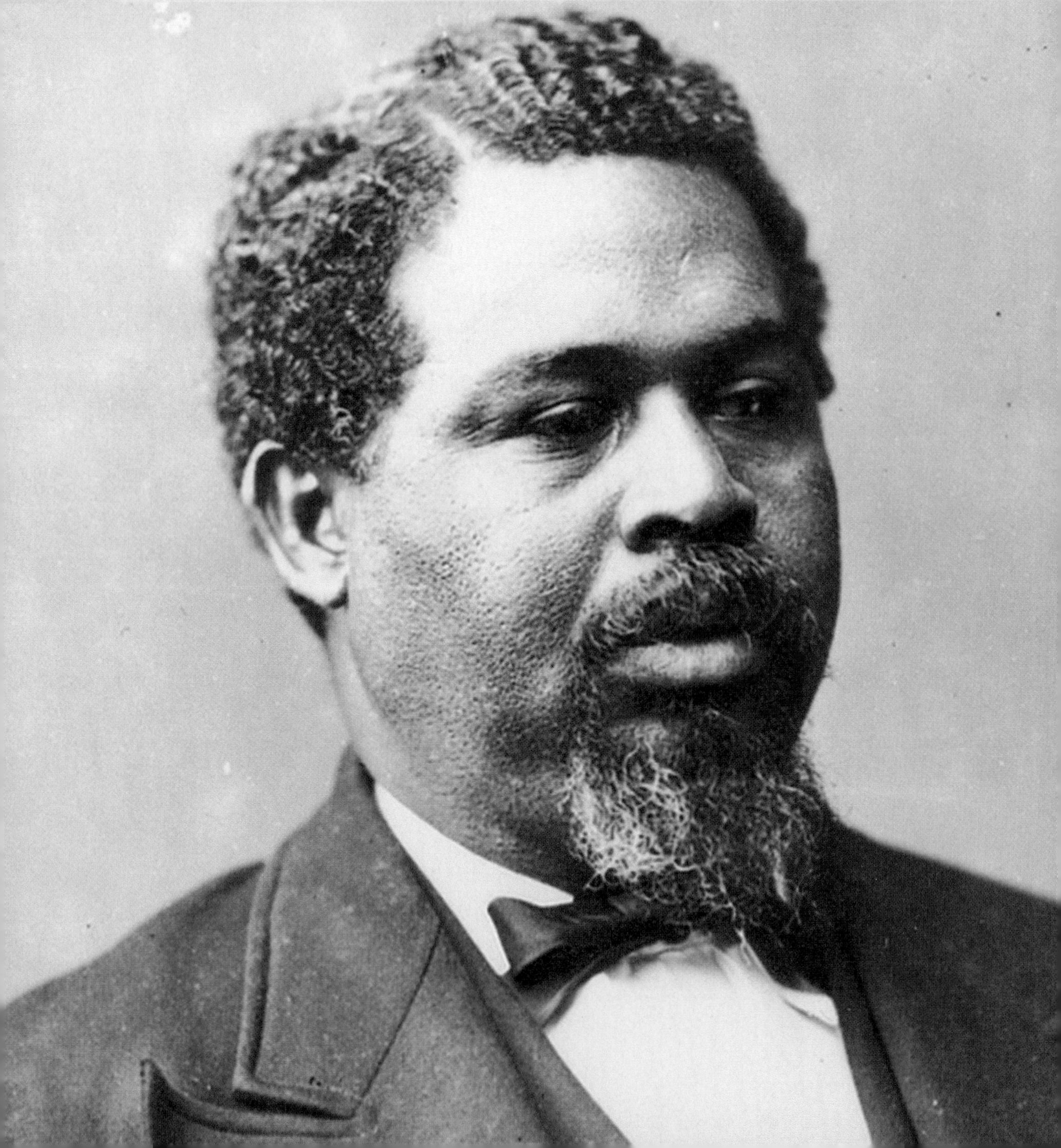

Contents and Spotlight Questions

THE PRESIDENT VERSUS CONGRESS PG. 389

What conflicts arose among Lincoln, Johnson, and Congress during Reconstruction?

RECONSTRUCTING SOUTHERN SOCIETY PG. 397

What problems did southern society face during Reconstruction?

RETREAT FROM RECONSTRUCTION PG. 405

Why did Reconstruction end?

REUNION AND THE NEW SOUTH PG. 408

Who benefited and who suffered from the reconciliation of the North and South?

((•—⌐ **Listen** to the **Chapter Audio** for Chapter 16 on **myhistorylab.com**

ROBERT SMALLS AND BLACK POLITICIANS DURING RECONSTRUCTION

During the Reconstruction period immediately following the Civil War, African Americans struggled to become equal citizens of a democratic republic. Remarkable black leaders won public office. Robert Smalls of South Carolina was perhaps the most famous and widely respected southern black leader of the era.

Born a slave in 1839, Smalls was allowed as a young man to live and work independently, hiring his own time from a master who may have been his half brother. Smalls worked as a sailor and trained

Robert Smalls With the help of several black crewmen, Robert Smalls—then twenty-three years old—commandeered the Planter, a Confederate steamship used to transport guns and ammunition, and surrendered it to the Union vessel, USS Onward. Smalls provided distinguished service to the Union during the Civil War and after the war went on to become a successful politician and businessman.

himself to be a pilot in Charleston Harbor. When the Union navy blockaded Charleston in 1862, Smalls, who was working on a Confederate steamship called the *Planter*, saw a chance to win his freedom. At three o'clock in the morning on May 13, 1862, when the white officers were ashore, he took command of the vessel and its slave crew, sailed it out of the fortified harbor, and surrendered it to the Union navy. Smalls immediately became a hero to antislavery northerners who were seeking evidence that the slaves were willing and able to serve the Union. The *Planter* became a Union army transport, and Smalls was made its captain after being commissioned as an officer. During the remainder of the war, he rendered conspicuous and gallant service as captain and pilot of Union vessels off the coast of South Carolina.

Like other African Americans who fought for the Union, Smalls had a distinguished political career during Reconstruction, serving in the South Carolina constitutional convention, the state legislature, and the U.S. Congress. He was also a shrewd businessman and owned extensive properties in Beaufort, South Carolina, and its vicinity. The electoral organization Smalls established was so effective that he controlled local government and was elected to Congress even after the election of 1876 had placed the state under the control of white conservatives bent on depriving blacks of political power. Organized mob violence defeated him in 1878, but he bounced back to win a contested congressional election in 1880. He did not leave the House of Representatives for good until 1886, when he lost another contested election.

To defeat him, Smalls's white opponents charged that he had a hand in the corruption that was allegedly rampant in South Carolina during Reconstruction. But careful historical investigation shows that he was, by the standards of the time, an honest and responsible public servant. In the South Carolina convention of 1868 and in the state legislature, he championed free and compulsory public education. In Congress, he fought for federal civil rights laws. Not especially radical on social questions, he sometimes bent over backward to accommodate what he regarded as the legitimate interests and sensibilities of South Carolina whites. Like other middle-class black political leaders in Reconstruction-era South Carolina, he can perhaps be faulted for not doing more to help poor blacks gain access to land of their own. But in 1875, he sponsored congressional legislation that opened for purchase at low prices the land in his own district that the federal government had confiscated during the war. As a result, blacks soon owned three-fourths of the land in the Beaufort area.

Robert Smalls spent the later years of his life as U.S. collector of customs for the port of Beaufort, a beneficiary of the patronage that the Republican party continued to provide for a few loyal southern blacks. But the loss of real political clout for Smalls and men like him was a tragic consequence of the fall of Reconstruction.

For a few years, black politicians such as Robert Smalls exercised more power in the South than they would for another century. But political developments on the national and regional stage made Reconstruction "an unfinished revolution," promising but not delivering true equality for newly freed African Americans. National party politics; shifting priorities among northern Republicans; white southerners' commitment to white supremacy, which was backed by legal restrictions and massive extralegal violence against blacks, all combined to stifle the promise of Reconstruction.

Yet during the Reconstruction era, American society was transformed—new ways of organizing labor and family life, new institutions within and outside the government, and new ideologies about the role of institutions and government in social and economic life. Many of the changes begun during Reconstruction would revolutionize American life.

THE PRESIDENT VERSUS CONGRESS

Reconstructing the Union after the South's defeat was one of the most difficult challenges American policymakers ever faced. The Constitution provided no firm guidelines, for the Framers had not anticipated that the country would divide into warring sections. After emancipation became a northern war aim, a new issue compounded the problem: How far should the federal government go to secure freedom and civil rights for 4 million former slaves?

What conflicts arose among Lincoln, Johnson, and Congress during Reconstruction?

The debate led to a major political crisis. Advocates of a minimal Reconstruction policy favored quickly restoring the Union with no protection for the freed slaves except prohibiting slavery. Proponents of a more radical policy demanded guarantees that "loyal" men would displace the Confederate elite in power and that blacks would acquire basic rights of American citizenship as preconditions for readmitting the southern states. The White House favored the minimal approach. Congress came to endorse the more radical and thoroughgoing form of Reconstruction. The resulting struggle between Congress and the chief executive was the most serious clash between two branches of government in the nation's history.

Wartime Reconstruction

Tension between the president and Congress over how to reconstruct the Union began during the war. Preoccupied with achieving victory, Lincoln never set forth a final and comprehensive plan to bring rebellious states back into the fold. But he favored a lenient and conciliatory policy toward southerners who would give up the struggle and repudiate slavery. In December 1863, he issued a Proclamation of Amnesty and Reconstruction, which offered a full pardon to all southerners (except certain Confederate leaders) who would take an oath of allegiance to the Union and accept emancipation. This Ten Percent Plan provided that once ten percent or more of the voting population of any occupied state had taken the oath, they could set up a loyal government. By 1864, Louisiana and Arkansas, states that Union troops occupied, had established Unionist governments. Lincoln's policy was meant to shorten the war. He hoped to weaken the southern cause by making it easy for disillusioned or lukewarm

Confederates to switch sides and support emancipation by insisting that the new governments abolish slavery.

Congress was unhappy with Lincoln's Reconstruction experiments and in 1864 refused to seat the Unionists that Louisiana and Arkansas elected to the House and Senate. A minority of congressional Republicans—the strongly antislavery Radical Republicans—favored protection for black rights (especially black male suffrage) as a precondition for readmitting southern states. But a larger group of congressional moderates opposed Lincoln's plan because they did not trust the repentant Confederates who would play a major role in the new governments. Congress also believed the president was exceeding his authority by using executive powers to restore the Union. Lincoln operated on the theory that secession, being illegal, did not place the Confederate states outside the Union in a constitutional sense. Since individuals and not states had defied federal authority, the president could use his pardoning power to certify a loyal electorate, which could then function as the legitimate state government.

After refusing to recognize Lincoln's ten percent governments, Congress passed a Reconstruction bill of its own in July 1864. Known as the Wade-Davis Bill, it required that 50 percent of the voters take a loyalty oath before the restoration process could begin. Once this had occurred, those who could swear they had never willingly supported the Confederacy could vote in an election for delegates to a constitutional convention. The bill did not require black suffrage, but it gave federal courts the power to enforce emancipation. Faced with this attempt to nullify his own program, Lincoln exercised a pocket veto by refusing to sign the bill before Congress adjourned. He said that he did not want to be committed to any single Reconstruction plan. The bill's sponsors responded angrily, and Lincoln's relations with Congress reached their low point.

Congress and the president remained stalemated on the Reconstruction issue for the rest of the war. During his last months in office, however, Lincoln showed a willingness to compromise. He tried to obtain recognition for the governments he had nurtured in Louisiana and Arkansas but seemed receptive to setting other conditions—perhaps including black suffrage—for readmitting those states in which wartime conditions had prevented execution of his plan. However, he was assassinated before he made his intentions clear, leaving historians to speculate whether his quarrel with Congress would have been resolved. Given Lincoln's record of flexibility, the best bet is that he would have come to terms with the majority of his party.

Quick Check

✓ On what matters did Lincoln and Congress disagree?

Andrew Johnson at the Helm

Andrew Johnson, the man an assassin's bullet suddenly made president, attempted to put the Union back together on his own authority in 1865. But his policies set him at odds with Congress and the Republican party and provoked the most serious crisis in the history of relations between the executive and legislative branches of the federal government.

Johnson's background shaped his approach to Reconstruction. Born in poverty in North Carolina, he migrated to eastern Tennessee, where he worked as a tailor. Lacking formal schooling, he was illiterate until adult life. Entering politics as a Jacksonian Democrat, his railing against the planter aristocracy made him the spokesman for Tennessee's non-slaveholding whites and the most successful politician in the state. He advanced from state legislator to congressman to governor and then the U.S. Senate in 1857.

In 1861, Johnson was the only senator from a Confederate state who remained loyal to the Union and continued to serve in Washington. But his Unionism and defense of the common people did not include antislavery sentiments. Nor was he friendly to blacks. In Tennessee, he had objected only to the fact that slaveholding was the privilege of a wealthy minority. He wished that "every head of family in the United States had one slave to take the drudgery and menial service off his family."

During the war, while acting as military governor of Tennessee, Johnson endorsed Lincoln's emancipation policy to destroy the power of the hated planter class rather than as a recognition of black humanity. He was chosen as Lincoln's running mate in 1864 because a pro-administration Democrat, who was a southern Unionist in the bargain, would strengthen the ticket. No one expected this fervent white supremacist to become president. Radical Republicans initially welcomed Johnson's ascent to the nation's highest office. Their hopes made sense given Johnson's fierce loyalty to the Union and his apparent agreement with the Radicals that ex-Confederates should be severely treated. Unlike Lincoln, who had spoken of "malice toward none and charity for all," Johnson seemed likely to punish southern "traitors" and prevent them from regaining political influence. Only gradually did the deep disagreement between the president and the Republican congressional majority become evident.

View the Image
Andrew Johnson Brady on
myhistorylab.com

The Reconstruction policy that Johnson initiated on May 29, 1865, created uneasiness among the Radicals, but most Republicans were willing to give it a chance. Johnson placed North Carolina, and eventually other states, under appointed provisional governors chosen mostly from among prominent southern politicians who had opposed the secession movement and had rendered no conspicuous service to the Confederacy. The governors were responsible for calling constitutional conventions and ensuring that only "loyal" whites could vote for delegates. Participation required taking the oath of allegiance that Lincoln had prescribed earlier. Confederate leaders and officeholders had to apply for individual presidential pardons to regain their political and property rights. Johnson made one significant addition to the list of the excluded: all those possessing taxable property exceeding $20,000 in value. He thus sought to prevent his longtime adversaries—the wealthy planters—from participating in the Reconstruction of southern state governments.

Johnson urged the convention delegates to declare the ordinances of secession illegal, repudiate the Confederate debt, and ratify the Thirteenth Amendment abolishing slavery. After governments had been reestablished under constitutions meeting these conditions, the president assumed that the Reconstruction process would be complete and that the ex-Confederate states could regain their full rights under the Constitution.

Read the
Document
*The Mississippi Black
Code (1865)* on
myhistorylab.com

The results of the conventions, which prewar Unionists and backcountry yeoman farmers dominated, were satisfactory to the president but troubling to many congressional Republicans. Delegates in several states approved Johnson's recommendations only grudgingly or with qualifications. Furthermore, all the constitutions limited suffrage to whites, disappointing the many northerners who hoped, as Lincoln had, that at least some African Americans—perhaps those who were educated or had served in the Union army—would be given the vote. Republican uneasiness turned to anger when the new state legislatures passed Black Codes restricting the freedom of former slaves. Especially troubling were vagrancy and apprenticeship laws that forced African Americans to work and denied them a free choice of employers. Blacks in some states could not testify in court on the same basis as whites and were subject to a separate penal code. The Black Codes looked like slavery under a new guise. More upsetting to northern public opinion in general was the election of prominent ex-Confederates to Congress in 1865.

Johnson himself was partly responsible for these events. Despite his lifelong feud with the planter class, he was generous in granting pardons to members of the old elite who came to him, hat in hand, and asked for them. When former Confederate Vice President Alexander Stephens and other proscribed ex-rebels were elected to Congress even though they had not been pardoned, Johnson granted them special amnesty so they could serve.

Quick Check

✓ Why did Northerners and Republicans grow uneasy and disillusioned with Johnson's approach to reconstruction?

The growing rift between the president and Congress came into the open in December, when the House and Senate refused to seat the recently elected southern delegations. Instead of recognizing the state governments Johnson had called into being, Congress established a joint committee to review Reconstruction policy and set further conditions for readmitting the seceded states.

Congress Takes the Initiative

The struggle over how to reconstruct the Union ended with Congress setting policy all over again. The clash between Johnson and Congress was a matter of principle and could not be reconciled. Johnson, an heir of the Democratic states' rights tradition, wanted to restore the prewar federal system as quickly as possible and without change except that states would not have the right to legalize slavery or to secede.

Most Republicans wanted guarantees that the old southern ruling class would not regain regional power and national influence by devising new ways to subjugate blacks. They favored a Reconstruction policy that would give the federal government authority to limit the political role of ex-Confederates and protect black citizenship.

Republican leaders—except for a few extreme Radicals such as Charles Sumner—lacked any firm conviction that blacks were inherently equal to whites. They did believe, however, that in a modern democratic state, all citizens must have the same basic rights and opportunities, regardless of natural abilities. Principle coincided with political expediency; southern blacks, whatever their alleged shortcomings, were likely to be loyal to the Republican party that had emancipated them and thus increase that party's power in the South.

The disagreement between the president and Congress became irreconcilable in early 1866, when Johnson vetoed two bills that had passed with overwhelming Republican support. The first extended the life of the Freedmen's Bureau—a temporary agency set up to provide relief, education, legal help, and assistance in obtaining land or work to former slaves. The second was a civil rights bill to nullify the Black Codes and guarantee to freedmen "full and equal benefit of all laws and proceedings for the security of person and property as is enjoyed by white citizens."

Johnson's vetoes shocked moderate Republicans. He succeeded in blocking the Freedmen's Bureau bill, although a modified version later passed. But his veto of the Civil Rights Act was overridden, signifying that the president was now hopelessly at odds with most of the legislators from what was supposed to be his own party. Congress had not overridden a presidential veto since Franklin Pierce was president in the early 1850s.

Johnson soon revealed that he intended to place himself at the head of a new conservative party uniting the few Republicans who supported him with a reviving Democratic party that was rallying behind his Reconstruction policy. In preparation for the elections of 1866, Johnson helped found the National Union movement to promote his plan to readmit the southern states to the Union without further qualifications. A National Union convention in Philadelphia called for electing men to Congress who endorsed the presidential plan for Reconstruction.

Meanwhile, the Republican majority on Capitol Hill, fearing that Johnson would not enforce civil rights legislation or that the courts would declare such laws unconstitutional, passed the Fourteenth Amendment. This, perhaps the most important of all the constitutional amendments, gave the federal government responsibility for guaranteeing equal rights under the law to all Americans. Section 1 defined national citizenship for the first time as extending to "all persons born or naturalized in the United States." The states were prohibited from abridging the rights of American citizens and could not "deprive any person of life, liberty, or property, without due process of law; nor deny to any person ... equal protection of the laws." The amendment was sent to the states with the understanding that southerners would have no chance of being readmitted to Congress unless their states ratified it. (See Table 16.1)

The congressional elections of 1866 served as a referendum on the Fourteenth Amendment. Johnson opposed the amendment on the grounds that it created a "centralized" government and denied states the right to manage their own affairs; he also counseled southern state legislatures to reject it, and all except Tennessee followed his advice. But bloody race riots in New Orleans and Memphis weakened the president's case for state autonomy. These and other atrocities against blacks made it clear that the southern state governments were failing abysmally to protect the "life, liberty, or property" of the ex-slaves.

Read the
Document
*Thirteenth, Four-
teenth, and Fifteenth
Amendments* on
myhistorylab.com

TABLE 16.1   Reconstruction Amendments, 1865–1870

Amendment	Main Provisions	Congressional Passage (2/3 majority in each house required)	Ratification Process (3/4 of all states required, including ex-Confederate states)
13	Slavery prohibited in United States	January 1865	December 1865 (27 states, including 8 southern states)
14	National citizenship; state representation in Congress reduced proportionally to number of voters disfranchised; former Confederates denied right to hold office; Confederate debt repudiated	June 1866	Rejected by 12 southern and border states, February 1867; Radicals make readmission of southern states hinge on ratification; ratified July 1868
15	Denial of franchise because of race, color, or past servitude explicitly prohibited	February 1869	Ratification required for readmission of Virginia, Texas, Mississippi, Georgia; ratified March 1870

Johnson further hurt his cause by taking the stump on behalf of candidates who supported his policies. In his notorious "swing around the circle," he toured the nation, slandering his opponents in crude language and engaging in undignified exchanges with hecklers. Enraged by southern inflexibility and the antics of a president who acted as if he were still campaigning in the backwoods of Tennessee, northern voters repudiated the administration. The Republican majority in Congress increased to a solid two-thirds in both houses, and the Radical wing of the party gained strength at the expense of moderates and conservatives.

Quick Check

✓ What events caused Congress to take the initiative in passing the Fourteenth Amendment?

Congressional Reconstruction Plan Enacted

Congress now implemented its own plan of Reconstruction. In 1867 and 1868, it nullified the president's initiatives and reorganized the South. Generally referred to as Radical Reconstruction, the measures actually represented a compromise between genuine Radicals and more moderate Republicans.

Radicals such as Senator Charles Sumner of Massachusetts and Congressmen Thaddeus Stevens of Pennsylvania and George Julian of Indiana wanted to reshape southern society before readmitting ex-Confederates to the Union. Their program of "regeneration before Reconstruction" required an extended period of military rule, confiscation and redistribution of large landholdings among the freedmen, and federal aid for schools to educate blacks and whites for citizenship. But most Republican congressmen found such a program unacceptable because it broke too sharply with American traditions of federalism and regard for property rights, and might take decades.

The First Reconstruction Act, passed over Johnson's veto on March 2, 1867, reorganized the South into five military districts. (See Map 16.1.) But military rule would last for only a short time. Subsequent acts allowed for quickly readmitting any state that framed and ratified a new constitution providing for black suffrage. Ex-Confederates disqualified from holding federal office under the Fourteenth Amendment were prohibited from voting for delegates to the constitutional conventions or in the elections to ratify the conventions' work. Since blacks could participate in this process, Republicans thought they had ensured that "loyal" men would dominate the new governments. Radical Reconstruction was based on the dubious assumption that once blacks had the vote, they would be able to protect themselves against white supremacists' efforts to deny them their rights. The Reconstruction Acts thus signaled a retreat from the true Radical position that sustained federal authority was needed to complete the transition from slavery to freedom and prevent the resurgence of the South's old ruling class Most Republicans were unwilling to embrace centralized government and an extended period of military rule over civilians. Yet a genuine spirit of democratic idealism did give legitimacy and

View the **Map**
Reconstruction on
myhistorylab.com

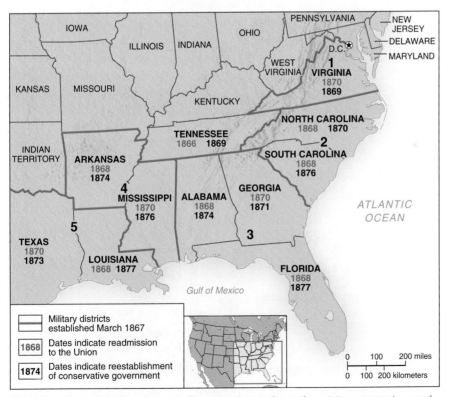

Map 16.1 *Reconstruction* During the Reconstruction era, the southern state governments passed through three phases: control by white ex-Confederates; domination by Republican legislators, both white and black; and, finally, the regaining of control by conservative white Democrats.

Quick Check

✓ What was "Radical
Reconstruction", and
how did it differ from
previous plans?

fervor to the cause of black male suffrage. Enabling people who were so poor and downtrodden to have access to the ballot box was a bold and innovative application of the principle of government by the consent of the governed. The problem was enforcing equal suffrage under conditions then existing in the postwar South.

The Impeachment Crisis

The first obstacle to enforcing Congressional Reconstruction was resistance from the White House. Johnson sought to thwart the will of Congress by obstructing the plan. He dismissed officeholders who sympathized with Radical Reconstruction and countermanded the orders of generals in charge of southern military districts who zealously enforced the new legislation. Conservative

THE PAROQUET OF THE WH—E HO—E.

Impeached Andrew Johnson's successful defense against conviction in his impeachment case centered on his invocation of the Constitution to defend his presidential rights and powers. Impeached in 1868, Johnson escaped conviction by a single vote.

Democrats replaced Radical generals. Congress then passed laws to limit presidential authority over Reconstruction. The Tenure of Office Act required Senate approval for the removal of officials whose appointment had needed the consent of the Senate. Another measure limited Johnson's authority to issue orders to military commanders.

Johnson objected that the restrictions violated the constitutional doctrine of the separation of powers. When it became clear that the president was resolute in fighting for his powers and using them to resist establishing Radical regimes in the southern states, congressmen began to call for his impeachment. A preliminary effort foundered in 1867, but when Johnson tried to discharge Secretary of War Edwin Stanton—the only Radical in the cabinet—and persisted in his efforts despite the disapproval of the Senate, the pro-impeachment forces gained in strength.

In January 1868, Johnson ordered General Grant, who already commanded the army, to replace Stanton as head of the War Department. But Grant had his eye on the Republican presidential nomination and refused to defy Congress. General Lorenzo Thomas then agreed to serve. Faced with this violation of the Tenure of Office Act, the House impeached the president on February 24, and he went on trial before the Senate.

Because seven Republican senators broke with the party leadership and voted for acquittal, the effort to convict Johnson and remove him from office fell one vote short of the necessary two-thirds. This outcome resulted in part from a skillful defense. Attorneys for the president argued that the constitutional provision that a president could be impeached only for "high crimes and misdemeanors" referred only to indictable offenses and that the Tenure of Office Act did not apply to Stanton because Lincoln, not Johnson, had appointed him.

The core of the prosecution case was that Johnson had abused the powers of his office to sabotage congressional Reconstruction. Obstructing the will of the legislative branch, they claimed, was grounds for conviction even if no crime had been committed. The Republicans voting for acquittal could not endorse such a broad view of the impeachment power. They feared that removing a president for essentially political reasons would threaten the constitutional balance of powers and allow legislative supremacy over the executive.

Failure to remove Johnson from office embarrassed Republicans, but the episode did ensure that Reconstruction in the South would proceed as the majority in Congress intended. Johnson influenced the verdict by pledging to enforce the Reconstruction Acts, and he held to this promise during his remaining months in office. Unable to depose the president, the Radicals had at least neutralized his opposition to their program.

> **Quick Check**
>
> ✓ What Prompted Congress to initiate impeachment against Johnson, and what was the outcome of that action?

RECONSTRUCTING SOUTHERN SOCIETY

The Civil War left the South devastated, demoralized, and destitute. Slavery was dead, but what this meant for future relationships between whites and blacks was unclear. Most southern whites wanted to keep blacks adrift between slavery and freedom—without rights, like the "free Negroes" of the Old South. Blacks

> **What** problems did southern society face during Reconstruction?

sought to be independent of their former masters and viewed acquiring land, education, and the vote as the best means of achieving this goal. The thousands of northerners who went south after the war for materialistic or humanitarian reasons hoped to extend Yankee "civilization" to what they considered an unenlightened and barbarous region. For most of them, this meant aiding the freed slaves.

Read the
Document
*Carl Schurz, Report
on the Condition of
the South (1865)* on
myhistorylab.com

The struggle between these groups bred chaos, violence, and instability. This was scarcely an ideal setting for an experiment in interracial democracy, but one was attempted nonetheless. Its success depended on massive and sustained federal support. To the extent that this was forthcoming, progressive reform could be achieved. When it faltered, the forces of reaction and white supremacy were unleashed.

Reorganizing Land and Labor

The Civil War scarred the southern landscape and wrecked its economy. One devastated area—central South Carolina—looked to an 1865 observer "like a broad black streak of ruin and desolation." Atlanta, Columbia, and Richmond were gutted by fire. Factories were dismantled or destroyed. Railroads were torn up.

Investment capital for rebuilding was inadequate. The wealth represented by Confederate currency and bonds had melted away, and emancipation had divested the propertied classes of their most valuable and productive assets—the slaves. According to some estimates, the South's per capita wealth in 1865 was only about half what it had been in 1860.

Watch the **Video**
*The Schools the Civil
War and Reconstruc-
tion Created* on
myhistorylab.com

Recovery could not begin until a new labor system replaced slavery. Most northerners and southerners assumed that southern prosperity still depended on cotton and that the plantation was the most efficient unit for producing the crop. Hindering efforts to rebuild the plantation economy were lack of capital, the conviction of southern whites that blacks would work only under compulsion, and the freedmen's resistance to labor conditions that recalled slavery.

Blacks preferred to determine their own economic relationships, and for a time they had reason to hope the federal government would support their ambitions. The freed slaves were, in effect, fighting a two-front war. Although they were grateful for federal aid in ending slavery, freed slaves' ideas about freedom often contradicted the plans of their northern allies. Many ex-slaves wanted to hold on to the family-based communal work methods that they used during slavery. Freed slaves in South Carolina, for example, attempted to maintain the family task system rather than adopt the individual piecework system northern capitalists pushed. Many ex-slaves opposed plans to turn them into wage laborers who produced exclusively for a market. Finally, freed slaves often wanted to stay on the land their families had spent generations farming rather than move elsewhere to occupy land as individual farmers.

While not guaranteeing all of the freed slaves' hopes for economic self-determination, the northern military attempted to establish a new economic base for them. General Sherman, hampered by the many black fugitives that followed his army on its famous march, issued an order in January 1865 that set aside the islands and coastal areas of Georgia and South Carolina for exclusive black occupancy on 40-acre plots. Furthermore, the Freedmen's Bureau was given control of hundreds of thousands of acres of abandoned or confiscated land and was authorized to make 40-acre grants to black settlers for three-year periods, after which they could buy at low prices. By June 1865, 40,000 black farmers were working on 300,000 acres of what they thought would be their own land.

But for most of them, the dream of "40 acres and a mule," or some other arrangement that would give them control of their land and labor, was not to be realized. President Johnson pardoned the owners of most of the land Sherman and the Freedmen's Bureau consigned to the ex-slaves, and Congress rejected proposals for an effective program of land confiscation and redistribution. Among the considerations prompting congressional opposition to land reform were a

Sharecropping The Civil War brought emancipation to slaves, but the sharecropping system kept many of them economically bound to their employers. At the end of a year the sharecropper tenants might owe most—or all—of what they had made to their landlord. Here, a sharecropping family poses in front of their cabin. Ex-slaves often built their living quarters near woods in order to have a ready supply of fuel for heating and cooking. The cabin's chimney lists away from the house so that it can be easily pushed away from the living quarters should it catch fire.

tenderness for property rights, fear of sapping the freedmen's initiative by giving them something they allegedly had not earned, and the desire to restore cotton production as quickly as possible to increase agricultural exports and stabilize the economy. Consequently, most blacks in physical possession of small farms failed to acquire title, and the mass of freedmen did not become landowners. As an ex-slave later wrote, "they were set free without a dollar, without a foot of land, and without the wherewithal to get the next meal even."

Despite their poverty and landlessness, ex-slaves were reluctant to settle down and commit themselves to wage labor for their former masters. Many took to the road, hoping to find something better. Some were still expecting land, but others were simply trying to increase their bargaining power. One freedman recalled that an important part of being free was that "we could move around [and] change bosses." By the end of 1865, many freedmen had still not signed up for the coming season; anxious planters feared that blacks were plotting to seize land by force. Within weeks, however, most holdouts signed for the best terms they could get.

One common form of agricultural employment in 1866 was a contract labor system. Under this system, workers committed themselves for a year in return for fixed wages, much of which was withheld until after the harvest. Since many planters drove hard bargains, abused their workers, or cheated them at the end of the year, the Freedmen's Bureau reviewed and enforced the contracts. But bureau officials had differing notions of what it meant to protect African Americans from exploitation. Some stood up for the rights of the freedmen; others served as allies of the planters.

An alternative capital–labor relationship—sharecropping—eventually replaced the contract system. First in small groups known as "squads" and later as individual families, black sharecroppers worked a piece of land for a fixed share of the crop, usually one-half. Credit-starved landlords liked this arrangement because it did not require much expenditure before the harvest, and the tenant shared the risks of crop failure or a fall in cotton prices.

African Americans initially viewed sharecropping as a step toward landowner-ship. But during the 1870s, it evolved into a new kind of servitude. Croppers had to live on credit until their cotton was sold, and planters or merchants "provisioned" them at high prices and exorbitant interest. Creditors deducted what was owed to them out of the tenant's share of the crop. This left most sharecroppers with no net profit at the end of the year—and often with a debt they had to work off in subsequent years.

Read the **Document**
A Sharecrop Contract (1882) on **myhistorylab.com**

Quick Check

✓ What were the conflicting visions of the planters, the Freedmen's Bureau agents, and the freed slaves with regard to what a new labor system should look like?

Black Codes: A New Name for Slavery?

While landless rural blacks were being reduced to economic dependence, those in towns and cities were living in an increasingly segregated society. The Black Codes of 1865 attempted to require separation of the races in public places and facilities; when federal authorities overturned most of the codes as violations of the Civil Rights Act of 1866, private initiative and community pressure often achieved the same end. In some cities, blacks resisted being consigned to separate streetcars by appealing to the military when it still exercised authority or by organizing boycotts. But they found it almost impossible to gain admittance to most hotels, restaurants, and other private establishments catering to whites. Although separate black, or "Jim Crow," cars were not yet the rule on railroads, African Americans were often denied first-class accommodations. After 1868, black-supported Republican governments required equal access to public facilities, but made little effort to enforce the legislation.

The Black Codes had other onerous provisions to control African Americans and return them to quasi-slavery. Most codes made black unemployment a crime, which meant blacks had to make long-term contracts with white employers or be arrested for vagrancy. Others limited the rights of African Americans to own property or engage in occupations other than those of servant or laborer. Congress, the military, and the Freedmen's Bureau set the codes aside, but vagrancy laws remained in force across the South.

Furthermore, private violence and discrimination against blacks continued on a massive scale, unchecked by state authorities. Whites murdered hundreds, perhaps thousands, of blacks in 1865–1866, and few perpetrators were brought to justice. Military rule was designed to protect former slaves from such violence and intimidation, but the task was beyond the capacity of the few thousand troops stationed in the South. When new constitutions were approved and states readmitted to the Union under the congressional plan in 1868, the problem became more severe. White opponents of Radical Reconstruction adopted systematic terrorism and mob violence to keep blacks from the polls.

The freed slaves, in the face of opposition from both their Democratic enemies and some Republican allies, tried to defend themselves by organizing their own militia groups and to assert their political rights. However, the militias were too weak to overcome the anti-Republican forces. And as the military presence was reduced, the new Republican regimes fought a losing battle against armed white supremacists.

> **Quick Check**
>
> ✓ What were the Black Codes, and how did they compare to the conditions of slavery?

Republican Rule in the South

Hastily organized in 1867, the southern Republican party dominated the constitution-making of 1868 and the regimes it produced. The party was an attempted coalition of three social groups (which varied in their relative strength from state to state). One was the same class that was becoming the backbone of the Republican party in the North—businessmen who wanted government aid for private enterprise. Many Republicans of this stripe were recent arrivals from the North—the so-called carpetbaggers—but some were scalawags, former Whig planters or merchants who were born in the South or had immigrated there before the war and now saw a chance to realize their dreams for commercial and industrial development.

Poor white farmers, especially those from upland areas where Unionist senti-ment had been strong during the Civil War, were a second element in the original coalition. These owners of small farms expected the party to favor their inter-ests at the expense of the wealthy landowners and pass special legislation when—as often happened in this period of economic upheaval—creditors attempted to seize their homesteads. Newly enfranchised blacks were the third group to which the Republicans appealed. Blacks formed most of the Republican rank and file in most states and were concerned mainly with education, civil rights, and landownership.

Under the best conditions, these coalitions would have been fragile. Each group had its own goals and did not fully support those of the others. White yeomen, for example, had a deep resistance to black equality. And for how long would essen-tially conservative businessmen support costly measures to elevate or relieve the lower classes of either race? In some states, astute Democrats exploited these divi-sions by appealing to disaffected white Republicans.

But during the relatively brief period when they were in power in the South—from one to nine years depending on the state—the Republicans chalked up notable achievements. They established (on paper at least) the South's first adequate sys-tems of public education, democratized state and local government, and expanded public services and responsibilities.

As important as these social and political reforms were, they took second place to the Republicans' major effort—fostering economic development and restoring prosperity by subsidizing the construction of railroads and other in-ternal improvements. But the policy of aiding railroads turned out to be di-sastrous, even though it addressed the region's real economic needs and was initially popular. Extravagance, corruption, and routes laid out in response to political pressure rather than on sound economic grounds increased public debt and taxation.

The policy did not produce the promised payoff of efficient, cheap trans-portation. Subsidized railroads went bankrupt, leaving the taxpayers holding the bag. When the Panic of 1873 brought many southern state governments to the verge of bankruptcy, and railroad building ended, it was clear the Republi-cans' "gospel of prosperity" through state aid to private enterprise had failed. Their political opponents, many of whom had favored such policies, now took advantage of the situation, charging that Republicans had ruined the southern economy.

In general, the Radical regimes failed to conduct public business honestly and efficiently. Embezzlement of public funds and bribery of state lawmakers or offi-cials were common. State debts and tax burdens rose enormously, mainly because governments had undertaken heavy new responsibilities, but also because of waste and graft. The situation varied from state to state: Ruling cliques in Louisiana and South Carolina were guilty of much wrongdoing; Mississippi had a relatively honest and frugal regime.

Furthermore, southern corruption was not exceptional, nor was it a result of extending suffrage to uneducated African Americans, as critics of Radical

Reconstruction have claimed. It was part of a national pattern during an era when private interests considered buying government favors as part of the cost of doing business, and politicians expected to profit by obliging them.

Many Reconstruction-era scandals started at the top. President Grant's first-term vice president, Schuyler Colfax of Indiana, was directly involved in the notorious Credit Mobilier scandal. Credit Mobilier was a construction company that actually served as a fraudulent device for siphoning off profits that should have gone to the stockholders of the Union Pacific Railroad, which had received massive federal land grants. Credit Mobilier distributed stock to influential congressmen, including Colfax before he became vice president, in order to keep Congress from inquiring into this shady arrangement. In 1875, during President Grant's second administration, his private secretary was indicted in a conspiracy to defraud the government of millions of dollars in liquor taxes, and his secretary of war was impeached for taking bribes. While there is no evidence that Grant profited personally from these misdeeds, he failed to take firm action against the wrongdoers and participated in covering up their crimes.

The new African American public officials were only minor participants in this rampant corruption. Although 16 blacks served in Congress—two in the Senate—between 1869 and 1880, only in South Carolina were blacks a majority of even one house of the legislature. Furthermore, no black governors were elected during Reconstruction (although Pinckney B. S. Pinchback was acting governor of Louisiana in 1872–1873). The biggest grafters were opportunistic whites. Businessmen offering bribes included members of the prewar gentry who were staunch opponents of Radical programs. Some black legislators went with the tide and accepted "loans" from railroad lobbyists who would pay most for their votes, but the same men would usually vote the will of their constituents on civil rights or education.

Blacks served or supported corrupt and wasteful regimes because the alternative was dire. Although the Democrats, or Conservatives as they called themselves in some states, made sporadic efforts to attract African American voters, it was clear that if they won control, they would strip blacks of their civil and political rights. But opponents of Radical Reconstruction capitalized on racial prejudice and persuaded many Americans that "good government" was synonymous with white supremacy.

Contrary to myth, the few African Americans elected to state or national office during Reconstruction demonstrated on the average more integrity and competence than their white counterparts. Most were fairly well educated, having been free or unusually privileged slaves before the war. Among the most capable were Robert Smalls (whose career was described earlier); Blanche K. Bruce of Mississippi, elected to the U.S. Senate in 1874 after rising to prominence in the Republican party of his home state; Congressman Robert Brown Elliott of South Carolina, an adroit politician who was also a consistent champion of civil rights; and Congressman James T. Rapier of Alabama, who stirred the nation in 1873 with his appeals for federal aid to southern education and new laws to enforce equal rights for African Americans.

Quick Check

✓ What were the three social groups that made up the southern Republican party?

Claiming Public and Private Rights

The ways that freed slaves claimed rights for themselves were as important as party politics to the changing political culture of the Reconstruction South. Ex-slaves fought for their rights not only in negotiations with employers and in public meetings and convention halls, but also through the institutions they created and, perhaps most important, the households they formed.

Some ex-slaves used institutions formerly closed to them like the courts to assert rights they considered part of citizenship. Many ex-slaves rushed to formalize their marriages before the law, and they used their new status to fight for custody of children who had been taken from them under the apprenticeship provisions of the Black Clodes. Ex-slaves sued white people and other blacks over domestic violence, child support, assault, and debt. Freed women sued their husbands for desertion and alimony and enlisted the Freedmen's Bureau to help them claim property from men. Immediately after the war, freed people created institutions that had been denied to them under slavery: churches, fraternal and benevolent associations, political organizations, and schools. Many joined all-black denominations such as the African Methodist Episcopal (AME) church, which provided freedom from white dominance and more congenial worship. Black women formed all-black chapters

📖 **Read the Document**
Slave Narrative, "The Story of Mattie J. Jackson" on **myhistorylab.com**

Freedmen's Schools A Freedmen's school, one of the more successful endeavors the Freedmen's Bureau supported. The bureau, working with teachers from northern abolitionist and missionary societies, founded thousands of schools for freed slaves and poor whites.

of organizations such as the Women's Christian Temperance Union and created their own women's clubs to oppose lynching and promote "uplift" in the black community.

A top priority for most ex-slaves was education for their children; the first schools for freed people were all-black institutions the Freedmen's Bureau and northern missionary societies established. Having been denied education during the antebellum period, most blacks viewed separate schooling as an opportunity rather than as a form of discrimination. However, these schools were precursors to the segregated public school systems first instituted by Republican governments. Only at city schools in New Orleans and the University of South Carolina were serious attempts made during Reconstruction to bring white and black students together in the same classrooms.

In many ways, African American men and women during Reconstruction asserted freedom in the "private" realm and the public sphere by claiming rights to their own families and building their own institutions. They did so despite the efforts of their former masters and the new government agencies to control their private lives and shape their new identities as husbands, wives, and citizens.

> **Quick Check**
> ✓ What new rights and institutions did free blacks create and use following emancipation?

RETREAT FROM RECONSTRUCTION

The era of Reconstruction began to end almost before it got started. Although it was only three years after the end of the Civil War, the impeachment crisis of 1868 was the high point of popular interest in Reconstruction. That year, Ulysses S. Grant, a popular general, was elected president. Many historians blame Grant for the corruption of his administration and for the inconsistency and failure of his southern policy. He had neither the vision nor the sense of duty to tackle the difficult challenges the nation faced. From 1868 on, political issues other than southern Reconstruction moved to the forefront of national politics, and the plight of African Americans in the South receded in white consciousness.

> **Why** did Reconstruction end?

Final Efforts of Reconstruction

The Republican effort to make equal rights for blacks the law of the land culminated in the Fifteenth Amendment. Passed by Congress in 1869 and ratified by the states in 1870, it prohibited any state from denying a male citizen the right to vote because of race, color, or previous condition of servitude. A more radical version, requiring universal manhood suffrage, was rejected partly because it departed too sharply from traditional federal–state relations. States therefore could still limit the suffrage by imposing literacy tests, property qualifications, or poll taxes allegedly applying to all racial groups; such devices would eventually be used to strip southern blacks of the right to vote. But the authors of the amendment did not foresee this. They believed it would prevent future

> ◗ **View** the **Closer Look**
> *The First Vote* on **myhistorylab.com**

Black Voting *The First Vote*, drawn by A. H. Ward for *Harper's Weekly*, November 16, 1867.

Congresses or southern constitutional conventions from repealing or nullifying the provisions for black male suffrage included in the Reconstruction Acts.
A secondary aim was to enfranchise African Americans in northern states that
still denied them the vote.

Many feminists were bitter that the amendment did not extend the vote to
women. A militant wing of the women's rights movement, led by Elizabeth Cady
Stanton and Susan B. Anthony, was so angered that the Constitution was being
amended to, in effect, make gender a qualification for voting that they campaigned
against ratification of the amendment. Other feminists led by Lucy Stone supported
the amendment, saying this was "the Negro's hour" and that women could afford to
wait a few years for the vote. This disagreement divided the woman suffrage movement for a generation.

The Grant administration was charged with enforcing the amendment and protecting black men's voting rights in the reconstructed states. Since survival of the
Republican regimes depended on African American support, political partisanship
dictated federal action, even though the North's emotional and ideological commitment to black citizenship was waning.

Read the
Document
*The State of the
South (1872)* on
myhistorylab.com

Quick Check

✓ What did the Fifteenth
Amendment stipulate,
and whom did it
benefit?

A Reign of Terror Against Blacks

Between 1868 and 1872, the Ku Klux Klan and other secret societies bent on restoring white supremacy by intimidating blacks who sought to exercise their political rights were the main threat to Republican regimes. Founded in Tennessee in 1866, the Klan spread rapidly, adopting lawless and brutal tactics. A grassroots vigilante movement, not a centralized conspiracy, the Klan thrived on local initiative and support from whites of all social classes. Its secrecy, decentralization, popular support, and ruthlessness made it difficult to suppress. As soon as blacks had been granted the right to vote, hooded "night riders" began to visit the cabins of active Republicans. Some victims were only threatened. Others were whipped or murdered.

Such methods were first used effectively in the presidential election of 1868. Grant lost in Louisiana and Georgia mainly because the Klan—or the Knights of the White Camellia, as the Louisiana variant was called—launched a reign of terror to prevent blacks from voting. In Louisiana, political violence claimed more than 1,000 lives. In Arkansas, which Grant did carry, more than 200 Republicans, including a congressman, were killed.

Thereafter, Klan terrorism was directed mainly at Republican state governments. Virtual insurrections broke out in Arkansas, Tennessee, North Carolina, and parts of South Carolina. Republican governors called out the state militia to fight the Klan, but only the Arkansas militia brought it to heel. In Tennessee, North Carolina, and Georgia, Klan activities enabled Democrats to come to power by 1870.

In 1870–1871, Congress provided federal protection for black suffrage and authorized using the army against the Klan. The Force Acts, also known as the Ku Klux Klan acts, made interference with voting rights a federal crime and provided for federal supervision of elections. The legislation also empowered the president to call out troops and suspend the writ of habeas corpus to quell insurrection. In 1871–1872, the military or U.S. marshals arrested thousands of suspected Klansmen, and the writ was suspended in nine counties of South Carolina that the Klan had virtually taken over. Although most of the accused Klansmen were never tried, were acquitted, or received suspended sentences, the enforcement effort did put a damper on hooded terrorism and ensure relatively fair and peaceful elections in 1872.

A heavy black turnout in these elections enabled the Republicans to hold on to power in most of the Deep South, despite Democratic-Conservative efforts to cut into the Republican vote by taking moderate positions on racial and economic issues. This setback prompted the Democratic-Conservatives to change their strategy and ideology. They stopped trying to take votes away from the Republicans by proclaiming support for black suffrage and government aid to business. Instead they began to appeal openly to white supremacy and the traditional Democratic and agrarian hostility to government promotion of economic development. They were thus able to attract part of the white Republican electorate, mostly small farmers.

Read the Document
Hannah Irwin Describes Ku Klux Klan Ride on myhistorylab.com

Ku Klux Klan This 1868 photograph shows typical regalia of members of the Ku Klux Klan, a secret white supremacist organization. Before elections, hooded Klansmen terrorized African Americans to discourage them from voting.

This new strategy dovetailed with a resurgence of violence to reduce Republican, especially black Republican, voting. Its agents no longer wore masks but acted openly. They were effective because the northern public was increasingly disenchanted with federal intervention to prop up what were widely viewed as corrupt and tottering Republican regimes. Grant used force in the South for the last time in 1874 when an overt paramilitary organization in Louisiana, known as the White League, tried to overthrow a Republican government accused of stealing an election. When another unofficial militia in Mississippi instigated bloody race riots before the state elections of 1875, Grant refused the governor's request for federal troops. As a result, black voters were intimidated—one county registered only seven Republican votes where there had been a black majority of 2,000—and Mississippi fell to the Democratic-Conservatives.

By 1876, partly because of Grant's hesitant and inconsistent use of presidential power, but mainly because the northern electorate would no longer tolerate military action to sustain Republican governments and black voting rights, Radical Reconstruction was collapsing.

> **Quick Check**
> ✓ How important was the Ku Klux Klan in influencing elections and policies in the South?

REUNION AND THE NEW SOUTH

The end of Radical Reconstruction in 1877 opened the way to a reconciliation of North and South. But the costs of reunion were high for less privileged groups in the South. The civil and political rights of African Americans, left unprotected, were relentlessly stripped away by white supremacist regimes. Lower-class whites saw their interests sacrificed to those of capitalists and landlords. Despite the rhetoric hailing a prosperous "New South," the region remained poor and open to exploitation by northern business interests.

> **Who** benefited and who suffered from the reconciliation of the North and South?

The Compromise of 1877

The election of 1876 pitted Rutherford B. Hayes of Ohio, a Republican governor untainted by the scandals of the Grant era, against Governor Samuel J. Tilden of New York, a Democratic reformer who had fought corruption in New York City. Honest government was apparently the electorate's highest priority. When the returns came in, Tilden had won the popular vote and seemed likely to win a narrow victory in the electoral college. But the returns from the three southern states the Republicans still controlled—South Carolina, Florida, and Louisiana—were contested. If Hayes were awarded these three states, plus one contested electoral vote in Oregon, Republican strategists realized, he would triumph in the electoral college by a single vote. (See Map 16.2)

The election remained undecided for months, plunging the nation into a political crisis. To resolve the impasse, Congress appointed a 15-member commission to determine who

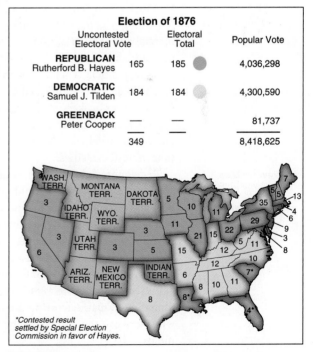

Map 16.2

Election of 1876			
	Uncontested Electoral Vote	Electoral Total	Popular Vote
REPUBLICAN Rutherford B. Hayes	165	185	4,036,298
DEMOCRATIC Samuel J. Tilden	184	184	4,300,590
GREENBACK Peter Cooper	—	—	81,737
		349	8,418,625

Contested result settled by Special Election Commission in favor of Hayes.

would receive the votes of the disputed states. Originally composed of seven Democrats, seven Republicans, and an independent, the commission fell under Republican control when the independent member resigned to run for the Senate and a Republican replaced him. The commission split along party lines and voted eight to seven to award Hayes all the disputed votes. But both houses of Congress still had to ratify the decision, and in the House, there was strong Democratic opposition. To ensure Hayes's election, Republican leaders struck an informal bargain with conservative southern Democrats that historians have dubbed the Compromise of 1877. What precisely was agreed to and by whom remains in dispute, but both sides understood that Hayes would be president and that southern blacks would be abandoned to their fate. President Hayes immediately ordered the army not to resist a Democratic takeover of state governments in South Carolina and Louisiana. Thus fell the last of the Radical governments. White Democrats firmly controlled the entire South. The trauma of the war and Reconstruction had destroyed the chances for renewing two-party competition among white southerners.

Quick Check

✓ Who agreed upon the Compromise of 1877, and why?

"Redeeming" a New South

The men who took power after Radical Reconstruction fell in one southern state after another are usually referred to as the Redeemers. Their backgrounds and previous loyalties differed. Some were members of the Old South's ruling planter class who had supported secession and now sought to reestablish the old order with as few changes as possible. Others, of middle-class origin or outlook, favored commercial and industrial interests over agrarian groups and called for a New South committed to diversified economic development. A third group consisted of professional politicians bending with the prevailing winds.

The Redeemers subscribed to no single coherent ideology but are best characterized as power brokers mediating among the dominant interest groups of the South to serve their own political advantage. The "rings" that they established on the state and county level were analogous to the political machines developing at the same time in northern cities.

View the **Map**
The Rise of Tenancy in the South, 1880 on
myhistorylab.com

Redeemers did, however, endorse two basic principles: laissez-faire and white supremacy. Laissez-faire could unite planters, frustrated at seeing direct state support going to businessmen, and capitalist promoters, who realized that low taxes and freedom from government regulation were even more advantageous than state subsidies. The Redeemers responded only to privileged and entrenched interest groups, especially landlords, merchants, and industrialists, and offered little or nothing to tenants, small farmers, and working people. As industrialization gathered steam in the 1880s, Democratic regimes became increasingly accommodating to manufacturing interests and hospitable to agents of northern capital who were gaining control of the South's transportation system and its extractive industries.

White supremacy was the rallying cry that brought the Redeemers to power. Once in office, they stayed there by charging that opponents of ruling Democratic cliques were trying to divide "the white man's party" and open the way for a return to "black domination." Appeals to racism also deflected attention from the economic grievances of groups without political clout.

The new governments were more economical than those of Reconstruction, mainly because they drastically cut appropriations for schools and other public services. But they were scarcely more honest—embezzlement and bribery remained rife. The Redeemer regimes of the late 1870s and 1880s neglected small white farmers. Whites, as well as blacks, were suffering from the notorious crop lien system, which gave local merchants who advanced credit at high interest during the growing season the right to take possession of the harvested crop on terms that buried farmers deeper and deeper in debt. As a result, many whites lost title to their homesteads and were reduced to tenancy. When a depression of world cotton prices added to the burden of a ruinous credit system, agrarian protesters began to challenge the ruling elite, first through the Southern Farmers' Alliance of the late 1880s and then by supporting its political descendant—the Populist party of the 1890s (see Chapter 20).

Quick Check

✓ Which principles divided, and which united, the new "Redeemer" governments?

The Rise of Jim Crow

The new order imposed the greatest hardships on African Americans. The dark night of racism fell on the South. From 1876 to 1910, southern states imposed restrictions on black civil rights known as Jim Crow laws. The term "Jim Crow" came from an antebellum minstrel show figure first popularized by Thomas "Daddy" Rice, who blackened his face and sang a song called "Jump Jim Crow." By the 1850s, Jim Crow was a familiar figure in minstrel shows, and had become a synonym for a black person in popular white speech. It was a short step to referring to segregated railroad cars for black people as Jim Crow cars. While segregation and disfranchisement began as informal arrangements in the immediate aftermath of the Civil War, they culminated in a legal regime of separation and exclusion that took firm hold in the 1890s. (See Chapter 19.)

The rise of Jim Crow in the political arena was especially bitter for southern blacks who realized that only political power could ensure other rights. The Redeemers promised, as part of the understanding that led to the end of federal intervention in 1877, that they would respect the rights of blacks as set forth in the Fourteenth and Fifteenth Amendments. Governor Wade Hampton of South Carolina pledged that the new regimes would not reduce African Americans to second-class citizenship. But when blacks tried to vote Republican in the "redeemed" states, they encountered violence and intimidation. "Bulldozing" African American voters remained common in state elections during the late 1870s and early 1880s; those blacks who withstood the threat of losing their jobs or being evicted from tenant farms if they voted for the party of Lincoln were

Watch the **Video**
The Promise and Failure of Reconstruction on **myhistorylab.com**

visited at night and literally whipped into line. The message was clear: Vote Democratic, or vote not at all.

Furthermore, white Democrats now controlled the electoral machinery and manipulated the black vote by stuffing ballot boxes, discarding unwanted votes, or reporting fraudulent totals. Some states imposed complicated voting requirements to discourage black participation. Full-scale disfranchisement did not occur until literacy tests and other legalized obstacles to voting were imposed from 1890 to 1910, but by then, less formal and comprehensive methods had already made a mockery of the Fifteenth Amendment.

Nevertheless, blacks continued to vote freely in some localities until the 1890s; a few districts, like the one Robert Smalls represented, even elected black Republicans to Congress during the immediate post-Reconstruction period. The last of these, Representative George H. White of North Carolina, served until 1901. His farewell address eloquently conveyed the agony of southern blacks in the era of Jim Crow (strict segregation):

These parting words are in behalf of an outraged, heart-broken, bruised, and bleeding but God-fearing people, faithful, industrious, loyal people—rising people, full of potential force.... The only apology that I have to make for the earnestness with which I have spoken is that I am pleading for the life, the liberty, the future happiness, and manhood suffrage of one-eighth of the entire population of the United States.

Quick Check

✓ What aspects of southern society did the Jim Crow Laws regulate?

CONCLUSION: HENRY MCNEAL TURNER AND THE "UNFINISHED REVOLUTION"

The career of Henry McNeal Turner sums up the bitter side of the black experience in the South during and after Reconstruction. Born free in South Carolina in 1834, Turner became a minister of the AME Church just before the Civil War. During the war, he recruited African Americans for the Union army and served as chaplain for black troops. After the war, he went to Georgia to work for the Freedmen's Bureau but encountered racial discrimination from white officers and left government service for church work and Reconstruction politics. Elected to the 1867 Georgia constitutional convention and to the state legislature in 1868, he was one of many black clergymen who became leaders among the freedmen. But whites won control of the Georgia legislature and expelled all the black members. As the inhabitant of a state in which blacks never gained the power that they achieved in other parts of the South, Turner was one of the first black leaders to see the failure of Reconstruction as the betrayal of African American hopes for citizenship.

Becoming a bishop of the AME Church in 1880, Turner emerged as the era's leading proponent of black emigration to Africa. Because he believed that white Americans would never grant blacks equal rights, Turner became

Henry McNeal Turner, who was born in freedom, became a bishop of the African Methodist Episcopal Church and was elected to the Georgia legislature.

an early advocate of black nationalism and a total separation of the races. Emigration became popular among southern blacks, who were especially hard hit by terror and oppression just after the end of Reconstruction. Still, most blacks in the nation as a whole and even in Turner's own church refused to give up the hope of eventual equality on American soil. But Bishop Turner's anger and despair were the understandable responses of a proud man to how he and his fellow African Americans had been treated in the post–Civil War period.

By the late 1880s, the wounds of the Civil War were healing, and white Americans were seized by the spirit of sectional reconciliation and their common Americanism. But whites could reunite only because northerners had tacitly agreed to give southerners a free hand to reduce blacks to servitude. The "outraged, heartbroken, bruised, and bleeding" African Americans of the South paid the heaviest price for sectional reunion.

16 STUDY RESOURCES

((•—Listen to the **Chapter Audio** for
Chapter 16 on **myhistorylab.com**

TIMELINE

1863 Lincoln sets forth 10 percent Reconstruction plan, p. 389

1864 Lincoln pocket vetoes Wade–Davis Bill, p. 390

1865 President Andrew Johnson moves to reconstruct the South on his own initiative, p. 391
- Congress refuses to seat representatives and senators from states reestablished under presidential plan (December), p. 392
- **1866** Johnson vetoes Freedmen's Bureau Bill (February), p. 392
- Civil Rights Act passed over Johnson's veto (April), p. 393
- Congress passes Fourteenth Amendment (June), p. 393
- Republicans increase their congressional majority, p. 393

1867 First Reconstruction Act passed over Johnson's veto (March), p. 395

1868 Johnson is impeached but avoids conviction by one vote (February–May), p. 396
- Southern blacks vote and serve in constitutional conventions, p. 405
- Ulysses S. Grant elected president, p. 405

1869 Congress passes Fifteenth Amendment, p. 405

1870–1871 Force Acts protect black voting rights in the South, p. 407

1872 Grant reelected president, p. 407

1876–1877 Disputed presidential election resolved in favor of Republican Rutherfrod B. Hayes, p. 409

1877 Compromise of 1877 ends Reconstruction, p. 409

CHAPTER REVIEW

THE PRESIDENT VERSUS CONGRESS

What conflicts arose between Lincoln and Johnson and Congress during Reconstruction?

Both Lincoln and Johnson had their own notions of how Reconstruction should be governed. Radical Republicans who sought more protection for black rights challenged Lincoln's Ten Percent Plan. Later, when Johnson hesitated to renew the Freedmen's Bureau and fight the Black Codes, Congress passed the Fourteenth Amendment to ensure equal rights to all Americans. *(p. 389)*

RECONSTRUCTING SOUTHERN SOCIETY

What problems did southern society face during Reconstruction?

The immediate problems facing the South were economic and physical devastation, and providing for the mass of freed slaves. While former slaveholders hoped to reduce ex-slaves to conditions not unlike slavery, northern Republicans wanted to reorganize southern land and labor on a northern free-labor model. Freedmen's Bureau agents emphasized that ex-slaves had to sign contracts and work for wages. The freed slaves hoped instead to own land. Sharecropping was a compromise. *(p. 397)*

RETREAT FROM RECONSTRUCTION

Why did Reconstruction end?

Although intended to protect civil rights, the Fifteenth Amendment allowed states to limit local suffrage through difficult voting prerequisites. Further, the

Ku Klux Klan intimidated black voters and representation. By 1876, these tactics had defeated the Republicans in most southern states and Reconstruction was nearly dead. *(p. 405)*

REUNION AND THE NEW SOUTH

Who benefited and who suffered from the reconciliation of North and South?

Reunion came at the expense of African Americans. The Compromise of 1877 restored autonomous government in the South to resolve the 1876 election. The North would no longer enforce unpopular civil rights, allowing the Redeemers to bring back laissez-faire economics and restore white supremacy through the Jim Crow laws. *(p. 408)*

KEY TERM QUESTIONS

1. Why was Congress unhappy with the Ten Percent Plan proposed by Lincoln? (p. 389)

2. What were the core beliefs of the Radical Republicans? (p. 390)

3. How did the Wade–Davis Bill passed by Congress in 1864 differ from the Ten Percent Plan? (p. 390)

4. Why did President Johnson assume that the Thirteenth Amendment would, almost on its own, be enough to end the Reconstruction process? (p. 391)

5. Why were the southern states able to pass Black Code laws so easily? (p. 392)

6. What were the successes and failures of the Freedmen's Bureau? (p. 393)

7. Why is the Fourteenth Amendment regarded as perhaps the most important of all the constitutional amendments? (p. 393)

8. How did Radical Reconstruction differ from previous plans? (p. 394)

9. How did sharecropping work in practice to keep many blacks from ever owning land? (p. 400)

10. Why were many feminists disappointed with the passage of the Fifteenth Amendment? (p. 405)

11. Why did Ku Klux Klan members disguise themselves in hoods and robes? (p. 406)

12. How did the Force Acts attack the Ku Klux Klan? (p. 407)

13. What was the most significant result of the Compromise of 1877? (p. 409)

14. Which principles divided, and which united, the new Redeemer governments? (p. 409)

15. How did the Jim Crow laws come to serve as a second racial caste system? (p. 410)

MYHISTORYLAB CONNECTIONS

Visit **www.myhistorylab.com** for a customized Study Plan to build your knowledge of *The Agony of Reconstruction*

Question for Analysis

1. What was the significance of The Mississippi Black Code?

   Read the **Document** *Mississippi Black Code, 1865* p. 392

Other Resources from this Chapter

View the **Image** *Andrew Johnson, Brady Photo*

Read the **Document** *Thirteenth, Fourteenth, and Fifteenth Amendments*

2. How were the Southern states readmitted to the Union during Reconstruction?

   View the **Map** *Reconstruction* p. 395

3. How did the nature of education change in America during Reconstruction?

   Watch the **Video** *The Schools that the Civil War and Reconstruction Created* p. 398

4. Why was the federal government unable to protect African American civil rights despite the passage of the Civil Rights Act of 1875?

   View the **Closer Look** *The First Vote* p. 405

5. Why did Reconstruction ultimately fail?

   Watch the **Video** *The Promise and Failure of Reconstruction* p. 410

Read the **Document** *Carl Schurz, Report on the Condition of the South*

Read the **Document** *Sharecrop Contract, 1882*

Read the **Document** *Slave Narrative, The Story of Mattie Jackson*

Read the **Document** *State of the South, 1872*

Read the **Document** *Hannah Irwin Describes KKK Ride*

View the **Map** *The Rise of Tenancy in the South, 1880*

Appendix

THE DECLARATION OF INDEPENDENCE

THE ARTICLES OF CONFEDERATION

THE CONSTITUTION OF THE UNITED STATES OF AMERICA

AMENDMENTS TO THE CONSTITUTION

PRESIDENTIAL ELECTIONS

PRESIDENTS AND VICE PRESIDENTS

For additional reference material, go to
www.pearsonamericanhistory.com
The on-line appendix includes the following:

The Declaration of Independence
The Articles of Confederation
The Constitution of the United States of America
Amendments to the Constitution
Presidential Elections
Vice Presidents and Cabinet Members by
    Administration

Supreme Court Justices
Presidents, Congresses, and Chief Justices,
    1789–2001
Territorial Expansion of the United States (map)
Admission of States of the Union
U.S. Population, 1790–2000
Ten Largest Cities by Population, 1700–1900
Birthrate, 1820–2000 (chart)
Death Rate, 1900–2000 (chart)
Life Expectancy, 1900–2000 (chart)
Urban/Rural Population, 1750–1900 (chart)
Women in the Labor Force, 1890–1990
United States Physical Features (map)
United States Native Vegetation (map)
Ancient Native American Communities (map)
Native American Peoples, c. 1500 (map)
Present-Day United States (map)

≈ ≈ ≈

THE DECLARATION OF INDEPENDENCE
In Congress, July 4, 1776

The Unanimous Declaration of the Thirteen United States of America,
When, in the course of human events, it becomes necessary for one people to dissolve the political bonds which have connected them with another, and to assume, among the powers of the earth, the separate and equal station to which the laws of nature and of nature's God entitle them, a decent respect to the opinions of mankind requires that they should declare the causes which impel them to the separation.

We hold these truths to be self-evident: That all men are created equal; that they are endowed by their Creator with certain unalienable rights; that among these are life, liberty, and the pursuit of happiness; that, to secure these rights, governments are instituted among men, deriving their just powers from the consent of the governed; that whenever any form of government becomes destructive of these ends, it is the right of the people to alter or to abolish it, and to institute new government, laying its foundation on such principles, and organizing its powers in such form, as to them shall seem most likely to effect their safety and happiness. Prudence, indeed, will dictate that governments long established should not be changed for light and transient causes; and accordingly all experience hath shown that mankind are more disposed to suffer, while evils are sufferable, than to right themselves by abolishing the forms to which they are accustomed. But when a long train of abuses and usurpations, pursuing invariably the same object, evinces a design to reduce them under absolute despotism, it is their right, it is their duty, to throw off such government, and to provide new guards for their future security. Such has been the patient sufferance of these colonies; and such is now the necessity which constrains them to alter their former systems of government. The history of the present King of Great Britain is a history of repeated injuries and usurpations, all having in direct object the establishment of an absolute tyranny over these states. To prove this, let facts be submitted to a candid world.

He has refused his assent to laws, the most wholesome and necessary for the public good.

He has forbidden his governors to pass laws of immediate and pressing importance, unless suspended in their operation till his assent should be obtained; and, when so suspended, he has utterly neglected to attend to them.

He has refused to pass other laws for the accommodation of large districts of people, unless those people would relinquish the right of representation in the legislature, a right inestimable to them, and formidable to tyrants only.

He has called together legislative bodies at places unusual, uncomfortable, and distant from the depository of their public records, for the sole purpose of fatiguing them into compliance with his measures.

He has dissolved representative houses repeatedly, for opposing, with manly firmness, his invasions on the rights of the people.

He has refused for a long time, after such dissolutions, to cause others to be elected; whereby the legislative powers, incapable of annihilation, have returned to the people at large for their exercise; the state remaining, in the mean time, exposed to all the dangers of invasions from without and convulsions within.

He has endeavored to prevent the population of these states; for that purpose obstructing the laws for naturalization of foreigners; refusing to pass others to encourage their migration hither, and raising the conditions of new appropriations of lands.

He has obstructed the administration of justice, by refusing his assent to laws for establishing judiciary powers.

He has made judges dependent on his will alone, for the tenure of their offices, and the amount and payment of their salaries.

He has erected a multitude of new offices, and sent hither swarms of officers to harass our people and eat out their substance.

He has kept among us, in times of peace, standing armies, without the consent of our legislatures.

He has affected to render the military independent of, and superior to, the civil power.

He has combined with others to subject us to a jurisdiction foreign to our constitution, and unacknowledged by our laws, giving his assent to their acts of pretended legislation:

For quartering large bodies of armed troops among us;

For protecting them, by a mock trial, from punishment for any murder which they should commit on the inhabitants of these states;

For cutting off our trade with all parts of the world;

For imposing taxes on us without our consent;

For depriving us, in many cases, of the benefits of trial by jury;

For transporting us beyond seas, to be tried for pretended offenses;

For abolishing the free system of English laws in a neighboring province, establishing therein an arbitrary government, and enlarging its boundaries, so as to render it at once an example and fit instrument for introducing the same absolute rule into these colonies;

For taking away our charters, abolishing our most valuable laws, and altering fundamentally the forms of our governments;

For suspending our own legislatures, and declaring themselves invested with power to legislate for us in all cases whatsoever.

He has abdicated government here, by declaring us out of his protection and waging war against us.

He has plundered our seas, ravaged our coasts, burned our towns, and destroyed the lives of our people.

He is at this time transporting large armies of foreign mercenaries to complete the works of death, desolation, and tyranny already begun with circumstances of cruelty and perfidy scarcely paralleled in the most barbarous ages, and totally unworthy the head of a civilized nation.

He has constrained our fellow-citizens, taken captive on the high seas, to bear arms against their country, to become the executioners of their friends and brethren, or to fall themselves by their hands.

He has excited domestic insurrection among us, and has endeavored to bring on the inhabitants of our frontiers the merciless Indian savages, whose known rule of warfare is an undistinguished destruction of all ages, sexes, and conditions.

In every stage of these oppressions we have petitioned for redress in the most humble terms; our repeated petitions have been answered only by repeated injury. A prince, whose character is thus marked by every act which may define a tyrant, is unfit to be the ruler of a free people.

Nor have we been wanting in our attentions to our British brethren. We have warned them, from time to time, of attempts by their legislature to extend an unwarrantable jurisdiction over us. We have reminded them of the circumstances of our emigration and settlement here. We have appealed to their native justice and magnanimity; and we have conjured them, by the ties of our common kindred, to disavow these usurpations, which would inevitably interrupt our connections and correspondence. They, too, have been deaf to the voice of justice and of consanguinity. We must, therefore, acquiesce in the necessity which denounces our separation, and hold them, as we hold the rest of mankind, enemies in war, in peace friends.

We, therefore, the representatives of the United States of America, in General Congress assembled, appealing to the Supreme Judge of the world for the rectitude of our intentions, do, in the name and by the authority of the good people of these colonies, solemnly publish and declare, that these United Colonies are, and of right ought to be, FREE AND INDEPENDENT STATES; that

John Hancock

Button Gwinnett	George Wythe	Geo. Ross	Saml. Adams
Lyman Hall	Richard Henry Lee	Caesar Rodney	John Adams
Geo. Walton	Th. Jefferson	Geo. Read	Robt. Treat Paine
Wm. Hooper	Benj. Harrison	Tho. M'kean	Elbridge Gerry
Joseph Hewes	Thos. Nelson, Jr.	Wm. Floyd	Step. Hopkins
John Penn	Francis Lightfoot Lee	Phil. Livingston	William Ellery
Edward Rutledge	Carter Braxton	Frans. Lewis	Roger Sherman
Thos. Heyward, Junr.	Robt. Morris	Lewis Morris	Sam'el Huntington
Thomas Lynch, Junr.	Benjamin Rush	Richd. Stockton	Wm. Williams
Arthur Middleton	Benja. Franklin	Jno. Witherspoon	Oliver Wolcott
Samuel Chase	John Morton	Fras. Hopkinson	Matthew Thornton
Wm. Paca	Geo. Clymer	John Hart	
Thos. Stone	Jas. Smith	Abra. Clark	
Charles Carroll of	Geo. Taylor	Josiah Bartlett	
Carrollton	James Wilson	Wm. Whipple	

they are absolved from all allegiance to the British crown, and that all political connection between them and the state of Great Britain is, and ought to be, totally dissolved; and that, as free and independent states, they have full power to levy war, conclude peace, contract alliances, establish commerce, and do all other acts and things which independent states may of right do. And for the support of this declaration, with a firm reliance on the protection of Divine Providence, we mutually pledge to each other our lives, our fortunes, and our sacred honor.

THE ARTICLES OF CONFEDERATION

Between the States of New Hampshire, Massachusetts Bay, Rhode Island and Providence Plantations, Connecticut, New York, New Jersey, Pennsylvania, Delaware, Maryland, Virginia, North Carolina, South Carolina, Georgia

ARTICLE 1

The stile of this confederacy shall be "The United States of America."

ARTICLE 2

Each State retains its sovereignty, freedom and independence, and every power, jurisdiction, and right, which is not by this confederation expressly delegated to the United States, in Congress assembled.

ARTICLE 3

The said states hereby severally enter into a firm league of friendship with each other for their common defence, the security of their liberties and their mutual and general welfare; binding themselves to assist each other against all force offered to, or attacks made upon them, or any of them, on account of religion, sovereignty, trade, or any other pretence whatever.

ARTICLE 4

The better to secure and perpetuate mutual friendship and intercourse among the people of the different states in this union, the free inhabitants of each of these states, paupers, vagabonds, and fugitives from justice excepted, shall be entitled to all privileges and immunities of free citizens in the several states; and the people of each State shall have free ingress and regress to and from any other State, and shall enjoy therein all the privileges of trade and commerce, subject to the same duties, impositions, and restrictions, as the inhabitants thereof respectively; provided, that such restrictions shall not extend so far as to prevent the removal of property, imported into any State, to any other State of which the owner is an inhabitant; provided also, that no imposition, duties, or restriction, shall be laid by any State on the property of the United States, or either of them.

If any person guilty of, or charged with treason, felony, or other high misdemeanor in any State, shall flee from justice and be found in any of the United States, he shall, upon demand of the governor or executive power of the State from which he fled, be delivered up and removed to the State having jurisdiction of his offence.

Full faith and credit shall be given in each of these states to the records, acts, and judicial proceedings of the courts and magistrates of every other State.

ARTICLE 5

For the more convenient management of the general interests of the United States, delegates shall be annually appointed, in such manner as the legislature of each State shall direct, to meet in Congress, on the 1st Monday in November in every year, with a power reserved to each State to recall its delegates, or any of them, at any time within the year, and to send others in their stead for the remainder of the year.

No State shall be represented in Congress by less than two, nor by more than seven members; and no person shall be capable of being a delegate for more than three years in any term of six years; nor shall any person, being a delegate, be capable of holding any office under the United States, for which he, or any other for his benefit, receives any salary, fees, or emolument of any kind.

Each State shall maintain its own delegates in a meeting of the states, and while they act as members of the committee of the states.

In determining questions in the United States, in Congress assembled, each State shall have one vote.

Freedom of speech and debate in Congress shall not be impeached or questioned in any court or place out of Congress: and the members of Congress shall be protected in their persons from arrests and imprisonments, during the time of their going to and from, and attendance on Congress, except for treason, felony, or breach of the peace.

ARTICLE 6

No State, without the consent of the United States, in Congress assembled, shall send any embassy to, or receive any embassy from, or enter into any conference, agreement, alliance, or treaty with any king, prince, or state; nor shall any person, holding any office of profit or trust under the United States, or any of them, accept of any present, emolument, office or title, of any kind whatever, from any king, prince, or foreign state; nor shall the United States, in Congress assembled, or any of them, grant any title of nobility.

No two or more states shall enter into any treaty, confederation, or alliance, whatever, between them, without the consent of the United States, in Congress assembled, specifying accurately the purposes for which the same is to be entered into, and how long it shall continue.

No State shall lay any imposts or duties which may interfere with any stipulations in treaties entered into by the United States, in Congress assembled, with any king, prince, or state, in pursuance of any treaties already proposed by Congress to the courts of France and Spain.

No vessels of war shall be kept up in time of peace by any State, except such number only as shall be deemed necessary by the United States, in Congress assembled, for the defence of such State or its trade; nor shall any body of forces be kept up by any

State, in time of peace, except such number only as, in the judgment of the United States, in Congress assembled, shall be deemed requisite to garrison the forts necessary for the defence of such State; but every State shall always keep up a well regulated and disciplined militia, sufficiently armed and accoutred, and shall provide, and constantly have ready for use, in public stores, a due number, of field pieces and tents, and a proper quantity of arms, ammunition and camp equipage.

No State shall engage in any war without the consent of the United States, in Congress assembled, unless such State be actually invaded by enemies, or shall have received certain advice of a resolution being formed by some nation of Indians to invade such State, and the danger is so imminent as not to admit of a delay till the United States, in Congress assembled, can be consulted; nor shall any State grant commissions to any ships or vessels of war, nor letters of marque or reprisal, except it be after a declaration of war by the United States, in Congress assembled, and then only against the kingdom or state, and the subjects thereof, against which war has been so declared, and under such regulations as shall be established by the United States, in Congress assembled, unless such States be infested by pirates, in which case vessels of war may be fitted out for that occasion, and kept so long as the danger shall continue, or until the United States, in Congress assembled, shall determine otherwise.

ARTICLE 7

When land forces are raised by any State for the common defence, all officers of or under the rank of colonel, shall be appointed by the legislature of each State respectively, by whom such forces shall be raised, or in such manner as such State shall direct; and all vacancies shall be filled up by the State which first made the appointment.

ARTICLE 8

All charges of war and all other expences, that shall be incurred for the common defence or general welfare, and allowed by the United States, in Congress assembled, shall be defrayed out of a common treasury, which shall be supplied by the several states, in proportion to the value of all land within each State, granted to or surveyed for any person, as such land and the buildings and improvements thereon shall be estimated according to such mode as the United States, in Congress assembled, shall, from time to time, direct and appoint.

The taxes for paying that proportion shall be laid and levied by the authority and direction of the legislatures of the several states, within the time agreed upon by the United States, in Congress assembled.

ARTICLE 9

The United States, in Congress assembled, shall have the sole and exclusive right and power of determining on peace and war, except in the cases mentioned in the 6th article; of sending and receiving ambassadors; entering into treaties and alliances, provided that no treaty of commerce shall be made, whereby the legislative power of the respective states shall be restrained from imposing such imposts and duties on foreigners as their own people are subjected to, or from prohibiting the exportation or importation of any species of goods or commodities whatsoever; of establishing rules for deciding, in all cases, what captures on land or water shall be legal, and in what manner prizes, taken by land or naval forces in the service of the United States, shall be divided or appropriated; of granting letters of marque and reprisal in times of peace; appointing courts for the trial of piracies and felonies committed on the high seas, and establishing courts for receiving and determining, finally, appeals in all cases of captures; provided, that no member of Congress shall be appointed a judge of any of the said courts.

The United States, in Congress assembled, shall also be the last resort on appeal in all disputes and differences now subsisting, or that hereafter may arise between two or more states concerning boundary, jurisdiction or any other cause whatever; which authority shall always be exercised in the manner following: whenever the legislative or executive authority, or lawful agent of any State, in controversy with another, shall present a petition to Congress, stating the matter in question, and praying for a hearing, notice thereof shall be given, by order of Congress, to the legislative or executive authority of the other State in controversy, and a day assigned for the appearance of the parties by their lawful agents, who shall then be directed to appoint, by joint consent, commissioners or judges to constitute a court for hearing and determining the matter in question; but, if they cannot agree, Congress shall name three persons out of each of the United States, and from the list of such persons each party shall alternately strike out one, in the petitioners beginning, until the number shall be reduced to thirteen; and from that number not less than seven, nor more than nine names, as Congress shall direct, shall, in the presence of Congress, be drawn out by lot; and the persons whose names shall be drawn, or any five of them, shall be commissioners or judges to hear and finally determine the controversy, so always as a major part of the judges who shall hear the cause shall agree in the determination; and if either party shall neglect to attend at the day appointed, without shewing reasons which Congress shall judge sufficient, or, being present, shall refuse to strike, the Congress shall proceed to nominate three persons out of each State, and the secretary of Congress shall strike in behalf of such party absent or refusing; and the judgment and sentence of the court to be appointed, in the manner before prescribed, shall be final and conclusive; and if any of the parties shall refuse to submit to the authority of such court, or to appear or defend their claim or cause, the court shall nevertheless proceed to pronounce sentence or judgment, which shall, in like manner, be final and decisive, the judgment or sentence and other proceedings being, in either case, transmitted to Congress, and lodged among the acts of Congress for the security of the parties concerned: provided, that every commissioner, before he sits in judgment, shall take an oath, to be administered by one of the judges of the supreme or superior court of the State where the cause shall be tried, "well and truly to hear and determine the matter in question, according to the best of his judgment, without favor, affection, or hope of reward": provided, also, that no State shall be deprived of territory for the benefit of the United States.

All controversies concerning the private right of soil, claimed under different grants of two or more states, whose jurisdictions, as they may respect such lands and the states which passed such grants, are adjusted, the said grants, or either of them, being at the same time claimed to have originated antecedent to such settlement of jurisdiction, shall, on the petition of either party to the Congress of the United States, be finally determined, as near as may be, in the same manner as is before prescribed for deciding disputes respecting territorial jurisdiction between different states.

The United States, in Congress assembled, shall also have the sole and exclusive right and power of regulating the alloy and value of coin struck by their own authority, or by that of the respective states; fixing the standard of weights and measures throughout the United States; regulating the trade and managing all affairs with the Indians not members of any of the states; provided that the legislative right of any State within its own limits be not infringed or violated; establishing and regulating post offices from one State to another throughout all the United States, and exacting such postage on the papers passing through the same as may be requisite to defray the expences of the said office; appointing all officers of the land forces in the service of the United States, excepting regimental officers; appointing all the officers of the naval forces, and commissioning all officers whatever in the service of the United States; making rules for the government and regulation of the said land and naval forces, and directing their operations.

The United States, in Congress assembled, shall have authority to appoint a committee to sit in the recess of Congress, to be denominated "a Committee of the States," and to consist of one delegate from each State, and to appoint such other committees and civil officers as may be necessary for managing the general affairs of the United States, under their direction; to appoint one of their number to preside; provided that no person be allowed to serve in the office of president more than one year in any term of three years; to ascertain the necessary sums of money to be raised for the service of the United States, and to appropriate and apply the same for defraying the public expences; to borrow money or emit bills on the credit of the United States, transmitting, every half year, to the respective states, an account of the sums of money so borrowed or emitted; to build and equip a navy; to agree upon the number of land forces, and to make requisitions from each State for its quota, in proportion to the number of white inhabitants in such State; which requisitions shall be binding; and, thereupon, the legislature of each State shall appoint the regimental officers, raise the men, and cloathe, arm, and equip them in a soldier-like manner, at the expence of the United States; and the officers and men so cloathed, armed, and equipped, shall march to the place appointed and within the time agreed on by the United States, in Congress assembled; but if the United States, in Congress assembled, shall, on consideration of circumstances, judge proper that any State should not raise men, or should raise a smaller number than its quota, and that any other State should raise a greater number of men than the quota thereof, such extra number shall be raised, officered, cloathed, armed, and equipped in the same manner as the quota of such State, unless the legislature of such State shall judge that such extra number cannot be safely spared out of the same, in which case they shall raise, officer, cloathe, arm, and equip as many of such extra number as they judge can be safely spared. And the officers and men so cloathed, armed, and equipped, shall march to the place appointed and within the time agreed on by the United States, in Congress assembled.

The United States, in Congress assembled, shall never engage in a war, nor grant letters of marque and reprisal in time of peace, nor enter into any treaties or alliances, nor coin money, nor regulate the value thereof, nor ascertain the sums and expences necessary for the defence and welfare of the United States, or any of them: nor emit bills, nor borrow money on the credit of the United States, nor appropriate money, nor agree upon the number of vessels of war to be built or purchased, or the number of land or sea forces to be raised, nor appoint a commander in chief of the army or navy, unless nine states assent to the same; nor shall a question on any other point, except for adjourning from day to day, be determined, unless by the votes of a majority of the United States, in Congress assembled.

The Congress of the United States shall have power to adjourn to any time within the year, and to any place within the United States, so that no period of adjournment be for a longer duration than the space of six months, and shall publish the journal of their proceedings monthly, except such parts thereof, relating to treaties, alliances or military operations, as, in their judgment, require secrecy; and the yeas and nays of the delegates of each State on any question shall be entered on the journal, when it is desired by any delegate; and the delegates of a State, or any of them, at his, or their request, shall be furnished with a transcript of the said journal, except such parts as are above excepted, to lay before the legislatures of the several states.

ARTICLE 10

The committee of the states, or any nine of them, shall be authorized to execute, in the recess of Congress, such of the powers of Congress as the United States, in Congress assembled, by the consent of nine states, shall, from time to time, think expedient to vest them with; provided, that no power be delegated to the said committee for the exercise of which by the articles of confederation, the voice of nine states, in the Congress of the United States assembled, is requisite.

ARTICLE 11

Canada acceding to this confederation, and joining in the measures of the United States, shall be admitted into and entitled to all the advantages of this union; but no other colony shall be admitted into the same, unless such admission be agreed to by nine states.

ARTICLE 12

All bills of credit emitted, monies borrowed and debts contracted by, or under the authority of Congress before the assembling of the United States, in pursuance of the present confederation, shall be deemed and considered as a charge against the United States, for payment and satisfaction whereof the said United States and the public faith are hereby solemnly pledged.

ARTICLE 13

Every State shall abide by the determinations of the United States, in Congress assembled, on all questions which, by this confederation, are submitted to them. And the articles of this confederation shall be inviolably observed by every State, and the union shall be perpetual; nor shall any alteration at any time hereafter be made in any of them, unless such alteration be agreed to in a Congress of the United States, and be afterwards confirmed by the legislatures of every State.

These articles shall be proposed to the legislatures of all the United States, to be considered, and if approved of by them, they are advised to authorize their delegates to ratify the same in the Congress of the United States; which being done, the same shall become conclusive.

THE CONSTITUTION OF THE UNITED STATES OF AMERICA

PREAMBLE

We the People of the United States, in Order to form a more perfect Union, establish Justice, insure domestic Tranquility, provide for the common defence, promote the general Welfare, and secure the Blessings of Liberty to ourselves and our Posterity, do ordain and establish this Constitution for the United States of America.

ARTICLE 1

Section 1

All legislative Powers herein granted shall be vested in a Congress of the United States, which shall consist of a Senate and House of Representatives.

Section 2

The House of Representatives shall be composed of Members chosen every second Year by the People of the several States, and the Electors in each State shall have the Qualifications requisite for Electors of the most numerous Branch of the State Legislature.

No Person shall be a Representative who shall not have attained to the Age of twenty five Years, and been seven Years a Citizen of the United States, and who shall not, when elected, be an inhabitant of that State in which he shall be chosen.

Representatives and direct Taxes shall be apportioned among the several States which may be included within this Union, according to their respective Numbers, *which shall be determined by adding to the whole Number of free Persons, including those bound to Service for a Term of Years, and excluding Indians not taxed, three fifths of all other Persons.* The actual Enumeration shall be made within three Years after the first Meeting of the Congress of the United States, and within every subsequent Term of ten Years, in such Manner as they shall by Law direct. The Number of Representatives shall not exceed one for every thirty Thousand, but each State shall have at Least one Representative; *and until such enumeration shall be made, the State of New Hampshire shall be entitled to chuse three, Massachusetts eight, Rhode-Island and Providence Plantations one, Connecticut five, New York six, New Jersey four, Pennsylvania eight, Delaware one, Maryland six, Virginia ten, North Carolina five, South Carolina five, and Georgia three.*

When vacancies happen in the Representation from any State, the Executive Authority thereof shall issue Writs of Election to fill such Vacancies.

The House of Representatives shall chuse their Speaker and other Officers; and shall have the sole Power of Impeachment.

Section 3

The Senate of the United States shall be composed of two Senators from each State, *chosen by the Legislature thereof,* for six Years; and each Senator shall have one Vote.

Immediately after they shall be assembled in Consequence of the first Election, they shall be divided as equally as may be into three Classes. The Seats of the Senators of the first Class shall be vacated at the Expiration of the second Year, of the second Class at the Expiration of the fourth Year, and of the third Class at the Expiration of the sixth Year so that one third may be chosen every second Year; and if Vacancies happen by Resignation, or otherwise, during the Recess of the Legislature of any state, the Executive thereof may make temporary Appointments until the next Meeting of the Legislature, which shall then fill such Vacancies.

No Person shall be a Senator who shall not have attained to the Age of thirty Years, and been nine Years a Citizen of the United States, and who shall not, when elected, be an Inhabitant of that State for which he shall be chosen.

The Vice President of the United States shall be President of the Senate, but shall have no Vote, unless they be equally divided.

The Senate shall chuse their other Officers, and also a President *pro tempore,* in the Absence of the Vice President, or when he shall exercise the Office of President of the United States.

The Senate shall have the sole Power to try all Impeachments. When sitting for that Purpose, they shall be on Oath or Affirmation. When the President of the United States is tried the Chief Justice shall preside: And no Person shall be convicted without the Concurrence of two thirds of the Members present.

Judgment in Cases of Impeachment shall not extend further than to removal from Office, and disqualification to hold and enjoy any Office of honor, Trust or Profit under the United States: but the Party convicted shall nevertheless be liable and subject to Indictment, Trial, Judgment and Punishment, according to Law.

Section 4

The Times, Places and Manner of holding Elections for Senators and Representatives, shall be prescribed in each State by the Legislature thereof; but the Congress may at any time by Law make or alter such Regulations, except as to the Places of chusing Senators.

*Passages no longer in effect are printed in italic type.

The Congress shall assemble at least once in every Year, *and such Meeting shall be on the first Monday in December, unless they shall by Law appoint a different Day.*

Section 5

Each House shall be the Judge of the Elections, Returns and Qualifications of its own Members, and a Majority of each shall constitute a Quorum to do Business; but a smaller Number may adjourn from day to day, and may be authorized to compel the Attendance of absent Members, in such Manner, and under such Penalties as each House may provide.

Each House may determine the Rules of its Proceedings, punish its Members for disorderly Behaviour, and, with the Concurrence of two thirds, expel a Member.

Each House shall keep a Journal of its Proceedings, and from time to time publish the same, excepting such Parts as may in their Judgment require Secrecy; and the Yeas and Nays of the Members of either House on any question shall, at the Desire of one fifth of those Present, be entered on the Journal.

Neither House, during the Session of Congress, shall, without the Consent of the other, adjourn for more than three days, nor to any other Place than that in which the two Houses shall be sitting.

Section 6

The Senators and Representatives shall receive a Compensation for their Services, to be ascertained by Law, and paid out of the Treasury of the United States. They shall in all Cases, except Treason, Felony and Breach of the Peace, be privileged from Arrest during their Attendance at the Session of their respective Houses, and in going to and returning from the same; and for any Speech or Debate in either House, they shall not be questioned in any other Place.

No Senator or Representative shall, during the Time for which he was elected, be appointed to any civil Office under the Authority of the United States, which shall have been created, or the Emoluments whereof shall have been encreased during such time, and no Person holding any Office under the United States, shall be a Member of either House during his Continuance in Office.

Section 7

All Bills for raising Revenue shall orginate in the House of Representatives; but the Senate may propose or concur with Amendments as on other Bills.

Every Bill which shall have passed the House of Representatives and the Senate, shall, before it become a Law, be presented to the President of the United States; If he approve he shall sign it, but if not he shall return it, with his Objections to the House in which it shall have originated, who shall enter the Objections at large on their Journal, and proceed to reconsider it. If after such Reconsideration two thirds of that House shall agree to pass the Bill, it shall be sent, together with the Objections, to the other House, by which it shall likewise be reconsidered, and if approved by two thirds of that House, it shall become a Law. But in all such Cases the Votes of both Houses shall be determined by yeas and Nays, and the Names of the Persons voting for and against the Bill shall be entered on the Journal of each House respectively. If any Bill shall not be returned by the President within ten Days (Sundays excepted) after it shall have been presented to him, the Same shall be a Law, in like Manner as if he had signed it, unless the Congress by their Adjournment prevent its Return, in which Case it shall not be a Law.

Every Order, Resolution, or Vote to which the Concurrence of the Senate and House of Representatives may be necessary (except on a question of Adjournment) shall be presented to the President of the United States; and before the Same shall take Effect, shall be approved by him, or being disapproved by him, shall be repassed by two thirds of the Senate and House of Representatives, according to the Rules and Limitations prescribed in the Case of a Bill.

Section 8

The Congress shall have Power To lay and collect Taxes, Duties, Imposts and Excises, to pay the Debts and provide for the common Defence and general Welfare of the United States; but all Duties, Imposts and Excises shall be uniform throughout the United States;

To borrow Money on the credit of the United States;

To regulate Commerce with foreign Nations, and among the several States, and with the Indian Tribes;

To establish an uniform Rule of Naturalization, and uniform Laws on the subject of Bankruptcies throughout the United States;

To coin Money, regulate the Value thereof, and of foreign Coin, and fix the Standard of Weights and Measures;

To provide for the Punishment of counterfeiting the Securities and current Coin of the United States;

To establish Post Offices and post Roads;

To promote the Progress of Science and useful Arts, by securing for limited Times to Authors and Inventors the exclusive Right to their respective Writings and Discoveries;

To constitute Tribunals inferior to the supreme Court;

To define and punish Piracies and Felonies committed on the high Seas, and Offences against the Law of Nations;

To declare War, grant Letters of Marque and Reprisal, and make Rules concerning Captures on Land and Water;

To raise and support Armies, but no Appropriation of Money to that Use shall be for a longer Term than two Years;

To provide and maintain a Navy;

To make Rules for the Government and Regulation of the land and naval Forces;

To provide for calling forth the Militia to execute the Laws of the Union, suppress Insurrections and repel Invasions;

To provide for organizing, arming, and disciplining, the Militia, and for governing such Part of them as may be employed in the Service of the United States, reserving to the States respectively, the Appointment of the Officers, and the Authority of training the Militia according to the discipline prescribed by Congress;

To exercise exclusive Legislation in all Cases whatsoever, over such District (not exceeding ten Miles square) as may, by Cession of particular States, and the Acceptance of Congress, become the Seat of the Government of the United States, and to exercise like Authority over all Places purchased by the Consent of the Legislature of the State in which the Same

shall be, for the Erection of Forts, Magazines, Arsenals, dock-Yards, and other needful Buildings;—And

To make all Laws which shall be necessary and proper for carrying into Execution the foregoing Powers, and all other Powers vested by this Constitution in the Government of the United States, or in any Department of Officer thereof.

Section 9

The Migration or Importation of such Persons as any of the States now existing shall think proper to admit, shall not be prohibited by the Congress prior to the Year one thousand eight hundred and eight, but a Tax or duty may be imposed on such Importation, not exceeding ten dollars for each Person.

The Privilege of the Writ of Habeas Corpus shall not be suspended, unless when in Cases of Rebellion or Invasion the public Safety may require it.

No Bill of Attainder or ex post facto Law shall be passed.

No Capitation, or other direct, Tax shall be laid, unless in Proportion to the Census or Enumeration herein before directed to be taken.

No Tax or Duty shall be laid on Articles exported from any State.

No Preference shall be given by any Regulation of Commerce or Revenue to the Ports of one State over those of another: nor shall Vessels bound to, or from, one State, be obliged to enter, clear, or pay Duties in another.

No Money shall be drawn from the Treasury, but in Consequence of Appropriations made by Law; and a regular Statement and Account of the Receipts and Expenditures of all public Money shall be published from time to time.

No Title of Nobility shall be granted by the United States: And no Person holding any Office of Profit or Trust under them, shall, without the Consent of the Congress, accept of any present, Emolument, Office, or Title, of any kind whatever, from any King, Prince, or foreign State.

Section 10

No State shall enter into any Treaty, Alliance, or Confederation; grant Letters of Marque and Reprisal;

coin Money; emit Bills of Credit; make any Thing but gold and silver Coin a Tender in Payment of Debts; pass any Bill of Attainder, ex post facto Law, or Law impairing the obligation of Contracts, or grant any Title of Nobility.

No State shall, without the Consent of the Congress, lay any Imposts or Duties on Imports or Exports, except what may be absolutely necessary for executing its inspection Laws: and the net Produce of all Duties and Imposts, laid by any State on Imports or Exports, shall be for the Use of the Treasury of the United States; and all such Laws shall be subject to the Revision and Controul of the Congress.

No State shall, without the Consent of Congress, lay any Duty of Tonnage, keep Troops, or Ships of War in time of Peace, enter into any Agreement or Compact with another State, or with a foreign Power, or engage in War, unless actually invaded, or in such imminent Danger as will not admit of delay.

ARTICLE 2

Section 1

The executive Power shall be vested in a President of the United States of America. He shall hold his Office during the Term of four Years, and, together with the Vice President, chosen for the same Term, be elected, as follows:

Each State shall appoint, in such Manner as the Legislature thereof may direct, a Number of Electors, equal to the whole Number of Senators and Representatives to which the State may be entitled in the Congress: but no Senator or Representative, or Person holding an Office of Trust or Profit under the United States, shall be appointed an Elector.

The Electors shall meet in their respective States, and vote by Ballot for two Persons, of whom one at least shall not be an Inhabitant of the same State with themselves. And they shall make a List of all the Persons voted for, and of the Number of Votes for each; which List they shall sign and certify, and transmit sealed to the Seat of the Government of the United States, directed to the President of the Senate. The President of the Senate shall, in the Presence of the Senate and House of Representatives, open all the

Certificates, and the Votes shall then be counted. The Person having the greatest Number of Votes shall be the President, if such Number be a Majority of the whole number of Electors appointed; and if there be more than one who have such Majority, and have an equal Number of Votes, then the House of Representatives shall immediately chuse by Ballot one of them for President; and if no Person have a Majority, then from the five highest on the List the said House shall in like Manner chuse the President. But in chusing the President, the Votes shall be taken by States, the Representation from each State having one Vote; A quorum for this Purpose shall consist of a Member or Members from two thirds of the States, and a Majority of all the States shall be necessary to a Choice. In every Case, after the Choice of the President, the Person having the greatest Number of Votes of the Electors shall be the Vice President. But if there should remain two or more who have equal Votes, the Senate shall chuse from them by Ballot the Vice President.

The Congress may determine the time of chusing the Electors, and the Day on which they shall give their Votes; which Day shall be the same throughout the United States.

No person except a natural born Citizen, *or a Citizen of the United States, at the time of the Adoption of this Constitution,* shall be eligible to the Office of President; neither shall any Person be eligible to that Office who shall not have attained to the Age of thirty five Years, and been fourteen Years a Resident within the United States.

In Case of the Removal of the President from Office, or of his Death, Resignation, or Inability to discharge the Powers and Duties of the said Office, the Same shall devolve on the Vice President, and the Congress may by Law provide for the Case of Removal, Death, Resignation or Inability, both of the President and Vice President, declaring what Officer shall then act as President, and such Officer shall act accordingly, until the Disability be removed, or a President shall be elected.

The President shall, at stated Times, receive for his Services, a Compensation, which shall neither be increased nor diminished during the Period for which he shall have been elected, and he shall not receive within that period any other Emolument from the United States, or any of them.

Before he enter on the Execution of his Office, he shall take the following Oath or Affirmation:—"I do solemnly swear (or affirm) that I will faithfully execute the Office of President of the United States, and will to the best of my Ability, preserve, protect and defend the Constitution of the United States."

Section 2

The President shall be Commander in Chief of the Army and Navy of the United States, and of the Militia of the several States, when called into the actual Service of the United States; he may require the Opinion, in writing, of the principal Officer in each of the executive Departments, upon any Subject relating to the Duties of their respective Offices, and he shall have Power to grant Reprieves and Pardons for Offences against the United States, except in Cases of Impeachment.

He shall have Power, by and with the Advice and Consent of the Senate, to make Treaties, provided two thirds of the Senators present concur; and he shall nominate, and by and with the Advice and Consent of the Senate, shall appoint Ambassadors, other public Ministers and Consuls, Judges of the supreme Court, and all other Officers of the United States, whose Appointments are not herein otherwise provided for, and which shall be established by Law: but the Congress may by Law vest the Appointment of such inferior Officers, as they think proper in the President alone, in the Courts of Law, or in the Heads of Departments.

The President shall have Power to fill up all Vacancies that may happen during the Recess of the Senate, by granting Commissions which shall expire at the End of their next Session.

Section 3

He shall from time to time give to the Congress Information of the State of the Union, and recommend to their Consideration such Measures as he shall judge necessary and expedient; he may, on extraordinary Occasions, convene both Houses, or either of them, and in Case of disagreement between them, with Respect to the Time of Adjournment, he may adjourn them to such Time as he shall think proper; he shall receive Ambassadors and other public Ministers; he shall take Care that the Laws be faithfully executed, and shall Commission all the officers of the United States.

Section 4

The President, Vice President and all civil Officers of the United States, shall be removed from Office on Impeachment for, and Conviction of, Treason, Bribery or other high Crimes and Misdemeanors.

ARTICLE 3

Section 1

The judicial Power of the United States, shall be vested in one supreme Court, and in such inferior Courts as the Congress may from time to time ordain and establish. The Judges, both of the supreme and inferior Courts, shall hold their offices during good Behaviour, and shall, at stated Times, receive for their Services, a Compensation, which shall not be diminished during their Continuance in Office.

Section 2

The judicial Power shall extend to all Cases, in Law and Equity, arising under this Constitution, the Laws of the United States, and Treaties made, or which shall be made, under their Authority;—to all Cases affecting Ambassadors, other public Ministers and Consuls;—to all Cases of admiralty and maritime Jurisdiction;—to Controversies to which the United States shall be a Party;—to Controversies between two or more States;—*between a State and Citizens of another State;*—between Citizens of different States;—between Citizens of the same State claiming Lands under Grants of different States, and between a State, or the Citizens thereof, and foreign States, Citizens or Subjects.

In all Cases affecting Ambassadors, other public Ministers and Consuls, and those in which a State shall be Party, the supreme Court shall have original Jurisdiction. In all the other Cases before mentioned, the supreme Court shall have appellate Jurisdiction, both as to Law and Fact, with such Exceptions, and under such Regulations as the Congress shall make.

The Trial of all Crimes, except in Cases of Impeachment, shall be by Jury; and such Trial shall be held in the State where the said Crimes shall have been committed, but when not committed within any State, the Trial shall be at such Place or Places as the Congress may by Law have directed.

Section 3

Treason against the United States, shall consist only in levying War against them, or in adhering to their Enemies, giving them Aid and Comfort. No person shall be convicted of Treason unless on the Testimony of two Witnesses to the same overt Act, or on Confession in open Court.

The Congress shall have Power to declare the Punishment of Treason, but no Attainder of Treason shall work Corruption of Blood, or Forfeiture except during the Life of the Person attainted.

ARTICLE 4

Section 1

Full Faith and Credit shall be given in each State to the public Acts, Records, and judicial Proceedings of every other State. And the Congress may by general Laws prescribe the Manner in which such Acts, Records and Proceedings shall be proved, and the Effect thereof.

Section 2

The Citizens of each State shall be entitled to all Privileges and Immunities of Citizens in the several States.

A Person charged in any State with Treason, Felony, or other Crime, who shall flee from Justice, and be found in another State, shall on Demand of the executive Authority of the State from which he fled, be delivered up, to be removed to the State having Jurisdiction of the Crime.

No Person held to Service or Labour in one State, under the Laws thereof, escaping into another, shall, in Consequence of any Law or Regulation therein, be discharged from such Service or Labour, but shall be delivered up on Claim of the Party to whom such Service or Labour may be due.

Section 3

New States may be admitted by the Congress into this Union; but no new State shall be formed or erected within the Jurisdiction of any other State; nor any State be formed by the Junction of two or more States, or Parts of States, without the Consent of the Legislatures of the States concerned as well as of the Congress.

The Congress shall have Power to dispose of and make all needful Rules and Regulations respecting the Territory or other Property belonging to the United States; and nothing in this Constitution shall be so construed as to Prejudice any Claims of the United States, or of any particular States.*

Section 4

The United States shall guarantee to every State in this Union a Republican Form of Government, and shall protect each of them against Invasion; and on Application of the Legislature, or of the Executive (when the Legislature cannot be convened) against domestic violence.

ARTICLE 5

The Congress, whenever two thirds of both Houses shall deem it necessary, shall propose Amendments to this Constitution, or, on the Application of the Legislatures of two thirds of the several States, shall call a Convention for proposing Amendments, which, in either Case, shall be valid to all Intents and Purposes, as Part of this Constitution, when ratified by the Legislatures of three fourths of the several States, or by Conventions in three fourths thereof, as the one or the other Mode of Ratification may be proposed by the Congress; Provided *that no Amendment which may be made prior to the Year One thousand eight hundred and eight shall in any Manner affect the first and fourth Clauses in the Ninth Section of the first Article;* and that no State, without its Consent, shall be deprived of its equal Suffrage in the Senate.

---

*The Constitution was submitted on September 17, 1787, by the Constitutional Convention, was ratified by the Convention of several states at various dates up to May 29, 1790, and became effective on March 4, 1789.

ARTICLE 6

All Debts contracted and Engagements entered into, before the Adoption of this Constitution, shall be as valid against the United States under this Constitution, as under the Confederation.

This Constitution, and Laws of the United States which shall be made in Pursuance thereof; and all Treaties made, or which shall be made, under the Authority of the United States, shall be the supreme Law of the Land; and the Judges in every State shall be bound thereby, any Thing in the Constitution or Laws of any State to the Contrary notwithstanding.

The Senators and Representatives before mentioned, and the Members of the several State Legislatures, and all executive and Judicial Officers, both of the United States and of the several States, shall be bound by Oath or Affirmation, to support this Constitution; but no religious Test shall ever be required as a Qualification to any Office of public Trust under the United States.

ARTICLE 7

The Ratification of the Conventions of nine States, shall be sufficient for the Establishment of this Constitution between the States so ratifying the Same.

Done in Convention by the Unanimous Consent of the States present the Seventeenth Day of September in the Year of our Lord one thousand seven hundred and Eighty seven and of the Independence of the United States of America the Twelfth* IN WITNESS whereof We have hereunto subscribed our Names,

George Washington President and Deputy from Virginia

Delaware
George Read
Gunning Bedford, Jr.
John Dickinson
Richard Bassett
Jacob Broom

Maryland
James McHenry
Daniel of St. Thomas Jenifer
Daniel Carroll

Virginia
John Blair
James Madison, Jr

North Carolina
William Blount
Richard Dobbs Spraight
Hugh Williamson

South Carolina
John Rutledge
Charles Cotesworth Pinckney
Charles Pinckney
Pierce Butler

Georgia
William Few
Abraham Baldwin

New Hampshire
John Langdon
Nicholas Gilman

Massachusetts
Nathaniel Gorham
Rufus King

Connecticut
William Samuel Johnson
Roger Sherman

New York
Alexander Hamilton

New Jersey
William Livingston
David Brearley
William Paterson
Jonathan Dayton
Pennsylvania
Benjamin Franklin
Thomas Mifflin
Robert Morris
George Clymer
Thomas FitzSimons
Jared Ingersoll
James Wilson
Gouverneur Morris

*The Constitution was submitted on September 17, 1787, by the Constitutional Convention, was ratified by the Convention of several states at various dates up to May 29, 1790, and became effective on March 4, 1789.

AMENDMENTS TO THE CONSTITUTION

AMENDMENT I

Congress shall make no law respecting an establishment of religion, or prohibiting the free exercise thereof; or abridging the freedom of speech, or of the press; or the right of the people peaceably to assemble, and to petition the Government for a redress of grievances.

AMENDMENT II

A well regulated Militia being necessary to the security of a free State, the right of the people to keep and bear Arms, shall not be infringed.

AMENDMENT III

No Soldier shall, in time of peace be quartered in any house, without the consent of the Owner, nor in time of war, but in a manner to be prescribed by law.

AMENDMENT IV

The right of the people to be secure in their persons, houses, papers, and effects, against unreasonable searches and seizures, shall not be violated, and no Warrants shall issue, but upon probable cause, supported by Oath or affirmation, and particularly describing the place to be searched, and the persons or things to be seized.

AMENDMENT V

No person shall be held to answer for a capital, or otherwise infamous crime, unless on a presentment or indictment of a Grand Jury, except in cases arising in the land or naval forces, or in the Militia, when in actual service in time of War or public danger; nor shall any person be subject for the same offense to be twice put in jeopardy of life or limb; nor shall be compelled in any criminal case to be a witness against himself, nor be deprived of life, liberty, or property, without due process of law; nor shall private property be taken for public use, without just compensation.

AMENDMENT VI

In all criminal prosecutions, the accused shall enjoy the right to a speedy and public trial, by an impartial jury of the State and district wherein the crime shall have been committed, which district shall have been previously ascertained by law, and to be informed of the nature and cause of the accusation; to be confronted with the witnesses against him; to have compulsory process for obtaining witnesses in his favor, and to have the Assistance of Counsel for his defence.

AMENDMENT VII

In Suits at common law, where the value in controversy shall exceed twenty dollars, the right of trial by jury shall be preserved, and no fact tried by a jury, shall be otherwise reexamined in any Court of the United States, than according to the rules of the common law.

AMENDMENT VIII

Excessive bail shall not be required, nor excessive fines imposed, nor cruel and unusual punishments inflicted.

AMENDMENT IX

The enumeration in the Constitution, of certain rights, shall not be construed to deny or disparage others retained by the people.

AMENDMENT X*

The powers not delegated to the United States by the Constitution, nor prohibited by it to the States, are reserved to the States respectively, or to the people.

AMENDMENT XI [ADOPTED 1798]

The Judicial power of the United States shall not be construed to extend to any suit in law or equity, commenced or prosecuted against one of the United States by Citizens of another State, or by Citizens or Subjects of any Foreign State.

*The first ten amendments (the Bill of Rights) were ratified and their adoption was certified on December 15, 1791.

AMENDMENT XII [ADOPTED 1804]

The Electors shall meet in their respective states, and vote by ballot for President and Vice President, one of whom, at least, shall not be an inhabitant of the same state with themselves; they shall name in their ballots the person voted for as President, and in distinct ballots the person voted for as Vice President, and they shall make distinct lists of all persons voted for as President, and of all persons voted for as Vice President, and of the number of votes for each, which lists they shall sign and certify, and transmit sealed to the seat of the government of the United States, directed to the President of the Senate;—The President of the Senate shall, in the presence of the Senate and House of Representatives, open all the certificates and the votes shall then be counted;—The person having the greatest number of votes for President, shall be the President, if such number be a majority of the whole number of Electors appointed; and if no person have such majority, then from the persons having the highest numbers not exceeding three on the list of those voted for as President, the House of Representatives shall choose immediately, by ballot, the President. But in choosing the President, the votes shall be taken by states, the representation from each state having one vote; a quorum for this purpose shall consist of a member or members from two-thirds of the states, and a majority of all the states shall be necessary to a choice. And if the House of Representatives shall not choose a President whenever the right of choice shall devolve upon them, before *the fourth day of March* next following, then the Vice President shall act as President, as in the case of the death or other constitutional disability of the President.—The person having the greatest number of votes as Vice President, shall be the Vice President, if such number be a majority of the whole number of Electors appointed, and if no person have a majority, then from the two highest numbers on the list, the Senate shall choose the Vice President; a quorum for the purpose shall consist of two-thirds of the whole number of Senators, and a majority of the whole number shall be necessary to a choice. But no person constitutionally ineligible to the office of President shall be eligible to that of Vice President of the United States.

AMENDMENT XIII [ADOPTED 1865]

Section 1

Neither slavery nor involuntary servitude, except as a punishment for crime whereof the party shall have been duly convicted, shall exist within the United States, or any place subject to their jurisdiction.

Section 2

Congress shall have power to enforce this article by appropriate legislation.

AMENDMENT XIV [ADOPTED 1868]

Section 1

All persons born or naturalized in the United States, and subject to the jurisdiction thereof, are citizens of the United States and of the State wherein they reside. No State shall make or enforce any law which shall abridge the privileges or immunities of citizens of the United States; nor shall any State deprive any person of life, liberty, or property, without due process of law; nor deny to any person within its jurisdiction the equal protection of the laws.

Section 2

Representatives shall be apportioned among the several States according to their respective numbers, counting the whole number of persons in each State, excluding Indians not taxed. But when the right to vote at any election for the choice of electors for President and Vice President of the United States, Representatives in Congress, the Executive and Judicial officers of a State, or the members of the Legislature thereof, is denied to any of the male inhabitants of such State, being twenty-one years of age, and citizens of the United States, or in any way abridged, except for participation in rebellion, or other crime, the basis of representation therein shall be reduced in the proportion which the number of such male citizens shall bear to the whole number of male citizens twenty-one years of age in such State.

Section 3

No person shall be a Senator or Representative in Congress, or elector of President and Vice President, or hold any office, civil or military, under the United States, or under any State, who, having previously taken an oath, as a member of Congress, or as an officer of the United States, or as a member of any State legislature, or as an executive or judicial officer of any State, to support the Constitution of the United States, shall have engaged in insurrection or rebellion against the same, or given aid or comfort to the enemies thereof. But Congress may by a vote of two-thirds of each House, remove such disability.

Section 4

The validity of the public debt of the United States, authorized by law, including debts incurred for payment of pensions and bounties for services in suppressing insurrection or rebellion, shall not be questioned. But neither the United States nor any State shall assume or pay any debt or obligation incurred in aid of insurrection or rebellion against the United States, or any claim for the loss or emancipation of any slave; but all such debts, obligations and claims shall be held illegal and void.

Section 5

The Congress shall have power to enforce, by appropriate legislation, the provisions of this article.

AMENDMENT XV [ADOPTED 1870]

Section 1

The right of citizens of the United States to vote shall not be denied or abridged by the United States or by any State on account of race, color, or previous condition of servitude.

Section 2

The Congress shall have power to enforce this article by appropriate legislation.

AMENDMENT XVI [ADOPTED 1913]

The Congress shall have power to lay and collect taxes on incomes, from whatever source derived, without apportionment among the several States, and without regard to any census or enumeration.

AMENDMENT XVII [ADOPTED 1913]

The Senate of the United States shall be composed of two Senators from each State, elected by the people thereof, for six years; and each Senator shall have one vote. The electors in each State shall have the qualifications requisite for electors of the most numerous branch of the State legislatures.

When vacancies happen in the representation of any State in the Senate, the executive authority of such State shall issue writs of election to fill such vacancies: *Provided*, That the legislature of any State may empower the executive thereof to make temporary appointments until the people fill the vacancies by election as the legislature may direct.

This amendment shall not be so construed as to affect the election or term of any Senator chosen before it becomes valid as part of the Constitution.

AMENDMENT XVIII [ADOPTED 1919, REPEALED 1933]

Section 1

After one year from the ratification of this article the manufacture, sale, or transportation of intoxicating liquors within, the importation thereof into, or the exportation thereof from the United States and all territory subject to the jurisdiction thereof for beverage purposes is hereby prohibited.

Section 2

The Congress and the several States shall have concurrent power to enforce this article by appropriate legislation.

Section 3

This article shall be inoperative unless it shall have been ratified as an amendment to the Constitution by the legislatures of the several States, as provided in the Constitution, within seven years from the date of the submission hereof to the States by the Congress.

AMENDMENT XIX [ADOPTED 1920]

The right of citizens of the United States to vote shall not be denied or abridged by the United States or by any State on account of sex.

Congress shall have power to enforce this article by appropriate legislation.

AMENDMENT XX [ADOPTED 1933]

Section 1

The terms of the President and Vice President shall end at noon on the 20th day of January, and the terms of Senators and Representatives at noon on the 3d day of January, of the years in which such terms would have ended if this article had not been ratified and the terms of their successors shall then begin.

Section 2

The Congress shall assemble at least once in every year, and such meeting shall begin at noon on the 3d day of January, unless they shall by law appoint a different day.

Section 3

If, at the time fixed for the beginning of the term of the President, the President elect shall have died, the Vice President elect shall become President. If a President shall not have been chosen before the time fixed for the beginning of his term, or if the President elect shall have failed to qualify, then the Vice President elect shall act as President until a President shall have qualified; and the Congress may by law provide for the case wherein neither a President elect nor a Vice President elect shall have qualified, declaring who shall then act as President, or the manner in which one who is to act shall be selected, and such person shall act accordingly until a President or Vice President shall have qualified.

Section 4

The Congress may by law provide for the case of the death of any of the persons from whom the House of Representatives may choose a President whenever the right of choice shall have devolved upon them, and for the case of the death of any of the persons from whom the Senate may choose a Vice President whenever the right of choice shall have devolved upon them.

Section 5

Sections 1 and 2 shall take effect on the 15th day of October following the ratification of this article.

Section 6

This article shall be inoperative unless it shall have been ratified as an amendment to the Constitution by the legislatures of three fourths of the several States within seven years from the date of its submission.

AMENDMENT XXI [ADOPTED 1933]

Section 1

The eighteenth article of amendment to the Constitution of the United States is hereby repealed.

Section 2

The transportation or importation into any State, Territory, or possession of the United States for delivery or use therein of intoxicating liquors in violation of the laws thereof, is hereby prohibited.

Section 3

This article shall be inoperative unless it shall have been ratified as an amendment to the Constitution by conventions in the several States, as provided in the Constitution, within seven years from the date of the submission hereof to the States by the Congress.

AMENDMENT XXII [ADOPTED 1951]

Section 1

No person shall be elected to the office of the President more than twice, and no person who has held the office of President, or acted as President, for more than two years of a term to which some other person was elected President shall be elected to the office of the President more than once. But this Article shall not apply to any person holding the office of President when this Article was proposed by the Congress, and shall not prevent any person who may be holding the office of President, or acting as President, during the term within which this Article becomes operative from holding the office of President or acting as President during the remainder of such term.

Section 2

This article shall be inoperative unless it shall have been ratified as an amendment to the Constitution by the legislatures of three-fourths of the several States within seven years from the date of its submission to the States by the Congress.

AMENDMENT XXIII [ADOPTED 1961]

Section 1

The District constituting the seat of Government of the United States shall appoint in such manner as the Congress shall direct:

A number of electors of President and Vice President equal to the whole number of Senators and Representatives in Congress to which the District would be entitled if it were a State, but in no event more than the least populous State; they shall be in addition to those appointed by the States, but they shall be considered, for the purposes of the election of President and Vice President, to be electors appointed by a State; and they shall meet in the District and perform such duties as provided by the twelfth article of amendment.

Section 2

The Congress shall have power to enforce this article by appropriate legislation.

AMENDMENT XXIV [ADOPTED 1964]

Section 1

The right of citizens of the United States to vote in any primary or other election for President or Vice President, for electors for President or Vice President, or for Senator or Representative in Congress, shall not be denied or abridged by the United States or any state by reason of failure to pay any poll tax or other tax.

Section 2

The Congress shall have the power to enforce this article by appropriate legislation.

AMENDMENT XXV [ADOPTED 1967]

Section 1

In case of the removal of the President from office or his death or resignation, the Vice President shall become President.

Section 2

Whenever there is a vacancy in the office of the Vice President, the President shall nominate a Vice President who shall take the office upon confirmation by a majority vote of both houses of Congress.

Section 3

Whenever the President transmits to the President pro tempore of the Senate and the Speaker of the House of Representatives his written declaration that he is unable to discharge the powers and duties of his office, and until he transmits to them a written declaration to the contrary, such powers and duties shall be discharged by the Vice President as Acting President.

Section 4

Whenever the Vice President and a majority of either the principal officers of the executive departments or of such other body as Congress may by law provide, transmit to the President pro tempore of the Senate and the Speaker of the House of Representatives their written declaration that the President is unable to discharge the powers and duties of his office, the Vice President shall immediately assume the powers and duties of the office as Acting President.

Thereafter, when the President transmits to the President pro tempore of the Senate and the Speaker of the House of Representatives his written declaration that no inability exists, he shall resume the powers and duties of his office unless the Vice President and a majority of either the principal officers of the executive department or of such other body as Congress may by law provide, transmit within four days to the President pro tempore of the Senate and the Speaker of the House of Representatives their written declaration that the President is unable to discharge the powers and duties of his office. Thereupon Congress shall decide the issue, assembling within 48 hours for that purpose if not in session. If the Congress, within 21 days after receipt of the latter written declaration, or, if Congress is not in session, within 21 days after Congress is required to assemble, determines by two-thirds vote of both houses that the President is unable to discharge the powers and duties of his office, the Vice President shall continue to discharge the same as Acting President; otherwise, the President shall resume the powers and duties of his office.

AMENDMENT XXVI [ADOPTED 1971]

Section 1

The right of citizens of the United States, who are 18 years of age or older, to vote shall not be denied or abridged by the United States or any state on account of age.

Section 2

The Congress shall have the power to enforce this article by appropriate legislation.

AMENDMENT XXVII [ADOPTED 1992]

No law, varying the compensation for the services of the Senators and Representatives shall take effect, until an election of Representatives shall have intervened.

Presidential Elections

Year	Candidates	Parties	Popular Vote	Electoral Vote	Voter Participation
1789	George Washington		*	69	
	John Adams			34	
	Others			35	
1792	George Washington		*	132	
	John Adams			77	
	George Clinton			50	
	Others			5	
1796	John Adams	Federalist	*	71	
	Thomas Jefferson	Democratic-Republican		68	
	Thomas Pinckney	Federalist		59	
	Aaron Burr	Dem.-Rep.		30	
	Others			48	
1800	Thomas Jefferson	Dem.-Rep.	*	73	
	Aaron Burr	Dem.-Rep.		73	
	John Adams	Federalist		65	
	C. C. Pinckney	Federalist		64	
	John Jay	Federalist		1	
1804	Thomas Jefferson	Dem.-Rep.	*	162	
	C. C. Pinckney	Federalist		14	
1808	James Madison	Dem.-Rep.	*	122	
	C. C. Pinckney	Federalist		47	
	George Clinton	Dem.-Rep.		6	
1812	James Madison	Dem.-Rep.	*	128	
	De Witt Clinton	Federalist		89	
1816	James Monroe	Dem.-Rep.	*	183	
	Rufus King	Federalist		34	
1820	James Monroe	Dem.-Rep.	*	231	
	John Quincy Adams	Dem.-Rep.		1	
1824	John Quincy Adams	Dem.-Rep.	108,740 (30.5%)	84	26.9%
	Andrew Jackson	Dem.-Rep.	153,544 (43.1%)	99	
	William H. Crawford	Dem.-Rep.	46,618 (13.1%)	41	
	Henry Clay	Dem.-Rep.	47,136 (13.2%)	37	

(continued)

Presidential Elections *(continued)*

Year	Candidates	Parties	Popular Vote	Electoral Vote	Voter Participation
1828	Andrew Jackson	Democratic	647,286 (56.0%)	178	57.6%
	John Quincy Adams	National Republican	508,064 (44.0%)	83	
1832	Andrew Jackson	Democratic	688,242 (54.2%)	219	55.4%
	Henry Clay	National Republican	473,462 (37.4%)	49	
	John Floyd	Independent		11	
	William Wirt	Anti-Mason	101,051 (7.8%)	7	
1836	Martin Van Buren	Democratic	762,198 (50.8%)	170	57.8%
	William Henry Harrison	Whig	549,508 (36.6%)	73	
	Hugh L. White	Whig	145,342 (9.7%)	26	
	Daniel Webster	Whig	41,287 (2.7%)	14	
	W. P. Magnum	Independent		11	
1840	William Henry Harrison	Whig	1,274,624 (53.1%)	234	80.2%
	Martin Van Buren	Democratic	1,127,781 (46.9%)	60	
	J. G. Birney	Liberty	7069	—	
1844	James K. Polk	Democratic	1,338,464 (49.6%)	170	78.9%
	Henry Clay	Whig	1,300,097 (48.1%)	105	
	J. G. Birney	Liberty	62,300 (2.3%)	—	
1848	Zachary Taylor	Whig	1,360,967 (47.4%)	163	72.7%
	Lewis Cass	Democratic	1,222,342 (42.5%)	127	
	Martin Van Buren	Free-Soil	291,263 (10.1%)	—	
1852	Franklin Pierce	Democratic	1,601,117 (50.9%)	254	69.6%
	Winfield Scott	Whig	1,385,453 (44.1%)	42	
	John P. Hale	Free-Soil	155,825 (5.0%)	—	
1856	James Buchanan	Democratic	1,832,955 (45.3%)	174	78.9%
	John C. Frémont	Republican	1,339,932 (33.1%)	114	
	Millard Fillmore	American	871,731 (21.6%)	8	
1860	Abraham Lincoln	Republican	1,865,593 (39.8%)	180	81.2%
	Stephen A. Douglas	Democratic	1,382,713 (29.5%)	12	
	John C. Breckinridge	Democratic	848,356 (18.1%)	72	
	John Bell	Union	592,906 (12.6%)	39	
1864	Abraham Lincoln	Republican	2,213,655 (55.0%)	212†	73.8%
	George B. McClellan	Democratic	1,805,237 (45.0%)	21	
1868	Ulysses S. Grant	Republican	3,012,833 (52.7%)	214	78.1%
	Horatio Seymour	Democratic	2,703,249 (47.3%)	80	

Presidential Elections *(continued)*

Year	Candidates	Parties	Popular Vote	Electoral Vote	Voter Participation
1872	Ulysses S. Grant	Republican	3,597,132 (55.6%)	286	71.3%
	Horace Greeley	Dem.; Liberal Republican	2,834,125 (43.9%)	66‡	
1876	Rutherford B. Hayes§	Republican	4,036,298 (48.0%)	185	81.8%
	Samuel J. Tilden	Democratic	4,300,590 (51.0%)	184	
1880	James A. Garfield	Republican	4,454,416 (48.5%)	214	79.4%
	Winfield S. Hancock	Democratic	4,444,952 (48.1%)	155	
1884	Grover Cleveland	Democratic	4,874,986 (48.5%)	219	77.5%
	James G. Blaine	Republican	4,851,981 (48.2%)	182	
1888	Benjamin Harrison	Republican	5,439,853 (47.9%)	233	79.3%
	Grover Cleveland	Democratic	5,540,309 (48.6%)	168	
1892	Grover Cleveland	Democratic	5,556,918 (46.1%)	277	74.7%
	Benjamin Harrison	Republican	5,176,108 (43.0%)	145	
	James B. Weaver	People's	1,029,329 (8.5%)	22	
1896	William McKinley	Republican	7,104,779 (51.1%)	271	79.3%
	William Jennings Bryan	Democratic People's	6,502,925 (47.7%)	176	
1900	William McKinley	Republican	7,207,923 (51.7%)	292	73.2%
	William Jennings Bryan	Dem.-Populist	6,358,133 (45.5%)	155	
1904	Theodore Roosevelt	Republican	7,623,486 (57.9%)	336	65.2%
	Alton B. Parker	Democratic	5,077,911 (37.6%)	140	
	Eugene V. Debs	Socialist	402,400 (3.0%)	—	
1908	William H. Taft	Republican	7,678,908 (51.6%)	321	65.4%
	William Jennings Bryan	Democratic	6,409,104 (43.1%)	162	
	Eugene V. Debs	Socialist	402,820 (2.8%)	—	
1912	Woodrow Wilson	Democratic	6,293,454 (41.9%)	435	58.8%
	Theodore Roosevelt	Progressive	4,119,538 (27.4%)	88	
	William H. Taft	Republican	3,484,980 (23.2%)	8	
	Eugene V. Debs	Socialist	900,672 (6.0%)	—	
1916	Woodrow Wilson	Democratic	9,129,606 (49.4%)	277	61.6%
	Charles E. Hughes	Republican	8,538,221 (46.2%)	254	
	A. L. Benson	Socialist	585,113 (3.2%)	—	
1920	Warren G. Harding	Republican	16,152,200 (60.4%)	404	49.2%
	James M. Cox	Democratic	9,147,353 (34.2%)	127	
	Eugene V. Debs	Socialist	917,799 (3.4%)	—	
1924	Calvin Coolidge	Republican	15,725,016 (54.0%)	382	48.9%
	John W. Davis	Democratic	8,386,503 (28.8%)	136	
	Robert M. La Follette	Progressive	4,822,856 (16.6%)	13	

(continued)

Presidential Elections *(continued)*

Year	Candidates	Parties	Popular Vote	Electoral Vote	Voter Participation
1928	Herbert Hoover	Republican	21,391,381 (58.2%)	444	56.9%
	Alfred E. Smith	Democratic	15,016,443 (40.9%)	87	
	Norman Thomas	Socialist	267,835 (0.7%)	—	
1932	Franklin D. Roosevelt	Democratic	22,821,857 (57.4%)	472	56.9%
	Herbert Hoover	Republican	15,761,841 (39.7%)	59	
	Norman Thomas	Socialist	884,781 (2.2%)	—	
1936	Franklin D. Roosevelt	Democratic	27,751,597 (60.8%)	523	61.0%
	Alfred M. Landon	Republican	16,679,583 (36.5%)	8	
	William Lemke	Union	882,479 (1.9%)	—	
1940	Franklin D. Roosevelt	Democratic	27,244,160 (54.8%)	449	62.5%
	Wendell L. Willkie	Republican	22,305,198 (44.8%)	82	
1944	Franklin D. Roosevelt	Democratic	25,602,504 (53.5%)	432	55.9%
	Thomas E. Dewey	Republican	22,006,285 (46.0%)	99	
1948	Harry S Truman	Democratic	24,105,695 (49.5%)	304	53.0%
	Thomas E. Dewey	Republican	21,969,170 (45.1%)	189	
	J. Strom Thurmond	State-Rights Democratic	1,169,021 (2.4%)	38	
	Henry A. Wallace	Progressive	1,157,326 (2.4%)	—	
1952	Dwight D. Eisenhower	Republican	33,778,963 (55.1%)	442	63.3%
	Adlai E. Stevenson	Democratic	27,314,992 (44.4%)	89	
1956	Dwight D. Eisenhower	Republican	35,575,420 (57.6%)	457	60.6%
	Adlai E. Stevenson	Democratic	26,033,066 (42.1%)	73	
	Other	—	—	1	
1960	John F. Kennedy	Democratic	34,227,096 (49.9%)	303	62.8%
	Richard M. Nixon	Republican	34,108,546 (49.6%)	219	
	Other	—	—	15	
1964	Lyndon B. Johnson	Democratic	43,126,506 (61.1%)	486	61.7%
	Barry M. Goldwater	Republican	27,176,799 (38.5%)	52	
1968	Richard M. Nixon	Republican	31,770,237 (43.4%)	301	60.6%
	Hubert H. Humphrey	Democratic	31,270,533 (42.7%)	191	
	George Wallace	American Indep.	9,906,141 (13.5%)	46	

Presidential Elections

Year	Candidates	Parties	Popular Vote	Electoral Vote	Voter Participation
1972	Richard M. Nixon	Republican	46,740,323 (60.7%)	520	55.2%
	George S. McGovern	Democratic	28,901,598 (37.5%)	17	
	Other	—	—	1	
1976	Jimmy Carter	Democratic	40,828,587 (50.0%)	297	53.5%
	Gerald R. Ford	Republican	39,147,613 (47.9%)	241	
	Other	—	1,575,459 (2.1%)	—	
1980	Ronald Reagan	Republican	43,901,812 (50.7%)	489	52.6%
	Jimmy Carter	Democratic	35,483,820 (41.0%)	49	
	John B. Anderson	Independent	5,719,437 (6.6%)	—	
	Ed Clark	Libertarian	921,188 (1.1%)	—	
1984	Ronald Reagan	Republican	54,455,075 (59.0%)	525	53.3%
	Walter Mondale	Democratic	37,577,185 (41.0%)	13	
1988	George H. W. Bush	Republican	48,886,097 (53.4%)	426	57.4%
	Michael S. Dukakis	Democratic	41,809,074 (45.6%)	111	
1992	William J. Clinton	Democratic	44,908,254 (43%)	370	55.0%
	George H. W. Bush	Republican	39,102,343 (37.5%)	168	
	H. Ross Perot	Independent	19,741,065 (18.9%)	—	
1996	William J. Clinton	Democratic	45,590,703 (50%)	379	48.8%
	Robert Dole	Republican	37,816,307 (41%)	159	
	Ross Perot	Reform	7,866,284	—	
2000	George W. Bush	Republican	50,456,167 (47.88%)	271	51.2%
	Al Gore	Democratic	50,996,064 (48.39%)	266"	
	Ralph Nader	Green	2,864,810 (2.72%)	—	
	Other	834,774 (less than 1%)	—		
2004	George W. Bush	Republican	60,934,251 (51.0%)	286	50.0%
	John F. Kerry	Democratic	57,765,291 (48.0%)	252	
	Ralph Nader	Independent	405,933 (less than 1%)	—	
2008	Barack Obama	Democractic	69,456,897 (52.9%)	365	62%
	John McCain	Republican	59,934,814 (45.7%)	173	

*Electors selected by state legislatures.

†Eleven secessionist states did not participate.

‡Greeley died before the electoral college met. His electoral votes were divided among the four minor candidates.

§Contested result settled by special election.

"One District of Columbia Gore elector abstained. Popular Vote

Presidents and Vice Presidents

	President	Vice President	Term
1.	George Washington	John Adams	1789–1793
	George Washington	John Adams	1793–1797
2.	John Adams	Thomas Jefferson	1797–1801
3.	Thomas Jefferson	Aaron Burr	1801–1805
	Thomas Jefferson	George Clinton	1805–1809
4.	James Madison	George Clinton (d. 1812)	1809–1813
	James Madison	Elbridge Gerry (d. 1814)	1813–1817
5.	James Monroe	Daniel Tompkins	1817–1821
	James Monroe	Daniel Tompkins	1821–1825
6.	John Quincy Adams	John C. Calhoun	1825–1829
7.	Andrew Jackson	John C. Calhoun	1829–1833
	Andrew Jackson	Martin Van Buren	1833–1837
8.	Martin Van Buren	Richard M. Johnson	1837–1841
9.	William H. Harrison (d. 1841)	John Tyler	1841
10.	John Tyler	—	1841–1845
11.	James K. Polk	George M. Dallas	1845–1849
12.	Zachary Taylor (d. 1850)	Millard Fillmore	1849–1850
13.	Millard Fillmore	—	1850–1853
14.	Franklin Pierce	William R. King (d. 1853)	1853–1857
15.	James Buchanan	John C. Breckinridge	1857–1861
16.	Abraham Lincoln	Hannibal Hamlin	1861–1865
	Abraham Lincoln (d. 1865)	Andrew Johnson	1865
17.	Andrew Johnson	—	1865–1869
18.	Ulysses S. Grant	Schuyler Colfax	1869–1873
	Ulysses S. Grant	Henry Wilson (d. 1875)	1873–1877
19.	Rutherford B. Hayes	William A. Wheeler	1877–1881
20.	James A. Garfield (d. 1881)	Chester A. Arthur	1881
21.	Chester A. Arthur	—	1881–1885
22.	Grover Cleveland	Thomas A. Hendricks (d. 1885)	1885–1889
23.	Benjamin Harrison	Levi P. Morton	1889–1893
24.	Grover Cleveland	Adlai E. Stevenson	1893–1897
25.	William McKinley	Garret A. Hobart (d. 1899)	1897–1901
	William McKinley (d. 1901)	Theodore Roosevelt	1901
26.	Theodore Roosevelt	—	1901–1905
	Theodore Roosevelt	Charles Fairbanks	1905–1909
27.	William H. Taft	James S. Sherman (d. 1912)	1909–1913
28.	Woodrow Wilson	Thomas R. Marshall	1913–1917
	Woodrow Wilson	Thomas R. Marshall	1917–1921

Presidents and Vice Presidents

	President	Vice President	Term
29.	Warren G. Harding (d. 1923)	Calvin Coolidge	1921–1923
30.	Calvin Coolidge	—	1923–1925
	Calvin Coolidge	Charles G. Dawes	1925–1929
31.	Herbert Hoover	Charles Curtis	1929–1933
32.	Franklin D. Roosevelt	John N. Garner	1933–1937
	Franklin D. Roosevelt	John N. Garner	1937–1941
	Franklin D. Roosevelt	Henry A. Wallace	1941–1945
	Franklin D. Roosevelt (d. 1945)	Harry S Truman	1945
33.	Harry S Truman	—	1945–1949
	Harry S Truman	Alben W. Barkley	1949–1953
34.	Dwight D. Eisenhower	Richard M. Nixon	1953–1957
	Dwight D. Eisenhower	Richard M. Nixon	1957–1961
35.	John F. Kennedy (d. 1963)	Lyndon B. Johnson	1961–1963
36.	Lyndon B. Johnson	—	1963–1965
	Lyndon B. Johnson	Hubert H. Humphrey	1965–1969
37.	Richard M. Nixon	Spiro T. Agnew	1969–1973
	Richard M. Nixon (resigned 1974)	Gerald R. Ford	1973–1974
38.	Gerald R. Ford	Nelson A. Rockefeller	1974–1977
39.	Jimmy Carter	Walter F. Mondale	1977–1981
40.	Ronald Reagan	George H. W. Bush	1981–1985
	Ronald Reagan	George H. W. Bush	1985–1989
41.	George H. W. Bush	J. Danforth Quayle	1989–1993
42.	William J. Clinton	Albert Gore, Jr.	1993–1997
	William J. Clinton	Albert Gore, Jr.	1997–2001
43.	George W. Bush	Richard Cheney	2001–2005
	George W. Bush	Richard Cheney	2005–2009
44.	Barack Obama	Joe Biden	2009-

Glossary

Abolitionist movement (p. 303) Reform movement dedicated to the immediate and unconditional end of slavery in the United States.

Adams–Onís Treaty (p. 223) Signed by Secretary of State John Quincy Adams and Spanish minister Luis de Onís in 1819, this treaty allowed for U.S. annexation of Florida.

African Methodist Episcopal (AME) Church (p. 148) Richard Allen founded the African Methodist Episcopal Church in 1816 as the first independent black-run Protestant church in the United States. The AME Church was active in the abolition movement and founded educational institutions for free blacks.

Agricultural Revolution (p. 7) The gradual shift from hunting and gathering to cultivating basic food crops that occurred worldwide from 7,000 to 9,000 years ago.

Alamo (p. 317) In 1835, Americans living in Mexican-ruled Texas fomented a revolution. Mexico lost the resulting conflict, but not before its troops defeated and killed a group of American rebels at the Alamo, a fortified mission in San Antonio.

Albany Plan (p. 106) Plan of intercolonial cooperation proposed by prominent colonists including Benjamin Franklin at a conference in Albany, New York, in 1754. The plan called for a Grand Council of elected delegates from the colonies that would have powers to tax and provide for the common defense. Although rejected by the colonial and British governments, it was a prototype for colonial union.

Alien and Sedition Acts (p. 191) Collective name given to four laws Congress passed in 1798 to suppress criticism of the federal government and curb liberties of foreigners living in the United States.

American Colonization Society (p. 282) Founded in 1817, the society advocated the relocation of free blacks and freed slaves to the African colony of Monrovia, present-day Liberia.

Antifederalists (p. 163) Critics of the Constitution who were concerned that it included no specific provisions to protect natural and civil rights.

Antinomianism (p. 46) Religious belief rejecting traditional moral law as unnecessary for Christians who possess saving grace and affirming that a person could experience divine revelation and salvation without the assistance of formally trained clergy.

Articles of Confederation (p. 153) Ratified in 1781, this document was the United States' first constitution, providing a framework for national government. The articles limited central authority by denying the national government any taxation or coercive power.

Backcountry (p. 87) In the eighteenth century, the edge of settlement extending from western Pennsylvania to Georgia. This region formed the second frontier as settlers moved west from the Atlantic coast into the interior.

Bacon's Rebellion (p. 77) An armed rebellion in Virginia (1675–1676) led by Nathaniel Bacon against the colony's royal governor, Sir William Berkeley. Although some of his followers called for an end to special privilege in government, Bacon was chiefly interested in gaining a larger share of the lucrative Indian trade.

Bank of the United States (p. 179) National bank proposed by Secretary of the Treasury Alexander Hamilton and established in 1791. It served as a central depository for the U.S. government and had the authority to issue currency.

Bank War (p. 259) Between 1832–1836, Andrew Jackson used his presidential power to fight and ultimately destroy the second Bank of the United States.

Battle of New Orleans (p. 218) Battle that occurred in 1815 at the end of the War of 1812 when U.S. forces defeated a British attempt to seize New Orleans.

Benevolent empire (p. 296) Collection of missionary and reform societies that sought to stamp out social evils in American society in the 1820s and 1830s.

Beringia (p. 5) Land bridge formerly connecting Asia and North America that is now submerged beneath the Bering Sea.

Bill of Rights (p. 167) The first ten amendments to the Constitution, adopted in 1791 to preserve the rights and liberties of individuals.

Black Codes (p. 392) Laws passed by southern states immediately after the Civil War to maintain white supremacy by restricting the rights of the newly freed slaves.

Boston Massacre (p. 124) A violent clash between British troops and a Boston mob on March 5, 1770. Five citizens were killed when the troops fired into the crowd. The incident inflamed anti-British sentiment in Massachusetts.

Boston Tea Party (p. 126) Raid on British ships in which Patriots disguised as Mohawks threw hundreds of chests of tea owned by the East India Company into Boston Harbor to protest British taxes.

Coercive Acts (p. 126) Also known as the Intolerable Acts, the four pieces of legislation passed by Parliament in response to the Boston Tea Party to punish Massachusetts.

Columbian Exchange (p. 12) The exchange of plants, animals, and diseases between Europe and the Americas from first contact throughout the era of exploration.

Committee of correspondence (p. 125) Communication network formed in Massachusetts and other colonies to communicate grievances and provide colonists with evidence of British oppression.

***Common Sense* (p. 129)** Revolutionary tract written by Thomas Paine in 1776. It called for independence and a republican government in America.

Compromise of 1850 (p. 339) Five federal laws that temporarily calmed the sectional crisis. The compromise made California a free state, ended the slave trade in the District of Columbia, and strengthened the Fugitive Slave Law.

Compromise of 1877 (p. 410) Compromise struck during the contested presidential election of 1876, in which Democrats accepted the election of Rutherford B. Hayes (Republican) in exchange for the withdrawal of federal troops from the South and the end of Reconstruction.

Conquistadores (p. 16) Sixteenth-century Spanish adventurers, often of noble birth, who subdued the Native Americans and created the Spanish empire in the New World.

Consumer revolution (p. 96) Period between 1740 and 1770 when English exports to the American colonies increased by 360 percent to satisfy Americans' demand for consumer goods.

Cooperationists (p. 361) Southerners in 1860 who advocated secession by the South as a whole rather than unilateral secession by each state.

Copperheads (p. 376) Northern Democrats suspected of being indifferent or hostile to the Union cause in the Civil War.

Cotton gin (p. 285) Invented by Eli Whitney in 1793, this device for separating the seeds from the fibers of short-staple cotton enabled a slave to clean fifty times more cotton as by hand, which reduced production costs and gave new life to slavery in the South.

***Coureurs de bois* (p. 21)** Fur trappers in French Canada who lived among the Native Americans.

Crittenden compromise (p. 363) Introduced by Kentucky Senator John Crittenden in 1861 in an attempt to prevent seccession and civil war, it would have extended the Missouri Compromise line west to the Pacific.

Cult of Domesticity (p. 297) Term used to characterize the dominant gender role for white women in the antebellum period. It stressed the virtue of women as guardians of the home, which was considered their proper sphere.

Dartmouth College v. Woodward (p. 237) In this 1819 case, the Supreme Court ruled that the Constitution protected charters given to corporations by states.

Dominion of New England (p. 78) Incorporation of the New England colonies under a single appointed royal governor that lasted from 1686–1689.

Eastern Woodland Cultures (p. 9) Term given to Indians from the Northeast region who lived on the Atlantic coast and supplemented farming with seasonal hunting and gathering.

Emancipation Proclamation (p. 373) On January 1, 1863, President Abraham Lincoln proclaimed that the slaves of the Confederacy were free. Since the South had not yet been defeated, the proclamation did not immediately free anyone, but it made emancipation an explicit war aim of the North.

Embargo Act (p. 213) In response to a British attack on an American warship off the coast of Virginia, this 1807 law prohibited foreign commerce.

Encomienda system (p. 19) An exploitative system by Spanish rulers that granted conquistadors control of Native American villages and their inhabiatants' labor.

Enlightenment (p. 93) Philosophical and intellectual movement that began in Europe during the eighteenth century. It stressed the use of reason to solve social and scientific problems.

Enumerated goods (p. 74) Raw materials, such as tobacco, sugar, and rice, that were produced in the British colonies and under the Navigation Acts had to be shipped only to England or its colonies.

Era of Good Feeling (p. 234) A description of the two terms of President James Monroe (1817–1823) during which partisan conflict abated and federal initiatives suggested increased nationalism.

Farewell Address (p. 186) In this 1796 document, President George Washington announced his intention not to seek a third term. He also stressed federalist interests and warned Americans against political factions and foreign entanglements.

Federalist (p. 163) Supporter of the Constitution who advocated its ratification.

Fifteenth Amendment (p. 393) Ratified in 1870, it prohibits the denial or abridgment of the right to vote by the federal or state governments on the basis of race, color, or prior condition as a slave. It was intended to guarantee African Americans the right to vote in the South.

First Continental Congress (p. 127) A meeting of delegates from 12 colonies in Philadelphia in 1774, the Congress denied Parliament's authority to legislate for the colonies, condemned British actions toward the colonies, created the Continental Association, and endorsed a call to take up arms.

Force Acts (p. 407) Designed to protect black voters in the South from the Ku Klux Klan in 1870–1871, these laws placed state elections under federal jurisdiction and imposed fines and punished those guilty of interfering with any citizen exercising his right to vote.

Fourteenth Amendment (p. 393) Ratified in 1868, it provided citizenship to ex-slaves after the Civil War and constitutionally protected equal rights under the law for all citizens. Radical Republicans used it to enact a congressional Reconstruction policy in the former Confederate states.

Freedmen's Bureau (p. 393) Agency established by Congress in March 1865 to provide freedmen with shelter, food, and medical aid and to help them establish schools and find employment. The Bureau was dissolved in 1872.

French Revolution (p. 182) A social and political revolution in France (1789–1799).

Fugitive Slave Law (p. 340) Passed in 1850, this federal law made it easier for slaveowners to recapture runaway slaves; it also made it easier for kidnappers to take free blacks. The law became an object of hatred in the North.

Gibbons v. Ogden (p. 238) In this 1824 case, the Supreme Court expanded the power of the federal government to regulate interstate commerce.

Glorious Revolution (p. 78) Replacement of James II by William III and Mary II as English monarchs in 1688, marking the beginning of constitutional monarchy in Britain.

Great Awakening (p. 98) Widespread evangelical religious revival movement of the mid-1700s. It divided congregations and weakened the authority of established churches in the colonies.

Great Migration (p. 44) Migration of 16,000 Puritans from England to the Massachusetts Bay Colony during the 1630s.

Greenbacks (p. 368) Paper currency issued by the Union during the Civil War.

Hartford Convention (p. 218) An assembly of New England Federalists who met in Hartford, Connecticut, in December 1814 to protest President James Madison's foreign policy in the War of 1812, which had undermined commercial interests in the North. They proposed amending the Constitution to prevent future presidents from declaring war without a two-thirds majority in Congress.

Headright (p. 37) System of land distribution in which settlers were granted a 50-acre plot of land from the colonial government for each servant or dependent they transported to the New World. It encouraged the recruitment of a large servile labor force.

House of Burgesses (p. 37) The elective representative assembly in colonial Virginia.

Implied powers (p. 179) Powers the Constitution did not explicitly grant the federal government, but that it could be interpreted to grant.

Indentured servants (pp. 37) Persons who agreed to serve a master for a set number of years in exchange for the cost of transport to America. Indentured servitude was the dominant form of labor in the Chesapeake colonies before slavery.

Itinerant preachers (p. 99) These charismatic preachers spread revivalism throughout America during the Great Awakening.

Jay's Treaty (p. 183) Treaty with Britain negotiated by Chief Justice John Jay in 1794. Though the British agreed to surrender forts on U.S. territory, the treaty provoked a storm of protest in America.

Jim Crow laws (p. 411) Segregation laws enacted by southern states after Reconstruction.

Joint-stock company (p. 33) Business enterprise that enabled investors to pool money for commerce and funding for colonies.

Judicial review (p. 206) The authority of the Supreme Court to determine the constitutionality of statutes.

Kansas-Nebraska Act (p. 343) This 1854 act repealed the Missouri Compromise, split the Louisiana Purchase into two territories, and allowed its settlers to accept or reject slavery by popular sovereignty.

Kentucky and Virginia Resolutions (p. 192) Statements penned by Thomas Jefferson and James Madison to mobilize opposition to the Alien and Sedition Acts, which they argued were unconstitutional. Jefferson's statement (the Kentucky Resolution) suggested that states could declare null and void congressional acts they deemed unconstitutional. (See **Nullification**.)

Ku Klux Klan (p. 407) A secret terrorist society first organized in Tennessee in 1866. The original Klan's goals were to disfranchise African Americans, stop Reconstruction, and restore the prewar social order of the South. The Ku Klux Klan re-formed in the twentieth century to promote white supremacy and combat aliens, Catholics, and Jews.

Lewis and Clark Expedition (p. 207) Overland expedition to the Pacific coast (1804–1806) led by Meriwether Lewis and William Clark. Commissioned by President Thomas Jefferson, it collected scientific data about the country and its resources.

Louisiana Purchase (p. 207) U.S. acquisition of the Louisiana Territory from France in 1803 for $15 million. The purchase secured American control of the Mississippi River and doubled the size of the nation.

Loyalists (p. 117) Colonists sided with Britain during the American Revolution.

Manifest Destiny (p. 315) Coined in 1845, this term referred to a doctrine in support of territorial expansion based on the belief that the United States should expand to encompass all of North America.

***Marbury v. Madison* (p. 209)** In this 1803 landmark decision, the Supreme Court first asserted the power of judicial review by declaring an act of Congress uncstitutional.

Mayflower Compact (p. 41) Agreement among the Pilgrims aboard the Mayflower in 1620 to create a civil government at Plymouth Colony.

***McCulloch v. Maryland* (p. 238)** This 1819 ruling asserted the supremacy of federal power over state power and the legal doctrine that the Constitution could be broadly interpretated. (See **Implied powers**.)

Mercantilism (p. 73) An economic theory that shaped imperial policy throughout the colonial period, mercantilism assumed that the supply of wealth was fixed. To increase its wealth, a nation needed to export more goods than it imported. Favorable trade and protective economic policies and colonial possessions rich in raw materials were important in achieving this balance.

Mexican-American War (p. 321) Conflict (1846–1848) between the United States and Mexico after the U.S. annexation of Texas. As victor, the United States acquired vast new territories from Mexico.

Middle ground (p. 90) A geographical area where two distinct cultures meet and merge with neither bolding a clear upper hand.

Missouri Compromise (p. 235) A sectional compromise in 1820 that admitted Missouri to the Union as a slave state and Maine as a free state. It also banned slavery in the remainder of the Louisiana Purchase territory above the latitude of 36°30′.

Monroe Doctrine (p. 240) A key foreign policy declaration made by President James Monroe in 1823, it declared the Western Hemisphere off limits to new European colonization; in return, the United States promised not to meddle in European affairs.

Natural rights (p. 151) Fundamental rights over which the government should exercise no control.

Navigation Acts (p. 74) Commercial restrictions that regulated colonial commerce to favor England's accumulation of wealth. (See **Mercantilism**.)

Northwest Ordinance (p. 155) Legislation in 1787 that established governments in America's northwest territories, defined a procedure for their admission to the Union as states, and prohibited slavery north of the Ohio River.

Nullification (p. 258) The supposed right of any state to declare a federal law inoperative within its boundaries. In 1832, South Carolina nullified the federal tariff.

Ostend Manifesto (p. 344) Written by American diplomats in 1854, this secret memorandum urged acquiring Cuba by any means necessary. When it became public, northerners claimed it was a plot to extend slavery, and the manifesto was disavowed.

Panic of 1837 (p. 262) A financial depression that lasted until the 1840s.

Parliamentary sovereignty (p. 116) Principle that emphasized Parliament's power to govern colonial affairs.

Peace of Paris of 1763 (p. 108) Treaty ending the French and Indian War by which France ceded Canada to Britain.

Perfectionism (p. 294) The doctrine that a state of freedom from sin is attainable on earth.

Popular sovereignty (p. 338) The concept that the settlers of a newly organized territory had the right to decide (through voting) whether to accept slavery.

Preemption (p. 225) The right of first purchase of public land. Settlers enjoyed this right even if they squatted on the land in advance of government surveyors.

Protestant Reformation (p. 21) Sixteenth-century religious movement to reform and challenge the spiritual authority of the Roman Catholic Church.

Puritans (p. 42) Members of a reformed Protestant sect in Europe and America that insisted on removing all vestiges of Catholicism from religious practice.

Quakers (p. 51) Members of a radical religious group, formally known as the Society of Friends, that rejects formal theology and stress each person's "inner light," a spiritual guide to righteousness.

Quasi-war (p. 188) Undeclared war between the United States and France in the late 1790s.

Radical Reconstruction (p. 394) The Reconstruction Acts of 1867 divided the South into five military districts. They required the states to guarantee black male suffrage and to ratify the **Fourteenth Amendment** as a condition of their readmission to the Union.

Radical Republicans (p. 390) Congressional Republicans who insisted on black suffrage and federal protection of civil rights of African Americans.

Redeemers (p. 410) A loose coalition of prewar Democrats, Confederate veterans, and Whigs who took over southern state governments in the 1870s, supposedly "redeeming" them from the corruption of Reconstruction. They shared a commitment to white supremacy and laissez-faire economics.

Republicanism (p. 144) Concept that ultimate political authority is vested in the citizens of the nation.

Royal African Company (p. 70) Slaving company created to meet colonial planters' demands for black laborers.

Sanitary Commission (p. 380) An association chartered by the government during the Civil War to promote health in the northern army's camps though cleanliness, nutrition, and medical care.

Second Continental Congress (p. 128) A gathering of colonial representatives in Philadelphia in 1775 that organized the Continental Army and began requisitioning men and supplies for the war effort.

Second Great Awakening (p. 292) Evangelical Protestant revivals that swept over America in the early nineteenth century.

Second-party system (p. 263) Historians' term for the national two-party rivalry between Democrats and **Whigs**. The second-party system began in the 1830s and ended in the 1850s with the demise of the Whigs and the rise of the Republican party.

Seneca Falls Convention (p. 308) An 1848 gathering of women's rights advocates that culminated in the adoption of a Declaration of Sentiments demanding voting and property rights for women.

Seven Years' War (p. 106) Worldwide conflict (1756–1763) that pitted Britain against France. With help from the American colonists, the British won the war and eliminated France as a power on the North American continent. Also known as the French and Indian War. (See **Peace of Paris of 1763**.)

Sharecropping (p. 400) After the Civil War, the southern states adopted a sharecropping system as a compromise between former slaves who wanted land of their own and former slave owners who needed labor. The landowners provided land, tools, and seed to a farming family, who in turn provided labor. The resulting crop was divided between them, with the farmers receiving a "share" of one-third to one-half of the crop.

Shays's Rebellion (p. 158) Armed insurrection of farmers in western Massachusetts led by Daniel Shays. Intended to prevent state courts from foreclosing on debtors unable to pay their taxes, the rebellion was put down by the state militia. Nationalists used the event to call a constitutional convention to strengthen the national government.

Spectral evidence (p. 79) In the Salem witch trials, the court allowed reports of dreams and visions in which the accused appeared as the devil's agent to be introduced as testimony. The accused had no defense against this kind of "evidence." When the judges later disallowed this testimony, the executions for witchcraft ended.

Stamp Act Congress (p. 121) Meeting of colonial delegates in New York City in October 1765 to protest the Stamp Act, a law passed by Parliament to raise revenue in America.

Stamp Act of 1765 (p. 120) Placed a tax on newspapers and printed matter produced in the colonies, causing mass opposition by colonists.

Tariff of abominations (p. 252) An 1828 protective tariff, or tax on imports, that angered southern free traders.

Ten Percent Plan (p. 389) Reconstruction plan proposed by President Abraham Lincoln as a quick way to readmit the former Confederate States. It called for pardon of all southerners except Confederate leaders, and readmission to the Union for any state after 10 percent of its voters signed a loyalty oath and the state abolished slavery.

The Spanish Armada (p. 25) Spanish fleet sent to invade England in 1588.

Thirteenth Amendment (p. 391) Ratified in 1865, it prohibits slavery and involuntary servitude.

Three-fifths rule (p. 160) Constitutional provision that for every five slaves a state would receive credit for three free voters in determining seats for the House of Representatives.

Trail of Tears (p. 256) In the winter of 1838–1839, the Cherokee were forced to evacuate their lands in Georgia and travel under military guard to present-day Oklahoma. Exposure and disease killed roughly one-quarter of the 16,000 forced migrants en route.

Treaty of Guadalupe Hidalgo (p. 322) Signed in 1848, this treaty ended the Mexican-American War. Mexico relinquished its claims to Texas and ceded an additional 500,000 square miles to the United States for $15 million.

Treaty of Paris of 1783 (p. 138) Agreement establishing Ameican independence after the Revolutionary War. It also transferred territory east of the Mississippi River, except for Spanish Florida, to the new republic.

Treaty of Tordesillas (p. 17) Treaty negotiated by the pope in 1494 that divided the world along a north–south line in the middle of the Atlantic Ocean, granting Spain all lands west of the line and Portugal lands east of the line.

Underground Railroad (p. 274) A network of safe houses organized by abolitionists (usually free blacks) to help slaves escape to the North or Canada.

Vesey conspiracy (p. 274) An unsuccessful 1822 plot to burn Charleston, South Carolina, and initiate a general slave revolt, led by a free African American, Denmark Vesey.

Virgin of Guadelupe (p. 20) Apparition of the Virgin Mary that has become a symbol of Mexican nationalism.

Virginia Plan (p. 159) Offered by James Madison and the Virginia delegation at the Constitutional Convention, this proposal called for a strong executive office and two houses of Congress, each with representation proportional to a state's population.

War Hawks (p. 216) Congressional leaders who, in 1811 and 1812, called for war against Britain.

War of 1812 (p. 217) War between Britain and the United States. U.S. justifications for war included British violations of American maritime rights, impressment of seamen, provocation of the Indians, and defense of national honor.

Whigs (p. 115) In mid-eighteenth century Britain, the Whigs were a political faction that dominated Parliament. Generally, they opposed royal influence in government and wanted to increase the power of Parliament. In America, a Whig party coalesced in the 1830s in opposition to President Andrew Jackson. The American Whigs supported federal power and internal improvements but not territorial expansion. The Whig party collapsed in the 1850s.

Whiskey Rebellion (p. 185) Protests in 1794 by western Pennsylvania farmers against a federal tax on whiskey. The uprising was suppressed when President George Washington called an army of 15,000 troops to the area.

Wilmot Proviso (p. 337) In 1846, shortly after outbreak of the **Mexican-American War**, Congressman David Wilmot of Pennsylvania introduced this amendment banning slavery in any lands won from Mexico.

XYZ Affair (p. 189) A diplomatic incident in which American peace commissioners sent to France by President John Adams in 1797 were insulted with bribe demands from their French counterparts, dubbed X, Y, and Z in American newspapers. The incident heightened war fever against France.

Yeomen (p. 65) Southern small landholders who owned no slaves, and who lived primarily in the foothills of the Appalachian and Ozark mountains. They were self-reliant and grew mixed crops, although they usually did not produce a substantial amount to be sold on the market.

Yorktown (p. 137) Virginia market town on a peninsula bounded by the York and James rivers, where Lord Cornwallis's army was trapped by the Americans and French in 1781.

Young America (p. 313) In the 1840s and early 1850s, many public figures—especially younger members of the Democratic party—used this term to describe their program of territorial expansion and industrial growth.

Credits

Chapter 1

2 North Wind Picture Archives/Alamy 7 Scala/Art Resource, NY 14 AP Photo/Clement N'Taye 21 From Theodor d Bry, "America" New York Public Library, Astor, Lenox, and Tilden Foundations 22 The Granger Collection, NYC. All rights reserved. 27 The Trustees of the British Museum

Chapter 2

30 MPI/Archive Photos/Getty Image 35 Ashmolean Museum, University of Oxford 38 Historic St. Mary's City 44 Eliot Elisofon/Time Life Pictures/Getty Images 50 Lebrecht Music and Arts Photo Library/Alamy 53 Mary Evans Picture Library / The Image Works

Chapter 3

60 © Fine Arts Museums of San Francisco 70 Colonial Williamsburg Foundation 72T © National Maritime Museum Greenwich, UK 72B © National Maritime Museum Greenwich, UK 73 Abby Aldrich Rockefeller Folk Art Museum, The Colonial Williamsburg Foundation, Williamsburg, Va. 79 Art Resource, NY

Chapter 4

82 William Byrd II (oil on canvas), Hysing, Hans (1678-1753)/Virginia Historical Society, Richmond, Virginia, USA/The Bridgeman Art Library 90 Richard Cummins/CORBIS 92 Oil on canvas, 36 × 27", Charles Willson Peale, 1789, Gift of James J. Barclay, 1852, Historical Society of Pennsylvania Collection, Portrait/Science, The Philidelphia History Museum at the Atwater Kent. 93 New York Public Library/Art Resource, 96 © National Portrait Gallery, London 102 The British Library 104 Library of Congress

Chapter 5

110 New Hampshire Historical Society 114 Courtesy of the John Carter Brown Library at Brown University 121 Library of Congress 122 Library of Congress 128 Atwater Kent Museum of Philadelphia 135 Anne S. K. Brown Military Collection, Brown University Library

Chapter 6

140 The Granger Collection, NYC. All rights reserved. 143 Library of Congress Rare Books and Special Collections 146 Art Resource, NY/The New York Public Library, Rare Book Division 148 Abigail Smith Adams, c.1766 (pastel on paper), Blyth, Benjamin (fl.1740-87)/© Massachusetts Historical Society, Boston, MA, USA/The Bridgeman Art Library 156 National Portrait Gallery, Smithsonian Institution/Art Resource, NY

Chapter 7

168 MPI/Getty Images 177 Art Resource, NY 183 North Wind/North Wind Picture Archives 185 U.S. Department of the Interior 187 Library of Congress

Chapter 8

194 National Museum of American History/Smithsonian Institution 197 Senator John Heinz Pittsburgh Regional History Center 198 Library of Congress 199 Library of Congress 207 Colonial Williamsburg Foundation 215 MPI/Getty Images

Chapter 9

220 Courtesy, Winterthur Museum, Funds provided by H.F. DuPont 226 Library of Congress 227 Library of Congress 229 The New York Public Library/Art Resource, NY 230 The Granger Collection, NYC. All rights reserved. 233T Colonial Williamsburg Foundation 233B American Textile History Museum, Lowell, MA

Chapter 10

244 Courtesy, Winterthur Museum, Funds provided by H.F. DuPont 250 Stump Speaking (oil on canvas), Bingham, George Caleb (1811–79)/Private Collection/The Bridgeman Art Library 255 Library of Congress 256 Woolaroc Museum 261 The New-York Historical Society

Chapter 11

268 Library of Congress 271 The New-York Historical Society 273 Library of Congress 277 The Collection of the Shadows-On-The-Teche, New Iberia, Louisiana. A National Trust Historic Site 282 Daughters of the Republic of Texas Library 284 Colonial Williamsburg Foundation 288 Library of Congress

Chapter 12

290 The Granger Collection, NYC. All rights reserved 296 Published courtesy of Fruitlands Museum, Harvard, MA 306 National Portrait Gallery, Smithsonian Institution/Art Resource, NY 307 Sophia Smith Collection, Smith College 308 Bettmann/CORBIS

Chapter 13

312 Harvard University, Houghton Library 314 The New York Public Library/Art Resource, NY 318 World History Archive/Newscom 326 Neg.# ICHi-00013/Chicago History Museum 330 Bettmann/CORBIS

Chapter 14

334 Art Resource, NY/The New York Public Library 339 The Granger Collection, NYC. All rights reserved. 341 Library of Congress 350 Library of Congress 352 Library of Congress

Chapter 15

358 Library of Congress **362** Library of Congress 366 Library of Congress **371** Library of Congress **372** Francis G. Mayer/Corbis Art/CORBIS **374** Library of Congress **375** The New-York Historical Society

Chapter 16

386 Library of Congress **396** Stock Montage, Inc./Historical Pictures Collection **399** Collection of The New-York Historical Society, negative number 50475 **404** Valentine Richmond History Center **406** The Granger Collection, NYC. All rights reserved. **408** Rutherford B. Hayes Presidential Center **413** Time & Life Pictures/Getty Images

Index

Key terms and the text page on which the term is defined are highlighted in boldface type.

A

Abenaki Indians, 9

Abolitionist movement, 303; antebellum South and, 275, 282–284, 306; under Articles of Confederation, 145; black abolitionists and, 305–307; rise of radical, 303–305; yeomen and, 281–282

Abortion and abortion rights, 300

"Act Concerning Religion" (Maryland), 40

Act of Supremacy (England, 1534), 25

Adams, Abigail, 147, *148*

Adams, John: American Revolution and, 115, 116, 124, 125; death of, 222; Declaration of Independence and, 128, *128;* diplomacy and, 157; presidency of, 183–190, *185, 205;* as vice president, 169–170, 171; on women's rights, 147

Adams, John Quincy, 202; presidency of, 240, 251–252, 253; as secretary of state, 223, 239–240

Adams, Samuel, 123, 124, 125, 142

Adams-Onís Treaty, 223, *224,* 239

Adet, Pierre, 184

Africa. *See* West Africa

African Americans: in American Revolution, 130; under Articles of Confederation, 145–147; as black abolitionists, 305–307; in Civil War, *374,* 374–375, *375,* 387–388; constructing identify of, 71–73, 80; evangelicalism and, 98; farming and, 399, 400; as free blacks in antebellum South, 275–276; in Jacksonian era, 246; in Jim Crow South, 411–412; in Reconstruction, 387–388, 389–392, 394–396, 397–401, 403–405. *See also* Ku Klux Klan; Segregation; Slaves and slavery

African Methodist Episcopal (AME) Church, 98, 146, 404, 412

Africans, in Americas, 4–5, 15–16, 27. *See also* African Americans

Agricultural colleges, 382

Agricultural Revolution, 6–7

Agriculture: Civil War and, 368; early nineteenth century, 231–232, 234; Eastern Woodland cultures and, 9; in Jeffersonian America, 199; technology and, 326. *See also* Planters and plantations

"Air-boiling process," *327*

Alabama, 147, 223, 255, 286, 361

Alamo, battle of, **317**

Albany (NY), 48, 132

Albany Plan, 103–104, *104*

Alexander I (Czar of Russia), 239–240

Algonquian Indians, 9, 12

Alien and Sedition Acts (1798), 187–188

Alien Enemies Law (1798), 187

Alien Law (1798), 187

Allen, Richard, 98, 146

Alliance, French, in American Revolution, 133–134

Alton (IL), 304

Amendments, Constitutional. *See* specific amendments

American and Foreign Anti-Slavery Society, 305

American Anti-Slavery Society, 303–305

American Bible Society, 295

American Board of Customs Commissioners, 121

American Colonization Society, 282, 303

American Crisis (Paine), 130

American Fur Company, 223

American Indians. *See* Native Americans

American party, 346, 348

American Plan, 246

American Revolution, 110–141, *127;* Boston Massacre and, 122–123; Boston Tea Party and, 123–125; boycotts in, 119, 121, *121,* 122; commitment and sacrifice in, 111–112; eroding bonds of empire and, 116–125, 138; fighting for independence in, 128–136, *131,* 138; fueling the crisis and, 121–122; independence and, 125–128, 138; loyalists in, 136; political cartoons and, *114;* protests in, 118–121; structure of colonial society and, 113–119, 138; taxation without representation and, 114–115

American Society (Philadelphia), 91–92

American System (Clay), 253

American Temperance Society, 296

American Tract Society, 295

America(s). *See* New World

Ames, Fisher, 201

Amherst, Jeffrey, 105

Amnesty, for Confederates, 389

Anasazi Indians, 7

Anderson, Alexander, *210*

Anderson, Robert, 364

Andros, Edmund, 77–78

Anglican Church. *See* Church of England (Anglican Church)

Anglo-American identity, 84–85

Annapolis meeting, 155–156

Antebellum era. *See under* South

Anthony, Susan B., 406

Anti-Catholicism, 345

Anti-colonialism, 322

Antietam, battle of, 371, *371*

Antifederalists, 161–165; Bill of Rights and, 163–165

Anti-Masonic party, 262

Antinomianism, 46, 51

Antislavery movement, 145–146, 303–307

Apalachee Indians, 4

Appalachian region, 197, 222, 223–225

Appeal... to the Colored Citizens of the World (Walker), 270, 306

Appleton, Nathan, 232–233

Appomattox Courthouse surrender, 378

Arawak Indians, 13

Aristocracy, early republic and, 143–144

Ark (ship), 39

Arkansas, 286

Army Corps of Engineers, 201

Articles of Capitulation (New Netherland), 49
Articles of Confederation, 150–151; western land and, 151–153
Artisans, 250
Art(s), 248–249
Ashley River, 53
Assassination(s), Lincoln, 378, 380
Assemblies, colonial, 99–100, 115. *See also* House of Burgesses (VA)
Astor, John Jacob, 223
Astor House, *244–245,* 246
Atlanta (GA), 378
Attorneys. *See* Legal system and profession
Attorneys general, first, 172
Austin, Stephen F., 315
Autobiography (Franklin), 92, 94
Aztec Indians, 7, *7,* 9, 19

B

Backcountry, 85; tension in, 85–88, 108, 117; yeomen in, 281
Backus, John, 148
Bacon, Nathaniel, 76
Bacon's Rebellion, 76–77
Bagley, Sarah, 233
Baltimore (MD), 214
Baltimore City Hotel, 246
Baltimore & Ohio Railroad, 324
Bank of the United States, 175; 1790s controversy over, 175–176; Bank War and, 259–261, *261,* 266; *McCulloch v. Maryland* and, 238
Banks and banking: Civil War and, 382; in Jacksonian era, 250–251, 259–261
Bank War, 259–261, *261,* 266
Banneker, Benjamin, 145
Baptists, 293, 347–348
Barbados, 53–54, 70
Barré, Isaac, 118
Battle of New Orleans, 214, *215*
Bayard, James A., 190
Bay Colony. *See* Massachusetts Bay Colony
Bear Flag Republic, 321
Beecher, Catherine, 299
Beecher, Henry Ward, 348
Beecher, Lyman, 294–295

Bell, John, 352
"Benevolent empire", 296
Benin, 14, 15
Bennington, battle of, 132
Beringia, 5
Berkeley, John, 50–51
Berkeley, William, 32, 76–77
Berlin Decree (France, 1806), 209, 211
Bethel Church for Negro Methodists, 146
Biddle, Nicholas, 260–261
Bight of Benin and Biafra, 15
Bill of Rights (U.S.), **163–165;** absence of, in Constitution, 160; due process and, 393; first civil liberties crisis and, 187–188
Bill of Rights, English, 78
Bill of rights, in Northwest Ordinance, 153
Bill of rights, in states, 146, 160
Bingham, George Caleb, 249, *250*
Birney, James G., 319
Birth control, 300
Birth rates, 300
Black belts, 231
Black Codes, 392, 400–401, 404
Black Hawk (chief), 227
Blacks. *See* African Americans
Black Seminoles, 227, 274
Blair, Francis P., 253, 260
"Bleeding Kansas" slogan, 346
Block House, New Braunfels (Von Iwonski), *282*
Board of Commissioners for Foreign Missions, 295
Board of Trade (British), 75, 99, 100
Boleyn, Anne, 25
Boone, Daniel, 153, 198
Booth, John Wilkes, 378
Border states, secession and, 365
Boston (MA): in American Revolution, 122–126; colonial, 46, 78, *93*
Boston Manufacturing Company, 232
Boston Massacre, 122, **122–123**
Boston Tea Party (1773), **123–125**
Boudinot, Elias, 226
Boycotts, in American Revolution, 119, 121, *121,* 122
Braddock, Edward, 104

Bradford, William, 41, 42
Bradstreet, Anne, 64
Brady, Mathew, *358–359*
Brahmin poets, 249
Breckinridge, John, 352
Breed's Hill. *See* Bunker Hill
Br'er Rabbit stories, 275
Britain. *See* England
British East India Company, 123–124
British Empire, American colonies in, 73–75, 79–80, 82–109; Anglo-American identity and, 84–85; backcountry tension and, 85–88, 108; clash of political cultures and, 98–100, 108; economic transformation and, 93–95; impact of European ideas on, 91–95, 108; imperial war and, *101,* 101–107, *103, 105, 106,* 108; national debt and, 116–118; Spanish borderlands and, *89,* 89–91, 108
Brooks, Preston, *334–335,* 335–336
Brown, Henry ("Box"), 274
Brown, John, 346, 351
Brown, William Wells, 305
Brown University, 97
Bruce, Blanche K., 403
Buchanan, James: election of 1856 and, 346–347; presidency of, 348–349, 364
"Bulldozing" voters, 409
Bull Run, first battle of, 370
Bunker Hill, battle of, 126
Burgis, William, *93*
Burgoyne, John, *131,* 132
Burke, Aedanus, 143
Burke, Edmund, 124
Burnside, Ambrose E., 371
Burr, Aaron, 190
Business. *See* Corporations
Bute, Earl of (John Stuart), 88, 113, *114,* 116
Butler, Andrew, 335
Byrd, William, II, 84–85

C

Cabot, John and Sebastian, 24
Calhoun, John C.: Jackson and, 252, 254, 258; nullification and, 257–258, 261; Texas annexation and, 318; War of 1812 and, 212

California, 90, 223, 321–322, 324, 338

Calvert family, 39–40

Calvinism, 43, 293

Campaigning, political, 249–250, *250*, 253, 260

Camp meetings, 293

Canada, 22–23, 213–214

Canals, 230, *230*, 324

Canary Islands, 17

Cane Ridge (KY), 292

Canning, George, 240

Capital (financial), 324–325. *See also* Finances and financing

Capitalism. *See* Corporations

Caravan trade, 14

Caribbean region, 19, 69–70

Carolinas, colonial, 53–54, *56*, 70, 87

Carpetbaggers, 401

Carteret, George, 50–51

Cartier, Jacques, 22–23

Cass, Lewis, 338

Catawba Indians, 12

Catherine of Aragon, 24–25

Catholicism: in colonial Maryland, 39; in French America, 23; Protestant Reformation and, 24–25; in Spanish America, 21; Texas and, 316

Cayuga Indians, 132

Ceramics, grain storage and, 7

Cerro Gordo, battle at, 321

Champlain, Samuel de, 23

Chancellorsville, battle of, 376

Charles I (King of England), 33, 40, 43, 114

Charles II (King of England), 47, 49, 52, 53, 76, 77

Charleston (SC), 53, *53*, 134, 361

Charleston and Hamburg Railroad, 324

Charles Town, 53, *53*

Chase, Samuel, 162, 206

Chatham, Earl of. *See* Pitt, William

Chattanooga, battle of, 377

Chauncy, Charles, 97

Cheever, George B., 348

Chenaworth, Richard B., *327*

Cherokee Indians, 88, 117, 132, 225–330, *226*; National Council of, 226; Trail of Tears and, 255–256, *256, 257*

Cherokee Phoenix, 226

Chesapeake (ship), 209

Chesapeake region, colonial, 31–41, *38, 39*, 66–69, 80

Chickasaw Indians, 88, 225, 228, *257*

Childhood, 299–302

Children. *See* Childhood; Families

China trade, 233

Chippewa Indians, 180

Choctaw Indians, 88, 132, 225, 255–256

Christian Commissions, 382

Christianity: evangelical, 96–98, 292–296, 310, 348, 354; Native Americans and, 11, 23. *See also* by denomination

Chrysler's Farm, battle of, 214

Church and state: under Articles of Confederation, 144; under Constitution, 153, 163

Church of England (Anglican Church), 77, 144

Cincinnati (OH), 197

Cities and towns, 180, 199–200

Citizenship, Fourteenth Amendment and, 393

"City on a Hill" (Massachusetts Bay), 44–45, 77–78

Civil liberties: Bill of Rights and, 163–165; Civil War and, 369; first national crisis over, 187–188; Fourteenth Amendment and, 393; writ of habeas corpus and, 369, 407

Civil Rights Act(s) of 1866, 393, 400–401

Civil War, 358–385; African-Americans and, *374*, 374–375, *375*; beginning of, 364–367, *366*; casualties of, 371, 380, *380*; effects of, 380–382, *384*; emancipation and, *372*, 372–374, 384; emergence of Lincoln and, 359–361; fight to the finish in, 371–380, *379, 380*; political leadership in, 368–370, 382; secession and, 361–366, *365*, 383; total war and, 367–371, 383

Clark, William, 203

Classes: in antebellum South, 276–282, 287–288; under Articles of Confederation, 144; colonial, 65–66, 67–69; early nineteenth century

and, 246–248, 299–300, 301–302; mid-nineteenth century and, 330–331

Clay, Cassius M., 283

Clay, Henry: 1824 election and, 251; 1844 election and, 319; "American System" of, 253; Compromise of 1850 and, 338–339, *339*; Jackson and, 258, 260–261; Missouri Compromise and, 236; Monroe Doctrine and, 239; War of 1812 and, 212; Whigs and, 261, 263

Clement VII (Pope), 25

Clermont (steamboat), 229, *229*

Clermont on the Hudson, The (Pensee), *229*

Clinton, De Witt, 212

Clinton, George, 177

Clinton, Henry, 134–135

Clothing, 232, 247

Coal and coal industry, 326

Cobb, Thomas Reade, 278

Codfish, 23–24

Coercive Acts (Intolerable Acts) **(1774)**, **124**, 125, *127*

Coins. *See* Currency

Cold Harbor, battle of, 377

Colfax, Schuyler, 403

College of New Jersey. *See* Princeton University

College of William and Mary, 11

Colleges and universities, 382. *See also* by specific names

Colonies, English, 30–81, *56*; Anglo-American identity and, 84–85; backcountry tension in, 85–88, 108; breaking away to, 32–41, 58; in the Chesapeake region, 33–41, 61–62, 66–69, 80; economy of, 93–95, *95*, 113, *120*; Empire and, 73–75, 79–80, *101*, 101–107, *103, 105, 106*; European impact on American culture in, 91–95, 108; families in, 61–63; government in, 98–100, 108, 115; immigrants in, 85–87, *86*; Middle, 48–53, 58; New England, 41–48, 58, 63–66, 80; political revolts in, 75–79, 81; population in, 85, 93, 113; religion in, *96*, 96–98, 108; Southern, 53–57, 58, 71–73

Colonization movement, 303, 373

Colt, Samuel, *327*

Columbian Exchange, 12–13, *13*

Columbus, Christopher, 16, 17–18

Commerce, 95, 199–200

Commerce clause, 238–239

Committee of correspondence, 123

Common school movement, 301

Common Sense (Paine), 127–128

Commonwealthmen, 116

Compromise of 1850, 336–343, *340,* 354

Compromise of 1877, 409–410

Concord, battle at, 125–126

Confederacy, 361–382; battles and, 370–371, 376–378, *379;* formation of, 361–362; home front of, 367–368; leadership of, 368–370

Congregational Church, 44–45, 144, 293–295

Congress (U.S.): Reconstruction and, 389–397, 414; in U.S. Constitution, 158–159. *See also* specific issues; specific legislation

Connecticut, 47–48, *56,* 115, 116, 144, 145, 149

Conquest. *See* New World

Conquistadores, 17, 19, 21

Conscription. *See* Draft (military)

Conspiracies theories, 251

Constitution (ship), 213

Constitution (U.S.): amendments to (*see* specific amendments); Bill of Rights (*see* Bill of Rights); commerce clause and, 238–239; compared to Articles of Confederation, *162;* contract clause of, 237–238; development of, 153–161; federal-state relations and (*see* Federal *vs.* state governments); implied powers of, 175, 238; loose construction of, 175, 237–238; ratification of, 160–165, *164;* strict construction of, 177, 196, 252, 381

Constitutional Convention, 157–161

Constitutional conventions during: Reconstruction, 390–392

Constitutional Union party, 352

Constitutions, state, 149

Consumer revolution, 94

Continental Army, 129–130, 132–133

Continental Congress. *See* First Continental Congress; Second Continental Congress

Continental System (Napoleon), 209

Contraband, slaver and, 373

Contraception. *See* Birth control

Contract clause, 237–238

Contract labor system, 400

Convention of 1818, *224*

Convention of Mortefontaine, 189

Cooper, Anthony Ashley (Earl of Shaftesbury), 53

Cooper, Peter, *327*

Cooperationists, 361

Cooper River, 54

"Cooper Union Portrait" (Brady), *358–359*

Copperheads, 376

Corinth (MS), 370

Cornwallis, Charles (Lord), 134–135

Corporations: Civil War and, 382; railroads and, 324–325

Corruption: New South and, 411; Reconstruction and, 402–403

Cortés, Hernán, 19, 21

Cotton and cotton industry, 231–232, 271, 285–287, *288,* 289

Cotton Belt, 271, 276–277

Cotton gin, 147, 231, **285**

Cotton Kingdom, 277, 285–287, *288,* 361

Coureurs de bois, 23

Courts. *See* Judicial branch

Cowpens, battle at, 135

Crawford, William, 251

Creative adaptations, 4

Credit Mobilier scandal, 403

Creek Indians, 88, 117, 132, 198, 225, 228; removal of, 255, *257*

Creole languages, 71–72

Creole society, 68

Criollos, 22

Crittenden, John, 362–363

Crittenden compromise, 363

Crockett, Davy, 317

Cromwell, Oliver, 40

Crop lien system, 411

Culpeper (Lord), 77

Cult of Domesticity, 297–299, 310; slavery and, 348

Culture, colonial, 62–63

Continental System (Napoleon), 209

Cumberland Gap, 151

Currency, paper, 368, 382

D

Dale, Thomas, 36, 37

Dartmouth College, 97

Dartmouth College* v. *Woodward, **237–238**

Davenport, John, 47

Davie, William, 189

Davies, K. G., 70

Davis, Jefferson, *362,* 369–370, 376

Death rates. *See* Mortality rates

Debates, Lincoln-Douglas, 349–351

Debt: assumption of state, 174–175; Hamilton and, 173–176

Declaration of Independence, 128, *128*

Declaration of Sentiments (Seneca Falls), 308

Declaratory Act (1766), 121, *127*

Deere, John, 326, *327*

Delaware, 52, 53, *56,* 151

Delaware Indians, 88

Delaware Prophet. *See* Neolin (Delaware Prophet)

Democracy: Civil War and, 360–361; and dissent (1788-1800), 176–184; Jacksonian politics of, 251–265, *266;* Jacksonian theory and practice of, 247–251, *266;* Tocqueville's wisdom and, 265

Democratic party: in Civil War, 369, 378; election of 1860 and, 351–352; in Jacksonian era, 250, 252–254, *254, 260, 263,* 264–264; in the New South, 410; in Reconstruction era, 407, 409; sectional crisis and, 338–346, 346–347, 354. *See also* Democratic presidents by name

Departments of government. *See* specific department names

Depression(s). *See* Panic(s)

Detroit (MI), 213

De Vaca, Álvar Núñez Cabeza, 3–4

Díaz del Castillo, Bernal, 7, 19, 21

Dickinson, John, 150, 151, 157

Discovery (ship), 34

Discrimination, 146. *See also* Segregation

Disease: colonial, 34, 38, 42; Native Americans and, 5, 12–13, 36, 42, 88

Dissent: 1790s party politics and, 176–184; Civil War and, 369; Jefferson presidency and, 203, 205–206

District of Columbia (DC). *See* Washington (DC)

Diversity, colonial, 52, 57, 58

Divorce, 64, 148

Dixon, Jeremiah, 39

Doctors. *See* Medicine

Domesticity, Cult of, 297–299, 310; slavery and, 348

Domestic work, 298, 300

Dominion of New England, 77

Douglas, Stephen A., 331, 339, 346, *350;* in 1860 election, 351–352; in debates with Lincoln, 349–351; Kansas-Nebraska Act and, 343–346; secession and, 365

Douglass, Frederick, 305–306, *306*

Dove (ship), 39

Draft (military), in Civil War, 375–376

Draft riots, 375–376

Drake, Edwin L., *327*

Drake, Francis, 26

Drama. *See* Theater

Dred Scott v. *Sandford*, 348–349

Dunmore, Lord (John Murray), 126

Dunn, Richard, 54

Dutch West India Company, 48–49

Dwight, Timothy, 293

E

Eastern Woodland Cultures, 9–10

East India Company. *See* British East India Company

Eaton, John, 254

Eaton, Joseph Oriel, 313

Eaton, Peggy O'Neale, 254

Eaton, Theophilus, 47

Economic cycles, 250–251. *See also* Panic(s)

Economic inequality. *See* Classes; Poverty

Economy: Civil War and, *367,* 367–368, 381; colonial, 73–75; early nineteenth century, 228–234; Embargo Act and, 209–210; railroads and, 324–325; slavery and Southern, 277, 278–279, 284–287, *287,* 289. *See also* Agriculture; Banks and banking; Commerce; Finances and financing; Industrialization, early; Panic(s); Trade

Economy policy: Civil War and, 382; in Jacksonian era, 250–251, 259–261, 263–264. *See also* Tariff(s)

Education: freedmen and, *404,* 405; nineteenth century, 300–302

Edwards, Jonathan, 96

Edward VI (King of England), 25

Election(s): of 1788, 171; of 1796, 183–184, *184;* of 1800, 189–191, *190,* 195; of 1804, 203, *205;* of 1808, 210, *211;* of 1812, 212, *212;* of 1816, 222; of 1820, 239; of 1824, 240, 251, *252;* of 1828, 252–254, *254;* of 1832, *259,* 259–260; of 1836, 262, *262;* of 1840, 250, 263, *263;* of 1844, 318–319; of 1848, 338, *338;* of 1852, 342–343, *343;* of 1856, 346–347, *347;* of 1860, 351–353, *353;* of 1864, 377–378, *378;* of 1876, *409,* 409–410

Electoral college, 160, 190

Elevators, *327*

Elizabeth I (Queen of England), 24–26

Elliott, Robert Brown, 403

Elliott, Stephen, 348

Ellsworth, Oliver, 189

Emancipation: abolitionist demand for, 303; Civil War and, 372–375

Emancipation Proclamation (1862), *372, 373*

Embargo Act, 209–210, *210*

Emerson, Ralph Waldo, 249, 302, 313, 348

Emigrants, African Americans and, 413

Empire, British. *See* British Empire, American colonies in

Empire, Spanish, *89,* 89–91

Employees. *See* Labor

Empresarios, 316

Encomienda system, 21

England (Britain): birth of Protestantism in, 24–26; exploration and conquest by, 23–26. *See also* British Empire, American colonies in

Enlightenment, 91; American, 91–92

Enrollment Act (1863), 375–376

Entail, 144

Enterprise (steamboat), 229

Enumerated goods, 74–75, 94

Environment, 6

Epidemics in Americas, 5, 12–13

Episcopalians, 348

Equality and inequality: under Articles of Confederation, 143–144; impact of Civil War on, 381; in Jacksonian era, 247; of opportunity *vs.* reward, 247; sectionalism and, 354–355. *See also* Race and racism; Segregation; Slaves and slavery; Women, rights of

Era of Good Feeling, 234, 241

Eric the Red, 16

Erie Canal, 230, *230*

Essex decision, 208

Ether, *327*

Ethnocentrism of European explorers, 11

Europe and Europeans, 16–18

Evangelicalism: colonial, 96–98; early nineteenth century, 292–296, 310; sectionalism and, 348, 354

Evans, Augusta Jane, 248

Evans, Oliver, *327*

Executive branch: under Articles of Confederation, 150; formation of, 171–172; under U.S. Constitution, 160, *162. See also* by name of departments; Presidency (U.S.)

Expansion and expansionism: cost of, 331; industrial revolution and, 325–331, 332; internal development and, 324–325, 332; Jeffersonian Republicans and, 196–199, 202–203, 217; Manifest Destiny and, 315, 318, 320, 323; Mexican-American War and, 320–323, *323;* by mid-nineteenth century, *315;* Native American resistance to, 198–199, 225–228; post War of 1812 migration and, 222–228, *224,* 241; spirit of Young America and, 313–315; Texas and, 315–320. *See also* West, trans-Appalachian; West, trans-Mississippi

Exploration: of New World, 16–27; voyages of European, *20;* West Africa and, 13–16

F

Factions, 1790s party politics and, 181

Factories and factory systems: early nineteenth century, 232–233; mid-nineteenth century, 325, 328, 330–331

Families: colonial, 61–64, 66–67; early nineteenth century, 297–302, 310; slave, 272–273, *273*, 283, 348

Family task system, 398

Far East. *See* China

Farewell Address (Washington), 182–183

Farms and farming. *See* Agriculture; Planters and plantations

Fashion. *See* Clothing

Federal agencies. *See* specific agencies

Federalist, The, 161

Federalist party, 170–171, 177, 179–180; Adam's presidency and, 183–190; demise of, 202, 214–216; Jefferson's presidency and, 203, 210; Madison's presidency and, 210, 212, 214–216; Whiskey Rebellion and, 182–183

Federalists, 161–163

Federal system, 152, 157–159, 165

Federal *vs.* state governments: Civil War and, 381–382; *Gibbons v. Ogden* and, 238–239; *McCulloch vs. Maryland* and, 238

Female Labor Reform Association, 330

Feminism: domestic, 299; early nineteenth century, 307–308

Ferdinand and Isabella (King and Queen of Spain), 16

Fertility rates. *See* Birth rates

Fifteenth Amendment, 405, 409

Fillmore, Millard, 346; presidency of, 339

Finances and financing: in Civil War, 368; railroads and, 324–325

Fink, Mike, 198

Finney, Charles G., 291–292, 294, 303

First Continental Congress, 125

First Vote, The (Ward), *406*

Fishing and fishing industry, 23–24, *28*

Fitch, John, 229, *327*

Fitzhugh, George, 283

Five Civilized Tribes, 225

Five Points district (New York), 329

Flatboat trade, 229

Florida, 223, 226, 274

Folklore, slave, 275

Folsom, David, 256

Force Acts, 407

Force Bill (1833), 258

Fort Crown Point, 105

Fort Donelson, 370

Fort Duquesne, 103–105

Fort Henry, 370

Fort McHenry, 214

Fort Moultrie, *366*

Fort Necessity, 103

Fort Niagara, 105

Fort Orange (Albany), 48

Fort Pickens, 364

Fort Sumter, siege of, 364–365, *365, 366*

Fort Ticonderoga, 105

Founding Fathers. *See* Constitutional Convention

Fourteenth Amendment, 393

France: in American Revolution, 133–134, 135, *135;* colonial conflicts with Britain and, 101–106, *103, 105;* exploration and conquest by, 22–23; Revolution in, 129, *177, 178*

Franchise. *See* Voting and voting rights

Franklin, Benjamin: Albany Plan of, 103–104; anti-slavery and, 145; Constitutional Convention and, 157–158; Declaration of Independence and, *128;* French alliance and, 133–134; on parliamentary sovereignty, 125; as Philadelphia administrator, 117; as *philosophe,* 92, 92–93; on presidential title, 170

Fredericksburg (VA), battle of, 371

Freedmen's Bureau, 393

Freedmen's Bureau, 399, 400, 405

Freedmen's schools, 404

Freedom(s), early republic and, 141–143. *See also* Liberties

Freedom's Journal, 306

Free markets, 73. *See also* Market economy

Freemen, 68, 76, 78

Freeport doctrine (Douglas), 350

Free-Soil movement, 337, 346, 354

Free-Soil party, 338, 342

Free trade. *See* Free markets; Market economy

Frémont, John C., 321, 347

French and Indian War. *See* Seven Years' War

French Revolution, 129, *177,* **178**

Friars. *See* Missions and missionaries

Friends. *See* Quakers

Frontier, 153. *See also* Expansion and expansionism; West, Trans-Appalachian; West, Trans-Mississippi

Fugitive Slave Law, 338, **340–341,** *341*

Fugitive slaves, 272, 274, 276, 340, 341

Fulton, Robert, 200, 229, *229*

Fundamental Orders (Connecticut), 47

Fur trade, 94, 223

G

Gadsden, Christopher, 125

Gadsden Purchase (1853), 322

Gage, Thomas, 124, 125–126, 129, 130

Gag rule, 306

Gallatin, Albert, 148, 200–201, 209, 216

Galloway, Joseph, 125

Gama, Vasco da, 17

Gardner, Alexander, *371*

Garnet, Henry Highland, 305

Garrison, William Lloyd, 270, 303–305, 307–308, 336

Gates, Horatio, 132

Gates, Thomas, 36

Gender: in Jacksonian era, 246, 297–299; Native Americans and, 11. *See also* Women

General Court (MA), 46, 78

George II (King of England), 55, 104, 113

George III (King of England), 113–114, *114,* 116, 123, 124, 125

Georgia: in American Revolution, 134; under Articles of Confederation, 144; Cherokees and, 255; in Civil War, 377, 378; colonial, 55, *56,* 72; cotton and, 285–286; slavery and, 271

German Americans, 86–87, 328, 329

Germantown (PA), 132–133

Gerry, Elbridge, 185, 188

Gettysburg, battle of, 376–377

Gettysburg Address, 360–361

Ghana, 14

Gibbons v. *Ogden,* **238–239**

Gibson (Mrs.), *197*

Glaciers, 5–6

Global warming, 6

Glorious Revolution, **77–78,** 114

Godspeed (ship), 34

Gold: in Spanish America, 19, 22; West Africa and, 13–16; western territories and, 315, 324

Gold Coast, 15

Gold Rush of 1849, 324

Goodyear, Charles, 326, *327*

Goose Creek Men, 54

GOP ("Grand Old Party"). *See* Republican party

Gorgas, Josiah, 368

"Gospel of prosperity," 402

Government (U.S.): formation of, 150–165; natural rights and, 149; written document for, 149. *See also* Executive branch; Judicial branch; Legislative branch

Government, colonial, 98–100; assemblies in, 99–100; in Chesapeake region, 37, 38, 40; governors councils in, 99–100; in Middle Colonies, 50, 52–53; in New England, 45–46, 47; in Southern Colonies, 54

Graebner, Norman, 322

Granada (Spain), 16

Grand Alliance, 239–240

Grand Banks region, 23–24

Grant, Ulysses S., 397; in Civil War, 370, 376–377; presidency of, 403–404, 407, 408

Grasse, Comte de, 135

Great Awakening, **96–98,** 115. *See also* Second Great Awakening

Great Lakes region: expansion and, 222, 230; Native Americans and, 180; Northwest Territory and, *152;* Seven Years' War and, 101–102, 105, *105;* War of 1812 and, 213

"Great Migration", **44**

Great Plains, Native Americans on, 7

Great Wagon Road, *95*

Greenbacks, **368**

Greene, Nathanael, 135

Greenland, 16

Grenville, George, 117

Grimké, Sarah and Angelina, 307

Guadeloupe, virgin of, 21, *22*

Guerriére (ship), 213

Guilford Courthouse, battle at, 135

Gulf Coast region, 83–84

Gulf of Saint Lawrence. *See* Saint Lawrence River region

Gullah language, 72

H

Habeas corpus, writ of: Civil War and, 369; Reconstruction and, 407

Haiti, 202

Hakluyt, Richard, the Younger, 26–27, 33

Hallam, Lewis, 141

Hamilton, Alexander: 1790s party politics and, 171–176, 178–180, 182–186, 189–190; bank controversy and, 175–176; Constitution and, 143, 157; *The Federalist* and, 161, 164; Manumission Society and, 145; prosperity and security plan of, 173–175, 201

Hampton, Wade, 411

Harmer, Josiah, 180

Harper, Frances, 305

Harpers Ferry, 351

Harrison, William Henry, 211, 214; presidency of, 263, 318

Hartford Convention, **214–216**

Hat and Felt Act (1732), 94

Hawkins, John, 26

Hawks, War of 1812 and, **212–213**

Hawthorne, Nathaniel, 249, 308–309

Hayes, Rutherford B., 1876 election and, 409–410

Headright system, **37**

Helper, Hinton R., 281, 284

Henry, Patrick, 118–119, 125, 157, 163

Henry VII (King of England), 24

Henry VIII (King of England), 24

Henson, Josiah, 306

Herttell, Thomas, 308

Hessian (German) mercenaries, 126, 128, 132

Highways. *See* Roads and highways

Hoe, Richard M., *327*

Holland. *See* Netherlands

Holmes, Oliver Wendell, Sr., 249

Homestead Act of 1862, 382

Hooker, Joseph, 376

Hooker, Thomas, 47

Horseshoe Bend, battle of, 199

Horses on the Great Plains, 6

Hotels and hotel culture, 245–246

"House divided" speech (Lincoln), 349–350

Households, yeoman, 281, *282*

House of Burgesses (VA), **37,** 38, 76, 100; Stamp Act and, 119

House of Commons (England), 99, 114, 118, 121

House of Lords (England), 99

House of Representatives (U.S.), 160, *162*

House of the Seven Gables, The (Hawthorne), 309

Houston, Sam, 317

Howard, Kenneth (Earl of Effingham), 77

Howe, Elias, 326, *327*

Howe, William, 130, 132, 134

Hudson, Henry, 48

Hudson Bay region, 24, 48–50

Hudson River, 200, 229, *229*

Huguenots, 54

Huitzilopochtli, 8

Hull, Isaac, 213

Hull, William, 213

Human sacrifice, 7, *7*

Hume, David, 91, 155

Hutchinson, Anne, 46–47, 48

Hutchinson, Thomas, 78, 114, 124, 136

I

Ice Age, 5, *6*

Iceland, 16

Ideology: American Revolution and, 115, 129, 136; women's rights and, 147–148

Illinois, 224

Illinois Central Railroad, 325

Illinois Territory, 197

Illiteracy. *See* Literacy and literacy tests

Immigrants and immigration: colonial, 85–87, *86;* mid-nineteenth century, 324, 328–329

Impeachment: Andrew Johnson and, 396–397; of federal judges, 206

Impending Crisis of the South, The (Helper), 284

Implied powers, 175; *McCullouch v. Maryland* and, 238

Impressment, 179, 208–209, 216

Inca peoples, 7

Indentured servants, 37, 66, 68

Independence, War of. *See* American Revolution

Indiana Territory, 197, 211

Indian Removal, 225, 254–256, *256, 257*

Indians. *See* Native Americans; *specific tribes*

Indigenous peoples. *See* Native Americans

Industrialization, early, 232–234, 247, 325–326, *327*

Industrial Revolution, 325–326, *327*

Inequality. *See* Equality and inequality

Infant mortality, 300

Interchangeable parts, 234, 325

Intercoastal trade, 95, 228

Internal improvements, 228, 253

Internal slave trade, 207, *207,* 284–285

International organizations. *See* specific organizations

International trade. *See* Tariff(s); *Trade*

Interstate commerce clause, 238–239

Intolerable Acts. *See* Coercive Acts (Intolerable Acts)

Inuit Indians, 7

Inventions and inventors: farming and, 326; nineteenth century, 231, 234, 326, *327*

Investment. *See* corporations

Ireland, 328

Irish Americans, 328–329

Iron Act (1750), 94

Iron and iron industry, 234, 324

Iroquois Indians, 11, 13, 103, 132

Isabella (Queen of Spain), 16

Islam, in West Africa, 13–14

Itinerant preachers, 97

J

Jackson, Andrew: in Battle of New Orleans, 214; Indian lands and, 228; Native Americans and, 199; presidency of, 245–246, 251–262, *255;* Seminole Indians and, 223; Texas and, 317

Jackson, Patrick Tracy, 232–233

Jackson, Rachel, 253

Jackson, Thomas J. (Stonewall), 370, 376

Jacksonian era (1824-1840), 244–267; bank war and second-party system in, 259–265, 266; democracy in theory and practice in, 247–251, 266; hotel culture and, 245–246; politics of democracy and, 251–259, 266; Tocqueville's wisdom and, 265

James (Duke of York), 49–51, 52

James I (King of England), 33–34, 36, 38, 43

James II (King of England), 77

Jamestown, 34–35

Jay, John, 145, 161, 172, 201

Jay's Treaty, 178–180, 184

Jefferson, Thomas: 1790s party politics and, 170–173, 175–176, 178, 180, 182–186, 188; in Articles of Confederation era, 143, 144, 151–152; Bill of Rights and, 165; death of, 222; Declaration of Independence and, 128, *128;* diplomacy and, 157; Native Americans and, 199, 225, 228; presidency of, 190, 196–210, 217; slaves and slavery and, 145, 147, 236; as vice president, 184; women's rights and, 149

Jeffersonian Republicans. *See* Republicans (Jeffersonians)

Jennings, Samuel, *140–141*

Jesuits, 23

Jesup, Thomas W., 227

Jews and Judaism, *Reconquista* and, 17

Jim Crow laws, 401, **411–412.** *See also* Segregation

Jobs. *See* Labor

Johnson, Andrew, 377; impeachment crisis and, *396,* 396–397; presidency of, 390–397, 399

Johnson, Richard, 199

Joint-stock company, 33–34, 35

Joloff (Africa), 14

Judicial branch: formation of, 172; under U.S. Constitution, 158, *162. See also* Supreme Court (U.S.)

Judicial review, 206

Judiciary Act of 1801, 205–206

Judiciary Acts of 1789, 172

Julian, George, 394

K

Kansas-Nebraska Act (1854), **343– 346,** *344,* 346

Kansas Territory, 343–346, *344*

Kearny, Stephen, 321

Kelly, William, *327*

Kendall, Amos, 253, 260

Kentucky, 153, 198, 365–366

Kentucky and Virginia Resolutions, 188–189

Key, Francis Scott, 214

King, Doris Elizabeth, 246

King, Rufus, 235

King Cotton, 271, 284, *288*

King George's War, *101,* 102–104

King Philip's War, 101

Kings Mountain, battle at, 135

King William's War, *101*

Kitchen Cabinet (Jackson), 260

Klan. *See* Ku Klux Klan

Knights of the White Camellia, 407

Know-Nothing party, 345, 348, 352

Knox, Henry, 147, 171, 186

Knox, Lucy, 147

Kongo, 14

Ku Klux Klan, 407–409, *408*

L

Labor: Civil War and, 381; immigrants and, 330–331; protests/unrest, 233; system, contract, 400

Labor unions, 330

Labrador, 23

Lady's Magazine and Repository of Entertaining Knowledge, 143

Lafayette, Marquis de, 133, 135, 177, 221–222

Laissez-faire, 325, 382, 410

Lake Erie, 213

Lake Ontario: battle on, 214

Land: headright, 37; quality of Southeastern, 231

Land, western: after American Revolution, 151–153, *152, 154;* quality of trans-Appalachian, 231. *See also* Expansion and expansionism

Land grants: Civil War and, 382; railroads and, 325

Land-grant universities, 382

Land Ordinance (1785), 152–153

Land systems, European, 12

Lane Theological Seminary, 304

La Salle, René Robert Cavalier (Sieur de), 23, 102

Las Casas, Bartolomé de (Fra), 21

Latin America, Monroe Doctrine and, 239–240

Latinos. *See* specific groups

Lawes and Liberties (Massachusetts Bay), 46

Lawrence (KS), 346

Lee, Richard Henry, 125, 165

Lee, Robert E., 366, 370–371, 376–377, 378

Legal system and profession: colonial, 100; in Jacksonian era, 248

Legislative branch: under Articles of Confederation, 150; under U.S. Constitution, 158–159, *162. See also* House of Representatives (U.S.); *Senate (U.S.)*

Leopard (ship), 209

Letters from a Farmer in Pennsylvania (Dickinson), 150

Lewis, Meriwether, 203

Lewis and Clark Expedition, 203, *204*

Lexington, battle at, 125–126

Liberator, The (newspaper), 270, 303

Liberties: American Revolution and, 112, 115–116, 124; Antifederalists and, 162–163; under Articles of Confederation, 143, 153, 154–155; colonial, 100; government constraints and, 150. *See also* Civil liberties; *Freedom(s)*

Liberty Displaying the Arts and Sciences (Jennings), *140–141*

Liberty party, 305, 319, *319*

Library Company, 93

Life expectancy, 64, 66–67, 68

Lincoln, Abraham, *352, 358;* assassination of, 378, 380; Civil War and, 364–382; in debates with Douglas, 349–351; election of, 351–352; emancipation and, 372–375; emergence of, 359–361; presidential leadership of, 369; Reconstruction and, 389–390; secession and, 361–365, *365*

Lincoln, Benjamin, 134

Lincoln-Douglas debates, 349–351

Lindneux, Robert, *256*

Lippard, George, 150

Literacy and literacy tests: Cherokee, 226, *226;* in Jacksonian era, 248

Literary World, 314

Livingston, Robert, *128,* 202, 229

Livingston, William, 155

Locke, John, 91, 115–116, 147

London Company, 34

Long, Crawford W., *327*

Longfellow, Henry Wadsworth, 249

Long Island, colonial, 47, 50

Loose construction (of Constitution), 175, 237–238

Louisbourg, 102–103, 105

Louisiana, 23, 102, 222, 271, 273, 285–286

Louisiana Purchase, 202–203, *204*

Louis XIV (King of France), 101–102

Louis XVI (King of France), 133, 177–178

Lovejoy, Elijah, 304

Lowell (MA), 233, *233,* 330

Lowell, Francis Cabot, 232–233

Lowell, James Russell, 249, 348

Lowell Female Labor Reform Association, 233

Loyalists (Tories), **115,** 134–135, 136

"Loyal opposition," 250

Lumber trade, 328

Lutherans, 87

Lynchings, 405

M

Machines (political). *See* Political machines/ organizations

Machine tools, 326

Macon, Nathaniel, 211

Macon's Bill Number Two (1810), 211

Madison, James, 156–157; 1790s party politics and, 170–171, 174–176, 179, 188; American Revolution and, 125; Constitution and, 142, 143, 154–160, 164–165; *The Federalist* and, 161; Jefferson presidency and, 200, 205, 210; presidency of, 211–216, 228

Magazines, 248

Maine, 235

Mali, 14

Mammals, 5

Manassas Junction, 370

Manifest Destiny, 315, 318, 320, 323, 324

Mann, Horace, 301

Manufacturing, "continuous process," 325

Manumission Society (New York), 145

Marbury, William, 205

***Marbury* v. *Madison,* 205–206**

Marcy, William, 344

Market economy: emergence of, 230–232; Jacksonian era and, 264; transportation and, 228–230

Maroon communities, in Florida, 226

Marquette, Père Jacques, 23

Marriage, 22, 63

Marshall, John, 185, 188, 190, 205–206, 237–239, 256

Martial law, in Civil War, 376

Mary I (Queen of England), 25

Mary II (Queen of England), 78

Maryland: under Articles of Confederation, 151–152; in Civil War, 366, 371; colonial, 38–41, *56,* 66–69, 70; in War of 1812, 214

Mason, Charles, 39

Mason, George, 157, 160, 164

Mason-Dixon line, 353

Mason family, *60–61*

Massachusetts: in American Revolution, 119, 122–126, 130; anti-slavery movement and, 146; under Articles of Confederation, 144, 149, 156; common school movement in, 301; factory system and, 232–233

Massachusetts Bay Colony, 44–47, *56;* Glorious Revolution and, 77–78; social stability in, 63–66, 80; witchcraft and, 78–79

Massasoit, 42

Mass production, 325–326

Mather, Cotton, 64, 79, *79*

Mather, Increase, 78, 79

Mayan Indians, 7

Mayflower (ship), 41

Mayflower Compact, 41–42

McArdle, H. A., *318*

McClellan, George, 370–371, 378

McCormick, Cyrus, 326, *326, 327*

McCormick, Richard P., 253

***McCulloch* v. *Maryland*, 238**

McDowell, Irvin, 370

McGuffey's Eclectic Readers, 302

McHenry, James, 186

McLoughlin, William, 225–226

Mechanical reaper, 326, *326*

Mechanization. *See* Industrialization, early; Industrial Revolution

Medicine and medical science, 248

Meetinghouses, *44, 45*

Melodramas, 248

Melville, Herman, 249, *312–313,* 314, 348

Memorable Providences, Relating to Witchcrafts and Possessions (Cotton Mather), *79*

Memphis (TN), 393

Menéndez de Avilés, Pedro, 90

Mennonites, colonial, 86

Mercantilism, 73

Merk, Frederick, 322

Mestizos, 22

Metacomet (King Philip), **77**

Methodists, 293, 347–348

Mexican-American War, 320–323, *323*

Mexican cession, 336–337

Mexico: independence of, 89, 315; Texas and, 316–317, *317, 318,* 320–323

Mexico City, siege of, 321

Miami Indians, 117, 180

Michigan, 224

Michigan Territory, 197

Michilimackinac, 213

Middle class: "child-centered," 299–300; redeeming, 291–292, 294

Middle Colonies, 48–53, *49,* 58

Middle ground, 88–89

"Midnight judges," 190, 205–206

Migrants and migration. *See* West, trans-Appalachian; West, trans-Mississippi

Milan Decree (France, 1807), 209, 211

Military districts in Reconstruction South, 395, *395,* 396

Militia, 112, 126, 129, 130, 132, 136, 138

Miller, Arthur, 284

Mills, Samuel John, 295

Mines and mining, 324

Minutemen, at Lexington and Concord, 126

Missions and missionaries, 4, 11, 21, 23

Mississippi, 147, 224, 286, 376

Mississippi River region, 180, 198, 214

Mississippi Territory, 222

Missouri, 235, 255, 366

Missouri Compromise (1820), **235–236,** *236,* 337; Crittenden compromise and, 363; Dred Scott case and, 348–349

Moby-Dick (Melville), 249, 314

Mohawk Indians, 132

Molasses Act (1733), 94

Money, paper, 368, 382

Monroe, James: Jefferson's presidency and, 209; presidency of, 222, 223, 234, 239–240

Monroe Doctrine, 239–240

Montcalm, Louis-Joseph de (Marquis de), 105

Montesquieu, Baron de (Charles-Louis de Secondat), 155, 161

Montezuma (Aztec emperor), 19

Montgomery (AL), 361–362

Montreal (Quebec), War of 1812 and, 213–214

Moors, *Reconquista* and, 17

Morality: alcohol and, 295–296; political, 141–142; public education and, 301–302; women and, 296, 299

Morgan, Daniel, 135

Morris, Gouverneur, 159–160

Morris, Robert, 157

Morse, Samuel F. B., 324, *327*

Mortality rates, childhood, 300

Mott, Lucretia, 308

Mount, William Sidney, 249

Mountain men, 223

Mühlenberg, Henry Melchior, 87

Mulattoes, 22, 71

"Mulatto King" (Seminole leader), 227

Murray, William Vans, 189

Muslims, in West Africa, 14

N

Napoleon I (Bonaparte) (Emperor of France), 189, 202–203, 208–210, 211

Narragansett Bay, colonial, 48

Narragansett Indians, 9, 77

National debt: Hamilton and, 173–175; Jefferson and, 201

National government. *See* Government (U.S.)

National Hotel, 245–246

Nationalism (1815-1825), 220–243; era of good feeling and, 234, 241; expansion and migration in, 222–228, *224;* politics of nation building and, 234–240, 234–242, *236;* transportation and market economy and, 228–234, *229, 230, 233,* 241–242

National Republicans, 251, *254,* 260, 261

National Road, 228

National Union movement, 393

Nation building: after American Revolution, 137; after War of 1812, 222, 234–240, *236*

Native Americans: colonial backcountry tensions and, 87–88, 117; conditions of conquest of, 10–13; before the conquest, 5–10, *8;* conquest of (1788-1825), 180–181, *181,* 198–199, 211, 225–228; cultural independence of, 88; disease and, 5, 12–13, 36, 42, 88; Removal policy and, 225, 254–256, *256, 257;* routes of, *6;* Spanish borderlands and, 90–91; western land grab and, 151. *See also* Paleo-Indians; specific tribes

Nativism, 345

Nat Turner's rebellion, 269–270, 274

Natural aristocracy, 162, 247

Naturalization Law (1798), 187

Natural rights, 149

Navigation Acts, 74–75, 78, 94, 117–118

Nebraska Territory, *344*

"Negative liberal state," 263

Negro Convention movement, 305

Neolin (Delaware Prophet), 117

Netherlands (Dutch), 41, 48–50, 52, 74–75

Neutrality, 177–178

New Amsterdam (New York City), 48–49, *50, 56*

New England, 210, 214, 233

New England, colonial, 31–32, 41–48, *47,* 58; Dominion of, 78; Glorious Revolution and, 77–78; Navigation Acts and, 74–75; social stability in, 63–66, 80; witchcraft and, 78–79

Newfoundland, 16

New France, 101–102, *103*

New Hampshire, 47, *56,* 144, 145

New Haven (CT), 47

New Jersey, 50–51, *56,* 132, 151

New Jersey Plan, 158

"New Lights," 97–98

New Mexico Territory, *344*

New Netherland colony, 48–49, 70

New Orleans (LA): Battle of, 214, *215;* in Civil War, 370; French settlement of, 23; as market, 231; race riot in, 393; Spanish control of, 198

New Orleans (steamboat), 229

New Salem (IL), 360

New Spain, 19, 22

Newspapers: colonial, 100, 116; in Jacksonian era, 248

New Sweden, 52

Newton, Isaac, 91

New World: conditions of conquest and, 10–13, 28; England and, 24–26, 28; Europe on eve of conquest of, 16–18, 28; France and, 22–23, 28; pre-conquest diverse cultures in, 3–10, 28; Spain and, 16–22, 28; West Africa and, 13–16, 28

New York (NY): in American Revolution, 130; in Civil War, *375, 375–*376

New York (state), 130, 132, 144

Nicolls, Richard, 49, 50

"Night riders"of Ku Klux Klan, 407

Niña (ship), 18

Nominating conventions, 260

Norsemen. *See* Vikings

North: Civil War home front in, 367–368, *375,* 375–376; Civil War lead-ership in, 368–370; Civil War "organizational revolution" and, 382; factory system in, 232–233; impact of Civil War on, 380–381; sectionalism and, 348, 353; slavery and, 337, 348; wheat as cash crop of, 231. *See also* Civil War; Sectionalism

North, Frederick (Lord), 123, 126, 128, 135

North, Simeon, 234

North Carolina, 53–54, *56,* 135, 144, 151–152

North Star, 305

Northwest Ordinance (1787), *152,* **153**

Northwest Passage, 48

Northwest Territory, 151–153, *152;* British occupation of, 177; Native Americans and, 227–228

Novels, 248

Nueces River, 320, 322

Nullification, 258; crisis, 257–259

Nursing in Civil War, 380–381

O

Oberlin College, 304

Of Plymouth Plantation (Bradford), 41

Oglethorpe, James, 55

Ohio, 197

Ohio River region: colonial war and, 103–105; Native Americans and, 180, 198, 227; Northwest Ordinance and, 151–153

Oil and oil industry, *327*

Old Plantation (painting), *73*

Olmsted, Frederick Law, 287–288

Oñate, Juan de, 89

Oneida Indians, 132

Onís, Louis de, 223

Onondaga Indians, 132

Opportunity: American belief in, 247; early nineteenth century and, 196, 246–247, 251

Orders in Council (Britain), 211

Ordinance of 1787. *See* Northwest Ordinance (1787)

Oregon Territory, 319–320, *344*

"Organizational revolution," 382

Organized labor. *See* Labor unions

Ostend Manifesto (1854), **344**

O'Sullivan, Timothy H., *273*

Otis, Elisha G., 327

Otis, James, 118

Ottawa Indians, 117

Overseers, 271, 279–280

P

Pacific Coast region, 223

Paddle wheelers, 229–230

Paine, Thomas, 126–127, 130, 142, 178

Pakenham, Edward, 214, *215*

Paleo-Indians, 5, 6

Panic(s): of 1819, 250; **of 1837, 262,** 317; of 1873, 402

Paper money. *See* Money, paper

Parker, Theodore, 348

Parliamentary sovereignty, 114, 118, 125

Party politics (1788-1800), 168–193, *187;* Adam's presidency, mistrust and, 183–190, 192; establishing new government and, 171–173, 192; foreign affairs, treason and, 176–185, 192; Hamilton's plan and, 173–176, 192; political culture and, 181–183, 192; political extremism and, 191

Pastorius, Francis Daniel, 52, 86

Paternalism, planters and, 278–280

Paterson, William, 158

Patronage, 201, 254. *See also* Corruption

Patten family, 111–112

Patuxet Indians, 42

Paul, Jeremiah, *294–295*

Paxton Boys, 117

Peaceable coercion policy, 209

Peace Democrats, 369

Peace of Paris: of 1763, 105, *106*

"Peculiar institution." *See* Slaves and slavery

Peninsulares, 22

Penn, William, 48, 51–52

Pennsylvania: in American Revolution, 125, 126, 128, 130, 132–133; antislavery movement and, 146; under Articles of Confederation, 144, 151; in Civil War, 376–377; colonial, 51–53, *56,* 86

Pennsylvania Dutch, 87

Pennsylvania Packet, 165

Pensee, Charles, *229*

Pepperell, William, 102–103

Percy (Lord), 126

Perfectionism, 294; counterpoint to, 308–309; radical abolitionism and, 303

Perry, Oliver Hazard, 214

Persac, Adrien, *277*

Petersburg, siege of, 377

Petroleum. *See* Oil and oil industry

Philadelphia (PA): in American Revolution, 125, 126, 128, 132; colonial, 52, 87; Constitutional Convention in, 157–161

Philanthropy, Civil War and, 382

Philip II (King of Spain), 26

Philosophes, 92

Physicians. *See* Medicine

Pickering, John, 206

Pickering, Timothy, 153, 202

Pierce, Franklin, presidency of, 342, 344, 348

Pilgrims, 41

Pinchback, P. B. S., 403

Pinckney, Charles Cotesworth, 159, 162, 184, 203, 210

Pinckney, Thomas, 180–181, 184–185

Pinckney, William, 209–210

Pine, Robert Edge, *128*

Pinta (ship), 18

Pitt, William, 104–105

Pittsburgh (PA), 197, *197*

Plains. *See* Great Plains

Planter (ship), 387

Planter (steamship), 387–388

Planters and plantations: in antebellum South, 276–280, *277;* colonial, 37–38, 53–54, 67–69; Reconstruction and, 391–392, 400–401

Plows: cast-iron, *327;* steel, 231, 326, *327*

Plymouth Colony, 41–42, *56*

Pocahontas, 36

Poe, Edgar Allan, 348

Poems on Various Subjects, Religious and Moral (Wheatley), *146*

Poets and poetry, 348

Political ideology. *See* Ideology

Political machines/organizations, 250–251, 252–253

Political parties: second-party system and, 250, 253, 259–265, 344; sectionalism and upheaval of, 341–347. *See also* American party; Constitutional Union party; Democratic party; Federalist party; Free-Soil party; Know-Nothing party; Liberty party; National Republicans; Party politics (1788-1800); Republicans (Jeffersonians); Republican party; Whigs

Politics: after War of 1812, 234–240; colonial, revolts in, 75–79; early party (1788-1800), 168–193; in Jacksonian era, 249–259

Polk, James K., presidency of, 314, 319–322, 337–338

Polk, Leonidas L., 348

Poll tax, 405–406

Pontiac (Ottawa), 117

Pontiac's Rebellion, 117

Popé, El, 89

Popular sovereignty, 247, 249, **338,** 339, 360

Population: colonial, 85, 93, 113; nineteenth century, 196–197, 199, 224; slave, *286*

Portolá, Gaspar de, 90

Port Royal, SC, 53

Portsmouth (RI), 48

Portugal, exploration and conquest by, 13, 17

"Positive liberal state," 263

Pottawatomie Massacre, 346

Poverty, in Reconstruction, 400–401

Power (political): 1800 transfer of, 191; Antifederalists on, 161–163; danger of, 150. *See also* Separation of powers

Powhatan (Chief), 36

Powhatan Indians, 9, *35,* 36, 38

Prairie. *See* Great Plains

Prairie du Chien (WI), *227*

Preemption, 225

Presbyterians, 86, 97, 293–295, 348

Presidency (U.S.), 160, *162. See also under* names of presidents

Presidential debates. *See* Debates

Presidential elections. *See* Election(s)

Presidios (forts), Spanish, 90

Press. *See* Newspapers

Primogeniture, 144

Princeton, battle of, 132

Princeton University, 97

Principall Navigations, Voyages, and Discoveries of the English Nation, The (Hakluyt), 26–27

Proclamation of Amnesty and Reconstruction, 389

Production. *See* Factories and factory systems; Mass production

Productivity, farm, 231

Professors of the Light. *See* Quakers

Progressivism, Civil War roots of, 382

Prohibitory Act (1775), 126, *127*

Property rights: Indians and, 227–228; Mann on, 301; Marshall court and, 237

Proportional representation, 157–158

Proprietary colonies, 53–54

Proslavery arguments, 278–279, 348

Prosser, Gabriel, 273

Prostitution, 295

Protestant ethic, 302

Protestant Reformation, 24–25

Protestants and Protestantism. *See by* denomination; Evangelicalism

Providence (RI), 46, 48

Providence Plantations, 48

Public education. *See* Education

Public virtue. *See* Virtue, republican government and

Pueblo Indians, 89, 90–91

Pullman, George M., *327*

Pullman passenger car, *327*

Puritans, English, 40

Puritans, New England, 42–43; in Massachusetts Bay, 32, *44,* 44–47, 63–66; witchcraft and, 78–79

Purvis, Robert, 305

Putting-out system, 232–233

Q

Quakers, 51, 141

Quartering Act (1765), 122, *127*

Quasi-War, 184, 189

Quebec, Canada, 102, 105, *105, 131*

Queen Anne's War, *101*

R

Race and racism: abolitionist movement and, 304; in antebellum South, 275–276, 278–280; colonial, 70–71; colonization movement and, 303; emancipation and, 372–375; in Jacksonian America, 246, 265; in Jeffersonian America, 196, 203, 205–208; in Lincoln-Douglas debates, 350; Mexican-American War and, 322; Native Americans and, 117. *See also* Jim Crow laws; Ku Klux Klan; Segregation; Slaves and slavery

Radical Reconstruction, 389–390, **394–396,** 409; white opposition to, 401, 403

Radical Republicans, 389–390

Railroads: Civil War and, 368; early, 230; mid-nineteenth century, 324–325, *325, 326, 332;* Reconstruction and, 403; strikes and, 361

Ralegh, Walter, 26

Randolph, Edmund, 157–158, 164, 172

Randolph, John, 203, 206

Randolph, Richard, 146

Rapier, James T., 403

Ratification of U.S. Constitution, 160–165, *164*

Reapers, mechanical, 326, *326*

Recollects (French priests), 23

Reconquista (Spain), 16–17

Reconstruction,   386–416,   *395;* Amendments and, 393, *394;* Black Codes and, 392, 399–400; president *vs.* Congress in, 389–397, 414; radical, 389–390, 394–396, 409; reign of terror during, 407–409; retreat from, 405–409, 414–415; reunion and the New South, 409–412, 416; southern society and, 397–409, 414; unfinished revolution and, 412–413

Reconstruction Acts, 395

Redcoats (British), 122, 126, 129–130, 134

Redeemers, 410–411, 411

Reed, Ester DeBerdt, 148

Reform and reform movements, 294–296, 302–308, 310. *See also* Antislavery movement

Relacion, La (De Vaca), 4

Religion: slave, 275. *See also* Christianity; *Evangelicalism; Missions and missionaries; Protestant Reformation; Revivalism; specific religious groups and denominations*

Religious toleration: in Bill of Rights, 153, 163; in colonial Maryland, 39–40; in colonial New England, 46–47

Remond, Charles, 305

Removal policy. *See* Indian removal

Report on Manufactures (Hamilton), 176

Report on the Public Credit (Hamilton), 173–174

Representation, virtual, 115

Representative government, 150, 155, 157–158, 160, 161–162, *162*

Republicanism, 1780s experiment in, 140–170, **142;** adding Bill of Rights and, 163–165; under Articles of Confederation, 150–153, 166; defining culture of, 142–149, 166; development of the Constitution and, 153–161, 166; Native Americans and, 180–181; ratification of the Constitution and, 160–165, *164,* 166; state constitutions and, 149; western land and, 151–153, *152, 154*

Republican party: African Americans and, 388–389, 400–401, 406, 407; election of 1860 and, 351–353, *353;* emancipation and, 373; emergence of, 343, 345–347, 354; Lincoln-Douglas debates and, 350–351; in Reconstruction era, 389–390, 392–397, 401–403, 405–409. *See also* Republican presidents by name

Republicans (Jeffersonians), 194–223; Adam's presidency and, 183–190; commercial life of cities and, 199–200; embarrassment overseas and, 208–212, 217; expansion and, 196–199, 217; Jefferson presidency and, 196–210, 217; limits of equality under, 195–196; Madison presidency and, 211–216; race and dissent under, 203, 205–208, 217; War of 1812 and, 213–215, 218; Washington presidency and, 170–171, 177, 179

Revenue Act (1764), 117

Revere, Paul, *122,* 123, 126

Revivalism: abolitionist movement and, 303; colonial, *96,* 96–98, 108;

early nineteenth century, *290–291,* 291–296

Revival Meeting (Paul), 290–291

Revolutionary War in America. *See* American Revolution

Revolver, *327*

Rhode Island: in American Revolution, 118, 130; under Articles of Confederation, 155, 157; colonial, 46, 48, *56,* 70, 149

Rice, Thomas "Daddy," 411

Rice and rice industry, 54, 71–72, 95, 231, 271, 285

Richmond (VA), 365, 370–371, 377

Rights. *See* Bill of Rights; Freedom(s); Liberties; Women, rights of

Rights, natural, 149

Rillieux, Norbert, *327*

Rio Grande River region, 320–322

Riverboats, 198

Rivers, 198; cotton industry and, 232; Ohio-Mississippi system of, 229; steamboats and, 229–230

Roads and highways: colonial, 95, *95;* early nineteenth century, 228–229

Roanoke colony, 26

Rochambeau Comte de, 135

Rochester (NY), 291–292

Rocky Mountain Fur Company, 223

Rolfe, John, 36

Roman Catholicism. *See* Catholicism

Rose, Ernestine, 308

Ross, John (Cherokee), 225, 226, 255

Rotary printing press, *327*

Royal African Company, 70

Royal colonies, 38, 99

Royal Navy (Britain), 178–179, 208–209

Rubber, vulcanizing, 326

Runaway slaves. *See* Fugitive slaves

Rush, Benjamin, 137

Rush, Richard, 240

Rutgers University, 97

S

Sacagawea, 203

Sac and Fox Indians, 227

"Sack of Lawrence," 346

Saint Lawrence River region, 23, 102

St. Augustine (FL) 55, 90

St. Clair, Arthur, 180

Salem (MA), 78–79

San Antonio (TX), 316–317

Sandys, Edwin, 37

Sanitary Commission, 380, 382

San Jacinto River, battle at, 317, *318*

Santa Anna, Antonio López de, 316–317, 321

Santa Fe (NM), 321

Santa Maria (ship), 18

San Xavier del Bac mission, *90*

Saratoga (NY), in American Revolution, 132, *133*

Savage, Edward, *128*

Savannah (GA), 55, 134, 378

Scalawags, 401

Scarlet Letter, The (Hawthorne), 249, 309

School(s), 300–302

Scorched-earth policy, 378

Scots-Irish immigration, 86–87

Scott, Dred, 348–349

Scott, Winfield, 321, 342, 370

Scrooby Manor, 41

Secession, 361–366, *365*

Second Continental Congress, 126, 149

Second Great Awakening, 292–294, 302–303

Second-party system, 263–264, 266; Bank War and, 259–263; end of, 344, 354

Sectionalism, 172, 334–357; 1860 election and, 351–353; bitterness of, 335–336; causes of, 353–355; Compromise of 1850 and, 336–343, *340,* 355; cultural, 347–348; Dred Scott case and, 348–349; Kansas and Nebraska and, 343–346; Lincoln-Douglas debates and, 349–351; political party upheaval and, 341–347, 356; secession and, 361–363, *365*

Sedgwick, Theodore, 186

Sedition Law (1798), 187–188

Segregation: Black Codes and, 392, 400–401, 404; Jim Crow and, 411–412

"Self-government" (childrearing), 300, 302

Self-made men, 247

Seminole Indians, 223, 225, 226–227; removal of, 256, *257;* wars of, 223, 227, 256, 274

Senate (U.S.), 159

Seneca Falls Convention, 308

Seneca Indians, 117, 132

Senegambia, 13

Separate spheres doctrine, 297

Separation of powers: Constitution and, 157–159, *162;* Johnson impeachment and, 397

Separatists and separatism, 41–43, 46, *56*

Sequoyah (Cherokee), 226

Serra, Junípero, 90

Seven Years' War, *101,* 104–106, *105;* perception of, 106–107

Seward, William H., 342, 351, 364

Sewing machine, 326

Sexual equality. *See* Women, rights of

Shadrack (slave), 306

Shaftesbury, Earl of. *See* Cooper, Anthony Ashley (Earl of Shaftesbury)

Sharecropping, *399,* **400**

Shattucks, Jacob, *156*

Shawnee Indians, 88, 132, 180

Shays, Daniel, 156, *156*

Shays's Rebellion, 156

Sheep raising, 231

Shenandoah Valley, 87

Sherman, Roger, *128,* 158–159

Sherman, William Tecumseh, 378, 398–399

Shiloh, battle of, 370

Ships and shipping, 74, 228

Shirley, William, 100

Simms, William Gilmore, 348

Simon Legree (fictional), 348

Sims, Thomas, *341*

Slater, Samuel, 200

Slave auctions, *284,* 285, 338–339

Slave codes, 70

Slaveholders, 276–280

Slave market, 278–279

Slave rebellions, 73

Slave Sale, Virginia (Miller), *284*

Slaves and slavery, 268–289; apologists for, 282–284; under Articles of Confederation, 145–147, 153; Cherokees and, 225; colonial, 53–54, 68, 69–73, 80; Compromise of 1850 and, 336–343; Constitution and, 158–159; cotton industry and, 232, 271, *271,* 284–287, 289; emancipation and, *372,* 372–375; free blacks in Old South and, 275–276; Indian, *21;* life and culture of, 270–273, 275, 288–289; Lincoln-Douglas debates on, 349–351; Missouri Compromise and, 235–236; population of, *286;* racism, paternalism and abuses of, 278–280; resistance and rebellion of, 269–270, 273–275; roots of, 69–70; Seminoles and, 226; Texas and, 316, 318, 322; Underground Railroad and, 274, 306, *307;* West African factories and, *14;* white society and, 276–284; yeomen and, 281–282

Slave trade, 69, 70, *71, 72;* internal, 207, *207,* 284–285; prohibition of importation and, 207–208; West Africa and, 14–15

Slidell, John, 320

Slums, 329

Smalls, Robert, *386,* 387–388, 403

Smith, John, 34–36, 57

Smith, Thomas, 34, 37

Social order. *See* Classes

Society, colonial, 61–80; African American identity and, 71–73; in Chesapeake region, 37–38, 40, 62, 66–69; in French America, 22–23; in New England, 44–45, 62, 63–66; preconquest Native American, 9–10; in Southern colonies, 61–62; in Spanish America, 19, 21–22

Society for the Relief of Free Negroes, Unlawfully Held, 145

Society of Friends. *See* Quakers

Society of the Cincinnati, 143–144

Soldiers. *See* Civil War; *Militia*

Some Thoughts Concerning Education (Locke), 147

"Song of the Open Road" (Whitman), 314

Sons of Liberty, 118, 122

South: abolitionism and, 275, 282–284, 306; antebellum white society in, 276–284; Civil War home front in, 367–368, 375; Civil War leadership in, 368–370; economy (slave) of, 277, 278–279, 284–287, *287,* 289; election of 1860 and, 353; impact of Civil War on, 380–381; railroads and, 368; Reconstruction and, 397–409; reunion and the New, 409–412; secession of, 361–366, *365;* sectionalism and, 348, 353; segregation in, 411–412; slavery in, 268–276; staple production in, 231; tariffs and, 252, 257–259.*See also* Civil War; Ku Klux Klan; Sectionalism

South, colonial, 53–57, *54,* 58, 71–73

South America. *See* Latin America

South Carolina: in American Revolution, 134–135; under Articles of Confederation, 144; in Civil War, 364–365, *365, 366,* 378; colonial, 53–54, *56,* 71–73; cotton and, 285–286; nullification crisis and, 257–259; Robert Smalls and, 387–388; secession convention in, 361; slavery and, 271, 273–274

Southern Farmers' Alliance, 410

Southworth, E. D. E. N. (Mrs.), 248

Spain: in American Revolution, *133;* empire of, *89,* 89–91; exploration and conquest by, 16–22; holdings of, 223; opening of Mississippi River and, 180–181

Spanish Armada, The, 26

Spanish Borderlands, *89,* 89–91, *90,* 108

Spectral evidence, 79

Spinning mills, *199,* 200, 232

Spirit of the Laws, The (Montesquieu), 155, 161

Spoils system, 254

Spotswood, Alexander, 100

Spotsylvania, battle of, 377

Springfield (IL), 360

Squanto, 42

Squatters, trans-Appalachian, 225

Squatter sovereignty, 338

Stamp Act (1765), **118–119,** 121, *127*

Stamp Act Congress (1765), **119**

Standing armies, Jefferson and, 201

Stanton, Edwin, 397

Stanton, Elizabeth Cady, 308, *308,* 406

Staple Act (1663), 74

Stark, John, 132

"Star-Spangled Banner, The" (Key), 214

State, U.S. Department of, 171

States' rights: Civil War and, 381–382; nullification crisis and, 257–259; tenth Amendment and, 165; Virginia and Kentucky Resolutions and, 188–189

Steamboats/ships, 200, *229,* 229–230

Steam power, *327*

Stephens, Alexander, 362, 392

Stevens, Thaddeus, 394

Stewart, Maria, 305

Stocks, development of, 325

Stoddert, Benjamin, 186

Stone, Lucy, 406

Stono Uprising, 73

Stowe, Harriet Beecher, 280, 348

Strict construction (of Constitution), 177, 196, 252, 381–382

Strikes, railroad, 361

Stuart, John. *See* Bute, Earl of (John Stuart)

Stuart dynasty (England), 33, 114

Stump Speaking (Bingham), *250*

Stuyvesant, Peter, 49

Subcultures in 1810, 197

Suburbs, 329

Suffolk Resolves, 125

Suffrage. *See* Voting and voting rights

Sugar Act, 94, 117, *127*

Sugar and sugar industry, 231, 285

Sullivan, Louis H., 320

Sumner, Charles, *334–335,* 335–336, 392, 394

Superiority, narrative of, 4

Supreme Court (U.S.): formation of, 172; Jackson and, 256; Marshall Court and, 237–239, 256; Taney Court and, 348–349. *See also* specific cases

Susan Constant (ship), 34

Sweden, 52

T

Talleyrand-Périgord, Charles-Maurice de, 185, 189, 202

Tallmadge, James, 235

Tallmadge amendment, 235

Taney, Roger B., 260–261, 349

Tappan, Lewis and Arthur, 303–304

Tariff of abominations (1828), **252**

Tariff(s): Civil War and, 382; first (1789), 172; Hamilton on, 176; in Jacksonian era, 252; New England and, 233; South and, 252, 257–259. *See also* by names of tariff laws

Taxation: Articles of Confederation and, 150; Jefferson and, 201; Whiskey Rebellion and, 182

Taxation without representation, 114–115, 124

Taylor, John, 188

Taylor, Zachary: Mexican-American War and, 320–321; presidency of, 338–339, 360

Tea Act (1773), 123–124, *127*

Technology: farming, 326; nineteenth century, 231, 234, 326, *327. See also* Transportation

Tecumseh, 198–199, 211, 214

Telegraph, 324

Temperance movement, 295–296, *296*

Tempest, The (Shakespeare), 35

Tennent, Gilbert, 97

Tennessee, 198, 377, 378

Tenochtitlán, 9

Ten Percent Plan, 389–390

Tenskwatawa (the Prophet), 198, *198*

Tenure of Office Act, 397

Testing of the First Reaping Machine near Steele's Tavern, Virginia, 1831, The, 326

Texas, 286; annexation of, 318–320, 332; revolution, 315–318, *317, 318*

Textile industry, 200, 231, 232–233, *233,* 325

Thames River, battle of, 214

Thanksgiving Day, 41, 42

Theater, in Jacksonian era, 248–249

Theyanoguin (King Hendrick) (Mohawk), *102*

Thirteenth Amendment, 375, 391

Thomas, George, 366

Thomson, James, 107

Thoreau, Henry David, 348

Thornwell, James H., 348

Three-fifths rule, 158–160, 207, 235

Tilden, Samuel J., 409

Tippecanoe, battle of, 211

"Tippecanoe and Tyler, too" (campaign slogan), 263

Tobacco and tobacco industry, 76, 231, 285; colonial, 36–37, 67–69, 74–75, 94–95

Tocqueville, Alexis de, 247, 256, 265

Toleration. *See* Religious toleration

Toll roads, 228–229

Toltec peoples, 7

Tools, precision, 326

Tordesilla. *See* Treaty of Tordesillas

Tories. *See* Loyalists

Towns. *See* Cities and towns

Townshend, Charles, 121–122

Townshend Revenue Acts (1767), 121–122, 123, *127*

Trade: 1790s with Britain, 177; colonial, 73–75, 94–95, *95, 120*; early nineteenth century, 200, 228–232, 233; Embargo Act and, 209–210; immigration and, 328; internal, 324; Mississippi River and, 198; pre-conquest Native Americans and, 10–12. *See also* Tariff(s)

Trade routes, West Africa and, 13–16, *15*

Trail of Tears, 256, *257*

Trail of Tears, The (Lindneux), *256*

Trans-Appalachian West, 197–198, 222, 223–225

Transportation: after War of 1812, 228–230, 231, 232; regulation of, 230. *See also* Railroads

Treason: 1790s party politics and, 176–181; nullification and, 258

Treasury, U.S. Department of, 171–172

Treaty of Ghent, 216

Treaty of Greenville, 180

Treaty of Guadalupe Hidalgo, 322

Treaty of Moultrie Creek, 227

Treaty of Paris (1783), 136, 177

Treaty of San Lorenzo (Pinckney's Treaty), 181

Treaty of Tordesillas, 18

Tremont House, 246

Trenton, battle at, 132

Trist, Nicholas P., 321–322

Truth, Sojourner, 305

Tubman, Harriet, 306, *307*

Tudor dynasty (England), 24–25

Turner, Henry McNeal, 412–413, *413*

Turner, Nat, 269–270, 274, 275

Turnpikes. *See* Roads and highways

Tuscarora Indians, 132

Twelfth Amendment, 190

Two-party system, 250, 253, 259–265, 344

Two Treatises of Government (Locke), 115–116

Tyler, John: presidency of, 318; vice presidency of, 263

U

Uncle Tom's Cabin (Stowe), 280, 348

Underground Railroad, 274, 306, *307*

Union (in Civil War): African-Americans and, *374,* 374–375; battles and, 370–371, 376–378, *379;* home front of, *367,* 367–368; leadership in, 368–370

Union Pacific Railroad, 403

Unions. *See* Labor unions

Unitarians, 293

United States Magazine and Democratic Review, 320

Universities and colleges. *See* by specific names

Urbanization: colonial, 91; immigration and, 329

Utah Territory, 344

V

Vacuum evaporator, *327*

Vagrancy and vagrancy laws, 401

Vallandigham, Clement, 376

Valley Forge, 133

Van Buren, Martin: election of 1844 and, 318–319; election of 1848 and, 338; Jackson and, 253, 254; presidency of, 262–263; statewide political organizations and, 249–250

Veracruz campaign, 321

Vermont, 132, 152

Vernier caliper, 326

Verrazzano, Giovanni da, 22

Vesey conspiracy, 273–274

Vespucci, Amerigo, 18

Vicksburg, siege of, 376

View of the Great Treaty Held at Prairie du Chien, 227

Vigilantism, 407

Vikings, 16

Virginia: in American Revolution, 118–119, 135; under Articles of Confederation, 144, 146, 151–153; in Civil War, 365, 370–371, 376–377, 378

Virginia, colonial, 32, 33–41, *56,* 66–69, 70; Bacon's Rebellion in, 76–77; French and, 103; immigration and, 87; Navigation Acts and, 74; source of name of, 26

Virginia Company, 34–38, 41

Virginia Luxuries (painting), *70*

Virginia Plan, 157–158, 159

Virginia Resolutions, 188

Virginia Resolves, 118–119

Virgin of Guadalupe, 21, *22*

Virtue, republican government and, 141–142, 143, 147–148, 154–155, 158

Voltaire, 91, 145

Von Iwonski, Carl G., *282*

Voting and voting rights: under Articles of Confederation, 144; colonial, 99; in Jacksonian era, 249; in Jim Crow South, 411–412; Reconstruction and, 389, 391–392, 395–396, 405–409, *406*

W

Wade-Davis Bill, 390

Wadsworth, Benjamin, 63

Walker, David, 270, 306

Waltham (MA), 232–233

Wampanoag Indians, 77

War, U.S. Department of, 171

War for Independence. *See* American Revolution

War Hawks: War of 1812 and, **212–213**

War of 1812, *213,* **213–216;** background of, 208–212; Treaty of Ghent and, 216

Warren, Joseph, 122–123

Washington (DC): in Jeffersonian America, 200; slave auctions in, 340; in War of 1812, 214

Washington, George: after presidency of, 186, 189; under Articles of Confederation, 143, 153; Constitution and, 142, 157; Farewell Address of, 182–183; pre-Revolutionary War, 103; presidency of, 171–183; Revolutionary War and, 125, 126, 129–130, *131*, 132–133, 135, *168–169*; slaves of, 146

Washingtonian Society, 296

Waterways. *See* Canals; Rivers

Wayne, Anthony, 180

WCTU. *See* Women's Christian Temperance Union

Webster, Daniel, 233, 237, 261, *339*

Weld, Theodore Dwight, 303–304

West, trans-Appalachian, 197–198, 222, 223–225; conquest of (1790s), 180–181, *181*

West, trans-Mississippi, 223

West Africa, ancient societies of, 13–16

Western Reserve, 198

West Indies, 70, 285

West Point military academy, 201

Wheat, 231

Wheatley, Phillis, 145, *146*

Wheelock, Eleazar, 97

Whigs, 113; in Jacksonian era, 250, 251, 259, 261–265, *263*; sectional crisis and, 337–346, 354; Texas and, 318, 322

Whiskey Rebellion, 182, *182*

White, George H., 412

White, John, 27

Whitefield, George, *96*, 96–97

White League, 408

White Pines Act (1711), 94

White supremacy: in the New South, 407–412; Reconstruction and, 407–409

Whitman, Walt, 314, *314*

Whitney, Eli, 231, 234, *327*

Wilkinson, James, 214

Willard, Samuel, 78

William III (King of England), 75, 78

Williams, Roger, 46, 48

Williamsburg (VA), 84, 119

Wilmot, David, 337

Wilmot Proviso, 322, **337–338**

Wilson, James, 157–158

Winthrop, John, 31, 43, 44, 45, 77, 79

Witchcraft, colonial, 78–79

Witherspoon family, 61–63

Wolfe, James, 105

Wolsey, Thomas, 24

Women: colonial, 64–65, 67; cult of domesticity and, 297–299; factory system and, 233, *233*; impact of Civil War on, 380–381; in Jacksonian era, 246, 248; reform movements and, 296, 297–298; yeoman, 281

Women, rights of: under Articles of Confederation, *143*, 147–149, *148*; in early nineteenth century, 307–308, *308*; Fifteenth Amendment and, 406

Women's Christian Temperance Union (WCTU), black chapters of, 405

Woolman, John, 145

Worcester v. *Georgia*, 256

Workers. *See* Labor

Work ethic, 355

Working class, 330–331

Workplace. *See* Factories and factory systems; Labor; Labor Unions

World's Anti-Slavery Convention, 308

Wright, Henry C., 305

Wright, Wilbur and Orville, 52–521

X

XYZ Affair, 184–185

Y

Yamasee War, 12

Yaocomico Indians, 39

Yeager, Joseph, *215*

Yeomen (independent farmers), **65**, 68; in antebellum South, 277, 280–282, *282*; Jefferson and, 173

York, Duke of. *See* James (Duke of York)

Yorktown, Battle of, **135**, *135*

Young America, **313–315**, 324

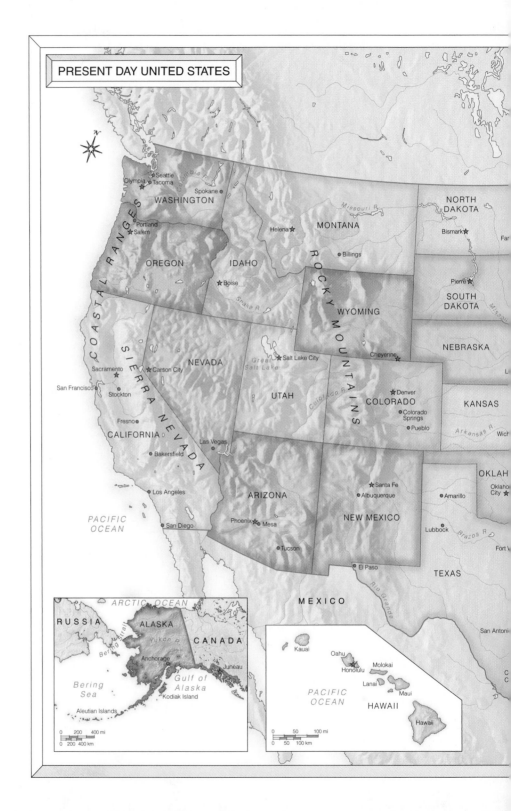

PRESENT DAY UNITED STATES

WASHINGTON
Seattle
Olympia ⭐ Tacoma
Spokane

Portland
⭐ Salem

OREGON

IDAHO
⭐ Boise

Snake R.

MONTANA
Helena ⭐
Billings

Missouri R.

NORTH DAKOTA
Bismark ⭐

SOUTH DAKOTA
Pierre ⭐

Missouri R.

WYOMING
Cheyenne ⭐

NEBRASKA

COASTAL RANGES

SIERRA NEVADA

NEVADA
Carson City ⭐

Sacramento ⭐
San Francisco
Stockton

Fresno

CALIFORNIA

Bakersfield

Los Angeles

San Diego

Great Salt Lake
⭐ Salt Lake City

UTAH

Colorado R.

ROCKY MOUNTAINS

Denver ⭐
COLORADO
Colorado Springs
Pueblo

KANSAS

Arkansas R.
Wich

Las Vegas

ARIZONA

Phoenix ⭐ Mesa

Tucson

Santa Fe ⭐
Albuquerque

NEW MEXICO

El Paso

Amarillo

Lubbock

Brazos R.

OKLAH
Oklahoma City ⭐

Rio Grande

TEXAS

PACIFIC OCEAN

MEXICO

San Antoni

ARCTIC OCEAN

RUSSIA
Bering Strait
ALASKA
Yukon R.
Anchorage
CANADA
Juneau

Bering Sea

Gulf of Alaska
Kodiak Island

Aleutian Islands

0   200   400 mi
0   200 400 km

Kauai
Oahu
Honolulu ⭐
Molokai
Lanai
Maui
HAWAII
Hawaii

PACIFIC OCEAN

0   50   100 mi
0   50 100 km

CANADA

MINNESOTA

Lake Superior

WISCONSIN

St. Paul
Minneapolis

Madison

Milwaukee

IOWA

Davenport

Des Moines

maha

MICHIGAN

Lake Michigan

Lake Huron

Grand
Rapids

Lansing

Detroit

Chicago

Gary

Toledo

Lake Erie

Lake Ontario

St. Lawrence R.

VERMONT

Montpelier

MAINE

Augusta

Portland

Concord

NEW
HAMPSHIRE

NEW YORK

Albany

Syracuse

Buffalo

Cleveland

Boston

MASSACHUSETTS

Providence

Hartford

RHODE ISLAND

CONNECTICUT

PENNSYLVANIA

Harrisburg

Pittsburgh

Newark

New York City

Trenton

Philadelphia

NEW JERSEY

OHIO

Columbus

ILLINOIS

Peoria

Springfield

INDIANA

Indianapolis

Cincinnati

WEST
VIRGINIA

Charleston

Baltimore

Dover

Annapolis

Washington D.C.

Richmond

DELAWARE

MARYLAND

Louisville

Frankfort

Lexington

St. Louis

Jefferson
City

Kansas
City

eka

KENTUCKY

VIRGINIA

Norfolk

Newport News

Ohio R.

MISSOURI

Nashville

Knoxville

Raleigh

NORTH
CAROLINA

Charlotte

TENNESSEE

Chattanooga

Memphis

Huntsville

Columbia

SOUTH
CAROLINA

ARKANSAS

Little
Rock

Atlanta

Charleston

ulsa

Birmingham

Columbus

GEORGIA

Savannah

MISSISSIPPI

ALABAMA

Jackson

Montgomery

LOUISIANA

Shreveport

Baton
Rouge

Mobile

Tallahassee

FLORIDA

Jacksonville

New Orleans

Houston

Gulf of
Mexico

Orlando

Tampa

St. Petersburg

Fort Lauderdale

Miami

Lake
Okeechobee

Key West

Straits of Florida

BAHAMAS

CUBA

ATLANTIC
OCEAN

APPALACHIAN MTS.

Tennessee R.

Mississippi

0   200   400 mi
0   200   400 km

ATLANTIC OCEAN

San Juan

Bayamon

Carolina

Isla de
Culebra

PUERTO RICO

Ponce

Isla de
Vieques

Carribbean
Sea

0   20   40 mi
0   20   40 km

— National boundary
— State boundary
⊕ National capital
★ State capital
• Other city

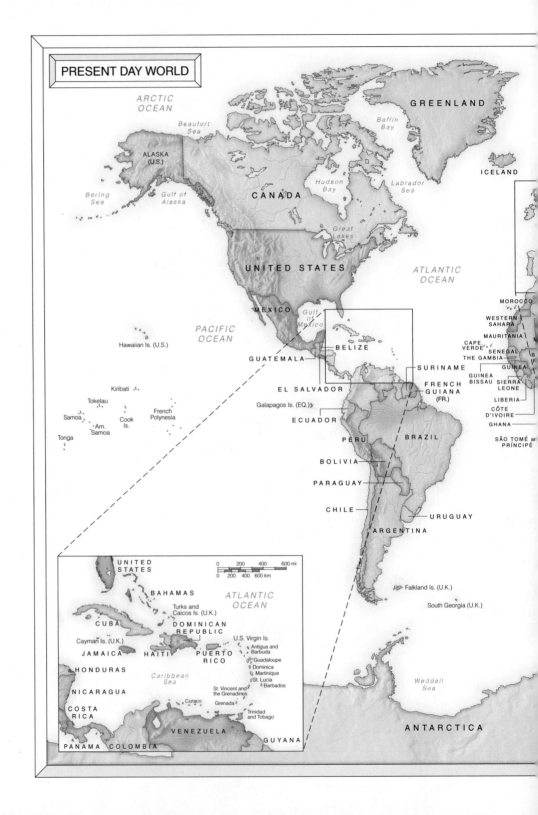

PRESENT DAY WORLD

ARCTIC OCEAN

GREENLAND

Baffin Bay

Beaufort Sea

ALASKA (U.S.)

ICELAND

Bering Sea

Gulf of Alaska

Hudson Bay

Labrador Sea

CANADA

Great Lakes

ATLANTIC OCEAN

UNITED STATES

MOROCCO

PACIFIC OCEAN

MEXICO

Gulf of Mexico

WESTERN SAHARA

MAURITANIA

Hawaiian Is. (U.S.)

BELIZE

GUATEMALA

CAPE VERDE

SENEGAL

THE GAMBIA

GUINEA

EL SALVADOR

SURINAME

GUINEA BISSAU

SIERRA LEONE

Kiribati

FRENCH GUIANA (FR.)

LIBERIA

CÔTE D'IVOIRE

Tokelau

Galapagos Is. (EQ.)

ECUADOR

French Polynesia

GHANA

Samoa

Cook Is.

Am. Samoa

PERU

BRAZIL

SÃO TOMÉ and PRÍNCIPE

Tonga

BOLIVIA

PARAGUAY

CHILE

URUGUAY

ARGENTINA

Falkland Is. (U.K.)

South Georgia (U.K.)

Weddell Sea

ANTARCTICA

UNITED STATES

200   400   600 mi

0   200   400   600 km

BAHAMAS

ATLANTIC OCEAN

Turks and Caicos Is. (U.K.)

CUBA

DOMINICAN REPUBLIC

Cayman Is. (U.K.)

U.S. Virgin Is.

Antigua and Barbuda

JAMAICA

HAITI

PUERTO RICO

Guadaloupe

Dominica

HONDURAS

Caribbean Sea

Martinique

St. Lucia

NICARAGUA

Barbados

St. Vincent and the Grenadines

COSTA RICA

Curaco

Grenada

Trinidad and Tobago

PANAMA   COLOMBIA

VENEZUELA

GUYANA